Tom Reuther

Traffic Engineering with MPLS

Eric Osborne, CCIE No. 4122
Ajay Simha, CCIE No. 2970

Cisco Press

Cisco Press
800 East 96th Street
Indianapolis, IN 46240 USA

Traffic Engineering with MPLS

Eric Osborne

Ajay Simha

Copyright © 2003 Cisco Systems, Inc.

Published by:
Cisco Press
800 East 96th Street
Indianapolis, IN 46240 USA

Printed in the United States of America 2 3 4 5 6 7 8 9 0

Second Printing   September 2004

Library of Congress Cataloging-in-Publication Number: 200-1086632

ISBN: 1-58705-031-5

Warning and Disclaimer

This book is designed to provide information about Multiprotocol Label Switching Traffic Engineering (MPLS TE). Every effort has been made to make this book as complete and as accurate as possible, but no warranty or fitness is implied.

The information is provided on an "as is" basis. The authors, Cisco Press, and Cisco Systems, Inc. shall have neither liability nor responsibility to any person or entity with respect to any loss or damages arising from the information contained in this book or from the use of the discs or programs that may accompany it.

The opinions expressed in this book belong to the author and are not necessarily those of Cisco Systems, Inc.

Trademark Acknowledgments

All terms mentioned in this book that are known to be trademarks or service marks have been appropriately capitalized. Cisco Press and Cisco Systems, Inc. cannot attest to the accuracy of this information. Use of a term in this book should not be regarded as affecting the validity of any trademark or service mark.

Feedback Information

At Cisco Press, our goal is to create in-depth technical books of the highest quality and value. Each book is crafted with care and precision, undergoing rigorous development that involves the unique expertise of members of the professional technical community.

Reader feedback is a natural continuation of this process. If you have any comments regarding how we could improve the quality of this book, or otherwise alter it to better suit your needs, you can contact us through e-mail at feedback@ciscopress.com. Please be sure to include the book title and ISBN in your message.

We greatly appreciate your assistance.

Corporate and Government Sales

Cisco Press offers excellent discounts on this book when ordered in quantity for bulk purchases or special sales.

For more information please contact: U.S. Corporate and Government Sales 1-800-382-3419 corpsales@pearsontechgroup.com

For sales outside the U.S. please contact: International Sales international@pearsoned.com

You can find additional information about this book, any errata, and Appendix B at www.ciscopress.com/1587050315.

Publisher	John Wait
Editor-In-Chief	John Kane
Cisco Systems Management	Michael Hakkert
	Tom Geitner
Executive Editor	Brett Bartow
Production Manager	Patrick Kanouse
Development Editor	Christopher Cleveland
Project Editor	Eric T. Schroeder
Copy Editor	Gayle Johnson
Technical Editors	Jim Guichard
	Alexander Marhold
	Jean-Philippe Vasseur
Team Coordinator	Tammi Ross
Book Designer	Gina Rexrode
Cover Designer	Louisa Klucznik
Compositor	Amy Parker
Indexer	Tim Wright

CISCO SYSTEMS

Corporate Headquarters
Cisco Systems, Inc.
170 West Tasman Drive
San Jose, CA 95134-1706
USA
www.cisco.com
Tel: 408 526-4000
        800 553-NETS (6387)
Fax: 408 526-4100

European Headquarters
Cisco Systems International BV
Haarlerbergpark
Haarlerbergweg 13-19
1101 CH Amsterdam
The Netherlands
www-europe.cisco.com
Tel: 31 0 20 357 1000
Fax: 31 0 20 357 1100

Americas Headquarters
Cisco Systems, Inc.
170 West Tasman Drive
San Jose, CA 95134-1706
USA
www.cisco.com
Tel: 408 526-7660
Fax: 408 527-0883

Asia Pacific Headquarters
Cisco Systems, Inc.
Capital Tower
168 Robinson Road
#22-01 to #29-01
Singapore 068912
www.cisco.com
Tel: +65 6317 7777
Fax: +65 6317 7799

Cisco Systems has more than 200 offices in the following countries and regions. Addresses, phone numbers, and fax numbers are listed on the
Cisco.com Web site at www.cisco.com/go/offices.

Argentina • Australia • Austria • Belgium • Brazil • Bulgaria • Canada • Chile • China PRC • Colombia • Costa Rica • Croatia • Czech Republic
Denmark • Dubai, UAE • Finland • France • Germany • Greece • Hong Kong SAR • Hungary • India • Indonesia • Ireland • Israel • Italy
Japan • Korea • Luxembourg • Malaysia • Mexico • The Netherlands • New Zealand • Norway • Peru • Philippines • Poland • Portugal
Puerto Rico • Romania • Russia • Saudi Arabia • Scotland • Singapore • Slovakia • Slovenia • South Africa • Spain • Sweden
Switzerland • Taiwan • Thailand • Turkey • Ukraine • United Kingdom • United States • Venezuela • Vietnam • Zimbabwe

About the Authors

Eric Osborne, CCIE No. 4122, has been doing Internet engineering of one sort or another since 1995. He's seen fire, he's seen rain, he's seen sunny days that he thought would never end. He joined Cisco in 1998 to work in the Cisco TAC, moved to the ISP Expert Team shortly after Ajay, and has been involved in MPLS since the Cisco IOS Software Release 11.1CT days. His BS degree is in psychology, which, surprisingly, is often more useful than you might think. He is a frequent speaker at the Cisco Networkers events in North America, having delivered the "Deploying MPLS Traffic Engineering" talk since 2000. He can be reached at eosborne@cisco.com.

Ajay Simha, CCIE No. 2970, graduated with a BS in computer engineering in India, followed by a MS in computer science. He joined the Cisco Technical Assistance Center in 1996 after working as a data communication software developer for six years. He then went on to support Tier 1 and 2 ISPs as part of the Cisco ISP Expert Team. His first exposure to MPLS TE was in early 1999. It generated enough interest for him to work with MPLS full-time. Simha has been working as an MPLS deployment engineer since October 1999. He has first-hand experience in trouble-shooting, designing, and deploying MPLS. He can be reached at asimha@cisco.com.

About the Technical Reviewers

Jim Guichard, CCIE No. 2069, is an MPLS deployment engineer at Cisco Systems. In recent years at Cisco, he has been involved in the design, implementation, and planning of many large-scale WAN and LAN networks. His breadth of industry knowledge, hands-on experience, and understanding of complex internetworking architectures have enabled him to provide a detailed insight into the new world of MPLS and its deployment. He can be reached at jguichar@cisco.com.

Alexander Marhold, CCIE No. 3324, holds an MSC degree in industrial electronics and an MBA. He works as a senior consultant and leader of the Core IP Services team at PROIN, a leading European training and consulting company focused on service provider networks. His focus areas are core technologies such as MPLS, high-level routing, BGP, network design, and implementation. In addition to his role as a consultant, Marhold is also a CCSI who develops and holds specialized training courses in his area of specialization. His previous working experience also includes teaching at a polytechnic university for telecommunications, as well as working as CIM project manager in the chemical industry.

Jean-Philippe Vasseur has a French engineer degree and a master of science from the SIT (New Jersey, USA). He has ten years of experience in telecommunications and network technologies and worked for several service providers prior to joining Cisco. After two years with the EMEA technical consulting group, focusing on IP/MPLS routing, VPN, Traffic Engineering, and GMPLS designs for the service providers, he joined the Cisco engineering team. The author is also participating in several IETF drafts.

Dedications

Ajay Simha: I want to dedicate this book to my dear wife, Anitha, and loving children, Varsha and Nikhil, who had to put up with longer working hours than usual. This book is also dedicated to my parents, who provided the educational foundation and values in life that helped me attain this level.

Eric Osborne: I want to dedicate this book to the many coffee shops within walking distance of my house; without them, this book may never have had enough momentum to get finished. I would also like to dedicate this book to my mother (who taught me to make lists), my father (who taught me that addition is, indeed, cumulative), and to anyone who ever taught me anything about networking, writing, or thinking. There's a bit of all of you in here.

Acknowledgments

There are so many people to thank. To begin with, we'd be remiss if we didn't extend heartfelt thanks to the entire MPLS development team for their continual sharing of expertise, often in the face of our daunting cluelessness. Special thanks go to Carol Itturalde, Rob Goguen, and Bob Thomas for answering our questions, no matter how detailed, how obscure, or how often we asked them.

We also want to thank our primary technical reviewers—Jim Guichard, Jean-Philippe Vasseur, and Alexander Marhold. Their guidance and feedback kept us on course.

We'd also like to thank the folks who reviewed parts of this book for accuracy and relevance. In alphabetical order: Aamer Akhter, Santiago Alvarez, Vijay Bollapragada, Anna Charny, Clarence Filsfils, Jim Gibson, Carol Iturralde, Francois Le Faucheur, Gwen Marceline, Trevor Mendez, Stefano Previdi, Robert Raszuk, Khalid Raza, Mukhtiar Shaikh, George Swallow, Dan Tappan, Mosaddaq Turabi, Siva Valliappan, Shankar Vemulapalli, and Russ White.

Eric wants to thank the members of PSU Local #1 for confirming and correcting his assumptions about how large Internet backbones really work.

Our last thanks go to the Cisco Press editing team—specifically, to Chris Cleveland and Brett Bartow for shepherding us through this process. It took over a year to do, and we couldn't have done it without them.

Contents at a Glance

Contents

Icons Used in This Book

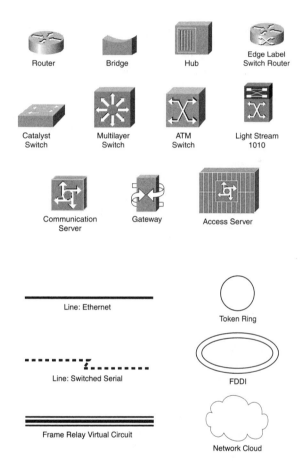

Command Syntax Conventions

The conventions used to present command syntax in this book are the same conventions used in the IOS Command Reference. The Command Reference describes these conventions as follows:

- Vertical bars (l) separate alternative, mutually exclusive elements.

- Square brackets ([ ]) indicate an optional element.

- Braces ({ }) indicate a required choice.

- Braces within brackets ([{ }]) indicate a required choice within an optional element.

- **Boldface** indicates commands and keywords that are entered literally as shown. In configuration examples and output (not general command syntax), boldface indicates commands that are manually input by the user (such as a **show** command).

- *Italic* indicates arguments for which you supply actual values.

Foreword

Tag Switching, the Cisco proprietary technology that evolved into MPLS began in March 1996. At that time, several major ISPs were operating two-tiered networks in order to manage the traffic in their network. You see, IP always takes the shortest path to a destination. This characteristic is important to the scalability of the Internet because it permits routing to be largely an automatic process. However, the shortest path is not always the fastest path or the most lightly loaded. Furthermore, in any non-traffic-engineered network, you find a distribution of link utilizations, with a few links being very heavily loaded and many links being very lightly loaded. You end up with many network users competing for the resources of the busy links, while other links are underutilized. Neither service levels nor operational costs are optimized. In fact, one ISP claims that, with Traffic Engineering, it can offer the same level of service with only 60 percent of the links it would need without Traffic Engineering.

Thus, Traffic Engineering becomes an economic necessity, enough of a necessity to build a whole separate Layer 2 network. To engineer traffic, an ISP would create a mesh of links (virtual circuits) between major sites in its IP network and would use the Layer 2 network, either Frame Relay or ATM, to explicitly route traffic by how they routed these virtual circuits.

By April 1996, it was recognized at Cisco that tag switching offered a means of creating explicit routes within the IP cloud, eliminating the need for a two-tiered network. Because this held the potential for major cost savings to ISPs, work began in earnest shortly thereafter. Detailed requirements and technical approaches were worked out with several ISP and equipment vendors.

Eric Osborne and Ajay Simha work in the development group at Cisco that built Traffic Engineering. They have been actively involved in the deployment of Traffic Engineering in many networks. They are among those with the greatest hands-on experience with this application. This book is the product of their experience. It offers an in-depth, yet practical, explanation of the various elements that make up the Traffic Engineering application: routing, path selection, and signalling. Throughout, these explanations are related back to the actual configuration commands and examples. The result is a book of great interest to anyone curious about Traffic Engineering and an invaluable guide to anyone deploying Traffic Engineering.

George Swallow

Cisco Systems, Inc.

Architect for Traffic Engineering and Co-Chair of the IETF's MPLS Working Group

Introduction

This book concentrates on real-world usage of MPLS TE. We spend most of our time discussing things you can configure, tools you can use to troubleshoot and manage MPLS TE, and design scenarios.

This is not an introduction to MPLS. There's enough literature out there, both Cisco and non-Cisco, that we didn't feel the need to spend time on an MPLS introduction. Although Chapter 2 reviews the basics, we generally assume that you're familiar with the three basic label operations (push, pop, and swap) and how an MPLS packet is forwarded through a network. But as soon as you're past that point, this book is for you.

You might already be using MPLS TE in your network. If so, this book is also for you. This book has many details that we hope will be useful as you continue to use and explore MPLS TE.

Or perhaps you are designing a new backbone and are considering MPLS TE for use in your network. If so, this book is also for you as well. Not only do you need to understand the protocol mechanisms to properly design a network, you also need to understand the ramifications of your design choices.

Who Should Read This Book?

Everybody! You, your friends, your grandmother, her knitting-circle friends, your kids, and their kindergarten classmates—everybody! Actually, we're not so much concerned with who *reads* this book as with who *buys* it, but to ask you to buy it and not read it is pretty crass.

In all seriousness, this book is for two kinds of people:

- **Network engineers**—Those whose job it is to configure, troubleshoot, and manage a network
- **Network architects**—Those who design networks to carry different types of traffic (voice and data) and support service-level agreements (SLAs)

We have friends who, in their respective jobs, fill both roles. To them, and to you if you do the same, we say, "Great! Buy two copies of this book!"

How This Book Is Organized

This book is designed to be read either cover-to-cover or chapter-by-chapter. It divides roughly into four parts:

- Chapters 1 and 2 discuss the history, motivation, and basic operation of MPLS and MPLS TE.
- Chapters 3, 4, and 5 cover the basic processes used to set up and build TE tunnels on your network.
- Chapters 6 and 7 cover advanced MPLS TE applications: MPLS TE and QoS, and protection using Fast Reroute (FRR).
- Chapters 8, 9, 10, and 11 cover network management, design, deployment, and troubleshooting—things you need to understand to be able to apply MPLS TE in the real world.

Here are the details on each chapter:

- **Chapter 1, "Understanding Traffic Engineering with MPLS"**—This chapter discusses the history of basic data networks and the motivation for MPLS and MPLS TE as the next step in the evolution of networks.
- **Chapter 2, "MPLS Forwarding Basics"**—This chapter is a quick review of how MPLS forwarding works. Although this book is not an introduction to MPLS, you might find it beneficial to brush up on some of the details, and that's what this chapter provides.

- **Chapter 3, "Information Distribution"** — This chapter begins the series of three chapters that are really the core of this book. The protocols and mechanisms of MPLS TE have three parts, and the first is distributing MPLS TE information in your IGP.

- **Chapter 4, "Path Calculation and Setup"** — This chapter is the second of the three core chapters. It covers what is done with information after it has been distributed by your IGP. The two prominent pieces covered in this chapter are Constrained SPF (CSPF) and Resource Reservation Protocol (RSVP).

- **Chapter 5, "Forwarding Traffic Down Tunnels"** — This chapter is the last of the three core chapters. It covers what is done with TE tunnels after they are set up. This chapter covers load sharing in various scenarios, announcing TE tunnels into your IGP as a forwarding adjacency, and automatic tunnel bandwidth adjustment using a Cisco mechanism called auto bandwidth.

- **Chapter 6, "Quality of Service with MPLS TE"** — This chapter covers the integration of MPLS and MPLS TE with the DiffServ architecture. It also covers DiffServ-Aware Traffic Engineering (DS-TE).

- **Chapter 7, "Protection and Restoration"** — This chapter covers various traffic protection and restoration mechanisms under the umbrella of Cisco's FRR — how to configure these services, how they work, and how to greatly reduce your packet loss in the event of a failure in your network.

- **Chapter 8, "MPLS TE Management"** — This chapter covers tools and mechanisms for managing an MPLS TE network.

- **Chapter 9, "Network Design with MPLS TE"** — This chapter predominantly covers scalability. It looks at different ways to deloy MPLS TE on your network, and how the various solutions scale as they grow.

- **Chapter 10, "MPLS TE Deployment Tips"** — This chapter covers various knobs, best practices, and case studies that relate to deploying MPLS TE on your network.

- **Chapter 11, "Troubleshooting MPLS TE"** — This chapter discusses tools and techniques for troubleshooting MPLS TE on an operational network.

Two appendixes are also provided. Appendix A lists all the major commands that are relevant to MPLS TE. Appendix B lists resources such as URLs and other books. Appendix B is also available at www.ciscopress.com/1587050315.

CHAPTER 1

Understanding Traffic Engineering with MPLS

Multiprotocol Label Switching (MPLS) has been getting a lot of attention in the past few years. It has been successfully deployed in a number of large networks, and it is being used to offer both Internet and virtual private network (VPN) services in networks around the world.

Most of the MPLS buzz has been around VPNs. Why? Because if you're a provider, it is a service you can sell to your customers.

But you can do more with MPLS than use VPNs. There's also an area of MPLS known as traffic engineering (TE). And that, if you haven't already figured it out, is what this book is all about.

Basic Networking Concepts

What is a data network? At its most abstract, a *data network* is a set of nodes connected by links. In the context of data networks, the nodes are routers, LAN switches, WAN switches, add-drop multiplexers (ADMs), and the like, connected by links from 64 Kb DS0 circuits to OC192 and 10 gigabit Ethernet.

One fundamental property of data networks is *multiplexing*. Multiplexing allows multiple connections across a network to share the same transmission facilities. Two main types of multiplexing to be concerned with are

- Time-division multiplexing (TDM)
- Statistical multiplexing (statmux)

Other kinds of multiplexing, such as frequency-division multiplexing (FDM) and wavelength-division multiplexing (WDM) are not discussed here.

TDM

Time-division multiplexing is the practice of allocating a certain amount of time on a given physical circuit to a number of connections. Because a physical circuit usually has a constant bit rate, allocating a fixed amount of time on that circuit translates directly into a bandwidth allocation.

A good example of TDM is the Synchronous Optical Network (SONET) hierarchy. An OC192 can carry four OC-48s, 16 OC-12s, 64 OC-3s, 192 DS-3s, 5376 DS-1s, 129,024 DS-0s, or various combinations. The Synchronous Digital Hierarchy (SDH) is similar.

TDM is a synchronous technology. Data entering the network is transmitted according to a master clock source so that there's never a logjam of data waiting to be transmitted.

The fundamental property of TDM networks is that they allocate a fixed amount of bandwidth for a given connection at all times. This means that if you buy a T1 from one office to another, you're guaranteed 1.544 Mbps of bandwidth at all times—no more, no less.

TDM is good, but only to a point. One of the main problems with TDM is that bandwidth allocated to a particular connection is allocated for that connection whether it is being used or not. Thirty days of T1 bandwidth is roughly 4 terabits. If you transfer less than 4 terabits over that link in 30 days, you're paying for capacity that you're not using. This makes TDM rather expensive. The trade-off is that when you want to use the T1, the bandwidth is guaranteed to be available; that's what you're paying for.

Statistical Multiplexing

The expense of TDM is one reason statistical multiplexing technologies became popular. *Statistical multiplexing* is the practice of sharing transmission bandwidth between all users of a network, with no dedicated bandwidth reserved for any connections.

Statistical multiplexing has one major advantage over TDM—it's much cheaper. With a statmux network, you can sell more capacity than your network actually has, on the theory that not all users of your network will want to transmit at their maximum bit rate at the same time.

There are several statmux technologies, but the three major ones in the last ten years or so have been

- IP
- Frame Relay
- ATM

MPLS is a fourth type of statmux technology. How it fits into the picture is explained later in this chapter.

Statmux technologies work by dividing network traffic into discrete units and dealing with each of these units separately. In IP, these units are called *packets*; in Frame Relay, they're called *frames*; in ATM, they're called *cells*. It's the same concept in each case.

Statmux networks allow carriers to oversubscribe their network, thereby making more money. They also allow customers to purchase network services that are less expensive than TDM circuits, thereby saving money. A Frame Relay T1, for example, costs far less than a

TDM T1 does. The ratio of bandwidth sold to actual bandwidth is the *oversubscription ratio*. If you have an OC-12 backbone and you sell 24 OC-3s off of it, this is a 6:1 oversubscription ratio. Sometimes, this number is expressed as a percentage—in this case, 600 percent oversubscription.

Issues That Statmux Introduces

Statmux introduces a few issues that don't exist in TDM networks. As soon as packets enter the network asynchronously, you have the potential for resource contention. If two packets enter a router at the exact same time (from two different incoming interfaces) and are destined for the same outgoing interface, that's resource contention. One of the packets has to wait for the other packet to be transmitted. The packet that's not transmitted needs to wait until the first packet has been sent out the link in question. However, the delay encountered because of simultaneous resource contention on a non-oversubscribed link generally isn't that big. If 28 T1s are sending IP traffic at line rate into a router with a T3 uplink, the last IP packet to be transmitted has to wait for 27 other IP packets to be sent.

Oversubscription greatly increases the chance of resource contention at any point in time. If five OC-3s are coming into a router and one OC-12 is going out, there is a chance of buffering because of oversubscription. If you have a sustained incoming traffic rate higher than your outgoing traffic capacity, your buffers will eventually fill up, at which point you start dropping traffic.

There's also the issue of what to do with packets that are in your buffers. Some types of traffic (such as bulk data transfer) deal well with being buffered; other traffic (voice, video) doesn't. So you need different packet treatment mechanisms to deal with the demands of different applications on your network.

Statmux technologies have to deal with three issues that TDM doesn't:

- Buffering
- Queuing
- Dropping

Dealing with these issues can get complex.

Frame Relay has the simplest methods of dealing with these issues—its concepts of committed information rate (CIR), forward and backward explicit congestion notification (FECN and BECN), and the discard eligible (DE) bit.

IP has DiffServ Code Point (DSCP) bits, which evolved from IP Precedence bits. IP also has random early discard (RED), which takes advantage of the facts that TCP is good at handling drops and that TCP is the predominant transport-layer protocol for IP. Finally, IP has explicit congestion notification (ECN) bits, which are relatively new and as of yet have seen limited use.

ATM deals with resource contention by dividing data into small, fixed-size pieces called cells. ATM also has five different service classes:

- CBR (constant bit rate)
- rt-VBR (real-time variable bit rate)
- nrt-VBR (non-real-time variable bit rate)
- ABR (available bit rate)
- UBR (unspecified bit rate)

Statmux Over Statmux

IP was one of the first statmux protocols. RFC 791 defined IP in 1981. The precursor to IP had been around for a number of years. Frame Relay wasn't commercially available until the early 1990s, and ATM became available in the mid-1990s.

One of the problems that network administrators ran into as they replaced TDM circuits with Frame Relay and ATM circuits was that running IP over FR or ATM meant that they were running one statmux protocol on top of another. This is generally suboptimal; the mechanisms available at one statmux layer for dealing with resource contention often don't translate well into another. IP's 3 Precedence bits or 6 DSCP bits give IP eight or 64 classes of service. Frame Relay has only a single bit (the DE bit) to differentiate between more- and less-important data. ATM has several different service classes, but they don't easily translate directly into IP classes. As networks moved away from running multiple Layer 3 protocols (DECnet, IPX, SNA, Apollo, AppleTalk, VINES, IP) to just IP, the fact that the Layer 2 and Layer 3 contention mechanisms don't map well became more and more important.

It then becomes desirable to have one of two things. Either you avoid congestion in your Layer 2 statmux network, or you find a way to map your Layer 3 contention control mechanisms to your Layer 2 contention control mechanisms. Because it's both impossible and financially unattractive to avoid contention in your Layer 2 statmux network, you need to be able to map Layer 3 contention control mechanisms to those in Layer 2. This is one of the reasons MPLS is playing an increasingly important part in today's networks—but you'll read more about that later.

What Is Traffic Engineering?

Before you can understand how to use MPLS to do traffic engineering, you need to understand what traffic engineering is.

When dealing with network growth and expansion, there are two kinds of engineering— network engineering and traffic engineering.

Network engineering is manipulating your network to suit your traffic. You make the best predictions you can about how traffic will flow across your network, and you then order the appropriate circuits and networking devices (routers, switches, and so on). Network engineering is typically done over a fairly long scale (weeks/months/years) because the lead time to install new circuits or equipment can be lengthy.

Traffic engineering is manipulating your traffic to fit your network. No matter how hard you try, your network traffic will never match your predictions 100 percent. Sometimes (as was the case in the mid- to late-1990s), the traffic growth rate exceeds all predictions, and you can't upgrade your network fast enough. Sometimes, a flash event (a sporting event, a political scandal, an immensely popular web site) pulls traffic in ways you couldn't have planned for. Sometimes, there's an unusually painful outage—one of your three cross-country OC-192s fails, leaving traffic to find its way from Los Angeles to New York via the other two OC-192s, and congesting one of them while leaving the other one generally unused.

Generally, although rapid traffic growth, flash events, and network outages can cause major demands for bandwidth in one place, at the same time you often have links in your network that are underutilized. Traffic engineering, at its core, is the art of moving traffic around so that traffic from a congested link is moved onto the unused capacity on another link.

Traffic engineering is by no means an MPLS-specific thing; it's a general practice. Traffic engineering can be implemented by something as simple as tweaking IP metrics on interfaces, or something as complex as running an ATM PVC full-mesh and reoptimizing PVC paths based on traffic demands across it. Traffic engineering with MPLS is an attempt to take the best of connection-oriented traffic engineering techniques (such as ATM PVC placement) and merge them with IP routing. The theory here is that doing traffic engineering with MPLS can be as effective as with ATM, but without a lot of the drawbacks of IP over ATM.

This book is about traffic engineering with MPLS; amazingly enough, that's also this book's title! Its main focus is the operational aspects of MPLS TE—how the various pieces of MPLS TE work and how to configure and troubleshoot them. Additionally, this book covers MPLS TE design and scalability, as well as deployment tips for how to effectively roll out and use MPLS TE on your network.

Traffic Engineering Before MPLS

How was traffic engineering done before MPLS? Let's look at two different statmux technologies that people use to perform traffic engineering—IP and ATM.

IP traffic engineering is popular, but also pretty coarse. The major way to control the path that IP takes across your network is to change the cost on a particular link. There is no reasonable way to control the path that traffic takes based on where the traffic is coming *from*—only where it's going *to*. Still, IP traffic engineering is valid, and many large networks use it successfully. However, as you will soon see, there are some problems IP traffic engineering cannot solve.

ATM, in contrast, lets you place PVCs across the network from a traffic source to a destination. This means that you have more fine-grained control over the traffic flow on your network. Some of the largest ISPs in the world have used ATM to steer traffic around their networks. They do this by building a full mesh of ATM PVCs between a set of routers and periodically resizing and repositioning those ATM PVCs based on observed traffic from the routers. However, one problem with doing things this way is that a full mesh of routers leads to $O(N^2)$ flooding when a link goes down and $O(N^3)$ flooding when a router goes down. This does not scale well and has caused major issues in a few large networks.

$O(N^2)$?

The expression $O(N^2)$ is a way of expressing the scalability of a particular mechanism. In this case, as the number of nodes N increases, the impact on the network when a link goes down increases roughly as the square of the number of nodes—$O(N^2)$. When a router goes down, the impact on the network increases $O(N^3)$ as N increases.

Where do $O(N^2)$ and $O(N^3)$ come from? $O(N^2)$ when a link goes down in a full-mesh environment is because the two nodes on either end of that link tell all their neighbors about the downed link, and each of those neighbors tells most of their neighbors. $O(N^3)$ when a node goes down is because all the neighbors of that node tell all other nodes to which they are connected that a node just went away, and nodes receiving this information flood it to their neighbors. This is a well-known issue in full-mesh architectures.

The Fish Problem

Let's make things more concrete by looking at a classic example of traffic engineering (see Figure 1-1).

Figure 1-1 *The Fish Problem*

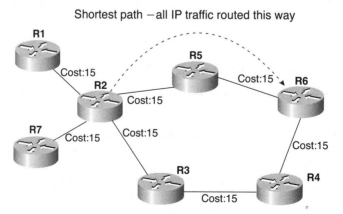

Shortest path — all IP traffic routed this way

In this figure, there are two paths to get from R2 to R6:

R2→R5→R6
R2→R3→R4→R6

Because all the links have the same cost (15), with normal destination-based forwarding, all packets coming from R1 or R7 that are destined for R6 are forwarded out the same interface by R2—toward R5, because the cost of the top path is lower than that of the bottom.

This can lead to problems, however. Assume that all links in this picture are OC-3—roughly 150 Mbps of bandwidth, after accounting for SONET overhead. And further assume that you know ahead of time that R1 sends, on average, 90 Mbps to R6 and that R7 sends 100 Mbps to R6. So what happens here? R2 tries to put 190 Mbps through a 150 Mbps pipe. This means that R2 ends up dropping 40 Mbps because it can't fit in the pipe. On average, this amounts to 21 Mbps from R7 and 19 Mbps from R1 (because R7 is sending more traffic than R1).

So how do you fix this? With destination-based forwarding, it's difficult. If you make the longer path (R2→R3→R4→R6) cost less than the shorter path, all traffic goes down the shorter path. You haven't fixed the problem at all; you just moved it.

Sure, in this figure, you could change link costs so that the short path and the long path both have the same cost, which would alleviate the problem. But this solution works only for small networks, such as the one in the figure. What if, instead of three edge routers (R1, R6, R7), you had 500? Imagine trying to set your link costs so that all paths were used! If it's not impossible, it is at least extremely difficult. So you end up with wasted bandwidth; in Figure 1-1, the longer path never gets used at all.

What about with ATM? If R3, R4, and R5 were ATM switches, the network would look like Figure 1-2.

Figure 1-2   *The Fish Problem in ATM Networks*

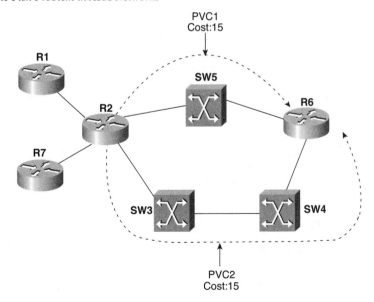

With an ATM network, the problem is trivial to solve. Just build two PVCs from R2 to R6, and set their costs to be the same. This fixes the problem because R2 now has two paths to R6 and is likely to use both paths when carrying a reasonably varied amount of data. The exact load-sharing mechanism can vary, but in general, CEF's per-source-destination load balancing uses both paths in a roughly equal manner.

Building two equal-cost paths across the network is a more flexible solution than changing the link costs in the ATM network, because no other devices connected to the network are affected by any metric change. This is the essence of what makes ATM's traffic engineering capabilities more powerful than IP's.

The problem with ATM TE for an IP network has already been mentioned—$O(N^2)$ flooding when a link goes down and $O(N^3)$ flooding when a router goes down.

So how do you get the traffic engineering capabilities of ATM with the routing simplicity of IP? As you might suspect, the answer is MPLS TE.

Enter MPLS

During mid-to-late 1996, networking magazine articles talked about a new paradigm in the IP world—*IP switching*. From the initial reading of these articles, it seemed like the need for IP routing had been eliminated and we could simply *switch* IP packets. The company that made these waves was Ipsilon. Other companies, such as Toshiba, had taken to ATM as a means of switching IP in their Cell-Switched Router (CSR). Cisco Systems came up with its own answer to this concept—*tag switching*. Attempts to standardize these technologies through the IETF have resulted in combining several technologies into Multiprotocol Label Switching (MPLS). Hence, it is not surprising that Cisco's tag switching implementation had a close resemblance to today's MPLS forwarding.

Although the initial motivation for creating such schemes was for improved packet forwarding speed and a better price-to-port ratio, MPLS forwarding offers little or no improvement in these areas. High-speed packet forwarding algorithms are now implemented in hardware using ASICs. A 20-bit label lookup is not significantly faster than a 32-bit IP lookup. Given that improved packet-forwarding rates are really not the key motivator for MPLS, why indulge in the added complexity of using MPLS to carry IP and make your network operators go through the pain of learning yet another technology?

The real motivation for you to consider deploying MPLS in your network is the applications it enables. These applications are either difficult to implement or operationally almost impossible with traditional IP networks. MPLS VPNs and traffic engineering are two such applications. This book is about the latter. Here are the main benefits of MPLS, as discussed in the following sections:

- Decoupling routing and forwarding
- Better integration of the IP and ATM worlds

- Basis for building next-generation network applications and services, such as provider-provided VPNs (MPLS VPN) and traffic engineering

Decoupling Routing and Forwarding

IP routing is a hop-by-hop forwarding paradigm. When an IP packet arrives at a router, the router looks at the destination address in the IP header, does a route lookup, and forwards the packet to the next hop. If no route exists, the packet is then dropped. This process is repeated at each hop until the packet reaches its destination. In an MPLS network, nodes also forward the packet hop by hop, but this forwarding is based on a fixed-length label. Chapter 2, "MPLS Forwarding Basics," covers the details of what a label is and how it is prepended to a packet. It is this capability to decouple the forwarding of packets from IP headers that enables MPLS applications such as traffic engineering.

The concept of being able to break from Layer 3-based (IP destination-based) forwarding is certainly not new. You can decouple forwarding and addressing in an IP network using concepts such as *policy-based routing* (PBR). Cisco IOS Software has had PBR support since Cisco IOS Software Release 11.0 (circa 1995). Some of the problems with using PBR to build end-to-end network services are as follows:

- The complexity in configuration management.
- PBR does not offer dynamic rerouting. If the forwarding path changes for whatever reason, you have to manually reconfigure the nodes along the new path to reflect the policy.
- The possibility of routing loops.

The limitations of PBR apply when PBR is used in an IP network to influence hop-by-hop routing behavior. PBR is easier to use in an MPLS TE-based network because PBR is used only at the tunnel headend. Using PBR in combination with MPLS does not overcome all PBR's limitations; see Chapter 5, "Forwarding Traffic Down Tunnels," for more information.

The advent of MPLS forwarding and MPLS TE enables successful decoupling of the *forwarding* process from the *routing* process by basing packet forwarding on labels rather than on an IP address.

Better Integration of the IP and ATM Worlds

From the get-go, the IP and ATM worlds seemed to clash. While ATM was being standardized, it envisioned IP coexisting with it, but always as a sideshow. Ever since the industry realized that we are not going to have our PCs and wristwatches running an ATM stack and that IP was here to stay, attempts have been made to map IP onto ATM. However, the main drawback of previous attempts to create a mapping between IP and ATM was that they either tried to keep the two worlds separate (carrying IP over ATM VCs) or tried to integrate IP and ATM with mapping services (such as ATM Address Resolution Protocol

[ARP] and Next-Hop Resolution Protocol [NHRP]). Carrying IP over ATM VCs (often called the *overlay model*) is useful, but it has scalability limits; using mapping servers introduces more points of failure into the network.

The problem with the overlay approach is that it leads to suboptimal routing unless a full mesh of VCs is used. However, a full mesh of VCs can create many routing adjacencies, leading to routing scalability issues. Moreover, independent QoS models need to be set up for IP and for ATM, and they are difficult to match.

MPLS bridges the gap between IP and ATM. ATM switches dynamically assign virtual path identifier/virtual channel identifier (VPI/VCI) values that are used as labels for cells. This solution resolves the overlay-scaling problem without the need for centralized ATM-IP resolution servers. This is called Label-Controlled ATM (LC-ATM). Sometimes it is called IP+ATM.

For further details on ATM's role in MPLS networks, read the section "ATM in Frame Mode and Cell Mode" in Chapter 2.

Traffic Engineering with MPLS (MPLS TE)

MPLS TE combines ATM's traffic engineering capabilities with IP's flexibility and class-of-service differentiation. MPLS TE allows you to build Label-Switched Paths (LSPs) across your network that you then forward traffic down.

Like ATM VCs, MPLS TE LSPs (also called TE tunnels) let the headend of a TE tunnel control the path its traffic takes to a particular destination. This method is more flexible than forwarding traffic based on destination address only.

Unlike ATM VCs, the nature of MPLS TE avoids the $O(N^2)$ and $O(N^3)$ flooding problems that ATM and other overlay models present. Rather than form adjacencies over the TE LSPs themselves, MPLS TE uses a mechanism called *autoroute* (not to be confused with the WAN switching circuit-routing protocol of the same name) to build a routing table using MPLS TE LSPs without forming a full mesh of routing neighbors. Chapter 5 covers autoroute in greater detail.

Like ATM, MPLS TE reserves bandwidth on the network when it builds LSPs. Reserving bandwidth for an LSP introduces the concept of a *consumable resource* into your network. If you build TE-LSPs that reserve bandwidth, as LSPs are added to the network, they can find paths across the network that have bandwidth available to be reserved.

Unlike ATM, there is no forwarding-plane enforcement of a reservation. A reservation is made in the control plane only, which means that if a Label Switch Router (LSR) makes a reservation for 10 Mb and sends 100 Mb down that LSP, the network attempts to deliver that 100 Mb unless you attempt to police the traffic at the source using QoS techniques.

This concept is covered in much more depth in Chapters 3, 4, 5, and 6.

Solving the Fish Problem with MPLS TE

Figure 1-3 revisits the fish problem presented in Figure 1-1.

Figure 1-3 *The Fish Problem with LSRs*

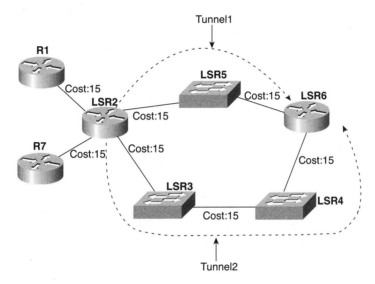

Like ATM PVCs, MPLS TE LSPs can be placed along an arbitrary path on the network. In Figure 1-3, the devices in the fish are now LSRs.

The three major differences between ATM and MPLS TE are

- MPLS TE forwards packets; ATM uses cells. It is possible to combine both MPLS TE and MPLS/ATM integration, but currently, this is not implemented and therefore is not covered here.

- ATM requires a full mesh of routing adjacencies; MPLS TE does not.

- In ATM, the core network topology is not visible to the routers on the edge of the network; in MPLS, IP routing protocols advertise the topology over which MPLS TE is based.

All these differences are covered throughout this book; Chapter 2, specifically, talks about the nuts and bolts of MPLS forwarding.

Building Services with MPLS

In addition to its penchant for traffic engineering, MPLS can also build services across your network. The three basic applications of MPLS as a service are

- MPLS VPNs
- MPLS quality of service (QoS)
- Any Transport over MPLS (AToM)

All these applications and services are built on top of MPLS forwarding. MPLS as a service is orthogonal to MPLS for traffic engineering: They can be used together or separately.

MPLS VPNs

VPNs are nothing new to internetworking. Since the mid-to-late 1990s, service providers have offered private leased lines, Frame Relay, and ATM PVCs as a means of interconnecting remote offices of corporations. IPSec and other encryption methods have been used to create intranets over public or shared IP networks (such as those belonging to an Internet service provider [ISP]). Recently, MPLS VPNs have emerged as a standards-based technology that addresses the various requirements of VPNs, such as private IP; the capability to support overlapping address space; and intranets, extranets (with optimal routing), and Internet connectivity, while doing so in a scalable manner. A detailed explanation of MPLS VPNs is outside the scope of this book. However, you are encouraged to read *MPLS and VPN Architectures* by Jim Guichard and Ivan Pepelnjak (Cisco Press) and the other references listed in Appendix B, "CCO and Other References."

MPLS QoS

In the area of QoS, the initial goal for MPLS was to simply be able to provide what IP offered—namely, Differentiated Services (DiffServ) support. When the MPLS drafts first came out, they set aside 3 bits in the MPLS header to carry class-of-service information. After a protracted spat in the IETF, these bits were officially christened the "EXP bits," or experimental bits, even though Cisco and most other MPLS implementations use these EXP bits as you would use IP Precedence. EXP bits are analogous to, and are often a copy of, the IP Precedence bits in a packet. Chapter 6, "Quality of Service with MPLS TE," covers MPLS QoS in greater detail.

Any Transport over MPLS (AToM)

AToM is an application that facilitates carrying Layer 2 traffic, such as Frame Relay (FR), Ethernet, and ATM, over an MPLS cloud. These applications include

- Providing legacy ATM and FR circuit transport
- Point-to-point bandwidth, delay, and jitter guarantees when combined with other techniques such as DS-TE and MPLS QoS
- Extending the Layer 2 broadcast domain

- Remote point of presence (POP) connectivity, especially for ISPs to connect to remote Network Access Points (NAPs)
- Support for multi-dwelling connections, such as apartment buildings, university housing, and offices within a building

Use the URLs provided in Appendix B if you want to learn more about AToM.

What MPLS TE Is Not

You just read a lot about what MPLS TE can do. It's important to understand what MPLS is *not* so that you don't take it for more than it is:

- MPLS TE is not QoS.
- MPLS TE is not ATM.
- MPLS TE is not magic.

MPLS TE Is Not QoS

"Quality of service" means different things to different people. At an architectural level, QoS is composed of two things:

- Finding a path through your network that can provide the service you offer
- Enforcing that service

Finding the path can be as simple as using your IGP metric to determine the best route to a destination. Enforcing that service can be as simple as throwing so much bandwidth at your network that there's no need to worry about any other sort of resource contention tools. This is sometimes called "quantity of service," but in the most generic sense, it is a method of providing good service quality, and therefore good quality of service.

Or you can make things complex. You can find a path through your network with an offline TE-LSP placement tool, much like ATM PVC placement. Enforcing that path can be done using DiffServ mechanisms such as policing, marking, queuing, and dropping. MPLS (specifically, MPLS TE) is only a tool you can use to help provide high-quality service.

There's a range of options in between these two choices. In general, the more time and money you spend on path layout, provisioning, and DiffServ mechanisms, the less money you need to spend on bandwidth and the associated networking equipment. Which direction you decide to go is up to you.

MPLS TE Is Not ATM

No, it's really not. MPLS TE (as a subset of all things MPLS) has some of ATM's traffic engineering properties, but MPLS TE is not ATM. MPLS as a whole is more like Frame

Relay than ATM, if for no other reason than both MPLS and Frame Relay carry entire packets with a switching header on them, and ATM divides things into cells. Although MPLS has been successfully used to replace ATM in some networks (replacing an ATM full mesh with an MPLS TE full mesh) and complement it in others (moving from IP over ATM to IP+ATM), MPLS is not a 1:1 drop-in replacement for ATM.

As mentioned earlier, it is possible to integrate MPLS TE with MPLS ATM forwarding (in Cisco parlance, the latter is called IP+ATM). This is still not the same as carrying IP over traditional ATM networks, as with IP+ATM (also called Label-Controlled ATM, or LC-ATM) and TE integration, there's still no full mesh of routing adjacencies.

MPLS TE Is Not Magic

That's right—you heard it here first. MPLS stands for Multiprotocol Label Switching, not "Magic Problem-solving Labor Substitute," as some would have you believe. As you might expect, adding a new forwarding layer between Layer 2 and IP (some call it Layer 2.5; we prefer to stay away from the entire OSI model discussion) does not come without cost. If you're going to tactically apply MPLS TE, you need to remember what tunnels you put where and why. If you take the strategic track, you have signed up for a fairly large chunk of work, managing a full mesh of TE tunnels in addition to IGP over your physical network. Network management of MPLS TE is covered in Chapter 8, "MPLS TE Management."

But MPLS TE solves problems, and solves them in ways IP can't. As we said a few pages back, MPLS TE is aware of both its own traffic demands and the resources on your network.

If you've read this far, you're probably at least interested in finding out more about what MPLS TE can do for you. To you, we say, "Enjoy!"

NOTE   Or maybe you're not interested. Maybe you're genetically predisposed to have an intense dislike for MPLS and all things label-switched. That's fine. To you we say, "Know thine enemy!" and encourage you to buy at least seven copies of this book anyway. You can always burn them for heat and then go back to the bookstore and get more.

Using MPLS TE in Real Life

Three basic real-life applications for MPLS TE are

- Optimizing your network utilization
- Handling unexpected congestion
- Handling link and node failures

Optimizing your network utilization is sometimes called the *strategic* method of deploying MPLS TE. It's sometimes also called the full-mesh approach. The idea here is that you build a full mesh of MPLS TE-LSPs between a given set of routers, size those LSPs according to how much bandwidth is going between a pair of routers, and let the LSPs find the best path in your network that meets their bandwidth demands. Building this full mesh of TE-LSPs in your network allows you to avoid congestion as much as possible by spreading LSPs across your network along bandwidth-aware paths. Although a full mesh of TE-LSPs is no substitute for proper network planning, it allows you to get as much as you can out of the infrastructure you already have, which might let you delay upgrading a circuit for a period of time (weeks or months). This translates directly into money saved by not having to buy bandwidth.

Another valid way to deploy MPLS TE is to handle unexpected congestion. This is known as the *tactical* approach, or *as needed*. Rather than building a full mesh of TE-LSPs between a set of routers ahead of time, the tactical approach involves letting the IGP forward traffic as it will, and building TE-LSPs only after congestion is discovered. This allows you to keep most of your network on IGP routing only. This might be simpler than a full mesh of TE-LSPs, but it also lets you work around network congestion as it happens. If you have a major network event (a large outage, an unexpectedly popular new web site or service, or some other event that dramatically changes your traffic pattern) that congests some network links while leaving others empty, you can deploy MPLS TE tunnels as you see fit, to remove some of the traffic from the congested links and put it on uncongested paths that the IGP wouldn't have chosen.

A third major use of MPLS TE is for quick recovery from link and node failures. MPLS TE has a component called Fast Reroute (FRR) that allows you to drastically minimize packet loss when a link or node (router) fails on your network. You can deploy MPLS TE to do just FRR, and to not use MPLS TE to steer traffic along paths other than the ones your IGP would have chosen.

Chapters 9 and 10 discuss strategic and tactical MPLS TE deployments; Chapter 7 covers Fast Reroute.

Summary

This chapter was a whirlwind introduction to some of the concepts and history behind MPLS and MPLS TE. You now have a feel for where MPLS TE came from, what it's modeled after, and what sort of problems it can solve.

More importantly, you also have a grasp on what MPLS is not. MPLS has received a tremendous amount of attention since its introduction into the networking world, and it has been exalted by some and derided by others. MPLS and MPLS TE are no more and no less than tools in your networking toolbox. Like any other tool, they take time and knowledge to apply properly. Whether you use MPLS TE in your network is up to you; the purpose of this book is to show you how MPLS TE works and the kinds of things it can do.

Although this book is not an introduction to MPLS as a whole, you might need to brush up on some MPLS basics. That's what Chapter 2 is for: It reviews basic label operations and label distribution in detail to prepare you for the rest of the book. If you're familiar with basic MPLS operation (push/pop/swap and the basic idea of LDP), you might want to skip to Chapter 3, "Information Distribution," where you can start diving into the nuts and bolts of how MPLS TE works and how it can be put to work for you.

This chapter covers the following topics:

- MPLS Terminology
- Forwarding Fundamentals
- Label Distribution Protocol
- Label Distribution Protocol Configuration

CHAPTER 2

MPLS Forwarding Basics

Chapter 1, "Understanding Traffic Engineering with MPLS," provided the history and motivation for MPLS. This chapter familiarizes you with the fundamental concepts of MPLS-based forwarding. It serves as a refresher if you are already familiar with MPLS and it is a good introduction if you are not. Chapters 3 through 11 deal with MPLS Traffic Engineering. You should read the MPLS drafts, RFCs, and other reference materials listed in Appendix B, "CCO and Other References," to obtain a more complete understanding of other MPLS topics.

MPLS Terminology

Before jumping into MPLS concepts, it is a good idea to familiarize yourself with the terminology and lingo used in MPLS.

Table 2-1 defines some common MPLS-related terms you must know in order to understand the concepts in this chapter and book.

Table 2-1 *MPLS Terminology*

Term	Definition
Upstream	A router that is closer to the source of a packet, relative to another router.
Downstream	A router that is farther from the source of a packet, relative to another router. As a packet traverses a network, it is switched from an upstream router to its downstream neighbor.
Control plane	Where control information such as routing and label information is exchanged.
Data plane/forwarding plane	Where actual forwarding is performed. This can be done only after the control plane is established.
Cisco Express Forwarding (CEF)[1]	The latest switching method used in Cisco IOS. It utilizes an *mtrie*-based organization and retrieval structure. CEF is the default forwarding method in all versions of Cisco IOS Software Release 12.0 and later.

continues

Table 2-1   *MPLS Terminology (Continued)*

Term	Definition
Label	A fixed-length tag that MPLS forwarding is based on. The term *label* can be used in two contexts. One term refers to 20-bit labels. The other term refers to the label header, which is 32 bits in length. For more details on labels, see the later section "What Is a Label?".
Label binding	An association of an FEC (prefix) to a label. A label distributed by itself has no context and, therefore, is not very useful. The receiver knows to apply a certain label to an incoming data packet because of this association to an FEC.
Label imposition	The process of adding a label to a data packet in an MPLS network. This is also referred to as "pushing" a label onto a packet.
Label disposition	The process of removing a label from a data packet. This is also referred to as "popping" a label off a packet.
Label swapping	Changing the value of the label in the MPLS header during MPLS forwarding.
Label Switch Router (LSR)	Any device that switches packets based on the MPLS label.
Label Edge Router (LER)	An LSR that accepts unlabeled packets (IP packets) and imposes labels on them at the ingress side. An LER also removes labels at the edge of the network and sends unlabeled packets to the IP network on the egress side.
Forwarding Equivalence Class (FEC)	Any set of properties that map incoming packets to the same outgoing label. Generally, an FEC is equivalent to a route (all packets destined for anything inside 10.0.0.0/8 match the same FEC), but the definition of FEC can change when packets are routed using criteria other than just the destination IP address (for example, DSCP bits in the packet header).
Label-Switched Path (LSP)	The path that a labeled packet traverses through a network, from label imposition to disposition.

Table 2-1   *MPLS Terminology (Continued)*

Term	Definition
Label stack	Apart from the label exchanged between LSRs and their neighbors, for applications such as MPLS-VPN, an end-to-end label is exchanged. As a result, a label stack is used instead of a single MPLS label. An important concept to keep in mind is that the forwarding in the core is based just on the top-level label. In the context of MPLS TE, label stacking is required when a labeled packet enters an MPLS TE tunnel.
Forwarding Information Base (FIB)[1]	The table that is created by enabling CEF on the Cisco routers.
Label Information Base (LIB)	The table where the various label bindings that an LSR receives over the LDP protocol are stored. It forms the basis of populating the FIB and LFIB tables.
Tag Information Base (TIB)	The older, "tag-switching" name for the LIB.
Explicit null	The opposite of implicit null. In the control plane, the last hop sends a label value of 0 (for IPv4) to the penultimate hop. The label value is never used for lookup. Explicit null provides some advantages that implicit null doesn't. It is used in network devices that don't support implicit null, or to carry EXP bits all the way to the tunnel tail.
Implicit null	The concept of not using a label on the last hop of an LSP in the forwarding plane. Implicit null has some performance advantages. In the control plane, the last hop of the LSP advertises a label value of 3 to indicate implicit null.
Penultimate Hop Popping (PHP)	After receiving the egress router, a labeled packet pops off the label and does an IP lookup in the CEF[1] table. This means that the egress router must do two lookups for every packet exiting the network. To reduce this burden placed on the egress router, PHP allows the penultimate hop router to remove the top-level label, which allows the LER to forward the packet based on a single lookup. The router that is immediately upstream of the tail of an MPLS TE tunnel also performs PHP.

continues

Table 2-1 *MPLS Terminology (Continued)*

Term	Definition
P/PE and C/CE	P and PE routers are LSRs and LERs in the context of MPLS-VPN. The term P comes from routers being in the provider network. C routers are routers found in the customer network. CE routers are the routers on the customer edge facing the provider. PE routers are provider edge routers, which connect to the CE routers. CE routers normally run plain IP (not required to be MPLS-aware).
Label Distribution Protocol (LDP)	One of the many protocols in place to distribute the label bindings between an LSR and its neighbor. Other mechanisms include RSVP, used in MPLS TE, and MP-BGP, used in MPLS-VPN.
Tag Distribution Protocol (TDP)	The predecessor of LDP, TDP is a Cisco-proprietary protocol that acts much like LDP. You can use TDP if interoperability between Cisco and non-Cisco devices is not important.
Resource Reservation Protocol (RSVP)	This protocol was originally intended as a signaling protocol for the Integrated Services (IntServ) quality of service (QoS) model, wherein a host requests a specific QoS from the network for a particular flow. This reservation could be within an enterprise network or over the Internet. RSVP with a few extensions has been adapted by MPLS to be the signalling protocol that supports MPLS TE within the core. RSVP theory is standardized in RFC 2205 and RFC 3209. It is covered in greater detail in Chapter 4, "Path Calculation and Setup."
Constrained Routing LDP (CR-LDP)	This is an alternative approach to RSVP that acts as a signalling protocol to achieve MPLS TE. Cisco routers support RSVP rather than CR-LDP for traffic engineering LSP setup. CR-LDP is not covered in this book.

[1]The terms *CEF* and *CEF table* are used interchangeably with *FIB*. Although CEF is the name given to the forwarding mechanism, FIB is the term used to reference the table and the internal data structures.

Forwarding Fundamentals

Table 2-1 provided an introductory glance at MPLS through terminology and definitions. This section goes into more depth about how all these concepts come together.

What Is a Label?

Labels, as you can probably guess, are an integral part of Multiprotocol *Label* Switching. The label allows the decoupling of routing from forwarding, which lets you do all sorts of neat things.

But what *is* a label? Before we define what a label is, you should know that MPLS can operate in one of two modes:

- Frame mode
- Cell mode

Frame Mode

Frame mode is the term used when you forward a *packet* with a label prepended to the packet in front of the Layer 3 header (the IP header, for example).

RFC 3031, "Multiprotocol Label Switching Architecture," defines a label as "a short fixed length physically contiguous identifier which is used to identify a FEC, usually of local significance."

Put simply, a label is a value prepended to a packet that tells the network where the packet should go. A label is a 20-bit value, which means that there can be 2^{20} possible label values, or just over 1,000,000.

A packet can have multiple labels, carried in what's known as a *label stack*. A label stack is a set of one or more labels on a packet. At each hop in a network, only the outermost label is considered. The label that an LSR uses to forward the packet in the data plane is the label it assigned and distributed in the control plane. Hence, the inner labels have no meaning as far as the midpoints are concerned.

When labels are placed on a packet, the 20-bit label value itself is encoded with some additional pieces of information that assist in the forwarding of the labeled packet through a network.

Figure 2-1 illustrates the encoded MPLS header packet format.

Figure 2-1 *MPLS Header Packet Format*

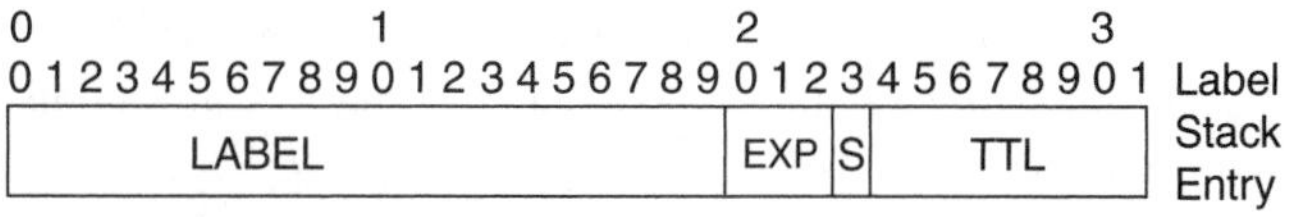

LABEL = 20 bits
EXP = Experimental, 3 bits
S = Bottom of stack, 1 bit
TTL = Time To Live, 8 bits

This 32-bit quantity is known as a *label stack entry*, but is often referred to as just a *label*. So, when labels are discussed, the discussion could be either about the 20-bit label value or the 32-bit label stack entry. The additional 12 bits are made up of the following:

- **EXP**—EXP bits are technically reserved for experimental use. Cisco IOS Software (and pretty much every MPLS implementation) uses these EXP bits to hold a QoS indicator—often a direct copy of the IP precedence bits in an underlying IP packet. When MPLS packets are queued up, it is possible to use EXP bits in the same way that IP precedence bits are used now. You'll read more about this in Chapter 6, "Quality of Service with MPLS TE."

- **S**—The S bit is the bottom-of-stack bit. It is possible (and common) to have more than one label attached to a packet. The bottommost label in a stack has the S bit set to 1; other labels have the S bit set to 0. The S bit is there because it's sometimes useful to know where the bottom of the label stack is, and the S bit is the tool to use to find it.

- **TTL**—Time To Live bits are often (but not always) a direct copy of the IP TTL header. They are decremented at every hop to prevent routing loops from creating infinite packet storms; this is just like IP. TTL bits can also be set to something *other* than the TTL on the IP packet. This is most often used when a network operator wants to hide the underlying network topology from traceroutes from the outside world.

NOTE	In some cases, such as for security concerns or to meet service-level agreements (SLAs) (although this might come across as a deception), you might need to hide the core of a service provider's network from the user community. You can do this on Cisco routers using the command **no mpls ip propagate-ttl** {**forwarded**	**local**}. This command, when used with the **forwarded** option, affects only traffic forwarded through the router. This lets TTL be used in **traceroute** commands to troubleshoot problems in the core.

Cell Mode

Cell mode is the term used when you have a network consisting of ATM LSRs that use MPLS in the control plane to exchange VPI/VCI information instead of using ATM signalling.

In cell mode, the label is said to be *encoded* in a cell's VPI/VCI fields (see Figure 2-2). After label exchange is done in the control plane, in the forwarding plane, the ingress router segments the packet into ATM cells, applying the appropriate VPI/VCI value that was exchanged in the control plane, and transmits the cells. Midpoint ATM LSRs behave like normal ATM switches—they forward a cell based on the incoming VPI/VCI and the incoming port information. Finally, the egress router reassembles the cells into a packet.

Cell mode is also called Label-Controlled ATM (LC-ATM). LC-ATM label distribution is discussed in more depth in the section "Label Distribution Concepts." The cell-mode discussion was included for the sake of completeness. It is not required for understanding MPLS traffic engineering concepts in this book because MPLS TE is not supported in cell mode on Cisco routers as of this writing.

NOTE	In some of the examples containing MPLS-related output in this chapter, you'll notice that ATM VPI/VCI values show up in the *outgoing tag* column. These are cases in which a VPI/VCI was exchanged in an MPLS control plane over an ATM interface and the downstream neighbor on that interface expects to see that VPI/VCI value on the cell it receives.

ATM in Frame Mode and Cell Mode

As you have seen so far, ATM switches can act as LSRs. When ATM switches are a part of the core, they can operate in two modes:

- Frame mode
- Cell mode

When a conventional ATM PVC is built to achieve classic IP over ATM (aal5snap encapsulation, for example) and MPLS is sent over that PVC, this is still called *frame-mode MPLS*. To understand this better, refer to the MPLS header format, also known as the label stack entry, illustrated in Figure 2-1.

Figure 2-2 shows the MPLS label in relation to Layer 2 and Layer 3 headers. The PPP and LAN headers show the label being inserted between the Layer 2 and Layer 3 headers (Ethernet and IP, for example). This is called a *shim* header. When operating in frame-mode MPLS, you always see a shim header. This is also applicable when you are simply connecting routers over ATM PVCs and doing MPLS in a classic IP-over-ATM environment.

Figure 2-2   *MPLS Layer 2 Encapsulation*

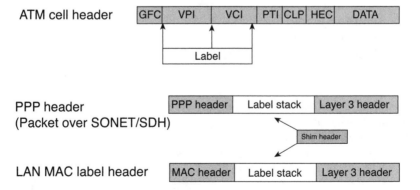

When running in cell mode, ATM LSRs act as routers in the control plane. In other words, they need to exchange routing information through IGP protocols, such as OSPF, and need to run a label distribution protocol, such as TDP or LDP.

NOTE   You might think that ATM switches forward only ATM cells, so whenever ATM switches are involved in the MPLS core, they *must* be acting as ATM LSRs, in cell mode. This is not true. The reason this is not always true is because the ATM switch could be used to build a conventional ATM point-to-point PVC between two routers. When this is done, the routers on either end of the PVC can be directly connected LSRs. When forwarding packets to each other, they would first have to build the IP packet and insert an MPLS header in front of it and then segment the entire packet (IP packet plus MPLS header) into ATM cells. When these cells reach the router at the other end of the PVC, they are reassembled into a packet. If further forwarding is required, the forwarding is based on the label value inside the label header. In this case, even though the MPLS packets were segmented into ATM cells, there was no mapping of MPLS label to the VPI/VCI fields of the ATM cell. Thus, this would be considered frame mode.

Control Plane Versus Data Plane

The control plane is where the routing information and other control information, such as label bindings, are exchanged between LSRs. MPLS is a control plane-driven protocol, meaning that the control information exchange must be in place before the first data packet can be forwarded. The forwarding of data packets is done in the data plane.

Classification

When an IP packet arrives at a LER (the ingress router), just as in the case of normal IP forwarding, a longest-match lookup is performed by comparing the entries in the FIB against the destination IP address of the received packet. In MPLS terminology, this process is called classifying the packet. This section explains the term FEC (Forwarding Equivalence Class), as well as where classification is performed and how it differs from classification in conventional IP networks.

FEC

When IP packets destined for the same subnet arrive at an ingress router, the classification for all these packets is the same—it is based on the longest-match lookup in the FIB. For example, assume you have an entry in the FIB for 171.68.0.0/16 with a next-hop address of 12.12.12.12. If you now receive two packets with destination IP addresses 171.68.1.1 and 171.68.23.5, both these packets are forwarded to the same next hop—12.12.12.12. In most cases, it could be said that 171.68.1.1 and 171.68.23.5 share the same FEC.

However, the classification into a particular FEC need not be restricted to the destination IP address of the received packet. Classification into a FEC could be based on the interface on which the packet arrived, the IP precedence values in the packet's IP header, the packet's destination port number, or any arbitrary scheme you can imagine. Regardless of the basis of the classification, all the packets that are classified into the same FEC receive the same treatment. This treatment can be forwarding the packet down a certain path, providing the packet some preferential treatment within the core, or even dropping the packet. The current Cisco IOS Software implementation classifies IP packets based on their destination IP address, in the absence of any tools such as policy-based routing.

Translating MPLS terminology into IP terminology, the FEC is nothing but the route (also called the prefix) found in the FIB that was the best match for the incoming packet.

Living on the Edge

In conventional IP networks, the forwarding of a packet is based on the packet's destination IP address. Each node along the packet's path can forward the packet only after examining the destination IP address contained in the packet. This means that each node along the packet's path classifies the packet. This is discussed in further detail in the section "MPLS Versus IP."

In MPLS-based forwarding, after the ingress LER at the edge of the network does the classification, it pushes a label on the data packet that matches that packet's FEC. This process is called *label imposition* or *label pushing*. The LSRs in the network's core are not required to reclassify the packet. When a core router receives a labeled packet, it does three things:

- It does a label lookup on the incoming label.
- It finds the outgoing interface and outgoing label for this packet.
- It swaps the received (incoming) label for the proper outgoing label and sends the packet out the outgoing interface.

This process is known as *label swapping*.

How an LSR knows what label the downstream LSR expects is based on the label bindings that are exchanged in the control plane using a label distribution protocol (LDP, RSVP, BGP, and so on) prior to forwarding packets.

When a packet reaches the end of the network, the packet's outermost label is removed, and the remainder of the packet is forwarded to the next hop. The act of removing a label from a packet is called *label popping* or *label disposition*.

The three fundamental label operations (push/impose, swap, and pop/dispose) are all that is needed for MPLS. Label imposition/disposition and forwarding allow for an arbitrarily complex classification scheme that needs higher processing power to be enforced at the edge, while keeping the core simply forwarding MPLS packets.

Control Planes in an MPLS Network

This section looks at the processes needed to get a packet through a network—first an IP network and then an MPLS network.

For both the IP network and the MPLS network, consider the topology shown in Figure 2-3. It represents a service provider network in which gateway routers 7200a and 7200b peer with external BGP peers 7500a and 12008c. The core routers in AS1 (12008a and 12008b) are only involved in IBGP peering.

Figure 2-3 *Packet Life: Both IP and MPLS*

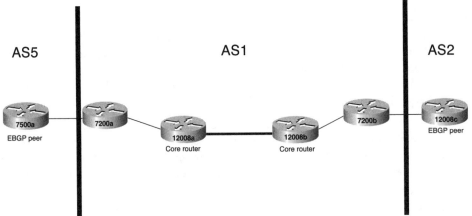

In order for any data packets to be passed through this network, first the control plane mechanisms have to be set up.

In an IP network, the control plane mechanisms consist of the following:

- **Interior Gateway Protocol (IGP)**—Most often OSPF or IS-IS in service provider networks. Can also be EIGRP, RIP, or just static routing.

- **Border Gateway Protocol (BGP)**—Used to advertise routes that are learned from external neighbors. External BGP (EBGP) is spoken between 7200b and 12008c, as shown in Figure 2-3. 7200b then communicates what it has learned to all other routers in AS1. In this example, 7200b has all other routers as IBGP neighbors; in real-life networks, a Route Reflector (RR) would probably be used. The important point here is that all the routers in AS1 need to learn the route from 7200b.

In an MPLS network, the control plane mechanisms are as follows:

- **IGP**—This is no different from the IGP used for an IP-only network. If the MPLS network were using traffic engineering, the IGP would have to be a link-state protocol, either OSPF or IS-IS. Because traffic engineering is not being considered in this example, the IGP doesn't matter.

- **Label distribution protocol**—The three principal label distribution protocols in an MPLS network are

  — Tag Distribution Protocol (TDP)

  — Label Distribution Protocol (LDP)

  — RSVP

  RSVP is used for traffic engineering and is not considered in this example. TDP and LDP are actually two different versions of the same thing; TDP is older, and LDP is standardized. So, assume that LDP is used to distribute labels.

  What exactly does *label distribution* mean? A *label binding* is an association of a label to a prefix (route). LDP works in conjunction with the IGP to advertise label bindings for all non-BGP routes to its neighbors. LDP neighbors are established over links enabled for LDP. So, when 12008a and 12008b in Figure 2-3 become LDP neighbors, they advertise labels for their IGP-learned routes to each other, but not the BGP routes learned from 7200b.

- **BGP**—Here's where the key difference is between MPLS and non-MPLS networks. Instead of needing to put BGP on every router, BGP is needed only at the edges of the network. Instead of 7200b having three BGP peers (7200a, 12008a, 12008b), it has only one—7200a.

  Why is BGP unnecessary in the core? Because an ingress LER, which has to have full BGP routes, knows the next hop for all BGP-learned routes. A label is put on the packet that corresponds to a packet's BGP next hop, and the packet is delivered across the network to that next hop using MPLS. The section "MPLS Versus IP" deals with this issue in great detail.

  Scaling issues because of large IBGP meshing can be solved using route reflectors or confederations; BGP scales well when deployed properly. However, some people like to totally avoid running BGP in the core. Route flaps outside the network can lead to instability in the core, and the fewer BGP speakers you have, the less you have to manage. In certain cases, the core routers might still need to run BGP for other reasons, such as for multicast.

Forwarding Mechanics

This section explains the differences between forwarding a packet in an IP network and forwarding a packet in an MPLS network. A sample service provider network is used to clarify this concept. So far, you have read about FIB and its role in forwarding packets in a Cisco router. This section covers the role of FIB, LIB, and LFIB tables in forwarding packets in an MPLS-enabled network.

MPLS Versus IP

RFC 3031 defines the MPLS architecture. The points where MPLS forwarding deviates from IP forwarding are as follows:

- IP forwarding is based on the destination IP address and the FIB.

- MPLS forwarding is based on the MPLS label and the Label Forwarding Information Base (LFIB).

- Both MPLS and IP forwarding are done hop-by-hop. IP forwarding involves packet classification at every hop, whereas in MPLS forwarding, the classification is done only by the ingress LSR.

Figure 2-4 illustrates a typical ISP backbone, in which external routes are learned through EBGP and are distributed to the core routers through full IBGP mesh. (Route reflectors or confederations are used in larger cores where a full IBGP mesh would not scale.) The route 171.68.0.0/16 is learned from an external peer by gateway router 7200b. All other routers in the core learn about this route through IBGP. Also, the core routers know how to reach each other from routes learned over IGP routing protocols, such as OSPF or IS-IS.

Figure 2-4 *Forwarding Table on Ingress Router 7200a*

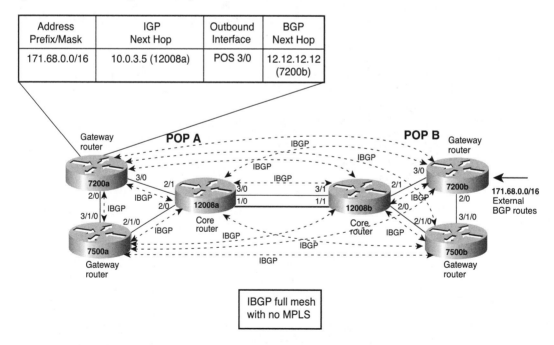

NOTE   Although OSPF and IS-IS seem to be the choice of IGP routing protocols in the service provider backbone, MPLS forwarding doesn't care what your IGP is. For traffic engineering, you need to run IS-IS or OSPF (see Chapter 3, "Information Distribution," for details on why), but if you're not using traffic engineering, you can use any IGP you want.

In Figure 2-4, 7200a is the ingress router that receives packets destined for network 172.68.0.0. Example 2-1 shows the output that displays the contents of the routing table (RIB) on 7200a. As you can see, the entry for 172.68.0.0/16 is the external route that 7200a learned through IBGP.

NOTE   You know that 172.168.0.0 is an IBGP-learned route, not an EBGP-learned route because the administrative distance field in the table shows 200, which indicates that it is an IBGP-learned route, not an EBGP-learned route, whose administrative distance is 20.

Example 2-1 *Router 7200a Routing Table*

```
7200a#show ip route
Codes: C - connected, S - static, I - IGRP, R - RIP, M - mobile, B - BGP
       D - EIGRP, EX - EIGRP external, O - OSPF, IA - OSPF inter area
       N1 - OSPF NSSA external type 1, N2 - OSPF NSSA external type 2
       E1 - OSPF external type 1, E2 - OSPF external type 2, E - EGP
       i - IS-IS, L1 - IS-IS level-1, L2 - IS-IS level-2, ia - IS-IS inter area
       * - candidate default, U - per-user static route, o - ODR

Gateway of last resort is 7.1.5.1 to network 0.0.0.0
B    171.68.0.0/16 [200/0] via 12.12.12.12, 01:10:44
       3.0.0.0/32 is subnetted, 1 subnets
```

When it comes to actually forwarding a data packet, 7200a consults the FIB that is built using the routing table. Example 2-2 shows the FIB entry for 171.68.0.0/16 on 7200a.

Example 2-2 *FIB Entry for 171.68.0.0/16 on 7200a*

```
7200a#show ip cef 171.68.0.0
171.68.0.0/16, version 69, cached adjacency to POS3/0
0 packets, 0 bytes, wccp tag 139
  via 12.12.12.12, 0 dependencies, recursive
    next hop 10.0.3.5, POS3/0 via 12.12.12.12/32
    valid cached adjacency
```

Now that you have examined the contents of the RIB and FIB on 7200a, you know that the control information has been exchanged and that 7200a is ready to forward data destined for network 171.68.0.0. Similarly, the forwarding tables are created on each of the routers in the core (12008a and 12008b in this example). Next, you need to know how forwarding works step by step.

Consider an IP packet with a destination IP address of 171.68.1.1 arriving at the ingress router (7200a in Figure 2-4). When the packet arrives at the ingress port, the router consults the FIB. The destination IP address of 171.68.1.1 is compared to the FIB entries, and the longest-match entry is selected. As a result of this operation, the ingress router (7200a) knows that the packet has to eventually reach 7200b (the egress router) to exit the network. This usually involves forwarding the packet to one of the immediately connected neighbors, which in this case happens to be 12008a. This process is repeated until the packet reaches the exit point. Figure 2-5 shows the next-hop router 12008a consulting the FIB in order to forward the packet. Note that 12008a has two outbound interface entries in the forwarding table, resulting in load sharing.

Figure 2-5   *Forwarding Table on Core Router 12008a*

Address Prefix/Mask	IGP Next Hop	Outbound Interface	BGP Next Hop
171.68.0.0/16	10.0.5.11 (12008b)	POS 1/0	12.12.12.12 (7200b)
171.68.0.0/16	10.0.4.11 (12008b)	ATM 3/0.1	12.12.12.12 (7200b)

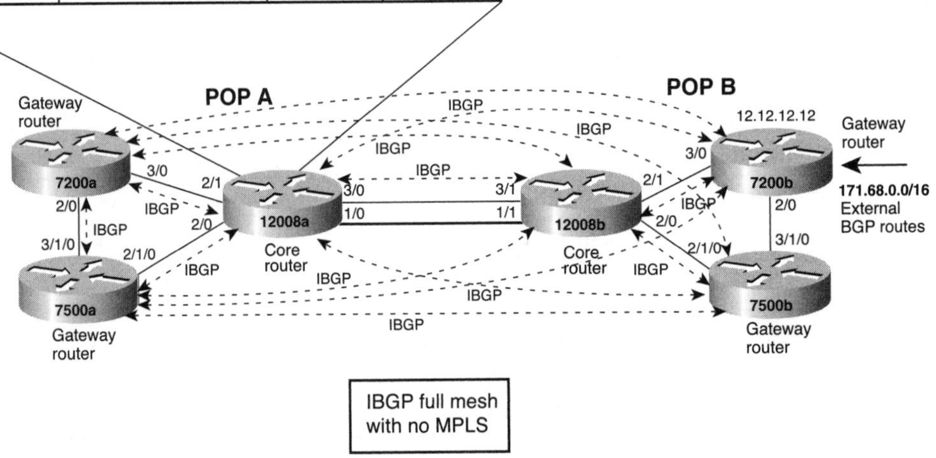

Because you are so accustomed to IP forwarding, you might take for granted how the packet reaches the network's exit point. On closer observation, this process of consulting the FIB for a longest match and mapping each set of destinations to a next-hop router happens on every router in the forwarding path.

Now take a look at Figure 2-6. MPLS forwarding is now turned on in the core. IBGP is now only between gateway routers and need not be run on the core routers. Right after the IGP converges, the loopback address of 7200b 12.12.12.12 has been learned by 7200a. At this time, LDP also converges. As a result, 7200a receives a label of 12323, corresponding to 7200b's loopback address 12.12.12.12 from 12008a. 12008a itself has received a similar label of 12324 from 12008b. 12008b has received a label of POP from 7200b because it is the penultimate hop router and is responsible for removing the top-level label.

Figure 2-6   *Internet Service Provider Backbone with MPLS Forwarding Enabled*

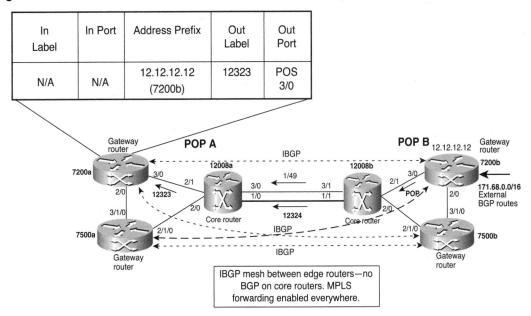

In Label	In Port	Address Prefix	Out Label	Out Port
N/A	N/A	12.12.12.12 (7200b)	12323	POS 3/0

NOTE   Labels distributed by TDP/LDP and RSVP are, in most cases, link-local—meaning it is between any two neighbors and not flooded like OSPF or ISIS. This means that the label value 12323 distributed by 12008a that maps to 12.12.12.12/32 has no relation to the label value 12324 that's received by 12008a, other than the fact that 12008a associated the incoming label value 12323 with the outgoing label value 12324. In other words, 12000b could have given 12008a the label value 42, 967, or 41243, and 12008a still could have distributed the label value 12323.

Next, focus your attention on the data plane. Consider the data packet destined for 171.68.1.1 entering the network at 7200a. 7200a still consults the FIB table because the incoming packet is an IP packet. The difference this time is that 7200a is responsible for label imposition. The longest-match IP lookup in the FIB table occurs. As in the case when MPLS forwarding was not turned on in the core, 7200a concludes that the packet needs to eventually reach 7200b—the exit point for this packet. However, now the FIB table has an entry for the label to be imposed for packets destined for 7200b. This is the value of the Out Label column in Figure 2-6, which happens to be 12323. Example 2-3 shows the FIB table on 7200a. If you focus your attention on the highlighted portion of the output, you'll notice the **tags imposed** field that is now present after MPLS forwarding was enabled in the core. This means that if 7200a receives either an IP packet that needs to be forwarded to 12.12.12.12 or an MPLS packet that has a label value of 36, 7200a switches that packet out as an MPLS packet on POS 3/0 with a label value of 12323.

Example 2-3   *FIB Entry for 171.68.0.0 on 7200a After MPLS Forwarding Has Been Turned On*

```
7200a#show ip cef 171.68.0.0 detail
171.68.0.0/16, version 1934, cached adjacency to POS3/0
0 packets, 0 bytes
  tag information from 12.12.12.12/32, shared
    local tag: 36
    fast tag rewrite with PO3/0, point2point, tags imposed {12323}
  via 12.12.12.12, 0 dependencies, recursive
    next hop 10.0.3.5, POS3/0 via 12.12.12.12/32
    valid cached adjacency
    tag rewrite with PO3/0, point2point, tags imposed {12323}
```

Figure 2-7 shows the packet as it enters 12008a, a core router. The packet is an MPLS packet with a label of 12323.

Figure 2-7   *LFIB on Core Router 12008a*

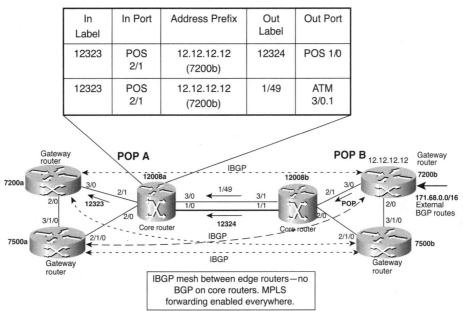

In Label	In Port	Address Prefix	Out Label	Out Port
12323	POS 2/1	12.12.12.12 (7200b)	12324	POS 1/0
12323	POS 2/1	12.12.12.12 (7200b)	1/49	ATM 3/0.1

People who are new to MPLS often wonder how a router knows that this is an MPLS packet and not an IP packet. If you ask yourself how a router knows an IP packet from an IPX packet, you have answered the question. The Layer 2 encapsulation that precedes the IP or IPX header contains a *protocol type* field. In LAN environments, this is *ethertype*. For PPP encapsulation, the Network Control Protocol (NCP) identified what type of Layer 3 packet was being carried, and so on. For MPLS packets, new ethertypes and NCPs have been defined. They are listed in Table 2-2.

Table 2-2   *Layer 2 MPLS Protocol Types*

Encapsulation	Value (in Hexadecimal)
MPLS Control Packet (MPLSCP) for PPP	0x8281
PPP Unicast	0x0281
PPP Multicast	0x0283
LAN Unicast	0x8847
LAN Multicast	0x8848

12008a no longer needs to look at the Layer 3 IP address. It simply consults the LFIB table and knows that there are two places to send an incoming MPLS packet with a label of 12323—POS 1/0 with a label of 12324, and ATM 3/0.1 on the VPI/VCI 1/49. Why are there two paths for this label? Because two equal-cost routes to the destination exist—one via POS and one via ATM. 12008a forwards the packet down POS 1/0 using frame mode. For the path down the ATM 3/0.1 interface, 12008a segments the packet into ATM cells, with each cell using a VPI/VCI value of 1/49. The following discussion focuses on forwarding the packet down the POS 1/0 interface in frame mode. The interesting aspects of cell-mode MPLS are discussed in the section "Label Distribution Concepts." In this chapter, the term *label*, when used in the context of cell-mode MPLS, refers to ATM VPI/VCI.

When the packet with label 12324 enters 12008b on POS1/1, it goes through the same exercise 12008a went through and consults the LFIB table, as shown in Figure 2-7. But because 12008b is the penultimate-hop router and has received a label of POP from 7200b, it removes the label of 12324, exposes the IP header, and forwards the packet to 7200b. It is important to note that all along, the packet's destination IP address was 171.68.1.1, for which neither 12008a nor 12008b had a RIB/FIB entry after BGP was removed from their configs. When the packet enters router 7200b, because the packet is IP, again the FIB is consulted. Because 7200b is a gateway (edge) router, it is running BGP and has learned 171.68.0.0/16 over the EBGP connection. Therefore, it can forward the packet.

Example 2-4 shows the LFIB table that router 12008a uses to forward labeled packets. To forward packets to the 171.68.0.0 network, packets need to be sent to 12.12.12.12 (7200b)—the egress router. Upstream routers, such as 7200a, impose a label 12323 that corresponds to the next-hop address 12.12.12.12 (7200b). Notice, in the highlighted part of Example 2-4, that label 12323 falls under the **Local** column because it was what 12008a assigned for FEC 12.12.12.12 and it distributed this label to 7200a—its upstream neighbor.

Example 2-4   *Displaying 12008a's LFIB Table on the Router*

```
12008a#show mpls forwarding
Local   Outgoing   Prefix         Bytes tag   Outgoing    Next Hop
tag     tag or VC  or Tunnel Id   switched    interface
12318   Pop tag    10.0.57.0/24   0           PO1/0       point2point
        1/43       10.0.57.0/24   0           AT3/0.1     point2point
12319   12320      10.0.86.0/24   0           PO1/0       point2point
        1/44       10.0.86.0/24   0           AT3/0.1     point2point
12320   12321      10.1.1.1/32    0           PO1/0       point2point
        1/45       10.1.1.1/32    0           AT3/0.1     point2point
12321   12322      10.1.1.2/32    0           PO1/0       point2point
        1/46       10.1.1.2/32    0           AT3/0.1     point2point
12322   12326      16.16.16.16/32 0           PO1/0       point2point
        1/51       16.16.16.16/32 0           AT3/0.1     point2point
12323   12324      12.12.12.12/32 575         PO1/0       point2point
        1/49       12.12.12.12/32 0           AT3/0.1     point2point
12324   12325      13.13.13.13/32 0           PO1/0       point2point
        1/50       13.13.13.13/32 0           AT3/0.1     point2point
12325   12327      17.17.17.17/32 144         PO1/0       point2point
```

As the output in Example 2-4 shows, 12008a has two ways of reaching 12.12.12.12 (the loopback interface of 7200b).

With MPLS forwarding, just as in IP forwarding, the CEF table (the same as FIB) is consulted. If there are multiple outbound links to the next hop, load sharing is possible, as demonstrated in Example 2-5. The highlighted portion shows that 12008a is doing per-destination load sharing.

Example 2-5 *Router 12008a's CEF Table Shows Load Sharing for Labeled Packets*

```
12008a#show ip cef 12.12.12.12 internal
12.12.12.12/32, version 385, per-destination sharing
0 packets, 0 bytes
  tag information set, shared
    local tag: 12323
  via 10.0.5.11, POS1/0, 0 dependencies
    traffic share 1
    next hop 10.0.5.11, POS1/0
    unresolved
    valid adjacency
    tag rewrite with PO1/0, point2point, tags imposed {12324}
  via 10.0.4.11, ATM3/0.1, 1 dependency
    traffic share 1
    next hop 10.0.4.11, ATM3/0.1
    unresolved
    valid adjacency
    tag rewrite with ATM3/0.1, point2point, tags imposed {1/49(vcd=65)}

  0 packets, 0 bytes switched through the prefix
  tmstats: external 0 packets, 0 bytes
           internal 0 packets, 0 bytes
  Load distribution: 0 1 0 1 0 1 0 1 0 1 0 1 0 1 0 1 (refcount 2)

  Hash  OK  Interface            Address         Packets  Tags imposed
  1     Y   POS1/0               point2point           0  {12324}
  2     Y   ATM3/0.1             point2point           0  {1/49}
  3     Y   POS1/0               point2point           0  {12324}
  4     Y   ATM3/0.1             point2point           0  {1/49}
  5     Y   POS1/0               point2point           0  {12324}
  6     Y   ATM3/0.1             point2point           0  {1/49}
  7     Y   POS1/0               point2point           0  {12324}
  8     Y   ATM3/0.1             point2point           0  {1/49}
  9     Y   POS1/0               point2point           0  {12324}
  10    Y   ATM3/0.1             point2point           0  {1/49}
  11    Y   POS1/0               point2point           0  {12324}
  12    Y   ATM3/0.1             point2point           0  {1/49}
  13    Y   POS1/0               point2point           0  {12324}
  14    Y   ATM3/0.1             point2point           0  {1/49}
  15    Y   POS1/0               point2point           0  {12324}
  16    Y   ATM3/0.1             point2point           0  {1/49}
  refcount 5
```

As shown in Example 2-5, packets destined for 12.12.12.12 on 12008a are load shared on the two outbound links. The load sharing is CEF's standard *per-source-destination* by default. This means that the packet's source and destination IP addresses are hashed. As a result, it uses one of the 16 buckets. You can also turn on *per-packet* load sharing by configuring the outbound interfaces in question.

FIB, LIB, and LFIB and Their Roles in MPLS Forwarding

If you are wondering how the FIB, LIB, and LFIB tables relate to each other, this section summarizes the roles of each of these tables and how they are populated.

The FIB table knows only about IP packets and therefore is consulted only when the incoming packet is an IP packet. Although the incoming packet is an IP packet, the outgoing packet might not be! If one or more label bindings have been received for the packet's destination, the packet is MPLS forwarded. Looking at the CEF table entry for destination 12.12.12.12 on 12008a (as in Example 2-5) tells you whether the outgoing packet is an IP packet or an MPLS packet. If it has an entry of **tags imposed** against the CEF entry, the outgoing packet is MPLS.

In the case of 7200a, destination 12.12.12.12 has an outgoing label of 12323. This results in the packet's entering the next-hop router—12008a with an MPLS label on it. This time, the LFIB table is consulted on 12008a. Example 2-6 shows that if an MPLS packet came in with a label of 12323, it would have to be switched out of the ATM 3/0.1 interface with a VPI/VCI value of 1/49 or with a label of 12324 on interface POS1/0.

Example 2-6 shows a segment of the LFIB table corresponding to 12.12.12.12.

Example 2-6 *Segment of 12008a's LFIB Table Corresponding to 12.12.12.12*

Local tag	Outgoing tag or VC	Prefix or Tunnel Id	Bytes tag switched	Outgoing interface	Next Hop
12323	12324	12.12.12.12/32	575	PO1/0	point2point
	1/49	12.12.12.12/32	0	AT3/0.1	point2point

Now consider the case of the packet being switched over the POS link with an MPLS label of 12324.

Where did all these labels come from? Labels can be distributed between LSRs using various methods. If LDP or TDP protocols are used, label bindings are exchanged between LSRs and their neighbors. This information is stored in the LIB. You can view the LIB's contents using the **show mpls ip bindings** *address* command. You can see in Example 2-7 the contents of the LIB that holds the label bindings for 12.12.12.12.

Example 2-7 *Viewing LIB Contents*

```
12008a#show mpls ip binding 12.12.12.12 32
  12.12.12.12/32
        in label:      12325
        out label:     36         lsr: 4.4.4.4:0
        out label:     12324      lsr: 11.11.11.11:0
        out label:     37         lsr: 3.3.3.3:0
        out vc label: 1/49        lsr: 11.11.11.11:2    ATM3/0.1
                       Active     ingress 1 hop (vcd 18)
```

Notice in Example 2-7 that several *remote bindings* exist in the LIB, but the forwarding table shows only two entries. This is because only the bindings that are received from the current IGP next-hop router are used, even though all the bindings are retained on the Cisco routers because they employ the liberal retention mode (discussed further in the section "Liberal and Conservative Retention Modes"). Look at 12008a's routing entry for 12.12.12.12 in Example 2-8.

Example 2-8 *RIB Entry for 12.12.12.12 on 12008a*

```
12008a#show ip route 12.12.12.12
Routing entry for 12.12.12.12/32
  Known via "ospf 100", distance 110, metric 3, type intra area
  Last update from 10.0.4.11 on ATM3/0.1, 00:41:50 ago
  Routing Descriptor Blocks:
  * 10.0.5.11, from 12.12.12.12, 00:41:50 ago, via POS1/0
      Route metric is 3, traffic share count is 1
    10.0.4.11, from 12.12.12.12, 00:41:50 ago, via ATM3/0.1
      Route metric is 3, traffic share count is 1
      Route metric is 3, traffic share count is 1
```

To figure out exactly how labels 12324 and 1/49 became the outgoing labels for 12.12.12.12, as shown in Example 2-6, you have to first look at the next hops for 12.12.12.12 from Example 2-8. They happen to be 10.0.5.11 and 10.0.4.11 (which are highlighted in Example 2-8). Incidentally, these next hops happen to be two links of 12008b, whose router ID is 11.11.11.11. Using this information, you can go back to the LIB (refer to Example 2-7) to look for what label bindings 12008a received from 11.11.11.11. You'll find labels 12324 and 1/49 over the two interfaces POS 1/0 and ATM 3/0.1, respectively.

Table 2-3 summarizes the input and output packet types and the table used for forwarding.

Table 2-3 *I/O Packet Types and Related Forwarding Tables*

Packet Type	Table Used for Packet Lookup	How to Look at This Table
IP to IP	FIB	**show ip cef**
IP to MPLS	FIB	**show ip cef**
MPLS to MPLS	LFIB	**show mpls forwarding-table**
MPLS to IP	LFIB	**show mpls forwarding-table**

Label Distribution Concepts

The preceding section elaborated on how forwarding works after the FIB and LFIB tables have been populated. This section covers the various methods of distributing label bindings.

When labels are distributed, what's actually distributed is a label, an IP prefix, and a mask length. Generally, this entire process is called *label distribution* rather than *label, prefix, and mask distribution*.

To understand how LSRs generate and distribute labels, you need to understand some terminology introduced in RFC 3031.

Ordered Versus Independent Control

As far as generating labels is concerned, regardless of what control method is applicable, the LSRs generate labels independently and have no relation to the received labels. As you would anticipate, there have to be *reserved* label values that are either used for control or have some special meaning.

The label values 0 to 15 are reserved. This means that the lowest label number you see that maps to an IP prefix is 16. Because the label space is 20 bits, the highest label you ever see advertised is $2^{20}-1$, or 1,048,575. This is subject to change, though. As long as an allocated label value is between 16 and 1,048,575, it's legal.

Only four out of the 16 reserved label values are currently defined in RFC 3032, "MPLS Label Stack Encoding":

0—IPv4 Explicit Null Label
1—Router Alert Label
2—IPv6 Explicit Null Label
3—Implicit Null Label

Except for MPLS edge applications, labels are generated only for IGP-learned prefixes (including static routes) in the routing. Why aren't labels allocated for BGP-learned routes? Because doing so is completely unnecessary. Again, for IPv4 routes (the non-MPLS-VPN case), if the egress LER set next-hop-self in BGP, all that is needed is a label and an IGP route for the next hop of the BGP-learned route. For example, consider the external route 171.68.0.0 that is learned by 7200b in Figure 2-6. By doing next-hop-self, 7200b sets the next hop for 171.68.0.0 to 12.12.12.12 (7200b's BGP router ID and Loopback0) before it advertises 171.68.0.0 to 7200a with IBGP. Because IGP routes have been exchanged and label distribution has occurred, 7200a has a label for 12.12.12.12. If it uses this label for packets destined for 171.68.0.0, the packet is delivered to 7200b as a result of MPLS forwarding. There is no need for a label for 171.68.0.0. Any packets destined for 171.68.0.0 are simply delivered to 12.12.12.12, which then routes the IP packet normally.

After LSRs have generated these labels that are associated with IP prefixes, two ways exist to distribute them:

- **Ordered LSP control mode**—The LSR waits to receive bindings from its downstream neighbors before sending the labels it generated to its upstream neighbors.

- **Independent LSP control mode**—LSRs are free to distribute the label bindings to all their neighbors (downstream and upstream) without waiting to receive bindings from their downstream neighbors.

LDP uses independent LSP control mode in frame-based networks and ordered LSP control mode in cell-mode networks; RSVP uses ordered LSP control mode.

Unsolicited Downstream Versus Downstream-on-Demand

In *unsolicited label distribution,* a router advertises labels for all prefixes in its IGP to all neighbors, whether or not they ask for them. Because the label advertisements are not used to make any routing decisions, it's OK for a router to send labels for all prefixes it knows about to all neighbors, even if those neighbors are not using the advertising router as the next hop for a route. LDP is not a routing protocol; it depends on the routing protocol to make loop-free routing decisions (although there are some loop detection and loop prevention measures in LDP). Figure 2-8 shows how routers 12008a and 12008b look up their RIB and assign labels for all IGP-derived routes. They then distribute these routes to their neighbors in an unsolicited manner.

Figure 2-8   *Unsolicited Downstream Distribution of Labels Destined for IGP-Derived Routes*

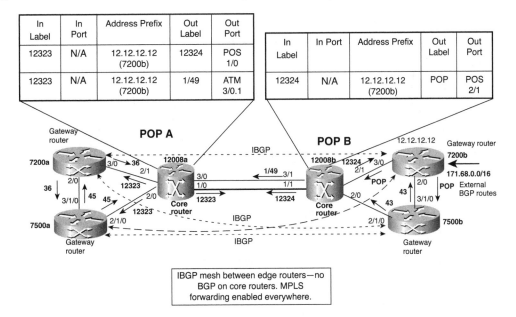

Unsolicited mode works fine in most cases. However, with label distribution over ATM, multiple labels might need to be distributed for the same destination IP address/mask, depending on the number of neighbors requiring these labels. This happens when an ATM switch cannot support something called *VC Merge* (discussed in the later section "VC Merge"). For now, just realize that rather than one label per destination prefix, an ATM LSR might need to distribute one label per destination prefix, multiplied by the number of neighbors. If an ATM LSR has 500 routes and 12 neighbors, it would have to distribute 500 * 12 = 6,000 labels. Remember that a *label* in cell mode is a VPI/VCI. Because of this, the VPI/VCI space can be depleted quickly on platforms that have limited VPI/VCI space. Therefore, ATM switches do not hand out labels for prefixes unless they are *asked* for labels for those prefixes. This is known as Downstream-on-Demand (DoD) label distribution.

With DoD label distribution, an LSR determines if it needs to obtain a label for a prefix. After this determination has been made, the LSR asks its next hop (downstream neighbor) for a label. The downstream neighbor, even though it might have generated a label for the prefix in question, abstains from sending its label bindings until it has received such a binding from its downstream neighbor. This process continues until the penultimate-hop LSR requests the LER (the egress LSR for this LSP) for a label binding. After this happens, label bindings flow from downstream to upstream LSRs—hence the term *downstream-on-demand*. Figure 2-9 illustrates an example of DoD label distribution.

Figure 2-9 *DoD and ATM*

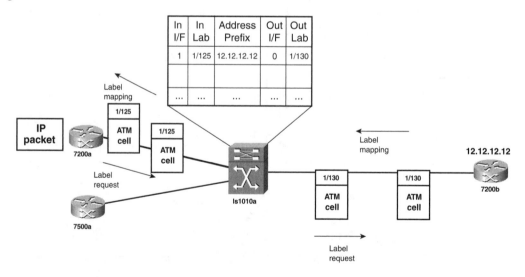

In Figure 2-9, the ingress router 7200a sends a label request for 12.12.12.12 to the ATM LSR ls1010a. ls1010a then sends a request to the egress LSR (router) 7200b on the right. The egress LSR replies with a label mapping with a label value of 1/130. After ls1010a receives this binding, it sends a label of 1/125 (label mapping) to 7200a. When an IP packet enters 7200a, it is segmented into ATM cells with a VPI/VCI value of 1/125 (exchanged in the MPLS control plane) and is sent to ls1010a. ls1010a swaps labels (VPI/VCIs) and switches out the cells with label values of 1/130.

The label range (VPI/VCI) and the VPI that each ATM LSR uses can be configured.

NOTE   There's no such thing as "MPLS cells" in an ATM network. ATM-LSRs don't distinguish MPLS-created ATM VPI/VCIs from those created with other ATM signalling protocols. To the ATM switching hardware, incoming cells are just ATM cells and are treated as such. If an incoming cell has a certain VPI/VCI value, it is switched out on a different port with a particular VPI/VCI value. The only place where a distinction is made between MPLS-derived ATM VPI/VCIs and VPI/VCIs derived from ATM signalling protocols is at the control plane level.

Liberal and Conservative Label Retention Modes

When LSRs receive label bindings from neighbors that are not routing next hops, they might choose to keep the bindings for future use in case the LSRs that sent these bindings become next hops. This approach is called *liberal label retention mode*. When LSRs choose to discard label bindings that are not currently useful, this is called *conservative label retention mode*. Liberal label retention mode uses more space in the LIB table but expedites convergence. This is because you don't have to wait for label bindings to arrive after routing converges in case of a link failure to an LSR that was previously the next hop. In conservative label retention mode, the opposite is true. This mode saves space in the LIB but suffers from slower convergence. Current Cisco IOS Software routers use liberal label retention mode.

Label Space

LSRs can generate labels that have either *global* space (sometimes known as *per-platform* space) or *interface* space. Sometimes, the word *scope* is substituted for *space,* so *global label space* and *global label scope* are interchangeable terms. *Global label space* is when a router generates a label that's unique to a particular destination FEC, but that is not associated with any particular incoming interface. An LSR could also choose to generate labels that are unique only to the interface or port used to send the label binding to the upstream node. This is called *per-interface label space*. Per-interface label space is not a problem as long as an LSR can differentiate between packets coming in on one interface and packets coming in on another. Cisco routers allocate labels from per-platform label space for frame-mode and per-interface label space for cell-mode; ATM switches use per-interface label space so as to conserve VCI/VPI space.

Keeping track of these concepts and in which environment they apply can be tricky. Understanding the label distribution methods is simple when you understand the underlying protocols, though. Table 2-4 summarizes this information.

Table 2-4   *Label Distribution Scheme Summary*

Label Distribution Method	Control	Distribution	Retention	Label Space
Frame Mode TDP and LDP	Unordered	Downstream unsolicited	Liberal	Per platform
Cell Mode (LC-ATM) TDP and LDP	Ordered	Downstream-on-Demand	Conservative	Per interface
RSVP-TE (Frame Mode Only)	Ordered	Downstream-on-Demand	Conservative	Per platform

Cell Mode Idiosyncrasies

Certain restrictions apply in cell-mode MPLS:

- The ATM header doesn't carry the TTL field.
- PHP is not supported.
- No route summarization can be done on ATM LSRs.

You might wonder how permanent packet loops are prevented without the use of TTLs when ATM LSRs are used in the core. The two pieces to solving this problem are

- A feature of LDP known as the *hop count* TLV is used in LSP signalling with LDP in cell-mode MPLS networks. Because ATM LSRs don't have a way to decrement the packet TTL at every hop, the router that is an ingress to a cell-mode MPLS cloud must decrement the packet TTL by the number of hops in the cell-mode cloud.

- A feature of LDP known as the *path vector* TLV contains a list of all hops an LSP traverses within a cell-mode cloud. The path vector can be used for loop detection in the control plane. For example, if the same LSR shows up twice in the path vector for a particular LSP, the LSP must be looping and must not be used.

NOTE   LDP path vector and hop count TLV are not used in frame-mode networks because the TTL in a label is decremented at every hop, just like an IP header. When the TTL value reaches 0, the packet is no longer forwarded.

If the ingress LSR determines that the packet would not make it through the core, it is the ingress LER's responsibility to send an "ICMP unreachable TTL expired" message to the source of the data packet.

PHP is not supported on ATM LSRs because it would require the ATM LSR to send out a packet without a top label on it, which would mean sending out the cells without a VPI/VCI. This makes no sense in an ATM environment.

Even though an ATM LSR is required to run a routing protocol in the control plane, it should not perform *route summarization*. The reason for this is that the LSR performing route summarization would be required to do an IP lookup. Although an ATM LSR is capable of doing an IP lookup, this would require reassembling a packet's cells back into an entire packet. This turns an ATM switch into a router, which is not what an ATM switch is best at.

When operating in cell mode, ATM LSRs set up a control VC (VCI/VPI 0/32 by default) to exchange all control information.

Example 2-9 shows output from a router that is speaking cell mode to an ATM switch.

Example 2-9 *ATM VC Table on a Router Operating in Cell Mode*

```
gsr4#show atm vc
                VCD /                                      Peak Avg/Min Burst
    Interface   Name     VPI   VCI   Type   Encaps   Kbps    Kbps   Cells Sts
    5/0.1       1         0    32    PVC    SNAP     622000 622000         UP
    5/0.1       84        1    61    TVC    MUX      622000 622000         UP
    5/0.1       85        1    62    TVC    MUX      622000 622000         UP
    5/0.1       86        1    63    TVC    MUX      622000 622000         UP
    5/0.1       87        1    64    TVC    MUX      622000 622000         UP
    5/0.1       88        1    65    TVC    MUX      622000 622000         UP
    5/0.1       89        1    66    TVC    MUX      622000 622000         UP
    5/0.1       90        1    67    TVC    MUX      622000 622000         UP
    5/0.1       91        1    68    TVC    MUX      622000 622000         UP
    5/0.1       92        1    69    TVC    MUX      622000 622000         UP
    5/0.1       93        1    70    TVC    MUX      622000 622000         UP
    5/0.1       94        1    71    TVC    MUX      622000 622000         UP
```

The highlighted text in Example 2-9 shows the MPLS control VC being set up on VPI/VCI 0/32. The others that show up as TVCs are *tag VCs* (also called Label Virtual Circuits [LVCs]) that are set up as a result of the label binding exchange that occurs on the control VC. A TVC is used to transport the data cells that make up an MPLS packet.

Example 2-10 is from an ATM switch (LS1010) that is connected to ATM5/0 of gsr4 from Example 2-9. The output from the LS1010 ATM switch is similar to that of gsr4. Again, the control VC setup on VPI/VCI 0/32 is highlighted.

Example 2-10 *ATM VC Table on ATM LSR*

```
ls1010-18#show atm vc interface a1/0/0
    Interface    VPI   VCI   Type    X-Interface    X-VPI  X-VCI  Encap  Status
    ATM1/0/0     0     32    PVC     ATM2/0/0       0      55     SNAP   UP
    ATM1/0/0     1     61    TVC(I)  ATM2/0/0       0      71     MUX    UP
    ATM1/0/0     1     62    TVC(I)  ATM1/1/0       42     81            UP
    ATM1/0/0     1     63    TVC(I)  ATM1/1/0       42     82            UP
```

continues

Example 2-10 *ATM VC Table on ATM LSR (Continued)*

ATM1/0/0	1	64	TVC(I) ATM1/1/0	42	83	UP
ATM1/0/0	1	65	TVC(I) ATM1/1/0	42	84	UP
ATM1/0/0	1	66	TVC(I) ATM1/1/0	42	85	UP
ATM1/0/0	1	67	TVC(I) ATM1/1/0	42	86	UP
ATM1/0/0	1	68	TVC(I) ATM1/1/0	42	87	UP
ATM1/0/0	1	69	TVC(I) ATM1/1/0	42	88	UP
ATM1/0/0	1	70	TVC(I) ATM1/1/0	42	89	UP
ATM1/0/0	1	71	TVC(I) ATM1/1/0	42	90	UP

VC Merge

Figure 2-10 illustrates an example in which an ATM LSR, ls1010a, has two upstream routers, 7200a and 7500a, and one downstream neighbor, 7200b. As a result of DoD, ls1010a receives a label binding of 1/130 for prefix 12.12.12.12 from 7200b. Because ls1010a has two upstream neighbors, it generates two labels, 1/125 and 1/128, for 12.12.12.12. ls1010a sends label 1/125 to 7200a and 1/128 to 7500a. However, when 7200a and 7500a send cells belonging to IP packets 1 and 2, the label swapping on ls1010a results in all these cells being switched out on interface 0 with a label value of 1/130. The problem that this creates is that router 7200b, which is responsible for reassembling the cells into IP packets, cannot do so correctly because the cells are out of order. 7200b has no way of telling which cells belong to packet 1 and which belong to packet 2.

Figure 2-10 *DoD Problem*

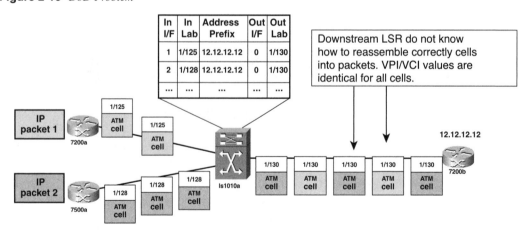

Figure 2-11 shows one approach to solving the problem illustrated in Figure 2-10. ls1010a could request two labels from 7200b and map each one to the labels it sends to the upstream neighbors. Now, when 7200b receives the cells belonging to IP Packet 1 and IP Packet 2, it has no problem reassembling them, because all cells that have a label value of 1/130 belong to IP Packet 1, and those that have a label value of 1/140 belong to IP Packet 2. The problem with this approach is that you would use additional VCs between ls1010a and 7200b, which would be a concern on ATM LSRs that have limited VPI/VCI space.

Figure 2-11 *DoD Nonmerge Solution*

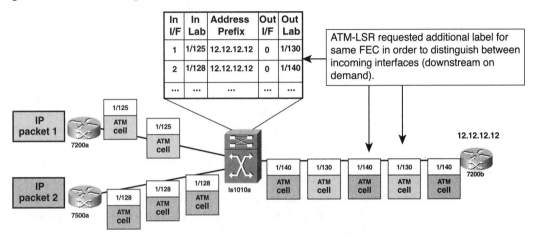

Figure 2-12 illustrates VC Merge. In this case, ls1010a buffers all the cells belonging to IP Packet 2 until IP Packet 1 is sent out. Now 7200b reassembles cells belonging to IP packet 1 first and then receives the cells belonging to IP Packet 2. There are no out-of-order cells.

Figure 2-12 *DoD VC Merge Solution*

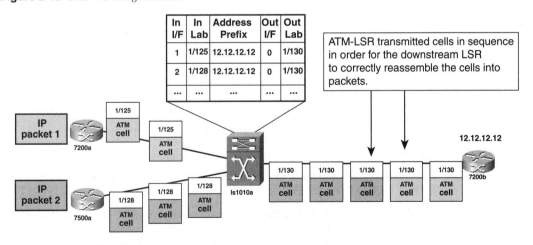

Note that ls1010a does not do an IP lookup on the cells it has received. ls1010a doesn't pay attention to the packet's contents; it just buffers them in order to achieve VC Merge.

Label Distribution Protocol

Standardized in RFC 3036, "LDP Specification," LDP exchanges labels for IGP and static routes. As mentioned earlier, Cisco's implementation of MPLS traffic engineering is not based on CR-LDP, which is an extension of LDP protocol for constrained based routing. However, understanding LDP is useful even in an MPLS TE network; often, MPLS-enabled networks run a mix of LDP and RSVP in different places.

Because this book is not really about LDP, and because RFC 3036 is more than 130 pages long, an exhaustive discussion of LDP is out of the scope of this chapter (and book). However, the following sections present enough details for you to understand the basics of LDP, as well as some of the packet format details. When you finish reading this section, you will know how to configure LDP, what it's used for, and some of how the protocol works.

LDP PDU Header

Before diving into the four major LDP functions, it is useful to understand the basic packet format behind LDP. LDP is carried in either UDP or TCP. Either way, an LDP packet always starts with a Protocol Data Unit (PDU) header, as illustrated in Figure 2-13.

Figure 2-13 *Generic LDP PDU Header Format*

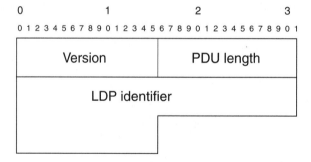

The LDP PDU header is comprised of the following fields:

- **Version**—Currently, the only version of LDP defined is 1.

- **PDU Length**—The length of the PDU, including any data carried in the packet after the PDU header.

- **LDP Identifier**—An LDP identifier is a six-octet string used to identify a particular label space. The first four octets of this LDP identifier are the LSR-ID. The value of the next two octets depends on the label space. If this LDP PDU pertains to global label space, these two octets are both 0. If this LDP PDU is per-interface label space, these two octets are a unique number assigned by the originator of the LDP PDU. By convention, this LDP identifier is written as *RouterID:space identifier*. So, global label space advertisements from a router with an LSR-ID of 1.2.3.4 are written as 1.2.3.4:0; per-interface label space is written as 1.2.3.4:1 or some other nonzero number.

LDP Message Format

The LDP PDU header is followed by one or more LDP messages, the general format of which is shown in Figure 2-14.

Figure 2-14 *Generic LDP Message Format*

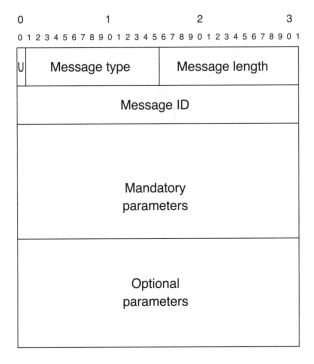

The Unknown (U) bit is set to 1 if the message type is Unknown. No messages defined in the LDP specification have a type of Unknown, so this bit is always 0.

Table 2-5 shows the possible values for the Message Type field.

Table 2-5   *Message Types*

Message Name	Message Number
Notification	0x0001
Hello	0x0100
Initialization	0x0200
Keepalive	0x0201
Address	0x0300
Address Withdraw	0x0301
Label Mapping	0x0400

continues

Table 2-5 *Message Types (Continued)*

Message Name	Message Number
Label Request	0x0401
Label Release	0x0403
Label Withdraw	0x0402
Label Abort Request	0x0404

The Message Length is the length of a set of fields after the message length (Message ID + Mandatory Parameters + Optional Parameters), in bytes.

The Message ID is sometimes used to associate some messages with others. For example, a message sent in response to another message uses the Message ID of the message to which it's responding.

The Mandatory Parameters and Optional Parameters depend on the types of message sent. They are covered in the upcoming sections about different LDP functions. The Mandatory and Optional Parameters are often TLV (Type/Length/Value) triplets, a common way of encoding arbitrary amounts of data in a packet.

When a TLV is used inside an LDP message, the generic format looks like Figure 2-15.

Figure 2-15 *LDP TLV Format*

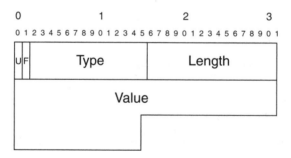

The U bit, if set to 1, means the receiving router should ignore it if it understands this message.

The Forward (F) bit is relevant only if the U bit is set to 1. Because these bits are always 0 in the messages defined in RFC 3036, we will not go into any more detail on them.

The Type field indicates the type of data carried in the Value portion of the TLV.

The Length field indicates the length of the data carried in the Value portion of the TLV. The actual values in the Type, Length, and Value fields depends on the Message Type and what exactly LDP is trying to accomplish with a particular message.

LDP's Major Functions

LDP has four major functions:

- Neighbor discovery
- Session establishment and maintenance
- Label advertisement
- Notification

Neighbor Discovery

Like most other network protocols, LDP has the concept of neighbors. LDP uses UDP/TCP ports 646 for discovery. LDP has two different types of neighbors:

- **Directly connected neighbors**—These neighbors have a Layer 2 connection between them. So, routers that are connected by any Layer 2 link—whether a POS link, an ATM PVC, an Ethernet connection, or a DS-3 interface—are considered directly connected for LDP. Neighbors connected by a logical connection such as GRE tunnel are also considered directly connected. The basic commonality over such connections is the fact that a neighbor is one IP hop away.

- **Non-directly connected neighbors**—These neighbors do not have a Layer 2 connection between them. More importantly, these neighbors are several IP hops away. Routers that are connected to each other by MPLS traffic engineering tunnels and that have LDP enabled on them are considered non-directly connected. Such an LDP session is called a *targeted* or *directed* LDP session.

NOTE   Although the use of LDP over directly connected neighbors might be obvious, the application of LDP between non-directly connected neighbors is not. Directed LDP sessions find use in any application in which an end-to-end LSP needs to be built, preserving an end-to-end application label. The section "LDP on a Tunnel Interface" in Chapter 10, "MPLS TE Deployment Tips," discusses this process in greater detail.

The only difference between directly and non-directly connected neighbors is in how they discover each other. LSRs discover directly connected neighbors by sending LDP hello messages encapsulated in UDP to the 224.0.0.2 multicast address (all routers on a subnet). These packets are known as *hello messages*.

Non-directly connected neighbors can't be reached through a multicast UDP packet. So, the same hello messages are sent as unicasts (also to UDP port 646). This requires that an LSR know ahead of time who it wants to have as a non-directly connected neighbor. This can be achieved through configuration.

Configuring directly connected neighbors is easy. All you need to do is enable **tag-switching ip** or **mpls ip** at the interface level. **mpls label protocol ldp** can be configured either on an interface, as demonstrated in Example 2-11, or at the global level, as shown in Example 2-12.

Example 2-11 *Configuring Directly Connected Neighbors for LDP*

```
interface POS3/0
 ip address 192.168.17.15 255.255.255.0
 mpls label protocol ldp
 tag-switching ip
end
```

tag-switching Versus mpls in the CLI

As mentioned earlier, Cisco's TDP is the predecessor to LDP. Migrating the TDP CLI commands to support LDP while still maintaining backward compatibility is a nontrivial problem. You often see some commands that say **tag-switching** and others that say **mpls**. These commands are often functionally identical; **tag-switching ip** and **mpls ip**, for example, do the same thing. Which protocol you use is controlled by the command **mpls label protocol {ldp | tdp}**. The command-line interface (CLI) might well have changed between the time this book was written and now. For the most up-to-date details, check the LDP documentation. Some online links are provided in Appendix B.

The command **mpls label protocol ldp** is necessary because the label protocol on an interface defaults to TDP. However, the CLI was designed to be flexible. Instead of overriding the default of TDP on every interface, you can instead configure **mpls label protocol ldp** at a *global* level, and then the interface default becomes LDP. Example 2-12 shows **mpls label protocol** specified only at the global level, which results in all the interfaces using LDP instead of TDP.

Example 2-12 *Configuring LDP for All Interfaces on the LSR*

```
!
mpls label protocol ldp
...
!
interface POS3/0
 ip address 192.168.17.15 255.255.255.0
 mpls ip
end
```

You can use the command **mpls label protocol tdp** on a per-interface basis to configure TDP if you need those interfaces to be TDP instead of LDP.

Use **show mpls interfaces** to verify that you have the proper interface configuration, as demonstrated in Example 2-13.

Example 2-13 *Verifying TDP/LDP Configuration on an Interface*

```
vxr15#show mpls interfaces
Interface            IP           Tunnel   Operational
FastEthernet0/0      Yes (tdp)    No       Yes
POS3/0               Yes (ldp)    Yes      Yes
```

You might notice that the **IP** column shows a Fast Ethernet interface that is configured to run TDP, whereas the POS interface is configured to run LDP. The **Operational** column should say Yes if the interface is up/up.

So, what do LDP hello packets look like?

After the PDU header, an LDP hello message is used. Its format is shown in Figure 2-16.

Figure 2-16 *LDP Hello Message Format*

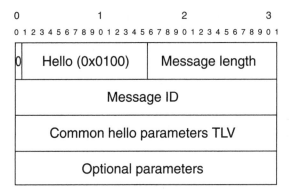

As Figure 2-16 shows, the hello message contains a Common Hello Parameters TLV. This TLV contains information about the type of LDP session that the LSR wants to establish. Figure 2-17 shows the Common Hello Parameters TLV format.

Hold Time is the hello holdtime in seconds. The default holdtime for directly connected sessions is 5 seconds. Hellos for directly connected sessions are sent every 5 seconds, whereas for targeted LDP neighbors, the holdtime is 180 seconds (hellos are still sent every 5 seconds). Hello messages are constantly being exchanged between a pair of LDP neighbors acting as link keepalives between the LDP neighbors.

The Targeted Hello (T) and Request Targeted Hello (R) bits are set to 1 when LSRs are forming non-directly connected LDP neighbors and are 0 otherwise.

Figure 2-17 *Common Hello Parameters TLV Format*

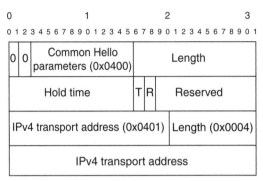

The IPv4 Transport Address TLV is optional, but it is implemented in Cisco's implementation of LDP. It is the IP address of the LSR initiating the LDP session over TCP. Generally, the transport address is the LSR ID of the transmitting router and it is most likely Loopback0.

All these packet formats might be confusing. Figure 2-18 shows you what an entire LDP packet looks like.

Figure 2-18 *Complete LDP Packet Format*

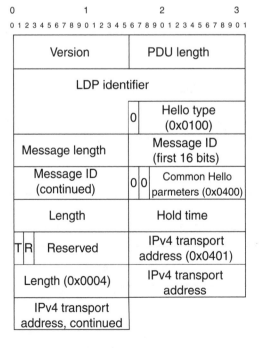

The LDP PDU Header is the Version, PDU Length, and LDP Identifier. The hello message starts immediately after the LDP Identifier. It consists of the Hello Type, Message Length, and Message ID. After the Message ID is the Common Hello Parameters TLV header, the Length of the Common Hello Parameters TLV, and other pieces of the Common Hello Parameters TLV.

Session Establishment and Maintenance

After discovering potential LDP neighbors, LDP session establishment can begin. LDP session establishment is a two-step procedure:

1 Determine who plays the *active* role and who plays the *passive* role in this establishment.

2 Initialize the session parameters.

Active or passive roles are determined by comparing the transport address (almost always the LSR-ID of the transmitter, which is Loopback0) in the hello packet. If the receiver determines that he is the one who should be active, he initiates a TCP session. If not, he waits for the sender to initiate it.

As shown in Figure 2-19, R1 receives hello R2:0 on link L1. R1 compares its transport address, 1.1.1.1, to that of R2, 2.2.2.2. Because R2's transport address is greater numerically, R1 plays the passive role and waits for R2 to establish the TCP connection. The TCP connection is initiated to well-known TCP port 646.

Figure 2-19 *LDP Session Establishment*

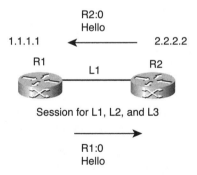

After the TCP session is established, the LSRs negotiate the session parameters through LDP initialization messages. These include version, label distribution method (unsolicited downstream or DoD), timer values (the hold-down time for the TCP connection), VPI/VCI ranges for label-controlled ATM, and so on.

After it is established, the session is maintained by sending periodic UDP discovery hellos and keepalive messages within the TCP session.

Various LDP timers can be checked with the **show mpls ldp parameters** command, as demonstrated in Example 2-14.

Example 2-14 *Checking LDP Timers*

```
gsr1#show mpls ldp parameters
Protocol version: 1
Downstream label pool: min label: 16; max label: 100000
Session hold time: 180 sec; keep alive interval: 60 sec
Discovery hello: holdtime: 15 sec; interval: 5 sec
Discovery targeted hello: holdtime: 180 sec; interval: 5 sec
Downstream on Demand max hop count: 255
TDP for targeted sessions
LDP initial/maximum backoff: 15/120 sec
LDP loop detection: off
```

The holdtime and hello interval can be changed with the following global configuration knob:

mpls ldp discovery {hello | targeted-hello} {holdtime | interval} *1-2147483 seconds*

Holding up an LDP session is dependent on receiving LDP keepalives on a regular basis. Changing the discovery holdtime changes the amount of time that can pass without a keepalive's being received from a neighbor. In other words, if the holdtime is increased, an LSR waits a little longer before declaring a neighbor down if it has not received keepalives from that neighbor.

The discovery interval is how often hellos are sent from a particular router. This value is not advertised in any LDP message; it is local to the receiver of the hellos.

As with so many other timers, don't change these unless you're sure you have a good reason to change them. However, there might be times when you know you have a congested link, and you want LDP to be more patient in receiving keepalives before declaring a neighbor down. Similarly, you might want LDP to detect neighbor failure faster, so you might want to turn the timers down, making them more sensitive to lost hellos. However, detecting failures is best left to the IGP or to link-specific alarm mechanisms.

As soon as an LDP neighbor comes up, you can view the neighbor relationship using the **show mpls ldp neighbor** command, as demonstrated in Example 2-15.

Example 2-15 *Viewing LDP Neighbor Relationships*

```
vxr15#show mpls ldp neighbor
    Peer LDP Ident: 192.168.1.8:0; Local LDP Ident 192.168.1.15:0
        TCP connection: 192.168.1.8.646 - 192.168.1.15.11056
        State: Oper; Msgs sent/rcvd: 41/39; Downstream
        Up time: 00:00:03
        Addresses bound to peer LDP Ident:
            192.168.1.8     192.168.13.8     192.168.3.8     192.168.17.8
            192.168.8.8
```

Example 2-15 shows an LDP neighbor relationship (because it says **Peer LDP Ident**) with neighbor 192.168.1.8. Output from **show tag-switching tdp neighbor** looks much the same, except it says **Peer TDP Ident** instead if the label protocol is TDP.

Figure 2-20 summarizes LDP session establishment. The number of sessions needed between LSRs depends on the label space. For frame-mode interfaces, even though there are multiple links between two LSRs, only one LDP session is established, because for frame-mode operation, a per-platform label space is used. When ATM interfaces are used, the LSR has to maintain a per-interface label space for each of them. RFC 3036 requires the use of one neighbor relationship per interface when using per-interface label space.

Figure 2-20 *LDP Session Establishment Summary*

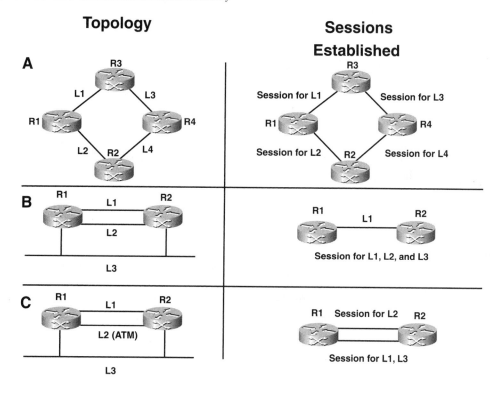

Case A in Figure 2-20 shows that four routers—R1, R2, R3, and R4—are connected by links L1 through L4. For each of the links, only one session needs to be established— assuming that these are frame-mode interfaces.

Case B shows multiple links between two routers, R1 and R2. Again, assuming frame-mode interfaces, only one LDP session is required.

Case C shows one ATM link between the two LSRs R1 and R2 doing cell mode. This calls for an additional session to be established.

What happens at the packet level? After deciding which LSR plays the active role in neighbor establishment, the active LSR sends an initialization message. Its format is illustrated in Figure 2-21.

Figure 2-21 *Initialization Message Format*

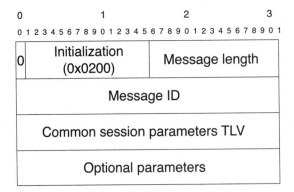

The initialization message contains a Common Session Parameters TLV. Its format is shown in Figure 2-22.

Figure 2-22 *Common Session Parameters TLV Format*

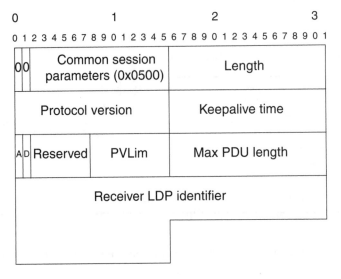

The initialization message might also contain optional parameters. These are not covered in this book; see RFC 3036, Sections 3.5.3, for more details.

The fields in the Common Session Parameters TLV are as follows:

- **Protocol Version**—Version 1.
- **Keepalive Time**—The proposed time in seconds after which the LDP neighbor relationship is torn down.
- **A**—Set to 0 for Downstream Unsolicited mode and 1 for DoD.
- **D**—Set to 0 if loop detection is disabled and 1 if loop detection is enabled. Loop detection is used with LC-ATM LDP relationships.
- **Reserved**—Not used.
- **PVLim**—Path vector limit. Also used with LC-ATM.
- **Max PDU Length**—The largest allowable LDP PDU between two neighbors. The default is 4096.
- **Receiver LDP Identifier**—The LDP Identifier, advertised back to the receiver.

Initialization messages are exchanged between two neighbors to determine parameters to be used for a session.

After neighbors are established, keepalive messages are sent between neighbors. Figure 2-23 shows the format for LDP keepalive messages.

Figure 2-23 *LDP Keepalive Message Format*

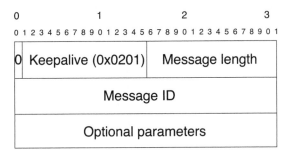

Keepalive messages are pretty straightforward. Optional parameters aren't covered here, and we've already defined the rest of the fields in the packet.

Keepalives are sent every 60 seconds by default; if a keepalive is not seen in 180 seconds, the LDP neighbor is torn down.

Hellos and Keepalives?

You might have noticed that LDP has both hello messages and keepalive messages. Both are necessary. As mentioned earlier in this chapter, LDP forms only one neighbor relationship if there are multiple frame-mode links between two LSRs. Hello messages are sent on each link via UDP multicast and are used to ensure that an LSR knows which interfaces a neighbor is over. Keepalives are sent between established neighbors on a TCP connection, and which interface the keepalives come in on isn't tracked. Hello messages are per-link keepalives, whereas keepalive messages are per-neighbor keepalives. Although perhaps a bit confusing, the separation of per-link and per-neighbor maintenance messages helps LDP scale more effectively.

Label Advertisement

As soon as LSRs have established an LDP neighbor relationship, they begin to advertise labels to each other. Seven different LDP message types are involved in label advertisement:

- Address
- Address Withdraw
- Label Request
- Label Mapping
- Label Withdraw
- Label Release
- Label Abort Request

Address Message

An LSR sends Address messages to advertise the interface addresses to which it is bound. Address messages are not *LDP label advertisement messages*. Address messages are also a form of advertisement and hence included here. Figure 2-24 shows the Address message format.

The Address message is the glue that creates an association between a label space and a next-hop. Without it, the LSR doesn't know which LDP ID to listen to if it wants to send a packet to particular next-hop. Refer to Figure 2-7, in which LSRs 12008a and 12008b have two links between them. If the ATM 3/0 link goes down, the route to 12.12.12.12 on 12008a is over the POS 1/0 link, and the next hop is the address of the POS 1/1 interface of 12008b. Now, because of receiving the Address message, 12008a can associate the binding it has from 12008b to this new next hop.

The command **show mpls ldp neighbor** shows the address bindings received from the neighbor, as demonstrated in Example 2-16.

Figure 2-24 *LDP Address Message Format*

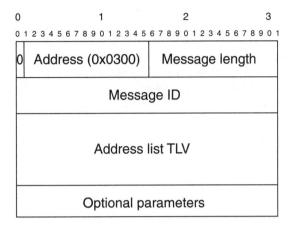

Example 2-16 *Viewing Address Bindings Received from LDP Neighbors*

```
12008a#show mpls ldp neighbors
Peer LDP Ident: 3.3.3.3:0; Local LDP Ident 5.5.5.5:0
        TCP connection: 3.3.3.3.646 - 5.5.5.5.11004
        State: Oper; Msgs sent/rcvd: 28881/28887; Downstream
        Up time: 2w3d
        LDP discovery sources:
          POS2/0
        Addresses bound to peer LDP Ident:
          7.1.5.113        10.0.1.3        3.3.3.3         10.0.2.3
Peer LDP Ident: 4.4.4.4:0; Local LDP Ident 5.5.5.5:0
        TCP connection: 4.4.4.4.646 - 5.5.5.5.11005
        State: Oper; Msgs sent/rcvd: 28894/28931; Downstream
        Up time: 2w3d
        LDP discovery sources:
          POS2/1
        Addresses bound to peer LDP Ident:
          7.1.5.110        10.0.1.4        4.4.4.4         10.0.3.4
Peer LDP Ident: 11.11.11.11:0; Local LDP Ident 5.5.5.5:0
        TCP connection: 11.11.11.11.11008 - 5.5.5.5.646
        State: Oper; Msgs sent/rcvd: 28904/28875; Downstream
        Up time: 2w3d
        LDP discovery sources:
          POS1/0
        Addresses bound to peer LDP Ident:
          10.0.19.11       10.0.17.11      10.0.4.11       7.1.5.100
          11.11.11.11      10.0.5.11
Peer LDP Ident: 11.11.11.11:1; Local LDP Ident 5.5.5.5:1
        TCP connection: 10.0.4.11.11009 - 10.0.4.5.646
        State: Oper; Msgs sent/rcvd: 5821/5821; Downstream on demand
        Up time: 3d12h
        LDP discovery sources:
          ATM3/0.1
```

The highlighted text in Example 2-16 shows the address bindings that 12008a received from its neighbor, whose LDP identifier is 11.11.11.11:0. The addresses listed under **Addresses bound** are those received by 12008a from the LSR 11.11.11.11:0 in the address-binding message. When it's time to install a label entry in the FIB/LFIB, 12008a consults the routing table. Only if a route's next-hop address is listed in the address bindings sent by a next-hop router does 12008a consider using the label bindings sent by that router. In Example 2-16, for 12008a to use label bindings from 11.11.11.11 for a prefix, the IGP next hop for that prefix must be one of the following addresses:

    10.0.9.11
    10.0.17.11
    10.0.4.11
    7.1.5.100
    11.11.11.11
    10.0.5.11

In liberal retention mode, if a route's next hop changes, as long as the next hop is one of the IP addresses listed under the **Address bound** portion for that neighbor, the LSR continues to use the previously received bindings it still holds.

NOTE   You don't see the address bindings over ATM3/0.1. This is because, by default, Cisco routers do not send Address messages over LC-ATM interfaces based on the fact that LC-ATM uses per-interface label space and there is no question of trying to map a next-hop to a different downstream interface for the same label space—there is one label space per interface. Also, Cisco routers and switches only use conservative retention mode for LC-ATM interfaces and if a next-hop changes, a new label request has to be made to be able to forward labeled packets over the new interface corresponding to the new next-hop. Adding the command **mpls ldp address-message** on the ATM interface would cause the address message to be sent over this interface.

Address Withdraw Message

The Address message and the Address Withdraw message share a similar format, as shown in Figure 2-25.

It contains a list of addresses that are being withdrawn in the Address List TLV.

NOTE   Whenever a new interface is added to an LSR, it is required to send an Address message. Conversely, when an interface is removed or shutdown it is required to send an Address Withdraw message.

Figure 2-25 *Address Withdraw Message Format*

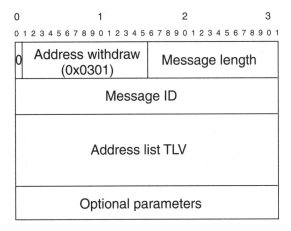

Label Request Message

When LSRs are acting in DoD/conservative retention mode, the upstream LSR requests a label from the downstream LSR. This request is sent as a Label Request message. It has the format shown in Figure 2-26.

Figure 2-26 *Label Request Message Format*

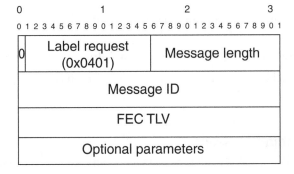

The FEC TLV contains the prefix for which the label binding is being requested.

NOTE   Sometimes, ATM-LSRs need to request multiple labels for the same prefix. This would be the case in the network shown in Figure 2-10 if ls1010a does not support VC Merge. In order for the downstream LSR to know to send a different label for the same FEC, the requesting LSR uses a different message ID.

Label Mapping Message

Label bindings are sent using the Label Mapping message. This is used for both DoD and Downstream Unsolicited distribution modes.

Figure 2-27 shows the format of the Label Mapping message.

Figure 2-27 *Label Mapping Message Format*

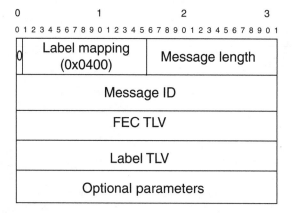

The Optional Parameters can be one of the following:

- **Label Request Message ID TLV**—Usually set to the message ID that was set in the request message.
- **Hop Count TLV**—Specifies the total number of hops along the LSP that would be set up by the label message.
- **Path Vector TLV**—Contains the list of LSRs of the LSP being set up.

Hop Count and Path Vector TLVs are both used for loop avoidance, almost always in LC-ATM networks.

Label Withdraw Message

An LSR sends the Label Withdraw message when it wants to withdraw the previous bindings it sent. Upon receipt of the Label Withdraw message, an LSR should stop using the label binding and should respond with a Label Release message to the sender of the Label Withdraw message.

Figure 2-28 shows the format of the Label Withdraw message.

The Label TLV field is optional because, if it is present, only the labels that are listed in the Label TLV are withdrawn. If it isn't, all labels corresponding to that FEC should be removed.

Figure 2-28 *Label Withdraw Message Format*

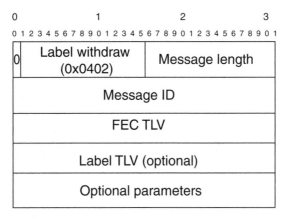

Label Release Message

This is identical to the Label Withdraw message in format, except for the Label Release (0x0403) field. A Label Release message confirms the release of the label bindings that was indicated in the Label Withdraw message. It is also used in conservative retention mode, to signal that the upstream LSR will no longer use this label—perhaps because it's next-hop has changed. If the Label TLV is present and contains labels, the message confirms withdrawal of only those label bindings. If the Label TLV is empty, all label bindings corresponding to the FEC are confirmed as withdrawn.

Label Abort Request Message

Label Abort Request, as the name suggests, aborts any outstanding requests made earlier. This could happen under a few circumstances:

- If the route for the prefix has changed since the LSR made a request.
- This LSR has received an abort from an upstream LSR that prompted the request in the first place.

The LSR that receives the Abort Request can respond in the following ways:

- If it has not already replied to the request with a Label Mapping message or an error notification, it needs to reply with a Label Request Aborted Notification message.
- If the LSR has already replied, just ignore the notification.

Notification

When an LSR needs to inform its peers of a problem, it uses a Notification message. Notifications can be

- Error notifications
- Advisory notifications

Error notifications are used when the LSR has encountered a fatal error and cannot recover from it. This results in tearing down the LDP session. By the same token, LSRs that receive the notification discard all the bindings associated with this session.

Advisory notifications are used like a warning. The LSR can recover from such problems. Notifications are carried in Status messages, the format of which is illustrated in Figure 2-29.

Figure 2-29 *LDP Status Message Format*

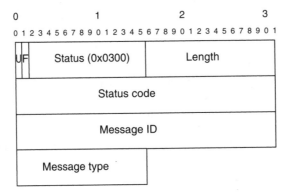

The Status Code field has the format shown in Figure 2-30.

Figure 2-30 *Status Code Field Format*

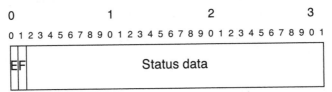

If the E bit is set to 1, a fatal error has occurred. If it is set to 0, it should be treated as a warning. The Status Data carries the Status Code of what actually went wrong.

Loop Detection

Loop detection is used only in DoD distribution mode, and therefore only in cell-mode ATM environments. This is because loop detection by nature requires *ordered* control mode. In ordered control mode, label requests are sent from upstream to downstream, and label bindings are sent in the opposite direction. This makes it natural for the LSRs along the path to add themselves to the path vector. If independent distribution mode is used, LSRs don't wait to receive label bindings from downstream neighbors before distributing labels to upstream neighbors. In DoD distribution, if an LSR receives a label mapping from its downstream neighbor in response to its own label request and the Label Mapping message contains a hop count TLV, the LSR simply updates the count. In Downstream Unsolicited (DU) distribution mode, no such communication occurs between neighbors. In a way, DoD can be considered stateful and DU stateless. Besides, in DU distribution, because the LSRs are routers and not ATM LSRs, the TTL field in the MPLS header is used to avoid infinite looping of packets.

TIP   On Cisco LSRs, loop detection is disabled by default and has to be configured using the command **mpls ldp loop-detection** globally.

If an LSR receives a Label Mapping message and the hop count TLV is out of range (more than the maximum), or if the path-vector TLV contains its own LSR ID, the LSR concludes that a loop is present within the LSP.

When an LSR detects a loop, it drops the label mapping and does not respond to the upstream neighbor's request. It also sends a notification message indicating a loop to the LSR that sent the Label Mapping message.

Label Distribution Protocol Configuration

This section gives you a basic understanding of how to configure LDP. The assumption is made that you already know how to configure the IGP routing protocols. Various aspects of configuring MPLS TE are dealt with in the remaining chapters of this book.

Configuration tasks for LDP include the following:

- Configuring CEF
- Configuring MPLS forwarding globally
- Interface-level configuration

Consider the service provider network shown in Figure 2-31. The goal here is to have an MPLS-enabled core. This section goes over the configuration of a core router 12008a to enable MPLS and thus act as an LSR. In order to enable MPLS in the entire network, you of course must enable CEF, MPLS forwarding globally, and MPLS forwarding per interface on every router you want to participate in MPLS.

Figure 2-31 *Enabling MPLS Forwarding in a Service Provider Network*

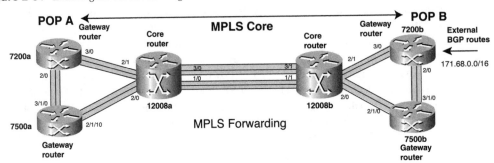

Configuring CEF

Example 2-17 shows how to enable CEF on a router. 12008a is used as an example.

Example 2-17 *Enabling CEF*

```
12008a#configure terminal
Enter configuration commands, one per line.  End with CNTL/Z.
mpls-12008a(config)#ip cef distributed
```

The keyword **distributed** applies only to distributed platforms such as the 12000 series router and the 7500 series router—not the 7200 series router.

NOTE   Example 2-17 shows how CEF is configured on a 12000-series router. In reality, 12000 series routers support CEF only as a forwarding mechanism, so there is no need to explicitly enable it. By default, distributed CEF is enabled on 12000 series routers.

CEF is a prerequisite for MPLS forwarding, no matter whether you're using LDP, TDP, RSVP, or BGP for label distribution.

Example 2-18 shows output generated from the **show ip interface** command.

Example 2-18 *Verifying That CEF Is Enabled on Inbound/Outbound Interfaces with the* **show ip interface** *Command*

```
12008a#show ip interface pos 2/1
POS2/1 is up, line protocol is up
  Internet address is 10.0.3.5/24
  Broadcast address is 255.255.255.255
  Address determined by non-volatile memory
  MTU is 4470 bytes
  Helper address is not set
```

Example 2-18 *Verifying That CEF Is Enabled on Inbound/Outbound Interfaces with the* **show ip interface** *Command (Continued)*

```
Directed broadcast forwarding is disabled
Multicast reserved groups joined: 224.0.0.5 224.0.0.6 224.0.0.2 224.0.0.14
Outgoing access list is not set
Inbound  access list is not set
Proxy ARP is enabled
Security level is default
Split horizon is enabled
ICMP redirects are always sent
ICMP unreachables are always sent
ICMP mask replies are never sent
IP fast switching is enabled
IP fast switching on the same interface is enabled
IP Flow switching is disabled
IP CEF switching is enabled
IP Null turbo vector
IP multicast fast switching is enabled
IP multicast distributed fast switching is disabled
IP route-cache flags are Fast, Distributed, CEF
Router Discovery is disabled
IP output packet accounting is disabled
IP access violation accounting is disabled
TCP/IP header compression is disabled
RTP/IP header compression is disabled
Probe proxy name replies are disabled
Policy routing is disabled
Network address translation is disabled
WCCP Redirect outbound is disabled
WCCP Redirect inbound is disabled
WCCP Redirect exclude is disabled
BGP Policy Mapping is disabled
```

show ip cef summary is another useful command to ensure that CEF is enabled, as demonstrated in Example 2-19. This is useful for global information about CEF, such as whether it is running in distributed mode, how many routing entries are present, and so on.

Example 2-19 *Verifying That CEF Is Enabled and Obtaining Statistics with the* **show ip cef summary** *Command*

```
mpls-12008a#show ip cef summary
IP Distributed CEF with switching (Table Version 170), flags=0x0, bits=8
  37 routes, 0 reresolve, 0 unresolved (0 old, 0 new)
  37 leaves, 34 nodes, 40724 bytes, 141 inserts, 104 invalidations
  8 load sharing elements, 2688 bytes, 8 references
  universal per-destination load sharing algorithm, id 5008782C
  2 CEF resets, 33 revisions of existing leaves
  34 in-place modifications
  refcounts:  8999 leaf, 8960 node

Adjacency Table has 9 adjacencies
```

Configuring MPLS Forwarding Globally

Example 2-20 shows the router-level configuration to enable MPLS forwarding.

Example 2-20 *Configuring MPLS Forwarding Globally*

```
mpls-12008a#configure terminal
Enter configuration commands, one per line.  End with CNTL/Z.
mpls-12008a(config)#mpls ip
mpls-12008a(config)#mpls label protocol ldp
mpls-12008a(config)#mpls ldp router-id loopback 0
```

The command **mpls label protocol ldp** specifies which label protocol to use. The choices are **ldp** and **tdp**.

The command **mpls ldp router-id loopback 0** ties the MPLS LSR ID to the IP address of the virtual interface Loopback0. This is recommended in order to avoid unpredictable results during session establishment.

Interface-Level Configuration

Apart from the router-level configuration presented in Example 2-20, you also have to explicitly configure each interface on which you want to run LDP by using the command **mpls ip** at the interface level.

Frame-Mode Interface Configuration

Example 2-21 shows the MPLS configuration options available at the interface level for a frame-mode interface.

Example 2-21 *Interface-Level MPLS Configuration*

```
12008a#configure terminal
Enter configuration commands, one per line.  End with CNTL/Z.
mpls-12008a(config)#interface ethernet 0
mpls-12008a(config-if)#mpls ip
mpls-12008a(config-if)#mpls mtu ?
  <64-65536>  MTU (bytes)
mpls-12008a(config-if)#mpls mtu 1504
mpls-12008a(config-if)#end
```

mpls label protocol can also be specified at the interface level. This is particularly useful when you have Cisco LSRs as neighbors on one set of interfaces and non-Cisco neighbors on other interfaces. This way, you can leave the label protocol as **tdp** (the default) on all interfaces connecting to other Cisco devices while specifying LDP on others.

The MPLS MTU size can also be set to values between 64 and 65,536 in order to accommodate situations in which label sizes have to be accounted for during MTU computation. This typically is an issue only on Ethernet interfaces.

For example, on an Ethernet interface, you'd normally have a maximum data size of 1500 bytes. After the Ethernet encapsulation has been added, this equals 1518 bytes (the maximum allowable size of an Ethernet frame). However, because of the fact that certain end-user applications don't use Path MTU Discovery to discover the maximum MTU size, you can receive 1500-byte IP packets with the Don't Fragment (DF) bit set. When this arrives at an ingress LER, the LER adds 4 or more bytes of MPLS header(s). The LER needs to fragment the packet, but it cannot do so because the DF bit is set. In such situations, if the LSR and the Layer 2 switches that are downstream from the LSR accommodate jumbo packets (also called baby giants), it is possible to transmit 1504-byte packets (with one MPLS label) or more on the Ethernet by setting the MPLS MTU to 1504. You compute the IP MTU by subtracting the number of labels from the MPLS MTU:

MPLS MTU = IP MTU + (4 * maximum number of labels)

The maximum number of labels in your network depends on several factors. For example, if an LSR is a PE in an MPLS-VPN network, it requires at least two labels. A third label is also imposed if the LSR is the headend of an MPLS TE tunnel. Using Fast ReRoute (see Chapter 7, "Protection and Restoration") might add another label to the mix, making your maximum label size 4. If the IP MTU on an interface is 1500, your best bet is to set the MPLS MTU to 1516 (1500 + (4 * 4)). Setting the MPLS MTU higher than you need doesn't hurt anything, so you might want to set the MPLS MTU to 1516 or 1520 on all Ethernet interfaces as a general practice.

The **show mpls forwarding** *a.b.c.d* **detail** command displays the label stack used to forward a data packet to subnet *a.b.c.d*. Example 2-22 shows the output of **show mpls forwarding detail** on 7200a when directed LDP is run on top of TE tunnel tunnel1. In this example, you can see the label stack containing two labels, 12335 and 43. 12335 is the tunnel label, and 43 is the result of LDP over it.

Example 2-22 *Label Stack Information Obtained Through* **show mpls forwarding detail**

```
7200a#show mpls forwarding 13.13.13.13 detail
Local  Outgoing    Prefix           Bytes tag  Outgoing   Next Hop
tag    tag or VC   or Tunnel Id     switched   interface
45     12326       13.13.13.13/32   0          PO3/0      point2point
         MAC/Encaps=4/8, MTU=4470, Tag Stack{12326}
         FF030281 03026000
         No output feature configured
      Per-destination load-sharing, slots: 0 2 4 6 8 10 12 14
         43          13.13.13.13/32   0          Tu1        point2point
         MAC/Encaps=4/12, MTU=4466, Tag Stack{12335 43}, via PO3/0
         FF030281 0302F0000002B000
         No output feature configured
      Per-destination load-sharing, slots: 1 3 5 7 9 11 13 15
```

Cell-Mode Interface Configuration

Example 2-23 shows the interface-level MPLS configuration for an ATM subinterface on a router for cell-mode operation.

Example 2-23 *Cell-Mode ATM Configuration for an ATM Subinterface on a Router*

```
12008a#configure terminal
Enter configuration commands, one per line.  End with CNTL/Z.
mpls-12008a(config)#interface atm 3/0
mpls-12008a(config-if)#no ip address
mpls-12008a(config-if)#no atm ilmi-keepalive
mpls-12008a(config-if)#exit
mpls-12008a(config)#interface atm 3/0.1 mpls
mpls-12008a(config-subif)#ip address 10.0.4.5 255.255.255.0
mpls-12008a(config-subif)#mpls ip
mpls-12008a(config-subif)#mpls ldp address-message
mpls-12008a(config)#mpls ldp atm ?
  control-mode  Select LSP setup control mode for MPLS VCs
  vc-merge      Select VC merge capability
```

Configuring MPLS forwarding and LDP on routers for cell-mode ATM is done on ATM subinterfaces. In addition to the commands done at the subinterface level, the following three router-level commands are specific to ATM:

- **mpls ldp address-message**—Cisco LSRs do not send address binding by default on ATM devices. This command enables sending the address binding.

- **mpls ldp atm [control | vc-merge]**—This global command can be used to specify ATM-related control. Both independent and ordered are supported. Configuring **vc-merge** allows the LSR to perform VC Merge. VC Merge is off by default.

- **mpls ldp loop-detection**—This router-level command enables loop detection, which is off by default on Cisco routers.

Verifying Your LDP Configuration

To verify the configuration, the following commands are useful:

- **show mpls ldp discovery**
- **show mpls ldp neighbor**
- **show mpls interfaces [detail]**

The **discovery** command option is useful to verify that hellos are being received from neighbors.

Example 2-24 shows the output from the **show mpls ldp discovery** command.

Example 2-24 **show mpls ldp discovery** *Command Output Shows a List of Interfaces Over Which the LDP Discovery Process Is Running*

```
12008a#show mpls ldp discovery
Local LDP Identifier:
    5.5.5.5:0
Discovery Sources:
    Interfaces:
        POS1/0 (ldp): xmit/recv
            LDP Id: 11.11.11.11:0
        POS2/0 (ldp): xmit/recv
            LDP Id: 3.3.3.3:0
        POS2/1 (ldp): xmit/recv
            LDP Id: 4.4.4.4:0
        ATM3/0.1 (ldp): xmit/recv
            LDP Id: 11.11.11.11:1; IP addr: 10.0.4.11
mpls-12008a#
```

If you don't see **recv** for an interface, hello packets were not received. In the context of serial interfaces using PPP encapsulation, this could mean that there is a PPP negotiation issue.

The **show mpls ldp neighbor** command, shown in Example 2-25, is useful to get more details, such as the addresses bound to a neighbor and the neighbor's LSR ID. If you have not explicitly configured the LDP identifier address using the **mpls ldp router-id** command, LDP might pick a different interface address than you intended. In such cases, the **Peer LDP Ident** field helps identify the problem.

Example 2-25 **show mpls ldp neighbor** *Command Output Shows the Status of LDP Sessions*

```
12008a#show mpls ldp neighbor
Peer LDP Ident: 4.4.4.4:0; Local LDP Ident 5.5.5.5:0
        TCP connection: 4.4.4.4.646 - 5.5.5.5.11000
        State: Oper; Msgs sent/rcvd: 67/65; Downstream
        Up time: 00:39:40
        LDP discovery sources:
          POS2/1
        Addresses bound to peer LDP Ident:
          7.1.5.110       10.0.1.4        4.4.4.4         10.0.3.4
Peer LDP Ident: 3.3.3.3:0; Local LDP Ident 5.5.5.5:0
        TCP connection: 3.3.3.3.646 - 5.5.5.5.11001
        State: Oper; Msgs sent/rcvd: 66/65; Downstream
        Up time: 00:39:40
        LDP discovery sources:
          POS2/0
        Addresses bound to peer LDP Ident:
          7.1.5.113       10.0.1.3        3.3.3.3         10.0.2.3
Peer LDP Ident: 11.11.11.11:0; Local LDP Ident 5.5.5.5:0
        TCP connection: 11.11.11.11.11011 - 5.5.5.5.646
        State: Oper; Msgs sent/rcvd: 65/63; Downstream
```

continues

Example 2-25 **show mpls ldp neighbor** *Command Output Shows the Status of LDP Sessions (Continued)*

```
                Up time: 00:38:24
                LDP discovery sources:
                  POS1/0
                Addresses bound to peer LDP Ident:
                  10.0.19.11      10.0.17.11      10.0.4.11      7.1.5.100
                  11.11.11.11     10.0.5.11
Peer LDP Ident: 11.11.11.11:1; Local LDP Ident 5.5.5.5:1
                TCP connection: 10.0.4.11.11013 - 10.0.4.5.646
                State: Oper; Msgs sent/rcvd: 43/43; Downstream on demand
                Up time: 00:24:20
                LDP discovery sources:
                  ATM3/0.1
```

The **TCP connection** information comes in handy when you are having problems with your session.

The **State** field is yet another place to check to see if everything is all right with the neighbor in question as far as your LDP session is concerned. Obviously, **Oper** (Operational) is good. If for any reason the session is not operational, you do not see an entry for this neighbor.

The **discovery sources** field is useful when you have multiple links between two LSRs. In such cases, losing one link between the LSRs does not result in the session's going down. You can observe this in the output of this **show** command.

Finally, the **show mpls interfaces detail** command is useful for checking things such as an interface's MPLS MTU size, as demonstrated in Example 2-26. The interesting information in this output is highlighted.

Example 2-26 **show mpls interfaces detail** *Command Output Displays Detailed Label Switching Information*

```
12008a#show mpls interfaces detail
Interface Ethernet0:
        IP labeling enabled (ldp)
        LSP Tunnel labeling not enabled
        MPLS Frame Relay Transport labeling not enabled
        BGP labeling not enabled
        MPLS operational
        MTU = 1504
Interface POS1/0:
        IP labeling enabled (ldp)
        LSP Tunnel labeling enabled
        MPLS Frame Relay Transport labeling not enabled
        MPLS operational
        MTU = 4470
Interface POS2/0:
        IP labeling enabled (ldp)
        LSP Tunnel labeling not enabled
        MPLS Frame Relay Transport labeling not enabled
        MPLS operational
```

Example 2-26 **show mpls interfaces detail** *Command Output Displays Detailed Label Switching Information (Continued)*

```
            MTU = 4470
Interface POS2/1:
        IP labeling enabled (ldp)
        LSP Tunnel labeling enabled
        MPLS Frame Relay Transport labeling not enabled
        MPLS operational
        MTU = 4470
Interface ATM3/0.1:
        IP labeling enabled (ldp)
        LSP Tunnel labeling not enabled
        MPLS Frame Relay Transport labeling not enabled
        MPLS operational
        MTU = 4470
        ATM labels: Label VPI = 1, Control VC = 0/32
```

IP labeling enabled shows **(ldp)**, meaning that the label imposition and switching are based on label bindings derived from LDP. This could be **(tdp)** if the TDP protocol were used on interface POS1/0. **LSP Tunnel labeling enabled** means that MPLS TE has been enabled on that interface. In Example 2-26, you can see that it is enabled for POS1/0 but not for POS2/0. This is a good place to see if MPLS MTU has been bumped up, as in the case of Ethernet/0, which has been increased from the default 1500 to 1504. Finally, for the LC-ATM interface ATM3/0.1, you can see the VPI being used and the control VC. In a multivendor environment, these default values might not be the same between two vendors and might have to be modified.

Configuring Session Attributes

In some cases, you might want to change the default LDP Hello and Holdtime parameters. Example 2-27 shows how you can find out what the current LDP parameter values are.

Example 2-27 *Verifying Hello and Holdtime Intervals*

```
12008a#show mpls ldp parameters
Protocol version: 1
Downstream label generic region: min label: 12304; max label: 100000
Session hold time: 180 sec; keep alive interval: 60 sec
Discovery hello: holdtime: 15 sec; interval: 5 sec
Discovery targeted hello: holdtime: 180 sec; interval: 5 sec
Downstream on Demand max hop count: 255
TDP for targeted sessions
LDP initial/maximum backoff: 15/120 sec
LDP loop detection: off
```

Example 2-28 shows how the default discovery hello holdtime can be changed.

Example 2-28 *Configuring Holdtime and Hello Intervals*

```
12008a#configure terminal
Enter configuration commands, one per line.  End with CNTL/Z.
12008a(config)#mpls ldp dis
12008a(config)#mpls ldp discovery hello ?
  holdtime  LDP discovery Hello holdtime
  interval  LDP discovery Hello interval
12008a(config)#mpls ldp discovery hello holdtime ?
  <1-2147483>  Holdtime in seconds
12008a(config)#mpls ldp discovery hello holdtime 240
```

Example 2-29 shows how you can verify the configuration changes you made.

Example 2-29 *Verifying LDP Parameters*

```
12008a#show mpls ldp parameters
Protocol version: 1
Downstream label generic region: min label: 12304; max label: 100000
Session hold time: 180 sec; keep alive interval: 60 sec
Discovery hello: holdtime: 240 sec; interval: 5 sec
Discovery targeted hello: holdtime: 180 sec; interval: 5 sec
Downstream on Demand max hop count: 255
TDP for targeted sessions
LDP initial/maximum backoff: 15/120 sec
LDP loop detection: off
```

As you can see from the highlighted text in Example 2-29, the discovery holdtime has been changed to 240.

Summary

You are probably familiar with switching concepts in an IP network. The fundamental problem with routing a packet based on the destination IP address is that every hop along the path has to route the packet. As a result, the forwarding table is based solely on the routing table and your IGP's shortest calculated path. If, for any reason, the forwarding path that is derived through the routing table is congested or is experiencing longer-than-expected delays, you have no choice but to forward the traffic down that path. MPLS-based forwarding and MPLS TE can be used to overcome this limitation.

MPLS forwarding is based on a fixed-length label. The label exchange happens in the control plane in much the same way that routing information is exchanged prior to the forwarding of IP packets. Label exchanges are done through a label distribution protocol such as TDP, LDP, RSVP, or BGP. With the exception of BGP-based label distribution, labels are assigned only to IGP-derived routes.

MPLS has two main modes—frame mode and cell mode. In frame mode, a label header is inserted between the Layer 2 encapsulation and the Layer 3 IP header. Cell mode is for ATM LSRs in which the control plane is MPLS and VPI/VCI values are exchanged between ATM LSRs in place of labels. As soon as the VPI/VCI values are in place, the ATM LSRs behave like normal ATM switches and switch cells.

In the forwarding plane, the ingress LER imposes one or more labels on the data packet. The core devices switch the packet to the egress LER based on the top label only. If the ingress LER imposes a single label, the egress LER usually sees a plain IP packet because of PHP.

IP packets that come into a router can be switched out with a label. When the incoming packet is IP, the FIB table is consulted to make the forwarding decision. If the incoming packet is labeled, the LFIB is consulted. The outgoing packet in this case can be either an MPLS or IP packet.

LDP is the standards-based label distribution protocol. It is the one used most commonly to build an MPLS core. It uses UDP multicast packets to discover directly connected neighbors. As soon as a neighbor is discovered, TCP is used to exchange label bindings. LDP can also be configured between nonadjacent neighbors. This is called directed or targeted LDP sessions. Like most routing protocols, LDP uses TLVs, which makes it flexible. LDP can be configured in conjunction with MPLS TE that is based on RSVP— they coexist.

The remainder of this book talks about MPLS TE. This chapter was provided as a foundation in case you are new to MPLS and as a refresher in case you are already familiar with MPLS basics.

CHAPTER 3

Information Distribution

From Chapter 1, "Understanding Traffic Engineering with MPLS," you understand the basic motivation behind MPLS Traffic Engineering. From Chapter 2, "MPLS Forwarding Basics," you understand label switching—how it works and how it's related to IP routing and switching.

But how does MPLS Traffic Engineering really work? What are the underlying protocols, and how do they all tie together? And, most importantly, what do you need to type on your router to make all this wonderful stuff come to life?

The answers to these questions can be broken down into three pieces:

- **Information distribution**—How routers know what the network looks like and what resources are available.

- **Path calculation and setup**—How routers decide to build TE tunnels, and how these TE tunnels are actually built and maintained.

- **Forwarding traffic down a tunnel**—After a tunnel is built, how is it used?

This chapter covers the information distribution piece. It covers the reason for information distribution, what information is distributed, and how the routers can take advantage of this information. This chapter also covers the configuration prerequisites before you can bring up MPLS Traffic Engineering on a router.

MPLS Traffic Engineering Configuration

Before diving into the what, when, and how of information distribution, you need to be aware of a few prerequisites. If your network doesn't have these enabled, you won't be able to get started in MPLS Traffic Engineering. You need the following:

- A release of the Cisco IOS Software that supports MPLS Traffic Engineering

- Cisco Express Forwarding (CEF) enabled in your network

- A link-state routing protocol (OSPF or IS-IS) as your Interior Gateway Protocol (IGP)

- Traffic engineering enabled globally on the router

- A loopback interface to use as your MPLS Traffic Engineering router ID (RID)

- Basic TE tunnel configuration

MPLS Traffic Engineering support for IS-IS was first included in Cisco IOS Software
Releases 12.0(5)S and 12.0(5)T; OSPF support was added in Cisco IOS Software Releases
12.0(7)S and 12.0(8)T. Most subsequent releases of Cisco IOS Software (including 12.0S,
12.1, 12.2, and later) also support MPLS Traffic Engineering. Not all features are in all code
versions; we will point out if a particular code level is needed for a particular feature.

Chapter 2 briefly covered CEF, and information on CEF is available in many other Cisco
publications. Refer to Chapter 2 for more information on CEF in the context of MPLS.

You also need a link-state routing protocol. The reason for this is covered in Chapter 4,
"Path Calculation and Setup." For now, just understand that if your network is not running
OSPF or IS-IS as its routing protocol, you won't be able to use MPLS Traffic Engineering.

In addition, you need an interface to use as your MPLS Traffic Engineering router ID. It
should be a loopback interface. Loopback interfaces are useful because they're always up,
no matter what the state of other interfaces in the box. This loopback interface should have
a /32 mask on it (a mask of 255.255.255.255 in dotted-quad notation); some things won't
work unless your loopback has a /32 mask. Odds are good that you already have a loopback
interface because these are useful for lots of other things as well. But just in case you've
never seen a loopback interface configuration before, it looks
like this:

```
interface Loopback0
 ip address 192.168.1.1 255.255.255.255
```

That's it. There's not much to it, but as you'll see, loopback addresses are an integral part
of MPLS Traffic Engineering. If you already have a loopback interface configured, you do
not need to create another one just for use with MPLS Traffic Engineering. In fact, we
strongly recommend that you use the same loopback interface for your IGP RID, your BGP
RID, and your MPLS TE RID. Although this is not necessary, it makes monitoring and
maintaining your network much cleaner. The rest of this book assumes that all routers in
your network are configured with a Loopback0 interface that has a /32 mask.

Finally, you need to enable MPLS Traffic Engineering on every router that you want to
participate in MPLS TE. This doesn't have to be every router in your network; it is typically
some or all routers in your core. In order to start the necessary traffic engineering
subsystems on the router, enter the following global configuration command:

```
gsr1(config)#mpls traffic-eng tunnels
```

Configuring **mpls traffic-eng tunnels** globally won't change anything in your network or
add any TE tunnels to a router, but if you don't configure it, most of the other commands
discussed in this book won't function.

After you configure MPLS TE globally, you also need to enable it on every interface that
might touch a TE tunnel. Every interface a TE tunnel goes out or comes in on must have
mpls traffic-eng tunnels enabled on it:

```
gsr1(config-if)#mpls traffic-eng tunnels
```

Do *not* enable **mpls traffic-eng tunnels** on interfaces that face your customers; if you want to run MPLS TE on a box your customers connect to, only enable TE on interfaces that connect to other devices in your network. If you enable **mpls traffic-eng tunnels** on a customer-facing interface, you are opening yourself up for some potential security problems.

A quick way to check to make sure everything is configured is with the first three lines of the command **show mpls traffic-eng tunnels summary**, as shown in Example 3-1.

Example 3-1 *Verifying MPLS TE Suppor*

```
gsr1#show mpls traffic-eng tunnels summary
Signalling Summary:
    LSP Tunnels Process:            running
    RSVP Process:                   running
    Forwarding:                     enabled
```

If these lines don't say **running**, **running**, and **enabled**, something is wrong. Double-check your configuration, and then refer to Chapter 11, "Troubleshooting MPLS TE," if things still don't look right.

Another thing that's useful to check is **show mpls interfaces**, as demonstrated in Example 3-2.

Example 3-2 **show mpls interfaces** *Command Output Verifies That MPLS TE Tunnels Are Configured*

```
gsr1#show mpls interfaces
Interface          IP          Tunnel    Operational
POS0/0             Yes (ldp)   Yes       Yes
POS3/0             Yes (ldp)   Yes       Yes
POS5/0             Yes (ldp)   Yes       Yes
```

If the Tunnel column says **Yes**, then **mpls traffic-eng tunnels** is configured on that interface.

Finally, you need to create a basic MPLS Traffic Engineering tunnel interface, as shown in Example 3-3.

Example 3-3 *Configuring a Basic MPLS TE Tunnel Interface*

```
interface Tunnel0
  ip unnumbered Loopback0
  tunnel mode mpls traffic-eng
  tunnel destination destination-ip
  tunnel mpls traffic-eng path-option 10 dynamic
```

Table 3-1 describes the key commands in this configuration.

Table 3-1 *Commands for Configuring a Basic MPLS TE Tunnel Interface*

Command	Description
interface Tunnel0	MPLS Traffic Engineering tunnels are represented as tunnel interfaces in the Cisco IOS Software. From this perspective, an MPLS Traffic Engineering tunnel is no different from a GRE tunnel or any other kind of tunnel you can configure.
ip unnumbered Loopback0	Cisco IOS Software does not forward traffic down an interface without an IP address on it, so you need to assign an IP address to the MPLS Traffic Engineering tunnel you've just created. However, because TE tunnels are unidirectional and don't have the concept of a link neighbor with which to communicate, it's a waste of addresses to put an additional IP address on the interface.
tunnel mode mpls traffic-eng	Tells the Cisco IOS Software that this tunnel interface is an MPLS Traffic Engineering tunnel. Other possible tunnel modes are GRE, DVMRP, and so on.
tunnel destination *destination-ip*	Tells the Cisco IOS Software what the tunnel's endpoint is. The IP address specified here is the MPLS Traffic Engineering RID (more on that later) of the router to which you want to build a tunnel. The *destination-ip* in this case is the Loopback0 interface on the tunnel's tailend router.
tunnel mpls traffic-eng path-option 10 dynamic	Tells the Cisco IOS Software how to generate the path from the tunnel headend to the tunnel tail. This command is covered in more detail in Chapter 4.

As you can see, a basic MPLS Traffic Engineering configuration is simple. You need to configure a few more things on your routers before MPLS Traffic Engineering tunnels will actually be set up and used, but not much more. You can tweak plenty of knobs to change how MPLS Traffic Engineering tunnels behave in your network.

What Information Is Distributed

So what's involved in information distribution? Information distribution is easily broken down into three pieces:

- *What* information is distributed and how you configure it
- *When* information is distributed and how you control when flooding takes place
- *How* information is distributed (protocol-specific details)

Chapter 4 details exactly how this information is used to calculate a TE tunnel path.

As discussed in previous chapters, the idea behind MPLS Traffic Engineering is to allow routers to build paths using information other than the shortest IP path. But what information is distributed to allow the routers to make more intelligent path calculations?

MPLS Traffic Engineering works by using OSPF or IS-IS to distribute information about available resources in your network. Three major pieces of information are distributed:

- Available bandwidth information per interface, broken out by priority to allow some tunnels to preempt others
- Attribute flags per interface
- Administrative weight per interface

Each of these three is advertised on a per-link basis. In other words, a router advertises available bandwidth, attribute flags, and administrative metric for all the links that are involved in MPLS Traffic Engineering.

Available Bandwidth Information

Perhaps the most appealing attribute of MPLS Traffic Engineering is the capability to reserve bandwidth across your network. You configure the amount of reservable bandwidth on a link using the following per-interface command:

```
router(config-if)#ip rsvp bandwidth [<1-10000000 total-reservable-bandwidth>
    [per-flow-bandwidth]]
```

This command can take two parameters. The first is the amount of total reservable bandwidth on the interface, in kbps. The second is the maximum amount of bandwidth that can be reserved per flow on the interface. The per-flow maximum is irrelevant to MPLS Traffic Engineering and is ignored. However, the **ip rsvp bandwidth** command is used for more than just MPLS Traffic Engineering, and the *per-flow-bandwidth* parameter has relevance to non-MPLS-related RSVP.

NOTE   Currently, RSVP for MPLS TE and "classic RSVP" (for IP microflows) do not play nicely together. You cannot enable an RSVP pool and have it reserved by both RSVP for MPLS TE and classic RSVP. The heart of the issue is that if you configure **ip rsvp bandwidth 100 100**, both MPLS TE and classic RSVP (as used for Voice over IP, DLSW+, and so on) *each* think they have 100 kbps of bandwidth available. This behavior is not a feature. If you're going to use RSVP, use it for MPLS TE *or* IP signalling; don't use both in your network at the same time.

If you don't configure the **ip rsvp bandwidth** command, the default reservable bandwidth advertised for that interface is 0. A common cause of tunnels not coming up during testing or initial deployment of MPLS Traffic Engineering is configuring a TE tunnel to require a certain amount of bandwidth but forgetting to configure available bandwidth on any link. See Chapter 11 for more details on how to detect this.

You don't have to specify a value for the *total-reservable-bandwidth* value in the **ip rsvp bandwidth** command. If you don't specify a value, the default is 75 percent of the link bandwidth. The link bandwidth is determined by the interface type or the per-interface **bandwidth** command.

The per-flow maximum defaults to being equal to the *total-reservable-bandwidth* parameter, but as previously mentioned, it's irrelevant anyway. So fuggetaboutit.

How much bandwidth do you allocate to the interface? That's a larger question than it might seem at first. It has to do with your oversubscription policies and how you enforce them; see Chapter 10, "MPLS TE Deployment Tips," for more information.

You can double-check your configuration using the command **show ip rsvp interface**, as demonstrated in Example 3-4.

Example 3-4 *Checking RSVP Bandwidth Status for an Interface*

```
gsr12>show ip rsvp interface
interface     allocated  i/f max  flow max  pct UDP  IP  UDP_IP  UDP M/C
POO/0         0M         116250K  116250K   0   0    0   0       0
POO/2         0M         116250K  116250K   0   0    0   0       0
PO4/2         233250K    466500K  466500K   50  0    1   0       0
```

The only columns that are relevant to MPLS TE are **interface**, **allocated**, **i/f max**, **pct**, and **IP**. **pct** is the percentage of reservable bandwidth that has actually been reserved across the link. **IP** is the number of IP tunnels (in this case, TE tunnels) reserved across that link.

In this example, a single tunnel across interface POS4/2 has reserved 233250 kbps, or 50 percent, of the total link bandwidth.

As MPLS Traffic Engineering tunnels reserve link bandwidth, the amount of allocated bandwidth changes, but the maximum available bandwidth does not. The amount of currently reservable bandwidth on an interface is the configured reservable interface bandwidth minus the currently allocated bandwidth. In addition to configuring the per-link available bandwidth, you also can configure the amount of bandwidth required by a tunnel. This sets one of the values the tunnel headend uses in its path calculation; see Chapter 4 for more details on how this calculation is performed.

Why do you need to configure both the per-interface and the tunnel bandwidth? It's simple. The per-interface configuration tells the network how much bandwidth is available on an interface, and the per-tunnel configuration at the headend tells the headend how much of the announced bandwidth to consume.

Example 3-5 shows the configuration on the tunnel headend.

Example 3-5   *Configuring the Desired Bandwidth on the Tunnel Headend*

```
interface Tunnel0
  ip unnumbered Loopback0
  tunnel mode mpls traffic-eng
  tunnel destination 192.168.1.8
  tunnel mpls traffic-eng path-option 10 dynamic
  tunnel mpls traffic-eng bandwidth kbps
```

Most commands that modify the behavior of a TE tunnel headend are configured on traffic engineering tunnels, as opposed to physical interfaces or in the global configuration. All the commands configured on a traffic engineering tunnel start with **tunnel mpls traffic-eng**. Keep this in mind as you learn more about how to configure tunnel interfaces.

You can verify the bandwidth setting on a tunnel interface using the **show mpls traffic-eng tunnels** *tunnel-interface* command. The output shown in Example 3-6 comes from a traffic engineering tunnel interface configured with **tunnel mpls traffic-eng bandwidth 97**.

Example 3-6   *Verifying Bandwidth Settings on a Tunnel Interface*

```
gsr1#show mpls traffic-eng tunnels Tunnel0

Name: gsr1_t0                             (Tunnel0) Destination: 192.168.1.8
  Status:
    Admin: up          Oper: up     Path: valid        Signalling: connected

    path option 10, type explicit bottom (Basis for Setup, path weight 40)

  Config Parameters:
    Bandwidth: 97        kbps (Global) Priority: 7  7   Affinity: 0x0/0xFFFF
    AutoRoute:  enabled   LockDown: disabled Loadshare: 97       bw-based
    auto-bw: disabled(0/218) 0  Bandwidth Requested: 97

  InLabel  :  -
  OutLabel : POS3/0, 35
```

The **Bandwidth: 97** under **Config Parameters** indicates that the tunnel is configured to request 97 kbps of bandwidth.

The **Loadshare** and **Bandwidth Requested** values are also 97. **Loadshare** has to do with sharing traffic among multiple tunnels; see Chapter 5, "Forwarding Traffic Down Tunnels," for more details. **Bandwidth Requested** is the amount of currently requested bandwidth. It is different from the **Bandwidth** value if you change the requested bandwidth and the new reservation has not yet come up.

Tunnel Priority

Some tunnels are more important than others. For example, you might have tunnels carrying VoIP traffic and tunnels carrying data traffic that are competing for the same resources. Or you might have a packing problem to solve (see Chapter 9, "Network Design with MPLS TE"). Or you might simply have some data tunnels that are more important than others. No matter what your motivation, you might be looking for a way to have some tunnels preempt others.

MPLS TE gives you a mechanism to do this. Each tunnel has a priority, and more-important tunnels take precedence over less-important tunnels. Less-important tunnels are pushed out of the way and are made to recalculate a path, and their resources are given to the more-important tunnel.

Priority Levels

A tunnel can have its priority set anywhere from 0 to 7. Confusingly, the *higher* the priority number, the *lower* the tunnel's importance! A tunnel of priority 7 can be preempted by a tunnel of any other priority, a tunnel of priority 6 can be preempted by any tunnel with a priority of 5 or lower, and so on down the line. A tunnel of priority 0 cannot be preempted.

To avoid confusion, the correct terminology to use is "better" and "worse" rather than "higher" and "lower." A tunnel of priority 3 has a *better* priority than a tunnel of priority 5. It's also valid to use "more important," meaning a numerically lower priority, and "less important," which is a numerically higher priority.

If you use this terminology, you won't get stuck on the fact that a tunnel of priority 3 has a *higher* priority (meaning it takes precedence) but a *lower* priority value (meaning it's numerically lower) than a tunnel of priority 5.

Preemption Basics

The basic idea is that some tunnels are more important than others. The more-important tunnels are free to push other tunnels out of their way when they want to reserve bandwidth. This is called *tunnel preemption*.

But how does it all really work?

Figure 3-1 shows the topology used in the examples in this section.

The link to pay attention to is the OC-3 between RouterC and RouterD. Currently, there is a 42-Mbps tunnel from RouterA to RouterD. This tunnel is configured with a default priority of 7.

For starters, consider IGP flooding. Both OSPF and IS-IS flood not only the available bandwidth on a link, but also the available bandwidth at each priority level. Example 3-7 shows the link information advertised for the RouterC to RouterD link.

Figure 3-1   *One Tunnel on a Network*

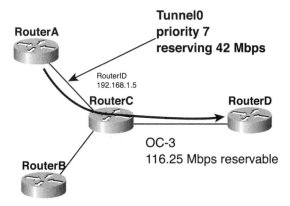

Example 3-7   *Link Information Advertised for the RouterC to RouterD Link with One Tunnel Reservation*

```
RouterC#show mpls traffic-eng topology 192.168.1.5

IGP Id: 0168.0001.0005.00, MPLS TE Id:192.168.1.5 Router Node  (isis  level-2) id 4
    link[0]: Point-to-Point, Nbr IGP Id: 0168.0001.0006.00, nbr_node_id:5, gen:33
        frag_id 0, Intf Address:192.168.10.5, Nbr Intf Address:192.168.10.6
        TE metric:10, IGP metric:10, attribute_flags:0x0
        physical_bw: 155000 (kbps), max_reservable_bw_global: 116250 (kbps)
        max_reservable_bw_sub: 0 (kbps)

                                   Global Pool     Sub Pool
                   Total Allocated Reservable      Reservable
                   BW (kbps)       BW (kbps)       BW (kbps)
                   --------------- -----------     ----------
           bw[0]:             0         116250              0
           bw[1]:             0         116250              0
           bw[2]:             0         116250              0
           bw[3]:             0         116250              0
           bw[4]:             0         116250              0
           bw[5]:             0         116250              0
           bw[6]:             0         116250              0
           bw[7]:         42000          74250              0
```

The highlighted portion of this output shows the available bandwidth at each priority level. Ignore the **Sub Pool Reservable** column; that's addressed in Chapter 6, "Quality of Service with MPLS TE."

This output shows that 42 Mbps (42,000 kbps) has been reserved at priority level 7. This bandwidth is used by the tunnel from RouterA to RouterD. This means that other TE tunnels that run SPF for this link and have their own priorities set to 7 see 74.25 Mbps available on this link (74,250 kbps). TE tunnels that have their priorities set to 6 or lower see 116.25 Mbps (116,259 kbps) reservable.

Figure 3-2 shows the same topology as in Figure 3-1, but with another TE tunnel at priority 5, for 74.250 Mbps, from RouterB to RouterD.

Figure 3-2 *Two Tunnels of Different Priorities*

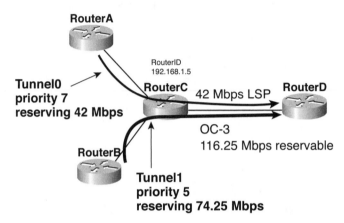

Example 3-8 shows the IGP announcement for the link between RouterC and RouterD.

Example 3-8 *Link Information Advertised with Two Tunnels*

```
RouterC#show mpls traffic-eng topology 192.168.1.5
IGP Id: 0168.0001.0005.00, MPLS TE Id:192.168.1.5 Router Node  (isis  level-2)
  id 4
      link[0]: Point-to-Point, Nbr IGP Id: 0168.0001.0006.00, nbr_node_id:5,
gen:55
          frag_id 0, Intf Address:192.168.10.5, Nbr Intf Address:192.168.10.6
          TE metric:10, IGP metric:10, attribute_flags:0x0
          physical_bw: 155000 (kbps), max_reservable_bw_global: 116250 (kbps)
          max_reservable_bw_sub: 0 (kbps)

                                    Global Pool     Sub Pool
                   Total Allocated  Reservable      Reservable
                   BW (kbps)        BW (kbps)       BW (kbps)
                   ---------------  ------------    ----------
          bw[0]:              0        116250                0
          bw[1]:              0        116250                0
          bw[2]:              0        116250                0
          bw[3]:              0        116250                0
          bw[4]:              0        116250                0
          bw[5]:          74250         42000                0
          bw[6]:              0         42000                0
          bw[7]:          42000             0                0
```

Figure 3-2 shows a tunnel of priority 5 that has reserved 74.25 Mbps and a tunnel of priority 7 that has reserved 42 Mbps. The **Global Pool Reservable** column tells how much bandwidth is available to a given priority level. So if a CSPF is run for a tunnel of priority 7, this link is seen to have 0 bandwidth available. For a tunnel of priority 5 or 6, this link has 42 Mbps available, and for a tunnel of priority 4 or less, this link has 116.25 Mbps left.

If the tunnel of priority 5 decides to increase its bandwidth request to 75 Mbps, the 42-Mbps tunnel can't fit on this link any more without disrupting Tunnel0, the tunnel from RouterA to RouterD. What happens?

Tunnel0 (the 42-Mbps tunnel with a priority of 7) will be torn down. After Tunnel0 is torn down, RouterA periodically tries to find a new path for the tunnel to take.

In Figure 3-3, there is no new path, and the tunnel remains down; in a real network, there can be an alternative path from RouterA to RouterD that has 42 Mbps available, and the tunnel will come up. Chapter 4 covers the details of the path calculation that RouterA goes through—a process often called Constrained Shortest Path First [CSPF].

Figure 3-3   *RouterA Searching for a New Tunnel Path*

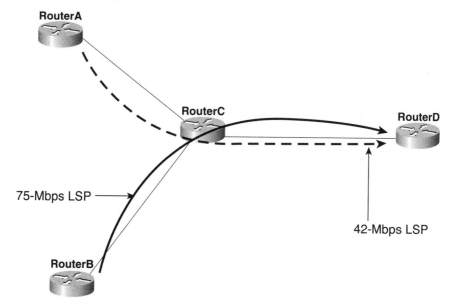

When setting up its 75-Mbps path with a priority of 5, RouterB does not take into account the possible existence of other tunnels at different priority levels; all it knows about is the bandwidth available at its priority level. If there was a path through this network that RouterB could take without disrupting RouterA's reservation, but that path was not the shortest path to meet all of RouterB's constraints, RouterB would *not* try to take that path. Tunnel preemption is not polite; it is aggressive and rude in trying to get what it wants. This makes sense. Higher-priority tunnels are more important and, therefore, are allowed to get whatever they want.

That's how preemption works. See the section "Packing Problem" in Chapter 9 for an idea of when and where you'd use priority.

Setup and Holding Priority

The preceding section explained that each tunnel has a priority. However, that's not quite true. Each tunnel has *two* priorities—a Setup priority and a Hold priority. They're almost always treated as a single priority, but it's worth understanding how they work and why there are two priorities instead of one.

RFC 3209 defines both a Setup priority and a Holding priority. It models them after the Preemption and Defending priorities in RFC 2751. The idea is that when a tunnel is first set up, its Setup priority is considered when deciding whether to admit the tunnel. When another tunnel comes along and competes with this first tunnel for link bandwidth, the Setup priority of the new tunnel is compared with the Hold priority of the first tunnel.

Allowing you to set the Setup priority differently from the Hold priority might have some real-life applications. For example, you could have a tunnel with a more-important Hold priority (say, 0) and a less-important Setup priority (maybe 7). A configuration like this means that this tunnel can't push any other tunnels out of its way to get resources it wants, because the tunnel has a Setup priority of 7. But it also means that as soon as the tunnel has been set up, it cannot be preempted by any other tunnels, because it has a Hold priority of 0.

One thing you cannot do is have a Setup priority that's better than the Hold priority for that tunnel. Why? Think about this for a second. If two tunnels (call them Tunnel1 and Tunnel2) are competing for the same resources, and both have a Setup priority of 1 and a Hold priority of 7, here's what happens:

  1 Tunnel1 comes up first and holds bandwidth with a Hold priority of 7.

  2 Tunnel2 comes up second and uses its Setup priority of 1 to push Tunnel1 off the link they're fighting over. Tunnel2 then holds the link with a Hold priority of 7.

  3 Tunnel1 comes along and uses its Setup priority of 1 to push Tunnel2 off the link they're fighting over. Tunnel2 then holds the link with a Hold priority of 7.

  4 Tunnel2 comes up second and uses its Setup priority of 1 to push Tunnel1 off the link they're fighting over. Tunnel2 then holds the link with a Hold priority of 7.

  5 Go back to Step 3, and repeat ad nauseum.

Any recent Cisco IOS Software version won't let you set the Setup priority to be lower than the Hold priority for a given tunnel, so you can't make this happen in real life. It's still worth understanding *why* this restriction is in place.

Having said all that, in real life, having Setup and Hold priorities differ is rare. It's perfectly OK to do if you can think of a good reason to do it, but it's not that common.

Configuring Tunnel Priority

The configuration is simple. The command is **tunnel mpls traffic-eng priority** *setup* [*holding*]. You don't have to specify a holding priority; if you don't, it's set to the same as the setup priority. Example 3-9 shows a sample configuration.

Example 3-9 *Configuring Tunnel Priority*

```
interface Tunnel0
 ip unnumbered Loopback0
 no ip directed-broadcast
 tunnel destination 192.168.1.6
 tunnel mode mpls traffic-eng
 tunnel mpls traffic-eng priority 5 5
 tunnel mpls traffic-eng path-option 10 explicit name top
```

That's it. Priority is automatically handled at the midpoint, so there's nothing to configure there. The default priority is 7 (for both Setup and Hold). As Example 3-10 demonstrates, **show mpls traffic-eng tunnels** tells you what the configured priority is on the headend.

Example 3-10 *Determining Where the Configured Priority Lies*

```
gsr4#show mpls traffic-eng tunnels

Name: gsr4_t0                              (Tunnel0) Destination: 192.168.1.6
  Status:
    Admin: up          Oper: up      Path: valid      Signalling: connected

    path option 10, type explicit top (Basis for Setup, path weight 3)

  Config Parameters:
    Bandwidth: 75000    kbps (Global)  Priority: 5  5   Affinity: 0x0/0xFFFF
    Metric Type: TE (default)
```

The shaded portion shows you the Setup and Hold priorities. In this case, both are 5.

Attribute Flags

Another property of MPLS Traffic Engineering that you can enable is attribute flags. An attribute flag is a 32-bit bitmap on a link that can indicate the existence of up to 32 separate properties on that link. The command on a link is simple:

```
router(config-if)#mpls traffic-eng attribute-flags attributes (0x0-0xFFFFFFFF)
```

attributes can be 0x0 to 0xFFFFFFFF. It represents a bitmap of 32 attributes (bits), where the value of an attribute is 0 or 1. 0x0 is the default, which means that all 32 attributes in the bitmap are 0.

You have the freedom to do anything you want with these bits. For example, you might decide that the second-least-significant bit in the attribute flag means "This link is routed over a satellite path and therefore is unsuitable for building low-delay paths across." In that case, any link that is carried over satellite would be configured as follows:

```
router(config-if)#mpls traffic-eng attribute-flags 0x2
```

Suppose for a minute that you're building an MPLS Traffic Engineering network to carry sensitive information that by regulation cannot leave the country. But, if you've got a global network, it might end up that your best path within a specific country is to leave that country and come back. For example, think about United States geography. It is entirely possible that the best path for data from Seattle to Boston would go through Canada. But, if you've got sensitive data that isn't allowed to enter Canada, what do you do?

One way to solve this problem is to decide that a bit in the attribute flag string means "This link leaves the country." Assume that you use bit 28 (the fourth bit from the right) for this purpose.

In that case, the link would be configured as follows:

```
router(config-if)#mpls traffic-eng attribute-flags 0x8
```

Now, suppose that you have a link that carries delay-sensitive traffic that cannot leave the country. Maybe you're a maker of high-tech hockey sticks based in Boston, and you have Voice over IP communications between your Boston office and your Seattle office. You don't want the VoIP traffic to transit any satellite links, because the voice quality would be unacceptable. But you also don't want that VoIP traffic to take a data path through Canada, because a jealous competitor of yours is known to be eavesdropping on your circuits as soon as they cross the U.S. border in order to steal your newest hockey stick design. In that case, any links that were satellite uplinks in Canada would be configured as follows:

```
router(config-if)#mpls traffic-eng attribute-flags 0xA
```

0xA is the logical ORing of **0x2** ("This link crosses a satellite") and **0x8** ("This link leaves the U.S.").

On the tunnel headend, the configuration is a little different. You configured both a desired bit string and a mask.

The short explanation for all this affinity/mask/attribute stuff is that if (AFFINITY && MASK) == (ATTRIBUTE && MASK), the link is considered a match.

If you are confused by the short explanation, here's how it works—in plain English.

Affinity and mask can be a bit tricky to understand. Look at the mask as a selection of "do-care" bits. In other words, if a bit is set to 1 in the mask, you care about the value in the affinity string.

Let's look at a quick example or two with affinities, masks, and link attributes. For the sake of brevity, pretend for a second that all the bit strings involved are only 8 bits long, rather than 32.

If a link has attribute flags of 0x1, in binary this is 0000 0001.

You might think that the affinity string alone is enough to specify whether you want to match this link. You could use the command **tunnel mpls traffic-eng affinity 0x1** and match the link attribute flags, right?

Sure, but only if you wanted to match all 8 bits. What if your link had three types of links:

> 0x1 (0000 0001)
> 0x81 (1000 0001)
> 0x80 (1000 0000)

and you wanted to match all links whose rightmost bit is 01?

To do that, you need to use a mask to specify which bits you want to match. As previously indicated, the mask is a collection of do-care bits; this means that if a bit is set to 1 in the mask, you *do* care that the bit set in the tunnel affinity string matches the link attribute flags. So, you would use the command **tunnel mpls traffic-eng affinity 0x1 mask 0x3**. A mask of 0x3 (0000 0011) means that you *do* care that the rightmost 2 bits of the link affinity string match the rightmost 2 bits of the tunnel affinity.

If you wanted to match all links with the leftmost bit set to (1000 0000), what affinity string and mask would you use?

```
tunnel mpls traffic-eng affinity 0x80 mask 0x80
```

What about if you wanted the leftmost 2 bits to be 10 and the rightmost 2 bits to be 01? What would you use then?

```
tunnel mpls traffic-eng affinity 0x81 mask 0xC3
```

This is because your affinity string is (1000 0001) and you care about the leftmost 2 bits (0xC) and the rightmost 2 bits (0x3). So, the mask is 0xC3.

Example 3-11 shows a sample configuration for the tunnel headend, including a mask. The mask is optional; if it is omitted, the default mask is 0xFFFF. (Remember, in hex, leading zeroes are removed, so the default mask is really 0x0000FFFF.)

Example 3-11 *Configuring Headend Affinity and Mask*

```
interface Tunnel0
  ip unnumbered Loopback0
  tunnel mode mpls traffic-eng
  tunnel destination 192.168.1.8
  tunnel mpls traffic-eng path-option 10 dynamic
  tunnel mpls traffic-eng affinity 0x0-0xFFFFFFFF string [mask <0x-0xFFFFFFFF>]
```

The mask is optional, and it defaults to 0xFFFF. Consider the earlier example, in which bit 0x2 indicated a satellite link and 0x8 indicated a non-U.S. link. If you want to build a tunnel that does not cross a satellite link, you need to make sure that any link the tunnel crosses has the satellite link bit set to 0. So, you would configure this:

```
tunnel mpls traffic-eng affinity 0x0 0x2
```

This says that the entire bit string for the link should be set to 0x0, but that we look only at bit 0x2. As long as bit 0x2 is set to 0x0, a link is acceptable for this tunnel. This means that this tunnel can cross links that have attribute flags of 0x0, 0xFFFFFFFD, or any other value where bit 0x2 is set to 0.

If you want only links that neither cross a satellite link (so bit 0x2 must be 0) nor leave the U.S. (so bit 0x8 must be 0), the configuration is

```
tunnel mpls traffic-eng affinity 0x0 0xA
```

Finally, if you want a link that does not leave the U.S. and that *does* cross a satellite, the configuration is

```
tunnel mpls traffic-eng affinity 0x2 0xA
```

This says that the 0x2 bit must be 1 and the 0x8 bit must be 0.

Tunnel affinities and link attributes can be confusing, but they become straightforward if you review them a few times. They let you easily exclude traffic from a given link without regard to link metric or other available resources.

Administrative Weight

One of the pieces of information that's flooded about a link is its cost, which the TE path calculation uses as part of its path determination process. Two costs are associated with a link—the TE cost and the IGP cost. This allows you to present the TE path calculation with a different set of link costs than the regular IGP SPF sees. The default TE cost on a link is the same as the IGP cost. To change only the TE cost without changing the IGP cost, use the following per-link command:

```
router(config-if)#mpls traffic-eng administrative-weight (0-4294967295)
```

Although the command is **mpls traffic-eng administrative-weight**, it is often referred to as a *metric* rather than a *weight*. Don't worry about it. Just remember that **administrative-weight** is the command you use to set the administrative weight or metric on an interface. This command has two uses:

- Override the metric advertised by the IGP, but only in traffic engineering advertisements
- As a delay-sensitive metric on a per-tunnel basis

What does it mean to override the metric advertised by the IGP, but only in traffic engineering advertisements? Consider that in either OSPF or IS-IS, when a link is advertised into the IGP, it has a link metric that goes along with it. The default link metric in IS-IS is 10, and it can be configured with the per-interface command **isis metric**. The default link metric in OSPF is 10^8 divided by the link bandwidth, and it can be configured with the per-interface command **ip ospf cost**.

If **mpls traffic-eng administrative-weight** is not configured on an interface, the cost advertised in the traffic engineering announcements is the same as the IGP cost for the link. However, there might be a situation in which you want to change the cost advertised for the link, but only for traffic engineering. This is predominantly useful in networks that have both IP and MPLS Traffic Engineering traffic. Consider Figure 3-4.

Figure 3-4   *Sample Network Using* **mpls traffic-eng administrative weight**

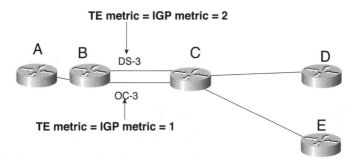

In OSPF, the IGP cost for the DS-3 link from B to C is 2, and the IGP cost for the OC-3 link is 1. Assume that B has a TE tunnel that terminates on D, but also has IP traffic destined for C. By default, both TE tunnels and IP traffic go over the OC-3 link whenever possible. However, if you want the DS-3 link to carry TE tunnel traffic in preference to the OC-3 link, one way to achieve this is to change the administrative metric on these links so that the DS-3 link is preferred for TE traffic.

You do this by setting the administrative weight on the OC-3 link to something higher than the metric on the DS-3 link. On the OC-3 link, if you configure this:

```
router(config-if)#mpls traffic-eng administrative-weight 3
```

the link cost is changed for TE only. Figure 3-4 shows what the IP routing sees on RouterA, but the MPLS Traffic Engineering on RouterA sees the information depicted in Figure 3-5.

Exactly how this path calculation works is considered in Chapter 4.

Another use of the **administrative weight** command is as a delay-sensitive metric on a per-tunnel basis. This is also covered in Chapter 4. The basic idea is that you configure the link administrative weight as a measure of the delay on the link and then use that number, rather than the IGP cost, to determine the path-of-least-delay to the destination. This brings awareness of delay to the network, which lets you differentiate between an OC-3 land line with a relatively small delay, and an OC-3 satellite link with a much higher delay, but with the same bandwidth.

Figure 3-5 *Network with TE Admin Weight and IGP Cost Set Differently*

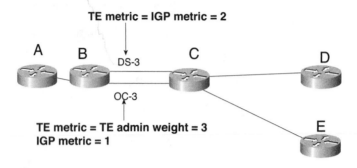

When Information Is Distributed

Now you understand what information is flooded. But *when* is it flooded? In a network that doesn't use MPLS Traffic Engineering, the IGP floods information about a link in three cases:

- When a link goes up or down
- When a link's configuration is changed (when link cost is modified, for example)
- When it's time to periodically reflood the router's IGP information

All sorts of timers are associated with these actions. They differ depending on which IGP you use.

However, MPLS Traffic Engineering adds another reason to flood information—when link bandwidth changes significantly.

As tunnels are set up and torn down across interfaces, the amount of available bandwidth on an interface changes in accordance with the reservations across an interface. As tunnels are set up across an interface, they consume bandwidth, and the amount of available bandwidth goes down; as tunnels are torn down across a particular interface, the amount of available bandwidth goes up.

But when should a router advertise this change in bandwidth?

The first answer that comes to mind might be "whenever a change happens." But that can lead to a tremendous amount of flooding. Some large MPLS Traffic Engineering networks have several thousand tunnels; reflooding whenever a tunnel changes is like adding several thousand links to your IGP. Reflooding TE changes isn't quite as bad as flooding the equivalent number of IGP links—you don't run a full SPF whenever you get new TE link-state information—but there can be a lot of information flooding in the network.

There could potentially be a tremendous amount of flooding—enough to consume bandwidth on the network and significant CPU resources on the router.

On the other hand, you want to make sure that the topology information advertised by the router is reasonably up to date. If all the bandwidth on a particular link is reserved, and this fact is not advertised to the rest of the network, the fact that the network is out of sync with reality can lead to setup failures and other suboptimalities. So, you must entertain ideas about when to flood changes. These are the three rules of flooding thresholds:

1 Flood significant changes immediately.

2 Flood insignificant changes periodically, but more often than the IGP refresh interval.

3 If a change that has not yet been flooded is known to cause an error, flood immediately.

Flood Significant Changes Immediately

The first rule seems simple. But how do you define *significant?* Is a 5-Mbps change in available link bandwidth significant? This depends on the link type. A 5-Mbps change might be significant if it happens on a DS-3 link which has a maximum reservable bandwidth of 45 Mbps. But a 5-Mbps change probably isn't worth flooding on an OC-192 link, which has more than 200 times the bandwidth of a DS-3 (a little less than 10 Gbps).

Significant is defined as a percentage of link bandwidth. But is that enough? You might not need to know immediately if your OC-192 goes from 6.483 Gbps of reservable bandwidth to 6.488 Gbps of reservable bandwidth. But you might want to know if your OC-192 gives up its last 100 Mbps of bandwidth and goes from 0.1 Gbps reservable bandwidth to 0 Gbps reservable bandwidth.

You might also need to care more about changes in one direction than in the other. So, it might be important to tell the world if you give away the last 5 Mbps on an OC-192 link, but it might not be important to tell the world if that 5 Mbps is freed up again.

Rules for when to advertise available bandwidth are different for every network, situation, and link. So Cisco IOS Software comes with a set of reasonable defaults, but also with a flexible scheme for determining what changes are *significant*.

Here is the command that controls when to flood information about a change on a particular link:

```
gsr12(config-if)#mpls traffic-eng flooding thresholds {up | down} list of threshold
    percentages
```

The percentages you configure are the percentages of bandwidth reserved on the link.

Configuring percentages in the **up** direction means that as more bandwidth is used and the thresholds are crossed, link bandwidth is flooded. Percentages configured in the **down** direction are crossed as bandwidth is freed up and reservations on the link decrease.

The default thresholds on all links are the same in both directions. They are 15, 30, 45, 60, 75, 80, 85, 90, 95, 96, 97, 98, 99, and 100. Currently, there is a limit of 16 flooding thresholds. There is no restriction on the numerical values used, but you cannot have more than 16 values in each direction.

You can view the current thresholds using the command **show mpls traffic-eng link-management bandwidth-allocation** [*interface-name*], as demonstrated in Example 3-12.

Example 3-12 *Viewing Available Bandwidth Thresholds*

```
gsr1#show mpls traffic-eng link-management bandwidth-allocation pos0/0
System Information::
    Links Count:        3
    Bandwidth Hold Time:  max. 15 seconds
Link ID::  PO0/0 (192.168.2.1)
    Link Status:
      Physical Bandwidth:    155000 kbits/sec
      Max Res Global BW:     116250 kbits/sec (reserved: 0% in, 0% out)
      Max Res Sub BW:        0 kbits/sec (reserved: 100% in, 100% out)
      BW Descriptors:        0
      MPLS TE Link State:    MPLS TE on, RSVP on, admin-up, flooded
      Inbound Admission:     allow-all
      Outbound Admission:    allow-if-room
      Admin. Weight:         10 (IGP)
      IGP Neighbor Count:    1
      Up Thresholds:         15 30 45 60 75 80 85 90 95 96 97 98 99 100 (default)
      Down Thresholds:       100 99 98 97 96 95 90 85 80 75 60 45 30 15 (default)
    Downstream Global Pool Bandwidth Information (kbits/sec):
      KEEP PRIORITY    BW HELD  BW TOTAL HELD    BW LOCKED  BW TOTAL LOCKED
                 0        0           0               0             0
                 1        0           0               0             0
                 2        0           0               0             0
                 3        0           0               0             0
                 4        0           0               0             0
                 5        0           0               0             0
                 6        0           0               0             0
                 7        0           0               0             0
```

Every time bandwidth is reserved on an interface, the reservation is considered. If the amount of bandwidth change is enough to cross a threshold, information about that link is reflooded immediately.

Flooding Links in IS-IS Versus OSPF

Flooding is a little different between IS-IS and OSPF. In OSPF, only information about the link that has changed is flooded, because a Type 10 LSA contains a single link advertisement. In IS-IS, information about *all* links on a node is flooded even if only one has changed, because the Type 22 TLV contains a list of all the links on the router. Ninety-nine percent of the time you're not going to care about the distinction, but it's worth noting. The trade-off is that on a router with many links doing MPLS Traffic Engineering, the flooding traffic from a single link change is more in IS-IS than the flooding traffic from a single link change in OSPF. But if multiple links change on the same router, IS-IS might be more efficient at encoding these changes in a single TLV. But again, most of the time you don't care.

Consider a link with 100 Mbps of reservable bandwidth. At time 0, the link has 0 Mbps reserved. As tunnels come and go, thresholds are inspected to see if any change in reservation crosses a threshold, and TE link-state information is flooded as necessary.

Consider the bandwidth changes caused by the tunnel reservations shown in Table 3-2. Positive bandwidth changes are due to reservations being made, and negative changes are due to reservations being torn down. Assuming that the default threshold is configured for the link, Table 3-2 lists bandwidth changes on the link at various points in time. The Flood? column shows whether the change caused flooding. The last column shows the thresholds crossed in each direction. Figure 3-6 illustrates the points in time where the bandwidth changes caused significant flooding. The arrows indicate points where TE information is flooded.

Table 3-2   *Crossing Flooding Thresholds*

Time	Bandwidth Change (%)	Bandwidth Remaining (%)	Bandwidth Consumed (%)	Flood?	Threshold Crossed, Direction?
0	0	100	0%	N/A	—
1	10	90	10%	N	—
2	1	89	11%	N	—
3	2	87	13%	N	—
4	2	85	15%	Y	15%, up
5	35	50	50%	Y	Both 30% and 45%, up
6	–8	58	42%	N	—
7	–20	78	22%	Y	30%, down
8	72	6	94%	Y	30%, 45%, up
9	1	5	95%	Y	95%, up
10	2	3	97%	Y	96%, 97%
11	–3	6	94%	Y	96%, 95%, down

Figure 3-6 *Significant Flooding Occurrences*

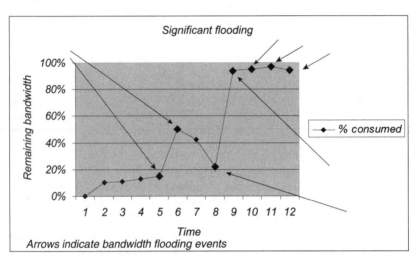

The important concept to take away from this example is that the default flooding values are more sensitive to changes when the link is almost full than when it's nearly empty.

Flood Insignificant Changes Periodically, But More Often Than the IGP Refresh Interval

How often is "periodically"? By default, it's every 180 seconds (3 minutes). But this too can be configured, using the following global command:

```
gsr1(config)#mpls traffic-eng link-management timers periodic-flooding 0-3600
    second interval
```

This is how often information is flooded if available bandwidth has changed and it hasn't already been flooded. The default behavior is to check with the TE Link Manager (see Chapter 4) every 3 minutes and, if reservable bandwidth has changed on any links, flood the new information about these links. MPLS Traffic Engineering information is *not* flooded every 3 minutes if there are no changes. Only if changes were made in the last 3 minutes are things flooded. Periodic flooding floods only information that has not yet been flooded (that is, a bandwidth change that did not cross a flooding threshold).

Setting **mpls traffic-eng link-management timers periodic-flooding** to 0 disables periodic flooding. This means that bandwidth information is flooded only on Rule 1 or Rule 3.

If a Change That Has Not Yet Been Flooded Is Known to Cause an Error, Flood Immediately

What's an *error?* RSVP sends an error when a path setup fails due to lack of bandwidth. Errors are covered in more detail in Chapter 4, but there's not much to understand from a flooding perspective. If a router receives a reservation request for more bandwidth than is currently available on a particular link, available link bandwidth has been changed since the last time flooding occurred, so the router receiving the reservation assumes that the router sending the reservation has stale information in its topology database, and it refloods.

When to Change the Flooding Timers

Don't.

Or, more specifically, don't change them unless you know you need to. It might be tempting to change the periodic flooding timer to 1 second so that all routers always have the most up-to-date information. But do you really need that level of accuracy? And at what cost do you achieve it? The default thresholds are useful; change them only if you know you need to.

How Information Is Distributed

You now have a good understanding of what information is flooded, and when. You might not understand exactly how that information is used, but that's covered in Chapter 4. This section covers the nuts and bolts: How do you configure the IGP to flood? What do the packet formats look like? How are MPLS Traffic Engineering attributes added to the IGP?

MPLS Traffic Engineering in OSPF

You need to enter only two commands to enable flooding of MPLS Traffic Engineering info in OSPF, as shown in Example 3-13.

Example 3-13 *Enabling MPLS TE in the OSPF Process*

```
router ospf 1
  mpls traffic-eng router-id Loopback0
  mpls traffic-eng area 0
```

mpls traffic-eng router-id Loopback0 sets the TE RID. This can be a different value than the OSPF RID, but it shouldn't be. See the discussion of loopback interfaces near the beginning of this chapter.

mpls traffic-eng area 0 configures the area in which traffic engineering is enabled. Generally, MPLS Traffic Engineering is enabled in only a single area. This does not have to be Area 0, but it almost always is. This single-area restriction can be lifted; see Chapter 9 and the "Interarea Tunnels" section of Chapter 4 for details.

One additional command might prove useful in OSPF. If you have a topology such as that shown in Figure 3-7, you might have a *virtual link* between ABR1 and ABR2.

Figure 3-7 *OSPF Network with a Virtual Link Between ABRs*

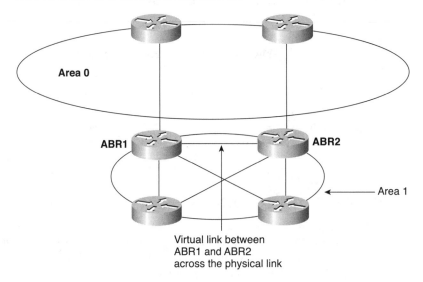

Virtual link between
ABR1 and ABR2
across the physical link

With a virtual link, the link between ABR1 and ABR2 is configured to be in Area 1, but the virtual link means that this link can be used in Area 0 to route across. MPLS TE doesn't understand virtual links, so in order to advertise the virtual link into Area 0, you need to use this command:

```
router ospf 1
  mpls traffic-eng interface interface-name area area
```

interface-name is the name of the interface the virtual link is on, and *area* is the area you want to advertise that link into. *area* should always be 0, unless you absolutely, positively, without a doubt know what you're doing.

That's it. If you add the first two lines shown in Example 3-13 to your IGP configuration and configure a basic TE tunnel as described in the earlier section "MPLS Traffic Engineering Configuration," TE tunnels start to come up. You won't actually route any traffic across them yet, but they'll come up.

In OSPF, the relevant data is encoded in an area-local opaque LSA (LSA Type 10). RFC 2370 defines opaque LSAs. The data inside these LSAs is defined in *draft-katz-yeung-ospf-traffic*.

Inside the Type 10 LSAs, the OSPF TE extensions define several TLV (Type/Length/Value) triplets. Each TLV is encoded as shown in Figure 3-8.

Figure 3-8   *TLV Encoding*

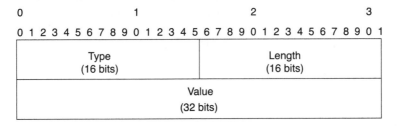

Two TLV types are defined:

- **Type 1**—The Router Address TLV. The Router Address TLV is 32 bits long and contains the configured MPLS Traffic Engineering router ID (see Chapter 4).

- **Type 2**—The Link TLV. The Link TLV is repeated once for each link the router describes. The Link TLV is composed of up to nine different sub-TLVs, as documented in Table 3-3. The terms used here correspond to the Cisco terminology; the names given to these sub-TLVs in the draft definition are sometimes different.

Table 3-3   *Sub-TLVs*

Sub-TLV Name	Sub-TLV ID	Size	Definition	Interface Configuration
Link type	1	1 byte	1 = point-to-point, 2 = multiaccess (for example, Ethernet)	N/A
Link ID	2	4 bytes	On point-to-point links, the neighbor's OSPF RID On multiaccess links, the designated router's (DR's) interface address	N/A
Local interface IP address	3	4 bytes	IP address of the advertising router on the link, or set to the advertiser's TE RID if unnumbered	**ip address** *address mask*

continues

Table 3-3 *Sub-TLVs (Continued)*

Sub-TLV Name	Sub-TLV ID	Size	Definition	Interface Configuration
Remote interface address	4	4 bytes	Interface address of the neighbor on the other end of this link, or the DR interface address if a multipoint interface	N/A
Traffic engineering metric	5	4 bytes	The link's OSPF cost, or a cost assigned by the TE code	**ip ospf cost** or **mpls traffic-eng administrative-weight**
Maximum link bandwidth	6	4 bytes	Maximum *physical* bandwidth on the interface, as seen in **show interface** and optionally set with the **bandwidth** command	**bandwidth** *x*
Maximum reservable bandwidth	7	4 bytes	Amount of bandwidth that can be reserved on the link	**ip rsvp bandwidth** *x*
Unreserved bandwidth (per priority level)	8	32 bytes	For each priority level, the difference between the maximum reservable bandwidth and the reserved bandwidth per priority level	N/A
Attribute flags	9	4 bytes	32-bit bitmask that puts the link in one or more administrative groups	**mpls traffic-eng attribute-flags**

MPLS Traffic Engineering Flooding in IS-IS

IS-IS floods exactly the same information as OSPF; however, it encodes the data a little differently. The Internet draft *draft-ietf-isis-traffic* was put forth not only to add MPLS TE information to IS-IS, but also to

- Expand the link metrics from 6 bits to 24 and the total path metric from 1023 to just over 4 billion

- Change some internal details of metric encoding

- Advertise a 32-bit router ID

These changes were made to make IS-IS more useful in large networks, which might contain many different types of links.

Expanding the link metrics also lets IS-IS advertise traffic engineering information. The other two modifications to IS-IS, changing the metric encoding and advertising a router ID, are not covered here; see the draft (or, eventually, RFC) for more details.

In order to use IS-IS traffic engineering, you first need to enable support for these new TLVs. These TLVs are collectively referred to as *wide metrics;* enabling them is called *wide metric support.*

The IS-IS configuration, shown in Example 3-14, is almost as simple as the OSPF configuration.

Example 3-14 *Enabling Wide Metric Support in IS-IS*

```
router isis name
  mpls traffic-eng router-id Loopback0
  mpls traffic-eng {level-1 | level-2}
  metric-style {narrow | transition | wide}
```

Like OSPF, IS-IS traffic engineering is generally enabled at only a single level, either Level 1 or Level 2. This restriction can be lifted, however, as discussed in the "Interarea Tunnels" section of Chapter 4.

Note the addition of the **metric-style** command.

When new IS-IS TLVs were defined to carry traffic engineering information, a TLV was also defined to carry larger metrics for IP links, whether those links were involved in MPLS Traffic Engineering or not. This additional TLV (TLV Type 135) increased the per-link metric range from 0 to 63 (a 6-bit link metric) to 0 to 1,677,214 (a 24-bit link metric). Type 135 TLVs are often called *IP-Extended TLVs.*

NOTE 2^{24} is 0 to 1,677,215, not 1,677,214! What gives?

If you configure the maximum link metric (where all 24 bits are set to 1), the link in question is not eligible for use as an MPLS TE link. As a safeguard, the highest numeric value you can configure is **isis metric 1677214** so that you don't accidentally remove links from your topology. If you want to remove a link from your topology on purpose, use the command **isis metric maximum**.

Although IP-Extended TLVs have nothing to do with MPLS Traffic Engineering per se, MPLS Traffic Engineering enhancements and IP-Extended TLVs go hand in hand. Before you can do MPLS Traffic Engineering, support for wide metrics must be enabled.

The problem is that many networks run code that does not understand the new TLVs. Advertising IP-Extended TLVs to routers that don't understand them can result in all sorts of routing problems. Routers that can understand both old- and new-style TLVs need to be able to gracefully transition from one style to the other—hence the **metric-style** command. You can use five different options with the **metric-style** command, as defined in Table 3-4.

Table 3-4   **metric-style** *Command Options*

Command	Description
metric-style narrow	Originates and accepts old-style TLVs only. Default behavior on code that understands old- and new-style TLVs.
metric-style narrow transition	Originates old-style TLVs and accepts both old- and new-style .TLVs.
metric-style transition	Originates and accepts both old- and new-style TLVs.
metric-style wide	Originates and accepts only new-style TLVs. The end goal of a move from old- to new-style metrics is to have all routers configured with **metric-style wide**.
metric-style wide transition	Originates only new-style metrics and accepts both old- and new-style metrics.

There are a few different ways to migrate from old to new, taking into consideration how much work you want to do and how perilous it might be to advertise both old- and new-style TLVs at the same time.

In order for MPLS Traffic Engineering to work, all routers that are participating in MPLS Traffic Engineering must have a metric style of **transition**, **wide**, or **wide transition** so that they can receive and originate wide metrics and MPLS Traffic Engineering TLVs.

Appendix B, "CCO and Other References," refers to a paper on CCO called "MPLS Traffic Engineering and Enhancements." It discusses migration from narrow to wide metrics in more detail.

The first point, expanding link metrics, is covered in this chapter because it is an integral part of MPLS Traffic Engineering. The other two points are not discussed here; see the drafts for full details.

IS-IS encodes MPLS Traffic Engineering information in an extended IS reachability TLV, TLV Type 22. Figure 3-9 shows the format of this TLV.

The field for systemID and pseudonode number is 7 bytes (56 bits) long. The default link metric is 3 bytes long. The sub-TLV length field is also 1 byte long. It indicates the length of the total number of sub-TLVs.

Figure 3-9 *TLV Type 22 Format*

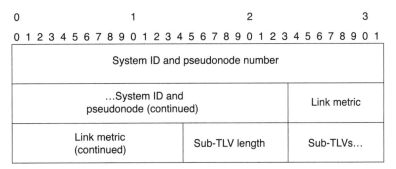

Table 3-5 describes the seven different sub-TLVs that carry MPLS Traffic Engineering link information.

Table 3-5 *Sub-TLVs That Carry MPLS Traffic Engineering Link Information*

Sub-TLV Name	Sub-TLV ID	Size	Definition	Interface Configuration
Attribute flags	3	4 bytes	32-bit bitmask that puts the link in one or more administrative groups	**mpls traffic-eng attribute-flags**
IPv4 interface address	6	4 bytes	Interface mask is in the Type-22 TLV	**ip address** *network mask*
IPv4 neighbor address	8	4 bytes	IP address of a neighbor on a p2p link; 0.0.0.0 if describing a broadcast link	N/A
Maximum link bandwidth	9	4 bytes	Maximum *physical* bandwidth on the interface, as seen in **sh int** and optionally set with the **bandwidth** command	**bandwidth** *x*
Maximum reservable bandwidth	10	4 bytes	Amount of bandwidth that can be reserved on the link	**ip rsvp bandwidth** *x*
Unreserved bandwidth (per priority level)	11	32 bytes	For each priority level, the difference between the maximum reservable bandwidth and the reserved bandwidth per priority	N/A
Traffic engineering metric	18	3 bytes	The IS-IS cost of the link, or a cost assigned by the TE code	**isis metric** or **mpls traffic-eng administrative-weight**

If you compare IS-IS to OSPF, you see that although the packet formats are different, both protocols advertise exactly the same information.

Summary

This chapter covered both bare-bones MPLS Traffic Engineering configuration and information flooding. We described what information is flooded, when this information is flooded, and in what format the information is carried. Now that you have reached the end of this chapter, you have enough information to bring up MPLS Traffic Engineering tunnels in a network. We're not recommending that you dash out and start bringing up TE tunnels quite yet. We have a few more things to cover before MPLS Traffic Engineering becomes useful to you. Chapter 4 covers path calculation and setup, and Chapter 5 covers forwarding traffic down tunnels. After you finish those chapters, you can start intelligently using MPLS Traffic Engineering!

Path Calculation and Setup

Chapter 3, "Information Distribution," asked these questions: How does MPLS Traffic Engineering really work? What are the underlying protocols, and how do they all tie together? And, most importantly, what do you need to type on your router to make all this wonderful stuff come to life?

Chapter 3 broke MPLS Traffic Engineering into three paths:

- Information distribution
- Path calculation and setup
- Forwarding traffic down a tunnel

This chapter, as you can tell from the title, is about the second part—path calculation and setup.

Path calculation and setup are two different things. Functionally, the code that decides what path a tunnel takes across your network is different from the code that actually sets up this tunnel; however, the two technologies are so closely related that it makes sense to discuss them in the same chapter.

First, this chapter discusses path calculation. This discussion is broken into three pieces:

- The basic Shortest Path First (SPF) calculation that OSPF and IS-IS use to build their routing tables in an IP network
- MPLS Traffic Engineering's Constrained SPF (CSPF) and how it differs from the traditional SPF performed by IP routing protocols
- Mechanisms you can use to influence CSPF's path calculation

After path calculation, this chapter covers MPLS Traffic Engineering Label-Switched Path (LSP) setup. The actual setup is done using a protocol called Resource Reservation Protocol (RSVP). RSVP plays a part not only in path setup, but also in error signalling and path teardown; that too is covered.

An alternative to RSVP for MPLS TE is Constrained Routing with LDP (CR-LDP). Cisco does not implement CR-LDP, so it is not covered further in this book.

How SPF Works

In a link-state routing protocol, each router knows about all other routers in a network and the links that connect these routers. In OSPF, this information is encoded as Link-State Advertisements (LSAs); in IS-IS, this information is Link-State Packets (LSPs). This chapter does not discuss the differences between these two protocols. See Appendix B, "CCO and Other Resources," for more information. Because the acronym LSP also stands for Label-Switched Path, the unit of information a router uses to flood its connectivity information will be called an LSA. Remember that IS-IS works much the same way that OSPF does.

As soon as a router knows about all other routers and links, it runs the *Dijkstra Shortest Path First* algorithm (named after Edsger W. Dijkstra, who first identified it) to determine the shortest path between the calculating router and all other routers in the network.

Because all routers run the same calculation on the same data, every router has the same picture of the network, and packets are routed consistently at every hop.

But how does the Dijkstra calculation actually work? It's actually quite simple. Understanding SPF is fundamental to understanding MPLS Traffic Engineering's CSPF, which is based on the basic Dijkstra SPF algorithm.

Suppose you have a simple network similar to the one shown in Figure 4-1.

Figure 4-1 *Simple Network Topology Demonstrating the SPF Algorithm*

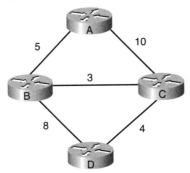

This example walks through what happens when Router A runs SPF and generates its routing table.

After each router has flooded its information to the network, all the routers know about all the other routers and the links between them. So the link-state database on every router looks like Table 4-1.

Table 4-1   *Class Map Matches*

Router	{neighbor, cost} Pairs
A	{B,5} {C,10}
B	{A,5} {C,3} {D,8}
C	{A,10} {B,3} {D,4}
D	{B,8} {C,4}

So what does Router A do with this information?

In SPF calculation, each router maintains two lists:

- A list of nodes that are known to be on the shortest path to a destination. This list is called the PATH list or sometimes the PATHS list. It is important to understand that the only things on the PATH list are paths to a destination that are known to be the shortest path to that destination.

- A list of next hops that might or might not be on the shortest path to a destination. This list is called the TENTatitve or TENT list.

Each list is a table of {router, distance, next-hop} triplets from the perspective of the calculating router.

Why a triplet? You need to know which router you're trying to get to in PATH and TENT lists, so the first part of the triplet is the name of the router in question. In reality, this is the router ID (RID) rather than the textual name, but for this example, we'll use the router name. The next hop is the router you go through to get to the node in question. The third item in the triplet is the distance, which is the cost to get to the node in question.

Why are the names of these lists in all capital letters? That's just how they're written. They're not acronyms; they're just written in capitals. Most other examples of SPF calculation, and many debugs involving the SPF calculations themselves, refer to these lists as PATH (or sometimes PATHS) and TENT.

The algorithm for computing the shortest path to each node is simple. Each router runs the following algorithm:

Step 1   Put "self" on the PATH list with a distance of 0 and a next hop of self. The router running the SPF refers to itself as either "self" or the *root node,* because this node is the root of the shortest-path tree.

Step 2   Take the node just placed on the PATH list, and call it the PATH node. Look at the PATH node's list of neighbors. Add each neighbor in this list to the TENT list with a next hop of the PATH node, unless the neighbor is already in the TENT or PATH list with a lower cost. Call the node just added to the TENT list the TENT node. Set the cost to reach the TENT node equal to the cost to get from the root node to the PATH node plus the cost to get from the PATH node to the TENT node. If the node just added to a TENT list already exists in the TENT list, but with a higher cost, replace the higher-cost node with the node currently under consideration.

Step 3 Find the neighbor in the TENT list with the lowest cost, add that neighbor to the PATH list, and repeat Step 2. If the TENT list is empty, stop.

This might seem complicated, but it's really straightforward. Consider the process that Router A in Figure 4-1 goes through to build its routing table:

Step 1 Put "self" on the PATH list with a distance of 0 and a next hop of self.

This means that Router A's databases look like Table 4-2.

Table 4-2 *PATH and TENT Lists for Router A*

PATH List	TENT List
{A,0,0}	(empty)

Step 2 Take the node just placed on the PATH list, and call it the PATH node. Look at that node's neighbor list. Add each neighbor in this list to the TENT list with a next hop of the PATH node, unless the neighbor is already in the TENT or PATH list with a lower cost. If the node just added to a TENT list already exists in the list, but with a higher cost, replace the higher-cost node with the node currently under consideration.

In this example, {B,5,B} and {C,10,C} get added to the TENT list, as reflected in Table 4-3.

Table 4-3 *PATH and TENT Lists for Router A After Step 2*

PATH List	TENT List
{A,0,0}	{B,5,B}
	{C,10,C}

Step 3 Find the neighbor in the TENT list with the lowest cost, add that neighbor to the PATH list, and repeat Step 2. If the TENT list is empty, stop.

{B,5,B} is moved to the PATH list, because that's the shortest path to B. Because {C,10,C} is the only other neighbor of Router A, and the cost to get to C is greater than the cost to get to B, it's impossible to ever have a path to B that has a lower cost than what's already known. Table 4-4 reflects the PATH and TENT lists at this point.

Table 4-4   *PATH and TENT Lists for Router A After Step 3*

PATH List	TENT List
{A,0,0}	{C,10,C}
{B,5,B}	

Step 4   Repeat Step 2. Take the node just placed on the PATH list and call it the PATH node. Look at that node's neighbor list. Add each neighbor in this list to the TENT list with a next hop of the PATH node, unless the neighbor is already in the TENT or PATH list with a lower cost. If the node just added to a TENT list already exists in the list, but with a higher cost, replace the higher-cost node with the node currently under consideration.

Router B's neighbors are examined. Router B has a link to C with a cost of 3 and a link to D with a cost of 8. Router C, with a cost of 5 (to get from "self" to B) + 3 (to get from B to C) = 8 (the total cost from A to C via B) and a next hop of B, is added to the TENT list, as is Router D, with a cost of 5 (the cost to get from the root node to B) + 8 (the cost to get from B to D) = 13 and a next hop of B. Because the path to C with a cost of 8 through B is lower than the path to C with a cost of 10 through C, the path to C with a cost of 10 is removed from the TENT list. Table 4-5 reflects the PATH and TENT lists at this point.

Table 4-5   *PATH and TENT Lists for Router A After Step 4*

PATH List	TENT List
{A,0,0}	~~{C,10,C}~~
{B,5,B}	{C,8,B}
	{D,13,B}

Step 5   Find the path in the TENT list with the lowest cost, add that path to the PATH list, and repeat Step 2. If the TENT list is empty, stop.

The path to C through {C,8,B} is moved from the TENT list to the PATH list, as reflected in Table 4-6.

Table 4-6   *PATH and TENT Lists for Router A After Step 5*

PATH List	TENT List
{A,0,0}	{D,13,B}
{B,5,B}	
{C,8,B}	

Step 6 Take the path just placed on the PATH list, and look at that node's neighbor list. For each neighbor in this list, add the path to that neighbor to the TENT list, unless the neighbor is already in the TENT or PATH list with a lower cost. If the node just added to a TENT list already exists in the list, but with a higher cost, replace the higher-cost path with the path currently under consideration.

Under this rule, the path to D through B (which is really B→C→D) with a cost of 12 replaces the path to D through B→D with a cost of 13, as reflected in Table 4-7.

Table 4-7 *PATH and TENT Lists for Router A After Step 6*

PATH List	TENT List
{A,0,0}	~~{D,13,B}~~
{B,5,B}	{D,12,B}
{C,8,B}	

Step 7 Find the neighbor in the TENT list with the lowest cost, add that neighbor to the PATH list, and repeat Step 2. If the TENT list is empty, stop.

The path to D is moved to the PATH list, as reflected in Table 4-8.

Table 4-8 *PATH and TENT Lists for Router A After Step 7: The TENT List Is Empty*

PATH List	TENT List
{A,0,0}	
{B,5,B}	
{C,8,B}	
{D,12,B}	

Step 8 Find the neighbor in the TENT list with the lowest cost, add that neighbor to the PATH list, and repeat Step 2. If the TENT list is empty, stop.

The TENT list is empty because D has no neighbors that are not already on the PATH list, so you stop. At this point, the PATH list becomes A's routing table, which looks like Table 4-9.

Table 4-9 *Router A's Routing Table*

Node	Cost	Next Hop
A	0	Self
B	5	B (directly connected)
C	8	B
D	12	B

So that's how the basic SPF algorithm works. After it's done, the topology (according to Router A's routing table) looks like Figure 4-2.

Figure 4-2   *Router A's View of the Network After Running the SPF Algorithm*

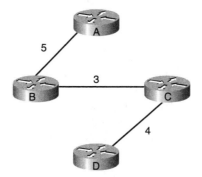

As you can see, traffic from Router A never crosses the links from A to C or the links from B to D.

Two things should jump out at you. The first is that the only traffic that crosses the link from B to D is traffic from Router A.

The second is that the link from Router A to Router C is not used at all, because its cost (10) is so high. In a real network, a link like this would end up being expensive dead weight, only being used when another link in the network fails. The actual SPF implementation is a bit more complex than what's been described here, but this is the general idea.

How CSPF Works

The process that generates a path for a TE tunnel to take is different from the regular SPF process, but not much. There are two major differences between regular SPF, done by routing protocols, and CSPF, run by MPLS Traffic Engineering.

For one thing, the path determination process is not designed to find the best route to all routers—only to the tunnel endpoint. This makes the SPF algorithm slightly different: You stop as soon as the node you're trying to get to is on the PATH list, rather than trying to calculate the shortest path to *all* nodes.

Also, there's now more than one metric at each node. Instead of just a single cost for a link between two neighbors, there's also

- Bandwidth
- Link attributes
- Administrative weight

So how does CSPF work? First, the triplet used in regular SPF needs to hold bandwidth, link attributes, and administrative weight. This turns the triplet into a sextuplet. See Chapter 3 for information on how to configure these properties.

Another subtle detail of CSPF is that because you're looking for a single path to an end node, there is no load sharing. There are a few tiebreakers when two paths have all the same attributes: minimum path bandwidth, the lowest IGP metric to a path, and the path's lowest hop count. So the sextuplet really becomes something of a nonet (nine items in the object).

To help you better understand this concept, let's run through a couple of examples. The first one, shown in Figure 4-3, is similar to Figure 4-1, but each link is advertising its available bandwidth. For simplicity, only four link properties are shown in the PATH/TENT lists {link, cost, next hop, and available bandwidth}. Assume that the other link attributes don't come into play in this example; you'll learn about those shortly.

Figure 4-3 *Simple Network Topology Demonstrating the CSPF Algorithm*

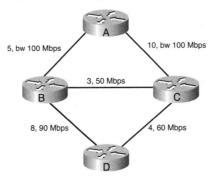

In the topology shown in Figure 4-3, Router A wants to build a TE tunnel to Router D with a bandwidth of 60 Mbps. Each link lists its metric (the same as in Figure 4-1) and its available bandwidth.

Without taking bandwidth into account, Router A's best path to Router D is A→B→C→D, with a total cost of 12. But the path A→B→C→D doesn't have 60 Mbps available. CSPF needs to calculate the shortest path that has 60 Mbps available.

This is actually quite simple. The steps for the CSPF algorithm are as follows:

Step 1 Put "self" on the PATH list with a distance of 0 and a next hop of self. Set the bandwidth to N/A.

Step 2 Take the node just placed on the PATH list, and call it the PATH node. Look at that node's neighbor list. Add each neighbor in this list to the TENT list with a next hop of the PATH node, unless the neighbor is already in the TENT or PATH list with a lower cost.

Do not add this path to the TENT list unless it meets all configured constraints for the desired tunnel—bandwidth and affinity. If the node just added to the TENT list already exists in the list, but with a higher cost or lower minimum bandwidth, replace the higher-cost path with the path currently under consideration.

Step 3   Find the neighbor in the TENT list with the lowest cost, add that neighbor to the PATH list, and repeat Step 2. If the TENT list is empty or the node that is the tail of the tunnel is on the PATH list, stop.

Given that the rules are similar, here's the SPF calculation for a path from A to D that needs 60 Mbps. Instead of {node, cost, next hop}, the PATH and TENT lists contain information encoded as {node, cost, next hop, minimum bandwidth}. You'll understand this better as you follow the next example. This example follows the same general format as the previous SPF example, but some of the basic steps are compressed into one (for example, moving a node from TENT to PATH and putting its neighbors on the TENT list.)

Step 1   Put "self" on the PATH list with a distance of 0 and a next hop of self. Set the bandwidth to N/A. The results are shown in Table 4-10.

Table 4-10   *Initial PATH and TENT Lists After Step 1*

PATH List	TENT List
{A,0,self,N/A}	(empty)

Step 2   Put Router A's neighbors in the TENT list. The results are shown in Table 4-11.

Table 4-11   *PATH and TENT Lists for Router A After Step 2*

PATH List	TENT List
{A,0,self,N/A}	{B,5,B,100}
	{C,10,C,100}

Step 3   Move B from the PATH list to the TENT list, and put B's neighbors in the TENT list. The results are shown in Table 4-12.

Table 4-12   *PATH and TENT Lists for Router A After Step 3*

PATH List	TENT List
{A,0,self,N/A}	{C,10,C,100}
{B,5,B,100}	{D,13,B,90}

{C,8,B,50} was not added to the TENT list because it doesn't meet the minimum bandwidth requirement.

Step 4 Put B's neighbors in the TENT list, and take C from TENT and put it in PATH. The results are shown in Table 4-13.

Table 4-13 *PATH and TENT Lists for Router A After Step 4*

PATH List	TENT List
{A,0,self,N/A}	{D,13,B,90}
{B,5,B,100}	
{C,10,C,100}	

{D,14,C,60} is not put on the TENT list because the cost to get to D through B is lower than the cost to get there through C.

Step 5 Take D off the TENT list. At this point, the best possible path to D is in the PATH list, so you're done. The fact that the TENT list happens to be empty is an artifact of the network topology; D happened to be the last node you encountered in the SPF. If you had reached the best path to D and there were still more nodes in the TENT list, you'd have stopped anyway. The results are shown in Table 4-14.

Table 4-14 *PATH and TENT Lists for Router A After Step 5*

PATH List	TENT List
{A,0,self,N/A}	
{B,5,B,100}	
{C,10,C,100}	
{D,13,B,90}	

In reality, the path calculation is more complex than what is covered here. CSPF has to keep track of all the nodes in the path, not just the next hop. Also, there's more than just bandwidth to consider—there are also link attributes and tiebreakers.

Tiebreakers in CSPF

In regular SPF (as used in OSPF and IS-IS), it's OK to use multiple paths to the destination that have the same cost. This is sometimes called Equal-Cost MultiPath (ECMP), and it's a good idea when talking about your regular Interior Gateway Protocol (IGP).

In CSPF, however, remember that you're not trying to calculate all the best paths to all possible destinations. You're looking for one path to one destination. What do you do when you go to put a node on the TENT list and the node in question is already on the TENT list, with the same cost? You need to find a way to differentiate these paths from each other.

Here are the tiebreakers between paths, in order:

1   Take the path with the largest minimum available bandwidth.

2   If there is still a tie, take the path with the lowest hop count (the number of routers in the path).

3   If there is still a tie, take one path at random.

NOTE   Things aren't really "random." When you get this far in the decision process, you take the top path on the PATH list. There's no "random" in the sense that every possible tied path has an equal chance of being chosen, but it's random in that which path ends up on the top of the PATH list is topology- and implementation-dependent, so it's not something that you, as the network administrator, control.

These tiebreakers are applied as a node is put on the TENT list. At any time, a given node should be listed only once on the TENT list. This is different from an IGP SPF, in which you can have multiple ways to get to a given node and can load share between them.

Assume that, in the network shown in Figure 4-4, you want to build a tunnel from RtrA to RtrZ with a bandwidth of 10 Mbps. Every path in this network fits that description. So which one do you choose?

Figure 4-4   *Sample Network in Which CSPF Tiebreakers Come into Play*

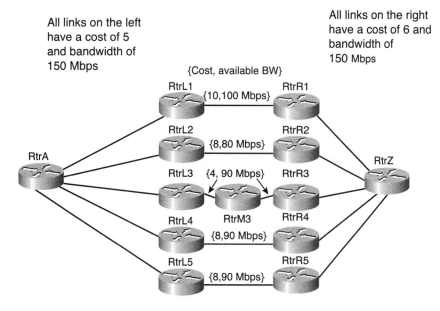

There are five possible paths from A to Z, referred to as P1 through P5 (from top to bottom). Table 4-15 lists the path attributes.

Table 4-15   *Attributes of the Five Possible Paths from RtrA to RtrZ*

Path Name	Routers in Path	Path Cost	Minimum Bandwidth on Path (in Mbps)
P1	RtrA→RtrL1→RtrR1→RtrZ	21	100
P2	RtrA→RtrL2→RtrR2→RtrZ	19	80
P3	RtrA→RtrL3→RtrM3→RtrR3→RtrZ	19	90
P4	RtrA→RtrL4→RtrR4→RtrZ	19	90
P5	RtrA→RtrL5→RtrR5→RtrZ	19	90

Here's the decision process that RtrA goes through to pick one of these paths:

- P1 is not used because it has a higher path cost than the other paths.
- P2 is not used because its minimum bandwidth is 80 Mbps, which is lower than the minimum bandwidths of the other paths.
- P3 is not used because it has a hop count of 5, whereas the other paths under consideration have a hop count of 4.
- RtrA picks either P4 or P5 off the top of the TENT list.

Other Things That Influence CSPF

Chapter 3 discussed the use and configuration of bandwidth, link attributes, and administrative weight in the context of information flooding. It also covered how to configure an MPLS Traffic Engineering tunnel to take advantage of these attributes.

How are these attributes used to influence CSPF? It's pretty straightforward.

Bandwidth has been pretty well covered. A path is not considered eligible for use for a particular MPLS TE tunnel if it does not have the bandwidth required.

Link attributes are similar to bandwidth, from a CSPF perspective. As covered in Chapter 3, you can optionally configure affinity bits on a tunnel so that it can be routed on or away from certain links. If a tunnel's affinity bits do not match the configured attribute string on a link, that link is not considered eligible for use for a particular MPLS Traffic Engineering tunnel.

Administrative weight is equally simple, although it is used a little differently. Administrative weight is what is propagated by the IGP when it floods traffic engineering information. By default, only the administrative weight is used to calculate a tunnel's path. However, just being able to change the administrative weight for a particular link might not give you the flexibility you need.

IGP metrics are usually derived from bandwidth. In OSPF, the default link metric is *reference-bandwidth/link bandwidth.* The default reference bandwidth (changeable through the command **auto-cost reference-bandwidth**) is 10^8, which means that any link of 100 Mbps or more has a cost of 1. You can also set the cost on an individual link with the **ip ospf cost** *cost* command.

In IS-IS, the default link cost is 10. You can change this cost with the command **isis metric**.

Both IS-IS and OSPF typically use their metric to encode some measure of link bandwidth. This is fine for data-only networks. TCP's congestion-control mechanisms, when combined with DiffServ queuing, take advantage of as much bandwidth as they can.

But what about voice? Voice tends to care less about bandwidth and more about delay. But there's no way to advertise *delay* on a link. Or is there?

You can always manipulate the IGP's link metric to represent delay rather than bandwidth. But the problem with this is that you then lose the ability to accurately route data traffic, which can seriously impact your network.

Consider the topology shown in Figure 4-5.

Figure 4-5   *Topology in Which Voice and Data Traffic Prefer Different Paths*

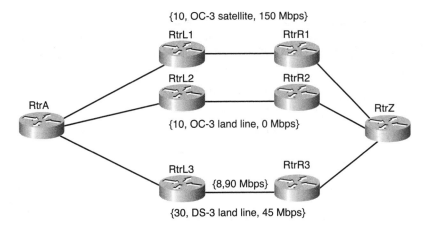

{IGP cost, link type, reservable BW}

{10, OC-3 satellite, 150 Mbps}

{10, OC-3 land line, 0 Mbps}

{8,90 Mbps}

{30, DS-3 land line, 45 Mbps}

The three paths between RtrA and RtrZ are

- P1 is an OC3 satellite path with 150 Mbps of available bandwidth and high delay.
- P2 is an OC3 land line, with correspondingly low delay. However, the OC3 land line has no bandwidth available—it's all reserved.
- P3 is a DS3 land line with 45 Mbps of available bandwidth and low delay.

Because the low-delay, high-bandwidth path is full, you could juggle priorities and shift traffic around so that the land-line OC3 path is no longer full, but that doesn't address what the example is trying to show you.

It comes down to a simple question: Do you want the high-bandwidth, high-latency path or the low-bandwidth, low-latency path? The answer to this question, like so many others, is, "It depends." Data is generally OK with the high-delay path, and voice has relatively lower bandwidth demand, so it is OK with the low-bandwidth path.

MPLS Traffic Engineering gives you the ability to consider both link bandwidth and link delay, so your voice tunnels can consider delay a separate cost from the metric your data tunnels use. To accomplish this, you must do the following:

Step 1 Configure the link delay using the command **mpls traffic-eng administrative-weight** *0-4294967295*, as covered in Chapter 3.

Step 2 Change the tunnel-decision process on the data tunnels to use the IGP metric, rather than the TE metric, as the measure of link cost. You can do this either globally, with the command **mpls traffic-eng path-selection metric igp**, or on a per-tunnel basis with **tunnel mpls traffic-eng path-selection metric igp**. If you set the global path-selection metric to IGP, you might want to have some TE tunnels refer to the TE metric link, in which case you configure those tunnels with **traffic-eng path-selection metric te**.

No inherent unit of measurement is associated with the configuration of administrative weight. If you configure **mpls traffic-eng administrative-weight 10**, the value 10 could be interpreted in all sorts of ways. Is 10 the propagation delay in microseconds? Hundredths of microseconds? Milliseconds? Seconds?

It's whatever you want it to be. Generally, it's a good idea to encode the delay in milliseconds for the following reasons:

- The TE metric is a 32-bit quantity, which means that you can encode delay from 0 to 4,294,967,295 milliseconds. 4,294,967,295 milliseconds is about seven weeks, which is probably more latency than you'll ever see.

- VoIP applications typically have delay budgets expressed in milliseconds, so there's no real need to be able to encode link delay in anything more specific (microseconds, or tens or hundreds of microseconds).

- It's hard to determine the amount of end-to-end latency across a particular circuit in any meaningful detail with a granularity finer than milliseconds.

To expand on that last point, how do you know how much latency to expect between two points?

Three ways exist to determine this number. In increasing order of complexity, they are as follows:

- Ping from one router to another across a circuit.
- Determine the expected latency based on route-miles.
- Use Cisco's Service Assurance Agent (SAA) to determine the latency.

Pinging from One Router to Another to Determine Expected Latency

This is by far the easiest way to determine a circuit's expected latency. It's pretty simple. You get on a router that's connected to a circuit you want to measure the latency on and then run some pings or traceroute to the other end.

Example 4-1 demonstrates a ping from a router in Massachusetts to a router in California.

Example 4-1 *Ping Results from a Massachusetts Router to a California Router*

```
chelmsford-gb1>ping sanjose-gb4
Type escape sequence to abort.
Sending 5, 100-byte ICMP Echos to 172.30.253.5, timeout is 2 seconds:
!!!!!
Success rate is 100 percent (5/5), round-trip min/avg/max = 80/80/80 ms
```

The round-trip time on this ping is 80 ms. It's a fair guess that the one-way latency on this circuit is half that, or 40 ms, but there's no guarantee for that estimate. In this case, the link between the two routers is an OC3. At the SONET level, this circuit can be routed differently in two directions, so the latency from Massachusetts to California might be 60 ms and the latency from California to Massachusetts is 40 ms. Because ping inherently tests two-way latency, there's no easy way to know for sure.

The other drawback of this approach is that ping runs at process level on the router. This means that when a router receives an ICMP echo request, it deals with it when it gets around to it, in between its more important jobs of maintaining routing protocol adjacencies, forwarding packets, and other such stuff. So if you ping a router that's under a high CPU load, it might have ping response times that are not representative of the actual latency, but more of the load on the router.

Despite these caveats, using ping to determine average latency is good enough most of the time. You might want to run an extended ping of 1000 packets or so, just so that any anomalous responses because of router processing are averaged out. You also want to make sure that the ping you're sending across a link does not encounter congestion because you want to measure transmission and propagation delay, not queuing delay.

Determining the Expected Latency Based on Route-Miles

The speed of light in a vacuum is roughly $3 * 10^8$ meters per second, which translates to about 3.3 ms to travel 1000 km. The speed of light over fiber is a little less than that, and you also need to account for various other kinds of delays in a real network. It's better to use an estimate of 6 to 9 ms per 1000 km when estimating delay across a network. Refer to the Cisco Press book *Integrating Voice and Data Networks* for more details on delay, jitter, and all sorts of fabulous stuff.

The other tricky piece is knowing the distance between two points. The *shortest* distance is easy to find. Attack your favorite map with a ruler, or see web sites such as the CIA World Factbook (www.odci.gov/cia/publications/factbook/) for maps. Using these maps, you can figure the latency that your circuit would take *if it took the shortest possible path,* and use that as a minimum expectation of delay.

For example, it's about 4500 km from Boston to San Francisco. Given that, the best possible one-way delay you should expect in an optical network is somewhere between 28 ms and 41 ms. It's important to realize that this is an estimate of the best possible delay. It does not take into account the fact that no circuits run from one end of the U.S. to the other as a single piece of fiber. But the upper end of the estimate (40.5 ms) correlates nicely with the ping testing from the preceding section (which suggests 40 ms one-way), so perhaps 40 ms is a good number to expect for average one-way latency on this link.

Using SAA

The best way to determine one-way latency across a circuit is to use Service Assurance Agent (SAA), because it was developed for just this purpose. Chapter 10, "MPLS TE Deployment Tips," covers SAA in greater detail.

CSPF Knobs

You should now understand how CSPF works. Also, between the preceding chapter and this one, you should have a good handle on the basic concept of link bandwidth. Three other major pieces to path calculation that you should understand are

- **path-option** configuration on the headend
- Various CSPF timers
- Various CSPF **show** commands

path-option Configuration

Example 4-2 repeats the basic MPLS TE tunnel configuration demonstrated in Chapter 3.

Example 4-2 *MPLS Traffic Engineering Tunnel Configuration*

```
interface Tunnel0
  ip unnumbered Loopback0
  tunnel mode mpls traffic-eng
  tunnel destination destination-ip
  tunnel mpls traffic-eng path-option 10 dynamic
```

One command you can use to influence CSPF on the headend is the **path-option** command. In addition to being able to control path properties such as requested link bandwidth, affinity and mask, and administrative weight for the tunnel, you also have control over which path the tunnel takes.

path-option lets you specify one or more possible paths that you want the tunnel to take, in the order you want to try them. The complete syntax is as follows:

```
tunnel mpls traffic-eng path-option preference [dynamic | explicit [identifier
    identifier | name name]] {lockdown}
```

Table 4-16 explains the syntax in better detail.

Table 4-16   **tunnel mpls traffic-eng path-option** *Command Syntax Explanation*

Keyword	Description
tunnel mpls traffic-eng path-option *preference*	Defines a **path-option** for this tunnel. *preference* is a number from 1 to 1000. Different **path-option** values are tried in preference order from lowest to highest.
dynamic	Tells the router that it is supposed to calculate the best path that fits the configured tunnel constraints, such as bandwidth and affinity bits.
explicit	Allows you to specify an explicit path (configured separately) across the network that the tunnel will take. The explicit path also has to match the configured tunnel constraints, and the tunnel headend will check the explicit path to make sure that these constraints are met before trying to signal the path.
identifier *identifier*	**name** *name*	When explicit paths are created, they're given names or numbers. This option specifies which path option to consider.
lockdown	Configuring **lockdown** prevents a TE tunnel from being periodically reoptimized. See the later section "Tunnel Reoptimization."

The most basic **path-option** configuration is **tunnel mpls traffic-eng path-option 10 dynamic**.

Why use 10 for the preference? There's no good reason why, really. Too much BASIC programming in the mid-1980s, perhaps. And it's a good idea to leave some space between your **path-option** preferences (10, 20, and so on), rather than using 1, 2, 3, 4 for successive **path-option** preferences. But the value 10 doesn't have any special meaning when compared to the value 9, other than an ordinal one.

Creating an Explicit Path

When you use an explicit **path-option**, you also need to define the **path-option** itself. You do this using the following configuration-level command:

```
ip explicit-path [identifier identifer | name name] {enable | disable}
```

When you enter the following command:

```
vxr15(config)#ip explicit-path name foo
vxr15(cfg-ip-expl-path)#
```

you enter a submode for **path-option** creation. In this submode, not only can you add nodes to the **path-option**, but you can also delete and change them. Example 4-3 demonstrates the possible options.

Example 4-3   *Possible Options for the* **path-option**

```
vxr15(config)#ip explicit-path name foo
vxr15(cfg-ip-expl-path)#?
Explicit-Path configuration commands:
  append-after     Append additional entry after specified index
  exclude-address  Exclude an address from subsequent partial path segments
  exit             Exit from explicit-path configuration mode
  index            Specify the next entry index to add, edit (or delete)
  list             Re-list all or part of the explicit path entries
  next-address     Specify the next (adjacent) address in the path
  no               Delete a specific explicit-path entry index
```

Explicit paths are usually a series of next addresses that list router hops (either TE RIDs or interface addresses) in the order you want the tunnel to traverse them.

You also have the option for **exclude-address**, which lets you specify a list of links or nodes to *not* be used in the tunnel path calculation. Not all code has this option.

How does this work? Consider Figure 4-6.

In Figure 4-6, each link has a cost of 10. Assume for now that all links can hold the tunnel you want to build (they all have enough bandwidth, the attribute bits match, and so forth). Note the two links from RtrB to RtrD.

The four paths from RtrA to RtrE are detailed in Table 4-17.

Table 4-17   *Path Details from RtrA to RtrE*

Path Number	Path	Cost
1	RtrA→RtrE	10
2	RtrA→RtrB→RtrD→RtrE	30 (through link 1)
3	RtrA→RtrB→RtrD→RtrE	30 (through link 2)
4	RtrA→RtrB→RtrC→RtrD→RtrE	40

Figure 4-6   *Finding the Lowest-Path Cost While Excluding Specific Links/Nodes*

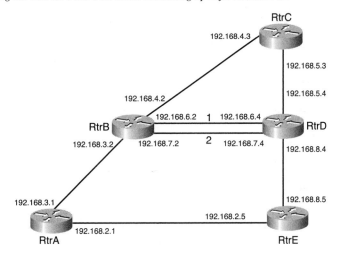

If you ask the router to dynamically calculate a path from RtrA to RtrE, the tunnel is placed across the A→E link because it is the lowest-cost path that meets your requirements.

Table 4-18 shows each router's TE RID.

Table 4-18   *Router TE RIDs*

Router	TE RID
RtrA	192.168.1.1
RtrB	192.168.1.2
RtrC	192.168.1.3
RtrD	192.168.1.4
RtrE	192.168.1.5

Figure 4-6 shows the link addresses between each router. Notice that the last octet of each interface address is the same as the RID's last octet. Although this might not be an entirely realistic addressing plan, it makes things easier to deal with in a lab setup; most of the examples in this book use that format.

If you wanted to build a tunnel from RtrA to RtrE over path 4, you could list the RIDs, as shown in Example 4-4.

Example 4-4 *Listing the RIDs for the Tunnel from RtrA to RtrE Over Path 4*

```
RtrA(cfg-ip-expl-path)#next-address 192.168.1.2
Explicit Path name foo:
    1: next-address 192.168.1.2
RtrA(cfg-ip-expl-path)#next-address 192.168.1.3
Explicit Path name foo:
    1: next-address 192.168.1.2
    2: next-address 192.168.1.3
RtrA(cfg-ip-expl-path)#next-address 192.168.1.4
Explicit Path name foo:
    1: next-address 192.168.1.2
    2: next-address 192.168.1.3
    3: next-address 192.168.1.4
RtrA(cfg-ip-expl-path)#next-address 192.168.1.5
Explicit Path name foo:
    1: next-address 192.168.1.2
    2: next-address 192.168.1.3
    3: next-address 192.168.1.4
    4: next-address 192.168.1.5
RtrA(cfg-ip-expl-path)#
```

As you can see, every time you enter a next address, you are shown the entire explicit path. You're actually shown the entire explicit path after every change to it, whether you are adding to or deleting from the **path-option** configuration. You can also list the explicit path with the **list** subcommand, as shown in Example 4-5.

Example 4-5 *Listing the Explicit Path*

```
RtrA(cfg-ip-expl-path)#list ?
  <1-65535>  List starting at entry index number
  <cr>

RtrA(cfg-ip-expl-path)#list
Explicit Path name foo:
    1: next-address 192.168.1.1
    2: next-address 192.168.1.2
    3: next-address 192.168.1.3
    4: next-address 192.168.1.4
    5: next-address 192.168.1.5
```

Example 4-5 defines the explicit path to be the list of RIDs. If you wanted to use path 3, which specifies a particular link between RtrB and RtrD, you'd have to specify the link address rather than the router ID. The explicit path would be something like the output from the **show ip explicit-paths name** command, as demonstrated in Example 4-6.

Example 4-6   *Using the* **show ip explicit-paths name** *Command*

```
RtrA#show ip explicit-paths name foo
PATH foo (strict source route, path complete, generation 28)
    1: next-address 192.168.1.2
    2: next-address 192.168.7.4
    3: next-address 192.168.1.5
```

As you can see, path option **foo** is a strict source route, it is a complete path (paths are almost always complete; incomplete paths are rare), and it is generation 28 of that path option. The generation number changes every time the path option is changed—in much the same way that the BGP table version changes when any updates happen.

If the explicit path in Example 4-6 had any loose subobjects specified in it (see "Interarea Tunnels" later in this chapter), you'd see *loose source route* rather than *strict source route* in the output of **show ip explicit-paths**.

This example uses the RID for RtrB and RtrE, but uses RtrD's incoming link address on link 2 to specify which link the tunnel crossed. The explicit path configuration can accept a mix of node addresses and link addresses; it's pretty flexible that way. Example 4-7 demonstrates another way to specify the explicit path.

Example 4-7   *Specifying an Explicit Path*

```
PATH foo (strict source route, path complete, generation 33)
    1: next-address 192.168.1.2
    2: next-address 192.168.7.2
    3: next-address 192.168.7.4
    4: next-address 192.168.8.5
```

Feel free to use any mix of interfaces and RIDs; as long as they are listed in the order you want them to traverse the network, you're fine.

In addition to **next-address**, you also have the option of **exclude-address**. The **exclude-address** option lets you specify nodes that are *not* to be used in the tunnel path calculation. Consider Figure 4-6 again. Assume that you want to build a tunnel from Router A to Router E, and you want it to *not* go through Router C, but to consider all other possible paths. To accomplish this, you could define a series of explicit paths from Router A to Router E, or you could just define a path option that excludes Router C from the path calculation using the following command sequence:

```
ip explicit-path name avoid-RtrC
  exclude-address 192.168.1.3
```

NOTE	Currently, an explicit path cannot contain both a next address and an exclude address; it's one or the other. You won't get any warnings if you create an explicit path that uses both **exclude-address** and **next-address**; it just won't work.

Table 4-19 describes some of the other commands in the explicit path submode.

Table 4-19 *Commands Available in Explicit Path Submode*

Command	Description
append-after	Appends an additional entry after the specified index.
index	Specifies the next entry index to add, edit, or delete.
list	Relists all or part of the explicit path entries.
no	Deletes a specific explicit-path entry index.

append-after and **index** are useful when you're editing an existing path option. You can insert new nodes in the list by specifying either a relative placement (through **append-after** *previous index number*) or an absolute placement (through **index** *index number*). **no index** *index* lets you delete a node in the path option list.

Using Multiple Path Options

Earlier in this chapter, you saw that you can specify a preference when selecting a path option for a TE tunnel. A TE tunnel can have multiple path options listed; they are tried in order of preference. For example, if you want to build a path from Router A to Router E, as in Figure 4-6, and you want the router to try using path 3, and then path 4 if path 3 is unavailable, and then path 2 if path 4 is unavailable, and then finally path 1, you could configure a tunnel as shown in Example 4-8.

Example 4-8 *Configuring a TE Tunnel with Multiple Path Options*

```
tunnel mpls traffic-eng path-option 30 explicit name Path3
tunnel mpls traffic-eng path-option 40 explicit name Path4
tunnel mpls traffic-eng path-option 20 explicit name Path2
tunnel mpls traffic-eng path-option 10 explicit name Path1
```

It is generally a good idea to have the last path option in your tunnel calculation be **dynamic**:

```
tunnel mpls traffic-eng path-option 50 dynamic
```

This is useful because putting **dynamic** as the last path option ensures that if it's at all possible for a TE tunnel to come up, it will. Although specifying a dynamic path option isn't strictly necessary in the topology depicted in Figure 4-6, it would be useful if a link were added between Router B and Router E. Router A's list of path options wouldn't need to be updated to allow Router A to take advantage of the A→B→E path.

Tunnel Reoptimization

What happens if, while a tunnel is up, a path appears that is a new best path from head to tail? Consider the network shown in Figure 4-7.

Figure 4-7 *New Path Is a More Optimal TE Tunnel Candidate*

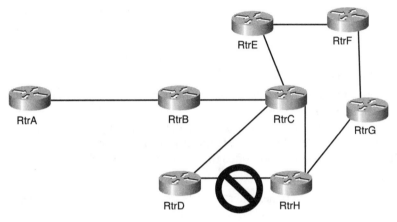

In Figure 4-7:

- All links start with 100-Mbps reservable bandwidth.
- Router A and Router D both want to build 60-Mbps tunnels to Router H.
- The link between Router D and Router H is down.

Assume that the following sequence of events happens:

1 Router D builds a tunnel D→C→H.

2 Router A builds a tunnel A→B→C→E→F→G→H.

3 Router D reduces its D→C→H bandwidth reservation to 30 Mbps, either by configuration or because of something like auto bandwidth adjustment.

At this point, the best possible path Router A could take to get to Router H is A→B→C→H. But Router A already has a tunnel established. Should Router A change its tunnel over to the B→C→H path? What if Router D needs to increase its tunnel bandwidth again? How long should Router A wait before cutting over to the best path? You can ask all kinds of questions along this line.

When a router looks to see if there is a better path for tunnels that are already up, this is known as *reoptimization*. Four things affect reoptimization:

- Periodic reoptimization
- Manual reoptimization
- Event-driven reoptimization
- Lockdown

It's important to understand that this reoptimization has nothing to do with the behavior when a tunnel goes down. If a tunnel goes down, you don't wait for the reoptimization timer to kick in before trying to find a better path for that tunnel; that calculation is done immediately.

Finally, realize that RSV-TE has what's called *make-before-break*, so that the act of making a new tunnel reservation does not disturb any existing reservations for that tunnel. This is covered in more detail in the "Resource Reservation Protocol (RSVP)" section.

Periodic Reoptimization

Cisco implements a periodic reoptimization timer, which can be configured on a global basis. After a tunnel comes up, an attempt is made to find a better path for it, given the tunnel's configured constraints. By default, this happens once an hour; this timer can be configured through the command **mpls traffic-eng tunnels reoptimize timers frequency** *0-604800*. *0-604800* is how often (in seconds) Cisco IOS Software looks for a better path for a tunnel.

Setting this timer to 0 means that tunnels are never reoptimized after they are up; on the other end of the scale, 604,800 is the number of seconds in 168 hours, or exactly one week. The default reoptimization timer is 3600 seconds, or one hour.

It's important to note that the reoptimization timer, although it can be configured only globally, is kept on a per-tunnel basis. What does this mean? Suppose you have 20 different tunnels, T1 through T20, that come up 2 minutes after each other (T1 comes up at 00:00, T2 at 00:02, T3 at 00:04, and so on). T20 comes up at 00:40. Twenty minutes after that, the global reoptimization timer *for T1* kicks in and tries to find a better path, but only for T1. T20 is not reoptimized until it has been up for an hour, or when the clock reads 1:40.

Manual Reoptimization

What if you know there's been a change in your network, and you don't want to wait for that tunnel's reoptimization timer to kick in before finding a better path? You can use the enable-level command **mpls traffic-eng reoptimize** [*tunnel-name*] to force the router to reoptimize a specific tunnel at any time.

Event-Driven Reoptimization

Finally, consider the link between RtrD and RtrH in Figure 4-7. If that link comes up, should RtrD reoptimize its D→H tunnel so that this tunnel flows over the directly connected link? Probably. But there are scenarios in which a link coming up should *not* trigger a reoptimization.

One scenario in which an up link should not trigger a reoptimization is if the link is flapping and the IGP timers aren't enough to hide the flapping from the network. Reoptimizing onto a flapping link and then calculating a path around that link when it fails again constantly changes the tunnel's path characteristics. Although RSVP's make-before-break leads to minimal data loss along this path, a constantly changing tunnel path could lead to large delay variation, which isn't good for either data (TCP) or voice.

For this reason, tunnels are not automatically reoptimized when a new link comes up. Tunnels are reoptimized onto a link that has just come up when the tunnel reoptimization timer goes off, but not until then. You can change this behavior with the following global configuration:

```
mpls traffic-eng reoptimize events link-up
```

Lockdown

You might have some tunnels that you don't ever want to reoptimize. You can specify this on a per-tunnel basis using the **lockdown** option in the path option specification:

```
tunnel mpls traffic-eng path-option preference {dynamic | explicit name name |
    identifier id>} {lockdown}
```

The reason for putting lockdown on a path option as opposed to a tunnel itself is that there might be some paths you never want to leave as long as the links underneath those paths are up, but if the underlying links are down, you want to fall back to another path until the preferred path is up.

To make that last sentence clearer, an example is in order.

In Figure 4-8, each link has 100 Mbps reservable to begin with.

Figure 4-8 *Sample Network for Lockdown Example*

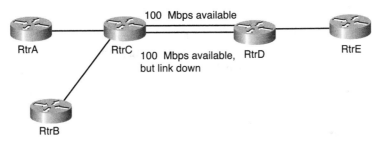

At some point in time, two tunnels were established; at that time, the lower link between RtrC and RtrD was down. At some point after these tunnels came up, the lower link also came up. A 60-Mbps tunnel from RtrA to RtrE crosses the top C→D link, and a 30-Mbps tunnel from RtrB to RtrE crosses the same link. Figure 4-9 shows this.

When a reoptimization happens on either of these tunnels (periodic, manually triggered, or because of the link-up event), whichever tunnel happens to reoptimize puts itself on the other link. Assume that it's the B→E tunnel. Figure 4-10 shows what things look like after that reoptimization.

Figure 4-9   *Two TE Tunnels Across the Top Link*

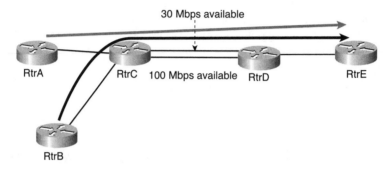

Figure 4-10   *B→E Tunnel Reoptimized to the Bottom Link*

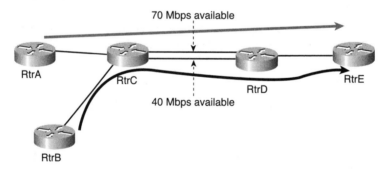

But what if you didn't want the B→E tunnel to reoptimize for some reason? If that tunnel had been configured with **tunnel mpls traffic-eng path-option ... lockdown**, it would not have reoptimized and shifted to the other link. It *will* reconverge on the bottom C→D link if the top C→D link goes down, however.

Resource Reservation Protocol (RSVP)

After a path is calculated with CSPF, that path needs to be signalled across the network for two reasons:

- To establish a hop-by-hop chain of labels that represent the path
- To consume any consumable resources (bandwidth) across that path

This signalling is accomplished using RSVP, along with RSVP extensions for MPLS TE. RSVP itself is specified in RFC 2205, with some pertinent extensions in RFC 2210. The MPLS TE extensions to RSVP are specified in RFC 3209.

The RSVP discussion in this chapter is divided into four parts:

- RSVP basics
- RSVP packets
- RSVP operation
- RSVP in the real world

The two most important sections to understand are "RSVP Basics" and "RSVP in the Real World." The "RSVP Packets" and "RSVP Operation" sections are useful for understanding exactly how RSVP does what it does.

RSVP Basics

RSVP is a signalling mechanism used to reserve resources throughout a network. It has its own protocol type (46), although it is possible to encapsulate RSVP in UDP. MPLS TE never encapsulates RSVP in UDP, so that isn't discussed further.

RSVP is not a routing protocol. Any routing decisions are made by the IGP (including TE extensions) and CSPF. RSVP's only job is to signal and maintain resource reservations across a network. In MPLS TE, RSVP reserves bandwidth at the control-plane layer; there is no forwarding-plane policing of traffic. When used for other purposes (such as VoIP or DLSW+ reservations), RSVP can be used to reserve Weighted Fair Queuing (WFQ) space or build ATM SVCs. Those uses are not discussed here.

RSVP has three basic functions:

- Path setup and maintenance
- Path teardown
- Error signalling

RSVP is a soft-state protocol. This means that it needs to periodically refresh its reservations in the network by resignalling them. This is different from a hard-state protocol, which signals its request once and then assumes that the request is up until it is explicitly taken down. With RSVP, a request goes away either if it is explicitly removed from the network by RSVP or if the reservation times out.

Table 4-20 lists the nine different defined RSVP message types.

Table 4-20 *RSVP Message Types*

Message Type	Description
Path	Used to set up and maintain reservations.
Resv (short for Reservation)	Sent in response to Path messages to set up and maintain reservations.
PathTear	Analogous to Path messages, but used to remove reservations from the network.
ResvTear	Analogous to Resv messages, but used to remove reservations from the network.
PathErr	Sent by a recipient of a Path message who detects an error in that message.
ResvErr	Sent by a recipient of a Resv message who detects an error in that message.
ResvConf	Optionally sent back to the sender of a Resv message to confirm that a given reservation actually got installed.
ResvTearConf	A Cisco-proprietary message analogous to a ResvConf. Used to confirm that a given reservation got removed from the network.
Hello	An extension defined in RFC 3209 that allows for link-local keepalives between two directly connected RSVP neighbors.

These message types are explained in more detail in the upcoming section "RSVP Packets."

Path Setup and Maintenance

Although path setup and maintenance are similar, they differ in a subtle way. Even though they use the same message formats do to what they do, it's worth explaining them separately the first time around.

Path Setup

After a tunnel headend completes its CSPF for a particular tunnel, it needs to signal this request to the network. The headend does this by sending a Path message to the next-hop node along the calculated path to the destination. The router that sent the Path message is called the *upstream* router, and the router that received the message is called the *down-stream* router. The upstream router is sometimes called the *previous hop* (*phop*).

After a downstream router receives a Path message, it does a few things. It checks the message's format to make sure everything is OK, and then it checks the amount of bandwidth the received Path message is asking for. This process is known as *admission control*.

If admission control is successful and the Path message is allowed to reserve the bandwidth it wants, the downstream router creates a new Path message and sends it to the next hop in the Explicit Route Object (ERO), which is covered later in this chapter. Path messages follow this chain until they reach the last node in the ERO—the MPLS TE tunnel tail.

The tunnel tail performs admission control on the Path message, just like any other downstream router. When the tail realizes that it is the destination of the Path message, it replies with a Resv message. Think of the Resv message as an ACK back to the upstream router. The Resv message not only contains an acknowledgment that the reservation made it all the way to the tunnel tail, but it also contains the incoming label that the upstream router should use to send packets along the TE LSP to the tail. Figure 4-11 shows the exchange of RSVP path and Resv messages during LSP setup.

Figure 4-11 *RSVP Path and Resv Messages During LSP Setup*

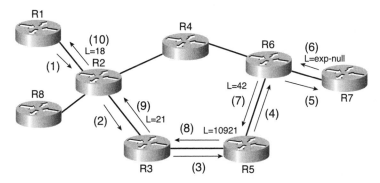

Figure 4-11 has 10 steps. The following is a walk-through of what happens with Path and Resv messages in those steps. Assume that R1 has done its CSPF already and knows that it wants to reserve bandwidth along the path R1→R2→R3→R5→R6→R7:

1 R1 sends a Path message to R2. R2 receives the path message, checks to make sure that the message is syntactically correct, and checks with the TE Link Manager to make sure that the bandwidth R1 requested is actually available. If anything is wrong (the Path message is incorrectly formed or is asking for more bandwidth than R2 can provide), R2 sends an error message back to R1. Assuming that everything is good, move on to Step 2.

2 R2 sends a Path message to R3. R3 goes through the same verification of the Path message that R2 did.

3 R3 sends a Path message to R5; the same checks happen.

4 R5 sends a Path message to R6; the same checks happen.

5 R6 sends a Path message to R7; the same checks happen.

6 R7, being the tunnel tail, sends a Resv message to R6. This Resv message indicates the label R7 would like to see on the packet for this tunnel; because R7 is the tail, it sends implicit-null.

7 R6 sends a Resv message to R5 and indicates that it wants to see incoming label 42 for this tunnel. This means that when R6 receives label 42, it removes that label (because of implicit-null) and sends the packet toward R7.

8 R5 sends a Resv message to R3, signalling label 10921. When R5 receives a packet with label 10921, it swaps that label for label 42 and sends the packet to R6.

9 R3 sends a Resv message to R2, signalling label 21.

10 R2 sends a Resv message to R1, signalling label 18.

At this point, R1 is done. It has received a Resv message for the tunnel to R7 it set up, and it knows which outgoing label to use. The Tunnel interface on R1 now comes up/up (until this point, the Tunnel interface is up/down).

Path Maintenance

At first glance, path maintenance looks just like path setup. Every 30 seconds (give or take 50 percent—see "RSVP Operation" later in this chapter), a headend sends one Path message per tunnel to its downstream neighbors. If a router sends out four Path messages in a row and does not see a Resv during that time, it considers the reservation gone and sends a message upstream, indicating that the reservation is gone.

However, there is one important thing to understand here. Path and Resv messages are both sent *independently* and *asynchronously* from one neighbor to another. Look again at Figure 4-11. Every 30 seconds, R1 sends a Path message for its one TE reservation to R2. And every 30 seconds, R2 sends a Resv message to R1 for that same reservation. The two messages, however, are not connected. A Resv message used to refresh an existing reservation is not sent in *response* to a Path message, as an ICMP Echo Reply would be sent in response to an ICMP Echo Request.

Why are things done this way? Largely to accommodate the merging of flows in "classic" RSVP (VoIP, DSLW+, that sort of thing), and these messages don't really apply to TE. If this doesn't make sense to you, don't worry about it. Just remember this when you start troubleshooting a TE problem and you don't see ping/ACK behavior with Path and Resv messages.

Path Teardown

Path teardown is pretty straightforward. If a node (usually the headend) decides that a reservation is no longer necessary in the network, it sends a PathTear along the same path that the Path message followed and a ResvTear along the same path that the Resv message followed.

PathTear messages are most commonly seen when the headend decides it no longer wants a reservation in the network (when a tunnel is shut down or reroutes off a certain path, for example). ResvTear messages are sent in response to PathTear messages to signal that the tunnel tail has removed the reservation from the network. Cisco IOS Software sends Resv messages and asks for confirmation that the reservation has been torn down; this results in a ResvTearConf message being sent back from the headend to the tail. PathTear and ResvTear messages can also be sent in response to an error condition in the middle of the network. You'll read more about this in the "RSVP Operation" section.

Much like refresh messages, PathTear messages don't have to go all the way downstream before taking effect. In Figure 4-11, if R1 sends a PathTear to R2, R2 immediately replies with a ResvTear and then sends its own PathTear downstream.

Error Signalling

Occasionally, there can be errors in RSVP signalling. These errors are signalled by PathErr or ResvErr messages. An error detected in a Path message is responded to with a PathErr message, and an error detected in a Resv message is responded to with a ResvErr message. Error messages are sent upstream toward the source of the error; a PathErr is sent toward the upstream from a downstream node, and a ResvErr is sent downstream from an upstream node. You'll read more about this in the next section.

RSVP Packets

The RSVP packet format is pretty straightforward. Every RSVP message is composed of a common header, followed by one or more objects. The number of objects in a message depends on exactly what the message is trying to accomplish.

RSVP Common Header

Figure 4-12 shows the RSVP common header format.

Figure 4-12 *RSVP Common Header Format*

0	1	2	3

0 1 2 3 4 5 6 7 8 9 0 1 2 3 4 5 6 7 8 9 0 1 2 3 4 5 6 7 8 9 0 1

Version (4 bits)	Flags (4 bits)	Message type (8 bits)	RSVP checksum (16 bits)
Send TTL (8 bits)		Reserved (8 bits)	RSVP length (16 bits)

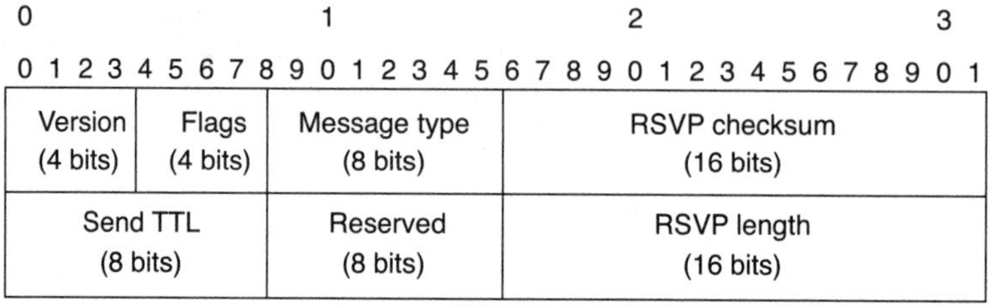

Table 4-21 explains the fields in the RSVP common header.

Table 4-21 *RSVP Common Header Format Fields*

Field	Description
Version	The RSVP protocol version. The current RSVP version is 1.
Flags	No flags are defined yet.
Message Type	1 = Path message
	2 = Resv message
	3 = PathErr message
	4 = ResvErr message
	5 = PathTear message
	6 = ResvTear message
	7 = ResvConf message
	10 = ResvTearConf message
	20 = Hello message
RSVP Checksum	The checksum of the RSVP message.
Send TTL	The TTL value on the IP packet this message was sent with.
Reserved	Not used.
RSVP Length	The length of the RSVP message in bytes, including the common header. RSVP Length, therefore, is always at least 8.

RSVP Object Class Formats

RSVP objects all have the same basic format, as illustrated in Figure 4-13.

Figure 4-13 *RSVP Object Format*

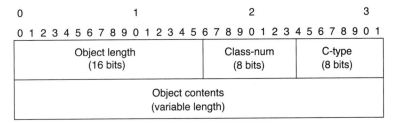

Table 4-22 describes the fields in the basic RSVP object format.

Table 4-22 *RSVP Object Format*

Field	Description
Object Length	The length of the RSVP object, including the object header. As such, this is always at least 4. It must be a multiple of 4.
Class-Num	The object's class.
C-Type	The object's class type. C-Type is a unique number within the class.
Object Contents	The object itself.

Twenty-three different object classes are defined. Not all of them are used in RSVP signalling for MPLS TE, but for the sake of completeness, they're all listed in Table 4-23.

Table 4-23 *RSVP Object Classes*

Object Class	Object Class Number	Used in MPLS TE?
NULL	0	No
SESSION	1	Yes
SESSION_GROUP	2	No
HOP	3	Yes
INTEGRITY	4	Optional
TIME_VALUES	5	Yes
ERROR_SPEC	6	Yes
SCOPE	7	No
STYLE	8	Yes
FLOWSPEC	9	Yes
FILTER_SPEC	10	Yes
SENDER_TEMPLATE	11	Yes
SENDER_TSPEC	12	Yes

continues

Table 4-23   *RSVP Object Classes (Continued)*

Object Class	Object Class Number	Used in MPLS TE?
ADSPEC	13	Yes
POLICY_DATA	14	No
RESV_CONFIRM	15	No
RSVP_LABEL	16	Yes
HOP_COUNT	17	No
LABEL_REQUEST	19	Yes
EXPLICIT_ROUTE	20	Yes
RECORD_ROUTE	21	Yes
HELLO	22	Yes
SESSION_ATTRIBUTE	207	Yes

Each class has its own C-Type number space. The C-Type numbers are unique within a class. For example, the SESSION class has four defined C-Types: IPv4, IPv6, LSP_TUNNEL_IPv4, and LSP_TUNNEL_IPv6. The numbers assigned to these C-Types are 1, 2, 7, and 8. LABEL_REQUEST has three C-Types defined: Without Label Range, With ATM Label Range, and With Frame Relay Label Range. The numbers assigned to these C-Types are 1, 2, and 3. You can see that a C-Type of 1 is not enough to uniquely identify a message's contents; you need to look at both the class and C-Type numbers.

NOTE   Yes, this is confusing. Think of RSVP classes and C-Types as any other type of hierarchical numbering scheme—such as phone numbers, for example. In RSVP, to identify exactly what's in the RSVP Message you received, you have to look at both the class *and* the C-Type of each object. It's like looking at a phone number—you need both the area code and the local number. Dialing 867-5309 isn't enough; you need to know that it's (701) 867-5309 to get through to the right person.

An RSVP message contains one or more objects. Not all messages contain all objects. The objects a message contains depends on the message definition.

Table 4-24 lists the classes and C-Types used in Cisco's implementation of RSVP-TE.

Table 4-24   *RSVP Object C-Types*

Object Class	C-Types Used in an Object	C-Type Number
SESSION	LSP Tunnel IPv4	4
TIME_VALUES	Refresh Period	1
ERROR_SPEC	IPv4 Error Spec	1
SCOPE	List of IPv4 Source Addresses	1
STYLE	Flags and Option Vector	1
FLOWSPEC	Intserv Flowspec	2
FILTER_SPEC	LSP Tunnel IPv4	7
SENDER_TEMPLATE	LSP Tunnel IPv4	7
SENDER_TSPEC	Intserv Sender Tspec	2
ADSPEC	Intserv Adspec	2
RESV_CONFIRM	IPv4 RevConfirm	1
RSVP_LABEL	Label	1
LABEL_REQUEST	Without Label Range	1
EXPLICIT_ROUTE	Explicit Route	1
RECORD_ROUTE	Record Route	1
HELLO	Request	1
HELLO	Acknowledgment	2
SESSION_ATTRIBUTE	LSP Tunnel	7

This table does not list all defined C-Types—only the ones Cisco IOS Software currently uses. For example, IPv5 C-Types are defined for various classes. Because MPLS TE for IPv6 isn't implemented (yet!), we have not listed the IPv6 C-Types.

To give you the complete picture, the following sections look at all the object formats. They might not make much sense in isolation. It's probably best to scan this section, read the sections about the various message formats later in this chapter, and then come back here if you're a glutton for details and/or punishment.

SESSION Class

Figure 4-14 shows the SESSION class object format.

The SESSION object is defined in RFC 2205. RFC 3209 defines C-Type 7 (LSP_TUNNEL_IPV4), which has the four fields described in Table 4-25.

Figure 4-14 *SESSION Class Format*

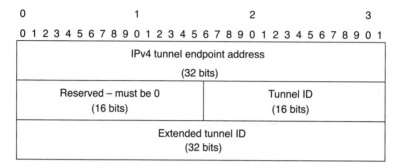

Table 4-25 *SESSION Class Fields*

Field	Contents
IPv4 Tunnel Endpoint Address	Router ID of the tunnel tail.
Reserved	Must be 0.
Tunnel ID	A 16-bit ID that uniquely identifies this tunnel. This is the interface number at the headend (so Tunnel8 has a Tunnel ID of 8).
Extended Tunnel ID	A 32-bit ID. Set to either all 0s or an interface IP address.

TIME_VALUES Class

Figure 4-15 shows the TIME_VALUES class object format.

Figure 4-15 *TIME_VALUES Class Format*

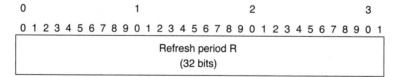

RFC 2205 defines the TIME_VALUES object as the refresh period (in milliseconds) used to send Path or Resv messages.

ERROR_SPEC Class

Figure 4-16 shows the ERROR_SPEC class object format.

Figure 4-16 *ERROR_SPEC Class Format*

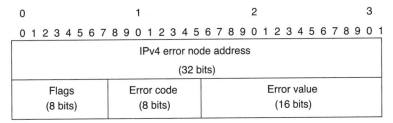

RFC 2205 defines the ERROR_SPEC object and also defines error codes 00 through 23. RFC 3209 defines error code 24, which holds errors specific to MPLS TE. In MPLS TE, you're most likely to see error code 00 (Confirmation—sent in response to receiving a message with a CONFIRMATION object) or error code 24.

When the error code is 00, the error value is also 00.

When the error code is 24, there are 10 possible error values, as documented in Table 4-26. There's also an error code 25 that generally only shows up when using Fast Reroute, and which is covered in more detail in Chapter 7.

Generally, the Flags field is 0 when you're using MPLS TE.

Table 4-26   *Error Values When the Error Code Is 24*

Error Value	Description
1	Bad EXPLICIT_ROUTE object
2	Bad strict node
3	Bad loose node
4	Bad initial subobject
5	No route available toward destination
6	Unacceptable label value
7	RRO indicated routing loops
8	MPLS being negotiated, but a non-RSVP-capable router stands in the path
9	MPLS label allocation failure
10	Unsupported L3PID

SCOPE Class

Figure 4-17 shows the SCOPE class object format.

RFC 2205 defines the SCOPE class. The SCOPE class is not used in Cisco's MPLS TE implementation because it implies a wildcard reservation style, whereas MPLS TE uses Shared Explicit or Fixed Filter (see the "Shared Explicit Reservation Style" section).

Figure 4-17 *SCOPE Class Format*

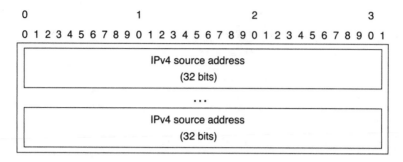

STYLE Class

Figure 4-18 shows the STYLE class object format.

Figure 4-18 *STYLE Class Format*

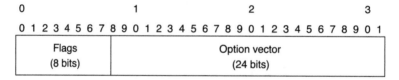

The STYLE class specifies the reservation style. The three possible styles are

- Wildcard Filter
- Fixed Filter
- Shared Explicit

Cisco IOS Software uses Shared Explicit for MPLS TE reservations.

The Flags field is unused. The Option Vector is always 0x12, indicating Shared Explicit style. See the "Shared Explicit Reservation Style" section for more details.

FLOWSPEC Class

Figure 4-19 shows the FLOWSPEC class object format.

The FLOWSPEC class is defined in RFC 2210. Cisco IOS Software requests Controlled-Load service when reserving a TE tunnel. The FLOWSPEC format is complex and has many things in it that RSVP for MPLS TE doesn't use.

The FLOWSPEC is used in Resv messages—Resv, ResvTear, ResvErr, ResvConf, ResvTearConf. Its only use in MPLS TE is to use the average rate section of the

FLOWSPEC to specify the bandwidth desired, in bytes. Not bits. Bytes. So if you configure a tunnel with **tunnel mpls traffic-eng 100000** to request 100 Mbps of bandwidth, this gets signalled as 12,500,000 bytes per second (100 Mb is 100,000 Kb is 100,000,000 bits, which is 12,500,000 bytes).

Figure 4-19 *FLOWSPEC Class Format*

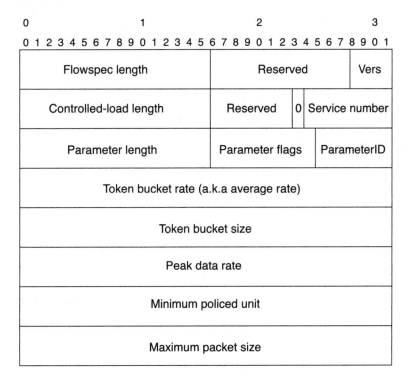

FILTER_SPEC Class

Figure 4-20 shows the FILTER_SPEC class object format.

The FILTER_SPEC class is defined in RFC 2205. RFC 3209 adds the C-Type 7, LSP Tunnel IPv4. The IPv4 Tunnel Sender Address field specifies the router ID of the TE tunnel headend, and the LSP ID field specifies the tunnel's LSP ID. The LSP ID changes when a tunnel's properties change (a bandwidth change or path change). See the "RSVP Operations" section for more information on how this is used. FILTER_SPEC is seen only in Resv and Resv-associated messages (ResvTear, ResvErr, and so on).

Figure 4-20   *FILTER_SPEC Class Format*

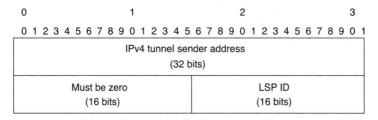

SENDER_TEMPLATE Class

Figure 4-21 shows the SENDER_TEMPLATE class object format.

Figure 4-21   *SENDER_TEMPLATE Class Format*

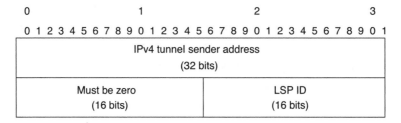

The SENDER_TEMPLATE is defined in RFC 2205, and RFC 3209 defines the C-Type 7, LSP Tunnel IPv4. It has the same format and purpose as the FILTER_SPEC class. Why does the same information have two different names, depending on direction? We have no idea. But it does.

SENDER_TSPEC Class

Figure 4-22 shows the SENDER_TSPEC class object format.

The SENDER_TSPEC class is generally seen only in Path messages. It's the same thing as FLOWSPEC, except that SENDER_TSPEC is seen in Path messages. Just like FLOWSPEC, the only part of SENDER_TSPEC that MPLS TE cares about is the average rate section.

Figure 4-22 *SENDER_TSPEC Class Format*

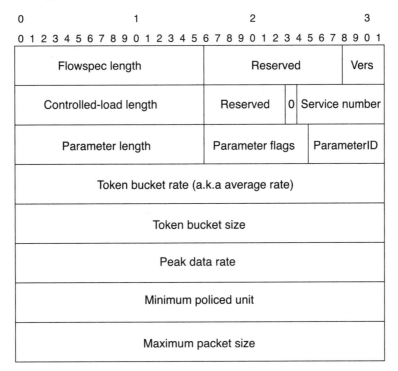

ADSPEC Class

Figure 4-23 shows the ADSPEC class object format.

ADSPEC is another of those complicated formats, as defined in RFC 2210. Like SENDER_TSPEC, ADSPEC is seen only in Path messages.

Figure 4-23 *ADSPEC Class Format*

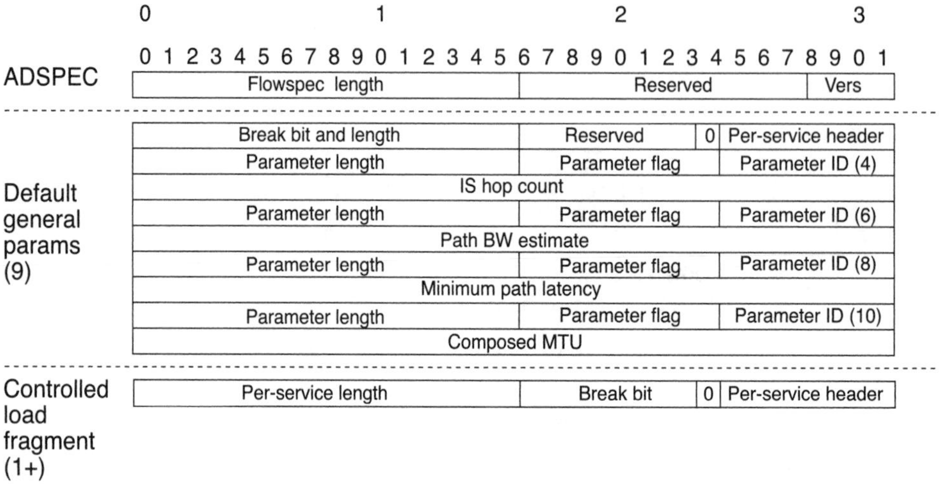

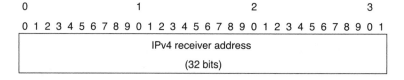

RESV_CONFIRM Class

Figure 4-24 shows the RESV_CONFIRM class object format.

Figure 4-24 *RESV_CONFIRM Class Format*

```
0                   1                   2                   3
0 1 2 3 4 5 6 7 8 9 0 1 2 3 4 5 6 7 8 9 0 1 2 3 4 5 6 7 8 9 0 1
+-------------------------------------------------------------+
|                   IPv4 receiver address                     |
|                      (32 bits)                              |
+-------------------------------------------------------------+
```

RESV_CONFIRM is defined in RFC 2205. It signals a request for confirmation; it appears in the Resv and ResvTear messages. The RESV_CONFIRM class sometimes shows up as CONFIRM; it's the same thing.

RSVP_LABEL Class

Figure 4-25 shows the RSVP_LABEL class object format.

The RSVP_LABEL class (sometimes just called LABEL) is defined in RFC 3209. It is a 32-bit quantity, in part because all RSVP objects must be a multiple of 4 bytes, but in frame mode, it carries the 20-bit label that the phop should use for a particular tunnel. The RSVP_LABEL class is seen only in Resv messages.

Figure 4-25 *RSVP_LABEL Class Format*

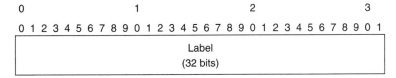

LABEL_REQUEST Class

Figure 4-26 shows the LABEL_REQUEST class object format.

Figure 4-26 *LABEL_REQUEST Class Format*

The LABEL_REQUEST object requests a label. An RSVP_LABEL object responds to it. The LABEL_REQUEST object is seen only in Path messages. It contains, in the upper 16 bits, the Layer 3 Protocol Identifier (L3PID) that is carried in the label. Cisco IOS always signals 0x800 (IP); the existence of the L3PID is somewhat historical. The fact that the LABEL_REQUEST object exists is enough to tell the downstream node that it is expected to provide a label.

EXPLICIT_ROUTE Class

Figure 4-27 shows the EXPLICIT_ROUTE class object format.

Figure 4-27 *EXPLICIT_ROUTE Class Format: IPv4 Subobject*

```
0                   1                   2                   3
0 1 2 3 4 5 6 7 8 9 0 1 2 3 4 5 6 7 8 9 0 1 2 3 4 5 6 7 8 9 0 1
┌─┬───────────┬───────────────┬───────────────────────────────┐
│L│   Type    │    Length     │         IPv4 address          │
│ │  (7 bits) │   (8 bits)    │        (First 16 bits)        │
├─┴───────────┴───────────────┼───────────────┬───────────────┤
│        IPv4 address         │ Prefix length │   Reserved    │
│       (Last 16 bits)        │   (8 bits)    │   (8 bits)    │
└─────────────────────────────┴───────────────┴───────────────┘
```

The EXPLICIT_ROUTE object defines the path that an MPLS TE tunnel takes. Often called the ERO, it is defined in RFC 3209. The ERO is seen only in Path messages.

The ERO is a collection of subobjects. The subobject is an 8-byte quantity pictured in Figure 4-27; the IPv4 Prefix subobject is the only one Cisco IOS currently supports. Table 4-27 shows the fields in the IPv4 subobject.

Table 4-27 *IPv4 Subobject Fields*

Field	Contents
L (Loose)	A bit to determine whether this is a Strict or Loose hop. See the "Strict Versus Loose ERO Subobject" section for more details.
Type	The type of object. Cisco IOS Software currently supports only the IPv4 type. IPv4 is Type 1. Other possible types are IPv6 and AS.
Length	The length of the subobject, in bytes.
IPv4 Address	The next IP address in the ERO—the hop to which a router should forward this Path message.
Prefix Length	The prefix length of the IPv4 Address. In Cisco IOS, this is always /32, independent of the destination's netmask.
Reserved	Reserved for future use.

RECORD_ROUTE Class

Figure 4-28 shows the RECORD_ROUTE class object format.

Figure 4-28 *RECORD_ROUTE Class Format*

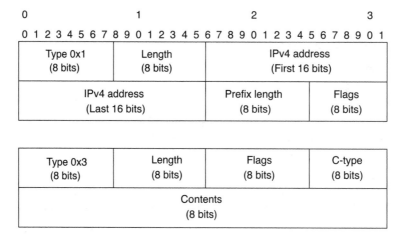

The RECORD_ROUTE object is defined in RFC 3209. There are two different RECORD_ROUTE subobjects; one is used to record the IP addresses at every hop, and the other is used to record the label used at every hop. Route recording can be configured by using the tunnel interface command **tunnel mpls traffic-eng record-route**.

RECORD_ROUTE allows you to do two things—record the IP address at each hop in the path, or record the label. The behavior is determined by the Label Recording bit in the SESSION_ATTRIBUTE flag string.

Table 4-28 describes the items in the RECORD_ROUTE object.

Table 4-28 *RECORD_ROUTE Object Fields*

Field	Contents
Type	0x1 for IPv4 Address. 0x3 for Label.
Length	Total length of the subobject.
IPv4 Address	An IP address that this LSP crossed.
Prefix Length	Always 32.
Flags (in the IPv4 subobject)	0x1 indicates Local Protection Available. 0x2 indicates Local Protection In Use. See Chapter 8, "MPLS TE Management," for more details.
Flags (in the Label subobject)	0x1 indicates that the label that's been recorded is from the recording router's global label space.
C-Type	The C-Type of the included label. This is the same as the C-Type for the RSVP_LABEL object. (Currently, the only defined value is 1.)
Contents	The label itself, as encoded in the RSVP_LABEL object.

HELLO Class

Figure 4-29 shows the HELLO class object format.

Figure 4-29 *HELLO Class Format*

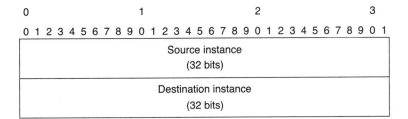

The HELLO class has two C-Types: Hello Request (Type 1) and Hello ACK (Type 2). They are both encoded the same. The Source Instance and Destination Instance are two counters used to track RSVP neighbor state; think of HELLO messages as RSVP-level keepalives. See RFC 3209 (particularly Section 5.3) for more details on HELLO messages.

SESSION_ATTRIBUTE Class

Figure 4-30 shows the SESSION_ATTRIBUTE class object format.

Figure 4-30 *SESSION_ATTRIBUTE Class Format*

```
0                   1                   2                   3
0 1 2 3 4 5 6 7 8 9 0 1 2 3 4 5 6 7 8 9 0 1 2 3 4 5 6 7 8 9 0 1
```

Setup priority (8 bits)	Holding priority (8 bits)	Flags (8 bits)	Name length (8 bits)
Session name (Variable length)			

The SESSION_ATTRIBUTE class is defined in RFC 3209. SESSION_ATTRIBUTE is seen only in Path messages.

SESSION_ATTRIBUTE has two types—with and without resource affinity (RA). Currently, Cisco IOS supports only the LSP Tunnel C-Type without RA (C-Type 7). This object has five fields, as listed in Table 4-29.

Table 4-29 *SESSION_ATTRIBUTE Object Fields*

Field	Contents
Setup Priority	The setup priority, as configured with **tunnel mpls traffic-eng priority**.
Holding Priority	The holding priority, also configured with **tunnel mpls traffic-eng priority**.
Flags	You can set three flags in the SESSION_ATTRIBUTE class: 0x1 = Local protection is desired. Configured with **tunnel mpls traffic-eng fast-reroute** on the headend tunnel interface. 0x2 = Label recording is desired. This can't be configured, but it is automatically enabled in some protection schemes. 0x4 = SE style is desired. Indicates that the headend wants an SE-style restriction rather than FF. In Cisco IOS, this flag is always set.
Name Length	The length of the Session Name string, in bytes.
Session Name	The session name assigned to this LSP. In Cisco IOS, this is either *RouterName_tTunnelNum* (so Tunnel5 from RouterA shows up as RouterA_t5) or a description entered on the tunnel interface with the **description** command.

RSVP Message Formats

This section examines message formats, both in theory and in practice. The objects dissected are as follows:

- Path
- Resv
- PathTear
- ResvTear
- PathErr
- ResvErr
- ResvConf
- ResvTearConf
- Hello

All the debugs in this section were captured with **debug ip rsvp path detail** or **debug ip rsvp resv detail**.

Figure 4-31 shows the basic topology used to gather all these debugs.

Figure 4-31 *Sample Network for Packet Examples*

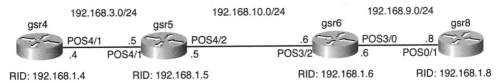

There is a single tunnel from gsr4 to gsr8. Its configuration is shown in Example 4-9.

Example 4-9 *gsr4 to gsr8 Tunnel Configuration*

```
interface Tunnel8
 ip unnumbered Loopback0
 no ip directed-broadcast
 tunnel destination 192.168.1.8
 tunnel mode mpls traffic-eng
 tunnel mpls traffic-eng priority 7 7
 tunnel mpls traffic-eng bandwidth 100000
 tunnel mpls traffic-eng path-option 10 dynamic
 end
```

Path Message

The Path message is defined in RFC 3209, as shown in Example 4-10.

Example 4-10 *Path Message*

```
<Path Message> :        <Common Header> [ <INTEGRITY> ]
                        <SESSION> <RSVP_HOP>
                        <TIME_VALUES>
                        [ <EXPLICIT_ROUTE> ]
                        <LABEL_REQUEST>
                        [ <SESSION_ATTRIBUTE> ]
                        [ <POLICY_DATA> ... ]
                        <SENDER_TEMPLATE>
                        <SENDER_TSPEC>
                        [ <ADSPEC> ]
                        [ <RECORD_ROUTE> ]
```

Example 4-11 shows a Path message as captured in **debug ip rsvp path detail**. The debug was run on the tunnel headend, gsr4.

NOTE	A note on the debug output: As this book was being written, the Cisco IOS Software's debug output was in the process of being reformatted. The debugs you see on your routers might be different in format from those shown here. However, the content, and the explanations therein, are the same.

Example 4-11 *Decoded Path Message*

```
1.  RSVP:        version:1 flags:0000 type:PATH cksum:1049 ttl:254 reserved:0
    length:200
2.  SESSION            type 7 length 16:
3.    Destination 192.168.1.8, TunnelId 8, Source 192.168.1.4
4.  HOP               type 1 length 12: C0A80304
5.                              : 00000000
6.  TIME_VALUES       type 1 length 8 : 00007530
7.  EXPLICIT_ROUTE    type 1 length 36:
8.    (#1) Strict IPv4 Prefix, 8 bytes, 192.168.3.5/32
9.    (#2) Strict IPv4 Prefix, 8 bytes, 192.168.10.6/32
10.   (#3) Strict IPv4 Prefix, 8 bytes, 192.168.9.8/32
11.   (#4) Strict IPv4 Prefix, 8 bytes, 192.168.1.8/32
12. LABEL_REQUEST     type 1 length 8 : 00000800
13. SESSION_ATTRIBUTE type 7 length 16:
14.   setup_pri: 7, reservation_pri: 7 MAY REROUTE
15.   SESSION_NAME:gsr4_t8
16. SENDER_TEMPLATE   type 7 length 12:
17.   Source 192.168.1.4, tunnel_id 1948
18. SENDER_TSPEC      type 2 length 36:
19.   version=0, length in words=7
20.   service id=1, service length=6
```

Example 4-11 *Decoded Path Message (Continued)*

```
21.      parameter id=127, flags=0, parameter length=5
22.      average rate=12500000 bytes/sec, burst depth=1000 bytes
23.      peak rate   = 12500000 bytes/sec
24.      min unit=0 bytes, max unit=0 bytes
25.  ADSPEC               type 2 length 48:
26.  version=0  length in words=10
27. General Parameters  break bit=0  service length=8
28.                                  IS Hops:1
29.              Minimum Path Bandwidth (bytes/sec):19375000
30.                  Path Latency (microseconds):0
31.                                  Path MTU:4470
32.  Controlled Load Service  break bit=0  service length=0
```

Table 4-30 analyzes, line by line, the output shown in Example 4-11.

Table 4-30   *Discussion of Example 4-11*

Line Number(s)	Description
1	This is the common header, seen in all RSVP messages. The TTL field is the TTL that the original RSVP message was sent with.
2 and 3	This is the SESSION object. It contains the message destination (192.168.1.8, the RID of the LSP tail), a Tunnel ID (8), and the tunnel source (192.168.1.4, the RID of the LSP headend).
	The Tunnel ID is the interface number on the headend tunnel, which is interface Tunnel8.
4 and 5	This is the RSVP_HOP object. It contains the IP address of the interface this message was just transmitted from. In this case, it's C0A80304, or 192.168.3.4, which is gsr4's interface address between gsr4 and gsr5.
6	The TIME_VALUES object. This is how often the headend refreshes the tunnel, in milliseconds. 0x7530 is 30,000 milliseconds, or 30 seconds.
7 through 11	These lines are the EXPLICIT_ROUTE object. EXPLICIT_ROUTE (often called the ERO) is the result of the CSPF calculation on the headend. It is a list of hops that this Path message needs to be propagated down. As each hop receives this ERO, it removes itself from the ERO; that's why you don't see any addresses for GSR1 in Figure 4-31.
12	The LABEL_REQUEST object. This is a signal from the headend that it would like a label returned to it in the RESV that comes back. 00000800 is the Layer 3 PID of the traffic that will be carried in the LSP; 0x0800 is IP, which is what the Cisco IOS Software always signals.

continues

Table 4-30 *Discussion of Example 4-11 (Continued)*

Line Number(s)	Description
13 through 15	The SESSION_ATTRIBUTE object is optional, but it is always sent by Cisco LERs. The setup and holding priorities are both given here, as are some flags. In this case, the only flag set is MAY REROUTE, which is set by default on all LSPs.
	SESSION NAME, although it looks like a separate object, is part of the SESSION_ATTRIBUTE object. It carries a text string describing the tunnel. By default, this string is *hostname_tifnum*. So you can tell that the tunnel you're looking at is interface Tunnel8 on gsr4. However, if the **description** command is used on the headend tunnel configuration, that description is carried in this field instead.
16 and 17	The SENDER_TEMPLATE object contains information about the originator of the Path message. Specifically, it contains the source RID and something labeled tunnel_id. This label is incorrect—it should be called the *LSP ID*. This ID is different from the tunnel ID carried in the SESSION object, but it is used in conjunction with it to do make-before-break. See the "What Is Make-Before-Break?" section for more details. Some **show** commands also call this number the *tunnel instance*—same thing, different name.
18 through 24	These are the SENDER_TSPEC. The SENDER_TSPEC is information from the tunnel headend about what kind of traffic it expects to send. Most of the information here is not used by MPLS Traffic Engineering. The only part that is used is the average rate, which is the amount of bandwidth the LSP wants to reserve. It's listed here as 12,500,000 bytes, which is 100,000,000 bits. So this tunnel is making a 100-Mbps bandwidth reservation, which matches the configuration shown for the tunnel.
25 through 32	The ADSPEC is an optional object, but it is always sent by Cisco IOS Software. It contains information about the path that the LSP is taking.

Resv Message

A Resv message contains information similar to that shown in a Path message. Example 4-12 provides the Resv message definition.

Example 4-12 *Resv Message*

```
<Resv Message> :     <Common Header> [ <INTEGRITY> ]
                     <SESSION>  <RSVP_HOP>
                     <TIME_VALUES>
                     [ <RESV_CONFIRM> ]  [ <SCOPE> ]
                     [ <POLICY_DATA> ... ]
                     <STYLE>
                     <FLOWSPEC>
```

Example 4-12 *Resv Message (Continued)*

```
                              <FILTER_SPEC>
                              <LABEL>
                            [ <RECORD_ROUTE> ]
```

Example 4-13 shows the message received on gsr4, as seen with **debug ip rsvp resv detail**.

Example 4-13 *Decoded Resv Message*

```
1.   RSVP:      version:1 flags:0000 type:RESV cksum:0000 ttl:255 reserved:0
       length:108
2.   SESSION            type 7 length 16:
3.     Destination 192.168.1.8, TunnelId 8, Source 192.168.1.4
4.   HOP                type 1 length 12: C0A80305
5.                               : 00000000
6.   TIME_VALUES        type 1 length 8 : 00007530
7.   STYLE              type 1 length 8 :
8.     RSVP_SE_OPTION
9.   FLOWSPEC           type 2 length 36:
10.    version = 0 length in words = 7
11.    service id = 5, service length = 6
12.    tspec parameter id = 127, tspec flags = 0, tspec length = 5
13.    average rate = 12500000 bytes/sec, burst depth = 1000 bytes
14.    peak rate   = 2147483647 bytes/sec
15.    min unit = 0 bytes, max unit = 0 bytes
16.  FILTER_SPEC        type 7 length 12:
17.    Source 192.168.1.4, tunnel_id 1955
18.  LABEL              type 1 length 8 : 00000017
```

As you can see, a Resv message looks much like a Path message. The major difference between the contents of a Resv message and the contents of a Path message is that Resv messages do not contain the following items found in a Path message:

- An Explicit Route object
- A Session Attribute object
- An AdSpec

The output in Example 4-13 also highlights some differences between Resv messages and Path messages, as documented in Table 4-31.

Table 4-31 *Things in a Resv Message But Not in a Path Message*

Line Number(s)	Significance
4	The HOP object is 192.168.3.5, or the downstream node's interface address, rather than the upstream node's interface address.
7	The STYLE object.
9 through 15	The Resv contains a FLOWSPEC rather than a SENDER_TSPEC.
18	The Resv message contains a LABEL object, in hex. 0x17 means that gsr5 has told gsr4 to use outgoing label 23 for this tunnel.

PathTear Message

The PathTear message is composed of messages you've seen before, as shown in Example 4-14.

Example 4-14 *PathTear Definition*

```
<PathTear Message> : <Common Header> [ <INTEGRITY> ]
                     <SESSION> <RSVP_HOP>
                     <SENDER_TEMPLATE>
                     <SENDER_TSPEC>
                     [ <ADSPEC> ]
```

A PathTear message was captured on gsr5 when Tunnel8 on gsr4 was shut down. Example 4-15 shows the debug results.

Example 4-15 *PathTear Message*

```
RSVP:      version:1 flags:0000 type:PTEAR cksum:0000 ttl:254 reserved:0 length:132
 SESSION             type 7 length 16:
   Destination 192.168.1.8, TunnelId 8, Source 192.168.1.4
 HOP                 type 1 length 12: C0A80304
                                     : 00000000
 SENDER_TEMPLATE     type 7 length 12:
   Source 192.168.1.4, tunnel_id 1955
 SENDER_TSPEC        type 2 length 36:
   version=0, length in words=7
   service id=1, service length=6
   parameter id=127, flags=0, parameter length=5
   average rate=12500000 bytes/sec, burst depth=1000 bytes
   peak rate   =12500000 bytes/sec
   min unit=0 bytes, max unit=0 bytes
 ADSPEC              type 2 length 48:
 version=0  length in words=10
 General Parameters  break bit=0  service length=8
                                     IS Hops:0
             Minimum Path Bandwidth (bytes/sec):2147483647
                    Path Latency (microseconds):0
                                     Path MTU:-1
 Controlled Load Service  break bit=0  service length=0
```

ResvTear Message

ResvTear also contains objects that might be familiar by now; there's nothing new under the sun here. The message shown in Example 4-16 was captured on gsr4. The ResvTear in question was sent by gsr5 in response to gsr4's PathTear when gsr4's Tunnel8 was shut down.

Example 4-16 *ResvTear Definition*

```
<ResvTear Message> : <Common Header> [<INTEGRITY>]
                     <SESSION>
                     <RSVP_HOP>
                     [ <SCOPE> ]
```

Example 4-16 *ResvTear Definition (Continued)*

```
                          <STYLE>
                          <FLOWSPEC>
                          <FILTER_SPEC>
```

Example 4-17 shows the decode.

Example 4-17 *ResvTear Message*

```
RSVP:       version:1 flags:0000 type:RTEAR cksum:9E95 ttl:255 reserved:0 length:
  100
SESSION             type 7 length 16:
  Destination 192.168.1.8, TunnelId 8, Source 192.168.1.4
HOP                 type 1 length 12: C0A80305
                                    : 00000000
STYLE               type 1 length 8 :
  RSVP_SE_OPTION
FLOWSPEC            type 2 length 36:
  version = 0 length in words = 7
  service id = 5, service length = 6
  tspec parameter id = 127, tspec flags = 0, tspec length = 5
  average rate = 12500000 bytes/sec, burst depth = 1000 bytes
  peak rate    = 2147483647 bytes/sec
  min unit = 0 bytes, max unit = 0 bytes
FILTER_SPEC         type 7 length 12:
  Source 192.168.1.4, tunnel_id 1956
CONFIRM             type 1 length 8 : C0A80305
```

About the only thing notable and new here is that this message contains a CONFIRM object. The CONFIRM object is a request for confirmation that the ResvTear actually took place. The node requesting the confirmation is 192.168.3.5, which is the interface address on gsr5 on the subnet between gsr4 and gsr5. A Cisco node responds to a ResvTear that contains a CONFIRM object by sending a ResvTearConfirm object. Interoperability with non-Cisco equipment isn't a problem; any device that doesn't understand what to do with a ResvTear with CONFIRM just ignores the CONFIRM message. For MPLS TE, not receiving a ResvTearConfirm won't hurt anything.

PathErr Message

Example 4-18 shows the PathErr message definition.

Example 4-18 *PathErr Definition*

```
<PathErr message> : <Common Header> [ <INTEGRITY> ]
                    <SESSION> <ERROR_SPEC>
                    [ <POLICY_DATA> ...]
                    <SENDER_TEMPLATE>
                    <SENDER_TSPEC>
                    [ <ADSPEC> ]
```

This error message was captured on gsr4. A PathErr with a bogus hop in the ERO was sent to gsr5, which forwarded it to gsr6. This error message is gsr6 complaining about that bad hop. Example 4-19 decodes this error message.

Example 4-19 *PathErr Decode*

```
1.   RSVP:         version:1 flags:0000 type:PERR cksum:0000 ttl:255 reserved:0
     length:132
2.   SESSION              type 7 length 16:
3.     Destination 192.168.1.8, TunnelId 8, Source 192.168.1.4
4.   ERROR_SPEC           type 1 length 12:
5.     Node 192.168.10.6
6.     Code 24
7.     Value 2
8.     Flags 0x00
9.   SENDER_TEMPLATE      type 7 length 12:
10.     Source 192.168.1.4, tunnel_id 8909
11.   SENDER_TSPEC         type 2 length 36:
12.        version=0, length in words=7
13.               Minimum Path Bandwidth (bytes/sec):2147483647
14.                    Path Latency (microseconds):0
15.                              Path MTU:-1
16.    Controlled Load Service  break bit=0  service length=0
```

ERROR_SPEC (lines 4 through 8) is a new object here. The Node field is the address of the node that detected the error—192.168.10.6 is gsr6's IP address on the subnet between gsr5 and gsr6. The Code of 24 indicates that this error is of type "Routing Problem," and the Value of 2 means that the specific routing problem is "Bad strict node."

ResvErr Message

Example 4-20 provides the ResvErr message definition.

Example 4-20 *ResvErr Definition*

```
<ResvErr Message> : <Common Header> [ <INTEGRITY> ]
                    <SESSION>
                    <RSVP_HOP>
                    <ERROR_SPEC>
                    [ <SCOPE> ]
                    [ <POLICY_DATA> ]
                    <STYLE>
                    <FLOWSPEC>
                    <FILTER_LIST>
```

Because of how RSVP signalling works, it's difficult to cause a ResvErr on purpose. Most errors that could be caught by a ResvErr would be caught first by a PathErr, so they'd never make it this far. A ResvErr looks a lot like a PathErr, though, so the decodes look similar.

ResvConf Message

ResvConf messages are sent in response to a Resv message containing a CONFIRM object. Currently, the Cisco IOS Software does not put the CONFIRM object in a ResvConf—at least, not for MPLS TE. Example 4-21 shows the message definition for a ResvConf.

Example 4-21 *ResvConf Definition*

```
<ResvConf message> : <Common Header> [ <INTEGRITY> ]
                     <SESSION> <ERROR_SPEC>
                     <RESV_CONFIRM>
                     <STYLE>
                     <FLOWSPEC>
                     <FILTER_LIST>
```

ResvTearConf Message

The ResvTearConf message is used by Cisco to confirm that a ResvTear took place. It's proprietary, but is easily identifiable in debugs. ResvTearConf is sent in response to a Resv message that contains a CONFIRM object.

Example 4-22 shows the message definition for the ResvTearConf message.

Example 4-22 *ResvTearConf Definition*

```
<ResvTearConf Message> : <Common Header>
                         <SESSION>
                         <ERROR_SPEC>
                         <CONFIRM>
                         <STYLE>
                         <FLOWSPEC>
                         <FILTER_SPEC>
```

Example 4-23 shows the decode of a ResvTearConf message.

Example 4-23 *ResvTearConf Decode*

```
RSVP:      version:1 flags:0000 type:RTEAR-CONFIRM cksum:0000 ttl:255 reserved:0
  length :100
 SESSION              type 7 length 16:
   Destination 192.168.1.8, TunnelId 8, Source 192.168.1.4
 ERROR_SPEC           type 1 length 12:
   Node 192.168.9.6
   Code 0
   Value 0
   Flags 0x00
 CONFIRM              type 1 length 8 : C0A80908
 STYLE                type 1 length 8 :
   RSVP_SE_OPTION
```

continues

Example 4-23 *ResvTearConf Decode (Continued)*

```
FLOWSPEC               type 2 length 36:
   version = 0 length in words = 7
   service id = 5, service length = 6
   tspec parameter id = 127, tspec flags = 0, tspec length = 5
   average rate = 12500000 bytes/sec, burst depth = 1000 bytes
   peak rate    = 2147483647 bytes/sec
   min unit = 0 bytes, max unit = 0 bytes
FILTER_SPEC            type 7 length 12:
   Source 192.168.1.4, tunnel_id 3992
```

Two things stand out in this decode. One is that the ResvTearConf contains an ERROR_SPEC message. An ERROR_SPEC with a Code of 0x0 is in fact a confirmation; this is what's sent in response to receiving a message with a CONFIRM request in it. The Node address is the node that is sending the ResvTearConf; the CONFIRM object contains the address of the node that the ResvTearConf message is being sent to. The Node address is 192.168.9.6, and the CONFIRM object turns out to be 192.168.9.8. This decode was captured on gsr8. It shows the incoming ResvTearConf that came from gsr6. A ResvTearConf acts much like a ResvErr, in that it is sent hop-by-hop from the headend to the tail.

Hello Message

The Hello message format is pretty straightforward. The Hello message itself is shown in Example 4-24.

Example 4-24 *Hello Definition*

```
<Hello Message> : <Common Header> [ <INTEGRITY> ]
                  <HELLO>
```

RSVP Operation

By now, you should have a pretty good grip on the RSVP components—at least as far as MPLS TE is concerned. A lot of RSVP stuff that doesn't apply to MPLS TE (more about the QoS specifications, flow merging, and so on) has been skipped over, but unless you run a non-TE RSVP network now, you'll never miss it.

You might be wondering how some of the protocol mechanisms fit together. This section is designed to answer these questions:

- What is make-before-break?
- How do the refresh mechanisms work?
- When, where, and to whom are messages sent?

- What good are strict and loose ERO subobjects?
- What about implicit and explicit null signalling at the penultimate hop?

What Is Make-Before-Break?

Make-before-break is an RSVP-TE mechanism that allows you to change some characteristics of a TE tunnel (namely, bandwidth and the path a tunnel takes) with virtually no data loss and without double-booking bandwidth. Consider Figure 4-32.

Figure 4-32 *Sample Network for Make-Before-Break*

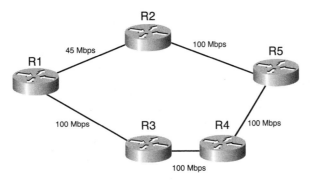

The bandwidths indicated are before any bandwidth is reserved from the network.

If R1 signals a 35 Mb request to the network, it goes over the top path, R1→R2→R5. That leaves the R1→R2 segment with 10 Mb available bandwidth and the R2→R5 segment with 65 Mb available bandwidth.

What if, at some point in the future, R1 wants to increase its reservation size to 80 Mb? This bandwidth has to come from the bottom path, because there's no way to get an 80 Mb reservation across the R1→R2→R5 path. So R1 reserves 80 Mb along the path R1→R3→R4→R5. This leaves 20 Mb available along each link in the bottom path. For a short while, R1 reserves bandwidth across both paths and therefore reserves a total of 115 Mb (35 Mb across the top and 80 Mb across the bottom) of bandwidth. However, the 35 Mb reservation is released soon after the 80 Mb reservation is made, and all is well. Make-before-break is simply the rule that a tunnel headend should not release an old reservation until the new reservation is in place; this minimizes data loss.

Sounds simple, right? It is. But there's a tricky piece to it. Look at Figure 4-33.

Figure 4-33 *The Need for Make-Before-Break*

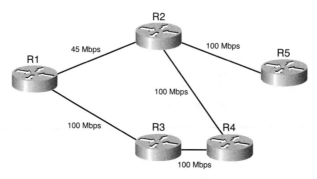

This looks like Figure 4-32, except that the link from R4 to R5 now goes from R4 to R2. R1 still makes its 35 Mb reservation across R1→R2→R5; nothing changes there.

Then what happens? R1 tries to make an 80 Mb reservation across R1→R3→R4→ R2→R5. But it can't! Because the first reservation from R1 to R5 has consumed 35 Mb of the 100 Mb from R2 to R5, that leaves the R2→R5 link with only 65 Mb of bandwidth! If R1 were to signal the reservation anyway, R2 would see an 80 Mb bandwidth request for a link that has only 65 Mb of capacity and would reject the reservation.

What to do now? R1 could tear down the R1→R2→R5 reservation and then build the R1→R3→R4→R2→R5 reservation. But that's stupid. During the window when the old reservation is gone and the new one is being established, traffic forwarded from R1 to R5 might not have particularly good service because it follows the shortest path, which in this case, means putting 80 Mb of data down a path whose smallest link is 45 Mb. This is bad. Even though R1 might not start out by sending that much data down the shortest path, the general idea of tearing down one reservation to make room for another is still not a good one. It's like tearing down your house in order to build a new one on the same lot: Where do you live in the meantime?

Shared Explicit Reservation Style

Fortunately, there is a better way to do this. You might recall that RSVP has a facility called *Shared Explicit (SE)*. SE is a reservation style that allows an existing LSP to share bandwidth with itself so that double booking doesn't happen. This avoids problems such as those shown in Figure 4-33, where, even if you allowed double booking, the second reservation would still never get established.

So how does SE work? SE reservations have two components:

- Requesting SE reservation style from the network

- Being able to identify that a given reservation is "the same" as an existing reservation, so the bandwidth should be shared

SE reservation style is requested by the tunnel headend using a flag in the SESSION_ATTRIBUTE object. The alternative to SE is something called Fixed Filter (FF), but it's never used by Cisco's MPLS TE implementation, so it's not discussed here. Suffice it to say, FF doesn't allow you to share bandwidth the way SE does, so an FF reservation would still leave you with the problem presented in Figure 4-33.

But how do you identify two reservations as the same one so that they can share bandwidth? As it turns out, this is relatively easy. All RSVP reservations are uniquely identified with a five-tuple of {Sender Address, LSP ID, Endpoint Address, Tunnel ID, Extended Tunnel ID}. The first two items in this five-tuple are found in the SENDER_TEMPLATE (and FILTER_SPEC) objects; the last three are found in the SESSION object. If two Path message are seen in which all five of these are the same, they are considered two representatives of the same reservation.

The Sender Address is the RID of the tunnel headend. The Endpoint Address is the RID of the tunnel tail. The Extended Tunnel ID is either all 0s or an IP address on the router; this is used in some protection schemes, but it doesn't matter for this discussion. And the Tunnel ID is the tunnel interface number at the headend.

Those four are pretty simple. But that leaves the LSP ID. Think of the LSP ID as an "instantiation counter": Every time the tunnel changes either its bandwidth requirement or the path it takes, the LSP ID increments by 1.

The rule of the SE reservation process for MPLS TE is that if two reservations are seen with the same five-tuple, except that they have different LSP IDs, the two reservations are for different LSPs, but they share bandwidth.

Assume that in Figure 4-33, R1's RID is 1.1.1.1 and R5's is 5.5.5.5. Table 4-32 shows what R1 sends out and what R4 does with the information it receives.

Table 4-32 *Steps in Make-Before-Break*

Step	R1 Transmission	R2 Action
1	Sends a reservation for {SA=1.1.1.1, LSP ID=1, EA=5.5.5.5, TID=8, XTID=0}, asking for 35 Mb along the path R1→R2→R5. Call this reservation Res1.	Forwards the reservation to R5. Marks the R2→R5 interface as having 35 Mb reserved for this tunnel and 65 Mb remaining reservable.
2	Sends a reservation for {SA=1.1.1.1, LSP ID=2, EA=5.5.5.5, TID=8} along the path R1→R3→R4→ R2→R5, asking for 80 Mb of bandwidth. Call this Res2.	Examines the reservation and realizes that this reservation is identical to the previous reservation except for the tunnel ID. Allows the new reservation to reuse the existing reserved bandwidth and allocates this tunnel 80 – 35 = 45 Mbps more bandwidth on the R2→R5 link. The R2→R5 link is marked with 80 Mbps reserved and 20 Mbps unreserved.

In this way, both Res1 and Res2 are allowed to coexist until Res1 is removed from the network. The implication is that after Res2 starts to share the reservation with Res1, Res1 will shortly no longer be active and will never try to compete with Res2 for bandwidth. In other words, after Res2 has shared the bandwidth with Res1, the implicit assumption is that Res1 will no longer try to use the bandwidth at the same time as Res2.

Wait a minute. Why does Res2 ask for 80 Mbps? Can't it just ask for 45 Mbps, leave the Res1 reservation in place, and get along just fine?

Well, sure. Except for the major holes in that plan, it works fine. Here are the two big holes in that idea:

- Keeping Res1 in place means consuming bandwidth across the R1→R2 link that's no longer going to be used.

- Asking for only 45 Mbps instead of 80 Mbps reserves only 45 Mbps across segments such as R1→R3, R3→R4, and R4→R2. This can lead to problems because Res2 might actually have 80 Mbps sent down it, and if someone else reserves the other 55 Mbps along any part of the R1→R3→R4→R2 path, there's likely to be unwarranted congestion.

But other than that, no, there are no problems whatsoever with this approach. None.

So that's make-before-break. SE reservation style is, as you can see, an integral part of the make-before-break strategy.

How Do the Refresh Mechanisms Work?

This can be confusing to most people. As you already know, RSVP is a soft-state protocol. As such, reservations are periodically refreshed. Reservations are sent using Path and Resv messages. There is no difference between the Path and Resv messages used to set up the LSP initially and the ones used to refresh it; the packet formats are the same. The way a router tells a new setup from a refresh is to see if it has an existing reservation with a five-tuple that matches the Path or Resv message in question.

Two major points to understand when talking about refresh mechanisms are

- The refresh timers are jittered.
- Path and Resv messages are sent independently between two routers

Refresh Timers Are Jittered

As you know, Path and Resv messages are sent every 30 seconds. They're not really sent every 30 seconds, however; they're sent on a 30-second timer with 50 percent jitter. So a given reservation has a Path message sent to refresh it every 15 to 45 seconds. It's the same deal with the Resv message for that reservation—every 15 to 45 seconds. And so it is for every refresh message.

The actual refresh formula is in RFC 2205, Section 3.7. The general idea is that a neighbor sends its refresh interval (R) to its neighbor in the TIME_VALUES object in its Path and Resv messages. Each router also knows how many messages it is willing to miss before declaring the reservation dead (call this K).

The neighbor computes a holdtime L for this message with the formula

$$L >= (K + 0.5) * 1.5 * R$$

In the current IOS implementation, R is 30 seconds and K is 3. So L is at least 157.5 seconds. This means that a router can go just under 157.5 seconds with no refresh before tearing down a neighbor. This is enough time that a router can have three consecutive intervals of worst-case jitter (with all packets lost) on the refresh timer (45 seconds) before timing out.

What this means is that, occasionally, you see something like Figure 4-34, in which the Path message refresh timer happened to fire at 00:00 and 00:45, and the Resv message refresh timer happened to fire at 00:15 and 00:30.

Figure 4-34 *Path and Resv Messages Are Sent Independently*

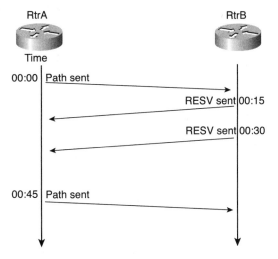

This is perfectly normal. It's important to understand that Path and Resv messages are not sent in ping/ACK fashion, but are sent independently from one another. This brings us to the next point.

Path and Resv Messages Are Sent Independently

Take a look at Figure 4-35.

Figure 4-35 *Sample Network for Path and Resv Messages*

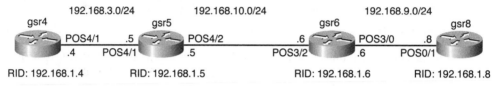

Assume that a single tunnel is set up from gsr4 to gsr8.

In addition to Path and Resv messages being on separate timers, when used for refreshes, they're not propagated hop-by-hop from the head to the tail, but instead are sent independently by each node. One possible refresh scenario might look like Figure 4-36.

Figure 4-36 *Possible Timing of Path and Resv Messages*

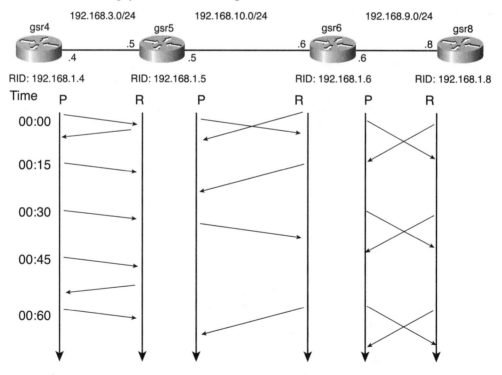

Figure 4-36 is a bit of an oversimplification; you won't see gsr4 send a Path message every 15 seconds five times in a row. Specifically, Rule 5 of section 3.7 of RFC 2205 limits the amount of time between any two consecutive refreshes. This figure, however, conveys the general idea. Path and Resv messages, when used for refresh, are independent of each other and are not propagated from head to tail.

When, Where, and to Whom Are Messages Sent?

As mentioned before, there are nine RSVP message types. Table 4-33 summarizes what messages are sent when and where.

This table has five columns:

- **Message**—The message type.
- **Function**—What the message is used for.
- **Direction**—The direction in which the message is sent. *Downstream* means "toward the tunnel tail, away from the head." *Upstream* means "toward the tunnel head, away from the tail."
- **Destination Address**—The destination IP address on the packet. Some RSVP messages carry the tunnel tail RID as their destination IP address, and others carry the IP address of the next-hop interface. All RSVP messages have their outgoing interface as the packet's source address.
- **Router Alert?**—Some RSVP messages carry the Router Alert option (as specified in RFC 2113), and others don't.

Table 4-33   *RSVP Message Types*

Message	Function	Direction	Destination Address	Router Alert?
Path	Signals a resource request to the network.	Downstream	Tail	Yes
Resv	Responds to a successful Path message.	Upstream	Next hop	No
PathErr	Sent toward the headend if there's an error with a Path message (for example, if a link goes down or you get a corrupted Path message).	Upstream	Next hop	No
ResvErr	Sent toward the tail if there's an error in processing a Path message.	Downstream	Next hop	No

continues

Table 4-33 *RSVP Message Types (Continued)*

Message	Function	Direction	Destination Address	Router Alert?
PathTear	Sent toward the tail to tear down an existing reservation.	Downstream	Tail	Yes
ResvTear	Sent toward the headend to tear down an existing reservation.	Upstream	Next hop	No
ResvConf	Sent in response to a Resv or ResvTear that has requested confirmation of message receipt.[*]	Downstream	Tail	Yes
ResvTearConf	Sent in response to a ResvTear that includes a Confirm message.	Downstream	Next hop	No
Hello	Sent to an RSVP neighbor on a directly connected link.	Upstream/ downstream	Next hop	No

Cisco IOS Software MPLS TE doesn't request confirmation of Resv messages, so you'll never see this message in an all-Cisco network. IOS sends a ResvConf if asked to, though.

NOTE   RFC 2113 introduced a new IP option called the *Router Alert* option. If this option is present in an IP header, it is a signal to every router it crosses that the router needs to take a close look at the packet. Router Alert is currently used in both IGMP and RSVP. It allows a router to examine certain packets that are in transit and gives a router the option of modifying that packet before passing it on.

To help understand the terminology (upstream/downstream, tail versus next-hop destination address, and the existence of Router Alert), see Figure 4-37.

Figure 4-37 *RSVP Terminology*

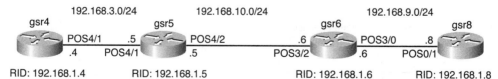

In Figure 4-37, gsr4 wants to signal an LSP from gsr4 to gsr8 along the path gsr4→gsr5→gsr6→gsr8.

After gsr4 computes the path it wants the tunnel to take, gsr4 sends a Path message out on the wire between gsr4 and gsr6. The Path message's contents are discussed in the next section. The destination IP address on the packet is gsr8's TE RID. This Path message has the Router Alert option.

Because the Router Alert option is set in the packet, gsr6 examines it. gsr6 makes some modifications to the packet (see the EXPLICIT_ROUTE object explanation in Table 4-27) and sends it out its top link to gsr8. gsr8 also examines the packet, modifies it, and sends it to gsr8.

At every hop in the path, the destination IP address on the Path message remains the same— gsr8. The Router Alert (RA) is always present in the Path message.

When gsr8 sends the Resv message upstream, the destination address is gsr6 (specifically, gsr6's address on the link between gsr6 and gsr8). Also, the Router Alert option is never present in the packet.

You might notice a pattern here:

- All messages that have the RA option set are sent in the downstream direction.
- All messages that have the RA option set have the tunnel tail as their destination IP address.
- All messages either have the Router Alert option set *or* put the next hop (either upstream or downstream) interface address as the destination address on the packet.

Why are things done this way? Largely for reasons that don't exist in an MPLS network. Controlling which messages carry the Router Alert option and which messages have the next hop as their destination address allows routers to detect the presence of non-RSVP routers in the path. But you can't build a TE tunnel through a router that doesn't speak RSVP, because MPLS Traffic Engineering needs not only a bandwidth reservation, but also a label allocation.

If you are interested, check out Section 2.9 of RFC 2205 for details on how this works.

Strict Versus Loose ERO Subobject

The discussion of the EXPLICIT_ROUTE object showed that an L (Loose) bit can be set on a hop in the ERO to indicate a Loose route. But what is a Loose route?

The ERO is encoded as a series of subobjects called *abstract nodes*. An abstract node can be either an IPv4 address, an IPv6 address, or an autonomous system. Cisco IOS Software currently supports only IPv4 addresses in the ERO.

Each subobject can be either a *strict hop* or a *loose hop*. Most of what Cisco IOS Software uses are strict hops, save some interarea traffic engineering uses and other specific cases.

When a router processes a strict hop, the IPv4 address in the subobject must be directly connected to the router doing the processing, or there is an error in the ERO.

Sometimes, though, the subobject is a loose hop. If a router processes an ERO subobject with a loose hop, it is the responsibility of that router to generate a set of strict hops to get this Path message to the destination and replace the single loose hop with the newly generated set of strict hops.

Implicit Versus Explicit Null

As you know, a tunnel tail can signal two kinds of labels—implicit null and explicit null. Explicit null is signalled by using the value 0 in the Label field of the LABEL object. Implicit null is signalled by using the value 3 in the Label field of the LABEL object.

By default, the tunnel tail node signals explicit null in its Resv message:

```
LABEL                 type 1 length 8 : 00000000
```

However, if you look at the penultimate hop, as demonstrated in Example 4-25, you see that the explicit-null value is interpreted as implicit null, on both the tail (gsr8) and the penultimate hop (gsr6).

Example 4-25 *Explicit Null Interpreted as Implicit Null*

```
gsr8#show mpls traffic-eng tunnels role tail
LSP Tunnel gsr4_t8 is signalled, connection is up
  InLabel  : POS0/1, implicit-null
  OutLabel :  -

gsr6#show mpls traffic-eng tunnels role middle
LSP Tunnel gsr4_t8 is signalled, connection is up
  InLabel  : POS3/2, 16
  OutLabel : POS3/0, implicit-null
```

How did we get into this state? It's a long story, and mostly historical. You can use a few knobs to control this behavior. On the tunnel tail, you can use the knob **mpls traffic-eng signalling advertise implicit-null** to make the tail advertise implicit null:

```
LABEL                 type 1 length 8 : 00000003
```

But no matter what you do on the tail, the penultimate hop still interprets the advertised label as implicit null, as confirmed by the output shown in Example 4-26.

Example 4-26 *Confirming Implicit-Null Interpretation on the Penultimate Hop*

```
gsr6#show mpls traffic-eng tunnels role middle
LSP Tunnel gsr4_t8 is signalled, connection is up
  InLabel  : POS3/2, 16
  OutLabel : POS3/0, implicit-null
```

If you care about sending explicit null from the penultimate hop to the tail, you need to enable the hidden command **mpls traffic-eng signalling interpret explicit-null verbatim** on the penultimate hop. After that, things look the way you'd expect them to, as shown in Example 4-27.

Example 4-27 *Interpreting Explicit Null Properly on the Penultimate Hop*

```
gsr6#show run | include verbatim
mpls traffic-eng signalling interpret explicit-null verbatim

gsr6#show mpls traffic-eng tunnels role middle
LSP Tunnel gsr4_t8 is signalled, connection is up
  InLabel  : POS3/2, 12304
  OutLabel : POS3/0, explicit-null
```

When you think about it, how often do you care if it's implicit null or explicit null? It makes little or no difference almost all the time. But the knob's there if you need to use it. One place you might have a need for explicit rather than implicit null is with QoS. See Chapter 6, "Quality of Service with MPLS TE"—specifically, the section "Label Stack Treatment"—for more details.

RSVP Message Pacing

When there is a disruption in the network (a link flap, a router reboot, and so on), this can result in a significant amount of signalling. If a link flaps, for example, a PathErr or ResvErr needs to be sent for every tunnel crossing that link. If there are 2000 TE tunnels across a link, that means 2000 PathErrs/ResvErrs. It is possible to send more messages out an interface than the next hop can handle.

When RSVP messages are sent out, they are sent either hop-by-hop or with the router alert bit set. This means that every router along the path for these RSVP messages needs to pay attention to them. Operationally, this means that every RSVP message that comes in on an interface goes through that interface's input queue. The input queue has a default size of 75 packets, as you can see in Example 4-28.

Example 4-28 *Displaying the Input Queue Size*

```
gsr5#show interfaces p5/0
POS5/0 is up, line protocol is up
  Hardware is Packet over SONET
  Internet address is 192.168.12.5/24
  MTU 4470 bytes, BW 622000 Kbit, DLY 100 usec, rely 255/255, load 1/255
  Encapsulation HDLC, crc 16, loopback not set
  Keepalive set (10 sec)
  Scramble disabled
  Last input 00:00:00, output 00:00:02, output hang never
  Last clearing of "show interface" counters never
  Queueing strategy: fifo
  Output queue 0/40, 0 drops; input queue 0/75, 0 drops
  5 minute input rate 7000 bits/sec, 0 packets/sec
  5 minute output rate 0 bits/sec, 0 packets/sec
     11687 packets input, 10119458 bytes, 0 no buffer
     Received 0 broadcasts, 16 runts, 0 giants, 0 throttles
              0 parity
     622 input errors, 606 CRC, 0 frame, 0 overrun, 0 ignored, 0 abort
     11674 packets output, 10141348 bytes, 0 underruns
     0 output errors, 0 applique, 0 interface resets
     0 output buffer failures, 0 output buffers swapped out
     1 carrier transitions
```

After messages go into the input queue, they are processed by the application they're destined for; in this case, RSVP is the focus of attention. All other applications that terminate on a router take their packets from the input queue—BGP, SNMP, Telnet, and so forth.

If there's enough signalling traffic in the network, it is possible for an interface to receive more packets for its input queue than it can hold. If a packet is received that is destined for the input queue, and the input queue for that interface is full, the packet is dropped.

This has unfortunate side effects on RSVP. If an RSVP message is lost, the node that sent it will not send it again until it's time to refresh that message—30 seconds, plus or minus 50% jitter.

One way to solve this problem is to make the input queue very large. You can adjust the input queue size with the command **hold-queue** *size* **input**. Making the input queue significantly bigger is a perfectly valid solution, especially on higher-end platforms that don't use the input queue to switch packets. However, no matter how much bigger you make the input queue, you run the risk of having a burst of signalling traffic that fills up the input queue, resulting in dropped packets and slower signalling convergence.

The best solution to this problem is RSVP message pacing. Message pacing controls the rate at which RSVP messages are sent so that the input queue on the other end of the link is not overloaded.

Message pacing is enabled with the global command **ip rsvp msg-pacing**, as demonstrated in Example 4-29.

Example 4-29 *Configuring RSVP Message Pacing*

```
gsr5(config)#ip rsvp msg-pacing ?
  burst    Configure a max burst of rsvp msgs queued to an output interface
  maxsize  Configure max number of rsvp msgs queued to an output interface
  period   Configure a period in msecs
  <cr>
```

Table 4-34 lists the three options available for the **ip rsvp msg-pacing** command.

Table 4-34 **ip rsvp msg-pacing** *Command Options*

Option	Function	Default
burst	The maximum number of RSVP messages that can be sent in a single burst	200
maxsize	The maximum number of messages that are queued up internally for transmission	500
period	The amount of time during which *burst* messages are sent	1

With the defaults for **burst**, **maxsize**, and **period**, this means that up to 200 messages per second can be sent out a given interface, and up to 500 messages (so 2.5 seconds of messages) can be queued.

Message pacing is disabled by default, but it's a good idea to enable it. If pacing doesn't kick in, nothing will be hurt, and it can only help if you end up generating a large burst of messages.

RSVP in the Real World

So far, this section has covered a lot of RSVP theory, but not much in the way of hands-on stuff. Although there's not much to configuring RSVP, there are a fair number of useful **show** commands you should know about.

All **show** commands in this section were captured on a router using the topology shown in Figure 4-38, which you should be familiar with by now.

Figure 4-38 *Sample Topology for RSVP in the Real World*

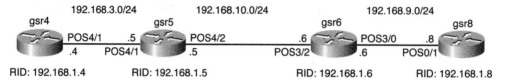

The tunnel topology has changed a bit. There are 50 TE tunnels from gsr4 to gsr8, each reserving 2 Mbps of bandwidth, and 50 TE tunnels from gsr8 to gsr4, each reserving 1 Mbps of bandwidth.

This section doesn't cover all the possible RSVP **show** commands (see the documentation for the relevant Cisco IOS Software release you're using, or just use **?** and check for yourself), but it covers the four most useful ones:

- **show ip rsvp counters**
- **show ip rsvp interface**
- **show ip rsvp neighbor**
- **show ip rsvp reservation**

show ip rsvp counters Command

show ip rsvp counters shows you counts, either per-interface or across the entire box, of the RSVP message types that have happened since the router has been up. Example 4-30 demonstrates all the possible options with this command.

Example 4-30 **show ip rsvp counters** *Options*

```
gsr5#show ip rsvp counters ?
  interface  RSVP statistics for interface
  summary    RSVP statistics summary
  |          Output modifiers
  <cr>
```

Example 4-31 shows the basic output from this command (with most interfaces removed for readability).

Example 4-31 **show ip rsvp counters** *Example*

```
gsr5#show ip rsvp counters
...
POS4/1                  Recv   Xmit                      Recv   Xmit
    Path                1956   1143   Resv              1137   1270
    PathError              0      0   ResvError            0      0
    PathTear               0     38   ResvTear            38      0
    ResvConfirm            0      0   ResvTearConfirm      0     38
    UnknownMsg             0      0   Errors               0      0
```

Example 4-31 show ip rsvp counters *Example (Continued)*

```
POS4/2              Recv   Xmit                        Recv   Xmit
   Path             1164   1277  Resv                  1294   1148
   PathError           0      0  ResvError                0      0
   PathTear           38      0  ResvTear                 0     38
   ResvConfirm         0      0  ResvTearConfirm         38      0
   UnknownMsg          0      0  Errors                   0      0
...
Non RSVP i/f's      Recv   Xmit                        Recv   Xmit
   Path                0      0  Resv                     0      0
   PathError           0      0  ResvError                0      0
   PathTear            0      0  ResvTear                 0      0
   ResvConfirm         0      0  ResvTearConfirm          0      0
   UnknownMsg          0      0  Errors                   0      0
All Interfaces      Recv   Xmit                        Recv   Xmit
   Path             3120   2420  Resv                  2431   2418
   PathError           0      0  ResvError                0      0
   PathTear           38     38  ResvTear                38     38
   ResvConfirm         0      0  ResvTearConfirm         38     38
   UnknownMsg          0      0  Errors                   0      0
```

Using the **interface** or **summary** option gives you counters for the specified interface or gives you only the All Interfaces output, shown at the bottom of Example 4-31.

show ip rsvp interface Command

show ip rsvp interface lists which interfaces have RSVP configured on them, how much bandwidth is currently allocated (reserved), and the interface and flow maximum. Example 4-32 shows typical output from this command.

Example 4-32 show ip rsvp interface *Example*

```
gsr5#show ip rsvp interface
interface   allocated  i/f max   flow max  sub max
PO0/0       0G         1866M     1866M     0G
PO1/0       0G         0G        0G        0G
PO3/0       0G         3169033K  3169033K  0G
PO4/0       0G         116250K   116250K   0G
PO4/1       50M        116250K   116250K   0G
PO4/2       100M       116250K   116250K   0G
PO5/0       0G         466500K   466500K   0G
```

You might recall from Chapter 3 that the command **ip rsvp bandwidth** *x y* configures an interface's reservable bandwidth. *x* is the i/f max, and *y* is the flow max, which MPLS TE doesn't use. In this output, POS4/2 is the interface on gsr5 that faces gsr6. RSVP reservations are always made from the bandwidth pool on the *outgoing* interface.

Note that 50 Mbps is reserved on POS4/1 (the interface facing gsr4) and 100 Mbps is reserved on POS4/2 (the interface facing gsr6). The 50 Mbps corresponds to the 50 1-Mbps tunnels from gsr8 to gsr4, and the 100 Mb corresponds to the 50 2-Mbps tunnels from gsr4 to gsr8.

show ip rsvp neighbor Command

As shown in Example 4-33, output from the **show ip rsvp neighbor** command is pretty easy to understand.

Example 4-33 **show ip rsvp neighbor** *Example*

```
gsr5#show ip rsvp neighbor
Interface  Neighbor       Encapsulation
PO4/1      192.168.3.4    RSVP
PO4/2      192.168.10.6   RSVP
```

One thing to remember is that RSVP does not have an explicit neighbor discovery phase. This means that if you enable RSVP on two interfaces, they will not see each other as RSVP neighbors until they start seeing Path and Resv messages from one another. Just having the interface RSVP enabled isn't enough.

The Encapsulation column can be either RSVP or UDP, but for MPLS TE it is always RSVP.

You can specify an interface as an optional parameter to this command, but this doesn't result in anything more exciting than the output of **show ip rsvp neighbor** for only one interface.

show ip rsvp reservation Command

This command is interesting. It has two distinct versions of output, **show ip rsvp reservation** and **show ip rsvp reservation detail**. Example 4-34 shows typical output from this command without the **detail** option.

Example 4-34 **show ip rsvp reservation** *Output*

```
gsr5#show ip rsvp reservation
To            From          Pro DPort Sport Next Hop      I/F     Fi Serv BPS Bytes
192.168.1.4   192.168.1.8   0   1     1     192.168.3.4   PO4/1   SE LOAD 1M  1K
192.168.1.4   192.168.1.8   0   2     1     192.168.3.4   PO4/1   SE LOAD 1M  1K
192.168.1.4   192.168.1.8   0   3     1     192.168.3.4   PO4/1   SE LOAD 1M  1K
192.168.1.4   192.168.1.8   0   4     1     192.168.3.4   PO4/1   SE LOAD 1M  1K
192.168.1.4   192.168.1.8   0   5     1     192.168.3.4   PO4/1   SE LOAD 1M  1K
192.168.1.4   192.168.1.8   0   6     1     192.168.3.4   PO4/1   SE LOAD 1M  1K
192.168.1.4   192.168.1.8   0   7     1     192.168.3.4   PO4/1   SE LOAD 1M  1K
192.168.1.4   192.168.1.8   0   8     1     192.168.3.4   PO4/1   SE LOAD 1M  1K
192.168.1.4   192.168.1.8   0   9     1     192.168.3.4   PO4/1   SE LOAD 1M  1K
192.168.1.4   192.168.1.8   0   10    1     192.168.3.4   PO4/1   SE LOAD 1M  1K
```

Example 4-34 show ip rsvp reservation *Output (Continued)*

```
...
192.168.1.8   192.168.1.4   0   41   15   192.168.10.6   PO4/2 SE LOAD 2M   1K
192.168.1.8   192.168.1.4   0   42   15   192.168.10.6   PO4/2 SE LOAD 2M   1K
192.168.1.8   192.168.1.4   0   43   16   192.168.10.6   PO4/2 SE LOAD 2M   1K
192.168.1.8   192.168.1.4   0   44   15   192.168.10.6   PO4/2 SE LOAD 2M   1K
192.168.1.8   192.168.1.4   0   45   15   192.168.10.6   PO4/2 SE LOAD 2M   1K
192.168.1.8   192.168.1.4   0   46   15   192.168.10.6   PO4/2 SE LOAD 2M   1K
192.168.1.8   192.168.1.4   0   47   15   192.168.10.6   PO4/2 SE LOAD 2M   1K
192.168.1.8   192.168.1.4   0   48   15   192.168.10.6   PO4/2 SE LOAD 2M   1K
192.168.1.8   192.168.1.4   0   49   15   192.168.10.6   PO4/2 SE LOAD 2M   1K
192.168.1.8   192.168.1.4   0   50   15   192.168.10.6   PO4/2 SE LOAD 2M   1K
```

If the full output from **show ip rsvp reservation** were printed here, it would have 100 lines—50 reservations from gsr4 to gsr8 and 50 from gsr8 to gsr4. Example 4-32 shows the first ten tunnels from gsr8 to gsr4 (to 192.168.1.4 and from 192.168.1.8) and the last ten tunnels from gsr4 to gsr8 (to 192.168.1.8 and from 192.168.1.4).

Table 4-35 documents the fields shown in Example 4-34.

Table 4-35 *Example 4-34 Fields of Interest*

Field	Description
To	Destination of the reservation. For RSVP-TE, the tunnel tail.
From	Source (headend) of the reservation.
Pro	Protocol type. 0 means raw RSVP, as opposed to UDP or TCP, both of which you should never see.
Dport	For RSVP-TE, this is the tunnel ID in the SESSION object.
Sport	For RSVP-TE, this is the LSP ID (aka Tunnel Instance) identifier, as found in the SENDER_TEMPLATE object.
Next Hop	Interface address of the device this tunnel crosses next.
I/F	Interface this tunnel goes out.
Fi	Filter type—either Shared Explicit (most often) or Fixed Filter (rare, but technically possible).
Serv	Type of QoS signalled for the reservation. For RSVP-TE, this is usually LOAD, for a Controlled Load service. Check out RFC 2210 and RFC 2215 if you're interested.
Bps	Bits per second reserved for the LSP.
Bytes	Burst parameter signalled in the QoS information in the Path message. Irrelevant for RSVP-TE.

show ip rsvp reservation also has a **detail** option. It provides information similar to the output shown in Example 4-35.

Example 4-0 show ip rsvp reservation detail *Output*

```
gsr5#show ip rsvp reservation detail

RSVP Reservation. Destination is 192.168.1.4, Source is 192.168.1.8,
  Protocol is 0  , Destination port is 1, Source port is 1
  Next Hop is 192.168.3.4, Interface is POS4/1
  Reservation Style is Shared-Explicit, QoS Service is Controlled-Load
  Average Bitrate is 1M bits/sec, Maximum Burst is 1K bytes
  Label is 0
```

Not only is this information easier to read, but it also contains the label that was received in the Resv for this tunnel. In this case, the label is 0 because this tunnel is destined for 192.168.1.4, and gsr5 is the penultimate hop. Look at a TE tunnel going from gsr4 to gsr8 in Example 4-36.

Example 4-0 show ip rsvp reservation detail *Output*

```
gsr5#show ip rsvp reservation detail 192.168.1.8
RSVP Reservation. Destination is 192.168.1.8, Source is 192.168.1.4,
  Protocol is 0  , Destination port is 1, Source port is 16
  Next Hop is 192.168.10.6, Interface is POS4/2
  Reservation Style is Shared-Explicit, QoS Service is Controlled-Load
  Average Bitrate is 2M bits/sec, Maximum Burst is 1K bytes
  Label is 12311
```

In this case, you see that the learned label for this tunnel is 12311. This matches the output of **show mpls traffic-eng tunnels** in Example 4-37, as it should.

Example 4-0 show mpls traffic-eng tunnels *Output*

```
gsr5#show mpls traffic-eng tunnels name gsr4_t1

LSP Tunnel gsr4_t1 is signalled, connection is up
  InLabel  : POS4/1, 12342
  OutLabel : POS4/2, 12311
  RSVP signalling Info:
      Src 192.168.1.4, Dst 192.168.1.8, Tun_Id 1, Tun_Instance 16
    RSVP Path Info:
      My Address: 192.168.3.5
      Explicit Route: 192.168.10.6 192.168.9.8 192.168.1.8
      Record   Route:  NONE
      Tspec: ave rate=2000 kbits, burst=1000 bytes, peak rate=2000 kbits
    RSVP Resv Info:
      Record   Route:  NONE
      Fspec: ave rate=2000 kbits, burst=1000 bytes, peak rate=Inf
```

show ip rsvp reservation gives you the option of an IP address or host name. Using that option shows you all tunnels destined for the specified router ID.

Interarea Tunnels

Up until now, you've seen TE tunnels that must start and end in the same area (or level, rather than area, if you're an IS-IS fan.) In fact, in older versions of Cisco IOS Software, a router was limited to a single TE database. This meant that not only could you not have a TE tunnel that spanned multiple areas, you couldn't have a router that was connected to multiple areas and had TE tunnels in each area independently. However, this restriction can be overcome using *interarea tunnels*.

IGP Terminology

Before diving into how interarea TE tunnels work, it's important to get the terminology straight. In OSPF, an *area* is a set of routers that share a common SPF tree. IS-IS, however, uses the term *level* to mean the same thing. Because the official Cisco term for the feature about to be discussed is *interarea tunnels,* this section uses the word *area* rather than *level*. However, realize that the feature under discussion is equally usable in both OSPF and IS-IS; there are no differences in what you can do based on the IGP you're running.

Another important term is the word used to describe the device that sits between SPF trees. In OSPF, this box is an Area Border Router (ABR). In IS-IS, this function is performed by the router with both an L1 and an L2 neighbor. Because we're using the term *area* already, we refer to this box as an ABR, regardless of whether the IGP is OSPF or IS-IS.

Figure 4-39 shows the terminology in use.

Figure 4-39 *Proper Terminology for Discussing Interarea TE*

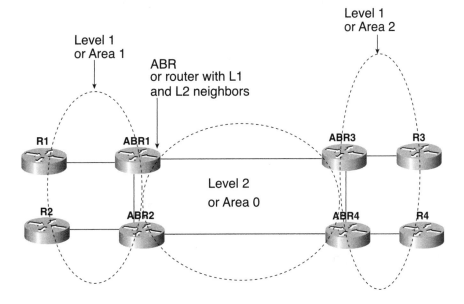

From the perspective of R1, ABR1 is the entrance to the backbone and is therefore called the *ingress ABR*. ABR3 and ABR4, because they are how an R1→R3 LSP gets to the other area, are called *egress ABRs*.

The IS-IS picture is slightly different because, in IS-IS, the area borders are built on the links, not on the routers. However, the terminology remains the same to make it easier to talk about interarea tunnels independent of your IGP.

What Interarea Tunnels Can Do

The interarea tunnels feature allows you to do two things:

- Build TE tunnels between areas (interarea tunnels)
- Build TE tunnels that start and end in the same area, on multiple areas on a router (intra-area tunnels)

Consider Figure 4-39. Without interarea tunnels, you can build TE tunnels in only one of the following areas:

- Area 1
- Area 0
- Area 2

You cannot build TE tunnels in any combination of these areas. ABR1 can't have a tunnel to R1 and a tunnel to ABR3 because it is limited to a single area's worth of topology in its traffic engineering database (TE-DB).

As soon as you are running code that supports interarea TE tunnels, you can build tunnels from R1 to R2, R1 to ABR1, ABR1 to ABR3, R3 to R4, R1 to R4, or any other combination. You have a tremendous amount of flexibility.

Most TE features work on an interarea TE tunnel. Any feature that is purely a local function of the headend works, because these features don't care if the tunnel crosses multiple areas. These features include the following (see Chapter 5, "Forwarding Traffic Down Tunnels" for more information):

- Static routing and policy routing onto tunnels
- Auto bandwidth

Additionally, most midpoint features don't care if a TE tunnel is single-area or multiarea. These features include

- Bandwidth reservation
- Fast Reroute (see Chapter 7, "Protection and Restoration")
- DiffServ-aware traffic engineering (see Chapter 6)

How Interarea Tunnels Work

Interarea tunnels are simple to configure, and intra-area tunnels are even easier.

To start with, there's the IGP configuration. In older versions of the Cisco IOS Software, if you try to enable MPLS TE in more than one area, you get a warning like the one shown in Example 4-38.

Example 4-38 *Attempting to Configure Interarea TE Tunnels in Older Code*

```
gsr1(config)#router isis
gsr1(config-router)#mpls traffic-eng level-2
gsr1(config-router)#mpls traffic-eng level-1
%MPLS TE already enabled, on isis level-2
gsr1(config-router)#
```

With code that supports interarea tunnels, you don't get this warning, as demonstrated in Example 4-39.

Example 4-39 *Successfully Configuring Interarea TE Tunnels*

```
gsr1(config)#router isis
gsr1(config-router)#mpls traffic-eng level-2
gsr1(config-router)#mpls traffic-eng level-1
gsr1(config-router)#
```

It's that simple. If all you want to do is have multiple intra-area tunnels (ABR1 to R1 and ABR1 to ABR3), you're done.

However, if you want to build true interarea tunnels, there's a bit of headend work to be done. You have to specify an explicit path for the tunnel to take. This explicit path must use the *loose* ERO subobject for hops outside its own area.

Why? When you configure an explicit path, each hop in that path is implicitly known as a *strict* hop. When a tunnel has an explicit route starting with strict hops, all the strict hops are checked against the TE database to make sure that they're valid. Because enabling interarea tunnels doesn't change the information flooding scheme, R1 does not know how to get to anything outside its area. Using the **next-address loose** command is a way of telling the next node in the ERO (the ABR, the one that has more than one TE database) that it needs to figure out what to do next.

Make sense? Look at Figure 4-40 before we look at this concept in a little more detail.

Figure 4-40 *Network Topology with Interarea Tunnels*

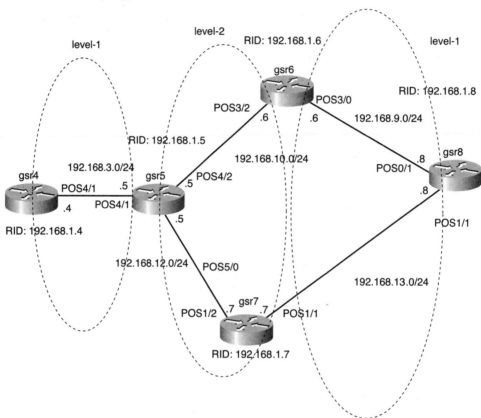

Example 4-40 shows the headend configuration on gsr4 when building a TE tunnel from gsr4 to gsr8.

Example 4-40 *gsr4 Headend Configuration*

```
interface Tunnel8
 ip unnumbered Loopback0
 no ip directed-broadcast
 tunnel destination 192.168.1.8
 tunnel mode mpls traffic-eng
 tunnel mpls traffic-eng path-option 10 explicit name interarea
end
...
ip explicit-path name interarea enable
 next-address 192.168.1.5
 next-address loose 192.168.1.6
 next-address loose 192.168.1.8
```

In Figure 4-40, the ABR is directly connected to the headend, so the explicit path has only a single next hop before specifying the loose hops. If the ABR were not directly connected to the tunnel headend, this path option would either specify the entire path to the ABR or would simply specify the first ABR with a loose path option.

In the configuration shown in Example 4-40, the tunnel tail is specified as a loose hop in the explicit path option. Although this is not strictly necessary, not specifying the tunnel tail as a loose hop can cause signalling problems.

The configuration shown in Example 4-40 says, "To build a TE tunnel to gsr8, first get to gsr5. Then tell gsr5 that it has to figure out how to get you to gsr6." gsr6 realizes that it is directly connected to gsr8 and forwards the Path message in that direction.

When an ABR receives an ERO with a loose subobject as the next object in the ERO, it is the ABR's job to resolve that loose object into a strict one. The ERO is then sent on its way.

At the tunnel headend, a loose subobject in the ERO results in slightly modified **show mpls traffic-eng tunnels** output, as demonstrated in Example 4-41.

Example 4-41 *Output of* **show mpls traffic-eng tunnels** *Showing a Loose ERO Subobject*

```
gsr4#show mpls traffic-eng tunnels Tunnel8
Name: gsr4_t8                         (Tunnel8) Destination: 192.168.1.8
  Status:
    Admin: up        Oper: up      Path: valid      signalling: connected

    path option 10, type explicit interarea (Basis for Setup, path weight 10)

  Config Parameters:
    Bandwidth: 100      kbps (Global) Priority: 7  7   Affinity: 0x0/0xFFFF
    Metric Type: TE (default)
    AutoRoute: disabled LockDown: disabled Loadshare 100      bw-based
    auto-bw: disabled(0/219) 0  Bandwidth Requested: 100

  InLabel  :  -
  OutLabel : POS4/1, 12309
  RSVP Signalling Info:
      Src 192.168.1.4, Dst 192.168.1.8, Tun_Id 8, Tun_Instance 390
    RSVP Path Info:
      My Address: 192.168.1.4
      Explicit Route: 192.168.3.5 192.168.1.5 192.168.1.6* 192.168.1.8*
      Record   Route:
      Tspec: ave rate=100 kbits, burst=1000 bytes, peak rate=100 kbits
    RSVP Resv Info:
      Record   Route: 192.168.3.5 192.168.10.6 192.168.9.8
      Fspec: ave rate=100 kbits, burst=1000 bytes, peak rate=Inf
  Shortest Unconstrained Path Info:
    Path Weight: UNKNOWN
    Explicit Route:  UNKNOWN
  History:
    Tunnel:
      Time since created: 1 hours, 31 minutes
```

continues

Example 4-41 *Output of* **show mpls traffic-eng tunnels** *Showing a Loose ERO Subobject (Continued)*

```
        Time since path change: 3 minutes, 9 seconds
      Current LSP:
        Uptime: 3 minutes, 9 seconds
      Prior LSP:
        ID: path option 10 [389]
        Removal Trigger: path error
```

In the Explicit Route line, you can see that the headend has resolved **next-address 192.168.1.5** into the path necessary to get to 192.168.1.5. 192.168.1.6, specified as **next-address loose 192.168.1.6** in the explicit-path configuration, has an asterisk to signify that that hop in the ERO is a loose hop. 192.168.1.8 is listed the same way.

When gsr5 gets the Path message for this LSP, it resolves the loose subobject 192.168.1.6 into a series of strict hops to get to 192.168.1.6 by running CSPF and taking into account this LSP's requested bandwidth.

When gsr6 gets the Path message for this LSP, it resolves the loose subobject 192.168.1.8 into a series of strict hops to get to 192.168.1.8 by running CSPF and taking into account this LSP's request bandwidth.

When gsr8 gets the Path message, it responds to this message by sending a Resv, just like it would in response to any other Path message. The Resv makes its way upstream, hop by hop, and when it reaches gsr4, the tunnel interface comes up.

Figure 4-41 is a more complicated topology, so perhaps it is a more realistic example.

NOTE Figure 4-41 has three kinds of routers—CRs (Customer Routers), DRs (Distribution Routers), and WRs (WAN Routers). The prefixes L-, C-, and R- stand for Left, Core, and Right. See Chapter 9, "Network Design with MPLS TE," for a discussion of router-naming syntax.

Here are some examples of how you might configure interarea tunnels between various routers. Rather than getting caught up in IP addressing schemes, the path options use router names rather than IP addresses.

Figure 4-41   *More Complex Interarea Tunnel Topology*

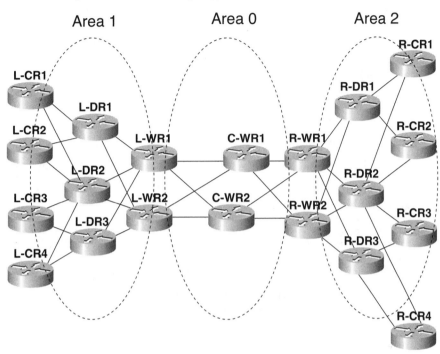

If you want to build a tunnel from L-CR1 to R-CR4, you might use the configuration shown in Example 4-42.

Example 4-42   *Sample Configuration for an Interarea TE Tunnel*

```
interface Tunnel4
 description Tunnel from L-CR1 to R-CR4
 ip unnumbered Loopback0
 tunnel destination R-CR4
 tunnel mode mpls traffic-eng
 tunnel mpls traffic-eng path-option 10 explicit name to-R-CR4


ip explicit-path name to-R-CR4
 next-address loose L-WR1
 next-address loose R-WR1
 next-address loose R-CR4
```

This configuration works fine. But what if L-WR1 or R-WR1 goes away? You don't want to have your interarea TE tunnels fail; you'd rather they reroute through L-WR2 or R-WR2. In the current implementation, if you have multiple permutations of ABRs to go through, you need to configure each one as a separate path option. Because there are two L-WRs and two R-WRs, this means you need to build four explicit paths:

- L-WR1→R-WR1
- L-WR1→R-WR2
- L-WR2→R-WR1
- L-WR2→R-WR2

Example 4-43 shows what a more thorough configuration on L-CR1 might look like.

Example 4-43 *Multiple Path Options in an Interarea Tunnel Configuration*

```
interface Tunnel4
 description Tunnel from L-CR1 to R-CR4
 ip unnumbered Loopback0
 tunnel destination R-CR4
 tunnel mode mpls traffic-eng
 tunnel mpls traffic-eng path-option 10 explicit name to-R-CR4.1
 tunnel mpls traffic-eng path-option 20 explicit name to-R-CR4.2
 tunnel mpls traffic-eng path-option 30 explicit name to-R-CR4.3
 tunnel mpls traffic-eng path-option 40 explicit name to-R-CR4.4


ip explicit-path name to-R-CR4.1
 next-address loose L-WR1
 next-address loose R-WR1
 next-address loose R-CR4


ip explicit-path name to-R-CR4.2
 next-address loose L-WR1
 next-address loose R-WR2
 next-address loose R-CR4


ip explicit-path name to-R-CR4.3
 next-address loose L-WR2
 next-address loose R-WR1
 next-address loose R-CR4


ip explicit-path name to-R-CR4.4
 next-address loose L-WR2
 next-address loose R-WR2
 next-address loose R-CR4
```

What order should you put the path options in? It's up to you. It makes sense to put them in the order that's most likely to succeed, although it really doesn't make much difference. It's hard to come up with a general rule. You need to take a look at your network and do whatever you find is best.

However, having to lay out multiple path options looks like it might not scale all that well, for the following reasons:

- Most multiarea network architectures have only two types of areas—a core area and several POP areas.

- Most areas only have two border routers between them.

It's reasonable to assume that the number of explicit path options you need to configure is no more than four.

What Interarea Tunnels Cannot Do

A few features currently are not supported with interarea traffic engineering:

- Autoroute and forwarding adjacency
- Tunnel affinity
- **tunnel mpls traffic-eng path-option dynamic**
- Reoptimization

Autoroute and Forwarding Adjacency

Autoroute and forwarding adjacency (both covered fully in Chapter 5) rely on the fact that the tunnel head and tunnel tail are in the same area. As such, you cannot build a tunnel across multiple areas and have either autoroute or forwarding adjacency work. To put packets down an interarea tunnel, you need to use static or policy routing.

If you are taking advantage of interarea code to build intra-area tunnels (R1 to ABR1, ABR1 to ABR4, ABR3 to R4, and so on), autoroute and forwarding adjacency will work. It's only when you have a TE tunnel spanning multiple areas that autoroute and forwarding adjacency don't work.

See Chapter 5 for a more detailed explanation of how autoroute and forwarding adjacency work, and why they don't work across areas.

Tunnel Affinity

The current Cisco MPLS TE implementation does not signal tunnel affinity in the LSP setup. Instead, it relies on the fact that the TE extensions for IGP propagate link attributes in their advertisements. Because the headend does not see the entire topology in interarea tunnel setup, and because there's no way to tell an ABR what the headend affinity string and bitmask are, tunnel affinity cannot be supported for interarea TE LSPs.

tunnel mpls traffic-eng path-option dynamic Command

A POP often has multiple exit points. One exit point might be much closer to the tunnel destination than another. Because the headend doesn't have the entire topology, it can't know which exit point is the best one to take. The same thing applies when going from the near-side ABR (for L-CR1, this is L-WR1 or L-WR2) to the far-side ABR: How does L-WR1 know what the best path is to get to R-CR4? In Figure 4-41, things are pretty symmetric, but that's not always the case in the real world. Because you need to tell the network which ABRs to go through from source to destination, you can't specify **path-option dynamic**. You need to specify explicit paths.

Reoptimization

This one is subtle. Reoptimization is the recalculation of a path from the head to the tail. What about that calculation is missing in multiarea TE?

Break the problem into pieces. Clearly, from the headend's perspective, two places that reoptimization could happen are

- Within the headend's area
- Outside the headend's area

Reoptimization within the headend's area happens normally. Only reoptimization outside the headend's area is different.

In Figure 4-42, an LSP goes from Router A to Router L.

Example 4-44 shows the configuration for this LSP's **explicit path-option**.

Example 4-44 *LSP* **explicit path-option** *Configuration*

```
ip explicit-path name to-L
  next-address loose E
next-address loose J
  next-address loose L
```

Figure 4-42 *Interarea Reoptimization*

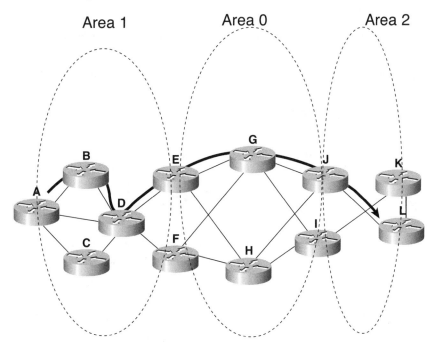

Router A knows the entire topology up to and including Router E. When reoptimization is triggered, either periodic, on demand, or driven by a link-up change in Area 1, Router L recalculates its path to Router E. However, the rest of the LSP (the part from E to L, through J) is never reoptimized. Why?

Because there's currently no method for the headend to tell the ingress ABR that it wants a reoptimization. Because Router E can't tell the difference between a reoptimize-driven Path message and a refresh-driven Path message, it can't know when to reoptimize the LSP. The same thing applies to Router J. You don't want ABRs reoptimizing every time they get a Path message, because that could cause quite a lot of signalling and CPU load on the router. In the future, there will probably be more-complex mechanisms that let the ABRs reoptimize interarea LSPs for which they are midpoints, but for right now, the only reoptimization is done by the headend, and only in the headend area.

Link Manager

Underneath a lot of externally visible RSVP and MPLS things is something called the *link manager*. The link manager's job is to track interface-related stuff with regard to MPLS Traffic Engineering. Specifically, the link manager keeps track of the following:

- **Flooding**—What information to flood and when to flood it
- **Admission control**—When an RSVP message comes in, whether to allow it or deny it

The link manager isn't really something you can configure. However, it's useful to know it's there.

The link manager has several things you can look at, as demonstrated in Example 4-45.

Example 4-45 *Displaying Link Manager Capabilities*

```
gsr2#show mpls traffic-eng link-management ?
  admission-control    Link Management admission-control
  advertisements       Link Management advertisements
  bandwidth-allocation Link Management bandwidth-allocation
  igp-neighbors        Link Management igp-neighbors
  interfaces           Link Management Traffic Engineering interfaces
  statistics           Link Management Traffic Engineering statistics
  summary              Link Management summary
```

The following sections provide output from each of these commands, along with some comments. Figure 4-43 shows the topology used in the link manager examples.

Figure 4-43 *Network Topology for the Link Manager Examples*

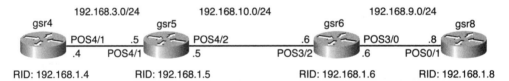

```
       192.168.3.0/24          192.168.10.0/24                192.168.9.0/24
 gsr4                    gsr5                           gsr6                    gsr8
        POS4/1    .5          POS4/2        .6                POS3/0     .8
        .4       POS4/1       .5          POS3/2              .6         POS0/1
RID: 192.168.1.4      RID: 192.168.1.5          RID: 192.168.1.6       RID: 192.168.1.8
```

There are 50 2-Mbps tunnels from gsr4 to gsr8 and 50 1-Mbps tunnels from gsr8 to gsr4.

All these commands were done on gsr4, so the link manager output is consistent with the other output in this chapter.

Most of these commands also take an interface as an optional argument, but the command output doesn't change other than showing you the interface you specify.

show mpls traffic-eng link-management admission-control Command

As Example 4-46 demonstrates, this command shows all the LSPs that the admission control portion of the link manager is aware of. The STATE of Resv Admitted means that a Resv for this tunnel has been sent, and everything is good. There can be other states for LSPs that are in the process of being set up or torn down. In the far-right column, the R means that the bandwidth has been reserved with a Resv. If the display has a tunnel that has an H instead of an R, this indicates that the bandwidth is being held. This means that the router has seen a Path message for a tunnel but has not yet seen the Resv.

The G next to the R means that the bandwidth reserved for this tunnel was reserved from the global pool rather than the subpool (see the section "DiffServ-Aware Traffic Engineering (DS-TE)" in Chapter 6).

Example 4-46 **show mpls traffic-eng link-management admission-control** *Command Output*

```
gsr5#show mpls traffic-eng link-management admission-control
System Information::
    Tunnels Count:        100
    Tunnels Selected:     100
TUNNEL ID            UP IF    DOWN IF  PRIORITY STATE           BW (kbps)
192.168.1.4 1_16     PO4/1    PO4/2    7/7      Resv Admitted   2000      RG
192.168.1.4 2_15     PO4/1    PO4/2    7/7      Resv Admitted   2000      RG
192.168.1.4 3_15     PO4/1    PO4/2    7/7      Resv Admitted   2000      RG
192.168.1.4 4_15     PO4/1    PO4/2    7/7      Resv Admitted   2000      RG
192.168.1.4 5_15     PO4/1    PO4/2    7/7      Resv Admitted   2000      RG
192.168.1.4 6_15     PO4/1    PO4/2    7/7      Resv Admitted   2000      RG
192.168.1.4 7_15     PO4/1    PO4/2    7/7      Resv Admitted   2000      RG
192.168.1.4 8_15     PO4/1    PO4/2    7/7      Resv Admitted   2000      RG
192.168.1.4 9_15     PO4/1    PO4/2    7/7      Resv Admitted   2000      RG
192.168.1.4 10_15    PO4/1    PO4/2    7/7      Resv Admitted   2000      RG
...
```

show mpls traffic-eng link-management advertisements Command

As demonstrated in Example 4-47, this command shows the information that the link manager floods when it asks the IGP to flood. Information for each link on the router is shown. On Link ID 0 (the link between gsr5 and gsr4), at priority 7, the reservable bandwidth is 66,250 Kbps, whereas it's 116,250 Kbps at every other priority. This is because of the 50 1-Mb tunnels from gsr8 to gsr2; these tunnels all have setup and holding priorities of 7, so tunnels with a better priority see the full 116,250 Kb available to them.

The same thing is true on Link ID 1 between gsr5 and gsr6. The 50 2-Mbps tunnels from gsr4 to gsr8 mean that the remaining bandwidth at priority 7 is 16,250 Kbps.

Example 4-47 **show mpls traffic-eng link-management advertisements** *Command Output*

```
gsr5#show mpls traffic-eng link-management advertisements
Flooding Status:        ready
Configured Areas:       3
IGP Area[1] ID:: isis  level-1
  System Information::
    Flooding Protocol:    ISIS
  Header Information::
    IGP System ID:        0168.0001.0005.00
    MPLS TE Router ID:    192.168.1.5
    Flooded Links:        2
  Link ID:: 0
    Link Subnet Type:     Point-to-Point
    Link IP Address:      192.168.3.5
```

continues

Example 4-47 *show mpls traffic-eng link-management advertisements Command Output (Continued)*

```
     IGP Neighbor:         ID 0168.0001.0004.00, IP 192.168.3.4
     TE metric:            10
     IGP metric:           10
     Physical Bandwidth:   155000 kbits/sec
     Res. Global BW:       116250 kbits/sec
     Res. Sub BW:          0 kbits/sec
     Downstream::
                                 Global Pool   Sub Pool
                                 -----------   ----------
        Reservable Bandwidth[0]:     116250         0 kbits/sec
        Reservable Bandwidth[1]:     116250         0 kbits/sec
        Reservable Bandwidth[2]:     116250         0 kbits/sec
        Reservable Bandwidth[3]:     116250         0 kbits/sec
        Reservable Bandwidth[4]:     116250         0 kbits/sec
        Reservable Bandwidth[5]:     116250         0 kbits/sec
        Reservable Bandwidth[6]:     116250         0 kbits/sec
        Reservable Bandwidth[7]:      66250         0 kbits/sec
     Attribute Flags:      0x00000000
  Link ID::  1
     Link Subnet Type:     Point-to-Point
     Link IP Address:      192.168.10.5
     IGP Neighbor:         ID 0168.0001.0006.00, IP 192.168.10.6
     TE metric:            10
     IGP metric:           10
     Physical Bandwidth:   155000 kbits/sec
     Res. Global BW:       116250 kbits/sec
     Res. Sub BW:          0 kbits/sec
     Downstream::
                                 Global Pool   Sub Pool
                                 -----------   ----------
        Reservable Bandwidth[0]:     116250         0 kbits/sec
        Reservable Bandwidth[1]:     116250         0 kbits/sec
        Reservable Bandwidth[2]:     116250         0 kbits/sec
        Reservable Bandwidth[3]:     116250         0 kbits/sec
        Reservable Bandwidth[4]:     116250         0 kbits/sec
        Reservable Bandwidth[5]:     116250         0 kbits/sec
        Reservable Bandwidth[6]:     116250         0 kbits/sec
        Reservable Bandwidth[7]:      16250         0 kbits/sec
     Attribute Flags:      0x00000000
```

show mpls traffic-eng link-management bandwidth-allocation Command

This command shows a few interesting things. Some of the output, as demonstrated in Example 4-48, is the same as **show mpls traffic-eng link-manager advertisements**, but not all of it. In particular, the flooding thresholds (discussed in Chapter 3) are displayed, as well as the amount of reserved bandwidth at each priority level. The 50 Mbps and 100 Mbps of reserved bandwidth from the tunnels between gsr4 and gsr8 show up here as well.

The BW HELD state is a temporary state that bandwidth is put in when a Path message has been seen for a tunnel, but not a Resv. It's difficult to see values in the BW HELD/TOTAL BW HELD columns in the real world, because tunnel setup takes only a few seconds at most. If you see bandwidth constantly in the HELD/TOTAL HELD columns, it's likely an indication of problems.

Example 4-48 show mpls traffic-eng link-management bandwidth-allocation *Command Output*

```
gsr5#show mpls traffic-eng link-management bandwidth-allocation
System Information::
    Links Count:            2
    Bandwidth Hold Time:  max. 15 seconds
Link ID::  PO4/1 (192.168.3.5)
    Link Status:
        Physical Bandwidth:    155000 kbits/sec
        Max Res Global BW:     116250 kbits/sec (reserved: 0% in, 43% out)
        Max Res Sub BW:        0 kbits/sec (reserved: 100% in, 100% out)
        BW Descriptors:        50
        MPLS TE Link State:    MPLS TE on, RSVP on, admin-up
        Inbound Admission:     allow-all
        Outbound Admission:    allow-if-room
        Admin. Weight:         10 (IGP)
        IGP Neighbor Count:    1
        Up Thresholds:         15 30 45 60 75 80 85 90 95 96 97 98 99 100 (default)
        Down Thresholds:       100 99 98 97 96 95 90 85 80 75 60 45 30 15 (default)
    Downstream Global Pool Bandwidth Information (kbits/sec):
        KEEP PRIORITY     BW HELD  BW TOTAL HELD   BW LOCKED  BW TOTAL LOCKED
                 0            0           0            0                 0
                 1            0           0            0                 0
                 2            0           0            0                 0
                 3            0           0            0                 0
                 4            0           0            0                 0
                 5            0           0            0                 0
                 6            0           0            0                 0
                 7            0           0        50000             50000
    Downstream Sub Pool Bandwidth Information (kbits/sec):
        KEEP PRIORITY     BW HELD  BW TOTAL HELD   BW LOCKED  BW TOTAL LOCKED
                 0            0           0            0                 0
                 1            0           0            0                 0
                 2            0           0            0                 0
                 3            0           0            0                 0
                 4            0           0            0                 0
                 5            0           0            0                 0
                 6            0           0            0                 0
                 7            0           0            0                 0
Link ID::  PO4/2 (192.168.10.5)
    Link Status:
        Physical Bandwidth:    155000 kbits/sec
        Max Res Global BW:     116250 kbits/sec (reserved: 0% in, 86% out)
        Max Res Sub BW:        0 kbits/sec (reserved: 100% in, 100% out)
        BW Descriptors:        50
        MPLS TE Link State:    MPLS TE on, RSVP on, admin-up
        Inbound Admission:     allow-all
        Outbound Admission:    allow-if-room
        Admin. Weight:         10 (IGP)
```

continues

Example 4-48 show mpls traffic-eng link-management bandwidth-allocation *Command Output (Continued)*

```
IGP Neighbor Count:    1
Up Thresholds:         15 30 45 60 75 80 85 90 95 96 97 98 99 100 (default)
Down Thresholds:       100 99 98 97 96 95 90 85 80 75 60 45 30 15 (default)
Downstream Global Pool Bandwidth Information (kbits/sec):
KEEP PRIORITY     BW HELD   BW TOTAL HELD     BW LOCKED   BW TOTAL LOCKED
     0               0            0               0               0
     1               0            0               0               0
     2               0            0               0               0
     3               0            0               0               0
     4               0            0               0               0
     5               0            0               0               0
     6               0            0               0               0
     7               0            0            100000            100000
Downstream Sub Pool Bandwidth Information (kbits/sec):
KEEP PRIORITY     BW HELD   BW TOTAL HELD     BW LOCKED   BW TOTAL LOCKED
     0               0            0               0               0
     1               0            0               0               0
     2               0            0               0               0
     3               0            0               0               0
     4               0            0               0               0
     5               0            0               0               0
     6               0            0               0               0
     7               0            0               0               0
```

show mpls traffic-eng link-management igp-neighbors Command

As the output in Example 4-49 demonstrates, this command just shows what neighbors exist on any links configured for traffic engineering. Information about a TE link is not flooded unless an IGP neighbor exists on that link. If a neighbor doesn't exist to send a Resv to, the rest of the network doesn't need to know about the link.

Example 4-49 show mpls traffic-eng link-management igp-neighbors *Command Output*

```
gsr5#show mpls traffic-eng link-management igp-neighbors
Link ID::  PO4/1
   Neighbor ID:  0168.0001.0004.00 (area: isis   level-1, IP: 192.168.3.4)
Link ID::  PO4/2
   Neighbor ID:  0168.0001.0006.00 (area: isis   level-1, IP: 192.168.10.6)
```

show mpls traffic-eng link-management interfaces Command

This command shows much the same information as the other commands. The only difference is that the flooding status for each link is also shown, as demonstrated in Example 4-50.

Example 4-50 show mpls traffic-eng link-management interfaces *Command Output*

```
gsr5#show mpls traffic-eng link-management interfaces
System Information::
    Links Count:          2
Link ID::  PO4/1 (192.168.3.5)
    Link Status:
        Physical Bandwidth:    155000 kbits/sec
        Max Res Global BW:     116250 kbits/sec (reserved: 0% in, 43% out)
        Max Res Sub BW:        0 kbits/sec (reserved: 100% in, 100% out)
        MPLS TE Link State:    MPLS TE on, RSVP on, admin-up
        Inbound Admission:     allow-all
        Outbound Admission:    allow-if-room
        Admin. Weight:         10 (IGP)
        IGP Neighbor Count:    1
        IGP Neighbor:          ID 0168.0001.0004.00, IP 192.168.3.4 (Up)
    Flooding Status for each configured area [1]:
        IGP Area[1]:  isis  level-1:  flooded
Link ID::  PO4/2 (192.168.10.5)
    Link Status:
        Physical Bandwidth:    155000 kbits/sec
        Max Res Global BW:     116250 kbits/sec (reserved: 0% in, 86% out)
        Max Res Sub BW:        0 kbits/sec (reserved: 100% in, 100% out)
        MPLS TE Link State:    MPLS TE on, RSVP on, admin-up
        Inbound Admission:     allow-all
        Outbound Admission:    allow-if-room
        Admin. Weight:         10 (IGP)
        IGP Neighbor Count:    1
        IGP Neighbor:          ID 0168.0001.0006.00, IP 192.168.10.6 (Up)
    Flooding Status for each configured area [1]:
        IGP Area[1]:  isis  level-1:  flooded
```

show mpls traffic-eng link-management statistics Command

As demonstrated in Example 4-51, this command shows some statistics about RSVP messages sent on each link. Up Path and Up Resv are Path and Resv messages received on the interface (from the upstream router), and Down Path and Down Resv are messages sent on the interface (to the downstream router). Because this router has only two links active in MPLS Traffic Engineering, any message received in Up Path on one link is also counted in Down Path on the other link, and vice versa.

This output was taken right after both tunnels came up for the first time. So you see two setup requests (both of which were admitted) on the Up interface and on the Down interface.

Example 4-51 show mpls traffic-eng link-management statistics *Command Output*

```
gsr5#show mpls traffic-eng link-management statistics
System Information::
  LSP Admission Statistics:
```

continues

Example 4-51 show mpls traffic-eng link-management statistics *Command Output (Continued)*

```
     Path:        138 setup requests, 138 admits, 0 rejects, 0 setup errors
                  38 tear requests, 0 preempts, 0 tear errors
     Resv:        138 setup requests, 138 admits, 0 rejects, 0 setup errors
                  38 tear requests, 0 preempts, 0 tear errors
Link ID:: PO4/1 (192.168.3.5)
  Link Admission Statistics:
    Up Path:     50 setup requests, 50 admits, 0 rejects, 0 setup errors
                 0 tear requests, 0 preempts, 0 tear errors
    Up Resv:     50 setup requests, 50 admits, 0 rejects, 0 setup errors
                 38 tear requests, 0 preempts, 0 tear errors
    Down Path:   88 setup requests, 88 admits, 0 rejects, 0 setup errors
                 38 tear requests, 0 preempts, 0 tear errors
    Down Resv:   88 setup requests, 88 admits, 0 rejects, 0 setup errors
                 0 tear requests, 0 preempts, 0 tear errors
Link ID:: PO4/2 (192.168.10.5)
  Link Admission Statistics:
    Up Path:     88 setup requests, 88 admits, 0 rejects, 0 setup errors
                 38 tear requests, 0 preempts, 0 tear errors
    Up Resv:     88 setup requests, 88 admits, 0 rejects, 0 setup errors
                 0 tear requests, 0 preempts, 0 tear errors
    Down Path:   50 setup requests, 50 admits, 0 rejects, 0 setup errors
                 0 tear requests, 0 preempts, 0 tear errors
    Down Resv:   50 setup requests, 50 admits, 0 rejects, 0 setup errors
                 38 tear requests, 0 preempts, 0 tear errors
```

show mpls traffic-eng link-management summary Command

As demonstrated in Example 4-52, this command shows a summary of link information. It also has much the same information as other links (commands), but not as much.

Example 4-52 show mpls traffic-eng link-management summary *Command Output*

```
gsr5#show mpls traffic-eng link-management summary
System Information::
    Links Count:         2
    Flooding System:     enabled
IGP Area ID:: isis  level-1
    Flooding Protocol:   ISIS
    Flooding Status:     data flooded
    Periodic Flooding:   enabled (every 180 seconds)
    Flooded Links:       2
    IGP System ID:       0168.0001.0005.00
    MPLS TE Router ID:   192.168.1.5
    IGP Neighbors:       2
Link ID:: PO4/1 (192.168.3.5)
    Link Status:
      Physical Bandwidth:   155000 kbits/sec
      Max Res Global BW:    116250 kbits/sec (reserved: 0% in, 43% out)
      Max Res Sub BW:       0 kbits/sec (reserved: 100% in, 100% out)
      MPLS TE Link State:   MPLS TE on, RSVP on, admin-up
      Inbound Admission:    allow-all
```

Example 4-52 *show mpls traffic-eng link-management summary Command Output (Continued)*

```
          Outbound Admission:   allow-if-room
          Admin. Weight:        10 (IGP)
          IGP Neighbor Count:   1
   Link ID:: PO4/2 (192.168.10.5)
      Link Status:
          Physical Bandwidth:   155000 kbits/sec
          Max Res Global BW:    116250 kbits/sec (reserved: 0% in, 86% out)
          Max Res Sub BW:       0 kbits/sec (reserved: 100% in, 100% out)
          MPLS TE Link State:   MPLS TE on, RSVP on, admin-up
          Inbound Admission:    allow-all
          Outbound Admission:   allow-if-room
          Admin. Weight:        10 (IGP)
          IGP Neighbor Count:   1
```

Summary

This chapter has quite a bit of information. However, RSVP is one of the largest and most complex pieces of MPLS TE. If you managed to absorb the entire chapter, great! If you managed to take away only a few points, here's what you should have learned from this chapter:

- How SPF and CSPF work, and how they differ

- How to control CSPF and manipulate the path a TE tunnel takes through a network

- How tunnel reoptimization works

- More than you ever wanted to know about RSVP—basics, packet formats, and some of the more complex operations

- What link manager does behind the scenes

Out of that list, the two most important pieces to understand are CSPF and RSVP. They are the cornerstones of MPLS TE, and a thorough understanding of both of these pieces is vital if you're going to successfully use MPLS TE on your network.

CHAPTER 5

Forwarding Traffic Down Tunnels

Chapter 3, "Information Distribution," covered information distribution through OSPF and IS-IS. Chapter 4, "Path Calculation and Setup" covered path calculation (CSPF) and path setup (RSVP).

If you have done everything in Chapters 3 and 4 successfully, at this point, any tunnel interface you have created comes up. But after a tunnel is up, what do you do with it?

You can use three methods to forward traffic down a tunnel interface:

- Static routes
- Policy routing
- Autoroute

This chapter covers these three methods, as well as information about load sharing across MPLS TE tunnels. Included is one of MPLS TE's more attractive properties—the capability to do fine-grained unequal-cost load sharing of traffic.

Forwarding Traffic Down Tunnels Using Static Routes

The easiest way to route traffic down an MPLS TE tunnel interface is to use static routes. There's nothing special about static routes over TE tunnels; they work just like static routes pointed down any other point-to-point interface. If you configure a route pointing down a tunnel interface, as in

```
ip route 10.0.0.0 255.0.0.0 Tunnel0
```

it's the exact same thing as if you had pointed the route out any other point-to-point interface, such as this:

```
ip route 10.0.0.0 255.0.0.0 POS0/0
```

Recursive static routes work normally as well. Basically, anything you can do with static routes down an interface, you can do with static routes down a TE tunnel interface.

Recursive Static Routes

A *recursive static route* is a static route that points not to an interface, but to a next hop:

```
ip route 10.0.0.0 255.0.0.0 192.168.1.1
```

This tells the router to send all packets for 10.0.0.0 255.0.0.0 to the same place it would send packets destined for 192.168.1.1. The router needs to have a route for 192.168.1.1 in the routing table.

Entering the following configuration sends all traffic for 10.0.0.0/8 down Tunnel0:

```
ip route 10.0.0.0 255.0.0.0 Tunnel0
```

If 192.168.1.1 is the tailend of your TE tunnel, entering the following command does the same:

```
ip route 192.168.1.1 255.255.255.255 Tunnel0
ip route 10.0.0.0 255.0.0.0 192.168.1.1
```

Forwarding Traffic Down Tunnels with Policy-Based Routing

You can also use policy-based routing (PBR) to forward traffic down a tunnel. This is not a new feature; the capability to forward traffic down a particular interface has been in policy routing for a while.

Suppose that Src in Figure 5-1 has two types of traffic to send to Dst—voice traffic and data traffic. If you want to carry only voice traffic across Tunnel0, you can do so with PBR.

PBR is enabled using policy route maps applied to the incoming interface. Under the **route-map** statement, simply match the voice traffic using the **match** statement and then use the **set interface Tunnel0** directive to send traffic down Tunnel0. PBR has the advantage that you can send specific types of traffic down a tunnel interface without modifying a router's routing table. For example, voice traffic entering Router A in Figure 5-1 can be forwarded down the tunnel using PBR with no changes to the routing table on Router A. Suppose that Src in Figure 5-1 is connected to Router A over the Ethernet 0/0 interface. Further suppose that voice traffic can be identified as traffic that is destined to IP address 5.5.5.5 (typically a voice gateway). Example 5-1 shows the configuration that's required to achieve this.

Example 5-1 *Policy-Routing Configuration on Router A*

```
interface Ethernet0/0
  ip policy route-map foo

route-map foo
 match ip address 101
```

Example 5-1 *Policy-Routing Configuration on Router A (Continued)*

```
set interface Tunnel0

access-list 101 permit ip any host 5.5.5.5
```

Figure 5-1 *Example of PBR*

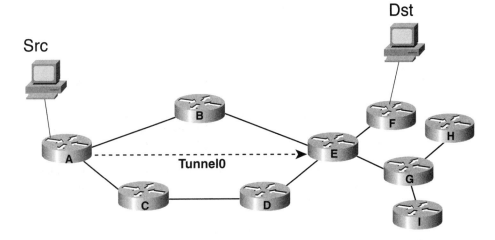

As you can see, there's nothing special about policy routing into a tunnel interface; it works just like policy routing down any other interface. For more information on policy routing, see Appendix B, "CCO and Other References."

Forwarding Traffic Down Tunnels with Autoroute

Autoroute is fairly detailed. Its behavior is intuitive, but you might have to stare at it for a while to understand *why* you need it. This section explains not only how it works, but also why you need it.

If you bring up most types of interfaces in Cisco IOS Software (a physical interface, subinterface, or GRE tunnel), you need to enable your Interior Gateway Protocol (IGP) on that interface in order to form routing protocol adjacency, learn routes, and build a routing table involving that interface. If you don't do this, you won't be able to dynamically figure out what traffic to send down that interface. Of course, you can point static routes down an interface without running your IGP on that interface, but that's not germane to this discussion.

You've probably noticed that enabling your IGP on a TE tunnel interface has not been mentioned. This is not an accidental omission; this step was left out on purpose. One of the attractive scaling properties of MPLS TE is that, unlike most other types of interfaces, you do not run an IGP over an MPLS TE tunnel. Two reasons for this are

- TE tunnels are unidirectional and thus can never receive any packets. If an interface can't receive any packets (such as routing updates), it's difficult to run an IGP over it.

- You don't need it. Because TE tunnels often originate and terminate in the same area, and because you already have the full link-state topology for that area, you don't need to flood another copy of the area's routing information (IS-IS LSPs or OSPF LSAs) over the tunnel. You'll get all the IGP information flooded over the underlying physical topology anyway, so there's no need to reflood over the TE tunnel.

Running a TE tunnel across multiple areas was covered in detail in Chapter 4.

The fact that you don't run a routing protocol over a TE interface has some attractive scaling properties, as you'll see later in Chapter 9, "Network Design with MPLS TE," and Chapter 10, "MPLS TE Deployment Tips." Not running a routing protocol over a TE interface also means that you need some other way of telling the router to provide the equivalent behavior. What you need is a knob that tells the tunnel headend the following:

> Treat this interface like the tunnel is a directly connected link to the tunnel tail, and send any packets down the tunnel that are destined for either the tunnel's tail or anything behind that tunnel tail.

The MPLS TE autoroute feature does precisely that. The basic configuration is simple: **tunnel mpls traffic-eng autoroute announce** on the tunnel headend. You can apply a few options to autoroute, as you will see in the section "How to Play with the TE Tunnel Metric."

Autoroute?

You might be familiar with a feature in Cisco's IGX/MGX/BPX WAN switch line of equipment called *autoroute*. That autoroute (a method of determining a path across the network) has nothing to do with the autoroute discussed here. The WAN switch feature called autoroute is similar to the MPLS TE CSPF. It's a method of calculating a path from one point to another point that meets a certain resource requirement.

To get a better grip on how MPLS TE autoroute works, consider Figure 5-2.

Figure 5-2   *Sample Network for Autoroute, Static Route, and PBR*

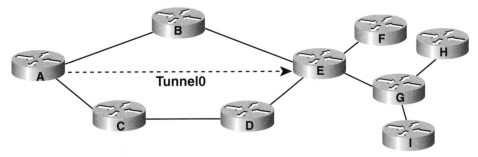

The following examples demonstrate the effects that autoroute, static routes, and policy routing have on Router A's routing table. Unless otherwise specified, all links in this network have a cost of 10.

Before TE tunnels are introduced, Router A's routing table looks like Table 5-1.

Table 5-1   *Router A's Routing Table Prior to TE Tunnel Configuration*

Node	Next Hop	Cost
A	Self	0
B	B	10
C	C	10
D	C	20
E	B	20
F	B	30
G	B	30
H	B	40
I	B	40

After the TE tunnel from Router A to Router E is up, you need to map traffic to Router E to Tunnel0. The effect of static routes on a routing table should be obvious. If you configure a static route for Router G pointing down the tunnel,

```
ip route router G's RID 255.255.255.255 Tunnel0
```

Router A's routing table will look like Table 5-2.

Table 5-2 *Router A's Routing Table After a Static Route Is Configured*

Node	Next Hop	Cost
A	Self	0
B	B	10
C	C	10
D	C	20
E	B	20
F	B	30
G	**Tunnel0**	0
H	B	40
I	B	40

Policy routing is arguably even simpler because it doesn't change the routing table at all. Packet forwarding decisions are made based on the configured policy and interface, not the routing table.

Autoroute is where things start to get interesting.

As mentioned earlier, autoroute tells a router to build its routing table so that anything behind the TE tunnel tailend is routed down that tunnel. How does this work? The IGP runs its regular SPF, but if it encounters a node that is either TE tunnel tail or located behind the TE tunnel tail, it installs the TE tunnel to that node rather than to the IGP path in the routing table.

To better understand this, walk through Router A's IGP SPF process, with autoroute enabled on the tunnel to Router E.

Router A starts by putting itself on the PATH list and its neighbors (Routers B and C) on the TENT list, with the following results:

PATH List	TENT List
{A,0,0}	{B,10,B}
	{C,10,C}

The next step is to take Router B from the TENT list, put it on the PATH list, and put Router B's neighbors on the TENT list, with the following results:

PATH List	TENT List
{A,0,0}	{C,10,C}
{B,10,B}	{E,20,B}

Router C is then moved to the PATH list, and its neighbors are put on the TENT list, with the following results:

PATH List	TENT List
{A,0,0}	{E,20,B}
{B,10,B}	{D,20,C}
{C,10,C}	

Because the tunnel tail ends on Router E, you replace Router E's next hop of B with Tunnel0. First, moving Router E to the PATH list results in the following:

PATH List	TENT List
{A,0,0}	{D,20,C}
{B,10,B}	
{C,10,C}	
{E,20,B}	

Next, replacing Router E's next hop with the tunnel to Router E results in the following table. Note that the cost to get to the tunnel tail has not changed—only the outgoing interface:

PATH List	TENT List
{A,0,0}	{D,20,C}
{B,10,B}	
{C,10,C}	
{E,20,**Tunnel0**}	

Then Router E's neighbors are added to the TENT list. When Router E's neighbors (Routers F and G) are put on the TENT list, they are given the next hop used to get to Router E, or Tunnel0:

PATH List	TENT List
{A,0,0}	{D,20,C}
{B,10,B}	{F,30,**Tunnel0**}
{C,10,C}	{G,30,**Tunnel0**}
{E,20,**Tunnel0**}	

To finish the SPF process, move {D,20,C} to the PATH list, with the following results:

PATH List	TENT List
{A,0,0}	{F,30,**Tunnel0**}
{B,10,B}	{G,30,**Tunnel0**}
{C,10,C}	
{E,20,**Tunnel0**}	
{D,20,C}	

Router D's only neighbor is Router E, but the cost to get to Router E through Router D is 30, which is higher than the cost to get to Router E on the PATH list. So, moving Router D to the PATH list adds no new nodes to the TENT list.

Move Router F to the PATH list, with the following results:

PATH List	TENT List
{A,0,0}	{G,30,**Tunnel0**}
{B,10,B}	
{C,10,C}	
{E,20,**Tunnel0**}	
{D,20,C}	
{F,30,**Tunnel0**}	

Router F has no new neighbors, so proceed to Router G, which has two neighbors, Routers H and I, and add them to the TENT list, as follows:

PATH List	TENT List
{A,0,0}	{H,40,**Tunnel0**}
{B,10,B}	{I,40,**Tunnel0**}
{C,10,C}	
{E,20,**Tunnel0**}	
{D,20,C}	
{F,30,**Tunnel0**}	
{G,30,**Tunnel0**}	

Routers H and I have no new neighbors, so they both end up on the PATH list and don't add anything to the TENT list.

Compressing these two steps into one, you end up with the following results:

PATH List	TENT List
{A,0,0}	<empty>
{B,10,B}	
{C,10,C}	
{E,20,**Tunnel0**}	
{D,20,C}	
{F,30,**Tunnel0**}	
{G,30,**Tunnel0**}	
{H,40,**Tunnel0**}	
{I,40,**Tunnel0**}	

This translates into the routing table shown in Table 5-3.

Table 5-3   *Router A's Routing Table After the IGP SPF Process, with Autoroute Enabled on the Tunnel to Router E*

Node	Next Hop	Cost
A	Self	0
B	B	10
C	C	10
D	C	20
E	Tunnel0	20
F	Tunnel0	30
G	Tunnel0	30
H	Tunnel0	40
I	Tunnel0	40

It's simple. The fundamental thing to understand is that, with autoroute enabled, the tunnel tail is always routed only through the tunnel. Even though Figure 5-2 shows multiple ways to get to Router E, the tunnel is the only route used. This is how the IGP SPF works; the tunnel tail can be reached only through the tunnel because of the replacement of the physical next hop with the tunnel interface during IGP SPF. Nodes *behind* the tunnel tail can generally be reached through the tunnel, although you can get to a node through both an IGP route and the TE tunnel route in some cases.

You have yet to explore a few subtleties:

- Load sharing between a TE tunnel path and an IGP path
- Load sharing between two TE tunnels
- Changing the metric used for the TE tunnel

The next two sections cover these subtleties, but what's just been covered is most of what you need to know to use autoroute successfully.

Much of what autoroute does is invisible to the user. The only **show** command autoroute has is **show mpls traffic-eng autoroute**, which can optionally take the RID of a TE tail as an argument. Example 5-2 shows the output from this command.

Example 5-2 **show mpls traffic-eng autoroute** *Command Output*

```
vxr15#show mpls traffic-eng autoroute
MPLS TE autorouting enabled
  destination 0168.0001.0008.00 has 1 tunnels
    Tunnel20    (traffic share 0, nexthop 192.168.1.8)
                (flags: Announce)
  destination 0168.0001.0011.00 has 3 tunnels
    Tunnel11    (traffic share 11111, nexthop 192.168.1.11)
                (flags: Announce)
    Tunnel12    (traffic share 11111, nexthop 192.168.1.11)
                (flags: Announce)
    Tunnel13    (traffic share 7352, nexthop 192.168.1.11)
                (flags: Announce)
```

The destination is the IGP RID (in this case, the CLNS NSAP) of the router that is the TE tunnel tail. The traffic share value is nonzero if bandwidth is configured on the TE tunnel and is 1,000,000 divided by the tunnel bandwidth. This traffic share value helps compute load sharing between multiple TE tunnels to the same destination.

Load Sharing

Equal-Cost Load Sharing

Load sharing can be done based on the packet's source and destination IP addresses or on a per-packet basis. Load sharing on the packet's source and destination addresses is often called (somewhat accurately) *per-flow* or *per-destination load sharing,* but it is more correctly called *per-src-dest load sharing*.

With MPLS and per-src-dest load sharing, when a packet enters the router, the packet underneath the label stack is examined. If the underlying data is an IP packet, it is load shared using the source and destination IP addresses of the underlying data, just like the router would do if it had received an unlabeled IP packet in the first place. If the packet underneath the received label stack is not an IP packet, load sharing is based on the bottommost label in the label stack.

Per-packet load sharing sends all packets in a round-robin fashion to the different next hops for a given route, without regard for the packet's contents. Per-packet load sharing is often undesirable, because the receiving end could receive packets out of order. For the following discussion, assume per-flow (also known as per-destination) load sharing. The next sections describe equal-cost load sharing between TE tunnels and IGP paths and between multiple TE paths leading to a destination.

Load Sharing Between the TE Tunnel Path and IGP Path

In the preceding section, you saw that the TE tunnel is used as the next hop as soon as you determine the cost of the shortest path to the tunnel tail. This approach has two ramifications:

- You will never load share between an IGP route and a TE route for the tunnel tail.
- You might load share between an IGP route and a TE route for nodes *behind* the tunnel tail.

Because the reasons behind these points might not be obvious, they deserve further discussion.

Load Sharing to the Tunnel Tail

Assume that you will never load share between an IGP route and a TE route for the tunnel tail. Why not? Because if you did, you'd lose the ability to explicitly route traffic down a tunnel that takes a suboptimal path.

Consider the network topology shown in Figure 5-3.

Suppose you have a TE tunnel between Router A and Router C. By default, this tunnel has a path cost of 20 because that's the IGP shortest-path cost between Routers A and C.

Two paths exist between Routers A and C, however, and they both have the same cost. There's A→B→C and A→C. If you didn't drop the other paths in favor of the TE tunnel, you would load share across these paths, which means that you can't steer traffic around your network the way you want to.

Depending on how you did things, you would share either between the TE tunnel and the A→C path (so that only 50 percent of the traffic destined for C goes down the TE tunnel) or between the TE tunnel, the A→C path, and the A→B→C path (so that only 33 percent of the traffic destined for Router C goes down the TE tunnel).

Neither of these scenarios is desirable because it's much harder to traffic-engineer your network if you don't have complete control over all your traffic.

Figure 5-3 *Load Sharing to a Tunnel Tail Through the Tunnel and the IGP Route*

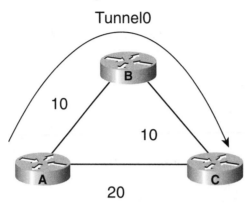

Suppose, however, that you *wanted* to send traffic across the A→C path and the A→B→C path. To accomplish this, you would build two TE tunnels, one across each path, and then load share between them, as illustrated in Figure 5-4.

Figure 5-4 *Load Sharing Across Two TE Tunnels*

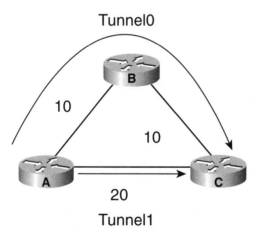

NOTE   You will never load share traffic to the TE tunnel tail between an IGP path and a TE tunnel path, but you *will* load share between multiple TE tunnels to the same tail.

When the Cisco IOS Software load shares IP packets between multiple paths to the same destination, it almost always does *equal-cost* load sharing between these paths. If no TE tunnels existed in 5-4, you'd share traffic in a 1:1 ratio between the top path and the bottom path from A→C. However, MPLS TE provides additional flexibility when you load share. See the upcoming section "Unequal-Cost Load Sharing" for details.

NOTE   EIGRP has something called *variance* that lets you use a limited form of unequal-cost load sharing. However, MPLS TE's load sharing is more flexible than EIGRP's. Also, because you can't do TE using EIGRP, you will see no more mention of variance.

Load Sharing to Nodes Behind the Tunnel Tail

Although you will never share between an IGP path and a TE tunnel to get to the tunnel tail, you *will* sometimes share between a TE tunnel path and an IGP path to get to destinations downstream of the tunnel tail.

You can end up load sharing between an IGP route and a TE tunnel to a node behind the TE tunnel if you have multiple paths to a given node and the TE tunnel is not on one or more of these paths.

This makes more sense when you consider the network shown in Figure 5-5.

Figure 5-5   *Load Sharing to Nodes Behind a Tunnel Tail*

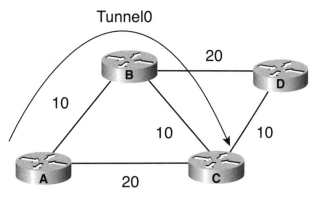

The following text walks you through all of Router A's SPF calculations. The gist of it is that if you find multiple paths to a given node, and that node is not the tunnel tail, you load share between these paths up to the max-paths limit in your IGP. Some of the "Move one node to the PATH list and then move its neighbors to the TENT list" stuff has been condensed into one step because by now you are either well-acquainted with how SPF works, or you're ignoring the SPF examples altogether because they don't make any sense!

Router A has a TE tunnel to Router C, across the top path.

As always, you start with Router A in the PATH list, as follows:

PATH List	TENT List
{A,0,0}	{B,10,B}
	{C,20,C}

Move Router B to the PATH list, and put its neighbors on TENT, with the following results:

PATH List	TENT List
{A,0,0}	{C,20,C}
{B,10,B}	{D,30,B}

Move Router C to the PATH list, change the next hop to Router C to Tunnel0, and put Router C's neighbors on TENT, with the following results:

PATH List	TENT List
{A,0,0}	{D,30,B}
{B,10,B}	{D,30,Tunnel0}
{C,20,Tunnel0}	

At this point, there are two paths to Router D—one through Router B and one through Tunnel0. If two paths exist with the *same* cost in the TENT list, you use them both; this rule is the same whether you're doing equal-cost forwarding with IP or with MPLS. So, leave both entries for Router D in the TENT list.

Next, move Router D to the PATH list. Router D has no new neighbors, so you don't add anything to the TENT list, as indicated in this table:

PATH List	TENT List
{A,0,0}	<empty>
{B,10,B}	
{C,20,Tunnel0}	
{D,30,B}	
{D,30,Tunnel0}	

Table 5-4 shows the routing table resulting from this SPF process.

Table 5-4   *Router A's Routing Table After IGP SPF*

Node	Next Hop	Cost
A	Self	0
B	B	10
C	Tunnel0	20
D	**Tunnel0**	30
	B	

That's how you can load share between TE tunnels and IGP paths to a destination behind a tunnel tail. Load sharing is equal-cost; you cannot get unequal-cost load sharing between a TE tunnel and a non-TE tunnel path. The next section tells you why.

Unequal-Cost Load Sharing

Normal IP routing has equal-cost load sharing. If there's more than one path between two nodes, and those two paths have equal cost, traffic is shared equally between those paths. Routing protocols currently are limited to installing either six or eight maximum parallel paths, depending on the level of code you're running.

Equal-cost load sharing is all well and good, but it's not very flexible. If you've ever tried to balance traffic on your network by changing link costs, you're probably aware that it's not as easy as you might think. Changing a link cost in one corner of your network often affects traffic in various other parts of your network in ways you didn't anticipate.

There's also the issue of unequal-cost load sharing. This is difficult to do while guaranteeing a loop-free topology. Consider the network topology shown in Figure 5-6.

The following example shows what can happen if a router is allowed to compute arbitrary non-shortest paths to send traffic over.

This example ignores many of the implementation-specific details of CEF. Those come later in this chapter, in the discussion of how load sharing works in real life.

Assume that unequal-cost paths are calculated based on path cost, with the amount of traffic forwarded down a particular path being inversely proportional to the cost of the path—*the lower the path cost, the more traffic is forwarded down that path.*

For example, if a router has three possible paths to a destination—two with a cost of 20 and one with a cost of 40—traffic is shared between these paths in a 40:40:20 ratio. This means that 40 percent of traffic to a destination goes down the first path, 40 percent goes down the second, and 20 percent goes down the third.

Figure 5-6 *Unequal-Cost Load Sharing with IP*

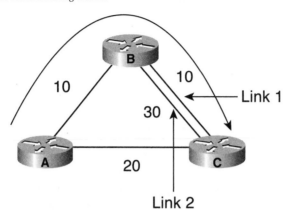

In Figure 5-6, Router A sends traffic roughly as shown in Table 5-5 and Table 5-6.

Table 5-5 *Router A's Routing Table*

Path	Cost	Amount of Traffic
A→C	20	40%
A→B(link1)→C	20	40%
A→B(link2)→C	40	20%

Table 5-6 *Router B's Routing Table*

Path	Cost	Amount of Traffic
B(link 1)→C	10	60%
B(link 2)→C	30	20%
B→A→C	30	20%

This example becomes more concrete when you add real traffic to the mix. Suppose that Router A has 100 Mbps of traffic to send to Router C. Forty Mbps of this 100 Mbps goes through path A→C and gets where it needs to go. The remaining 60 Mbps is given to Router B, with Router A assuming that Router B forwards the traffic along the path that Router A wants the traffic to follow.

But Router B has other ideas. Of the 60 Mbps received from Router A, Router B forwards 80 percent of that (approximately 48 Mb) over either link 1 or link 2, and the traffic arrives at Router C. But Router B then forwards the remaining 20 percent (approximately 12 Mb) back to Router A!

What happens next depends on the load sharing that Routers A and B are doing. If both routers make their packet forwarding decision based on some combination of source and destination IP addresses, the aforementioned 12 Mb of traffic loops indefinitely between Router A and Router B until its TTL times out.

If both routers are doing per-packet load sharing, odds are good that most of the traffic will eventually get to Router C, although the route it takes to get there might be time-consuming. 12 Mb goes from Router B to Router A, Router A sends 60 percent of this (approximately 7.2 Mb) back to Router B, Router B sends 20 percent of this (approximately 1.4 Mb) back to Router A, and so on until no more traffic is left.

This suboptimal situation occurs *because Router A couldn't tell Router B what to do with the packet*. Router A must assume that Router B shares in a way that makes sense for Router A, and Router B has other ideas.

What Router A needs is some way to identify a *path* that traffic needs to follow. Router A needs to be able to tell Router B which traffic should be forwarded across link 1 and which traffic should go across link 2, without giving Router B the chance to do an IP lookup on the packet and do something other than what Router A wants. Some sort of tag or label is needed to indicate the direction in which the traffic should flow.

This is why MPLS TE is so beneficial. Although the MPLS TE configuration model is currently less dynamic than the model in the preceding example, the important point is that it doesn't matter how Router A decides to send traffic. If a label is applied to a packet going from Router A to Router B, and that label came from an RSVP LSP setup, the traffic is forwarded to Router C without fear of potential looping at Router B.

This example might seem a bit contrived. Load sharing can be set up in this picture so that no loops occur. But the point is that you can't *guarantee* that a next hop will be as intelligent as you'd like it to be, so the odds of a loop are high.

How Unequal-Cost Load Sharing Works

Now that you've seen how unequal-cost load sharing is more feasible with MPLS than with IP, you need to know how it works.

It's simple, actually. It has two parts:

1 Setting up the load-sharing ratios

2 Installing these ratios in the FIB for CEF to use

MPLS TE load sharing works between multiple tunnels to the same destination. If there is more than one tunnel to a destination, you share between those tunnels. You decide what unequal-cost ratios to use through one of the following:

- Bandwidth (configured with **tunnel mpls traffic-eng bandwidth** *0-4294967295*)
- Load-share value (configured with **tunnel mpls traffic-eng load-share** *0-1000000*)

If the **load-share** value is configured, it is used as the ratio with which to share. Otherwise, you share traffic between multiple parallel tunnels in accordance with the configured bandwidth. Traffic share is directly proportional to bandwidth—the more bandwidth a tunnel has, the more traffic it receives. The **load-share** value works the same way. It's just a knob that lets you reserve the same bandwidth on multiple tunnels but share differently between them. For the following discussions, *bandwidth* refers to tunnel **bandwidth** or **load-share** value. In other words, the two tunnel configurations in Example 5-3 are treated exactly the same as far as load sharing goes; the only difference is that in the load-sharing case, no bandwidth is reserved in the network.

Example 5-3 *Tunnel Configurations with* **bandwidth** *and* **load-share** *Values Allocated*

```
interface Tunnel1
 ip unnumbered Loopback0
 no ip directed-broadcast
 tunnel destination 192.168.1.8
 tunnel mode mpls traffic-eng
 tunnel mpls traffic-eng bandwidth 20
 tunnel mpls traffic-eng path-option 10 dynamic
```

```
interface Tunnel1
 ip unnumbered Loopback0
 no ip directed-broadcast
 tunnel destination 192.168.1.8
 tunnel mode mpls traffic-eng
 tunnel mpls traffic-eng path-option 10 dynamic
 tunnel mpls traffic-eng load-share 20
```

If you like, you can configure both **tunnel mpls traffic-eng bandwidth** and **tunnel mpls traffic-eng load-share**. The configured **bandwidth** value is reserved through RSVP, and the configured **load-share** value is used for load sharing on the tunnel headend.

Consider the network topology shown in Figure 5-7.

This is the same topology as shown in Figure 5-6, but with TE tunnels set across the three paths from Router A to Router C. Table 5-7 shows the bandwidth and paths for each of the three tunnels in Figure 5-7.

Table 5-7 *Tunnel Bandwidth/Path Information*

Tunnel	Configured Bandwidth	Path
Tunnel1	20	A→B(link1)→C
Tunnel2	20	A→C
Tunnel3	40	A→B(link2)→C

Figure 5-7   *Unequal-Cost Load Sharing with MPLS TE*

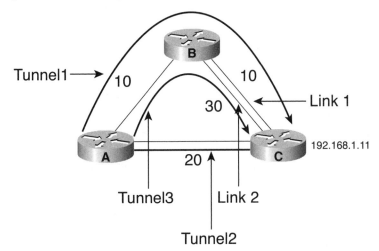

NOTE   It is important to understand that the amount of bandwidth you reserve for a tunnel is purely a control plane number. TE deals with reservations at the control plane only. No policing, fancy queuing, or shaping are established on an interface as a result of a TE bandwidth reservation. This means that, no matter how much traffic is sent from Router A to Router C, it is shared correctly between all three tunnels. You could have just as easily set the tunnel bandwidths to 2, 2, and 4, or 90, 90, and 180; it makes no difference.

Example 5-4 shows the routing table with autoroute enabled on these tunnels.

Example 5-4   *Unequal-Cost Load Sharing with MPLS TE Tunnels*

```
RouterA#show ip route 192.168.1.11
Routing entry for 192.168.1.11/32
  Known via "isis", distance 115, metric 40, type level-2
  Redistributing via isis
  Last update from 192.168.1.11 on Tunnel13, 00:01:55 ago
  Routing Descriptor Blocks:
  * 192.168.1.11, from 192.168.1.11, via Tunnel11
      Route metric is 40, traffic share count is 1
    192.168.1.11, from 192.168.1.11, via Tunnel12
      Route metric is 40, traffic share count is 1
    192.168.1.11, from 192.168.1.11, via Tunnel13
      Route metric is 40, traffic share count is 2
```

Even though the bandwidths are configured to share in the ratio 20:20:40, the routing table has boiled these down to 1:1:2. The routing table follows two rules when generating these traffic share counts:

1 Reduce until the lowest metric is 1.

2 Allow only whole numbers as traffic share counts.

The actual algorithm is more complex than that, but that's the basic idea.

A consequence of this algorithm is that sometimes bandwidth ratios aren't preserved exactly as they're inserted into the routing table. What if the bandwidth ratios were 20:20:30 instead of 20:20:40? The routing table would look the same as it does in Example 5-4—traffic share counts of 1, 1, and 2. Why? Because in 20:20:30, the steps are as follows:

1 Reduce 20 to 1.

2 Realize that 30:20 is 1.5:1, which isn't allowed.

3 Round 1.5 up to 2.

4 End up with traffic share counts of 1:1:2.

This has a subtle impact on your load sharing. If you have a tunnel with a bandwidth of 7 and a tunnel with a bandwidth of 9, 7:9 is reduced to 1:1 as it enters the RIB.

The routing table hands the traffic share count values down to CEF, which is the mechanism that actually does all the load sharing.

Chapter 2, "MPLS Forwarding Basics," covered the basics of how CEF works. When CEF is load sharing, it keeps an array of 16 possible next hops, in a data structure called a *loadinfo*. When a packet comes into the router and a switching lookup is done on it, CEF picks one of these loadinfo entries. CEF picks the loadinfo entry based on a combination of the source and destination IP addresses, so the default load sharing has no out-of-order packets. CEF can also be configured to load share per packet rather than in a source/destination hash. See Appendix B, "CCO and Other References," for more information on CEF and its load sharing.

The **show ip cef exact-route** command is helpful in that it lets you give CEF a source and destination IP address pair, and it tells you which way the router switches the packet. With a routing table like the one shown in Example 5-4, several routes exist for 192.168.1.11. Example 5-5 shows the output from **show ip cef exact-route** *src dst,* which shows you which way CEF switches packets of a given source/destination pair.

Example 5-5 **show ip cef exact-route** *Command Output*

```
RouterA#show ip cef exact-route 1.2.3.4 192.168.1.11
1.2.3.4          -> 192.168.1.11   : Tunnel11 (next hop 192.168.1.11)
RouterA#show ip cef exact-route 1.2.3.5 192.168.1.11
1.2.3.5          -> 192.168.1.11   : Tunnel11 (next hop 192.168.1.11)
RouterA#show ip cef exact-route 1.2.3.6 192.168.1.11
```

Example 5-5 show ip cef exact-route *Command Output (Continued)*

```
1.2.3.6          -> 192.168.1.11   : Tunnel12 (next hop 192.168.1.11)
RouterA#show ip cef exact-route 1.2.3.4 192.168.1.11
1.2.3.4          -> 192.168.1.11   : Tunnel11 (next hop 192.168.1.11)
```

Example 5-5 shows which path packets from three different sources (1.2.3.4, 1.2.3.5, and 1.2.3.6) take to get to 192.168.1.11. Example 5-5 shows the output for source 1.2.3.4 twice to emphasize that the same source/destination pair always takes the same interface, as long as all these tunnel interfaces are up.

You can see the load-sharing information by looking at the output of **show ip cef** *destination ip address* **internal**, as demonstrated in Example 5-6.

Example 5-6 show ip cef *Command Output*

```
RouterA#show ip cef 192.168.1.11 internal
192.168.1.11/32, version 80, per-destination sharing
...
  Load distribution: 0 1 2 0 1 2 0 1 2 0 1 2 0 0 0 0 (refcount 2)

  Hash  OK  Interface         Address          Packets  Tags imposed
  1     Y   Tunnel13          point2point          0    {50}
  2     Y   Tunnel11          point2point          0    {49}
  3     Y   Tunnel12          point2point          0    {48}
  4     Y   Tunnel13          point2point          0    {50}
  5     Y   Tunnel11          point2point          0    {49}
  6     Y   Tunnel12          point2point          0    {48}
  7     Y   Tunnel13          point2point          0    {50}
  8     Y   Tunnel11          point2point          0    {49}
  9     Y   Tunnel12          point2point          0    {48}
  10    Y   Tunnel13          point2point          0    {50}
  11    Y   Tunnel11          point2point          0    {49}
  12    Y   Tunnel12          point2point          0    {48}
  13    Y   Tunnel13          point2point          0    {50}
  14    Y   Tunnel13          point2point          0    {50}
  15    Y   Tunnel13          point2point          0    {50}
  16    Y   Tunnel13          point2point          0    {50}
```

The output in Example 5-6 shows the load sharing for CEF, populated in an 8:4:4 ratio. How do you know it's an 8:4:4 ratio? If you count all the occurrences of each tunnel in Example 5-6, Tunnel13 shows up eight times, and Tunnel11 and Tunnel12 each show up four times.

Unequal-cost load sharing works only when all the paths you're sharing between have a nonzero bandwidth.

Attempting to load share in the following situations forces reversion to equal-cost load sharing between these paths:

- Between a TE tunnel with nonzero bandwidth and a TE tunnel with zero bandwidth
- Between a TE tunnel and an IGP path (for load sharing to a node behind a TE tunnel tail)

This reversion occurs because in order to figure out the proper percentages to load share among *n* paths, you have to do something like the following:

1 Add up all the traffic-share counts to get the value T (in the preceding example, T = 1 + 1 + 2, or 4).

2 Divide each tunnel's traffic share count by the total tunnel traffic share count to get the percentage of load sharing each tunnel should receive. If you have a zero-bandwidth tunnel, this means you end up doing something like 0 / 4, which is 0.

3 Convert the percentage to 16ths by multiplying by 16. 16 * 0 is, as you know, 0.

This means that if you try to follow the load-sharing algorithm and include a path with a zero-traffic-share count, you'll have a path that you never end up using. The logic is that if there's a zero-traffic-share path anywhere in the set of paths to a given destination, you revert to equal-cost load sharing. So, if you change the sample network shown in Figure 5-7 to have four tunnels to 192.168.1.11, but you give the fourth tunnel (Tunnel14) zero bandwidth, the route for 192.168.1.11 looks like that shown in Example 5-7.

Example 5-7 *Router A's Route for 192.168.1.11 Sharing Across Four Tunnels, One with Zero Bandwidth*

```
RouterA#show ip route 192.168.1.11
Routing entry for 192.168.1.11/32
  Known via "isis", distance 115, metric 40, type level-2
  Redistributing via isis
  Last update from 192.168.1.11 on Tunnel14, 00:00:12 ago
  Routing Descriptor Blocks:
  * 192.168.1.11, from 192.168.1.11, via Tunnel13
      Route metric is 40, traffic share count is 1
    192.168.1.11, from 192.168.1.11, via Tunnel12
      Route metric is 40, traffic share count is 1
    192.168.1.11, from 192.168.1.11, via Tunnel11
      Route metric is 40, traffic share count is 1
    192.168.1.11, from 192.168.1.11, via Tunnel14
      Route metric is 40, traffic share count is 1
```

The output in Example 5-8 shows what the CEF loadinfo looks like.

Example 5-8 *Router A's CEF Entry for 192.168.1.11 Sharing Across Four Tunnels, One with Zero Bandwidth*

```
RouterA#show ip cef 192.168.1.11 internal
...
  Load distribution: 0 1 2 3 0 1 2 3 0 1 2 3 0 1 2 3 (refcount 4)
```

Example 5-8 *Router A's CEF Entry for 192.168.1.11 Sharing Across Four Tunnels, One with Zero Bandwidth (Continued)*

```
Hash  OK  Interface       Address       Packets  Tags imposed
 1    Y   Tunnel13        point2point      0      {22}
 2    Y   Tunnel12        point2point      0      {21}
 3    Y   Tunnel11        point2point      0      {20}
 4    Y   Tunnel14        point2point      0      {19}
 5    Y   Tunnel13        point2point      0      {22}
 6    Y   Tunnel12        point2point      0      {21}
 7    Y   Tunnel11        point2point      0      {20}
 8    Y   Tunnel14        point2point      0      {19}
 9    Y   Tunnel13        point2point      0      {22}
10    Y   Tunnel12        point2point      0      {21}
11    Y   Tunnel11        point2point      0      {20}
12    Y   Tunnel14        point2point      0      {19}
13    Y   Tunnel13        point2point      0      {22}
14    Y   Tunnel12        point2point      0      {21}
15    Y   Tunnel11        point2point      0      {20}
16    Y   Tunnel14        point2point      0      {19}
```

Because one tunnel has zero bandwidth, all tunnels now share equally between each other rather than in proportion to any bandwidths.

The IGP path is treated as though it has a bandwidth of 0, because you don't know the amount of available bandwidth along the path, just the path cost. In order to take advantage of unequal-cost load sharing, the following must be true:

- All paths to a destination have to be TE tunnels.

- All these paths have to have a nonzero bandwidth (or nonzero load-share metric).

How to Play with the TE Tunnel Metric

As mentioned earlier in the autoroute SPF example, the metric assigned to a tunnel interface when that interface is used in the IGP SPF is the shortest-cost path the IGP takes to get to the tunnel tail. Any routes behind the tunnel (such as the routes to Routers H and I in Figure 5-2) have the cost to transit the tunnel plus the cost to get from the tunnel tail to that node—just like your IGP.

However, you might want to change the metric. You can do so using the **tunnel mpls traffic-eng autoroute metric** command, as demonstrated in Example 5-9.

Example 5-9 *Changing the Autoroute Metric*

```
vxr15(config-if)#tunnel mpls traffic-eng autoroute metric ?
  <1-4294967295>  Set tunnel metric for autoroutes
  absolute        Set metric for all autoroutes over tunnel
  relative        Adjust tunnel metric for autoroutes relative to IGP
```

Changing the tunnel metric with the **tunnel mpls traffic-eng autoroute metric** command influences only the tunnel headend; other routers in the network don't know about the changed metric. You might want to advertise the tunnel into the IGP in some situations; see the later section "Forwarding Adjacency."

You would want to change the tunnel metric mainly if you want the IGP shortest-cost route to be preferred over the TE tunnel routes in some cases. Changing the metric isn't all that common, but it's worth understanding.

Fixing the Tunnel Metric

The first way you can tweak the tunnel metric is with the command **tunnel mpls traffic-eng autoroute metric** *1-4294967295*. Doing this overrides the IGP shortest-path cost and uses the configured cost instead. Setting this number influences the cost assigned to the tunnel interface in the IGP SPF, and thus the routing.

You typically do this if you want to use a TE tunnel only if the IGP shortest path is unavailable. Consider the network shown in Figure 5-8.

Figure 5-8 *Setting the Tunnel Metric to 25*

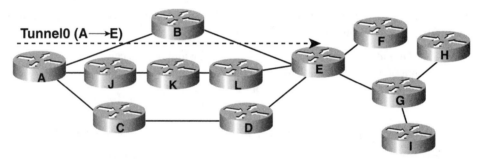

Based on Figure 5-2, Figure 5-8 adds Routers J, K, and L in the middle. Again, all links have a cost of 10.

For the sake of simplicity, Table 5-8 lists the three different paths Router A has to Router E.

Table 5-8 *Router A's Paths to Router E*

Path	Name	Cost
A→B→E	Top path	20
A→J→K→L→E	Middle path	40
A→C→D→E	Bottom path	30

By default, if the top path goes away, the next-best path to Router E is the bottom path. Assume that instead you want to use the middle path (cost: 40) if the top path goes away. You can do this by building a TE tunnel across the middle path and setting its metric to 25 with the command **tunnel mpls traffic-eng autoroute metric 25**. Table 5-9 lists the new path costs after you change this metric.

Table 5-9   *New Path Costs from Router A to Router E After Changing the Tunnel Metric and Path*

Path	Name	Cost
A→B→E	Top path	20
A→J→K→L→E	Middle path with a TE tunnel installed	25
A→C→D→E	Bottom path	30

If the top (IGP) path exists, it wins because the top path cost is the lowest at 20. However, if that goes away for some reason, the TE tunnel with a cost of 25 beats the bottom path (cost of 30) into the routing table. Because the TE tunnel terminates on Router E, Router A's cost is the cost to reach Router E (25, if the tunnel is used) plus 10 (the cost of E→G), or 35.

In all these examples, the cost to nodes *behind* the TE tunnel tail is increased by the cost to get from the tunnel tail to these nodes. So, if the middle path is used for the TE tunnel, and it has a cost of 25, the cost to get to Router F is 25 + 10, or 35. The cost to Router G is also 35, and the cost to Routers H and I is 45.

Absolute Tunnel Metric

Assume that you have a network topology that looks like Figure 5-9.

Figure 5-9   *Network Topology to Use with Absolute Metrics*

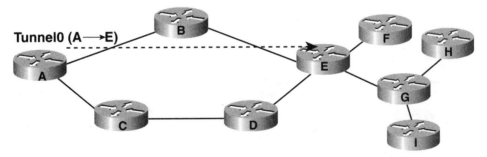

Suppose that you configure a TE tunnel from Router A to Router E with **tunnel mpls traffic-eng autoroute metric 17**.

Table 5-10 shows the resulting routing table for Router A after this configuration.

Table 5-10   *Router A's Routing Table After the TE Tunnel from Router A to Router E Is Configured with a Metric of 17*

Node	Next Hop	Cost
A	Self	0
B	B	10
C	C	10
D	C	20
E	Tunnel0	17
F	Tunnel0	27
G	Tunnel0	27
H	Tunnel0	37
I	Tunnel0	37

Another thing you can do is set the *absolute* tunnel metric, which assigns the same cost to the tunnel *and all nodes behind the tunnel.* Table 5-11 shows Router A's routing table if you configure **tunnel mpls traffic-eng autoroute metric absolute 17** on Tunnel0.

Only IS-IS supports **tunnel mpls traffic-eng autoroute metric absolute**; if you configure absolute metrics on an OSPF network, it's just ignored.

Table 5-11   *Router A's Routing Table After Tunnel0 Is Configured with an Absolute Metric of 17*

Node	Next Hop	Cost
A	Self	0
B	B	10
C	C	10
D	C	20
E	Tunnel0	17
F	Tunnel0	17
G	Tunnel0	17
H	Tunnel0	17
I	Tunnel0	17

Assigning an absolute metric is one way around the problem of sharing between IGP paths and TE paths. If every node behind the tunnel tail has the same cost as the tunnel tail, no matter what the topology looks like behind the tunnel tail, you'll always use the tunnel to forward traffic, no matter how many back doors exist. As long as the absolute cost on the tunnel is equal to or lower than the IGP cost to the tunnel tail, the tunnel carries all traffic for or behind the node.

Relative Tunnel Metric

The *relative metric* is yet another tool in the tunnel metric toolbox. Rather than setting the tunnel metric to a particular cost, you can set the tunnel metric *relative* to the IGP cost that the tunnel would normally have.

The CLI command to do this is as follows:

```
tunnel mpls traffic-eng autoroute metric relative -10 - 10
```

That is, **tunnel mpls traffic-eng autoroute metric relative** X, where X is any integer from -10 to 10.

Table 5-12 shows Router A's routing table if you set **tunnel mpls traffic-eng autoroute metric relative -8** on the tunnel interface on Router A's Tunnel0 in 5-9.

Table 5-12   *Router A's Routing Table After Tunnel0 Is Configured with a Relative Metric of –8*

Node	Next Hop	Cost
A	Self	0
B	B	10
C	C	10
D	C	20
E	Tunnel0	**12**
F	Tunnel0	**22**
G	Tunnel0	**22**
H	Tunnel0	**32**
I	Tunnel0	**32**

The cost to get to Router E through Tunnel0 is 12 because the IGP shortest-cost path to get to E is 20, and 20–8 (or 20 + –8, if you want to be precise) is 12.

If Router B goes away, the IGP shortest path to Router E becomes 30 (A→C→D→E). Configuring **tunnel mpls traffic-eng autoroute metric relative -8** means that the tunnel to Router E has a cost of 22, and all nodes behind Router E inherit this cost as they are accounted for in the IGP SPF.

Conversely, if you use a positive offset (**tunnel mpls traffic-eng autoroute metric relative 8**), the tunnel gets installed with a metric of 28 (A→B→E has a cost of 20+8 for the tunnel offset). If Router B goes away, the tunnel is given a cost of 38.

Applying Negative Offsets to Tunnel Costs

If you try to apply a negative offset to a TE tunnel path, and that offset would make the cost to get to the TE tunnel tail negative, the cost to the TE tunnel tail is instead set to 1. So if the IGP shortest cost to get to Router E is 6, and you apply **tunnel mpls traffic-eng autoroute metric relative -8**, the cost used for the A→E tunnel is 1 rather than –2.

From this discussion, you might note that, if a tunnel is given a positive offset metric, it is never installed in the routing table. So there's not any reason to use the positive offset.

Just like setting the TE tunnel to a different cost or an absolute cost, setting a negative relative metric allows you to set a preferred TE tunnel path in some cases when you wouldn't otherwise.

To better clarify this concept, read through the following example of how the different metric types work. Figure 5-10 shows a single tunnel and the routing tables if different techniques are used to change the metric. All link costs are 10, and there's a TE tunnel from Router A to Router E.

Figure 5-10 *Network Topology to Demonstrate Different Metric Types*

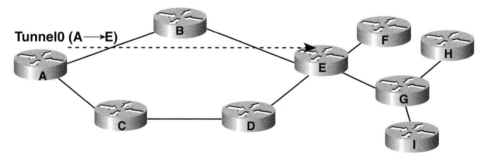

Table 5-13 shows Router A's routing table with no special metrics applied.

Table 5-13 *Router A's Routing Table with No Metric Changes*

Node	Next Hop	Cost
A	Self	0
B	B	10
C	C	10
D	C	20
E	Tunnel0	20
F	Tunnel0	30

Table 5-13 *Router A's Routing Table with No Metric Changes (Continued)*

Node	Next Hop	Cost
G	Tunnel0	30
H	Tunnel0	40
I	Tunnel0	40

Table 5-14 shows Router A's routing table after **tunnel mpls traffic-eng autoroute metric 12** is applied to Tunnel0.

Table 5-14 *Router A's Routing Table After Tunnel0 Is Configured with an Autoroute Metric of 12*

Node	Next Hop	Cost
A	Self	0
B	B	10
C	C	10
D	C	20
E	Tunnel0	12
F	Tunnel0	22
G	Tunnel0	22
H	Tunnel0	32
I	Tunnel0	32

Table 5-15 shows Router A's routing table after **tunnel mpls traffic-eng autoroute metric absolute 4** is applied to Tunnel0 instead.

Table 5-15 *Router A's Routing Table After Tunnel0 Is Configured with an Autoroute Absolute Metric of 4*

Node	Next Hop	Cost
A	Self	0
B	B	10
C	C	10
D	C	20
E	Tunnel0	4
F	Tunnel0	4
G	Tunnel0	4
H	Tunnel0	4
I	Tunnel0	4

Finally, Table 5-16 shows Router A's routing table after **tunnel mpls traffic-eng autoroute metric relative -3** is applied to Tunnel0.

Table 5-16   *Router A's Routing Table After Tunnel0 Is Configured with an Autoroute Relative Metric of –3*

Node	Next Hop	Cost
A	Self	0
B	B	7
C	C	7
D	C	17
E	Tunnel0	17
F	Tunnel0	27
G	Tunnel0	27
H	Tunnel0	37
I	Tunnel0	37

As with most knobs in the Cisco IOS Software, don't play with this one unless you know that you must. Most of the time, leaving the metrics at their defaults (where they track the IGP shortest cost) is fine.

How Changing the Metric Works

No matter which mechanism you use to change the metric, they all work the same in SPF. The key thing to remember is that any metrics are changed *after* SPF is run. Figure 5-11 shows a scenario in which changing the metric *after* SPF, rather than before, makes a difference.

Figure 5-11   *Sample Network for the SPF Processing Example*

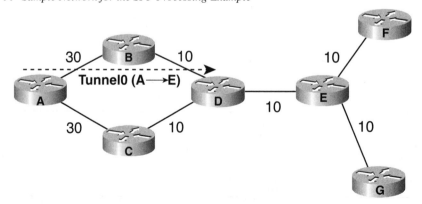

Links A→B and A→C have a cost of 30; all other links have a cost of 10. The tunnel from Router A to Router E has been configured with **tunnel mpls traffic-eng autoroute metric 1**. This means that the cost to get to Router E is 1, the cost to get to Router F is 11, and the cost to get to Router G is also 11.

But what about the costs to Routers B, C, and D? If the tunnel from Router A to Router E had a metric of 1 when the tunnel was put in the TENT list, the SPF would look something like this:

PATH List	TENT List
{A,0,0}	{E,1,Tunnel0}
	{B,30,B}
	{C,30,C}

PATH List	TENT List
{A,0,0}	{D,11,Tunnel0}
{E,1,Tunnel0}	{F,11,Tunnel0}
	{G,11,Tunnel0}
	{B,30,B}
	{C,30,C}

In the next table, {B,30,B} and {C,30,C} are removed from the TENT list because, as far as SPF is concerned, {B,21,Tunnel0} and {C,21,Tunnel0} are the shortest paths to Routers B and C.

PATH List	TENT List
{A,0,0}	{F,11,Tunnel0}
{E,1,Tunnel0}	{G,11,Tunnel0}
{D,11,Tunnel0}	{B,21,Tunnel0}
	{C,21,Tunnel0}
	{B,30,B}
	{C,30,C}

PATH List	TENT List
{A,0,0}	\<Empty\>
{E,1,Tunnel0}	
{D,11,Tunnel0}	
{B,21,Tunnel0}	
{C,21,Tunnel0}	
{F,11,Tunnel0}	
{G,11,Tunnel0}	

Table 5-17 shows the resulting routing table.

Table 5-17   *Router A's Routing Table After Tunnel0 Is Configured with an Autoroute Metric of 1 if Metric Modification Happened Before SPF*

Node	Next Hop	Cost
A	Self	0
E	Tunnel0	1
D	Tunnel0	11
F	Tunnel0	11
G	Tunnel0	11
B	Tunnel0	21
C	Tunnel0	21

This is extremely suboptimal. To get from Router A to Router B, the packets go across Router A's Tunnel0 to Router E, back to Router D, and then to Router B. This is a physical path of A→B→D→E→D→B. Nodes B and D show up twice in the path—once carrying the TE tunnel, and once carrying the IP packet after it reaches Router E.

Because you can give the tunnel a cost of less than the physical path to get to the tunnel tail, putting the tunnel metric in the SPF means you can easily have problems like this. Just think about how much worse it could become on a larger network if you used **tunnel mpls traffic-eng autoroute metric absolute 1** instead! If you did that, every node more than halfway across the network would be suboptimally routed down the TE tunnel instead of on the physical path.

It's important to realize that these problems can happen in real life. In order to avoid these problems, metrics are changed *after* the SPF run is complete. This means that you don't end up with extremely silly routes like those shown in Table 5-17. It also means that changing the tunnel metric doesn't influence what routes are installed through the tunnel, only the cost to get to those routes. The SPF run for the network in Figure 5-11 actually looks like this:

PATH List	TENT List
{A,0,0}	{B,30,B}
	{C,30,C}

PATH List	TENT List
{A,0,0}	{C,30,C}
{B,30,B}	{D,40,B}

PATH List	TENT List
{A,0,0}	{D,40,B & C}
{B,30,B}	
{C,30,C}	

PATH List	TENT List
{A,0,0}	{E,50,B & C}
{B,30,B}	
{C,30,C}	
{D,40,B & C}	

PATH List	TENT List
{A,0,0}	{F,60,Tunnel0}
{B,30,B}	{G,60,Tunnel0}
{C,30,C}	
{D,40,B & C}	
{E,50,Tunnel0}	

PATH List	TENT List
{A,0,0}	<Empty>
{B,30,B}	
{C,30,C}	
{D,40,B & C}	
{E,50,Tunnel0}	
{F,60,Tunnel0}	
{G,60,Tunnel0}	

Then the routing table is built, and any metric changes are made. With a configuration of **tunnel mpls traffic-eng autoroute metric 1**, the routing table looks like Table 5-18.

Table 5-18 *Router A's Routing Table After Tunnel0 Is Configured with an Autoroute Metric of 1*

Node	Next Hop	Cost
A	Self	0
B	B	30
C	C	30
D	B,C	40
E	Tunnel0	1
F	Tunnel0	11
G	Tunnel0	11

As you can see, this is far more sensible than the previous example.

The final thing to consider about SPF metric processing is that it might not always do what you want. Consider the network topology shown in Figure 5-12.

Figure 5-12 *Sample Topology for Autoroute Metric*

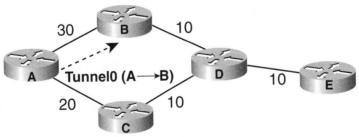

In Figure 5-12, the A→B link has a cost of 30, and the A→C link has a cost of 20. Without any TE tunnels, the routing table for this network looks like Table 5-19.

Table 5-19 *Routing Table Without TE Tunnels*

Node	Next Hop	Cost
A	Self	0
B	B	30
C	C	20
D	C	30
E	C	40

Table 5-20 shows what you might expect the routing table to look like if you add a TE tunnel between Routers A and B and configure it with **tunnel mpls traffic-eng autoroute metric 1**.

Table 5-20 *Expected Routing Table After a TE Tunnel Is Configured Between Routers A and B with a Metric of 1*

Node	Next Hop	Cost
A	Self	0
B	Tunnel0	1
C	C	20
D	Tunnel0	11
E	Tunnel0	21

But this is not what happens. The SPF looks like this:

PATH List	TENT List
{A,0,0}	{B,30,B}
	{C,20,C}
{A,0,0}	{B,30,B}
{C,20,C}	{D,30,C}
{A,0,0}	{D,30,C}
{C,20,C}	
{B,30,Tunnel0}	
{A,0,0}	{E,40,C}
{C,20,C}	
{B,30,Tunnel0}	
{D,30,C}	

After the SPF process, the routing table looks like Table 5-21.

Routers D and E can't be reached through the TE tunnel to Router B because when the IGP SPF is finished, the TE tunnel from Routers A to B has a cost of 30, not 1, so the shortest paths to Routers D and E are still through Router C. Remember, it's only *after* the SPF is done that any autoroute metric modifications are applied.

Table 5-21   *Routing Table After the SPF Process*

Node	Next Hop	Cost
A	Self	0
B	Tunnel0	1
C	C	20
D	C	30
E	C	40

The moral of the story is that you should follow a few rules when deploying MPLS TE, including

- Don't change tunnel metrics unless you know you need to.

- Become familiar with how SPF works.

- If routing isn't doing what you expect it to, work it out by hand and see if you can figure out what's happening.

Forwarding Adjacency

Earlier in this chapter, you learned how to change the metric on a TE tunnel. But sometimes, changing the metric isn't enough to steer traffic the way you want it to go.

As mentioned earlier, TE tunnels are not advertised in your IGP. This means that if you change the metric on a TE tunnel, other routers will not see this changed metric and won't be able to take advantage of it.

All links shown in Figure 5-13 have a cost of 10, and all routers are at the same IS-IS level. This example uses Level-2 adjacencies between routers; forwarding adjacency also works across a Level-1 cloud.

Traffic goes from Router A to Router G. With no MPLS TE, all A→G traffic goes across A→C→F→G. What if you want to send A→G traffic across both A→C→F→G and A→B→D→E→G?

One way to do this is to place two TE tunnels from Router A to Router F—one across the B→D→E→F path and one across the C→E→F path. These tunnels are both installed with the shortest cost to the IGP tail, and Router A load shares between them.

But what if you don't want to extend TE tunnels all the way to Router A? Extending TE tunnels all the way to the edge works OK in a small network, but most real-world networks have more than seven routers. If you have 50 POPs with 15 routers in each POP, that's a total of 750 routers; a full mesh of TE tunnels between 750 routers is 561,750 TE LSPs, and two tunnels between each router means 1,123,500 TE LSPs. That's pretty big.

Figure 5-13 *Network Without MPLS TE*

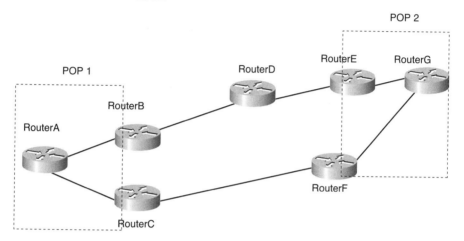

Obviously, things scale better if you move the TE tunnels up one level in the network hierarchy, toward the core. If you deploy a full mesh of TE tunnels between the POP-facing core routers (B, C, E, and F), only 12 tunnels are necessary in Figure 5-13. If your 50 POPs have two core routers each, that's 100 * 99 TE tunnels, for a total of 9900. A total of 9900 is a big number, but it's much lower than 1,123,500.

Figure 5-14 shows the same topology as Figure 5-13, but with TE tunnels.

Figure 5-14 *Network with MPLS TE and Without Forwarding Adjacency*

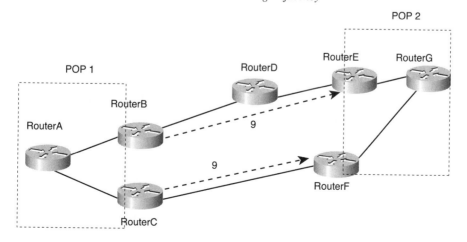

Now you've got two TE tunnels—B→E and C→F. Each of these tunnels has been configured with **tunnel mpls traffic-eng autoroute metric 9**, which means that the tunnel headends assign these tunnels a metric of 9.

Problem solved, right?

Wrong!

Router A doesn't know about those TE tunnels. It makes its SPF decision based on the IGP metrics alone, which means it still sends all its A→G traffic to Router C. You haven't solved anything yet!

You need a way to advertise the TE tunnels into the IGP so that Router A can see them and take advantage of them. You do this using the command **tunnel mpls traffic-eng forwarding-adjacency** on the tunnel interface, as shown in Example 5-10.

Example 5-10 *Advertising TE Tunnels into the IGP*

```
interface Tunnel1
 ip unnumbered Loopback0
 no ip directed-broadcast
 tunnel destination 192.168.1.8
 tunnel mode mpls traffic-eng
 tunnel mpls traffic-eng forwarding-adjacency
 tunnel mpls traffic-eng path-option 10 dynamic
 isis metric 9 level-2
```

NOTE **forwarding-adjacency** and the IGP metric are configured on both the tunnel from Router B to Router E and from Router C to Router F. Another way to solve this problem is to only build a TE tunnel from Router B to Router E, not from Router C to Router F, and give the B→E tunnel a cost of 10. Because 10 is a link's default IS-IS cost, there is no need to configure an IS-IS metric on the tunnel interface. This example was done with a metric of 9 so that you can see that you control the tunnel's cost by changing the IGP metric rather than the autoroute metric.

Note that an IS-IS metric is also configured on the tunnel interface. This metric is what's announced into the IGP.

When you configure **forwarding-adjacency**, the tunnel headend advertises that tunnel in its IGP. The IS-IS database looks like Example 5-11.

Example 5-11 *IS-IS Database After* **forwarding-adjacency** *Is Configured*

```
RouterB#show isis database detail RouterB.00-00
IS-IS Level-2 LSP RouterB.00-00
LSPID                 LSP Seq Num  LSP Checksum  LSP Holdtime    ATT/P/OL
RouterB.00-00      * 0x0000023D   0xEDD2        1122            0/0/0
  Area Address: 47.0001.0192
```

Example 5-11 *IS-IS Database After* **forwarding-adjacency** *Is Configured (Continued)*

```
NLPID:          0x81 0xCC
Hostname: RouterB
Router ID:      192.168.1.5
IP Address:     192.168.1.5
Metric: 10         IP 192.168.10.0/24
Metric: 10         IS-Extended RouterD.00
Metric: 9          IS-Extended RouterE.00
Metric: 10         IP 192.168.1.5/32
```

After this IS-IS LSP is announced, all other routers see the TE tunnel as a regular link. It's not a link that TE tunnels can be signalled across, but it is available for regular IGP traffic. It's important to understand that any router that sees this advertisement has no idea that the forwarding adjacency from Router B to Router E is a forwarding adjacency; all any other router sees is a link of cost 9.

From Router A's perspective, the topology looks like Figure 5-15.

Figure 5-15 *Network with Forwarding Adjacency*

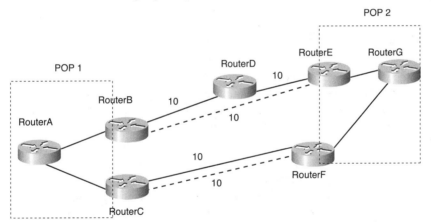

Forwarding adjacency optionally allows you to configure a holdtime. Here is the full **forwarding-adjacency** command syntax:

```
tunnel mpls traffic-eng forwarding-adjacency {holdtime 0-4294967295 milliseconds}
```

The holdtime is used when a TE tunnel goes down. If the link a TE tunnel is on fails, the tunnel might go down and come back up quickly as it finds a new path. This is not the sort of thing you want to advertise into your IGP because the link would be removed and readvertised, causing unnecessary IGP churn. The holdtime is how long the TE tunnel must be down before its status is advertised in the IGP. The holdtime is configured in milliseconds, so **tunnel mpls traffic-eng forwarding-adjacency holdtime 12000** waits until a TE tunnel has been down for 12 seconds before telling the IGP that the tunnel is down.

The default forwarding adjacency holdtime is 0 ms.

Forwarding adjacency has a few restrictions:

- You must have IS-IS as your IGP; OSPF does not currently support forwarding adjacency.

- When a forwarding adjacency is advertised in the IGP, it is advertised as an IP link only, not as a TE link. This means that you cannot send a TE reservation from Router A to Router G across the *tunnel* from Router C to Router F.

- Because of the nature of forwarding adjacency, the tunnel headend and tail must be in the same area.

Note that IS-IS's bidirectional check is not removed. This means that if you have a TE tunnel from Router B to Router E that you've configured with **tunnel mpls traffic-eng forwarding-adjacency**, you also need to have a similarly configured tunnel from Router E to Router B in order for forwarding adjacency to be considered in Router A's IGP SPF. If you don't, even after receiving IS-IS LSPs about the tunnel link, Router A will not install it in the routing table because only one of the links is up.

Automatic Bandwidth Adjustment

As you've seen, MPLS TE tunnels can be configured to reserve bandwidth. But in everything you've seen so far, reservations require manual intervention to change. What happens if the traffic patterns in your network change several times during the day? One way to handle this situation is to use an offline tool to figure out how much bandwidth to give each tunnel and to send new configurations to your routers with the new configuration information. See Chapter 9 for more on the issues involved.

Offline tunnel calculation has a decided advantage in that you can also use this offline tool to calculate the paths your TE LSPs flow over, which leads to a more efficient use of bandwidth. However, an offline tool is a lot of work. If you want to give your network a fair degree of autonomy without having to run an offline tool, consider a mechanism called *auto bandwidth*.

Auto bandwidth is a simple concept. You configure it on a per-LSP basis at the headend. Periodically, the headend looks at the bandwidth actually *used* by the auto bandwidth-configured LSPs and changes the configuration of those LSPs to reflect a more recent bandwidth requirement.

The devil, of course, is in the details.

How Auto Bandwidth Works

The general idea behind auto bandwidth is that it watches the traffic rate on a tunnel interface and periodically resizes the bandwidth on the tunnel interface to more closely align with the traffic that's actually going down the tunnel.

Table 5-22 lists several auto bandwidth variables with which you must concern yourself.

Table 5-22 *Auto Bandwidth Variables*

Variable	Name	Description	Default Value
A	Application frequency	How often a tunnel's bandwidth is changed	24 hours (86,400 seconds)
B	Tunnel bandwidth	The value of **tunnel mpls traffic-eng bandwidth** that is configured on a tunnel	0 Kbps
C	Collection frequency	How often a tunnel's output rate is polled	5 minutes (300 seconds)
H	Highest collected bandwidth	The highest collected bandwidth in the last A seconds	N/A
D	Delta	H–B—the difference between a tunnel's highest recorded bandwidth and its configured bandwidth	N/A

When a tunnel is first configured with auto bandwidth, a timer A is started. After this timer is started, every C seconds, the output rate on that tunnel interface is collected, and D is calculated. When A expires, the tunnel is reconfigured (the value of B is modified) in accordance with D.

For example, suppose you enable auto bandwidth on an interface that has no bandwidth configured. Over A seconds, the highest bandwidth seen on that tunnel is 30 Mbps. The value of D is therefore 30 Mbps. The tunnel is resized to 30 Mbps, and the A timer starts again.

What if you enable auto bandwidth on a tunnel whose highest observed bandwidth is 30 Mbps but that is configured for 45 Mbps? In this case, as soon as A expires, D is 15 Mbps, and the tunnel is resized to 45 Mbps – 15 Mbps, or 30 Mbps.

There are a few cases in which auto bandwidth doesn't change B to be the same as H:

- If the tunnel has been up for less than 5 minutes, don't apply all the D value to B. Instead, use the values listed in Table 5-23. If B is less than 50 kbps, change it only if D is 10 kbps or more. Otherwise, pretend that no change happened. The idea is to not constantly resignal relatively small changes in a tunnel.

- If B is greater than 50 kbps and less than 100 kbps, change the bandwidth only if D is 10 percent or more of B.

- If D is more than 100 kbps, apply the change no matter what percentage of B it is. This is done because even if you have tunnels large enough that a D of 100 kbps is less than 10 percent (tunnels of more than 1 Mbps), 100 kbps is still a significant-enough difference to warrant a change.

- If you have configured minimum or maximum bandwidth values for a tunnel, obey them.

Table 5-23   *Percentage of D Applied to New Bandwidth Request*

Tunnel Uptime, in Minutes	Percentage of D to Apply to B
5+	100%
4	80%
3	60%
2	40%
1	20%
0	10%

Auto Bandwidth Configuration

Auto bandwidth has one globally configurable knob:

```
gsr3(config)#mpls traffic-eng auto-bw timers frequency ?
  <1-604800>  seconds between auto-bw
```

This is the *collection frequency* (C) referred to in Table 5-22. The default for this timer is 300 seconds, or 5 minutes. Whenever this timer expires, the output rate on all tunnel interfaces (as seen in **show interface**) is recorded. Nothing is actually done with this information until **auto-bandwidth** is enabled on a TE tunnel.

How the Interface Bandwidth Is Calculated

Auto bandwidth checks the interface output rate on a tunnel the same way you would—it looks at the output rate counter in **show interfaces**:

```
gsr3#show interfaces tunnel0
Tunnel0 is up, line protocol is up
...
  30 second output rate 2791000 bits/sec, 506 packets/sec
```

The output rate shown on any interface (and, for that matter, the input rate, but TE tunnels don't have an input rate) is an exponentially decaying average. It is calculated with the formula

$$\text{average\_traffic} = ((\text{average\_traffic} - \text{interval\_traffic}) * e^{(-t/C)}) + \text{interval\_traffic}$$

where *e* is approximately 2.718, *t* equals 5, *C* is the load interval in seconds, and interval_traffic is how much traffic (the number of bits or the number of packets) has passed in the last *t* seconds. *t* is always 5; it's an internal Cisco IOS Software timer thing that you shouldn't worry about. You can't configure values of *t*.

This formula applies for all input and output rates on all interfaces in a router, not just TE tunnels.

To converge on the actual interface load faster, you should set the load interval on the tunnel interface to 30 seconds using the command **load-interval 30**. This gives you a more accurate picture of what happened in the last 30 seconds. **auto-bw** has its own dampening built in, so using the default 5-minute load interval timer gives you less-recent results than using 30 seconds.

On an LSP, auto bandwidth is configured with the knob **tunnel mpls traffic-eng auto-bw**. That's all you need to do to turn on auto bandwidth with the default timers. This command has several options, as shown in Example 5-12.

Example 5-12 **auto-bw** *Options*

```
gsr3(config-if)#tunnel mpls traffic-eng auto-bw ?
  collect-bw  Just collect Bandwidth info on this tunnel
  frequency   Frequency to change tunnel BW
  max-bw      Set the Maximum Bandwidth for auto-bw on this tunnel
  min-bw      Set the Minimum Bandwidth for auto-bw on this tunnel
  <cr>
```

collect-bw does everything except actually change the tunnel bandwidth. It collects it so that you can see what bandwidth **auto-bw** would change the tunnel to if it were enabled.

frequency controls *A,* the application frequency. **frequency** needs to be the same size as or larger than *C,* the global collection frequency. This makes sense, because you can't change bandwidth faster than you check to see if it's changed. The lower you configure this frequency, the more often you change the tunnel bandwidth.

max-bw sets the maximum bandwidth to which **auto-bw** can go. It's the same idea as **min-bw**, but in the other direction. No matter what the traffic rate down a tunnel, if you configure **max-bw**, auto bandwidth never sets the tunnel's bandwidth to higher than that.

min-bw sets the minimum bandwidth to which **auto-bw** can go. No matter what the traffic rate down a tunnel, if you configure **min-bw**, auto bandwidth will never set the tunnel's bandwidth to lower than that.

Auto Bandwidth Operation

Auto bandwidth, like so many other things, displays its information in **show mpls traffic-eng tunnels**, as demonstrated in Example 5-13.

Example 5-13 *Displaying Auto Bandwidth Information*

```
Router-1# show mpls traffic-eng tunnels
Name:tagsw4500-9_t1 (Tunnel1) Destination:10.0.0.11
  Status:
    Admin:up Oper:up Path:valid Signalling:connected
    path option 10, type dynamic
  Config Parameters:
    Bandwidth:5000 kbps (Global) Priority:7 7 Affinity:0x0/0xFFFF
    AutoRoute: disabled LockDown:disabled Loadshare:500 bw-based
    auto-bw:(86400/85477) 765 Bandwidth Requested:500
```

Table 5-24 dissects the meaning of the fields in the highlighted output.

Table 5-24 *Understanding Auto Bandwidth Information*

Number	Description
86,400	The tunnel's *A*—application frequency.
85,477	The amount of time remaining in the current application frequency period.
765	The highest bandwidth sampled since the beginning of the application frequency period (in the last 86,400 – 85,477 = 923 seconds).
Bandwidth Requested: 500	The amount of bandwidth the tunnel currently is asking the network for. This is the value configured with **tunnel mpls traffic-eng bandwidth**.

One final thing to understand about **auto-bw** is that it actually *changes your tunnel configuration*. Suppose you start with a tunnel configured as shown in Example 5-14.

Example 5-14 *Basic Tunnel Configuration*

```
interface Tunnel0
  ip unnumbered Loopback0
  tunnel mode mpls traffic-eng
  tunnel destination 192.168.1.8
  tunnel mpls traffic-eng path-option 10 dynamic
  tunnel mpls traffic-eng auto-bw
```

If **auto-bw** decides that this tunnel should be resized with 750 kbps of bandwidth, the tunnel configuration changes to that shown in Example 5-15.

Example 5-15 *Tunnel Reconfigured by Auto Bandwidth*

```
interface Tunnel0
  ip unnumbered Loopback0
  tunnel mode mpls traffic-eng
  tunnel destination 192.168.1.8
  tunnel mpls traffic-eng path-option 10 dynamic
  tunnel mpls traffic-eng auto-bw
  tunnel mpls traffic-eng bandwidth 750
```

The configuration changes that auto bandwidth makes are like a configuration change you make by hand. The configuration is not saved, so unless you have saved it yourself, after the router is reloaded, the configured bandwidth is not there on reload.

Summary

This chapter can be looked at as the last in a three-part series. Chapter 3 covered information distribution. Chapter 4 covered path calculation and setup. This chapter covered forwarding traffic down a tunnel.

If you finished all three of these chapters, you have a good idea of how MPLS TE works. In fact, if you combine the information in Chapters 3, 4, and 5 with the introductory material in Chapters 1 and 2, you have enough information to start configuring and deploying MPLS TE in your network.

The next things to look at are some advanced features of MPLS and MPLS TE—Quality of Service with MPLS TE (Chapter 6), Protection and Restoration (Chapter 7), and MPLS TE Management (Chapter 8).

CHAPTER 6

Quality of Service with MPLS TE

Quality of service (QoS) and MPLS are, at a political level, similar. They're both technologies that have been gaining popularity in recent years. They both seem to be technologies that you either love or hate—some people are huge QoS fans, and others can't stand it. The same is true of MPLS—some people like it, and others don't.

At a technical level, though, QoS and MPLS are very different.

QoS is an umbrella term that covers network performance characteristics. As discussed in Chapter 1, "Understanding Traffic Engineering with MPLS," QoS has two parts:

- Finding a path through your network that can provide the service you offer
- Enforcing that service

The acronym QoS in respect to IP first showed up in RFC 1006, "ISO Transport Service on Top of the TCP: Version 3," published in 1987. The term QoS has been around for even longer, because it is a general term used to describe performance characteristics in networks. In the IP and MPLS worlds, the term QoS is most often used to describe a set of techniques to manage packet loss, latency, and jitter. QoS has been rather appropriately described as "managed unfairness": If you have contention for system resources, who are you unfair to, and why?

Two QoS architectures are in use today:

- Integrated Services (IntServ)
- Differentiated Services (DiffServ)

For various reasons, IntServ never scaled to the level it needed to get to for Internet-size networks. IntServ is fine for small- to medium-sized networks, but its need to make end-to-end, host-to-host, per-application microflows across a network means it can't grow to the level that large service provider networks need.

DiffServ, on the other hand, has proven quite scalable. Its use of classification on the edge and per-hop queuing and discard behaviors in the core means that most of the work is done at the edge, and you don't need to keep any microflow state in the core.

This chapter assumes that you understand QoS on an IP network. It concentrates on the integration of MPLS into the IP QoS spectrum of services. This means that you should be comfortable with acronyms such as CAR, LLQ, MDRR, MQC, SLA, and WRED in order to get the most out of this chapter. This chapter briefly reviews both the DiffServ architecture and the Modular QoS CLI (MQC), but see Appendix B, "CCO and Other References," if you want to learn more about the portfolio of Cisco QoS tools.

QoS, as used in casual conversation and in the context of IP and MPLS networks, is a method of packet treatment: How do you decide which packets get what service?

MPLS, on the other hand, is a switching method used to get packets from one place to another by going through a series of hops. Which hops a packet goes through can be determined by your IGP routing or by MPLS TE.

So there you have it—MPLS is about getting packets from one hop to another, and QoS (as the term is commonly used) is what happens to packets at each hop. As you can imagine, between two complex devices such as QoS and MPLS, a lot can be done.

This chapter covers five topics:

- The DiffServ architecture
- DiffServ's interaction with IP Precedence and MPLS EXP bits
- The treatment of EXP values in a label stack as packets are forwarded throughout a network
- A quick review of the Modular QoS CLI (MQC), which is how most QoS features on most platforms are configured
- Where DiffServ and MPLS TE intersect—the emerging DiffServ-Aware Traffic Engineering (DS-TE) devices and how they can be used to further optimize your network performance

---

DiffServ and MPLS TE

It is important to understand that the DiffServ architecture and the sections of this chapter that cover DiffServ and MPLS have nothing to do with MPLS TE. DiffServ is purely a method of treating packets differently at each hop. The DiffServ architecture doesn't care what control plane protocol a given label assignment comes from. Whether it's RSVP or LDP, or BGP, or something else entirely, the forwarding plane doesn't care. Why does this chapter exist then, if it's not about TE? Partly because MPLS TE and DiffServ treatment of MPLS packets go hand in hand in many network designs, and partly because of the existence of something called DS-TE, discussed later in this chapter.

The DiffServ Architecture

RFC 2475 defines an architecture for Differentiated Services—how to use DiffServ Code Point (DSCP) bits and various QoS mechanisms to provide different qualities of service in your network.

DiffServ has two major components:

- **Traffic conditioning**—Includes things such as policing, coloring, and shaping. Is done only at the edge of the network.
- **Per-hop behaviors**—Essentially consist of queuing, scheduling, and dropping mechanisms. As the name implies, they are done at every hop in the network.

Cisco IOS Software provides all sorts of different tools to apply these architecture pieces. You can configure most services in two ways—a host of older, disconnected, per-platform methods, and a newer, unified configuration set called the MQC. Only MQC is covered in this chapter. For information on the older configuration mechanisms, see Appendix B or the documentation on CCO. Not all platforms support MQC, so there might be times when you need to configure a service using a non-MQC configuration method; however, MQC is where all QoS configuration services are heading, so it's definitely worth understanding.

Traffic conditioning generally involves classification, policing, and marking, and per-hop behaviors deal with queuing, scheduling, and dropping. Each of these topics are discussed briefly.

Classification

The first step in applying the DiffServ architecture is to have the capability to classify packets. Classification is the act of examining a packet to decide what sort of rules it should be run through, and subsequently what DSCP or EXP value should be set on the packet.

Classifying IP Packets

Classifying IP packets is straightforward. You can match on just about anything in the IP header. Specific match capabilities vary by platform, but generally, destination IP address, source IP address, and DSCP values can be matched against. The idea behind DSCP is discussed in the section "DiffServ and IP Packets."

Classifying MPLS Packets

The big thing to keep in mind when classifying MPLS packets is that you can't match on anything other than the outermost EXP value in the label stack. There's no way to look past the MPLS header at the underlying IP packet and do any matching on or modification of that packet. You can't match on the label value in the top of the stack, and you can't match on TTL (just as you can't match on IP TTL). Finally, you can't do any matching of EXP values on any label other than the topmost label on the stack.

Policing

Policing involves metering traffic against a specified service contract and dealing with in-rate and out-of-rate traffic differently. One of the fundamental pieces of the DiffServ architecture is that you don't allow more traffic on your network than you have designed for, to make sure that you don't overtax the queues you've provisioned. This is generally done with policing, although it can also be done with shaping.

Policing is done on the edge of the network. As such, the packets coming into the network are very often IP packets. However, under some scenarios it is possible to receive MPLS-labeled packets on the edge of the network. For example, the Carrier Supporting Carrier architecture (see Appendix B) means that a provider receives MPLS-labeled packets from a customer.

Marking

The marking configuration is usually very tightly tied to the policing configuration. You can mark traffic as in-rate and out-of-rate as a result of policing traffic.

You don't need to police in order to mark. For example, you can simply define a mapping between the IP packet's DSCP value and the MPLS EXP bits to be used when a label is imposed on these packets. Another possibility is to simply mark all traffic coming in on an interface, regardless of traffic rate. This is handy if you have some customers who are paying extra for better QoS and some who are not. For those who are not, simply set the EXP to 0 on all packets from that customer.

Being able to set the EXP on a packet, rather than having to set the IP Precedence, is one of the advantages of MPLS. This is discussed in more detail in the sections "Label Stack Treatment" and "Tunnel Modes."

Queuing

Queuing is accomplished in different ways on different platforms. However, the good news is that you can treat MPLS EXP just like IP Precedence.

Multiple queuing techniques can be applied to MPLS, depending on your platform and code version:

- First In First Out (FIFO)
- Modified Deficit Round Robin (MDRR) (GSR platforms only)
- Class-Based Weighted Fair Queuing (CBWFQ) (most non-GSR platforms)
- Low-Latency Queuing (LLQ)

FIFO exists on every platform and every interface. It is the default on almost all of those interfaces.

MDRR, CBWFQ, and LLQ are configured using the MQC, just like most other QoS mechanisms on most platforms. Just match the desired MPLS EXP values in a class map and then configure a bandwidth or latency guarantee via the **bandwidth** or **priority** commands. The underlying scheduling algorithm (MDRR, CBWFQ/LLQ) brings the guarantee to life.

Queuing is one of two parts of what the DiffServ architecture calls *per-hop behaviors* (PHBs). A per-hop behavior is, surprisingly, a behavior that is implemented at each hop. PHBs have two fundamental pieces—queuing and dropping.

Dropping

Dropping is the other half of DiffServ's PHB. Dropping is important not only to manage queue depth per traffic class, but also to signal transport-level backoff to TCP-based applications. TCP responds to occasional packet drops by slowing down the rate at which it sends. TCP responds better to occasional drops than to tail drop after a queue is completely filled up. See Appendix B for more information.

Weighted Random Early Detection (WRED) is the DiffServ drop mechanism implemented on most Cisco platforms. WRED works on MPLS EXP just like it does on IP Precedence. See the next section for WRED configuration details.

As you can see, implementing DiffServ behavior with MPLS packets is no more and no less than implementing the same behavior with IP.

A Quick MQC Review

Over time, various Cisco IOS Software versions and hardware platforms have invented different ways to control QoS behaviors (policing, marking, queuing, and dropping). There have been many different CLIs that accomplish very similar things. A GSR QoS configuration was different from a 7200 configuration was different from a 7500 configuration, and so forth.

Along came MQC. MQC's goal is to unify all the QoS configuration steps into a single, flexible CLI that can be used across all IOS platforms.

This chapter covers only the MQC, because that is the preferred way to configure QoS. You can configure QoS services in other ways, but they are not covered here. If you have questions about a specific router model or software version, see the relevant documentation.

MQC is very powerful, and it can be a bit complex to the beginner. This section is a quick review of MQC. This is not a book on QoS, so this chapter doesn't go into great detail on the different types of services—merely how you can configure them with MQC.

MQC has three pieces:

- **Class map**—How you define what traffic you're interested in
- **Policy map**—What you do to the traffic defined in a class map
- **Service policy**—How you enable a policy map on an interface

The options you have within each of these pieces vary between code versions and platforms, so some of the options shown here might not be available to you. The basic idea remains constant, though.

Configuring a Class Map

The first step in using MQC is to build a class map. Not surprisingly, you do this with the **class-map** command:

```
vxr12(config)#class-map ?
  WORD       class-map name
  match-all  Logical-AND all matching statements under this classmap
  match-any  Logical-OR all matching statements under this classmapm
```

The **match-all** and **match-any** keywords let you specify whether traffic matches this class, if it matches *all* the rules in this class or *any* of them, respectively. The default is **match-all**.

You create a class by giving it a name. This puts you in a submode called config-cmap:

```
vxr12(config)#class-map voice
vxr12(config-cmap)#?
QoS class-map configuration commands:
  description  Class-Map description
  exit         Exit from QoS class-map configuration mode
  match        classification criteria
  no           Negate or set default values of a command
  rename       Rename this class-mapm
```

The most useful option under config-cmap is **match**, which lets you define the traffic you want to match with this class map. Its options are as follows:

```
vxr12(config-cmap)#match ?
  access-group     Access group
  any              Any packets
  class-map        Class map
```

```
cos                    IEEE 802.1Q/ISL class of service/user priority values
destination-address    Destination address
fr-de                  Match on Frame-relay DE bit
input-interface        Select an input interface to match
ip                     IP specific values
mpls                   Multi Protocol Label Switching specific values
not                    Negate this match result
protocol               Protocol
qos-group              Qos-group
source-address         Source addressm
```

There are a few interesting options here. Note that you can match a class map; this lets you define hierarchical classes. A class called "Business," for example, can match an "Email" class and a "Payroll" class you define so that all business-class e-mail and all traffic to or from the payroll department gets the same treatment. You can also match **not**, which lets you match everything *except* a specific thing. You might now start to understand the awesome power of MQC.

Table 6-1 lists the matches of interest here.

Table 6-1   *Class Map Matches*

Match Type	Function	Configuration Syntax
access-group	Matches a named or numbered access list.	**access-group** {**name** *acl-name* | *acl-number 1-2699*}
ip	Matches IP packets of a specific DSCP or IP Precedence value (or a range of RTP ports, but that's not addressed here).	**ip** {**dscp** *name-or-number* | **precedence** *name or number* | **rtp** *lower-bound range*}
mpls	Matches MPLS packets that have a particular EXP value.	**mpls experimental** *0-7*

For the example in this chapter, create a simple LLQ policy matching MPLS EXP 5 traffic, and assume it is Voice over IP (VoIP) traffic. The necessary configuration is as follows:

```
class-map match-all voice
  match mpls experimental  5
policy-map llq
  class voice
    priority percent 30
```

This defines a class that matches any MPLS traffic that has the EXP bits set to 5 and then defines a policy for that traffic that gives the traffic 30 percent of a link's bandwidth. The policy map hasn't been enabled on an interface yet; you'll see that in a minute.

You can match multiple values with the same line using the following command sequence:

```
class-map match-any bronze-service
  match mpls experimental  0  1
```

This matches any packets that have an MPLS EXP of 0 or 1. As with route maps, multiple values specified within the same match clause (such as **match mpls experimental 0 1**) are implicitly ORed together; a packet can't have both EXP 0 *and* EXP 1, so this implicit ORing makes sense.

You can also match more than one criteria within a class, and you can use the **match-any** and **match-all** statements to decide how you want to match traffic. For example, the following policy matches traffic that has MPLS EXP 5 *or* traffic that entered the router on interface POS3/0:

```
class-map match-any gold
  match mpls experimental  5
  match input-interface POS3/0
```

The following policy matches any traffic that has MPLS EXP 5 *and* that came in on interface POS3/0:

```
class-map match-all gold
  match mpls experimental  5
  match input-interface POS3/0
```

See the difference? The first class map is **match-any** (the default), and the second is **match-all**.

The output for **show class-map** {*class-map-name*} shows you the configured class maps, as demonstrated in Example 6-1.

Example 6-1 *Displaying the Configured Class Maps*

```
vxr12#show class-map
 Class Map match-all gold (id 2)
   Match mpls experimental  5
   Match input-interface POS3/0

 Class Map match-any class-default (id 0)
   Match any

 Class Map match-all voice (id 3)
   Match mpls experimental  5
```

Note the **class-default** class in this list. **class-default** is a predefined class; it can be used to match any traffic that doesn't match any other class. You'll read more about this in the next section.

Configuring a Policy Map

After you define the class maps you want to match, you need to associate the class of traffic with a behavior. You create the behavior with the **policy-map** command, which, like **class-map**, puts you in a special submode:

```
vxr12(config)#policy-map ?
  WORD  policy-map name

vxr12(config)#policy-map llq
vxr12(config-pmap)#?
```

```
QoS policy-map configuration commands:
  class          policy criteria
  description    Policy-Map description
  exit           Exit from QoS policy-map configuration mode
  no             Negate or set default values of a command
  rename         Rename this policy-map
```

Under the config-pmap submode, you specify the class you want to match. This puts you in the config-pmap-c submode:

```
vxr12(config)#policy-map llq
vxr12(config-pmap)#class voice
vxr12(config-pmap-c)#?
QoS policy-map class configuration commands:
  bandwidth      Bandwidth
  exit           Exit from QoS class action configuration mode
  no             Negate or set default values of a command
  police         Police
  priority       Strict Scheduling Priority for this Class
  queue-limit    Queue Max Threshold for Tail Drop
  random-detect  Enable Random Early Detection as drop policy
  service-policy Configure QoS Service Policy
  set            Set QoS values
  shape          Traffic Shaping
```

You can do all sorts of things here. Table 6-2 shows the options of interest for the purposes of this chapter.

Table 6-2 **policy-map** *Command Options*

Policy Type	Function	Configuration Syntax
bandwidth	Allocates the configured amount of bandwidth to the matched class. This is CBWFQ.	**bandwidth** {*bandwidth-kbps* | **remaining percent** *percentage* | **percent** *percentage*}
police	A token bucket policer that conforms to RFCs 2697 and 2698.	**police** {**cir** *cir*} [**bc** *conform-burst*] {**pir** *pir*} [**be** *peak-burst*] [**conform-action** *action* [**exceed-action** *action* [**violate-action** *action*]]]
priority	Allocates the configured amount of bandwidth to the matched class. This differs from the bandwidth option in that the priority keyword is LLQ.	**priority** {*bandwidth-kbps* | **percent** *percentage*} [*burst*]
random-detect	Sets the WRED parameters for this policy.	**random-detect** {**prec** *precedence min-threshold max-threshold* [*mark-probability-denominator*]
set	Sets IP Precedence, DSCP, or the EXP value on a packet.	**set** {**ip** {**dscp** *value* | **precedence** *value*} | {**mpls experimental** *value*}}
shape	Shapes the matched traffic to a certain profile.	**shape** {**average** *value* | **max-buffers** *value* | **peak** *value*}

The syntax for all those commands makes them look intimidating, but it's easy. Example 6-2 shows the LLQ policy you read about earlier, using the **voice** class map that's already been defined.

Example 6-2 *LLQ Policy with a Defined* **voice** *Class Map*

```
class-map match-any voice
  match mpls experimental  5
policy-map llq
  class voice
    priority percent 30
```

A predefined class called class-default implicitly matches anything not matched by a specific class; this gives you an easy way to give all unmatched packets the same treatment if you want to. For example, you can expand this class map to cover two types of service: voice and business. Business class is any data that has an MPLS EXP of 3 or 4, that is allocated 60 percent of the link bandwidth, and in which MPLS-based VoIP packets (EXP 5) get 30 percent of the link bandwidth. All other traffic is matched with **class-default**, which gets the remaining 10 percent of link bandwidth. This requires both a new class (to match the EXP 3 and 4 traffic) and a new policy map to define the treatment these classes get (see Example 6-3).

Example 6-3 *Defining a Policy Map with a Business Class*

```
class-map match-all business
  match mpls experimental  3  4
class-map match-all voice
  match mpls experimental  5
policy-map business-and-voice
  class voice
    priority percent 30
  class business
   bandwidth percent 60
  class class-default
   bandwidth percent 10
```

The **show policy-map** command gives you a fair amount of detail about the policy maps defined on a router and the class maps inside them. Example 6-4 shows two policy maps— llq and business-and-voice; the llq policy matches the voice class, and the business-and-voice policy matches the voice and business classes.

Example 6-4 *Displaying Policy Map Information*

```
vxr12#show policy-map
  Policy Map business-and-voice
    Class voice
      Weighted Fair Queuing
            Strict Priority
            Bandwidth 30 (%)
    Class business
```

Example 6-4 *Displaying Policy Map Information (Continued)*

```
              Weighted Fair Queuing
                    Bandwidth 60 (%) Max Threshold 64 (packets)
            Class class-default
              Weighted Fair Queuing
                    Bandwidth 10 (%) Max Threshold 64 (packets)

      Policy Map llq
        Class voice
          Weighted Fair Queuing
                    Strict Priority
                    Bandwidth 30 (%)
```

Configuring a Service Policy

This is the easiest part of the MQC. So far, you've seen a few class definitions and a policy definition. Now all that's left is to apply the policy to an interface, as shown in Example 6-5.

Example 6-5 *Applying a Service Policy to a Router Interface*

```
vxr12(config-if)#service-policy ?
  history  Keep history of QoS metrics
  input    Assign policy-map to the input of an interface
  output   Assign policy-map to the output of an interface

vxr12(config-if)#service-policy out
vxr12(config-if)#service-policy output ?
  WORD  policy-map name

vxr12(config-if)#service-policy output llq
```

That's it. Note that you can have both an inbound and an outbound service policy.

show policy-map interface *interface* gives you details about which policy maps are applied to an interface, as demonstrated in Example 6-6.

Example 6-6 *Determining Which Policy Maps Are Applied to an Interface*

```
vxr12#show policy-map interface pos3/0
 POS3/0

  Service-policy output: llq

    Class-map: voice (match-all)
      0 packets, 0 bytes
      5 minute offered rate 0 bps, drop rate 0 bps
      Match: mpls experimental  5
      Weighted Fair Queuing
        Strict Priority
        Output Queue: Conversation 264
        Bandwidth 30 (%)
        Bandwidth 46500 (kbps) Burst 1162500 (Bytes)
```

continues

Example 6-6 *Determining Which Policy Maps Are Applied to an Interface (Continued)*

```
            (pkts matched/bytes matched) 0/0
            (total drops/bytes drops) 0/0

    Class-map: class-default (match-any)
      21 packets, 15744 bytes
      5 minute offered rate 3000 bps, drop rate 0 bps
      Match: any
```

If you're still not comfortable with either MQC or the underlying QoS concepts such as CBWFQ and LLQ, it is highly recommended that you check out the references in Appendix B.

DiffServ and IP Packets

QoS markings in the IP packet have evolved over time. The IP header has always contained a byte known as the *type of service* (ToS) byte. The 8 bits within this byte have evolved and have been redefined over time. It's a little confusing to start with, because the ToS *byte* has contained multiple things, some of which were called ToS *bits*.

Figure 6-1 shows the first four bytes of the IP header as defined in the original IP header (RFC 791, circa 1981) and as redefined in RC 1349 (circa 1992), RFC 2474 (circa 1998), and RFC 3168 (circa 2001).

Figure 6-1 *Evolution of the First 4 Bytes of the IP Header*

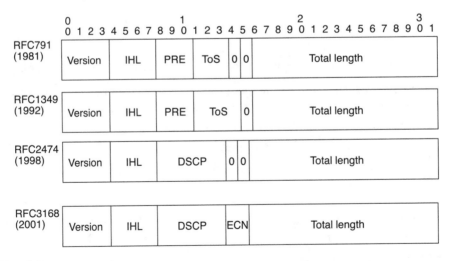

Originally, the IP header had 3 precedence bits and 3 ToS bits, as well as 2 unused bits. The precedence bits were (and still are) used to make various decisions about packet treatment. Precedence values 0 through 5 are designated for user data; precedence values 6 and 7 are reserved to make network control traffic. RFC 1349 reassigned one of the unused bits to the ToS bits, giving the IP header a total of 3 precedence bits, 4 ToS bits, and one unused bit.

Use of ToS bits was never well-defined or well-deployed. The original intent was to be able to mark packets that preferred low delay, high throughput, or high-reliability paths, but service architectures were never designed or built around these bits.

The DiffServ set of RFCs (RFCs 2474 and 2475) redefined the entire ToS byte. The ToS byte now contains 6 bits of information that declare desired packet treatment—DSCP bits. The remaining two bits in the ToS byte are used for a TCP mechanism called Explicit Congestion Notification (ECN), which isn't addressed here but is defined in RFC 3168.

When discussing QoS and the ToS byte, some people use IP Precedence terminology, and others use DiffServ terminology. This chapter uses DiffServ terminology, but we recognize that not everyone is familiar with DiffServ and its code points. If you are familiar with IP Precedence but are new to DiffServ, two things you should know are

- How to map DSCP bits to IP Precedence bits, and vice versa
- What services DSCP offers above and beyond mapping to IP Precedence

The first part is easy—how to map DSCP bits to IP Precedence bits. See Table 6-3.

Table 6-3   *Mapping DSCP Bits to IP Precedence Bits*

IP Precedence (Decimal)	IP Precedence (Bits)	DSCP (Decimal)	DSCP (Bits)
0	000	0	000000
1	001	8	001000
2	010	16	010000
3	011	24	011000
4	100	32	100000
5	101	40	101000
6	110	48	110000
7	111	56	111000

If you're accustomed to dealing with IP Precedence values 0, 1, 2, and 5 (for example), you just need to refer to them as DSCP values 0, 8, 16, and 40. It's easy: To convert IP Precedence to DSCP, just multiply by 8.

The terminology is simple, too. The eight IP Precedence values are called *classes,* and the DSCP bits that map to them (in Table 6-3) are called *Class Selector Code Points* (CSCP). Sometimes you see these class selectors abbreviated as CS (CS1, CS2, CS5, and so on). These are referred to simply as *class selectors;* the term Class Selector Code Point isn't all that widely used.

In addition to the eight class selectors that are defined, RFCs 2597 and 2598 define 13 additional DSCP values—12 Assured Forwarding (AF) values and an Expedited Forwarding (EF) value (see Table 6-4). The decimal values are shown for reference only; almost all discussions of DSCP use the names given in the Name column.

Table 6-4   *Additional DSCP Values in RFCs 2597 and 2598*

Name	DSCP (Decimal)	DSCP (Bits)
Default	0	000000
AF11	10	001010
AF12	12	001100
AF13	14	001110
AF21	18	010010
AF22	20	010100
AF23	22	010110
AF31	26	011010
AF32	28	011100
AF33	30	011110
AF41	34	100010
AF42	36	100100
AF43	38	100110
EF	46	101110

There are 12 AF values, all in the format AFxy, where x is the class number and y is the drop precedence. There are four classes (AF1y through AF4y), each of which has three drop precedences (AFx1 through AFx3). AF is a method of providing low packet loss within a given traffic rate, but it makes minimal guarantees about latency.

EF is a defined behavior that asks for low-delay, low-jitter, low-loss service. EF is typically implemented using some form of LLQ. Only one EF class is defined, because it doesn't make sense to have more than one class whose goals are minimal delay and jitter. These two classes would compete with each other for the same resources.

DiffServ would be extremely simple if it weren't for all the confusing terminology, not all of which is covered here. If you want to learn more about the full set of DiffServ terminology and the DiffServ architecture, see the references in Appendix B.

DiffServ and MPLS Packets

One thing you might have noticed is that there are 6 DSCP bits and only 3 EXP bits. Because only eight possible EXP values and 64 possible DSCP values (21 of which are currently defined) exist, how do you offer DSCP services over MPLS?

On a frame-mode network (as opposed to a cell-mode network), you are stuck with the 3 EXP bits; you need to map multiple DSCP classes to these EXP bits. However, this has operationally not yet proven to be an issue in production networks, because hardly any QoS deployments offer services that can't be provisioned with the 3 MPLS EXP bits.

Work is being done to define something called L-LSPs (Label-Only Inferred PSC LSPs) that will help alleviate this problem. The basic idea behind L-LSPs is that you use both the EXP bits and the label to define different service classes. This is actually how label-controlled ATM MPLS mode with multi-VC works. However, this book doesn't cover cell mode, because, as of this writing, there is no MPLS TE cell mode implementation available.

L-LSPs for frame-mode MPLS aren't discussed in this chapter because they're not yet implemented or even fully defined. See RFC 3270, "Multiprotocol Label Switching (MPLS) Support of Differentiated Services," for more details on how L-LSPs work.

Label Stack Treatment

As mentioned earlier in this book, MPLS has 3 EXP bits in the label header that are used in much the same way as IP Precedence bits or the DSCP CS bits.

You should consider three cases. The first case is when IP packets enter an MPLS network. This is known as the *ip-to-mpls* case, often written as *ip2mpls*.

The second case is when packets that already have one or more labels have their label stack manipulated. This is known as the *mpls-to-mpls* case, or *mpls2mpls*.

The third case is when packets exit an MPLS network and have all their labels removed. This is known as the *mpls-to-ip* path, or *mpls2ip*.

ip2mpls

Packets entering an MPLS network have one or more labels applied to an underlying IP packet. This is an *ip2mpls push,* because labels are pushed onto an unlabeled IP packet.

By default, when Cisco IOS Software pushes labels onto an IP packet, the most significant bits in the DiffServ field (the IP Precedence bits) are copied to the EXP field of all imposed labels.

Figure 6-2 shows an ip2mpls push.

Figure 6-2   *ip2mpls Push*

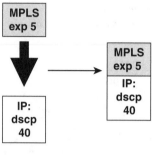

ip2mpls push

mpls2mpls

Similarly, when a label is pushed onto a packet that already has a label, the EXP value from the underlying label is copied into the EXP field of the newly imposed label. This is known as the *mpls2mpls* path.

Three actions are possible in the mpls2mpls path:

- **Push**—An mpls2mpls push is when one or more labels are added to an already-labeled packet.

- **Swap**—An mpls2mpls swap is when the topmost label on a packet is swapped for another label.

- **Pop**—An mpls2mpls pop is when one or more labels are removed from a packet, but at least one label is left.

Figure 6-3 illustrates these three cases.

Figure 6-3   *mpls2mpls Operations*

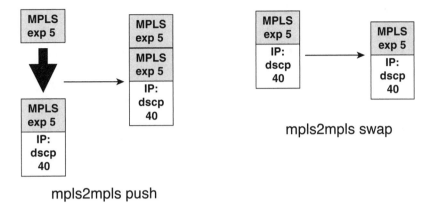

mpls2mpls push

mpls2mpls swap

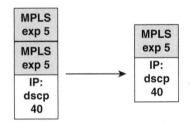

mpls2mpls pop

mpls2ip

Packets leaving an MPLS network have their label stack removed; this is known as the *mpls-to-ip* operation, or *mpls2ip*. The only operation in the mpls2ip case is a pop, as illustrated in Figure 6-4.

Figure 6-4   *mpls2ip Pop*

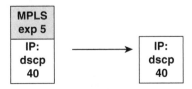

mpls2ip pop

EXP and DSCP Are Independent

As you can see, the default Cisco IOS Software behavior is to propagate the IP Precedence bits (the three most significant DSCP bits) through your network.

NOTE   To avoid confusion and to make things simpler, this chapter calls the bits that are copied from the IP header to the EXP field the "IP Precedence bits." This is deliberate; there is no DiffServ term that means "only the three most significant bits of the DSCP field." There are CSs, but to talk about copying the DSCP CS to EXP isn't accurate, because CS definitions cover all six of the DSCP bits. So, when you see text such as "IP Precedence is copied to EXP," this reminds you that only the three most significant DSCP bits are copied to the MPLS EXP field.

Two things interact to define the basic EXP and IP Precedence interaction:

- Cisco IOS Software allows you to set the EXP value on a label independently of any IP or EXP values that might already be set.

- In both the ip2mpls and mpls2mpls pop cases, nothing is done to the lower-level packet when labels are removed.

These two facts, when considered together, mean that if you set a packet's EXP values differently from the underlying IP packet, or if you change EXP values on the top of a label stack midway through your network, these changes are not propagated downward. Figure 6-5 shows this in action, by default, in both the mpls2mpls pop and mpls2ip.

Figure 6-5   *Default EXP Treatment When Popping*

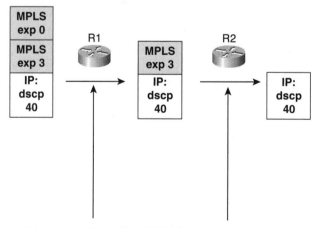

Topmost label removed, modified EXP value not propagated downward

Generally, this is acceptable. However, you might want to do things differently in some cases.

In Figure 6-5, you might want to preserve the fact that the outermost label has an EXP value of 0, even after that outermost label is removed and the underlying label (with an EXP of 3) is exposed.

This means copying the value of EXP 0 *down* and overwriting the value of EXP 3 in the underlying label. The motivation and mechanics of this scenario are explained in the upcoming "Tunnel Modes" section.

Per-Hop Behaviors in the ip2mpls and mpls2ip Cases

Another thing to consider is how your packets are treated if the outermost label on a packet has its EXP value set to something other than the EXP or IP Precedence underneath it. If you push a label of EXP 0 onto a packet with EXP 3 (or IP Precedence 3), how do you treat the packet as it leaves the box? Is the packet given PHB treatment as if it has EXP 0, or as if it has IP Precedence 3/DSCP 24? Figure 6-6 illustrates this question.

Figure 6-6   *PHB Decision on Label Push*

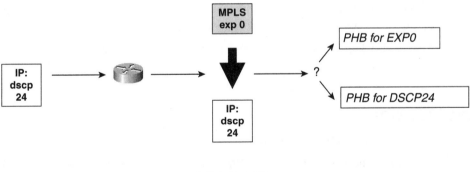

ip2mpls push

As it turns out, the case of label imposition is an easy one. The router doing the imposition always treats the packet according to the new outgoing PHB indicator. In Figure 6-6, this means that the packet is given PHB treatment for EXP 0.

The mpls2mpls and mpls2ip pop cases are not as straightforward. Figure 6-7 illustrates these cases.

Figure 6-7 *PHB Decision on Label Pop*

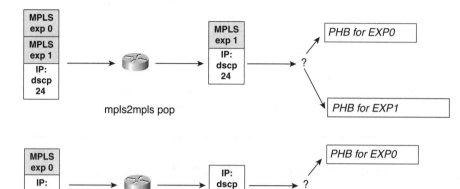

In some cases, you will want the resulting packet to receive treatment according to the label that was removed, and in other cases, you will want the resulting packet to receive treatment according to the outermost indicator in whatever remains after the POP (MPLS EXP in the case of mpls2mpls and IP DSCP in the case of mpls2ip).

All these label operations can be confusing. The next section aims to unify them and make things easier to understand.

Tunnel Modes

So far, you've seen two independent questions:

- How is the queuing indicator (IP Precedence or MPLS EXP) propagated up and down the label stack and upon exit from the MPLS network?

- In the mpls2mpls and mpls2ip pop cases, which PHB does the resulting packet get?

This section covers reasons why you might want to enforce different behaviors, as well as the mechanisms being defined to standardize those behaviors.

Currently, a set of behaviors are being defined that give you a set of mechanisms to control EXP values in various scenarios. These mechanisms are called *tunnel modes*. Three tunnel modes are defined in RFC 3270:

- Uniform

- Short-Pipe

- Pipe

These modes are defined in the same IETF draft that defines L-LSP—"MPLS Support of Differentiated Services" (*draft-ietf-mpls-diff-ext*), which might well be an RFC by the time you read this. Because this is a developing technology, this chapter does not cover CLI commands for configuring tunnel modes. However, it's worth understanding the concepts behind tunnel modes so that you can design your network accordingly. If you're interested in the current state of affairs regarding tunnel mode in Cisco IOS Software, check CCO for availability.

Uniform Mode

In Uniform mode, any changes made to the EXP value of the topmost label on a label stack are propagated both *upward* as new labels are added and *downward* as labels are removed. The idea here is that the network is a single DiffServ domain, so any changes made to the EXP values on the MPLS packet in transit are supposed to be applied to all labels underneath the packet, as well as to the underlying IP packet.

The rules for Uniform mode are as follows:

- On imposition, copy the DSCP/EXP upward.
- On disposition, copy the removed EXP downward to both IP packet and MPLS (if stacked).

The question of deciding which PHB is applied on label disposition is irrelevant; no matter when you apply the PHB according to the received EXP value or the outgoing EXP/DSCP value, they're both the same.

Table 6-5 shows the EXP treatment in Uniform mode.

Table 6-5   *EXP Manipulation in Uniform Mode*

	Push	Swap	Pop
ip2mpls	Copies the IP Precedence into the newly imposed label.	N/A	N/A
mpls2mpls	Copies the received EXP into the newly imposed EXP.	Copies the received EXP into the newly imposed EXP.	Copies the removed EXP into the newly revealed label.
mpls2ip	N/A	N/A	Copies the removed EXP into the DSCP.

Figure 6-8 illustrates a case where a new label is pushed onto the stack with EXP 0 and, as this label is popped off, the underlying label (previously EXP 3) is changed to EXP 0.

Figure 6-8 *Uniform Mode Packet Handling*

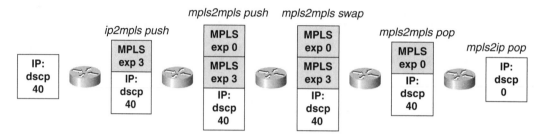

You would apply Uniform mode when both the IP and the MPLS network are in the same DiffServ domain. You use Uniform mode if you want a change in EXP somewhere in your network to affect how the IP packet is treated after it exits the MPLS portion of the network.

Short-Pipe Mode

Short-Pipe mode is useful for ISPs implementing their own QoS policy independent of their customer's QoS policy. The IP Precedence bits on an IP packet are propagated upward into the label stack as labels are added. When labels are swapped, the existing EXP value is kept. If the topmost EXP value is changed, this change is propagated downward only within the label stack, not to the IP packet.

Table 6-6 shows EXP treatment in Short-Pipe mode.

Table 6-6 *EXP Manipulation in Short-Pipe Mode*

	Push	**Swap**	**Pop**
ip2mpls	Copies the IP Precedence into the EXP.	N/A	N/A
mpls2mpls	Copies the received EXP into the newly imposed EXP.	Copies the received EXP into the newly imposed EXP.	Copies the removed EXP into the newly revealed EXP.
mpls2ip	N/A	N/A	Doesn't modify the DSCP; selects the PHB based on the DSCP.

Figure 6-9 illustrates this.

Figure 6-9 *Short-Pipe Mode Packet Handling*

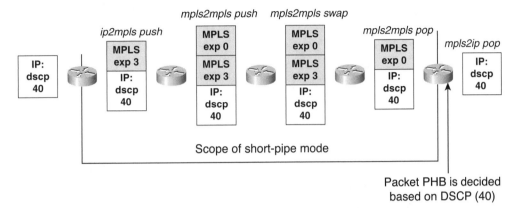

The only difference between Uniform and Short-Pipe mode is that any changes to the label stack EXP are propagated throughout the MPLS network, but—in Short-Pipe mode—the underlying IP packet DSCP is not touched.

What about PHBs? There are two rules in Short-Pipe mode:

- In the mpls2mpls pop case, the received EXP is propagated downward, so the question of which EXP value decides the PHB is moot.

- In the mpls2ip pop case, the PHB is decided based on the DSCP on the IP packet that's revealed after the label stack is removed.

The assumption in Short-Pipe mode is that the link between the provider and the customer is where the mpls2ip processing happens. Because the customer is paying for the link between the provider and the customer, the customer is the one in charge of the queuing on that link, so the outgoing packet in the mpls2ip case is queued according to the DSCP the customer sent the packet into the network with.

Pipe Mode

Pipe mode is just like Short-Pipe mode, except the PHB on the mpls2ip link is selected based on the removed EXP value rather than the recently-exposed DSCP value. The underlying DSCP in the packet is not touched, but the mpls2ip path does not consider the DSCP for queuing on the egress link.

Table 6-7 shows EXP treatment in Pipe mode.

Table 6-7   *EXP Manipulation in Pipe Mode*

	Push	Swap	Pop
ip2mpls	Copies the IP Precedence into the EXP.	N/A	N/A
mpls2mpls	Copies the received EXP into the newly imposed EXP.	Copies the received EXP into the newly imposed EXP.	Copies the removed EXP into the newly revealed EXP.
mpls2ip	N/A	N/A	Doesn't modify DSCP; selects the PHB based on the EXP.

Figure 6-10 illustrates this.

Figure 6-10   *Pipe Mode Packet Handling*

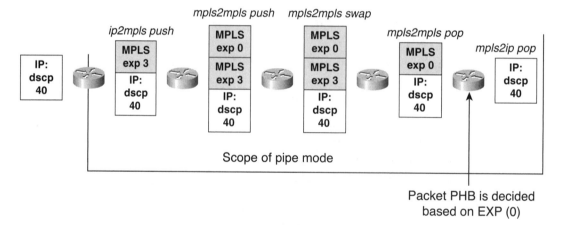

When might you want to use Pipe mode? Pipe mode is useful if the ISP is the one that decides what the PHB selection is on the link immediately exiting the MPLS network. Typically, this is in a managed CPE scenario, in which the ISP does not want to extend MPLS all the way out to the CPE but wants PHB selection control over the link to the CPE.

DiffServ-Aware Traffic Engineering (DS-TE)

So far, you've seen that DiffServ service with MPLS packets is basically the same thing as with IP packets, with a few differences in configuration. Overall, MPLS packets with a given EXP setting are treated just like IP packets with a given IP Precedence setting.

There's more to MPLS TE and DiffServ than just applying IP mechanisms to MPLS packets, though. The rest of this book spends a great deal of time showing you that there's benefit in making a headend resource-aware, because the headend can then intelligently pick paths through the network for its traffic to take. However, after you add QoS, you're almost back at square one. Things are better than they were—you can steer IP traffic away from the IGP shortest path in a resource-aware fashion. What you can't do is steer traffic *per QoS*. If you have traffic destined for a particular router, all that traffic follows the same path, regardless of the DSCP/EXP settings on that packet.

To expand on this point further, suppose you are a service provider offering four classes of service: Low latency, Gold, Silver, and Bronze. Low latency being self-explanatory, suppose Gold is defined as guaranteed delivery. Edge QoS is applied to mark EXP bits to differentiate your low-latency traffic from Gold and other traffic. Now, if the forwarding is based on IGP best path alone, all your traffic, regardless of what class it belongs to, is forwarded to a downstream neighbor dictated by your routing table. Even if you use MPLS TE and **mpls traffic-eng autoroute announce**, you are still limited by the routing table and how it decides to forward traffic.

The problem with this implementation is that when you have a congested link at a downstream node along the forwarding path, even though most low-latency traffic might get through, some of the Gold traffic might get dropped. This congestion knowledge is localized at the downstream node and is not propagated back to the edge devices that send traffic down that path. As a result, your edges continue to send traffic to the same downstream router that continues to drop some of your Gold traffic. What is needed to fix this situation is *per-class call admission control*—and this is exactly what you get when you combine DiffServ and TE. Surprisingly enough, this combination is called DS-TE.

This might lead you to believe that all you need to do is mark the EXP bits according to your QoS policy and let them ride over TE tunnels, conquering all the problems.

Not quite. The problem with TE, as it's been discussed so far, is that it doesn't do admission control on a per-QoS class basis.

TE certainly offers call admission control in addition to the PHB offered by DiffServ. This takes care of the first problem—sending more traffic down a certain path than there is available bandwidth—while queuing your higher-priority traffic ahead of your low-priority traffic.

A second problem is that there might be contention between different high-priority traffic streams. For example, if you sold two voice pipes to two customers, both with a low-latency requirement, if you forward both streams down the same path which is experiencing congestion, both streams might be affected. Remember, for voice, it is better to drop a call than to get degraded service. So how does DS-TE solve this problem?

DS-TE allows you to advertise more than one pool of available resources for a given link—a global pool and things called *subpools*. A subpool is a subset of link bandwidth that is available for a specific purpose.

The current DS-TE implementation allows you to advertise one subpool. Think of this as a pool with which you can advertise resources for a separate queue. The recommended use of the DS-TE subpool is to advertise bandwidth in your low-latency queue on a link, but you can do whatever you like with this subpool. The rest of this chapter assumes that you are advertising LLQ space using the subpool.

It's important to understand that DS-TE and its subpools are, like the rest of MPLS TE, control-plane mechanisms only. If you reserve 10 Mbps of global bandwidth, it's probably not a good idea to send 100 Mbps down that LSP. DS-TE behaves the same way. Building a separate control-plane reservation for a subpool doesn't mean that any special queuing policy is enforced as a result of this reservation. The actual queuing behavior at every hop is still controlled by regular DiffServ mechanisms such as LLQ; what DS-TE buys you is purely the ability to reserve queue bandwidth, rather than just link bandwidth, in the control plane. This ability lets you build TE-LSPs that specifically reserve subpool bandwidth and carry only LLQ traffic, and in effect build a second network on top of the one you already have. You have a network of physical interfaces and global pools and a network of subpools. This lets you get better resource utilization out of your network.

Going back to the example of two voice streams that might contend for the same low-latency bandwidth along the same path, this would not happen with DS-TE. When you try to build the second LSP requesting low-latency bandwidth and that bandwidth is not available along a certain path, the LSP is not signaled. If you used dynamic path options to configure your DS-TE tunnels, using CSPF on the router might find you an alternative path that meets the subpool reservation.

But how do you configure all this?

Configuring DS-TE

The best way to understand DS-TE is to see it in action. DS-TE is easy to configure. The configuration pieces provided in this section are for a 7200 series router with an OC-3 interface. The OC-3 interface is advertising 150 MB of global RSVP bandwidth. 45 Mbps (30 percent) of this is subpool bandwidth. The OC-3 also has 45 Mbps configured in a low-latency queue. Other configurations vary by platform and according to the goal you're trying to achieve.

There are five pieces to configuring DS-TE:

- Per-link subpool bandwidth availability
- Per-link scheduling
- Headend subpool bandwidth requirements

- Headend tunnel admission control
- Tunnel preemption

Per-Link Subpool Bandwidth Availability

On each hop that you want to advertise a subpool, you configure the following command:

```
ip rsvp bandwidth interface-kbps sub-pool kbps
```

This is merely an extension of the **ip rsvp bandwidth** command discussed in earlier chapters. The *interface-kbps* parameter is the amount of bandwidth (in Kbps) on the interface to be reserved. The range is 1 to 10,000,000. **sub-pool** *kbps* is the amount of bandwidth (in Kbps) on the interface to be reserved as a portion of the total. The range is from 1 to the value of *interface-kbps*.

For this specific example of an OC-3 with 150 Mbps in the global pool and 45 Mbps in the subpool, the necessary configuration is as follows:

```
ip rsvp bandwidth 150000 sub-pool 45000
```

Per-Link Scheduling

Advertising a subpool in DS-TE doesn't change any packet queuing behavior on an interface. You need to configure the forwarding-plane LLQ mechanisms in addition to the control-plane subpool mechanisms. The subpool advertisement and LLQ capacity are usually set to the same value, but you can set them differently if you want to do fancy things such as oversubscription or undersubscription.

Per-link scheduling is just whatever LLQ mechanism exists in your platform. With MQC, the **priority** keyword builds a low-latency queue. The MQC LLQ configuration for this example is as follows:

```
class-map match-all voice
  match mpls experimental  5
policy-map llq
  class voice
    priority percent 30
interface POS3/0
  service-policy output llq
```

Headend Subpool Bandwidth Requirements

On the tunnel headend, you use the following command:

```
tunnel mpls traffic-eng bandwidth sub-pool kbps
```

This is the same thing as the **tunnel mpls traffic-eng bandwidth** *kbps* command that was covered earlier in this book, except that you are telling the headend to do its path calculation and bandwidth reservation based on the advertised subpool bandwidth.

You are allowed to have only one type of reservation per tunnel. If you try to configure a tunnel with the command **tunnel mpls traffic-eng bandwidth** followed by the command **tunnel mpls traffic-eng bandwidth sub-pool**, the **sub-pool** command overwrites the global pool command.

Headend Tunnel Admission Control

The next piece is controlling what traffic goes down the tunnel. There are three steps to this:

Step 1   Make sure no more traffic enters your network than you have sold.

Step 2   Make sure that the only traffic to enter the DS-TE tunnel is traffic that belongs there.

Step 3   Make sure your TE tunnel reservation accurately matches your traffic requirements.

The first step is a generic DiffServ architecture component; it has nothing to do with MPLS TE. You can't have any kind of QoS guarantees if you provision your network for a certain amount of traffic and then send to that network far more traffic than you have provisioned for.

The second step is where things start getting TE-specific. The general idea is that if you've decided that your DS-TE subpool is for EXP 5 traffic, you send only EXP 5 traffic down the DS-TE tunnel. Why? Because if you send nonsubpool traffic down a DS-TE tunnel, this traffic interferes with other traffic at every hop. Let's say you have a tunnel for 10 Mbps of subpool bandwidth that you're mapping to a low-latency queue for EXP 5 traffic. If you send 100 Mbps of EXP 0 traffic down this DS-TE tunnel, that EXP 0 traffic is put into the same queue as other EXP 0 traffic, but it is not reserved from the network. You'll read more about this in the section "Forwarding DS-TE Traffic Down a Tunnel."

The reason for the third step should be obvious: If you don't reserve bandwidth in accordance with what you're actually sending, and your reservations are designed to track LLQ capacity at every hop, you run the risk of overloading the LLQ and providing poor service. One way to make this adjustment is to size your DS-TE tunnels based on the amount of DS-TE tunnel bandwidth you have provisioned for. The other way is to use something such as auto-bandwidth (see Chapter 5, "Forwarding Traffic Down Tunnels") to adjust tunnel size based not on the provisioned load, but on the real-life traffic load.

Tunnel Preemption

The last thing you have to do is make sure that the subpool tunnel can preempt nonsubpool tunnels. This is done with the command **tunnel mpls traffic-eng priority**, which was covered in Chapter 3, "Information Distribution." Why do you have to allow DS-TE tunnels to preempt non-DS-TE tunnels? Because of the way subpool bandwidth is advertised. The subpool is, as the name implies, a *subset* of the global bandwidth pool on an interface, not a separate bandwidth pool. If you don't allow the DS-TE LSP to preempt a global LSP, the global LSP can reserve bandwidth that would then no longer be available for the subpool.

If the subpool bandwidth were advertised as a *separate* bandwidth pool, rather than as a *subset* of existing bandwidth, you could easily end up with bandwidth fragmentation, as the following example shows.

If you have a link configured with **ip rsvp bandwidth 150000 sub-pool 45000**, this means that you are advertising that you have 150 Mbps (150,000 Kbps) of global reservable bandwidth on the link, and 45 Mbps of that 150 Mbps is subpool bandwidth. At this point, the link is advertising the output shown in Example 6-7.

Example 6-7 *Available Bandwidth Before Any Reservations Have Been Made*

```
vxr12#show mpls traffic-eng topology 192.168.1.12

IGP Id: 0168.0001.0012.00, MPLS TE Id:192.168.1.12 Router Node  id 2
    link[0 ]:Nbr IGP Id: 0168.0001.0001.00, nbr_node_id:3, gen:1
        frag_id 0, Intf Address:2.3.4.12, Nbr Intf Address:2.3.4.1
        TE metric:10, IGP metric:10, attribute_flags:0x0
        physical_bw: 155000 (kbps), max_reservable_bw_global: 150000 (kbps)
        max_reservable_bw_sub: 45000 (kbps)


                                    Global Pool      Sub Pool
                     Total Allocated Reservable      Reservable
                     BW (kbps)       BW (kbps)       BW (kbps)
                     --------------- -----------     ----------
        bw[0]:             0             150000          45000
        bw[1]:             0             150000          45000
        bw[2]:             0             150000          45000
        bw[3]:             0             150000          45000
        bw[4]:             0             150000          45000
        bw[5]:             0             150000          45000
        bw[6]:             0             150000          45000
        bw[7]:             0             150000          45000
```

This shows a link with no reservations across it, a global pool of 150 Mbps, and a subpool of 45 Mbps.

Let's send three reservations across this link: a reservation for 60 Mbps from the global pool, 20 Mbps from the subpool, and 50 Mbps for the global pool, in that order. After the first reservation, the router advertises the bandwidth displayed in the output of **show mpls traffic-eng topology**, as shown in Example 6-8. All LSPs are set up with the default priority of 7.

Example 6-8 *Available Bandwidth with 60 Mbps Reserved*

```
vxr12#show mpls traffic-eng topology 192.168.1.12

IGP Id: 0168.0001.0012.00, MPLS TE Id:192.168.1.12 Router Node  id 2
    link[0 ]:Nbr IGP Id: 0168.0001.0001.00, nbr_node_id:3, gen:3
        frag_id 0, Intf Address:2.3.4.12, Nbr Intf Address:2.3.4.1
```

continues

Example 6-8 *Available Bandwidth with 60 Mbps Reserved (Continued)*

```
        TE metric:10, IGP metric:10, attribute_flags:0x0
        physical_bw: 155000 (kbps), max_reservable_bw_global: 150000 (kbps)
        max_reservable_bw_sub: 45000 (kbps)

                                Global Pool      Sub Pool
                 Total Allocated Reservable       Reservable
                 BW (kbps)       BW (kbps)        BW (kbps)
                 --------------- -----------      ----------
        bw[0]:          0          150000             45000
        bw[1]:          0          150000             45000
        bw[2]:          0          150000             45000
        bw[3]:          0          150000             45000
        bw[4]:          0          150000             45000
        bw[5]:          0          150000             45000
        bw[6]:          0          150000             45000
        bw[7]:      60000           90000             45000
```

This is because 60 Mbps was reserved from the global pool (at the default setup and holding priorities of 7/7), leaving 90 Mbps available on the link. Of that 90 Mbps, 45 Mbps can be reserved as subpool bandwidth should anybody want it.

The next reservation to come across takes 20 Mbps from the subpool. This means that the available bandwidth on the interface is now as advertised in Example 6-9.

Example 6-9 *Available Bandwidth with an Additional 20 Mbps of Subpool Bandwidth Reserved*

```
vxr12#show mpls traffic-eng topology 192.168.1.12

IGP Id: 0168.0001.0012.00, MPLS TE Id:192.168.1.12 Router Node  id 2
     link[0 ]:Nbr IGP Id: 0168.0001.0001.00, nbr_node_id:3, gen:4
        frag_id 0, Intf Address:2.3.4.12, Nbr Intf Address:2.3.4.1
        TE metric:10, IGP metric:10, attribute_flags:0x0
        physical_bw: 155000 (kbps), max_reservable_bw_global: 150000 (kbps)
        max_reservable_bw_sub: 45000 (kbps)

                                Global Pool      Sub Pool
                 Total Allocated Reservable       Reservable
                 BW (kbps)       BW (kbps)        BW (kbps)
                 --------------- -----------      ----------
        bw[0]:          0          150000             45000
        bw[1]:          0          150000             45000
        bw[2]:          0          150000             45000
        bw[3]:          0          150000             45000
        bw[4]:          0          150000             45000
        bw[5]:          0          150000             45000
        bw[6]:          0          150000             45000
        bw[7]:      80000           70000             25000
```

The available bandwidth on the interface is an important point to understand. 20 Mbps of additional bandwidth is reserved from the available link bandwidth. This brings the total allocated bandwidth from 60 Mbps to 80 Mbps and decreases the total available link bandwidth from 90 Mbps to 70 Mbps. It just so happens that the 20 Mbps reserved was taken from the subpool, which means that the available subpool bandwidth is now 25 Mbps. This is because the subpool is considered a subset of the global pool, rather than a whole separate pool.

The third reservation for 50 Mbps from the global pool brings the available link bandwidth down to that advertised in Example 6-10.

Example 6-10 *Available Bandwidth with an Additional 50 Mbps of Subpool Bandwidth Reserved*

```
vxr12#show mpls traffic-eng topology 192.168.1.12

IGP Id: 0168.0001.0012.00, MPLS TE Id:192.168.1.12 Router Node  id 2
     link[0 ]:Nbr IGP Id: 0168.0001.0001.00, nbr_node_id:3, gen:5
          frag_id 0, Intf Address:2.3.4.12, Nbr Intf Address:2.3.4.1
          TE metric:10, IGP metric:10, attribute_flags:0x0
          physical_bw: 155000 (kbps), max_reservable_bw_global: 150000 (kbps)
          max_reservable_bw_sub: 45000 (kbps)


                                       Global Pool      Sub Pool
                      Total Allocated  Reservable       Reservable
                      BW (kbps)        BW (kbps)        BW (kbps)
                      ---------------  -----------      ----------
            bw[0]:               0        150000            45000
            bw[1]:               0        150000            45000
            bw[2]:               0        150000            45000
            bw[3]:               0        150000            45000
            bw[4]:               0        150000            45000
            bw[5]:               0        150000            45000
            bw[6]:               0        150000            45000
            bw[7]:          130000         20000            20000
```

The total allocated bandwidth is 130 Mbps (60 Mbps + 20 Mbps + 50 Mbps). 20 Mbps of that 130 Mbps is allocated from the subpool, and 110 Mbps (60 Mbps + 50 Mbps) is allocated from the rest of the global pool.

If you ponder this for a while, making the subpool a subset of the global pool rather than a whole separate pool makes sense. If the global pool and the subpool bandwidth were segregated, instead of advertising a pool of 150 Mbps available bandwidth (45 Mbps of which is in a subpool), the router would advertise a 105 Mbps pool and a 45 Mbps pool.

If you then have the same reservations, in the same order as before, the bandwidth reservations and availability look like what is shown in Table 6-8.

Table 6-8 *What If You Advertised Global and Subpool as Separate Pools?*

Reservation	Global Available Bandwidth	Subpool Available Bandwidth
No reservations	105 Mbps	45 Mbps
60 Mbps global	45 Mbps	45 Mbps
20 Mbps subpool	45 Mbps	25 Mbps
50 Mbps global	?????	??????

But what about the third reservation for 50 Mbps from the global bandwidth pool? It fails to get through, even though a total of 70 Mbps of bandwidth (45 + 25) is available.

Advertising DS-TE bandwidth as a subpool rather than as a separate pool means that you can reserve *up to* 45 Mbps for the subpool, but if it's not in use, other nonsubpool tunnels can use it.

If you want subpool tunnels to be able to take up to 45 Mbps of bandwidth no matter what else is reserved on the link, the subpool tunnels need to be able to preempt other tunnels on the link. However, see the section in Chapter 9, "Network Design with MPLS TE," titled, "The Packing Problem," before you start messing with tunnel priorities.

Forwarding DS-TE Traffic Down a Tunnel

Chapter 5 covered three different methods of forwarding traffic down a tunnel:

- Static routes
- Policy-based routing (PBR)
- Autoroute

How do you forward traffic down a DS-TE tunnel? The only thing different between regular TE tunnels and DS-TE tunnels is the subpool from which they reserve bandwidth. However, there are some things you need to think about when trying to get traffic to a DS-TE tunnel.

All three of these methods work the same way on DS-TE tunnels as they do on regular TE tunnels. Out of the three, autoroute is generally the easiest method to use; it requires only one command on the headend, and all traffic destined for or behind the tail is sent down the tunnel.

The problem with autoroute and DS-TE is that autoroute is not always granular enough to do what you need to do. If you have both TE and DS-TE tunnels to the same destination, you can't autoroute on them both and have them do what you probably want.

Consider the topology shown in Figure 6-11.

Figure 6-11 *Topology in Which You Can't Enable Autoroute on a DS-TE Tunnel*

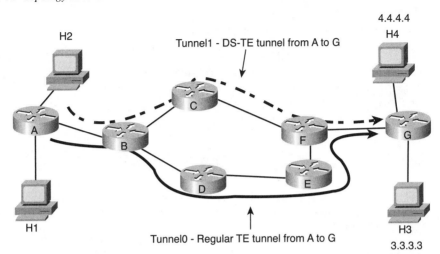

In Figure 6-11, H2 has VoIP traffic destined for H4, and H1 has regular data traffic destined for H3. This network has two TE tunnels. Tunnel0 is a regular TE tunnel that follows the path A→B→D→E→F→G, and Tunnel1 is a DS-TE tunnel from A to G that follows the path A→B→C→F→G. You want all traffic for H4 to go down Tunnel1 and all other traffic to go down Tunnel0.

What happens if you enable autoroute on both tunnels? Both H3 and H4 become reachable over *both* TE tunnels, as shown in Example 6-11.

Example 6-11 *H3 and H4 Can Be Reached Over Both TE Tunnels*

```
RouterA#show ip route 3.3.3.3
Routing entry for 3.3.3.3/32
  Known via "isis", distance 115, metric 50, type level-2
  Redistributing via isis
  Last update from 192.168.1.1 on Tunnel0, 00:00:19 ago
  Routing Descriptor Blocks:
  * 192.168.1.1, from 192.168.1.1, via Tunnel1
      Route metric is 50, traffic share count is 10
    192.168.1.1, from 192.168.1.1, via Tunnel0
      Route metric is 50, traffic share count is 1

RouterA#show ip route 4.4.4.4
Routing entry for 4.4.4.4/32
  Known via "isis", distance 115, metric 50, type level-2
  Redistributing via isis
  Last update from 192.168.1.1 on Tunnel0, 00:00:31 ago
  Routing Descriptor Blocks:
  * 192.168.1.1, from 192.168.1.1, via Tunnel1
      Route metric is 50, traffic share count is 10
    192.168.1.1, from 192.168.1.1, via Tunnel0
      Route metric is 50, traffic share count is 1
```

This is not what you want. The only way to solve this problem is with a static route—something like this:

```
ip route 3.3.3.3 255.255.255.255 Tunnel1
```

This gives you the routing table shown in Example 6-12.

Example 6-12 *Routing Table for Router A After Configuring a Static Route*

```
RouterA#show ip route 3.3.3.3
Routing entry for 3.3.3.3/32
  Known via "static", distance 1, metric 0 (connected)
  Routing Descriptor Blocks:
  * directly connected, via Tunnel1
      Route metric is 0, traffic share count is 1
```

But what happens if you have lots of hosts that receive VoIP traffic? Static routes are a reasonable solution for a small-scale problem, but managing large numbers of static routes can be a nightmare.

You can try to solve the static route problem by aggregating your VoIP devices into shared subnets. Instead of 200 VoIP devices and a /32 route for each device, number all the VoIP devices into the same /24. Then you have only one static route.

Even then, you still have the same problem of scale. It's not always possible to summarize all your devices so neatly. Plus, you need to consider the issue of multiple sources. Consider the network shown in Figure 6-12.

Figure 6-12 *Topology in Which You Can't Enable Autoroute on a DS-TE Tunnel*

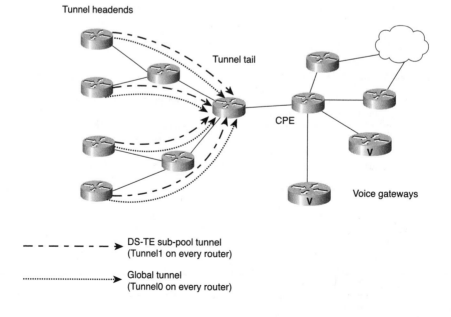

Figure 6-12 shows four routers that each have two TE tunnels terminating on the same tail node. Behind the tunnel tail is a CPE router, behind the CPE are two VoIP gateways and two routers, and behind the two routers is the rest of the customer network. You can't enable autoroute on the headends, because you only want to send traffic to the VoIP gateways down the subpool tunnels. Managing this network with static routes is messy. You need to have two static routes on each tunnel headend, and every time you add a new VoIP gateway, you need to add static routes to every headend.

Luckily, you can more easily manage this routing. You can use recursive routes and route maps to manipulate the next hop of a given route based on whether the route is for a VoIP gateway. The procedure is as follows:

Step 1 Configure a second loopback address on the tunnel tail.

Step 2 Have the CPE advertise separate routes for the VoIP routers via BGP to the tunnel tail, with a different community for the VoIP routes.

Step 3 The tunnel tail changes the next hop for the VoIP routes to be its second loopback address.

Step 4 All the tunnel headends point to a route to the second loopback address down their DS-TE subpool tunnels.

Step 5 Recursive routing ensures that the forwarding works properly.

Figure 6-13 illustrates this scenario.

Figure 6-13 *Topology in Which You Can't Enable Autoroute on a DS-TE Tunnel*

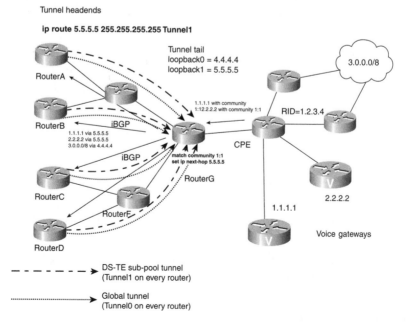

Figure 6-13 is pretty busy, so Example 6-13 shows the necessary configuration snippets.

Example 6-13 *Key Configurations for the Network Shown in Figure 6-13*

```
On the CPE:
router bgp 100
 neighbor 4.4.4.4 route-map setcom-voice out

route-map setcom-voice
  match ip address 101
  set community 1:1

access-list 101 permit ip host 1.1.1.1 host 255.255.255.255

On RouterG (the tunnel tail)
router bgp 100
  neighbor 1.2.3.4 route-map set-nh in

route-map set-nh
 match community 1
 set ip next-hop 5.5.5.5

ip community-list 1 permit 1:1

On Routers A, B, C, and D
ip route 5.5.5.5 255.255.255.255 Tunnel1
```

Doing things this way means that the only one who needs to know which routers are VoIP routers and which aren't is the CPE; the administration of any static configuration is limited to the CPE. As more VoIP and CPE routers are added off RouterG, the tunnel headends don't need to change anything. As more tunnel tails are added, the tunnel headends need to add only a single static route per DS-TE tunnel to that tail.

You can also be more flexible than using a community. RouterG can change the next hop based on any criteria, because BGP is flexible in what it supports. Rather than a community, you could change the next hop based on the destination AS, for example, or perhaps a transit AS. The choice is up to you.

Summary

This chapter covered several things—a brief look at the DiffServ architecture and its interaction with IP and MPLS packets, the MQC, and DS-TE.

Many tools are available to help you build QoS policies on your network. Here are the two main points to take away from this chapter:

- Applying the DiffServ architecture to MPLS packets is not much different from applying it to IP packets.

- DS-TE helps you solve the same problem for QoS that "regular" MPLS TE solves for link bandwidth, and in the same manner.

You can put as much or as little work as you like into your QoS policy. Whatever you can do with IP, you can do with MPLS. The resource awareness and source-based forwarding that MPLS TE gives you let you do even more with QoS in your network.

This chapter covers the following topics:

- The Need for Fast Reroute
- What Is Protection?
- Link Protection
- Node Protection
- Path Protection
- Advanced Protection Issues

CHAPTER 7

Protection and Restoration

Networks fail. More precisely, pieces of networks fail. Lots of things can cause something to fail in a network. They run the gamut from loosely connected cables to fiber cuts. Router crashes are another form of failure.

From a router's perspective, there are two kinds of failures in a network—link failures and node failures. It doesn't matter what the underlying cause is. A link failure can be a fiber cut, an ADM problem, or any number of other things. A node failure can be anything from a power problem to a router crash to a router being taken down for scheduled maintenance. No matter what the cause, all failures are either a link failure or a node failure.

It is highly desirable to reduce the negative effects of such failures, such as packet loss. As it turns out, MPLS TE and its ability to steer traffic away from the IGP-derived shortest path helps mitigate packet loss associated with link or node failures in the network. MPLS TE's ability to do this is known as Fast Reroute (FRR) or simply MPLS TE Protection.

This chapter covers the aspects of MPLS TE that deal with fast recovery from failures— what they are, how they work, and how you can configure them using Cisco IOS Software.

The Need for Fast Reroute

Network administrators have been dealing with link and node failures for as long as there have been networks. It has traditionally fallen to the Interior Gateway Protocol (IGP) to quickly route around failures, converging on the remaining topology. However, there are a few things the IGP doesn't do that well when it comes to convergence:

- In a large network, your IGP can take quite a few seconds to converge; until the entire network is converged, there is packet loss. It's not uncommon to see 5 to 10 seconds of packet loss when a core link flaps in a large network.

- A link failure can lead to congestion in some parts of the network while leaving other parts free of congestion.

- Configuring the IGP to converge quickly can make it overly sensitive to minor packet loss, causing false negatives and IGP convergence for no reason.

Also, assuming that the IGP is a link-state protocol, SPF has to be run once when the link goes down and then again when it comes back up. This problem is exacerbated with MPLS TE: If a link that is a part of an LSP fails, the LSP is torn down. After the headend recomputes a new path, SPF has to be run again for prefixes routed over the tunnel when autoroute is in place, thus making convergence times even worse than in a pure IP network.

IP networks that use SONET can also employ automatic protection switching (APS) to aid in quick recovery from link failures. The goal of APS is to switch over from an active link to a standby link within 50 milliseconds upon failure of the active link. However, if APS is run directly on a router, even after APS switches traffic over to the standby link, the IGP still needs to converge with the new neighbor on the other end of the link. Until the new IGP neighbors come up, packets might still be dropped.

APS also does not come without additional cost—the hardware cost of the add/drop multiplexer (ADM) required to achieve APS.

Luckily, there's an alternative to all this. You can use MPLS TE's FRR capabilities to minimize packet loss, without all the drawbacks of APS or fast IGP convergence.

RFC 2702, "Requirements for Traffic Engineering Over MPLS," describes the "resilience attribute" as the behavior of a traffic trunk under fault conditions:

A basic resilience attribute indicates the recovery procedure to be applied to traffic trunks whose paths are impacted by faults.

This is called *headend LSP reroute* or simply *headend reroute*.

At its simplest, headend rerouting is calculating a new path for an LSP after its existing path goes down. However, during the time required to perform this basic reroute, there can be significant traffic loss; the packet loss is potentially worse than with regular IP routing if you are autorouting over the TE tunnel. This is because you first need to signal a new TE LSP through RSVP and run SPF for destinations that need to be routed over the tunnel. It is desirable to be able to deal with a link or node failure in a way that has less loss than the basic headend LSP reroute.

Normally, when a link or node fails, this failure is signalled to the headends that had LSPs going through the failed link or node. The headends affected attempt to find new paths across the network for these tunnels.

Although a few seconds of loss is generally acceptable for data traffic, real-time applications such as voice, video, and some legacy applications might not be so forgiving. Many attempts have been made and drafts submitted to the IETF to solve this problem.

Within Cisco, the question arose as to how to make MPLS TE tunnels resistant to failures within the network. Mechanisms were developed to address this question, and they are collectively known as FRR, fast restoration mechanisms, or simply protection. Although it's impossible to have a completely lossless failure recovery mechanism, it's certainly possible to have mechanisms that minimize loss as much as possible.

Generally speaking, the goal for the different FRR mechanisms is to achieve as little packet loss as possible. Practically, this translates into anything from SONET-like recovery times (50 ms or less) to a few hundred milliseconds of loss before FRR kicks in.

What Is Protection?

Protection, in the context of fast restoration, is having procedures in place that, when applied to selected resources, ensures minimal loss of traffic upon failure. Protected resources could either be viewed as physical resources (link or nodes) or logical resources (the LSPs that cross a link or node). Regardless of how you look at it, network failures are always physical in origin—a link or a node goes down, taking some LSPs with it. What protection boils down to is protection of logical resources (LSPs) from physical failures (links or nodes).

For all subsequent discussions in this chapter (or, for that matter, anywhere in MPLS), the term *protection* should be associated with the fact that backup resources are *preestablished* and are not signalled after a failure has occurred, as you'd see in the case of headend LSP reroute. The preestablishment of protection resources is fundamental for any protection strategy. If protection resources weren't preestablished, they'd have to be set up after the failure was detected; by then, it's too late.

This chapter calls this preestablished LSP a *backup tunnel* or *protection tunnel.* They mean the same thing.

NOTE	Many people have asked, "When I have multiple path-option statements under my tunnel configuration, and a link/node failure causes my headend to pick the next path option in the list, isn't this protection?" No; no backup resources are precomputed or signalled before failure. Configuring multiple path options is merely a way to influence basic LSP rerouting. Unless the backup resources are signalled *before* any failure, there can be no fast protection.

Types of Protection

This section provides an overview of the three different types of protection schemes.

Protection can be broken into

- Path protection (sometimes called end-to-end protection)
- Local protection, which can be broken into two types:
  — Link protection
  — Node protection

Path Protection

Path protection is not currently available on Cisco routers. It is provided here for the sake of completeness and is not discussed further in this chapter. It is, however, discussed again in Chapter 9, "Network Design with MPLS TE," where the scalability of path protection is compared with that of link and node protection.

Path protection is essentially the establishment of an additional LSP in parallel with an existing LSP, where the additional LSP is used only in case of failure. This LSP is sometimes called the *backup, secondary,* or *standby* LSP. The backup LSP is not used to carry traffic except during a failure condition—hence, the term *standby.*

The backup LSP is built along paths that are as diverse as possible from the LSP they're protecting. This ensures that a failure along the path of the primary LSP does not also affect the backup LSP. Path protection is simple in concept. Each primary LSP is backed up by a standby LSP. Both the primary and backup LSPs are configured at the headend. Both are signalled ahead of time in the control plane.

The primary and backup LSPs might have the same constraints. If the primary LSP has a bandwidth reservation of 100 Mbps, the backup LSP can also reserve 100 Mbps. This way, the end-to-end characteristics essentially remain the same, no matter whether the LSP used to carry traffic is the primary LSP or the protection LSP.

As mentioned in the preceding section, simply having a second path option under the tunnel interface does not make it path protection—it would be an LSP reroute. Path protection has better convergence than IGP convergence in an IP network or MPLS TE LSP reroute because it makes use of a presignalled LSP that is ready to go in case the primary LSP fails. With path protection, the relationship between the backup LSP and the number of primary LSPs it is protecting is 1:1. This makes the path protection scheme less scalable.

In other words, for every LSP you want to protect, you have to signal another LSP. If you want the primary and backup LSPs to share the same bandwidth characteristics, they need to reserve the same amount of bandwidth. Protection LSPs kick in only when there's a failure, and hopefully your network failure rate is far less than 50 percent, so you end up reserving backup bandwidth that you won't use most of the time and keeping other LSPs in the network from being able to use that bandwidth.

Figure 7-1 shows a primary tunnel going from 7200a to 7200c over 12008a and 12008c. The path protection tunnel is also from the headend 7200a to tail 7200c but goes over a diverse path (7200a→7500a→12008b→12008d→7500c→7200c).

Figure 7-1   *Path Protection*

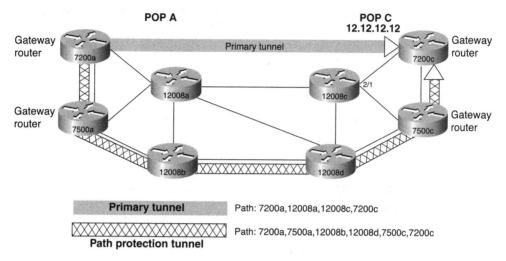

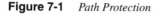

| Primary tunnel | Path: 7200a,12008a,12008c,7200c |
| Path protection tunnel | Path: 7200a,7500a,12008b,12008d,7500c,7200c |

Local Protection

Local protection is the term used when the backup or protection tunnel is built to cover only a segment of the primary LSP. Local protection, like path protection, requires the backup LSP to be presignalled.

In local protection, the backup LSP is routed around a failed link (in link protection) or node (in node protection), and primary LSPs that would have gone through that failed link or node are instead encapsulated in the backup LSP. Local protection has several advantages over path protection—faster failure recovery, 1:N scalability, and the consumption of less network state, to name a few.

Local Protection Terminology

Cisco's implementation of local protection is based on the bypass section of the IETF *draft-ietf-mpls-rsvp-lsp-fastreroute,* "Fast Reroute Extensions to RSVP-TE for LSP Tunnels," which might be an RFC by now.

Unlike path protection, for local protection, the relationship between the backup LSP and the number of primary LSPs it is protecting is 1:N. In other words, a single backup LSP can protect N primary LSPs, making it more scalable than path protection. This scalability makes the local protection scheme extremely attractive.

Before going any further into local protection, it is important to stop and understand some of the terminology. Figure 7-2 shows 12008a as the headend as of two backup tunnels—tunnel0, which terminates on 12008c, and tunnel1, which terminates on 7200c. Table 7-1 defines some of the commonly used terms.

Figure 7-2 *Elements of Local Protection*

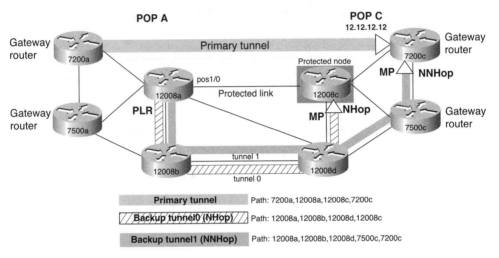

In addition to the terms "backup tunnel" and "protection tunnel," you might see the terms "FRR tunnel" and "bypass tunnel" being used to refer to this presignalled tunnel. They all mean the same thing.

Table 7-1 *Local Protection Terminology*

Term	Definition
PLR	Point of Local Repair—The headend of the backup tunnel. In Figure 7-2, 12008a is the PLR.
MP	Merge Point—The merge point is where the backup tunnel terminates. In Figure 7-2, the merge point for tunnel0 is 12008c, and the merge point for tunnel1 is 7200c.
NHop	Next-hop router—A router that is one hop away from the PLR. This bypasses the protected link (12008a→12008c). 12008c in Figure 7-2 is the NHop for PLR 12008a.
NNHop	Next-next-hop router—A router that is two hops away from the PLR. 7200c is the NNHop for PLR 12008a in Figure 7-2. The NNHop bypasses a protected node (12008c).

NOTE	The material presented so far might give you the impression that the primary tunnel headend and the PLR have to be two distinct things. This is not necessarily true in every case, even if it is the common situation. You might have configured link protection, protecting the link between the primary tunnel headend and its downstream neighbor. In this case, the primary tunnel headend is also the PLR. Basically, the PLR is where the backup tunnel begins.

The Need for Label Stacking

Consider Figure 7-3. It has two tunnels: *primary* and *backup*. The primary tunnel goes from 7200a to 7200c, whereas the backup tunnel goes from 12008a to 12008c, protecting link 12008a→12008c. Labels are distributed downstream to upstream (from 7200c toward 7200a). For the primary tunnel, routers 7200a, 12008a, and 12008c receive labels 16, 33, and POP (implicit null), respectively, in RSVP Resv messages from their downstream neighbors. Similarly for the backup tunnel, 12008a receives label 38 from 12008b. 12008b receives label 35 from 12008d, and 12008d receives the POP label from 12008c.

Figure 7-3   *Label Forwarding Over the Primary Tunnel*

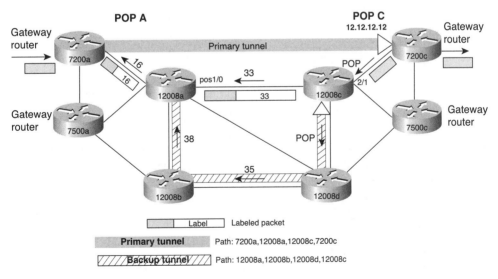

In the forwarding plane, when the ingress router 7200a forwards a packet down the primary tunnel, it imposes a label of 16 and transmits the packet to 12008a. 12008a label-swaps 16 to 33 and sends it to 12008c. Because 12008c performs Penultimate Hop Popping (PHP), the top label 33 is removed, and the packet is sent to 7200c, which is the egress router.

If you now focus your attention on the link 12008a→12008c (the protected link), you'll notice that primary tunnel packets that are carried on this link have a label value of 33 as they enter 12008c.

Now consider Figure 7-4.

Figure 7-4 *Label Stacking Over the Backup Tunnel After Failure of Protected Link*

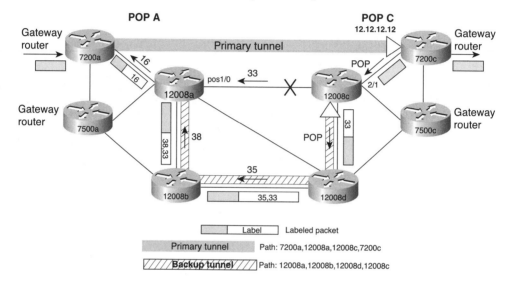

Before the protected link failed, the primary tunnel traffic entered 12008a with a label of 33.

When the protected link fails, if the primary tunnel traffic entering 12008a somehow reached 12008c with a label of 33, it would be as though the protected link never failed. 12008c would simply POP label 33 and send the packet to 7200c. This is because all routers in this figure are allocating labels from global label space. One of the benefits of global label space is that a router does the same thing with a label no matter what interface it comes in on.

This is exactly what happens with local protection. Because the backup tunnel is presignalled and is ready to carry traffic to 12008c, when the protected link fails, 12008a switches the traffic onto the backup path. Because 12008c is expecting the packets to arrive with a label value of 33, 12008a takes the packets destined for 12008c with a label value of 33 and stacks another label, 38, on top.

Label 38 is what 12008a is expected to impose on any packets entering the backup tunnel. As you can see in Figure 7-4, the packet leaving 12008a toward 12008b has a label stack {38,33}. As you'd expect, 12008b switches the packet based on the top-level label, 38. The packet leaving 12008b now has a label stack of {35,33} because 12008b label swapped the top label, 38, with label 35. When this packet reaches 12008d, PHP is performed, removing the top label. 12008d performs PHP for the backup tunnel. With the top label removed, the packet has a single label of 33 as it enters 12008c. From the labels exchanged for the primary tunnel, 12008c performs PHP when it receives packets with a label of 33, and the packet is forwarded to 7200c.

Notice that the packet with label 33 enters 12008c over a different interface than it would have if the protected link did not go down. This is not an issue for 12008c because it is using global label space. 12008c does not care on which interface the packet enters. If it comes in with a label value of 33, it performs PHP and forwards the packet to 7200c. As you can see, for this scheme to work, both label stacking and global label space are required.

The other assumption made in local protection is that the failure is temporary. 12008a forwards the traffic down the backup tunnel upon failure and then informs the primary tunnel's headend (7200a) of the failure and its subsequent protection. 7200a then performs a make-before-break headend LSP reroute using normal CSPF.

NOTE   Because of the assumption that restoration in local protection is temporary, there is no need to reserve bandwidth on the backup tunnel. Reserving bandwidth for backup tunnels not only takes bandwidth away from primary tunnels, but also might influence the placement of other backup tunnels, and as such, should be avoided.

As previously mentioned, there are two types of local protection—*link* protection and *node* protection. They're similar in concept, but node protection is more complex than link protection.

This section briefly summarizes link and node protection. The rest of this chapter examines each of them in more detail.

Link Protection Overview

In many networks that are deployed today, it is common to see high-bandwidth links carrying traffic belonging to "important" flows and other flows that are not so important. If MPLS TE is deployed in such networks, "important flows" translates to "important LSPs." These LSPs might be carrying critical information or time-sensitive data that requires a real-time response. In such cases, it would be nice if all the "important LSPs" could be protected while ignoring the less-important LSPs. FRR allows you to protect some of your TE tunnels (just the ones you deem important) or all of your TE tunnels. With link protection, you can protect links that are carrying these important LSPs by using presignalled backup tunnels that bypass the protected link. Figure 7-5 depicts one such sample network.

Figure 7-5 *Link Protection*

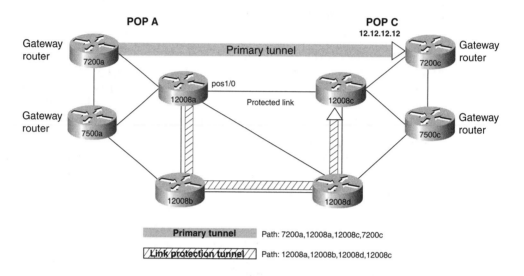

Here, link 12008a→12008c is considered the crucial link over which a primary tunnel is signalled. This link is called the *protected link*. In order to protect this link and the primary tunnel over it, a backup tunnel is signalled around the link so that the headend of the backup tunnel is the node that is immediately upstream of the protected link, and the tail of the backup tunnel is the node that is immediately downstream of the protected link. In Figure 7-5, the headend of the backup tunnel is 12008a (PLR), and the tail is 12008c (MP). As described in the preceding section, when the protected link fails, label stacking delivers the primary tunnel packets to 12008c so that 12008c sees the label it is expecting. Link protection relies on the fact that, although a protected link has gone down, the router at the other end of that protected link is still up. Link protection uses NHop backup tunnels; the backup tunnels terminate on the node on the other end of the protected link. As you can imagine, this allows you to protect against a link failure but not a node failure. If the node you terminate your backup tunnel on goes down, link protection can't help you.

Node Protection Overview

What if the node that is downstream of the protected link goes down, causing the protected link to fail? If this happens, it does you no good to try to deliver the packets to the node that just went down. In this case, you might want to safeguard the primary LSP from node failure on the other end of a link in addition to protecting the link itself.

Looking at this slightly differently, if you protect against failure of the downstream node, you have automatically protected against failure of the downstream link as well. Figure 7-6 shows the protection being moved to 12008c. 12008a is still the PLR, but the MP is now 7200c instead of 12008c. Node protection uses NNHop backup tunnels instead of NHop tunnels because it needs to protect against a failure of the NHop.

Figure 7-6   *Node Protection*

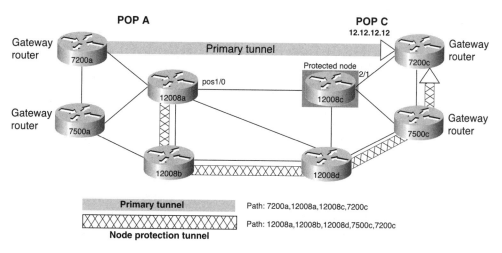

Node protection is similar to link protection in most ways. It differs from link protection in that the MP is not the NHop, but the NNHop. This has implications in label stacking as well. With link protection, the PLR knows what label the MP expects because it receives a label mapping directly from the MP for the primary tunnel. With node protection, however, the label the MP wants to see is never signalled through RSVP to the PLR. There has to be some other mechanism to learn about the label that MP is expecting for the primary tunnel. This mechanism is discussed in detail in the later section "Node Protection."

Link Versus Node Protection

Link and node protection scale differently, solve different problems, and have different restrictions. You don't always need to protect everything in your network. You might want to protect only resources you consider critical (perhaps only the most important core links) or consider protecting links that are not being protected by, say, APS. Perhaps you need to protect LSPs carrying Voice over IP (VoIP) traffic or specific types of traffic from specific customers with whom you have service-level agreements (SLAs).

Where you deploy protection, and what type of protection you deploy, is up to you. Whatever you end up doing, you need to understand the scalability of various protection schemes as part of deciding what to protect. See Chapter 9 for a discussion of protection scalability.

The next two sections examine link and node protection in more detail—how they work, how they're configured, and the differences between them.

All the figures in this chapter are based on the sample network shown in Figure 7-7. The router IDs (RIDs) (also loopback addresses) are in parentheses above or below the routers. For example, 7200a's RID is 4.4.4.4.

Figure 7-7 *IP Addressing Used in the Sample Network*

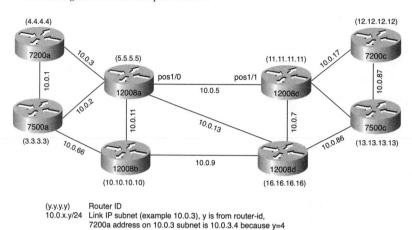

Each link's subnet address is of the form 10.0.*x.y*, and each link has a 24-bit mask. For example, the link between 7200a and 12008a is 10.0.3.0/24. The IP address of 7200a's side of the link is 10.0.3.4 because 7200a's RID is 4.4.4.4, and 12008a's side of the link has the address 10.0.3.5 because 12008a's RID is 5.5.5.5.

Link Protection

Link protection can be divided into four sections:

- Prefailure configuration
- Failure detection
- Connectivity restoration
- Post-failure signalling

The following sections examine each of these topics in detail.

Prefailure Configuration

You need to note one subtle point: Link protection, like all other TE applications, is unidirectional. In order to protect LSPs flowing from A to B across a link, you need protection in the A→B direction. To protect LSPs flowing from B to A across the same link, you also need to build a protection LSP in the B→A direction. Most of the configurations or concepts presented in this chapter are unidirectional unless specified otherwise.

There are two places where you have to configure things related to link protection:

- At the headend on the tunnel interface you want to protect
- At the PLR

Enabling Link Protection on a Tunnel Interface

You might not want to protect all your primary tunnels. Remember that link protection means that, when a link goes down, the LSPs that would have gone over that link are instead sent across some other path in the network. If you end up protecting too much traffic (protecting an OC-48 with an LSP that goes down an OC-3, for example), you might end up making things not much better than if there was no protection.

That's why TE tunnels don't request protection by default. In order to have a TE tunnel request protection, you need to explicitly configure the tunnel to ask for protection. You do this using the **tunnel mpls traffic-eng fast-reroute** configuration under the primary tunnel interface at the headend, as shown in Example 7-1.

Example 7-1   *Enabling Protection on 7200a*

```
7200a#configure terminal
Enter configuration commands, one per line. End with CNTL/Z.
7200a(config)#interface tunnel 1
7200a(config-if)#tunnel mpls traffic-eng fast-reroute
```

When you configure **tunnel mpls traffic-eng fast-reroute,** the headend sets the SESSION_ATTRIBUTE flag 0x01 ("Local protection desired") in the PATH message for that tunnel.

This can be observed in the output of **debug ip rsvp path detail** on the 7200a router, as demonstrated in Examples 7-2 and 7-3.

Example 7-2 shows the output *before* **tunnel mpls traffic-eng fast-reroute** is configured.

Example 7-2   **debug ip rsvp path detail** *Output Before FRR Configuration*

```
7200a#debug ip rsvp path detail
*Oct 16 14:38:56.460:  SESSION_ATTRIBUTE    type 7 length 24:
*Oct 16 14:38:56.460:   Setup Prio: 7, Holding Prio: 7
*Oct 16 14:38:56.460:   Flags: SE Style
*Oct 16 14:38:56.460:   Session Name: 7200a_t1
```

The only flag set is SE Style.

Example 7-3 shows the output *after* **tunnel mpls traffic-eng fast-reroute** is configured on the primary tunnel interface.

Example 7-3 **debug ip rsvp path detail** *Output After FRR Configuration*

```
7200a#debug ip rsvp path detail
*Oct 16 14:40:57.124:  SESSION_ATTRIBUTE    type 7 length 24:
*Oct 16 14:40:57.124:  Setup Prio: 7, Holding Prio: 7
*Oct 16 14:40:57.124:  Flags: Local Prot desired, Label Recording, SE Style
*Oct 16 14:40:57.124:  Session Name: 7200a_t1
```

After **tunnel mpls traffic-eng fast-reroute** is configured, three flags are now set, as detailed in Table 7-2.

Table 7-2 *Flags Set After FRR Is Configured on the Primary Tunnel Interface*

Flag	Description
Local Prot desired	This is how the headend indicates to any downstream nodes that it would like local protection of some sort (either link or node) for this LSP.
Label Recording	Not used in link protection, but as you will see later, it is used in node protection.
SE Style	Stays the same as before **tunnel mpls traffic-eng fast-reroute** was configured.

Enabling Link Protection at the PLR

Enabling FRR at the PLR involves two things:

- Creating a backup tunnel to the NHop
- Configuring the protected link to use the backup tunnel upon failure

Creating a Backup Tunnel to the NHop

In local protection, a backup tunnel needs to be built from the PLR to the MP. In link protection, the MP is the node on the other end of the protected link, as depicted in Figure 7-8. The primary LSP in Figure 7-8 goes from 7200a to 7200c. The midpoints are 12008a and 12008c. The link that is being protected in this example is the POS link that goes between 12008a and 12008c in the 12008a→12008c direction.

If this link fails, the LSPs that are traversing this link need to be protected and rerouted locally to 12008c, which is the downstream end of this link.

You need to be sure to configure the backup tunnel so that it doesn't attempt to cross the link it's protecting. This would defeat the entire concept of local protection. You can use one of two methods to build the path for this backup tunnel:

- Use an explicitly routed path option to route the backup tunnel away from the link it is protecting.
- Use the **exclude-address** knob to tell a backup LSP to use any path it can find that avoids the link it's protecting.

Figure 7-8 *Link Protection*

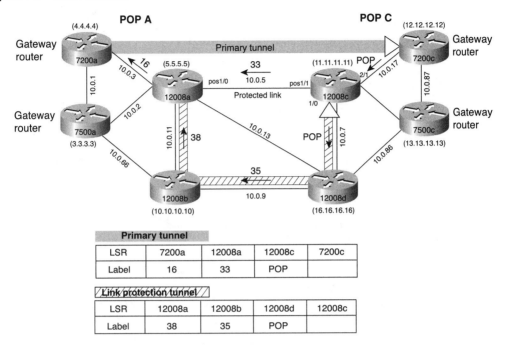

Primary tunnel			
LSR	7200a	12008a	12008c	7200c
Label	16	33	POP	

Link protection tunnel			
LSR	12008a	12008b	12008d	12008c
Label	38	35	POP	

NOTE   It is important to understand that, for link protection to work, the backup tunnel must
originate at the router on the upstream end of the protected link and terminate on the router
at the downstream end of the protected link. It is not important what path the protected link
takes, as long as the protection LSP doesn't try to go out the link it's trying to protect. You
might want to provision the backup LSP along a path that has available bandwidth
comparable to the resources it's protecting.

Example 7-4 shows how to build the path for the backup tunnel using the exclude-address
syntax.

Example 7-4 *Building a Path for the Backup Tunnel*

```
12008a#show running-config interface tunnel1
interface Tunnel1
 description Link Protection Tunnel (Backup)
 ip unnumbered Loopback0
 no ip directed-broadcast
 tunnel destination 11.11.11.11
 tunnel mode mpls traffic-eng
 tunnel mpls traffic-eng path-option 5 explicit name nhop
end
12008a#show ip explicit-paths name nhop
PATH link-protection-tunnel (loose source route, path complete, generation 8)
    1: exclude-address 10.0.5.11
```

Example 7-4 excludes 12008c's POS1/1 interface address (10.0.5.11) to ensure that the protected link 12008a→12008c is not included in CSPF for the backup tunnel on 12008a. As you can see from Example 7-5, the backup tunnel comes up. If you examine the ERO, you can see that the protected tunnel is not a part of it.

Example 7-5 **show mpls traffic-eng tunnel tunnel1** *Output Verifies that the Backup Tunnel Is Present*

```
12008a#show mpls traffic-eng tunnel tunnel1

Name: Link Protection Tunnel (Backup)      (Tunnel1) Destination: 11.11.11.11
  Status:
    Admin: up        Oper: up      Path: valid       Signalling: connected

    path option 5, type explicit nhop (Basis for Setup, path weight 3)

  Config Parameters:
    Bandwidth: 0        kbps (Global)  Priority: 7  7   Affinity: 0x0/0xFFFF
    Metric Type: TE (default)
    AutoRoute:  disabled  LockDown: disabled  Loadshare: 0        bw-based
    auto-bw: disabled(0/60) 0  Bandwidth Requested: 0

  InLabel  :  -
  OutLabel : POS1/1, 38
  RSVP Signalling Info:
      Src 5.5.5.5, Dst 11.11.11.11, Tun_Id 1, Tun_Instance 93
    RSVP Path Info:
      My Address: 5.5.5.5
      Explicit Route: 10.0.11.10 10.0.9.16 10.0.7.11 11.11.11.11
```

Tying the Protected Link to the Backup Tunnel

Just configuring the backup tunnel and calling the explicit path "backup" does not make traffic go over this tunnel when the protected link goes down. After you build the backup tunnel, you need to tell an interface to use that tunnel for protection.

How do you tie the protection of interface POS 1/0 (the outgoing interface of the protected link on 12008a) to this backup tunnel? You use the configuration highlighted in Example 7-6 on that interface.

Example 7-6 *Configuration for Backing Up Interface POS 1/0 with Tunnel1*

```
12008a#show running-config interface pos1/0
interface POS1/0
 ip address 10.0.5.5 255.255.255.0
 no ip directed-broadcast
 mpls traffic-eng tunnels
 mpls traffic-eng backup-path Tunnel1
 ip rsvp bandwidth 155000 155000
end
```

The command **mpls traffic-eng backup-path Tunnel1** protects 12008a's POS1/0 interface with Tunnel1.

The backup tunnel is now signalled and ready to go. If failure is detected on the protected link, all the traffic from LSPs requesting protection is forwarded over the backup tunnel. Until then, the backup LSP does not carry any traffic. Example 7-7 shows the output of **show mpls traffic-eng fast-reroute database** before any failure has occurred but after the backup tunnel is ready to protect the primary LSP.

Example 7-7 *Verifying the FRR State*

```
12008a#show mpls traffic-eng fast-reroute database
Tunnel head fast reroute information:
Prefix              Tunnel     In-label Out intf/label    FRR intf/label    Status
LSP midpoint frr information:
LSP identifier                 In-label Out intf/label    FRR intf/label    Status
4.4.4.4 1 [1520]               16       PO1/0:33          Tu1:33            ready
```

Here is a detailed explanation of the key fields in this output:

- **LSP identifier**—This column shows the source address of the primary LSP being protected (4.4.4.4), its tunnel ID (1), and its LSP ID (1520).

- **In-label**—This column shows the incoming label that is being protected. This label corresponds to the tunnel listed in the **LSP identifier** column.

- **Out intf/label**—This column shows the interface of the protected link (PO1/0) and the tunnel's outgoing label on that interface (33).

- **FRR intf/label**—This column shows the backup tunnel that is being used to back up the primary tunnel. When POS1/0 fails, the packet that would have gone out POS1/0 with label 33 is instead sent down the backup tunnel, but with that same label value.

- **Status**—This column shows **ready**, meaning that FRR protection is ready to back up the primary tunnel, and that a failure has not yet occurred. If the **Status** field shows **active**, the protected link is currently down, and protection is *active* (sometimes referred to as *in place*). The **Status** field can also show **partial**, meaning that all the pieces required to back up a primary LSP are not yet available. A tunnel that has requested protection is not protected, generally because the interface is not configured with **mpls traffic-eng backup-path**, or the backup tunnel is not up.

If the backup tunnel exists and is up, the PLR (12008a) responds by setting the RRO subobject IPv4 flags to 0x01, indicating "Local protection available." This is specified in RFC 3209. You can see this from the output of **debug ip rsvp resv detail** on 7200a, as demonstrated in Example 7-8.

Example 7-8 **debug ip rsvp resv detail** *Output on 7200a*

```
7200a#debug ip rsvp resv detail
*Oct 17 08:38:04.216: RSVP:     version:1 flags:0000 type:RESV cksum:0000 ttl:255
  reserved:0 length:152
*Oct 17 08:38:04.220: SESSION                 type 7 length 16:
*Oct 17 08:38:04.220:   Tun Dest 12.12.12.12 Tun ID 1 Ext Tun ID 4.4.4.4
*Oct 17 08:38:04.220: HOP                     type 1 length 12:
*Oct 17 08:38:04.220:   Hop Addr: 10.0.3.5 LIH: 0x0
```

continues

Example 7-8 **debug ip rsvp resv detail** *Output on 7200a (Continued)*

```
*Oct 17 08:38:04.220:  TIME_VALUES          type 1 length 8 :
*Oct 17 08:38:04.220:   Refresh Period (msec): 30000
*Oct 17 08:38:04.220:  STYLE                type 1 length 8 :
*Oct 17 08:38:04.220:   RSVP_SE_OPTION
*Oct 17 08:38:04.220:  FLOWSPEC             type 2 length 36:
*Oct 17 08:38:04.220:   version = 0 length in words = 7
*Oct 17 08:38:04.220:   service id = 5, service length = 6
*Oct 17 08:38:04.220:   tspec parameter id = 127, tspec flags = 0, tspec length = 5
*Oct 17 08:38:04.220:   average rate = 0 bytes/sec, burst depth = 1000 bytes
*Oct 17 08:38:04.220:   peak rate  = 2147483647 bytes/sec
*Oct 17 08:38:04.220:   min unit = 0 bytes, max unit = 0 bytes
*Oct 17 08:38:04.220:  FILTER_SPEC          type 7 length 12:
*Oct 17 08:38:04.220:   Tun Sender: 4.4.4.4, LSP ID 1520
*Oct 17 08:38:04.220:  LABEL                type 1 length 8 : 00000012
*Oct 17 08:38:04.220:  RECORD_ROUTE         type 1 length 44:
*Oct 17 08:38:04.220:   10.0.5.5/32, Flags:0x1 (Local Prot Avail/to NHOP)
*Oct 17 08:38:04.220:     Label record: Flags 0x1, ctype 1, incoming label 16
*Oct 17 08:38:04.220:   10.0.17.11/32, Flags:0x0 (No Local Protection)
*Oct 17 08:38:04.220:     Label record: Flags 0x1, ctype 1, incoming label 33
*Oct 17 08:38:04.220:   10.0.17.12/32, Flags:0x0 (No Local Protection)
*Oct 17 08:38:04.220:
*Oct 17 08:38:04.220: RSVP 4.4.4.4_1520-12.12.12.12_1: RESV message arrived from
   10.0.3.5 on POS3/0
```

The highlighted output in Example 7-8 also shows that protection is available to the PLR's NHop.

Entering **show ip rsvp sender detail** on 7200a and 12008a, as shown in Example 7-9, is useful to get a quick synopsis of the FRR states of the two routers.

Example 7-9 *Determining the FRR States on 7200a and 12008a*

```
7200a#show ip rsvp sender detail
PATH:
  Tun Dest 12.12.12.12 Tun ID 1 Ext Tun ID 4.4.4.4
  Tun Sender: 4.4.4.4, LSP ID: 1520
  Path refreshes being sent to NHOP 10.0.3.5 on POS3/0
  Session Attr::
    Setup Prio: 7, Holding Prio: 7
    Flags: Local Prot desired, Label Recording, SE Style
    Session Name: 7200a_t1
  ERO:
    10.0.3.5 (Strict IPv4 Prefix, 8 bytes, /32)
    10.0.5.11 (Strict IPv4 Prefix, 8 bytes, /32)
    10.0.17.12 (Strict IPv4 Prefix, 8 bytes, /32)
    12.12.12.12 (Strict IPv4 Prefix, 8 bytes, /32)
  RRO:
    Empty
  Traffic params - Rate: 0G bits/sec, Max. burst: 1K bytes
  Fast-Reroute Backup info:
    Inbound  FRR: Not active
    Outbound FRR: No backup tunnel selected
```

Example 7-9 *Determining the FRR States on 7200a and 12008a (Continued)*

```
12008a#show ip rsvp sender detail
PATH:
  Tun Dest 12.12.12.12 Tun ID 1 Ext Tun ID 4.4.4.4
  Tun Sender: 4.4.4.4, LSP ID: 1520
  Path refreshes arriving on POS2/1 from PHOP 10.0.3.4
  Path refreshes being sent to NHOP 10.0.5.11 on POS1/0
  Session Attr::
    Setup Prio: 7, Holding Prio: 7
    Flags: Local Prot desired, Label Recording, SE Style
    Session Name: 7200a_t1
  ERO:
    10.0.5.11 (Strict IPv4 Prefix, 8 bytes, /32)
    10.0.17.12 (Strict IPv4 Prefix, 8 bytes, /32)
    12.12.12.12 (Strict IPv4 Prefix, 8 bytes, /32)
  RRO:
    10.0.3.4/32, Flags:0x0 (No Local Protection)
  Traffic params - Rate: 0G bits/sec, Max. burst: 1K bytes
  Fast-Reroute Backup info:
    Inbound  FRR: Not active
    Outbound FRR: Ready -- backup tunnel selected
      Backup Tunnel: Tu1   (label 33)
      Bkup Sender Template:
        Tun Sender: 10.0.11.5, LSP ID: 506
      Bkup FilerSpec:
        Tun Sender: 10.0.11.5, LSP ID 506
```

Failure Detection

One of the most important pieces of any dynamic protocol is failure detection. This is doubly important in protection mechanisms because the longer it takes to detect a failure, the longer it takes to kick in the protection mechanism designed to circumvent that failure, and the less good your protection mechanism does you.

The methods for detecting these failures and the complexity involved in detecting them vary. It is easy to determine that a link has gone down if the PLR has had its interface administratively turned down, and harder to determine if the interface is down if there is a failure at or between the PLR and the other end of the circuit. Fortunately, detection of a failed link is nothing new. The mechanisms in place to aid the detection of these failures are

- Failure detection mechanisms specific to a particular physical layer, such as SONET
- For point-to-point links, PPP or HDLC keepalives
- RSVP hello extensions

Link protection needs to be able to detect that a directly connected link to the NHop has gone down. The next two sections examine detection using Layer 2 alarms and RSVP hellos in detail.

Failure Detection Using SONET Alarms

When link protection was designed, SONET APS 50-millisecond convergence was used as the metric. An important part of achieving this goal is rapid detection of an interface's failure. If it takes 10 seconds to figure out that a link is down, that's 10 seconds of lost traffic that was forwarded out that link, and that's not good. SONET's APS (and SDH's MSP) are triggered by various physical alarms; FRR merely hooks into those alarms and so detects interface failure as quickly as APS and MSP would.

NOTE   Although FRR can be triggered by SONET alarms, it is supported only on POS interfaces, not ATM SONET interfaces.

NOTE   Although FRR works off the same alarms that trigger APS, you do not need to configure APS to get FRR to work. They're two completely independent mechanisms that just happen to use the same failure trigger.

It is a good idea to enable **pos ais-shut** on both sides of any POS link; this sends a Line Alarm Indication Signal (LAIs) when the interface is administratively shut down. This is independent of whether you use FRR or not; **pos ais-shut** simply helps a router detect when the interface on the other side of a link has been shut down. Without **pos ais-shut**, the router needs to rely on PPP/HDLC keepalives timing out to figure out that an interface went down, and keepalive timeout can take a while.

Failure Detection Using RSVP Hellos

RFC 3209 defines RSVP hellos in Section 5. Here is part of the definition:

The RSVP Hello extension enables RSVP nodes to detect when a neighboring node is not reachable. The mechanism provides node to node failure detection. When such a failure is detected it is handled much the same as a link layer communication failure. This mechanism is intended to be used when notification of link layer failures is not available and unnumbered links are not used, or when the failure detection mechanisms provided by the link layer are not sufficient for timely node failure detection.

Physical layer alarms are not always available. For example, a Gigabit Ethernet interface that's connected to a switch doesn't always lose the link signal when a link in the same VLAN goes down.

If you want to detect failures on non-POS interfaces, you might want to use RSVP hellos. However, you need to know that RSVP hello-based failure detection is somewhat slower than Layer 2 alarm-based detection. It can take several hundred milliseconds to detect a neighbor failure using RSVP hellos, depending on how you tune them.

Even so, RSVP hello-based detection is considered sufficient for failure detection in local protection, and convergence is faster than plain IP or MPLS TE without FRR.

Figure 7-9 shows the configuration used for RSVP hellos.

Figure 7-9   *Failure Detection Using RSVP Hellos*

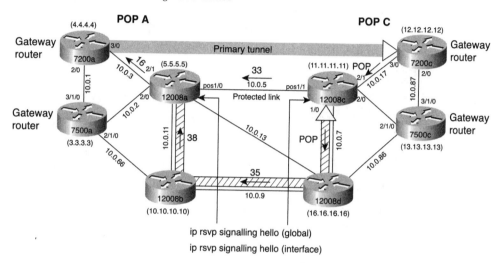

You need to configure RSVP hellos at both the global and interface levels, as shown in Example 7-10.

Example 7-10 *Configuring RSVP Hellos at the Global and Interface Levels*

```
12008a(config)#ip rsvp signalling hello
12008a(config)#interface pos 1/0
12008a(config-if)#ip rsvp signalling hello ?
  missed-acks       # missed Hello Acks which triggers neighbor down
  refresh-interval  Time between sending Hello Requests, msec.
  <cr>
12008a(config-if)#ip rsvp signalling hello missed-acks ?
  <2-10>  Hello missed
```

You control the refresh interval by entering the command shown in Example 7-11.

Example 7-11 *Determining the Refresh Interval Setting*

```
12008a(config-if)#ip rsvp signalling hello refresh-interval ?
  <10-10000>  Hello interval
  <cr>
```

If no refresh interval is specified, it defaults to 100 milliseconds. Keep this default unless you have a good reason to change it. RSVP hellos need to be configured on *both* sides of a link.

You can examine the configuration of RSVP hellos using the **show ip rsvp hello instance detail** command, as demonstrated in Example 7-12.

Example 7-12 *Determining RSVP Hello Configuration Information*

```
mpls-12008a#show ip rsvp hello instance detail
  Neighbor 10.0.5.11  Source  10.0.5.5
    State: LOST
    Type: ACTIVE   (sending requests)
    I/F: PO1/0
    LSPs protecting: 3
    Refresh Interval (msec)
      Configured: 100
      Statistics:
        no stats collected
    Src_instance 0xCFF52A98, Dst_instance 0x0
    Counters:
      Communication with neighbor lost:
        Num times: 0
        Reasons:
          Missed acks:              0
          Bad Src_Inst received:    0
          Bad Dst_Inst received:    0
          I/F went down:            0
          Neighbor disabled Hello: 0
        Msgs Received:   0
              Sent:        24
              Suppressed: 0

mpls-12008a#
```

Using the **missed-acks** knob, you can control how many acknowledgments should be missed before the neighbor is considered down. This defaults to 4 if it is not configured explicitly.

Connectivity Restoration

As soon as the failure is detected, the PLR is responsible for switching traffic to the backup tunnel. The internal processing performed on the PLR involves the following:

*   Making sure a presignalled backup LSP is in place. This includes the new label provided by a new downstream neighbor.

*   New adjacency information (Layer 2 encapsulation) is computed based on the backup tunnel's outgoing physical interface.

This information is precomputed and ready to be installed in the FIB/LFIB as soon as the failure is detected so as to minimize packet loss; this is referred to as the *ready* state, as shown in Example 7-13. After the failure is detected, FRR kicks and is said to be in *active* state (see Example 7-17). These states can only be observed on the PLR (12008a, in this example).

Example 7-13 *Verifying the FRR State*

```
12008a#show mpls traffic-eng fast-reroute database
Tunnel head fast reroute information:
Prefix              Tunnel     In-label Out intf/label   FRR intf/label   Status
LSP midpoint frr information:
LSP identifier                 In-label Out intf/label   FRR intf/label   Status
4.4.4.4 1 [1520]               16       PO1/0:33         Tu1:33           ready
```

The LSP identifier (4.4.4.4 1 [1520]) in Example 7-13 refers to the tunnel's source, the tunnel identifier, and the tunnel instance. This should agree with what you see in the output of **show mpls traffic-eng tunnel tunnel1** on 7200a, shown in Example 7-14.

Example 7-14 *Tunnel State on Primary Tunnel Headend 7200*

```
7200a#show mpls traffic-eng tunnel tunnel1
...
RSVP Signalling Info:
        Src 4.4.4.4, Dst 12.12.12.12, Tun_Id 1, Tun_Instance 1520
...
```

The output in Examples 7-13 and 7-14 demonstrates that protection is offered to the LSP originating from 7200a but not to the one originating from 7500a.

Figure 7-10 shows a tunnel from 7500a that is not requesting protection.

Figure 7-10 *Unprotected LSP Over a Protected Link*

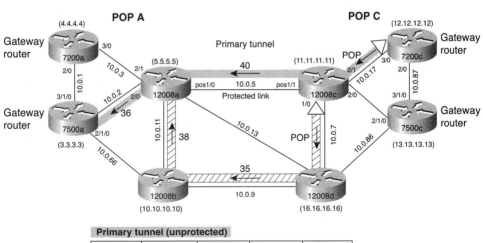

Primary tunnel (unprotected)			
LSR	7500	12008a	12008c	7200c
Label	36	40	POP	

Backup tunnel			
LSR	12008a	12008b	12008d	12008c
Label	38	35	POP	

You can see this in the configuration of the tunnel on 7500a in Example 7-15.

Example 7-15 *7500a Tunnel Configuration*

```
7500a#show running-config interface tunnel1
interface Tunnel1
 description Primary tunnel(7500a->12008a->12008c->7200c)
 ip unnumbered Loopback0
 no ip directed-broadcast
 ip route-cache distributed
 tunnel destination 12.12.12.12
 tunnel mode mpls traffic-eng
 tunnel mpls traffic-eng autoroute announce
 tunnel mpls traffic-eng path-option 5 explicit name primary
 tunnel mpls traffic-eng path-option 6 dynamic
 tunnel mpls traffic-eng record-route
end

7500a#show ip explicit-paths name primary
PATH primary (strict source route, path complete, generation 6)
    1: next-address 10.0.2.5
    2: next-address 10.0.5.11
    3: next-address 10.0.17.12
    4: next-address 12.12.12.12
```

Example 7-15 shows that FRR is not configured under tunnel1 on 7500a.

As soon as a failure is detected, FRR quickly reacts to send traffic down the protection tunnel. This can be seen in the output from **show mpls traffic-eng fast-reroute database** (see Example 7-17) and **show mpls traffic-eng fast-reroute log reroutes** (see Example 7-20).

Figure 7-11 depicts the flow of traffic over the *link protection tunnel*. It is important to note that for local protection mechanisms, while the protection is active and the backup tunnel is forwarding traffic, the primary LSP continues to stay up. This is different from the end-to-end path protection scheme, in which the primary LSP goes down after a failure, gracefully switching over to standby LSP to minimize packet loss. This results in the tunnel's staying up.

When local protection is active, if you just examine the state of the primary tunnel on 7200a using the **show mpls traffic-eng tunnels tunnel1** command, you might not notice that protection has kicked in because the primary LSP is still up and you see only the original ERO, which does not include the backup path. As you can see from Figure 7-11, the primary tunnel traffic now goes over the backup path. Doing a **traceroute** to the tunnel destination when FRR is active shows you that the backup path is actually taken. Example 7-16 shows the output of the **traceroute** from 7200a to 7200c. 10.0.3.5 is the first hop to 12008a, 10.0.11.10 is the second hop to 12008b, 10.0.9.16 is the third hop to 12008d, 10.0.7.11 is the forth hop to 12008c, and 10.0.17.12 is the final hop to 7200c. You can also observe the label stack in this output.

Figure 7-11 *Link Protection After the Protected Link Fails*

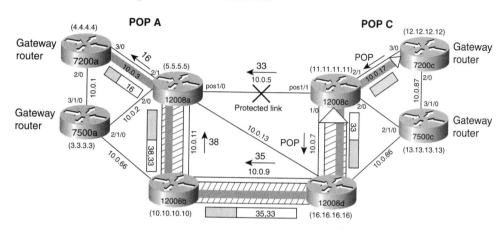

Primary tunnel   Path: 7200a,12008a,12008b,12008d,12008c,7200c

Label   Labeled packet

Link protection tunnel   Path: 12008a,12008b,12008d,12008c

Example 7-16 traceroute *Output*

```
7200a#traceroute 12.12.12.12

Type escape sequence to abort.
Tracing the route to 12.12.12.12

  1 10.0.3.5 [MPLS: Label 16 Exp 0] 0 msec 0 msec 0 msec
  2 10.0.11.10 [MPLS: Labels 38/33 Exp 0] 0 msec 0 msec 4 msec
  3 10.0.9.16 [MPLS: Labels 35/33 Exp 0] 0 msec 0 msec 0 msec
  4 10.0.7.11 [MPLS: Label 33 Exp 0] 0 msec 0 msec 0 msec
  5 10.0.17.12 4 msec *  0 msec
```

After failure, you can check if the FRR is active using the **show mpls traffic-eng fast-reroute** command at the PLR (12008a), as demonstrated in Examples 7-17 and 7-18.

Example 7-17 *Determining Whether FRR Is Active*

```
12008a#show mpls traffic-eng fast-reroute database
Tunnel head fast reroute information:
Prefix            Tunnel      In-label Out intf/label  FRR intf/label   Status
LSP midpoint frr information:
LSP identifier                In-label Out intf/label  FRR intf/label   Status
4.4.4.4 1 [1520]              16       PO1/0:33        Tu1:33           active
```

Example 7-18 *Details of the FRR Database*

```
12008a#show mpls traffic-eng fast-reroute database detail
LFIB FRR Database Summary:
  Total Clusters:      1
  Total Groups:        1
  Total Items:         1
Link 4: PO1/0 (Down, 1 group)
  Group 28: PO1/0->Tu1 (Up, 1 member)
    LSP identifier 4.4.4.4 1 [1520], active
       Input label 16, Output label PO1/0:33, FRR label Tu1:33
```

Another useful command for checking FRR information is **show ip rsvp sender detail**. It shows what the RSVP neighbors have sent. Example 7-19 shows the output of this command executed on 12008a.

Example 7-19 **show ip rsvp sender detail** *Output*

```
12008a#show ip rsvp sender detail
PATH:
  Tun Dest:   12.12.12.12  Tun ID: 1  Ext Tun ID: 4.4.4.4
  Tun Sender: 4.4.4.4  LSP ID: 1520
  Path refreshes arriving on POS2/1 from PHOP 10.0.3.4
  Path refreshes being sent to NHOP 11.11.11.11 on Tunnel1
  Session Attr::
    Setup Prio: 7, Holding Prio: 7
    Flags: Local Prot desired, Label Recording, SE Style
    Session Name:Primary tunnel 7200a->12008a->12008c->7200c
  ERO:
    11.11.11.11 (Strict IPv4 Prefix, 8 bytes, /32)
    10.0.17.12 (Strict IPv4 Prefix, 8 bytes, /32)
    12.12.12.12 (Strict IPv4 Prefix, 8 bytes, /32)
  RRO:
    10.0.3.4/32, Flags:0x0 (No Local Protection)
  Traffic params - Rate: 0G bits/sec, Max. burst: 1K bytes
  Fast-Reroute Backup info:
    Inbound  FRR: Not active
    Outbound FRR: Active -- using backup tunnel
    Backup Tunnel: Tu1       (label 33)
    Bkup Sender Template:
      Tun Sender: 10.0.11.5  LSP ID: 1632
    Bkup FilerSpec:
      Tun Sender: 10.0.11.5, LSP ID 1632
    Orig Output I/F: PO1/0
    Orig Output ERO:
      10.0.5.11 (Strict IPv4 Prefix, 8 bytes, /32)
      10.0.17.12 (Strict IPv4 Prefix, 8 bytes, /32)
      12.12.12.12 (Strict IPv4 Prefix, 8 bytes, /32)
```

The **show mpls traffic-eng fast-reroute database** and **show ip rsvp sender detail** commands are good when they are applied *when FRR is active.* However, if you want to get historical information about when FRR was active and for how long, you can use the **show mpls traffic-eng fast-reroute log reroutes** command, shown in Example 7-20.

Example 7-20 *Obtaining Historical Information for Fast Reroute*

```
12008a#show mpls traffic-eng fast-reroute log reroutes
When       Interface  Event  Rewrites      Duration    CPU msecs   Suspends  Errors
23:58:20   Tu1        Down          0      0 msecs             0          0       0
23:58:04   PO1/0      Down          1      0 msecs             0          0       0
23:57:54   PO1/0      Up            0      0 msecs             0          0       0
01:05:47   PO1/0      Down          1      0 msecs             0          0       0
01:01:12   PO1/0      Down          1      0 msecs             0          0       0
00:34:39   PO1/0      Down          1      0 msecs             0          0       0
00:00:41   PO1/0      Down          1      0 msecs             0          0       0
```

Some useful commands for debugging FRR are as follows:

- **debug ip rsvp fast-reroute**
- **debug mpls lfib fast-reroute database**
- **debug mpls lfib fast-reroute events**
- **debug mpls lfib fast-reroute reroutes**

Post-Failure Signalling

As you understand by now, much of RSVP-based MPLS TE revolves around RSVP signalling. Fast restoration is not an exception. FRR concepts and implementation depend heavily on making further extensions to what is already defined in RFC 3209. These extensions are specified in *draft-ietf-mpls-rsvp-lsp-fastreroute*. This section talks about RSVP signalling that happens after FRR protection has kicked in. This can be broken into the following:

- Upstream signalling
- IGP notification
- Downstream signalling

Upstream Signalling

Recall from Chapter 4, "Path Calculation and Setup," that when a link goes down along an LSP, the node that is upstream of the failed link signals a path error to the headends of the LSPs traversing the failed link. In Figure 7-12, after the link between 12008a and 12008c fails, it is the responsibility of 12008a to send a PathErr message to 7200a, which is the headend of the primary tunnel.

According to RFC 3209, "RSVP-TE: Extensions to RSVP for LSP Tunnels," with no local protection configured, a node that is upstream of a failed link needs to send a PathErr for each LSP that crossed this link. This PathErr contains an error code of 24 (meaning

"Routing Problem") with a value of 5 (indicating "No route available toward destination"), as shown in Figure 7-12. You can see this in the output of **debug ip rsvp path detail** on 7200a after shutting down the link between 12008a and 12008c, as demonstrated in Example 7-21.

Example 7-21 *Using RSVP Path Debug to Observe PathErr*

```
7200a#debug ip rsvp path detail
*Oct 16 12:54:09.469: RSVP:        version:1 flags:0000 type:PERR cksum:0000 ttl:25
*Oct 16 12:54:09.469: SESSION              type 7 length 16:
*Oct 16 12:54:09.469:   Tun Dest 12.12.12.12 Tun ID 1 Ext Tun ID 4.4.4.4
*Oct 16 12:54:09.469: ERROR_SPEC           type 1 length 12:
*Oct 16 12:54:09.469:   Error Node: 10.0.3.5
*Oct 16 12:54:09.469:   Error Code: 24 (Routing Problem)
*Oct 16 12:54:09.469:   Error Value: 0x5  (No route available toward destination)
```

Figure 7-12 *PathErr Without Local Protection*

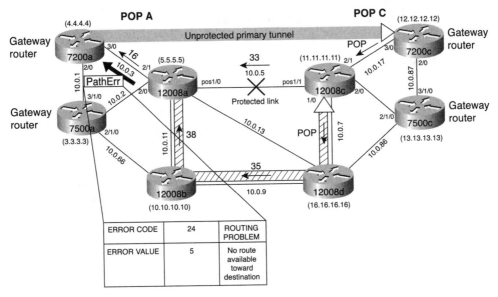

When an LSP's headend gets the error shown in Example 7-21, it brings the tunnel interface down and then tries to find a new path for the LSP. The headend ignores the fact that local protection might be available around the broken link.

As a result, traffic along that LSP is blackholed until the LSP can be rerouted. This makes the backup LSP completely useless. Hence, you need a mechanism for 12008a to tell 7200a something like this: "My downstream link along the LSP is broken. I am temporarily rerouting the traffic. This path might no longer be the optimal path to the destination. Please compute an alternative path if one is available." This is also referred to as the LSR 12008a *triggering reoptimization.*

To signal the nondestructive information, RFC 3209 specifies using a PathErr with an ERROR_SPEC containing error code 25, "Notification," and a subcode of 3, "Tunnel locally repaired."

When an LSP headend receives such a message, it knows that it does not need to immediately stop using its primary LSP, just that this LSP might be following a suboptimal path until it can be rerouted. The headend is free to reroute the LSP when it gets a chance to do so. What protection buys you here is that during the time before the headend can find a suitable alternative end-to-end path, traffic is still being delivered down the backup tunnel.

A headend that receives a notification of 25/3 attempts to calculate and signal a new path for that tunnel. After receiving the reservation (RESV) message for this new path, the label for the old path is replaced with the new label. Only then is the old LSP torn down. This achieves make-before-break and helps minimize packet loss.

If the headend cannot find a new path for an LSP that is currently being protected, the headend remains on the protected path. You might have an LSP that has an explicit path that doesn't allow it to get away from a failed link, or perhaps the necessary bandwidth for an LSP is available only along the link that has failed. As long as the protection tunnel is in place, the protected LSP remains up and passes traffic, and the headend periodically tries to find a new path for that tunnel to take.

Figure 7-13 shows the PathErr message when local protection has been enabled.

Figure 7-13 *PathErr with Local Protection*

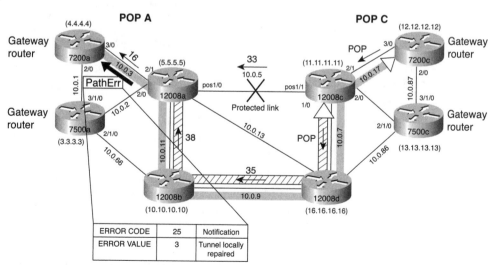

Figure 7-13 shows that 12008a (PLR) sends a PathErr to the primary tunnel headend 7200a. This is also captured in the debug output on 7200a using the **debug ip rsvp path detail** command, as shown in Example 7-22.

Example 7-22 *PathErr Sent from 12008a to 7200a*

```
7200a#debug ip rsvp path detail
*Oct 17 08:20:45.420: RSVP:     version:1 flags:0000 type:PERR cksum:0000 ttl:255
reserved:0 length:132
*Oct 17 08:20:45.420:  SESSION             type 7 length 16:
*Oct 17 08:20:45.420:   Tun Dest 12.12.12.12 Tun ID 1 Ext Tun ID 4.4.4.4
*Oct 17 08:20:45.420:  ERROR_SPEC          type 1 length 12:
*Oct 17 08:20:45.420:   Error Node: 10.0.3.5
*Oct 17 08:20:45.420:   Error Code: 25 (Notify)
*Oct 17 08:20:45.420:   Error Value: 0x3  (Tunnel locally repaired)
*Oct 17 08:20:45.420:  SENDER_TEMPLATE     type 7 length 12:
*Oct 17 08:20:45.420:   Tun Sender: 4.4.4.4, LSP ID: 1520
*Oct 17 08:20:45.420:  SENDER_TSPEC        type 2 length 36:
*Oct 17 08:20:45.420:   version=0, length in words=7
*Oct 17 08:20:45.420:   service id=1, service length=6
*Oct 17 08:20:45.420:   parameter id=127, flags=0, parameter length=5
*Oct 17 08:20:45.420:   average rate=0 bytes/sec, burst depth=1000 bytes
*Oct 17 08:20:45.420:   peak rate  =0 bytes/sec
*Oct 17 08:20:45.420:   min unit=0 bytes, max unit=0 bytes
*Oct 17 08:20:45.420:  ADSPEC              type 2 length 48:
*Oct 17 08:20:45.420:  version=0  length in words=10
*Oct 17 08:20:45.420:  General Parameters  break bit=0  service length=8
*Oct 17 08:20:45.420:                                    IS Hops:1
*Oct 17 08:20:45.420:            Minimum Path Bandwidth (bytes/sec):19375000
*Oct 17 08:20:45.420:                     Path Latency (microseconds):0
*Oct 17 08:20:45.420:                                 Path MTU:4470
*Oct 17 08:20:45.420:  Controlled Load Service  break bit=0  service length=0
*Oct 17 08:20:45.420:
*Oct 17 08:20:45.420: RSVP 4.4.4.4_1520-12.12.12.12_1: PATH ERROR message for
   12.12.12.12 (POS3/0) from 10.0.3.5
```

As shown in the highlighted output in Example 7-22, 10.0.3.5 happens to be the interface address of 12008a facing 7200a. This is highlighted so that you know where the RSVP messages are coming from.

When a protected link fails and is switched down the backup tunnel, the PLR also sends Path messages for the protected LSPs down the backup tunnel. This is so that the MP doesn't time out the protected tunnel, in the unlikely event that the protected tunnel headend can't reroute the LSP. See the later section "Downstream Signalling" for more details on why this is necessary.

Additionally, some changes are made to the body of the Path message itself. As you know, RSVP is a soft-state protocol. In order to keep sessions alive, RSVP refresh messages are sent periodically. These refresh messages are sent between RSVP neighbors by sending Path and Resv messages. LSP tunnels are identified by a combination of the SESSION and SENDER_TEMPLATE objects in these Path and Resv messages (see Chapter 4). The

SENDER_TEMPLATE object is modified by the PLR so that the sender IPv4 address now contains the PLR's IP address rather than that of the headend. Doing so allows the tail to see this Path message as coming from a new sender but still belonging to the same session.

From this point on, the refresh messages can flow over the backup tunnel. The original state maintained by the tail for this session is eventually torn down because of timeout (by any LSR downstream of the failed link, including the tail), but the altered Path message from the PLR is enough to effectively maintain the bandwidth reservation for as long as necessary. Example 7-23 shows the original ERO on 7200a before the protected link between 12008a and 12008c went down. Example 7-24 shows the change in ERO in the RSVP refresh message over the backup tunnel.

Example 7-23 *Original ERO on Headend Router 7200a*

```
7200a#show mpls traffic-eng tunnel tunnel1

Name: Primary tunnel 7200a->12008a->12... (Tunnel1) Destination: 12.12.12.12
  Status:
    Admin: up          Oper: up      Path: valid        Signalling: connected

    path option 5, type explicit primary (Basis for Setup, path weight 3)

  Config Parameters:
    Bandwidth: 100      kbps (Global)  Priority: 7  7    Affinity: 0x0/0xFFFF
    Metric Type: TE (default)
    AutoRoute: enabled   LockDown: disabled  Loadshare: 100      bw-based
    auto-bw: disabled(0/258) 0  Bandwidth Requested: 100

  InLabel  :  -
  OutLabel : POS3/0, 16
  RSVP Signalling Info:
       Src 4.4.4.4, Dst 12.12.12.12, Tun_Id 1, Tun_Instance 1520
    RSVP Path Info:
      My Address: 4.4.4.4
      Explicit Route: 10.0.3.5 10.0.5.11 10.0.17.12 12.12.12.12
```

Example 7-24 *Path Message for 7200c*

```
12008a#debug ip rsvp path detail
RSVP 4.4.4.4_1520-12.12.12.12_1: PATH message for 12.12.12.12(POS2/1) from 10.0.3.4
RSVP 4.4.4.4_1520-12.12.12.12_1: PATH: fastreroute in progress
RSVP:    version:1 flags:0000 type:PATH cksum:0000 ttl:254 reserved:0 length:216
  SESSION            type 7 length 16:
        Destination 12.12.12.12, TunnelId 3, Source 3.3.3.3
  HOP                type 1 length 12: 0A000203
                                     : 00000000
  TIME_VALUES        type 1 length 8 : 00007530
  EXPLICIT_ROUTE     type 1 length 52:
        (#1) Strict IPv4 Prefix, 8 bytes, 10.0.2.5/32
        (#2) Strict IPv4 Prefix, 8 bytes, 10.0.11.10/32
        (#4) Strict IPv4 Prefix, 8 bytes, 10.0.7.11/32
        (#5) Strict IPv4 Prefix, 8 bytes, 10.0.17.12/32
        (#6) Strict IPv4 Prefix, 8 bytes, 12.12.12.12/32
```

Related to the refresh messages is the fact that Path messages would have to be forwarded down the backup tunnel by the PLR. But if the PLR did so using the contents of the ERO, as it would normally do, it would fail because the next IP address in the ERO would point to the failed link. This behavior has to change to make FRR work. In addition to the ERO, the RRO and phop objects are modified for refresh messages flowing over the backup tunnel according to the IETF draft.

IGP Notification

Although in many cases, RSVP messages reach either the headend or tailend ahead of any IGP notification, this is not guaranteed to be the case. When IGP information (such as OSPF/IS-IS LSA declaring a link down) for some reason makes it before the RSVP message, what consequences does this have on TE signalling?

In the absence of FRR, if the primary tunnel headend receives a link-down LSA for a link that was part of the primary LSP, the headend tears down the primary tunnel. After that, the headend can, if configured correctly, attempt to reroute the LSP.

If the primary tunnel is configured for FRR, the link-down LSA has no effect. The headend tears down a protected LSP based only on RSVP error messages and ignores IGP's reporting a link down along the LSP. This is because a downed link doesn't necessarily mean a failed LSP because the LSP could be protected.

Downstream Signalling

You just saw the repercussions of link failure upstream of the failed link, both with and without local protection. This section examines what goes on downstream of the failed link.

Consider the topology shown in Figure 7-14.

Figure 7-14 *PathTear in the Absence of FRR*

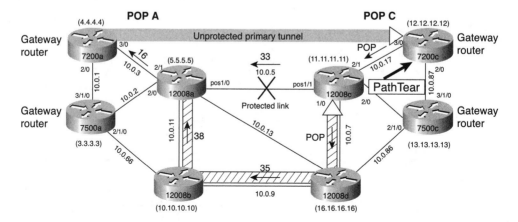

When the link between 12008a and 12008c goes down (when no local protection is in place), 12008c sends a PathTear message to 7200c, as demonstrated in Example 7-25.

Example 7-25 *PathTear Message from 12008c to 7200c*

```
12008c#debug ip rsvp path detail
*Oct 22 12:59:41.185: RSVP:     version:1 flags:0000 type:PTEAR cksum:6CF7 ttl:2
52 reserved:0 length:132
*Oct 22 12:59:41.185:  SESSION            type 7 length 16:
*Oct 22 12:59:41.189:   Tun Dest 12.12.12.12 Tun ID 1 Ext Tun ID 4.4.4.4
*Oct 22 12:59:41.189:  HOP                type 1 length 12:
*Oct 22 12:59:41.189:   Hop Addr: 10.0.17.11 LIH: 0x0
*Oct 22 12:59:41.189:  SENDER_TEMPLATE     type 7 length 12:
*Oct 22 12:59:41.189:   Tun Sender: 4.4.4.4, LSP ID: 1520
*Oct 22 12:59:41.189:  SENDER_TSPEC        type 2 length 36:
*Oct 22 12:59:41.189:   version=0, length in words=7
*Oct 22 12:59:41.189:   service id=1, service length=6
*Oct 22 12:59:41.189:   parameter id=127, flags=0, parameter length=5
*Oct 22 12:59:41.189:   average rate=0 bytes/sec, burst depth=1000 bytes
*Oct 22 12:59:41.189:   peak rate   =0 bytes/sec
*Oct 22 12:59:41.189:   min unit=0 bytes, max unit=0 bytes
*Oct 22 12:59:41.189:  ADSPEC             type 2 length 48:
*Oct 22 12:59:41.189:  version=0  length in words=10
*Oct 22 12:59:41.189:  General Parameters  break bit=0  service length=8
*Oct 22 12:59:41.189:                                 IS Hops:2
*Oct 22 12:59:41.189:             Minimum Path Bandwidth (bytes/sec):19375000
*Oct 22 12:59:41.189:                     Path Latency (microseconds):0
*Oct 22 12:59:41.189:                                 Path MTU:4470
*Oct 22 12:59:41.189:  Controlled Load Service  break bit=0  service length=0
*Oct 22 12:59:41.189:
```

But if the LSP were protected because of FRR, this kind of message would have an adverse effect. It would result in the LSP's being torn down even though the LSP were being locally protected by the PLR. To prevent this, the PathTear message needs to be suppressed for primary LSPs that have the "Local Protection Desired" flag on, in spite of the fact that you don't receive Path messages for the protected primary tunnel on the original incoming interface anymore. As long as 12008c receives Path messages belonging to the original RSVP session on any interface, it does not time out and sends a PathTear on its downstream interface. If you recall from the "Upstream Signalling" section, the PLR sends Path messages for all protected tunnels down the protection tunnel.

As the tail of the primary tunnel, 7200c does not know that the protected tunnel has failed unless one of the following things happens:

● It receives an IGP update about the link failure.

● It receives a PathTear from MD 12008c.

● It does not receive an RSVP refresh message (Path) that keeps the session alive within a certain period of time.

This wait on Cisco routers by default is four keepalive periods. (See Chapter 4 for more information on RSVP timers.)

If the tail receives an IGP update about the link failure, it does not take any action from an MPLS TE perspective.

If the RSVP signalling state times out, the LSP is declared dead, and a ResvTear message is sent to the headend. This means that, apart from preventing PathTear from being sent by MP 12008c, you somehow need to make sure that the tail continues to receive the RSVP refresh messages even though one of the links that constituted the primary LSP is now down. This is achieved by making sure that the MP (12008c) continues to receive PATH messages for the primary LSP over the backup tunnel.

Link Protection Configuration Summary

The earlier sections delved into the pieces that make up local protection. The configuration and **show** commands used for each piece were provided and the concepts explained. This section summarizes all the configuration pieces needed to configure link protection.

The sample topology shown in Figure 7-15 explains the link protection configuration. In Figure 7-15, 7200a is the head of the primary tunnel that needs to be protected against failure of the protected link 12008a→12008c. 12008a is the PLR, and 12008c is the MP.

Figure 7-15 *Link Protection Configuration*

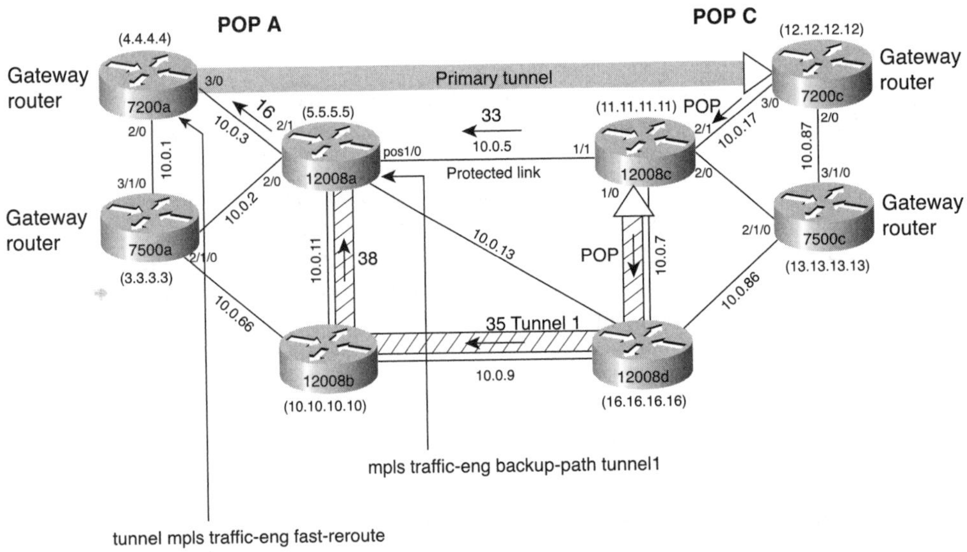

The configuration task for link protection can be broken into the following:

- Headend configuration
- PLR configuration

Headend Configuration

Example 7-26 shows the primary tunnel configuration for 7200a for enabling FRR.

Example 7-26 *7200a Tunnel Configuration Before Enabling FRR*

```
7200a#show running-config interface tunnel1
interface Tunnel1
 description Primary tunnel 7200a->12008a->12008c->7200c
 ip unnumbered Loopback0
 tunnel destination 12.12.12.12
 tunnel mode mpls traffic-eng
 tunnel mpls traffic-eng autoroute announce
 tunnel mpls traffic-eng path-option 5 explicit name primary
 tunnel mpls traffic-eng path-option 6 dynamic
 tunnel mpls traffic-eng fast-reroute

7200a#show ip explicit-paths name primary
PATH primary (strict source route, path complete, generation 6)
    1: next-address 10.0.3.5
    2: next-address 10.0.5.11
    3: next-address 10.0.17.12
    4: next-address 12.12.12.12
```

PLR Configuration

The PLR configuration consists of two pieces:

- Building a backup tunnel to NHop
- Configuring the protected interface to use the backup tunnel

Example 7-27 shows what the configuration of the backup tunnel on 12008a looks like.

Example 7-27 *12008a Backup Tunnel Configuration*

```
12008a#show running-config interface tunnel1
interface Tunnel1
 description Link Protection Tunnel (Backup)
 ip unnumbered Loopback0
 no ip directed-broadcast
 tunnel destination 11.11.11.11
 tunnel mode mpls traffic-eng
 tunnel mpls traffic-eng path-option 5 explicit name nhop

12008a#show ip explicit-paths name nhop
PATH nhop (strict source route, path complete, generation 24)
    1: next-address 10.0.11.10
    2: next-address 10.0.9.16
    3: next-address 10.0.7.11
```

Example 7-28 shows the configuration of protected interface POS 1/0, required for FRR.

Example 7-28 *POS 1/0 Configuration After the* **backup-path** *Statement Is Added*

```
12008a#show running-config interface pos 1/0
Building configuration...

Current configuration : 365 bytes
!
interface POS1/0
 ip address 10.0.5.5 255.255.255.0
 no ip directed-broadcast
 mpls label protocol ldp
 mpls traffic-eng tunnels
 mpls traffic-eng backup-path Tunnel1
 tag-switching ip
 crc 32
 clock source internal
 ip rsvp bandwidth 155000 155000
end
```

As you can see, enabling link protection is simple. It turns out that enabling node protection is just as easy, as you will see in the next section.

Node Protection

The earlier section "Node Protection Overview" provided you with a basic understanding of how node protection works. This section focuses on the details of node protection, particularly the areas in which node protection deviates from link protection.

Similarities Between Link Protection and Node Protection

Node protection and link protection share a few common characteristics and differ on a few others. The similarities are as follows:

- Enabling FRR at the primary tunnel headend
- Tying the protected link to the backup tunnel
- Failure detection
- Connectivity restoration
- Post-failure signalling

In node protection, although you are trying to protect against the failure of an NHop, the way you detect the failure is configured on the link connecting the PLR to the NHop, just as you would in case of link protection.

Differences Between Link Protection and Node Protection

This section examines the areas in which node protection differs from link protection:

- NNHop backup tunnel is configured at the PLR.
- Label recording is required for the NNHop backup tunnel.
- NNHop tunnel handles link and node failures.

NNHop Backup Tunnel Is Configured at the PLR

Creating a backup tunnel to the NNHop is similar to creating a backup tunnel to the NHop, except that an NNHop tunnel terminates on the NNHop instead of on the NHop. You have to build the backup tunnel to the NNHop instead of the NHop to protect against the failure of the NHop node. Example 7-29 shows the configuration of the NNHop backup tunnel on 12008a. This is depicted in Figure 7-16.

Example 7-29 *NNHop Backup Tunnel for Node Protection*

```
12008a#show running-config interface tunnel2
interface Tunnel2
 ip unnumbered Loopback0
 no ip directed-broadcast
 tunnel destination 12.12.12.12
 tunnel mode mpls traffic-eng
 tunnel mpls traffic-eng path-option 5 explicit name nnhop
 ip rsvp signalling dscp 0
end

12008a#show ip explicit-paths name nnhop
ip explicit-path name nnhop enable
 next-address 10.0.11.10
 next-address 10.0.9.16
 next-address 10.0.86.13
 next-address 10.0.87.12
 next-address 12.12.12.12
```

The hops specified in the explicit path list **nnhop** are as follows:

- **10.0.11.10**—The IP address of 12008b on link 12008a→12008b
- **10.0.9.16**—The IP address of 12008d on link 12008b→12008d
- **10.0.86.13**—The IP address of 7500c on link 12008d→7500c
- **10.0.87.12**—The IP address of 7200c on link 7500c→7200c

As you can see from Example 7-29, the destination of the tunnel is 12.12.12.12, which is the RID of 7200c, the NNHop node.

Figure 7-16 *Node Protection*

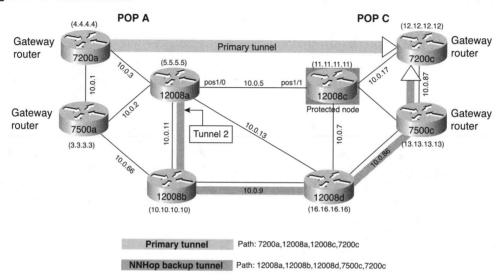

Primary tunnel	Path: 7200a,12008a,12008c,7200c
NNHop backup tunnel	Path: 12008a,12008b,12008d,7500c,7200c

Label Recording Is Required for the NNHop Backup Tunnel

The output in Example 7-30 shows the **Label Recording** flag turned on. This flag is turned on whenever the headend configures **tunnel mpls traffic-eng fast-reroute**.

Example 7-30 **debug ip path resv detail** *Output on 7200a Showing Label Recording*

```
7200a#debug ip path resv detail
*Oct 16 14:40:57.124:  SESSION_ATTRIBUTE    type 7 length 24:
*Oct 16 14:40:57.124:   Setup Prio: 7, Holding Prio: 7
*Oct 16 14:40:57.124:   Flags: Local Prot desired, Label Recording, SE Style
*Oct 16 14:40:57.124:   Session Name: 7200a_t1
```

When you build a tunnel to the NHop because you are this node's upstream neighbor, you know what label the downstream neighbor expects because you received the label from the RSVP Resv message along the reservation. However, if you want to build a backup tunnel to the NNHop node, you do not know what label this node expects for a given LSP.

This is what the Label Recording flag is for. It records the incoming label used at each hop for an LSP so that a PLR doing node protection knows what label to use on a protected LSP when it's switched down the backup tunnel. Here is a quote from RFC 3902:

The recording of the Label subobject in the ROUTE_RECORD object is controlled by the label-recording-desired flag in the SESSION_ATTRIBUTE object. Since the Label subobject is not needed for all applications, it is not automatically recorded. The flag allows applications to request this only when needed.

Also, if you examine the output of **show mpls traffic-eng tunnel tunnel1** on 7200a, you'll see this:

```
Record   Route:   10.0.5.5(16) 10.0.17.11(33)
                  10.0.17.12(0)
```

The numbers 16, 33, and 0 in parentheses refer to the label values from the record label object.

Having this information available is also useful during troubleshooting.

Note that requesting label recording is controlled by the tunnel headend. Because the headend doesn't know whether the network has link protection or node protection, label recording is turned on but is not used if the network has no node protection.

NNHop Tunnel Handles Link and Node Failures

If you consider Figure 7-16 again, the backup tunnel bypasses both the NHop and the link that connects the PLR to the NHop. Even though the tunnel is primarily in place to protect against the failure of 12008c, the protected node, if the link 12008a→12008c fails, there is no way for the PLR (12008a) to tell whether the link went down because link itself went down or the link went down because the entire NHop node went down.

If you used an NHop backup tunnel, it would only guard against link failures. With NNHop backup tunnels, the moment a failure is detected on the POS 1/0 interface on 12008a, protection kicks in, sending all the packets of the primary tunnel over the backup tunnel. As you can see, node protection is both link and node protection rolled into one.

Advanced Protection Issues

The previous sections described how link and node protection work. This section covers some advanced FRR features that you can configure to make the protection you are using more effective. Here are the topics covered:

- Multiple backup tunnels to the same MP
- Backup bandwidth reservation
- Backup tunnel selection
- Promotion

Multiple Backup Tunnels

There are two types of multiple backup tunnels:

- Multiple backup tunnels to the same MP
- NHop versus NNHop backup tunnels

Multiple Backup Tunnels to the Same MP

Figure 7-17 shows a link that is protected by backup tunnel1 and backup tunnel2. This link carries two primary tunnels—tunnel1 and tunnel2.

Figure 7-17 *Multiple Backup Tunnels to the Same MP*

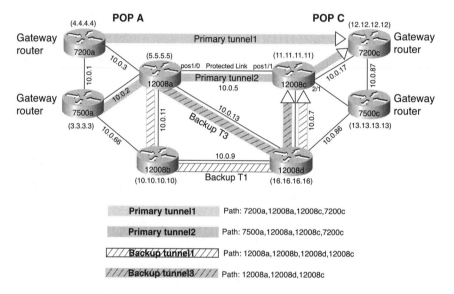

Suppose that the protected link—12008a→12008c in Figure 7-17—is an OC-12 link, but the other two downstream links from 12008a to 12008b and 12008d are only OC-3s. Suppose further that two LSPs exist that traverse the protected link: one from 7200a (Primary Tunnel1 in Figure 7-17) and one from 7500a (primary tunnel2 in Figure 7-17). Each LSP has a reservation of 150 Mbps, and both of them have FRR configured at the headend. If the protected link fails, it is not possible to offload both these LSPs onto a single backup tunnel without incurring traffic loss, because the two downstream links from 12008a over which you can build backup tunnels are both OC-3s. What can you do?

You can configure two backup tunnels from 12008a to 12008c—backup tunnel1 and backup tunnel3—such that each backup tunnel goes over diverse paths that have OC-3 worth of bandwidth. This protects the two primary tunnels without dropping traffic, as shown in Figure 7-17.

With multiple backup tunnels to the same MP, when the protected link or node fails, the traffic from primary tunnel1 and primary tunnel2 is assigned to these backup tunnels. This can be observed using the **show mpls traffic-eng fast-reroute database** command, as demonstrated in Example 7-31, which shows the FRR status on 12008a.

Example 7-31 *FRR Status Information with Multiple Backup Tunnels*

```
12008a#show mpls traffic-eng fast-reroute database
Tunnel head fast reroute information:
Prefix            Tunnel   In-label Out intf/label  FRR intf/label  Status
LSP midpoint frr information:
LSP identifier             In-label Out intf/label  FRR intf/label  Status
4.4.4.4 1 [1520]           16       PO1/0:33         Tu1:33          ready
3.3.3.3 1 [902]            28       PO1/0:12319      Tu3: 19         ready
```

The first line of output in Example 7-31 corresponds to Primary Tunnel1 (7200a), and the second one corresponds to primary tunnel2 (7500a). The out interface is POS1/0—the protected link/interface in both cases. Figure 7-18 illustrates the actual forwarding of the primary LSPs after failure.

Figure 7-18 *Load Balancing of Two Primary LSPs*

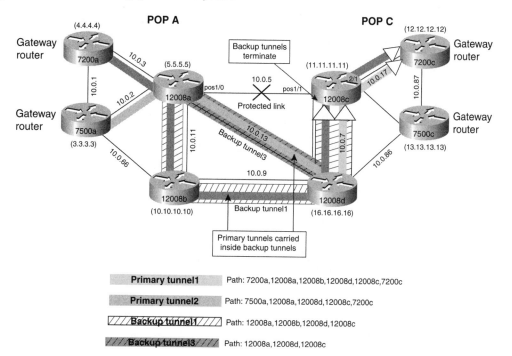

NOTE Parallel backup tunnels are meaningful only when they are destined for the same MP. Traffic belonging to a single primary tunnel is always carried on the same backup tunnel during failure. It is not split over multiple backup tunnels, even if they are configured. This is not CEF's load balancing, but instead merely a distribution of protected tunnels among protection tunnels. The later section "Backup Tunnel Selection Summary" covers this assignment in more detail.

NHop Versus NNHop Backup Tunnels

An NHop backup tunnel protects against failure of the link from the PLR to the NHop node, whereas an NNHop backup tunnel protects against both NHop node failure and the link connecting the PLR to the NHop. Hence, if both are configured, the PLR chooses the NNHop backup tunnel over the NHop backup tunnel when assigning protected LSPs to backup tunnels. Figure 7-19 depicts two backup tunnels configured on PLR 12008a—one going to NHop and the other going to NNHop.

Figure 7-19 *NHop Versus NNHop Backup Tunnels*

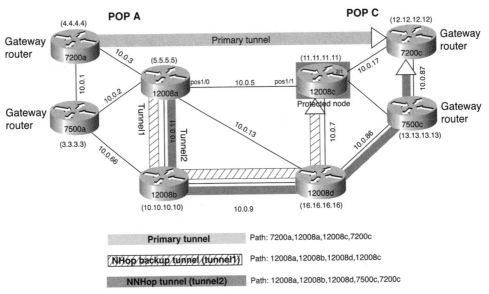

Example 7-32 shows that both primary LSPs are backed up using NNHop tunnel2, even though two backup tunnels are available—one to the NHop and the second to the NNHop. This can be observed by executing the **show mpls traffic-eng fast-reroute database** command.

Example 7-32 *NNHop Tunnel2 Being Used for Protection*

```
12008a#show mpls traffic-eng fast-reroute database
Tunnel head fast reroute information:
Prefix              Tunnel    In-label Out intf/label   FRR intf/label    Status
LSP midpoint frr information:
LSP identifier                In-label Out intf/label   FRR intf/label    Status
4.4.4.4 1 [1520]                 16      PO1/0:Pop tag   Tu2:tag-implicit ready
3.3.3.3 1 [902]                  28      PO1/0:19        Tu2:tag-implicit ready
```

Backup Bandwidth Reservation

The preceding section discussed the motivation for having multiple backup tunnels. This section discusses another FRR feature—*bandwidth* protection rather than just *link* (or node) protection. The idea is that, rather than placing all protected tunnels down a protection tunnel that might end up traversing a link that could be congested during failure, you can build bandwidth-aware protection tunnels. This is a fairly complex mechanism to employ on a large scale, but it gives you the best possible protection for your network.

Two new terms are introduced:

* Limited backup bandwidth
* Unlimited backup bandwidth

Limited backup bandwidth, as you might suspect, puts a limit on how much bandwidth can be allocated from a backup tunnel. It is a number that you need to configure, as shown in Example 7-33.

Example 7-33 *Backup Bandwidth Configuration for Global Pools and Subpools*

```
12008a(config-if)#tunnel mpls traffic-eng backup-bw ?
  <1-4294967295>  Amount of allocatable backup bw, any lsp may use
  global-pool     Enter Allocatable amount for Global-Pool bw
  sub-pool        Enter Allocatable amount for Sub-Pool bw
```

The limit can be a number between 1 and 4,294,967,295 specified in terms of kbps. The keywords **Global-Pool** and **Sub-Pool** refer to the dual pools created for DiffServ-Aware Traffic Engineering (DS-TE) (if you recall from Chapter 6, "Quality of Service with MPLS TE"). Again, for each of the pools, you can either limit the backup bandwidth using the configuration shown in Example 7-34, or you can use the keyword **unlimited**. If you enter a backup bandwidth without specifying the pool, the bandwidth protection offered by this backup tunnel is available to both types of primary LSPs. If you specify the pool type on the backup tunnel, only primary LSPs of that pool type can use the backup tunnel.

Example 7-34 *Configuring Limited Versus Unlimited Backup Bandwidth for the DS-TE Global Pool*

```
12008a(config-if)#tunnel mpls traffic-eng backup-bw global-pool ?
  <1-4294967295>  Amount of allocatable backup bw, only global-pool may use
  Unlimited       Unlimited amount for Global-Pool bw
```

Unlimited backup bandwidth, as the name suggests, has no limits on how much backup bandwidth can be allocated from the backup tunnel. The same terms apply to subpools as well. Example 7-35 shows the configuration for unlimited backup bandwidth.

Example 7-35 *Configuring Limited Versus Unlimited Backup Bandwidth for the DS-TE Subpool*

```
12008a(config-if)#tunnel mpls traffic-eng backup-bw sub-pool ?
  <1-4294967295>  Amount of allocatable backup bw, only sub-pool may use
  Unlimited       Unlimited amount for Sub-Pool bw
```

If you refer to Table 7-3 (in the next section), you can see that, if multiple backup tunnels are configured at a PLR, the backup tunnel selection process chooses a backup tunnel with *limited* backup bandwidth over one that has *unlimited* bandwidth configured. Among the tunnels that have *limited* bandwidth configured, the ones that terminate at NNHop are preferred over ones that terminate on NHop. It also prefers tunnels with subpool reservation over ones that have global pool reservation.

NOTE   It is important to understand that backup bandwidth is only an associated bandwidth. It is not actually signalled. In other words, this scheme does not require the backup tunnels to successfully reserve the amount of bandwidth they offer (by configuring the backup-bw on the backup tunnels). You can configure the backup tunnel to reserve bandwidth if you want (using the **tunnel mpls traffic-eng bandwidth** command), but reserving bandwidth is a separate issue from protecting bandwidth.

Consider the example shown in Figure 7-20. The primary LSP has 100 Mbps of bandwidth reserved (from either pool), and four backup tunnels terminate at the same destination (12008c—PLR). Backup tunnel T1 has been configured with *unlimited* backup bandwidth and three tunnels (T2, T3, and T4) with *limited* backup bandwidth—80 Mbps, 120 Mbps, and 150 Mbps, respectively.

During the backup selection process, tunnel T1 is eliminated because other *limited* backup tunnels are going to the same destination that fit the demand. Tunnel T2 is eliminated because it has 80 Mbps and does not fulfill the bandwidth requirement of the primary LSP (100 Mbps). Both tunnel T3 and T4 meet the bandwidth requirement of the primary LSP. Backup tunnel T3 is selected because it has the least leftover bandwidth. After the primary LSP is assigned to backup tunnel T3, the backup bandwidth on tunnel T3 is reduced by 100 Mbps, so it now has a remaining protection capacity of 20 Mbps.

If backup tunnel T4 were selected, 50 Mbps of bandwidth would be wasted because it is not required by the primary LSP. If tunnel T3 is selected, only 20 Mbps is wasted, thus making it the best fit. Assignment is done this way in an attempt to limit backup bandwidth fragmentation.

Figure 7-20 *Backup Tunnel Selection*

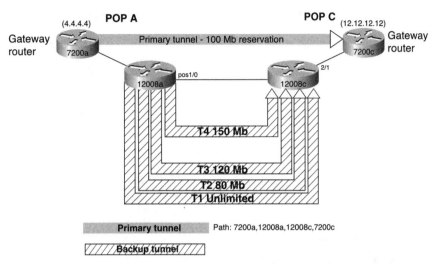

In the case of limited backup bandwidth, if more than one tunnel meets the bandwidth requirement, you choose the one that has the least *leftover* bandwidth. For unlimited, if you have more than one unlimited tunnel to choose from, you choose the one that has the least *assigned.*

Each primary LSP can reserve either global (best-effort) or subpool (premium/low-latency) bandwidth. As mentioned earlier, you can designate the pool type for the backup bandwidth—subpool to backup subpool primary LSPs, global-pool to backup global-pool primary LSPs and *any* pool (if you don't select either global or subpool). This means that the PLR tries to find a subpool backup tunnel for a subpool primary LSP with sufficient subpool bandwidth to cover the needs of that primary LSP. If such a subpool backup tunnel is not available, it tries to use the *any* pool (but not the global-pool tunnels). The same applies for global-pool backup tunnel selection. If a global-pool LSP needs backup, the PLR looks for a global-pool backup tunnel that meets its need. If it cannot find one, the PLR looks for an *any* pool tunnel but not subpool backup tunnels. Figure 7-21 shows two backup tunnels from the PLR (12008a) to the MP (7200c). One is a subpool backup tunnel and the other is a global-pool backup tunnel. Which one is used to backup the primary tunnel depends on the type of bandwidth being reserved by the primary tunnel.

Figure 7-21 *Global Versus Subpool NNHop Backup Tunnels*

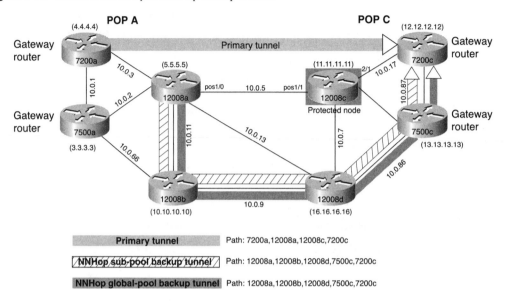

Backup Tunnel Selection Summary

When multiple backup tunnels are configured, keeping track of which backup the PLR chooses can be confusing. The process of backup tunnel selection is covered in Table 7-3 and Table 7-4. The first column shows, from best to worst, what the PLR prefers. For example, an NNHop subpool tunnel with limited bandwidth is the best, and the NHop backup tunnel with unlimited bandwidth configuration is the worst.

Table 7-3 *Tunnel Selection for Subpool Primary LSPs*

Preference	Backup Tunnel Destination	Bandwidth Pool	Bandwidth Amount
Best	NNHop	Subpool	Limited
	NNHop	Subpool	Unlimited
	NNHop	Any	Limited
	NNHop	Any	Unlimited
	NHop	Subpool	Limited
	NHop	Subpool	Unlimited
	NHop	Any	Limited
Worst	NHop	Any	Unlimited

Table 7-4   *Tunnel Selection for Global-Pool Primary LSPs*

Preference	Backup Tunnel Destination	Bandwidth Pool	Bandwidth Amount
Best	NNHop	Global-pool	Limited
	NNHop	Global-pool	Unlimited
	NNHop	Any	Limited
	NNHop	Any	Unlimited
	NHop	Global-pool	Limited
	NHop	Global-pool	Unlimited
	NHop	Any	Limited
Worst	NHop	Any	Unlimited

NOTE   Complete details on configuration and the enhancements that were implemented for node protection are available at the Cisco web site at www.cisco.com. You can obtain information relevant to node protection enhancement by searching for "Fast Reroute enhancement."

Promotion

Because multiple backup tunnels can now be configured, a backup LSP that was chosen as a result of the selection process described earlier might no longer be the best due to a change in the environment, such as the configuration of a new backup tunnel or a primary LSP's resource requirement changing. To address this issue, the PLR performs reoptimization periodically. This periodic reoptimization is called *promotion*. It is done every five minutes on the PLRs by default. You can change this default using the **mpls traffic-eng fast-reroute timers** command. Setting the value of this timer to 0 disables promotion.

You can observe when the next promotion is due by using **show mpls traffic-eng tunnels summary**, as demonstrated in Example 7-36.

Example 7-36 *Observing LSP Promotion Periods*

```
12008a#show mpls traffic-eng tunnels summary
Signalling Summary:
    LSP Tunnels Process:            running
    RSVP Process:                   running
    Forwarding:                     enabled
    Head: 3 interfaces, 2 active signalling attempts, 2 established
          10 activations, 8 deactivations
```

continues

Example 7-36 *Observing LSP Promotion Periods (Continued)*

```
Midpoints: 2, Tails: 0
Periodic reoptimization:      every 3600 seconds, next in 3367 seconds
Periodic fastreroute:         every 300 seconds, next in 67 seconds
Periodic auto-bw collection:  every 300 seconds, next in 67 seconds
```

Configuring Multiple Backup Tunnels to Multiple NNHops

When doing link protection, there is, of course, only one MP because there's only one neighbor—at least on point-to-point links. However, in the case of node protection (or link protection of a multipoint subnet, such as an Ethernet subnet), you might need to configure multiple backup tunnels to different nodes. Because multipoint Ethernet segments are rare in a network core, let's consider node protection.

If you want to configure node protection on a PLR, and the NHop across that link has three neighbors of its own, the PLR needs at least three NNHop tunnels—one to each of the NNHops. Of course, you can use more than one backup tunnel to the same NNHop if you want.

Figure 7-22 illustrates multiple backup tunnels to different NNHops. Three primary tunnels go from 7200a and 7500a to 7200c, 7500c, and 7500d. These are labeled primary tunnel 1, primary tunnel 2, and primary tunnel 3. The PLR is 12008a. The NHops that the PLR is trying to protect are 12008c, 12008b, and 12008d. Three backup tunnels—backup tunnel 1, backup tunnel 2, and backup tunnel 3—start at 12008a. Backup tunnel 1 terminates on 7200c, backup tunnel 2 terminates on 12008d, and backup tunnel 3 terminates on 12008d also. The rule you have to keep in mind when building these backup tunnels is that they need to

- Terminate on the PLR's NNHop node
- Avoid signalling the backup tunnel through the protected NHop

Notice that all the backup tunnels meet these criteria.

Figure 7-22 *Multiple Backup Tunnels to Multiple NNHops*

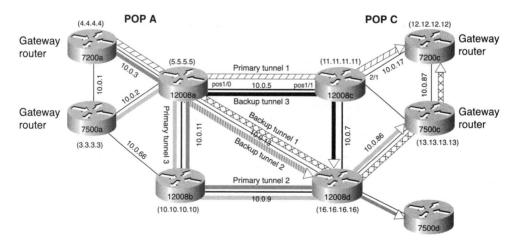

Multiple backup tunnels can be configured as shown in Example 7-37.

Example 7-37 *Multiple Backup Tunnel Configuration*

```
12008a#show running-config interface pos 1/0
interface POS1/0
 ip address 10.0.5.5 255.255.255.0
 no ip directed-broadcast
 mpls label protocol ldp
 mpls traffic-eng tunnels
 mpls traffic-eng backup-path Tunnel1
 mpls traffic-eng backup-path Tunnel2
 mpls traffic-eng backup-path Tunnel3
 crc 32
 clock source internal
 pos ais-shut
 ip rsvp bandwidth 155000 155000
end
```

Adding the second and third backup paths is no different from adding the first one. Example 7-38 shows the configuration for all the backup tunnels on 12008a.

Example 7-38 *Configuration for All the Backup Tunnels on 12008a*

```
12008a#show running-config interface tunnel1
interface Tunnel1
 description Link Protection Tunnel (Backup)
 ip unnumbered Loopback0
 no ip directed-broadcast
 tunnel destination 12.12.12.12
 tunnel mode mpls traffic-eng
 tunnel mpls traffic-eng backup-bw global-pool unlimited
 tunnel mpls traffic-eng path-option 5 explicit name backup1
end
12008a#show running-config interface tunnel2
interface Tunnel2
 ip unnumbered Loopback0
 no ip directed-broadcast
 tunnel destination 13.13.13.13
 tunnel mode mpls traffic-eng
 tunnel mpls traffic-eng backup-bw global-pool unlimited
 tunnel mpls traffic-eng path-option 5 explicit name backup2
end
12008a#show running-config interface tunnel3
interface Tunnel3
 ip unnumbered Loopback0
 no ip directed-broadcast
 tunnel destination 14.14.14.14
 tunnel mode mpls traffic-eng
 tunnel mpls traffic-eng backup-bw global-pool unlimited
 tunnel mpls traffic-eng path-option 5 explicit name backup3
end
12008a#show ip explicit paths
ip explicit-path name backup1 enable
```

continues

Example 7-38 *Configuration for All the Backup Tunnels on 12008a (Continued)*

```
next-address 10.0.13.16
next-address 10.0.87.13
next-address 10.0.86.12
next-address 12.12.12.12

ip explicit-path name backup2 enable
 next-address 10.0.13.16
next-address 16.16.16.16

ip explicit-path name backup3 enable
 next-address 10.0.5.7
 next-address 10.0.7.16
 next-address 16.16.16.16
```

As you can see, node protection configuration is similar to link protection. The only difference is in the protection tunnel (or tunnels) on the protected interface—how many there are and where they terminate.

Summary

Both IP and MPLS TE reroute if there's a failure somewhere in the network. However, IGP reroute is often not quick enough for real-time applications, and the MPLS TE headend reroute is, if anything, slower than IGP reroute because there's more work to be done.

Real-time applications might require subsecond convergence. FRR is the way to acheive this. Loss is minimized because of the ability to use local failure detection and repair. In the absence of local failure detection and repair, signalling propagation delay might result in packet loss that is unsuitable for real-time applications.

There are two types of local protection: link protection and node protection. Link protection can help only when the link that is downstream of the PLR fails. Node protection protects both the link and the node that are immediately downstream of the PLR.

Local repair is highly scalable because multiple LSPs are protected by a single backup tunnel, as opposed to path protection, which needs one backup tunnel per LSP.

Chapter 9 discusses design issues related to protection.

This chapter covers the following topics:

- MPLS LSR MIB
- MPLS TE MIB

CHAPTER 8

MPLS TE Management

The earlier chapters showed you how you can configure and manage MPLS TE using the CLI. Chapter 10, "MPLS TE Deployment Tips," covers some aspects of measurement and accounting that are useful for an MPLS TE-based network. This chapter covers the SNMP-based management available for MPLS that is useful for MPLS TE. Two topics are covered here:

- MPLS LSR Management Information Base (MIB)
- MPLS TE MIB

The LSR MIB is based on the IETF *draft-ietf-mpls-lsr-mib,* and the TE MIB is based on *draft-ietf-mpls-te-mib,* both of which are on their way to becoming RFCs.

A basic understanding of SNMP and MIBs is a prerequisite for understanding the underlying details of the LSR and the TE MIBs and their use. Using SNMP to manage your network is outside the scope of this discussion. See Appendix B, "CCO and Other References," for details on SNMP basics.

MPLS LSR MIB

The MPLS LSR MIB is currently defined in *draft-ietf-mpls-lsr-mib,* "Multiprotocol Label Switching (MPLS) Label Switch Router (LSR) Management Information Base." The LSR MIB is considered the foundation of other MIBs, such as the MPLS TE MIB, because label switching is common to all Label-Switched Paths (LSPs), regardless of how the labels are exchanged. Specific to TE, the mplsTunnelXCPointer link in the MPLS TE MIB points to the mplsXCTable (pronounced "MPLS cross-connect table") defined in the LSR MIB. This entry in the mplsXCTable identifies the MPLS TE LSP. This association will make more sense when you examine the TE MIB in detail. For now, the point is that it is important to have a basic understanding of the capabilities offered by the LSR MIB, because it is used in the TE MIB.

Before we get into exactly what is available in the LSR MIB, you need to understand the term *segment* in the context of MPLS MIBs. An LSP is broken into one or more incoming and outgoing segments as it crosses each LSR. The incoming segment is tied to outgoing segments using the cross-connect table (mplsXCTable). The terms *connection* and *LSP* are used interchangeably in these MIBs. Now you can proceed to the details of the LSR MIB.

The LSR MIB provides the following:

- Interface configuration table (mplsInterfaceConfTable), used to enable/disable MPLS on interfaces

- Interface performance table (mplsInterfacePerfTable), used to get performance statistics on a given interface

- Tables to actually define in-segments and out-segments for configuring LSP segments

- A cross-connect table that associates the in-segments and out-segments of LSPs

- Two other tables are defined in the draft that are not supported by Cisco IOS Software at this time—labelStackTable and trafficParamTable

The following sections examine the four tables that are currently supported.

Interface Configuration Table (mplsInterfaceConfTable)

Every LSR creates an entry for each MPLS-capable interface available on that LSR. The index into this table corresponds to the ifIndex, which is the interface index defined in the ifTable.

The interface MIB has been extended to include

- **ifType 150**—mplsTunnel

- **ifType 166**—MPLS

Figure 8-1 shows this extension.

Figure 8-1 *ifTable Extensions for MPLS*

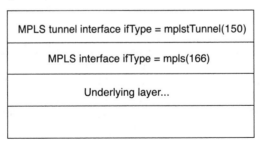

The Underlying Layer shown in Figure 8-1 is any Layer 2 that supports MPLS, such as Ethernet, Frame Relay, or ATM.

Figure 8-2 shows a Network Management System (NMS) attached to a sample network. You can either have a dedicated management network that attaches to each device you want to monitor, or simply place the NMS somewhere on your network and all management traffic to traverse the backbone.

Figure 8-2 *Network Management*

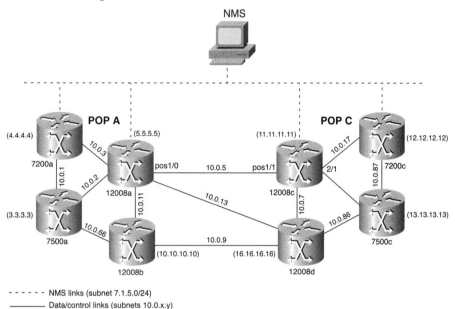

- - - - - - NMS links (subnet 7.1.5.0/24)
—————— Data/control links (subnets 10.0.x.y)

In the sample network shown in Figure 8-2, a computer running Linux is used as the NMS. The management subnet used is on 7.1.5.0/24. The host name of the Linux machine is linux1. The SNMP commands used to set or get information from the devices can be used with a GUI provided in management applications such as HP OpenView. In the examples used in this chapter, the commands were run on the command line using commands such as **snmpget** and **snmpwalk**. Example 8-1 shows the **snmpwalk** command used to retrieve the system table on node 12008a. **linux1>** is the system prompt. The command executed is shown in bold, and the output follows the command.

NOTE   The Object Identifiers (OIDs) for the MPLS LSR and the MPLS TE MIBs are currently branched off the org.dod.internet.experimental part of the OID tree. It is common practice to use the experimental branch for MIBs that are awaiting standardization. Currently, the LSR MIB uses the experimental.96 branch, and the MPLS TE MIB uses the experimental.95 branch. The OID files for the LSR and TE MIBs are available at www.cisco.com/public/mibs.

Example 8-1 *Sample Output of the* **snmpwalk** *Command Used to Get the System Table on 12008a*

```
linux1>snmpwalk -t 500 7.1.5.5 public system (system)
system.sysDescr.0 = Cisco Internetwork Operating System Software
IOS (tm) GS Software (GSR-P-M), Version 12.0(21.2)S, EARLY DEPLOYMENT MAINTENANCE
INTERIM SOFTWARE
```

continues

Example 8-1 *Sample Output of the* **snmpwalk** *Command Used to Get the System Table on 12008a (Continued)*

```
TAC Support: http://www.cisco.com/tac
Copyright (c) 1986-2002 by cisco Systems, Inc.
Compiled Tue 26-Mar-0
system.sysObjectID.0 = OID: enterprises.9.1.182
system.sysUpTime.0 = Timeticks: (15909997) 1 day, 20:11:39.97
system.sysContact.0 =
system.sysName.0 = mpls-12008a
system.sysLocation.0 =
system.sysServices.0 = 6
system.sysORLastChange.0 = Timeticks: (0) 0:00:00.00
```

Because the MPLS LSR and TE MIBs are branches of the experimental portion of the OID tree, examples shown in this chapter use the numerical OID string, such as .1.3.6.1.3.96. 1.1.1.3.8 for the MPLS LSR and .1.3.6.1.3.95.2.2.1.5 for the MPLS TE MIB. The command line where **snmpget** or **snmpwalk** is executed is annotated in parentheses for ease of reading to show which variable is being polled. For example:

```
linux1>snmpget -t 500 7.1.5.4 public .1.3.6.1.3.96.1.1.1.2.8
    (mplsInterfaceLabelMinIn)
```

means that the mplsInterfaceLabelMinIn variable is being polled.

Example 8-2 shows the results of polling for the ifType of 12008a. As you can see from the highlighted text, certain interfaces show up as type 150—mplsTunnel.

Example 8-2 *Polling 12008a for ifType Shows MPLS Extensions*

```
linux1>snmpwalk -t 500 7.1.5.5 public interfaces.iftable.ifentry.iftype (ifType)
interfaces.ifTable.ifEntry.ifType.8 = ppp(23)
interfaces.ifTable.ifEntry.ifType.9 = 171
interfaces.ifTable.ifEntry.ifType.13 = sonet(39)
interfaces.ifTable.ifEntry.ifType.17 = ethernetCsmacd(6)
interfaces.ifTable.ifEntry.ifType.31 = atm(37)
interfaces.ifTable.ifEntry.ifType.32 = atmSubInterface(134)
interfaces.ifTable.ifEntry.ifType.33 = aal5(49)
interfaces.ifTable.ifEntry.ifType.42 = softwareLoopback(24)
interfaces.ifTable.ifEntry.ifType.43 = softwareLoopback(24)
interfaces.ifTable.ifEntry.ifType.44 = mplsTunnel(150)
interfaces.ifTable.ifEntry.ifType.45 = mplsTunnel(150)
interfaces.ifTable.ifEntry.ifType.46 = mplsTunnel(150)
```

Example 8-3 shows the results of polling the ifDescr table for indexes 44, 45, and 46 that correspond to ifType 150—mplsTunnel. As you can see from the highlighted output in Example 8-3, the ifDescr for these indices shows tunnel interfaces.

Example 8-3 *Polling ifDescr for Indexes 44, 45, and 46 Shows Tunnel Interfaces*

```
linux1> snmpget 7.1.5.4 public interfaces.iftable.ifentry.ifdescr.44 (ifDescr)
interfaces.ifTable.ifEntry.ifDescr.44 = Tunnel1
linux1> snmpget 7.1.5.4 public interfaces.iftable.ifentry.ifdescr.45 (ifDescr)
```

Example 8-3   *Polling ifDescr for Indexes 44, 45, and 46 Shows Tunnel Interfaces (Continued)*

```
interfaces.ifTable.ifEntry.ifDescr.45 = Tunnel2
linux1> snmpget 7.1.5.4 public interfaces.iftable.ifentry.ifdescr.46 (ifDescr)
interfaces.ifTable.ifEntry.ifDescr.46 = Tunnel3
```

Table 8-1 shows the organization of the MPLS interface configuration table for each mplsInterfaceConfEntry.

Table 8-1   *mplsInterfaceConfEntry Organization*

Object	Syntax	Access	Description
mplsInterfaceConfIndex	InterfaceIndex OrZero	not-accessible	This field is meaningful only if it is nonzero. A nonzero value corresponds to the interface's ifIndex value.
mplsInterfaceLabelMinIn	MplsLabel	read-only	Minimum value that the LSR can receive on this interface.
mplsInterfaceLabelMaxIn	MplsLabel	read-only	Maximum value that the LSR can receive on this interface.
mplsInterfaceLabelMinOut	MplsLabel	read-only	Minimum label value that the LSR sends out this interface.
mplsInterfaceLabelMaxOut	MplsLabel	read-only	Maximum label value that the LSR sends out this interface.
mplsInterfaceTotalBandwidth	MplsBitRate	read-only	Total bandwidth in Kbps for this interface.
mplsInterfaceAvailableBandwidth	MplsBitRate	read-only	Available bandwidth in Kbps for this interface.
mplsInterfaceLabelParticipation Type	Perplatform (0), PerInterface (1)	read-only	Indicates the label space for this interface.
mplsInterfaceConfStorageType	StorageType	read-only	Storage type for this entry.

It should be noted that polling for parameters such as minimum and maximum label values should result in the same values for all interfaces that use per-platform label space. This is because the minimum and maximum labels that an LSR uses are controlled globally for all interfaces that don't use per-interface label scoping. This can be seen in the highlighted output of Example 8-4.

Example 8-4 *Polling the MinIn, MaxIn, MinOut, and MaxOut Variables of the MPLS Interface Configuration Table*

```
linux1>snmpwalk -t 500 7.1.5.5 public .1.3.6.1.3.96.1.1.1.2
   (mplsInterfaceLabelMinIn)
96.1.1.1.2.2 =  Gauge: 2
96.1.1.1.2.3 =  Gauge: 2
96.1.1.1.2.4 =  Gauge: 2
96.1.1.1.2.7 =  Gauge: 2
96.1.1.1.2.8 =  Gauge: 2
96.1.1.1.2.15 = Gauge: 2
96.1.1.1.2.45 = Gauge: 2
96.1.1.1.2.46 = Gauge: 2
96.1.1.1.2.48 = Gauge: 2

linux1>snmpwalk -t 500 7.1.5.5 public .1.3.6.1.3.96.1.1.1.3
   (mplsInterfaceLabelMaxIn)
96.1.1.1.3.2 =  Gauge: 12500
96.1.1.1.3.3 =  Gauge: 12500
96.1.1.1.3.4 =  Gauge: 12500
96.1.1.1.3.7 =  Gauge: 12500
96.1.1.1.3.8 =  Gauge: 12500
96.1.1.1.3.15 = Gauge: 12500
96.1.1.1.3.45 = Gauge: 12500
96.1.1.1.3.46 = Gauge: 12500
96.1.1.1.3.48 = Gauge: 12500

linux1>snmpwalk -t 500 7.1.5.5 public .1.3.6.1.3.96.1.1.1.4
   (mplsInterfaceLabelMinOut)
96.1.1.1.4.2 =  Gauge: 2
96.1.1.1.4.3 =  Gauge: 2
96.1.1.1.4.4 =  Gauge: 2
96.1.1.1.4.7 =  Gauge: 2
96.1.1.1.4.8 =  Gauge: 2
96.1.1.1.4.15 = Gauge: 2
96.1.1.1.4.45 = Gauge: 2
96.1.1.1.4.46 = Gauge: 2
96.1.1.1.4.48 = Gauge: 2

linux1>snmpwalk -t 500 7.1.5.5 public .1.3.6.1.3.96.1.1.1.5
   (mplsInterfaceLabelMaxOut)
96.1.1.1.5.2 =  Gauge: 12500
96.1.1.1.5.3 =  Gauge: 12500
96.1.1.1.5.4 =  Gauge: 12500
96.1.1.1.5.7 =  Gauge: 12500
96.1.1.1.5.8 =  Gauge: 12500
96.1.1.1.5.15 = Gauge: 12500
```

Example 8-4 *Polling the MinIn, MaxIn, MinOut, and MaxOut Variables of the MPLS Interface Configuration Table (Continued)*

```
96.1.1.1.5.45 = Gauge: 12500
96.1.1.1.5.46 = Gauge: 12500
96.1.1.1.5.48 = Gauge: 12500
```

Note that the last numbers in each line of the numerical OID string in the output—the 2, 3, 4, 7, 8, 15, 45, 46, and 48 that follow 96.1.1.1.5, for example—correspond to the ifIndex of interfaces on the router 12008a. You can poll the ifDescr corresponding to a specific interface if you are interested in finding out which interface has an mplsInterfaceLabelMaxOut value of 12500. For example, ifIndex 8, corresponding to POS2/1 on 12008a, is shown in Example 8-5.

Example 8-5 *ifDescr of Interface POS2/1*

```
linux1>snmpget 7.1.5.5 public interfaces.iftable.ifentry.ifdescr.8 (ifDescr)
interfaces.ifTable.ifEntry.ifDescr.8 = POS2/1
```

Interface Performance Table (mplsInterfacePerfTable)

As mentioned earlier, the mplsInterfacePerfTable has objects to measure MPLS perform-ance on a per-interface basis. Table 8-2 shows the organization of each entry within the table.

Table 8-2 *mplsInterfacePerfTable Organization*

Object	Syntax	Access	Description
mplsInterfaceInLabelsUsed	Gauge32	read-only	This counter provides a count of the number of incoming labels currently in use for the interface.
mplsInterfaceFailedLabelLookup	Counter32	read-only	This counter is incremented when a labeled packet enters this interface, but no match is found in the LFIB for the label.
mplsInterfaceOutLabelsUsed	Gauge32	read-only	This counter provides the number of top-level labels outbound on this interface.

continues

Table 8-2 *mplsInterfacePerfTable Organization (Continued)*

Object	Syntax	Access	Description
mplsInterfaceOutFragments	Counter32	read-only	This counter counts the number of outgoing MPLS packets that required fragmentation before transmission on this interface.
mplsInterfaceLabelMaxOut	MplsLabel	read-only	Maximum label value that the LSR sends out this interface.
mplsInterfaceTotalBandwidth	MplsBitRate	read-only	Total bandwidth in kbps for this interface.

Example 8-6 shows the 12008a being polled for mplsInterfaceInLabelsUsed. This variable is a count of how many labels to expect on a given interface. Because 12008a is using global label space, it is legal to receive a labeled packet with any of the 26 labels on each interface. As a result, polling this variable produces the same result on every interface. This can be observed in the highlighted text of Example 8-6.

Example 8-6 *Polling the mplsInterfaceInLabelsUsed Variable on 12008a*

```
linux1>snmpwalk -t 500 7.1.5.5 public .1.3.6.1.3.96.1.2.1.1
    (mplsInterfaceInLabelsUsed)
96.1.2.1.1.2 =  Gauge: 26
96.1.2.1.1.3 =  Gauge: 26
96.1.2.1.1.4 =  Gauge: 26
96.1.2.1.1.7 =  Gauge: 26
96.1.2.1.1.8 =  Gauge: 26
96.1.2.1.1.15 = Gauge: 26
96.1.2.1.1.45 = Gauge: 26
96.1.2.1.1.46 = Gauge: 26
96.1.2.1.1.48 = Gauge: 26
```

InSegment Table (mplsInSegmentTable)

As mentioned earlier in this chapter, from an LSR's point of view, an LSP consists of InSegments and OutSegments. InSegment is the segment of the LSP that is ingress to the LSR, and OutSegment is egress from the LSR. The LSR MIB has provisions to create and view these segments. Like other tables, the InSegmentTable has entries. Table 8-3 shows the organization of each mplsInSegmentEntry in the table.

Table 8-3   *mplsInSegmentEntry Organization*

Object	Syntax	Access	Description
mplsInSegmentIfIndex	InterfaceIndex OrZero	accessible-for-notify	A nonzero number represents the index into the mplsInSegmentTable. A 0 value represents the incoming label value for per-platform label space.
mplsInSegmentLabel	MplsLabel	accessible-for-notify	The incoming label for this segment (IPv4 is indicated by a 1).
mplsInSegmentNPop	Integer32	read-create	The number of labels to pop from the incoming segment.
mplsInSegmentAddrFamily	AddressFamily Numbers	read-create	The IANA address family of the incoming packet (IPv4 is indicated by a 1).
mplsInSegmentXCIndex	Integer32	read-only	The index into the mplsXCTable (Cross Connect Table).
mplsInSegmentOwner	MplsObject Owner	read-create	A placeholder to store the creator of this segment. If it is not set, it defaults to **unknown**.
mplsInSegmentTrafficParamPtr	RowPointer	read-create	A pointer to a traffic parameter table entry (set to the default 0.0) because it is not supported.
mplsInSegmentRowStatus	RowStatus	read-create	Used to create a row in the table.
mplsInSegmentStorageType	StorageType	read-create	Indicates the storage type.

In Table 8-3's Access column for the variables mplsInSegmentIfIndex and mplsInSegmentLabel, notice that the access is accessible-for-notify. This means that these variables are used only in the traps mplsXCUp and mplsXCDown and cannot be polled. Also note that both the mplsXCUp and mplsXCDown traps currently are not supported on the Cisco routers. So, you will never see a value for those variables when you poll the mplsInSegment table.

Example 8-7 shows the output after the mplsInSegmentNPop of the InSegment table is polled.

NOTE   The output from **snmpwalk** for each of the InSegment table variables polled actually produces 26 rows. Only the first three are shown to keep it concise. There are 26 rows because if you remember from Example 8-6, each interface can expect 26 different labels on an incoming packet.

Example 8-7   *Polling the mplsInSegmentNPop Variable of the InSegment Table*

```
linux1>snmpwalk -t 500 7.1.5.5 public .1.3.6.1.3.96.1.3.1.3.3 (mplsInSegmentNPop)
96.1.3.1.3.3.12304 = 1
96.1.3.1.3.3.12306 = 1
96.1.3.1.3.3.12307 = 1
```

The value of mplsInSegmentNPop is 1 for all labels because the router being polled (12008a) is a midpoint router and is expected to pop just one label.

Example 8-8 shows the output after the mplsInSegmentAddrFamily variable is polled.

Example 8-8   *Polling the mplsInSegmentAddrFamily Variable of the InSegment Table*

```
linux1>snmpwalk -t 500 7.1.5.5 public .1.3.6.1.3.96.1.3.1.4.3
  (mplsInSegmentAddrFamily)
96.1.3.1.4.3.12304 = 1
96.1.3.1.4.3.12306 = 1
96.1.3.1.4.3.12307 = 1
```

The IANA Address Family Numbers MIB defines the address family numbers, as demonstrated in Example 8-9.

Example 8-9   *IANA Definition of Address Families*

```
AddressFamilyNumbers ::= TEXTUAL-CONVENTION

    STATUS        current
    DESCRIPTION
        "The definition of this textual convention with the
        addition of newly assigned values is published
        periodically by the IANA, in either the Assigned
        Numbers RFC, or some derivative of it specific to
        Internet Network Management number assignments.
        (The latest arrangements can be obtained by
        contacting the IANA.)

        The enumerations are described as:

        other(0),    -- none of the following
        ipV4(1),     -- IP Version 4
```

As you can see from the highlighted output of Examples 8-8 and 8-9, the 1 in Example 8-8 corresponds to the IPv4 address family shown in Example 8-9.

mplsInSegmentXCIndex is the index into mplsXCTable (cross-connect table). Example 8-10 shows the output of polling this variable.

Example 8-10 *Polling the mplsInSegmentXCIndex Variable of the InSegment Table*

```
linux1>snmpwalk -t 500 7.1.5.5 public .1.3.6.1.3.96.1.3.1.5.3
  (mplsInSegmentXCIndex)
96.1.3.1.5.3.12304 = 1414595812
96.1.3.1.5.3.12306 = 1414588772
96.1.3.1.5.3.12307 = 1414586308
```

Example 8-11 provides the output of polling the mplsInSegmentOwner variable of the InSegment table.

Example 8-11 *Polling the mplsInSegmentOwner Variable of the InSegment Table*

```
linux1>snmpwalk -t 500 7.1.5.5 public .1.3.6.1.3.96.1.3.1.6.3 (mplsInSegmentOwner)
96.1.3.1.6.3.12304 = 1
96.1.3.1.6.3.12306 = 1
96.1.3.1.6.3.12307 = 1
```

Example 8-12 shows the definition of mplsInSegmentOwner.

Example 8-12 *mplsInSegmentOwner Definition*

```
MplsObjectOwner ::= TEXTUAL-CONVENTION
    STATUS      current
    DESCRIPTION
            "The entity which owns the object in question."
    SYNTAX    INTEGER {
                  other(1),
                  snmp(2),
                  ldp(3)
```

As you can see from the output in Examples 8-11 and 8-12, the segment owner is "other." Cisco IOS Software currently sets the owner field to "other."

Coverage of mplsInSegmentTrafficParamPtr is omitted here because the Cisco implementation currently does not support the label stack and traffic parameter tables. mplsInSegmentRowStatus also is not currently supported for the creation of InSegments using SNMP. However, it can be polled using the syntax shown in Example 8-13.

Example 8-13 *Polling the mplsInSegmentRowStatus Variable*

```
linux1>snmpwalk -t 500 7.1.5.5. public .1.3.6.1.3.96.1.3.1.8.3
  (mplsInSegmentRowStatus)
96.1.3.1.8.3.12304 = 1
96.1.3.1.8.3.12306 = 1
96.1.3.1.8.3.12307 =1
```

A value of 1 represents "active."

InSegment Performance Table (mplsInSegmentPerfTable)

The mplsInSegmentPerfTable contains mplsInSegmentPerfEntry elements—one per interface. Table 8-4 shows the organization of mplsInSegmentPerfEntry.

Table 8-4 *mplsInSegmentPerfEntry Organization*

Object	Syntax	Access	Description
mplsInSegmentOctets	Counter32	read-only	Bytes received on this input segment.
mplsInSegmentPackets	Counter32	not-implemented	Number of packets received on this input segment. Note that this is currently not implemented in Cisco IOS Software.
mplsInSegmentErrors	Counter32	not-implemented	Number of packets received with errors on this segment. Not currently implemented in Cisco IOS Software.
mplsInSegmentDiscards	Counter32	not-implemented	Number of packets received on this segment that were discarded even though there were no errors. Not currently implemented in Cisco IOS Software.
mplsInSegmentPerf DiscontinuityTime	TimeStamp	read-only	Currently set to 0 in Cisco IOS Software.

It is particularly useful to obtain the "Bytes tag switched" information to see if the packets are being MPLS switched, as demonstrated in Example 8-14.

Example 8-14 *Determining Whether Packets Are Being "Bytes Tag Switched"*

```
mpls-12008a#show mpls forwarding 12.12.12.12
Local  Outgoing    Prefix         Bytes tag  Outgoing    Next Hop
tag    tag or VC   or Tunnel Id   switched   interface
12318  12322       12.12.12.12/32   2347      PO1/0       point2point
```

You can obtain the same information through SNMP by polling the mplsInSegmentOctets variable for ifIndex 3 (POS1/0), as shown in Example 8-15.

Example 8-15 *Polling the mplsInSegmentOctets Variable*

```
linux1>snmpget -t 500 7.1.5.5 public .1.3.6.1.3.96.1.4.1.1.3.12318
 (mplsInSegmentOctets)
96.1.4.1.1.3.12318 = 2347
```

OutSegment Table (mplsOutSegmentTable)

The OutSegment table is similar to the InSegment table, except that it is the egress portion of the LSP. The objects contained in each mplsOutSegmentEntry are as shown in Table 8-5.

Table 8-5   *mplsOutSegmentEntry Organization*

Object	Syntax	Access	Description
mplsOutSegment Index	Unsigned 32	not-accessible	An instance of mplsOutSegmentEntry can be created using SNMP via an NMS. The value of this variable indicates which row is being created.
mplsOutSegmentIf Index	Interface IndexOr Zero	read-create	The interface index of the outgoing interface.
mplsOutSegment PushTopLabel	Truth Value	read-create	If the value of this variable is set to true, the top label in the packet is pushed.
mplsOutSegmentTop Label	Mpls Label	read-create	Holds the label value that needs to be pushed on the stack if the PushTopLabel is set to true.
mplsOutSegment NextHopIpAddrType	Inet Address Type	read-create	If the value of this variable is 1, the next-hop IP address is IPv4. A value of 2 indicates an IPv6 address.
mplsOutSegment NextHopIpv4Addr	Inet Address IPv4	read-create	The variable that holds the IPv4 address of the next hop if the NextHopIpAddrType is set to 1.
mplsOutSegment NextHopIpv6Addr	Inet Address IPv6	read-create	The variable that holds the IPv6 address of the next hop if the NextHopIpAddrType is set to 2.
mplsOutSegmentXC Index	Unsigned 32	read-only	The index into the cross-connect table that identifies this segment.
mplsOutSegment Owner	Mpls Initial Creation Source	read-create	Who is responsible for creating this Out Segment. 1 means other, 2 means snmp, 3 means ldp, 4 means rsvp, 5 means crldp, 6 means policyAgent, and 7 means unknown.

continues

Table 8-5 *mplsOutSegmentEntry Organization (Continued)*

Object	Syntax	Access	Description
mplsOutSegment TrafficParamPtr	Row Pointer	read-create	A pointer to the traffic parameter specification for this out segment.

In the OutSegmentTable, the following objects are most interesting:

- mplsOutSegmentPushTopLabel
- mplsOutSegmentTopLabel
- mplsOutSegmentNextHopIpAddrType
- mplsOutSegmentNextHopIpAddr

The following sections explain these objects in greater detail.

mplsOutSegmentPushTopLabel

Example 8-16 shows the output of polling the mplsOutSegmentPushTopLabel variable.

Example 8-16 *Polling the mplsOutSegmentPushTopLabel Variable*

```
linux1>snmpwalk -t 500 7.1.5.5 public .1.3.6.1.3.96.1.6.1.3
  (mplsOutSegmentPushTopLabel)
96.1.6.1.3.1414586308 = 2
96.1.6.1.3.1414586484 = 2
96.1.6.1.3.1414586660 = 2
```

SNMPv2-MIB-V1SMI.my defines true and false, as shown in Example 8-17.

Example 8-17 *Definitions of True and False Values Used in MIBs*

```
SYNTAX TruthValue
--     Rsyntax INTEGER {
--         true(1),
--         false(2)
--         }
```

Because Example 8-16 produced the value 2 (false), no top labels need to be pushed onto the stack.

mplsOutSegmentTopLabel

If mplsOutSegmentPushTopLabel is true, this represents the label that should be pushed onto the top of the outgoing packet's label stack. Example 8-18 provides an **snmpwalk** that reveals the top label values.

Example 8-18 *Polling the mplsOutSegmentTopLabel Variable*

```
linux1>snmpwalk -t 500 7.1.5.5 public .1.3.6.1.3.96.1.6.1.4
   (mplsOutSegmentTopLabel)
96.1.6.1.4.1414586308 = Gauge: 3
96.1.6.1.4.1414586484 = Gauge: 12304
96.1.6.1.4.1414586660 = Gauge: 3
96.1.6.1.4.1414586836 = Gauge: 3
96.1.6.1.4.1414587012 = Gauge: 12321
96.1.6.1.4.1414587188 = Gauge: 12320
96.1.6.1.4.1414587364 = Gauge: 3
```

mplsOutSegmentNextHopIpAddrType

The IP address type can assume values IPv4 or IPv6. Currently, only IPv4 is supported. Example 8-19 shows the output of **snmpwalk** polling mplsOutSegmentNextHopIpAddrType.

Example 8-19 *Polling the mplsOutSegmentNextHopIpAddrType Variable*

```
linux1>snmpwalk -t 500 7.1.5.5 public .1.3.6.1.3.96.1.6.1.5
   (mplsOutSegmentNextHopIpAddrType)
96.1.6.1.5.1414586308 = 1
96.1.6.1.5.1414586484 = 1
96.1.6.1.5.1414586660 = 1
```

The value 1 represents IPv4.

mplsOutSegmentNextHopIpAddr

This contains the IPv4 address of the next hop. Example 8-20 shows the output of **snmpwalk** on this variable.

Example 8-20 *Polling the mplsOutSegmentNextHopIpAddr Variable*

```
linux1>snmpwalk -t 500 7.1.5.5 public .1.3.6.1.3.96.1.6.1.6
   (mplsOutSegmentNextHopIpAddr)
96.1.6.1.6.1414586308 = "0000"
96.1.6.1.6.1414586484 = "0000"
96.1.6.1.6.1414586660 = "0000"
```

The NextHopIpAddr is set to 0 because the next hop is over a point-to-point (p2p) link.

OutSegment Performance Table (mplsOutSegmentPerfTable)

This is similar to the InSegmentPerfTable. It provides statistics about the outgoing segment. The mplsOutSegmentPerfTable contains mplsOutSegmentPerfEntry, which is organized as shown in Table 8-6.

Table 8-6 *mplsOutSegmentPerfEntry Organization*

Object	Syntax	Access	Description
mplsOutSegmentOctets	Counter32	read-only	The total number of bytes sent out on this segment.
mplsOutSegmentPackets	Counter32	read-only	The total number of packets sent out on this segment. This is not currently supported in Cisco IOS software.
mplsOutSegmentErrors	Counter32	read-only	Packets that were received with an error. Also not supported by Cisco IOS.
mplsOutSegmentDiscards	Counter32	read-only	Packets received without error that were discarded. This is another variable that is not supported in Cisco IOS.
mplsOutSegmentHCOctets	Counter64	read-only	Number of octets sent out on this segment. This is similar to mplsOutSegmentOctets but is used when a 32-bit counter is not enough.
mplsOutSegmentPerf DiscontinuityTime	TimeStamp	read-only	sysUpTime value when this segment's counter suffers a discontinuity.

mplsOutSegmentOctets is a useful variable. Example 8-21 shows the output of polling mplsOutSegmentOctets.

Example 8-21 *Polling the mplsOutSegmentOctets Variable*

```
linux1>snmpwalk -t 500 7.1.5.5 public .1.3.6.1.3.96.1.7.1 (mplsOutSegmentOctets)
96.1.7.1.1.1414590708 = 0
96.1.7.1.1.1414590884 = 351615
96.1.7.1.1.1414591060 = 0
96.1.7.1.1.1414592820 = 66971
```

Cross-Connect Table (mplsXCTable)

The cross-connect table associates InSegments (labels) with OutSegments (labels). This table can be indexed using one of the following indices:

- mplsXCIndex
- mplsInSegmentIfIndex
- mplsInSegmentLabel
- mplsOutSegmentIndex

mplsXCTable contains mplsXCEntry. The organization of mplsXCEntry is shown in Table 8-7.

Table 8-7   *mplsXCEntry Organization*

Object	Syntax	Access	Description
mplsXCIndex	Unsigned32	not-accessible	Index used to create an mplsXCEntry using an NMS.
mplsXCLspId	MplsLSPID	read-create	The LSP that this cross-connect entry belongs to.
mplsXCLabelStackIndex	Unsigned32	read-create	Index into mplsLabel StackTable.
mplsXCIsPersistent	TruthValue	read-create	If this is set to true, the in and out segments that correspond to this entry are restored automatically upon failure.
mplsXCOwner	MplsInitialCreationSource	read-create	Holds the creator of the cross-connect entry.
mplsXCRowStatus	RowStatus	read-create	Used to create, modify, or delete a cross-connect entry using an NMS.
mplsXCStorageType	StorageType	read-create	Storage type for this object.

continues

Table 8-7 *mplsXCEntry Organization (Continued)*

Object	Syntax	Access	Description
mplsXCAdminStatus	up(1), down(2), testing(3)	read-create	Administrative status of the segment.
mplsXCOperStatus	up(1), down(2), testing(3), unknown(4), dormant(5), notPresent(6), lowerLayerDown(7)	read-only	Operational status of the segment.

Consider the output shown in Example 8-22. It was produced using the CLI **show mpls forwarding 12.12.12.12**.

Example 8-22 show mpls forwarding 12.12.12.12 *on 7200a*

```
mpls-12008a#show mpls forwarding-table 10.0.22.0
Local  Outgoing    Prefix         Bytes tag Outgoing   Next Hop
tag    tag or VC   or Tunnel Id   switched  interface
12311  Pop tag     10.0.22.0/24   0         POS0/0     point2point
```

As you can see from Example 8-22, the prefix 12.12.12.12 is going over interface POS 0/0. The local label is 12311.

Now, using **snmpwalk**, poll the mplsXCLspId variable in the cross-connect table and filter the output to include label 12311—the local label on 12008a. Example 8-23 uses the UNIX **grep** command to filter the output. You can do it any way you want, including visually sorting through the output to find label 12311!

Example 8-23 *Filtering the Output of* **snmpwalk** *on the mplsXCLspId Variable to Find Label 12311*

```
linux1>snmpwalk -t 500 7.1.5.5 public .1.3.6.1.3.96.1.9.1.2 | grep 12311
96.1.9.1.2.1414584372.2.12311.1414584372 =  Hex: 0A 00 16 00
96.1.9.1.2.1414584372.3.12311.1414584372 =  Hex: 0A 00 16 00
96.1.9.1.2.1414584372.4.12311.1414584372 =  Hex: 0A 00 16 00
96.1.9.1.2.1414584372.7.12311.1414584372 =  Hex: 0A 00 16 00
96.1.9.1.2.1414584372.8.12311.1414584372 =  Hex: 0A 00 16 00
96.1.9.1.2.1414584372.15.12311.1414584372 =  Hex: 0A 00 16 00
96.1.9.1.2.1414584372.45.12311.1414584372 =  Hex: 0A 00 16 00
96.1.9.1.2.1414584372.46.12311.1414584372 =  Hex: 0A 00 16 00
96.1.9.1.2.1414584372.48.12311.1414584372 =  Hex: 0A 00 16 00
```

The LSP ID is 0A 00 16 00, which is hex for 10.0.22.0. From the highlighted output, you can see that the ifIndex for the outgoing interface for 10.0.22.0 is 2. You can check which interface ifIndex 2 corresponds to, as shown in Example 8-24.

Example 8-24 *Obtaining the Interface from ifIndex*

```
linux1>snmpwalk -t 500 7.1.5.5 public interfaces.iftable.ifentry.ifdescr
interfaces.ifTable.ifEntry.ifDescr.1 = Ethernet0
interfaces.ifTable.ifEntry.ifDescr.2 = POS0/0
```

Next you can find out what is the outgoing label on that interface by polling mplsOutSegmentTopLabel using the cross-connect index 1414584372, obtained from Example 8-23, as shown in Example 8-25.

Example 8-25 *Polling the mplsOutSegmentTopLabel Variable to Obtain the OutLabel for 10.0.22.0*

```
linux1>snmpwalk -t 500 7.1.5.5 public .1.3.6.1.3.96.1.6.1.4.1414584372
  (mplsOutSegmentTopLabel)
96.1.6.1.4.1414584724 = Gauge: 3
```

It yields label 3—POP. Examples 8-23 through 8-25 demonstrated how you can obtain all the information contained in Example 8-22 using SNMP.

This concludes the discussion of the LSR MIB. The next section describes the MPLS TE MIB.

MPLS TE MIB

As mentioned in the introductory section, the TE MIB is defined in *draft-ietf-mpls-te-mib*. Appendix B provides links to the Cisco online documentation for the MPLS TE MIB.

The following tables constitute the TE MIB:

- mplsTunnelTable
- mplsTunnelHopTable
- mplsTunnelResourceTable
- mplsTunnelCRLDPResTable

The mplsTunnelCRLDPResTable is not supported in the current Cisco implementation, because Cisco's MPLS TE does not support CR-LDP. The following sections examine each of the TE MIB tables in detail.

mplsTunnelTable

The purpose of the mplsTunnelTable is to create or modify tunnels. Using this table, you can tie an InSegment to an OutSegment in the cross-connect table, as described in the "MPLS LSR MIB" section.

As with the LSR MIB, the TE tunnel interface is included in the IFMIB as an extension.

You can see this when you perform **snmpwalk** on the ifType object on 7200a, as demonstrated in Example 8-26.

Example 8-26 *ifType Extensions for the MPLS TE Tunnel*

```
linux1>snmpwalk -t 500 7.1.5.4 public interfaces.iftable.ifentry.ifdescr (ifDescr)
...
interfaces.ifTable.ifEntry.ifType.15 = mplsTunnel(150)
interfaces.ifTable.ifEntry.ifType.16 = mplsTunnel(150)
...
```

Each mplsTunnelTable entry contains mplsTunnelEntry.

The organization of the mplsTunnelEntry table is shown in Table 8-8.

Table 8-8 *mplsTunnelEntry Organization*

Object	Syntax	Access	Description
mplsTunnel Index	Integer32	not-accessible	The key index into the Entry table.
mplsTunnel Instance	MplsTunnelInstanceIndex	not-accessible	Uniquely identifies a TE tunnel and can be used to index into the Entry table.
mplsTunnel IngressLSRId	MplsLsrIdentifier	not-accessible	Helps uniquely identify an LSP within the network, much like the extended TE ID in the session object of the RSVP message.
mplsTunnel EgressLSRId	MplsLsrIdentifier	not-accessible	Used to identify the Egress LSR.
mplsTunnel Name	DisplayString	read-create	Holds the tunnel name.
mplsTunnel Descr	DisplayString	read-create	Textual description of the tunnel.

Table 8-8   *mplsTunnelEntry Organization (Continued)*

Object	Syntax	Access	Description
mplsTunnelIs If	TruthValue	read-create	If this value is set to true, the ifName in the interface's MIB and the mplsTunnelName are the same.
mplsTunnelIf Index	InterfaceIndexOrZero	read-only	If the mplsTunnelIsIf is set to true, the mplsTunnelIfIndex is an index into the ifTable.
mplsTunnel XCPointer	RowPointer	read-create	Points to a row in the mplsXCTable defined in the LSR MIB.
mplsTunnel Signalling Proto	none(1), rsvp(2), crldp(3), other(4)	read-create	Holds the protocol responsible for creating the tunnel.
mplsTunnel SetupPrio	Integer32 (0...7)	read-create	Holds the tunnel's setup priority.
mplsTunnel HoldingPrio	Integer32 (0...7)	read-create	Holds the tunnel's holding priority.
mplsTunnel Session Attributes	fastReroute (0), mergingPermitted (1), isPersistent (2), isPinned (3), recordRoute (4)	read-create	A bitmask that can hold the values 0 through 4. These are attributes that correspond to the primary tunnel going through this LSR. If this is 0, the primary LSP might be rerouted for local repair. A value of 1 means that the transit LSRs can merge this RSVP session with other RSVP sessions to reduce refresh overhead. A value of 3 indicates that loose-routed hops should be pinned. A value of 4 means that a record route is requested.

continues

Table 8-8 *mplsTunnelEntry Organization (Continued)*

Object	Syntax	Access	Description
mplsTunnel Owner	admin(1), rsvp(2), crldp(3), policyAgent(4), other(5)	read-create	Holds the protocol that is responsible for creating this tunnel.
mplsTunnel LocalProtect InUse	TruthValue	read-create	If this variable is set to true, FRR is currently active.
mplsTunnel Resource Pointer	RowPointer	read-create	A pointer to the traffic parameter specification for this tunnel. It can point to either mplsTunnelResourceEntry or the traffic parameter specification table.
mplsTunnel Instance Priority	Unsigned32	read-create	Tunnel group priority.
mplsTunnel HopTable Index	MplsPathIndexOrZero	read-create	Holds the explicit path list defined in the mplsTunnelHopTable.
mplsTunnel ARHopTable Index	MplsPathIndexOrZero	read-only	Index into the mplsTunnelARHopTable. The mplsTunnelARHop Table is the user-defined table that holds the hops, strict or loose, for an MPLS tunnel similar to the IP explicit path list used in the CLI.
mplsTunnel CHopTable Index	MplsPathIndexOrZero	read-only	Index into the mplsTunnelCHopTable. The mplsTunnelCHop Table is the table that holds the hops, strict or loose, that come from CSPF computation.
mplsTunnel Primary Instance	MplsTunnelInstanceIndex	read-only	Specifies the instance index of this tunnel's primary instance.
mplsTunnel PrimaryTime Up	TimeTicks	read-only	Specifies the total time that this tunnel's primary instance has been active.

Table 8-8   *mplsTunnelEntry Organization (Continued)*

Object	Syntax	Access	Description
mplsTunnel PathChanges	Counter32	read-only	Specifies the number of times the path has changed for this tunnel.
mplsTunnel LastPath Change	Counter32	read-only	Specifies the time since the last path change for this tunnel.
mplsTunnel CreationTime	TimeStamp	read-only	Specifies the value of SysUpTime when the first instance of this tunnel came into existence.
mplsTunnel State Transitions	Counter32	read-only	Specifies the number of times the state of this tunnel instance has changed.
mplsTunnel IncludeAny Affinity	MplsTunnelAffinity	read-create	The MPLS TE MIB draft says, "A link satisfies the include-any constraint if and only if the constraint is zero, or the link and the constraint have a resource class in common."
mplsTunnel IncludeAll Affinity	MplsTunnelAffinity	read-create	The MPLS TE MIB draft says, "A link satisfies the include-all constraint if and only if the link contains all of the administrative groups specified in the constraint."
mplsTunnel ExcludeAll Affinity	MplsTunnelAffinity	read-create	The MPLS TE MIB draft says, "A link satisfies the exclude-all constraint if and only if the link contains none of the administrative groups specified in the constraint."
mplsTunnel PathInUse	MplsPathIndexOrZero	read-create	If this is nonzero, it holds the explicit path being used by the tunnel.
mplsTunnel Role	head(1), transit(2), tail(3)	read-create	Holds the tunnel's role.
mplsTunnel TotalUpTime	TimeTicks	read-create	Total uptime for all instances of the tunnel.

continues

Table 8-8 *mplsTunnelEntry Organization (Continued)*

Object	Syntax	Access	Description
mplsTunnel InstanceUp Time	TimeTicks	read-create	Total uptime for the current instance of the tunnel.
mplsTunnel AdminStatus	up(1), down(2), testing(3)	read-create	Administrative status of this tunnel.
mplsTunnel OperStatus	up(1), down(2), testing(3), unknown(4), dormant(5), notPresent(6), lowerLayerDown(7)	read-create	Operational status of this tunnel.
mplsTunnel RowStatus	RowStatus	read-create	Used to create, modify, or delete an instance in the mplsTunnelEntry table.
mplsTunnel StorageType	StorageType	read-create	Indicates the storage type for this object.

The first four variables—mplsTunnelIndex, mplsTunnelInstance, mplsTunnelIngressLSRId, and mplsTunnelEgressLSRId—are used only in the notifications—mplsTunnelUp, mplsTunnelDown, and mplsTunnelRerouted.

Example 8-27 shows the mplsTunnelUp and mplsTunnelDown traps captured by turning on **debug snmp packet** on 12008a. You can see the tunnel Index, Instance, IngressLSRId, AdminStatus, and OperStatus variables being used in these traps.

Example 8-27 *Tunnel Up and Tunnel Down Traps*

```
12008a#debug snmp packet
1d18h: SNMP: V1 Trap, ent mplsTeNotifications, addr 7.1.5.5, gentrap 6, spectrap
 1
 mplsTunnelIndex.3.0.0.185273099 = 3
 mplsTunnelInstance.3.0.0.185273099 = 0
 mplsTunnelIngressLSRId.3.0.0.185273099 = 0
 mplsTunnelEgressLSRId.3.0.0.185273099 = 185273099
 mplsTunnelAdminStatus.3.0.0.185273099 = 1
 mplsTunnelOperStatus.3.0.0.185273099 = 1
1d18h: SNMP: Packet sent via UDP to 7.1.5.254
mpls-12008a#configure terminal
Enter configuration commands, one per line.  End with CNTL/Z.
mpls-12008a(config)#interface tunnel 3
mpls-12008a(config-if)#shut
mpls-12008a(config-if)#end
1d19h: %SYS-5-CONFIG_I: Configured from console by console
1d19h: %LINK-5-CHANGED: Interface Tunnel3, changed state to administratively down
1d19h: %LINEPROTO-5-UPDOWN: Line protocol on Interface Tunnel3, changed state to
  down
1d19h: SNMP: Queuing packet to 7.1.5.254
1d19h: SNMP: V1 Trap, ent mplsTeNotifications, addr 7.1.5.5, gentrap 6,
  spectrap 2
```

Example 8-27 *Tunnel Up and Tunnel Down Traps (Continued)*

```
mplsTunnelIndex.3.0.0.185273099 = 3
mplsTunnelInstance.3.0.0.185273099 = 0
mplsTunnelIngressLSRId.3.0.0.185273099 = 0
mplsTunnelEgressLSRId.3.0.0.185273099 = 185273099
mplsTunnelAdminStatus.3.0.0.185273099 = 2
mplsTunnelOperStatus.3.0.0.185273099 = 2
1d19h: SNMP: Packet sent via UDP to 7.1.5.254
```

The following sections examine some of the mplsTunnelEntry objects that are interesting from a tunnel-management perspective.

mplsTunnelName

This object represents the tunnel's name. Example 8-28 shows the output generated from the CLI command **show ip interface brief**.

Example 8-28 **show ip interface brief** *Command Output Shows the Tunnel1 Interface*

```
mpls-12008a#show ip interface brief
Interface          IP-Address      OK? Method Status                Protocol
POS0/0             10.0.13.5       YES NVRAM  up                    up
POS1/0             10.0.5.5        YES NVRAM  up                    up
POS1/1             10.0.11.5       YES NVRAM  up                    up
POS1/2             unassigned      YES NVRAM  administratively down down
POS1/3             unassigned      YES NVRAM  administratively down down
POS2/0             10.0.2.5        YES NVRAM  up                    up
POS2/1             10.0.3.5        YES NVRAM  up                    up
POS2/2             unassigned      YES NVRAM  administratively down down
POS2/3             10.0.56.5       YES NVRAM  administratively down down
ATM3/0             unassigned      YES NVRAM  administratively down down
ATM3/0.2           unassigned      YES unset  administratively down down
ATM3/0.3           10.0.4.5        YES NVRAM  administratively down down
ATM3/1             unassigned      YES NVRAM  up                    up
ATM3/1.1           10.0.10.5       YES NVRAM  up                    up
ATM3/2             unassigned      YES NVRAM  administratively down down
ATM3/3             unassigned      YES NVRAM  administratively down down
FastEthernet4/0    100.100.100.100 YES NVRAM  up                    up
FastEthernet4/1    unassigned      YES NVRAM  administratively down down
FastEthernet4/2    unassigned      YES NVRAM  administratively down down
FastEthernet4/3    unassigned      YES NVRAM  administratively down down
FastEthernet4/4    unassigned      YES NVRAM  administratively down down
FastEthernet4/5    unassigned      YES NVRAM  administratively down down
FastEthernet4/6    unassigned      YES NVRAM  administratively down down
FastEthernet4/7    unassigned      YES NVRAM  administratively down down
Loopback0          5.5.5.5         YES NVRAM  up                    up
Loopback1          55.55.55.55     YES NVRAM  administratively down down
Loopback2          unassigned      YES NVRAM  administratively down down
Loopback3          55.55.55.56     YES NVRAM  administratively down down
Tunnel1            5.5.5.5         YES unset  up                    down
Tunnel2            5.5.5.5         YES unset  up                    up
Tunnel3            5.5.5.5         YES unset  up                    up
Ethernet0          7.1.5.5         YES NVRAM  up                    up
```

You can get the same information using **snmpwalk** on 7200, as shown in Example 8-29.

Example 8-29 *Polling the mplsTunnelName Variable Via SNMP*

```
linux1>snmpwalk -t 500 7.1.5.5 public .1.3.6.1.3.95.2.2.1.5 (mplsTunnelName)
95.2.2.1.5.1.0.84215045.185273099 = "Tunnel1"
95.2.2.1.5.1.8.67372036.202116108 = ""
95.2.2.1.5.1.500.50529027.202116108 = ""
95.2.2.1.5.2.0.84215045.202116108 = "Tunnel2"
95.2.2.1.5.2.48.84215045.202116108 = ""
95.2.2.1.5.3.0.84215045.185273099 = "Tunnel3"
95.2.2.1.5.3.758.84215045.185273099 = ""
```

mplsTunnelDescr

Example 8-30 shows the free text you would enter for the interface description.

Example 8-30 *Retrieving the Tunnel Interface Descriptions*

```
mpls-12008a#show running-config interface tunnel1
Building configuration...

Current configuration : 388 bytes
!
interface Tunnel1
 description Link Protection Tunnel (Backup)
 ip unnumbered Loopback0
 no ip directed-broadcast
 tunnel destination 11.11.11.11
 tunnel mode mpls traffic-eng
 tunnel mpls traffic-eng priority 7 7
 tunnel mpls traffic-eng bandwidth  10000
 tunnel mpls traffic-eng path-option 5 explicit name backup
 tunnel mpls traffic-eng record-route
 ip rsvp signalling dscp 0
end
```

Example 8-31 shows how you can obtain this information using **snmpwalk**.

Example 8-31 *Polling the mplsTunnelDescr Variable for a Tunnel Description Via SNMP*

```
linux1>snmpwalk -t 500 7.1.5.5 public .1.3.6.1.3.95.2.2.1.6 (mplsTunnelDescr)
95.2.2.1.6.1.0.84215045.185273099 = "Link Protection Tunnel (Backup)"
```

mplsTunnelIsIf

If the value of this object is set to true, the ifName for this tunnel should be the same as the mplsTunnelName. Example 8-32 shows the output of **snmpwalk** on mplsTunnelIsIf.

Example 8-32 *Polling the mplsTunnelIsIf Variable Via SNMP*

```
linux1>snmpwalk -t 500 7.1.5.5 public .1.3.6.1.3.95.2.2.1.7 (mplsTunnelIsIf)
95.2.2.1.7.1.0.84215045.185273099 = 1
```

mplsTunnelIfIndex

Again, if mplsTunnelIsIf is set to true, the value of this object should be the same as ifIndex. Example 8-33 shows the output of polling the mplsTunnelIfIndex variable.

Example 8-33 *Polling the mplsTunnelIfIndex Variable Via SNMP*

```
linux1>snmpwalk -t 500 7.1.5.5 public .1.3.6.1.3.95.2.2.1.8 (mplsTunnelIfIndex)
95.2.2.1.8.1.0.84215045.185273099 = 44
```

If you look at the ifDescr for index 44, as shown in Example 8-34, you'll notice from the highlighted text that index 44 corresponds to tunnel1.

Example 8-34 *ifDescr of ifIndex 44*

```
linux1>snmpget -t 500 7.1.5.5 public interfaces.iftable.ifentry.ifdescr.44
  (ifDescr)
interfaces.ifTable.ifEntry.ifDescr.44 = Tunnel1
```

mplsTunnelXCPointer

This object is what ties the mplsTunnelTable to the mplsXCTable defined in the LSR MIB. If the value is 0, no LSP is associated with this tunnel.

Polling for mplsTunnelXCPointer is meaningful only on midpoints, because the cross-connect table ties an incoming segment of an LSP to an outgoing segment. From the output shown in Example 8-35, you can see that no LSP is associated with this tunnel when you examine the headend (ingress LER—7200a).

Example 8-35 *Polling the mplsTunnelXCPointer Variable on Ingress LER 7200a*

```
linux1>snmpwalk -t 500 7.1.5.4 public .1.3.6.1.3.95.2.2.1.9 (mplsTunnelXCPointer)
95.2.2.1.9.1.0.67372036.202116108 = OID: .ccitt.nullOID
95.2.2.1.9.1.8.67372036.202116108 = OID: .ccitt.nullOID
95.2.2.1.9.55.0.67372036.202116108 = OID: .ccitt.nullOID
```

However, when this variable is polled on 12008a, it produces a non-null output, as shown in Example 8-36.

Example 8-36 *Polling the mplsTunnelXCPointer Variable on Midpoint 12008a*

```
linux1>snmpwalk -t 500 7.1.5.5 public .1.3.6.1.3.95.2.2.1.9 (mplsTunnelXCPointer)
95.2.2.1.9.1.0.84215045.185273099 = OID: .ccitt.nullOID
95.2.2.1.9.1.8.67372036.202116108 = OID: 96.1.9.1.2.1414582612.8.12326.1414582612
95.2.2.1.9.1.500.50529027.202116108 = OID:
  96.1.9.1.2.1414594228.7.12305.1414594228
95.2.2.1.9.2.0.84215045.202116108 = OID: .ccitt.nullOID
95.2.2.1.9.2.48.84215045.202116108 = OID: .ccitt.nullOID
95.2.2.1.9.3.0.84215045.185273099 = OID: .ccitt.nullOID
95.2.2.1.9.3.758.84215045.185273099 = OID: .ccitt.nullOID
```

The rows that have null output correspond to entries for which 12008a is the tunnel head. The non-null highlighted rows are for entries for which 12008a is the midpoint.

mplsTunnelSignallingProto

The signalling protocol can assume one of the following four values:

```
SYNTAX      INTEGER {
                  none(1),
                  rsvp(2),
                  crldp(3),
                  other(4)
```

In Cisco implementation, this is always set to 2 (RSVP), as shown in Example 8-37.

Example 8-37 *Polling the mplsTunnelSignallingProto Variable Via SNMP Yields RSVP*

```
linux1>snmpwalk -t 500 7.1.5.5 public .1.3.6.1.3.95.2.2.1.10
  (mplsTunnelSignallingProto)
95.2.2.1.10.1.0.84215045.185273099 = 2
95.2.2.1.10.1.8.67372036.202116108 = 2
95.2.2.1.10.1.500.50529027.202116108 = 2
95.2.2.1.10.2.0.84215045.202116108 = 2
95.2.2.1.10.2.48.84215045.202116108 = 2
95.2.2.1.10.3.0.84215045.185273099 = 2
95.2.2.1.10.3.758.84215045.185273099 = 2
```

mplsTunnelSetupPrio

This object represents the tunnel's setup priority. It should be 7—the default value—if it's not explicitly set.

According to the CLI command **show mpls traffic-eng tunnels t1**, you get the results shown in Example 8-38.

Example 8-38 **show mpls traffic-eng tunnels t1** *Command Output Isolates the Tunnel Setup and Holding Priority*

```
mpls-12008a#show mpls traffic-eng tunnels tunnel 1

Name: Link Protection Tunnel (Backup)     (Tunnel1) Destination: 11.11.11.11
  Status:
    Admin: up        Oper: down   Path: not valid   Signalling: Down
    path option 5, type explicit backup

  Config Parameters:
    Bandwidth: 10000    kbps (Global)   Priority: 7  7   Affinity: 0x0/0xFFFF
    Metric Type: TE (default)
    AutoRoute: disabled  LockDown: disabled  Loadshare: 10000   bw-based
    auto-bw: disabled
```

Example 8-38 **show mpls traffic-eng tunnels t1** *Command Output Isolates the Tunnel Setup and Holding Priority (Continued)*

```
Shortest Unconstrained Path Info:
  Path Weight: 1 (TE)
  Explicit Route: 10.0.5.11 11.11.11.11
History:
  Tunnel:
    Time since created: 2 days, 22 hours, 56 minutes
  Path Option 5:
    Last Error: PCALC:: Can't use link 0.0.0.0 on node 5.5.5.5
```

You can obtain the tunnel's setup priority via SNMP, as shown in Example 8-39.

Example 8-39 *Obtaining the Tunnel Setup Priority Via SNMP*

```
linux1>snmpwalk -t 500 7.1.5.5 public .1.3.6.1.3.95.2.2.1.11 (mplsTunnelSetupPrio)
95.2.2.1.11.1.0.84215045.185273099 = 7
95.2.2.1.11.1.8.67372036.202116108 = 7
95.2.2.1.11.1.500.50529027.202116108 = 7
95.2.2.1.11.2.0.84215045.202116108 = 7
95.2.2.1.11.2.48.84215045.202116108 = 7
95.2.2.1.11.3.0.84215045.185273099 = 7
95.2.2.1.11.3.758.84215045.185273099 = 7
```

mplsTunnelHoldingPrio

This object indicates the holding priority for this tunnel. Again, this should be 7, as shown in Example 8-40.

Example 8-40 *Obtaining a Tunnel's Holding Priority Via SNMP*

```
linux1>snmpwalk -t 500 7.1.5.5 public .1.3.6.1.3.95.2.2.1.12
  (mplsTunnelHoldingPrio)
95.2.2.1.12.1.0.84215045.185273099 = 7
95.2.2.1.12.1.8.67372036.202116108 = 7
95.2.2.1.12.1.500.50529027.202116108 = 7
95.2.2.1.12.2.0.84215045.202116108 = 7
95.2.2.1.12.2.48.84215045.202116108 = 7
95.2.2.1.12.3.0.84215045.185273099 = 7
95.2.2.1.12.3.758.84215045.185273099 = 7
```

mplsTunnelSessionAttributes

The tunnel's session attributes are one of the following values:

```
fastReroute (0),
mergingPermitted (1),
isPersistent (2),
isPinned (3),
recordRoute(4)
```

Because the record route was turned on for Tunnel1, you would get the results shown in Example 8-41.

Example 8-41 *Polling the mplsTunnelSessionAttributes Variable Via SNMP*

```
linux1>snmpwalk -t 500 7.1.5.5 public .1.3.6.1.3.95.2.2.1.13
  (mplsTunnelSessionAttributes)
95.2.2.1.13.1.0.84215045.185273099 =  Hex: 04
```

mplsTunnelOwner

The tunnel owner variable can assume one of the following values:

```
SYNTAX        INTEGER {
    admin(1),  -- represents all management entities
    rsvp(2),
    crldp(3),
    policyAgent(4),
    other(5)
  }
```

Example 8-42 shows that the mplsTunnelOwner is set to **admin** or **other**.

Example 8-42 *Polling the mplsTunnelOwner Variable Via SNMP*

```
linux1>snmpwalk -t 500 7.1.5.5 public .1.3.6.1.3.95.2.2.1.14 (mplsTunnelOwner)
95.2.2.1.14.1.0.84215045.185273099 = 1
95.2.2.1.14.1.9.67372036.202116108 = 5
95.2.2.1.14.1.500.50529027.202116108 = 5
95.2.2.1.14.2.0.84215045.202116108 = 1
95.2.2.1.14.2.48.84215045.202116108 = 5
95.2.2.1.14.3.0.84215045.185273099 = 1
95.2.2.1.14.3.758.84215045.185273099 = 5
```

mplsTunnelLocalProtectInUse

This variable, if set to true, indicates that a local repair mechanism is in use to maintain this tunnel. For details on local repair, refer to Chapter 7, "Protection and Restoration." Currently on 12000a, this variable is set to false because currently it is not implemented in Cisco IOS Software. Example 8-43 demonstrates how to poll for the value of this variable.

Example 8-43 *Polling the mplsTunnelLocalProtectInUse Variable Via SNMP*

```
linux1>snmpwalk -t 500 7.1.5.5 public .1.3.6.1.3.95.2.2.1.15
  (mplsTunnelLocalProtectInUse)
95.2.2.1.15.1.0.84215045.185273099 = 2
95.2.2.1.15.1.9.67372036.202116108 = 2
95.2.2.1.15.1.505.50529027.202116108 = 2
95.2.2.1.15.2.0.84215045.202116108 = 2
95.2.2.1.15.2.48.84215045.202116108 = 2
95.2.2.1.15.3.0.84215045.185273099 = 2
95.2.2.1.15.3.758.84215045.185273099 = 2
```

mplsTunnelResourcePointer

Note that TunnelResourcePointer is currently valid only for midpoints, not for headends. If you look at 12008a in Example 8-44, you see that all the non-null values correspond to midpoint entries. The nulls are for the tunnels for which the 12008a is the headend.

Example 8-44 *Polling the mplsTunnelResourcePointer Variable on 12008a*

```
linux1>snmpwalk -t 500 7.1.5.5 public .1.3.6.1.3.95.2.2.1.16
  (mplsTunnelResourcePointer)
95.2.2.1.16.1.0.84215045.185273099 = OID: .ccitt.nullOID
95.2.2.1.16.1.509.50529027.202116108 = OID: 95.2.6.1.1.1414391828
95.2.2.1.16.2.0.84215045.202116108 = OID: .ccitt.nullOID
95.2.2.1.16.2.48.84215045.202116108 = OID: 95.2.6.1.1.1414391236
95.2.2.1.16.3.0.84215045.185273099 = OID: .ccitt.nullOID
95.2.2.1.16.3.785.84215045.185273099 = OID: 95.2.6.1.1.1414391532
```

mplsTunnelInstancePriority

This object is not currently implemented in Cisco IOS Software.

mplsTunnelHopTableIndex

This object provides an index into the hop table. The hop table is basically where you can define the hops for an explicit path option. Example 8-45 shows the result of polling the mplsTunnelHopTableIndex variable.

Example 8-45 *Polling the mplsTunnelHopTableIndex Variable Via SNMP*

```
linux1>snmpwalk -t 500 7.1.5.5 public .1.3.6.1.3.95.2.2.1.18
  (mplsTunnelHopTableIndex)
95.2.2.1.18.1.0.84215045.185273099 = Gauge: 1
95.2.2.1.18.1.509.50529027.202116108 = Gauge: 0
95.2.2.1.18.2.0.84215045.202116108 = Gauge: 2
95.2.2.1.18.2.48.84215045.202116108 = Gauge: 0
95.2.2.1.18.3.0.84215045.185273099 = Gauge: 3
95.2.2.1.18.3.785.84215045.185273099 = Gauge: 0
```

mplsTunnelARHopTableIndex

This points to the ARHopTable, which is the hops reported by the signalling protocol—RSVP in the case of Example 8-46.

Example 8-46 *Polling the mplsTunnelARHopTableIndex Variable Via SNMP*

```
linux1>snmpwalk -t 500 7.1.5.5 public .1.3.6.1.3.95.2.2.1.19
  (mplsTunnelARHopTableIndex)
95.2.2.1.19.1.0.84215045.185273099 = Gauge: 0
95.2.2.1.19.1.509.50529027.202116108 = Gauge: 1414391828
95.2.2.1.19.2.0.84215045.202116108 = Gauge: 0
95.2.2.1.19.2.48.84215045.202116108 = Gauge: 1414391236
95.2.2.1.19.3.0.84215045.185273099 = Gauge: 0
95.2.2.1.19.3.785.84215045.185273099 = Gauge: 1414391532
```

The highlighted output shows the mplsTunnelARHopTableIndex value. From Table 8-8, you know that mplsTunnelARHopTableIndex is defined as MplsPathIndexOrZero, which in turn is defined as an Unsigned32. The **snmpwalk** program interprets these as Gauge.

Using the mplsTunnelARHopTableIndex value to index into the ARHopTable, you can obtain the Explicit Route Object (ERO) reported in the **show mpls traffic-eng tunnels** command. Currently, this is supported only for midpoints.

mplsTunnelCHopTableIndex

This index points to the CHopTable, which contains the hops as computed by CSPF. Example 8-47 shows the output of polling this variable.

Example 8-47 *Polling the mplsTunnelCHopTableIndex Variable Via SNMP*

```
linux1>snmpwalk -t 500 7.1.5.5 public .1.3.6.1.3.95.2.2.1.20
  (mplsTunnelCHopTableIndex)
95.2.2.1.20.1.0.84215045.185273099 = Gauge: 0
95.2.2.1.20.1.509.50529027.202116108 = Gauge: 1414391828
95.2.2.1.20.2.0.84215045.202116108 = Gauge: 0
95.2.2.1.20.2.48.84215045.202116108 = Gauge: 1414391236
95.2.2.1.20.3.0.84215045.185273099 = Gauge: 0
95.2.2.1.20.3.785.84215045.185273099 = Gauge: 1414391532
```

Using the numbers in the highlighted text, you can index the CHopTable to obtain information about the hops computed by CSPF.

This is applicable only to midpoints, not tunnel heads.

mplsTunnelPrimaryTimeUp

This variable provides the amount of time a tunnel has been up. It is meaningful to poll this on tunnel headends only. Example 8-48 shows this variable being polled.

Example 8-48 *Polling the mplsTunnelPrimaryTimeUp Variable Via SNMP*

```
linux1>snmpwalk -t 500 7.1.5.5 public .1.3.6.1.3.95.2.2.1.22
  (mplsTunnelPrimaryTimeUp)
95.2.2.1.22.1.0.84215045.185273099 = Timeticks: (0) 0:00:00.00
95.2.2.1.22.1.509.50529027.202116108 = Timeticks: (0) 0:00:00.00
95.2.2.1.22.2.0.84215045.202116108 = Timeticks: (513883) 1:25:38.83
95.2.2.1.22.2.48.84215045.202116108 = Timeticks: (0) 0:00:00.00
95.2.2.1.22.3.0.84215045.185273099 = Timeticks: (349972) 0:58:19.72
95.2.2.1.22.3.785.84215045.185273099 = Timeticks: (0) 0:00:00.00
```

The nonzero values correspond to tunnels for which 12008 (being polled) is the headend.

This corresponds to the output from **show mpls traffic-eng tunnels t1**, as demonstrated in Example 8-49.

Example 8-49 *Confirming a Tunnel's Uptime*

```
12008a#show mpls traffic-eng tunnel tunnel2 | begin History
History:
    Tunnel:
      Time since created: 3 days, 43 minutes
      Time since path change: 1 hours, 28 minutes
    Current LSP:
      Uptime: 1 hours, 28 minutes
```

Because the CLI output was captured a few minutes after the SNMP poll, a couple of minutes have elapsed.

mplsTunnelPathChanges

This variable provides the number of path changes. You can also observe this using the CLI command **show mpls traffic-eng tunnels tunnel2 statistics**, as demonstrated in Example 8-50.

Example 8-50 *Confirming the Number of Path Changes*

```
mpls-12008a#show mpls traffic-eng tunnels tunnel2 statistics
Tunnel2 (Destination 12.12.12.12; Name mpls-12008a_t2)
  Management statistics:
    Path:   46 no path, 1 path no longer valid, 0 missing ip exp path
            4 path changes
    State:  3 transitions, 0 admin down, 1 oper down
  Signalling statistics:
    Opens:  3 succeeded, 0 timed out, 0 bad path spec
            0 other aborts
    Errors: 0 no b/w, 0 no route, 0 admin
            0 bad exp route, 0 rec route loop, 0 frr activated
            0 other
```

Example 8-51 shows how you can obtain the same information using SNMP.

Example 8-51 *Obtaining mplsTunnelPathChanges Information Via SNMP*

```
linux1>snmpwalk -t 500 7.1.5.5 public .1.3.6.1.3.95.2.2.1.23
    (mplsTunnelPathChanges)
95.2.2.1.23.1.0.84215045.185273099 = 0
95.2.2.1.23.1.509.50529027.202116108 = 0
95.2.2.1.23.2.0.84215045.202116108 = 4
95.2.2.1.23.2.48.84215045.202116108 = 0
95.2.2.1.23.3.0.84215045.185273099 = 37
95.2.2.1.23.3.785.84215045.185273099 = 0
```

mplsTunnelLastPathChange

This variable provides the time since the last path change occurred. Again, this can be obtained using the CLI command **show mpls traffic-eng tunnels tunnel1**, which results in the output shown in Example 8-52.

Example 8-52 *Determining the Time Since the Last Path Change*

```
mpls-12008a#show mpls traffic-eng tunnels role head | include Time
        Time since created: 3 days, 55 minutes
        Time since created: 3 days, 55 minutes
        Time since path change: 1 hours, 41 minutes
        Time since created: 3 days, 55 minutes
        Time since path change: 1 hours, 13 minutes
```

The SNMP data agrees with the CLI, as shown in Example 8-53.

Example 8-53 *Obtaining the Time Since the Last Path Change Occurred Via SNMP*

```
linux1>snmpwalk -t 500 7.1.5.5 public .1.3.6.1.3.95.2.2.1.24
    (mplsTunnelLastPathChange)
95.2.2.1.24.1.0.84215045.185273099 = Timeticks: (26258001) 3 days, 0:56:20.01
95.2.2.1.24.1.509.50529027.202116108 = Timeticks: (0) 0:00:00.00
95.2.2.1.24.2.0.84215045.202116108 = Timeticks: (607730) 1:41:17.30
95.2.2.1.24.2.48.84215045.202116108 = Timeticks: (0) 0:00:00.00
95.2.2.1.24.3.0.84215045.185273099 = Timeticks: (443819) 1:13:58.19
95.2.2.1.24.3.785.84215045.185273099 = Timeticks: (0) 0:00:00.00
```

mplsTunnelCreationTime

The mplsTunnelCreationTime is actually set to the number of time ticks from when the system came up (sysUpTime) in Cisco IOS.

The LSP creation time can be obtained via CLI using the command **show mpls traffic-eng tunnel**, as shown in Example 8-54.

Example 8-54 *Obtaining LSP Creation Time Via CLI*

```
mpls-12008a#show mpls traffic-eng tunnels role head | include Time
        Time since created: 3 days, 55 minutes
        Time since created: 3 days, 55 minutes
        Time since path change: 1 hours, 41 minutes
        Time since created: 3 days, 55 minutes
        Time since path change: 1 hours, 13 minutes
```

To obtain this information via SNMP, first you have to poll the mplsTunnelCreationTime, and then you poll the system table for the sysUpTime. After this, you can compute the LSP creation time by subtracting the mplsTunnelCreationTime from the sysUpTime.

Example 8-55 shows the output of polling the mplsTunnelCreationTime variable.

Example 8-55 *Polling the mplsTunnelCreationTime Variable Via SNMP*

```
linux1>snmpwalk -t 500 7.1.5.5 public .1.3.6.1.3.95.2.2.1.25
  (mplsTunnelCreationTime)
95.2.2.1.25.1.0.84215045.185273099 = Timeticks: (2348) 0:00:23.48
95.2.2.1.25.1.509.50529027.202116108 = Timeticks: (0) 0:00:00.00
95.2.2.1.25.2.0.84215045.202116108 = Timeticks: (2350) 0:00:23.50
95.2.2.1.25.2.48.84215045.202116108 = Timeticks: (0) 0:00:00.00
95.2.2.1.25.3.0.84215045.185273099 = Timeticks: (2351) 0:00:23.51
95.2.2.1.25.3.785.84215045.185273099 = Timeticks: (0) 0:00:00.00
```

A walk on the system table provides the sysUpTime, as shown in Example 8-56.

Example 8-56 *Polling the System Table to Obtain the sysUpTime*

```
linux1>snmpwalk -t 500 7.1.5.5 public system (system)
system.sysDescr.0 = Cisco Internetwork Operating System Software
IOS (tm) GS Software (GSR-P-M), Version 12.0(21.2)S, EARLY DEPLOYMENT
  MAINTENANCE INTERIM SOFTWARE
TAC Support: http://www.cisco.com/tac
Copyright (c) 1986-2002 by cisco Systems, Inc.
Compiled Tue 26-Mar-0
system.sysObjectID.0 = OID: enterprises.9.1.182
system.sysUpTime.0 = Timeticks: (26280739) 3 days, 1:00:07.39
system.sysContact.0 =
system.sysName.0 = mpls-12008a
system.sysLocation.0 =
system.sysServices.0 = 6
system.sysORLastChange.0 = Timeticks: (0) 0:00:00.00
```

Of course, you also can obtain the sysUpTime via the CLI, as shown in Example 8-57.

Example 8-57 *Obtaining the Uptime on 12008a Using CLI*

```
mpls-12008a#show version | include uptime
mpls-12008a uptime is 3 days, 1 hour, 3 minutes
```

If you want to obtain the actual creation time, you have to subtract the value of mplsTunnelCreationTime from sysUpTime:

Actual LSP creation time = sysUpTime – mplsTunnelCreationTime = 26280739 – 2351 = 2625722

If you convert 2625722, which is in 1/100ths of a second, to seconds, you get the following result:

26257.22 seconds, which is 3.041 days

This is approximately what you saw in the CLI of the **show mpls traffic-eng tunnel** output.

mplsTunnelStateTransitions

This variable represents the number of times that the tunnel has changed state.

You can observe this on the CLI using the **show mpls traffic-eng tunnels tunnel2 statistics** command, as demonstrated in Example 8-58.

Example 8-58 *Determining the Number of Times the Tunnel Has Changed State*

```
mpls-12008a#show mpls traffic-eng tunnels tunnel2 statistics
Tunnel2 (Destination 12.12.12.12; Name mpls-12008a_t2)
  Management statistics:
    Path:   46 no path, 1 path no longer valid, 0 missing ip exp path
            4 path changes
    State:  3 transitions, 0 admin down, 1 oper down
  Signalling statistics:
    Opens:  3 succeeded, 0 timed out, 0 bad path spec
            0 other aborts
    Errors: 0 no b/w, 0 no route, 0 admin
            0 bad exp route, 0 rec route loop, 0 frr activated
            0 other
```

Using SNMP, you can obtain the same information. This is demonstrated in Example 8-59.

Example 8-59 *Obtaining Tunnel Transition Information Through SNMP*

```
linux1>snmpwalk -t 500 7.1.5.5 public .1.3.6.1.3.95.2.2.1.26
  (mplsTunnelStateTransitions)
95.2.2.1.26.1.0.84215045.185273099 = 2
95.2.2.1.26.1.517.50529027.202116108 = 0
95.2.2.1.26.2.0.84215045.202116108 = 3
95.2.2.1.26.2.48.84215045.202116108 = 0
95.2.2.1.26.3.0.84215045.185273099 = 42
95.2.2.1.26.3.844.84215045.185273099 = 0
```

The highlighted output corresponds to tunnel2. It shows the same number of transitions as the CLI—3.

mplsTunnelIncludeAnyAffinity

This object is not implemented on the Cisco routers.

mplsTunnelIncludeAllAffinity

This object represents the attribute bits that must be set for the tunnel to include a link in the CSPF. Example 8-60 shows the output of **snmpwalk** on the mplsTunnelIncludeAllAffinity variable.

Example 8-60 *Polling the mplsTunnelIncludeAllAffinity Variable to Get Affinity Bits*

```
linux1>snmpwalk -t 500 7.1.5.5 public .1.3.6.1.3.95.2.2.1.28
  (mplsTunnelIncludeAllAffinity)
95.2.2.1.28.1.0.84215045.185273099 = Gauge: 0
95.2.2.1.28.1.517.50529027.202116108 = Gauge: 0
95.2.2.1.28.2.0.84215045.202116108 = Gauge: 1
95.2.2.1.28.3.0.84215045.185273099 = Gauge: 0
95.2.2.1.28.3.844.84215045.185273099 = Gauge: 0
```

To see a nonzero value in the highlighted output, set the tunnel affinity for tunnel2 to 1, as shown in Example 8-61.

Example 8-61 *Setting the Tunnel Affinity of tunnel2 to 0x1*

```
mpls-12008a#configure terminal
Enter configuration commands, one per line.  End with CNTL/Z.
mpls-12008a(config)#interface tunnel 2
mpls-12008a(config-if)#tunnel mpls traffic-eng affinity 0x1 mask 0xff
mpls-12008a(config-if)#end
```

mplsTunnelExcludeAllAffinity

This variable refers to attribute bits that must be unset for the tunnel to include a link in the CSPF. Example 8-62 shows the **snmpwalk** output for this variable.

Example 8-62 *Polling the mplsTunnelExcludeAllAffinity Variable Via SNMP*

```
linux1>snmpwalk -t 500 7.1.5.5 public .1.3.6.1.3.95.2.2.1.29
  (mplsTunnelExcludeAllAffinity)
95.2.2.1.29.1.0.84215045.185273099 = Gauge: 65535
95.2.2.1.29.1.519.50529027.202116108 = Gauge: 0
95.2.2.1.29.2.0.84215045.202116108 = Gauge: 254
95.2.2.1.29.3.0.84215045.185273099 = Gauge: 65535
95.2.2.1.29.3.844.84215045.185273099 = Gauge: 0
```

mplsTunnelPathInUse

This variable represents the path option that is currently in use. Using the CLI command **show mpls traffic-eng tunnels tunnel2**, you can obtain the information shown in Example 8-63.

Example 8-63 *Determining the Path Option Currently in Use*

```
mpls-12008a#show mpls traffic-eng tunnels tunnel 2

Name: mpls-12008a_t2                    (Tunnel2) Destination: 12.12.12.12
   Status:
      Admin: up         Oper: up      Path: valid      Signalling: connected

      path option 5, type explicit backup2 (Basis for Setup, path weight 4)
      path option 10, type dynamic
```

The path option that is the basis of tunnel setup can also be retried using SNMP, as shown in Example 8-64.

Example 8-64 *Polling the mplsTunnelPathInUse Variable to Obtain the Path Option Used for Tunnel Setup*

```
linux1>snmpwalk -t 500 7.1.5.5 public .1.3.6.1.3.95.2.2.1.30 (mplsTunnelPathInUse)
95.2.2.1.30.1.0.84215045.185273099 = Gauge: 0
95.2.2.1.30.1.519.50529027.202116108 = Gauge: 0
95.2.2.1.30.2.0.84215045.202116108 = Gauge: 5
95.2.2.1.30.2.302.84215045.202116108 = Gauge: 0
95.2.2.1.30.3.0.84215045.185273099 = Gauge: 5
95.2.2.1.30.3.844.84215045.185273099 = Gauge: 0
```

mplsTunnelRole

An LSR has one of three roles for a given tunnel:

- Head
- Midpoint
- Tail

You can observe this on the CLI using **show mpls traffic-eng summary**, as demonstrated in Example 8-65.

Example 8-65 *Determining the LSR Role for a Tunnel*

```
mpls-12008a#show mpls traffic-eng tunnels summary
Signalling Summary:
    LSP Tunnels Process:            running
    RSVP Process:                   running
    Forwarding:                     enabled
    Head: 3 interfaces, 2 active signalling attempts, 2 established
          24 activations, 22 deactivations
    Midpoints: 1, Tails: 0
    Periodic reoptimization:        every 3600 seconds, next in 171 seconds
    Periodic FRR Promotion:         every 300 seconds, next in 171 seconds
    Periodic auto-bw collection:    disabled
```

You can obtain the same information via SNMP, as demonstrated in Example 8-66.

Example 8-66 *Determining a Tunnel's LSR Role Via SNMP*

```
linux1>snmpwalk -t 500 7.1.5.5 public .1.3.6.1.3.95.2.2.1.31 (mplsTunnelRole)
95.2.2.1.31.1.0.84215045.185273099 = 1
95.2.2.1.31.1.519.50529027.202116108 = 2
95.2.2.1.31.2.0.84215045.202116108 = 1
95.2.2.1.31.2.302.84215045.202116108 = 1
```

From the output shown in Example 8-66, you can see three 1s (headend) and one 2 (midpoint), which agrees with the CLI output.

mplsTunnelTotalUpTime

This object refers to the amount of time that the tunnel has been operationally up. Example 8-67 shows the output of polling mplsTunnelTotalUpTime.

Example 8-67 *Polling the mplsTunnelTotalUpTime Variable Via SNMP*

```
linux1>snmpwalk -t 500 7.1.5.5 public .1.3.6.1.3.95.2.2.1.32
  (mplsTunnelTotalUpTime)
95.2.2.1.32.1.0.84215045.185273099 = Timeticks: (0) 0:00:00.00
95.2.2.1.32.1.519.50529027.202116108 = Timeticks: (0) 0:00:00.00
95.2.2.1.32.2.0.84215045.202116108 = Timeticks: (27305450) 3 days, 3:50:54.50
95.2.2.1.32.2.302.84215045.202116108 = Timeticks: (0) 0:00:00.00
95.2.2.1.32.3.0.84215045.185273099 = Timeticks: (21297744) 2 days, 11:09:37.44
95.2.2.1.32.3.844.84215045.185273099 = Timeticks: (0) 0:00:00.00
```

This corresponds to what you see in Example 8-68 using the CLI.

Example 8-68 *Determining a Tunnel's Operational Uptime Via the Cisco IOS Software CLI*

```
mpls-12008a#show mpls traffic-eng tunnels tunnel1

Name: Link Protection Tunnel (Backup)      (Tunnel1) Destination: 11.11.11.11
  Status:
    Admin: up        Oper: down   Path: not valid   Signalling: Down
    path option 5, type explicit backup

  Config Parameters:
    Bandwidth: 10000    kbps (Global)  Priority: 7  7   Affinity: 0x0/0xFFFF
    Metric Type: TE (default)
    AutoRoute:  disabled  LockDown: disabled  Loadshare: 10000    bw-based
    auto-bw: disabled

  Shortest Unconstrained Path Info:
    Path Weight: 2 (TE)
    Explicit Route: 10.0.13.16 10.0.7.11 11.11.11.11
```

continues

Example 8-68 *Determining a Tunnel's Operational Uptime Via the Cisco IOS Software CLI (Continued)*

```
History:
  Tunnel:
    Time since created: 3 days, 3 hours, 51 minutes
  Path Option 5:
    Last Error: PCALC:: Can't use link 0.0.0.0 on node 5.5.5.5
```

mplsTunnelInstanceUpTime

This object is not currently supported in the Cisco IOS Software.

mplsTunnelAdminStatus

This object indicates a tunnel's administrative status. Example 8-69 shows the output of **snmpwalk** polling this variable.

Example 8-69 *Polling the mplsTunnelAdminStatus Variable Using SNMP*

```
linux1>snmpwalk -t 500 7.1.5.5 public .1.3.6.1.3.95.2.2.1.34
  (mplsTunnelAdminStatus)
95.2.2.1.34.1.0.84215045.185273099 = 1
95.2.2.1.34.1.519.50529027.202116108 = 1
95.2.2.1.34.2.0.84215045.202116108 = 1
95.2.2.1.34.2.302.84215045.202116108 = 1
95.2.2.1.34.3.0.84215045.185273099 = 1
95.2.2.1.34.3.844.84215045.185273099 = 1
```

1 is up and 2 is down.

mplsTunnelOperStatus

This object indicates a tunnel's administrative status. Example 8-70 shows the output of polling this variable.

Example 8-70 *Polling the mplsTunnelOperStatus Variable Via SNMP*

```
linux1>snmpwalk -t 500 7.1.5.5 public .1.3.6.1.3.95.2.2.1.35
  (mplsTunnelOperStatus)
95.2.2.1.35.1.0.84215045.185273099 = 2
95.2.2.1.35.1.519.50529027.202116108 = 1
95.2.2.1.35.2.0.84215045.202116108 = 1
95.2.2.1.35.2.302.84215045.202116108 = 1
95.2.2.1.35.3.0.84215045.185273099 = 1
95.2.2.1.35.3.844.84215045.185273099 = 1
```

1 is up and 2 is down.

mplsTunnelHopTable

The HopTable specifies hops that constitute an explicitly defined path. Table 8-9 shows the organization of the objects defined for each entry of the table (mplsTunnelHopEntry).

Table 8-9   *mplsTunnelHopEntry Organization*

Object	Syntax	Access	Description
mplsTunnelHopListIndex	MplsPathIndex	not-accessible	Primary index into the HopListEntry table.
mplsTunnelHopPath OptionIndex	MplsPathIndex	not-accessible	Secondary index into the HopListEntry table.
mplsTunnelHopIndex	MplsPathIndex	not-accessible	Secondary index used to identify a hop.
mplsTunnelHopAddrType	ipV4(1), ipV6(2), asNumber(3), lspid(4)	read-create	Address type of the tunnel hop.
mplsTunnelHopIpv4Addr	InetAddressIPv4	read-create	If mplsTunnelHopAddr Type is set to 1, mplsTunnelHopIpv4 Addr holds the IPv4 address of the current hop.
mplsTunnelHopIpv4 PrefixLen	Unsigned32	read-create	Prefix length of the IPv4 address. This is valid only if mplsTunnelHopAddrT ype is set to 1.
mplsTunnelHopIpv6Addr	InetAddressIPv6	read-create	If mplsTunnelHopAddr Type is set to 2, mplsTunnelHopIpv4 Addr holds an IPv6 address of the current hop.
mplsTunnelHopIpv6 PrefixLen	Unsigned32	read-create	If mplsTunnelHopAddr Type is set to ipV6(2), this value contains the prefix length for this hop's IPv6 address.

continues

Table 8-9 *mplsTunnelHopEntry Organization (Continued)*

Object	Syntax	Access	Description
mplsTunnelHopAsNumber(3)	Unsigned32	read-create	Holds the AS number of the hop if mplsTunnelHopAddr Type is set to asNumber.
mplsTunnelHopLspId	MplsLSPID	read-create	If mplsTunnelHopAddr Type is set to lspid(4), this value contains the LSPID of a tunnel of this hop.
mplsTunnelHopType	strict(1), loose(2)	read-create	Denotes whether this tunnel hop is routed in a strict or loose fashion.
mplsTunnelHopInclude Exclude	include(1), exclude(2)	read-create	Determines whether a hop is included or excluded in the CSPF calculation for that tunnel.
mplsTunnelHopPath OptionName	DisplayString	read-create	Name of the path option.
mplsTunnelHopEntryPath Comp	dynamic(1), explicit(2)	read-create	If set to dynamic, CSPF figures out the path. If set to explicit, the user specifies the path.
mplsTunnelHopRowStatus	RowStatus	read-create	Used to create, modify, and/or delete a row in this table.
mplsTunnelHopStorage Type	StorageType	read-create	Storage type for this object.

Walking the HopTable provides the same information as displaying the explicit path list using the CLI command **show ip explicit-paths**, as demonstrated in Example 8-71.

Example 8-71 *Determining the Hops That Constitute an Explicitly Defined Path*

```
mpls-7200a#show ip explicit-paths name primary
PATH primary (strict source route, path complete, generation 6)
    1: next-address 10.0.3.5
    2: next-address 10.0.5.11
    3: next-address 10.0.17.12
    4: next-address 12.12.12.12
```

The following sections describe the objects that constitute the HopTable. Coverage of the first three objects has been omitted because they are not accessible via SNMP.

mplsTunnelHopAddrType

This variable provides the tunnel hop's type of address. The possible values are

* IPv4 (1)
* IPv6 (2)
* AS number (3)
* LSPID (4)

In the current Cisco IOS Software implementation, all explicit paths are IPv4. Example 8-72 gives an example.

Example 8-72 *Polling the mplsTunnelHopAddrType Variable Using SNMP*

```
linux1>snmpwalk -t 500 7.1.5.4 public .1.3.6.1.3.95.2.4.1.4.1.5
  (mplsTunnelHopAddrType)
95.2.4.1.4.1.5.1 = 1
95.2.4.1.4.1.5.2 = 1
95.2.4.1.4.1.5.3 = 1
95.2.4.1.4.1.5.4 = 1
```

mplsTunnelHopIpv4Addr

This variable holds the actual IPv4 address of the hops, as demonstrated in Example 8-73.

Example 8-73 *Polling the mplsTunnelHopIpv4Addr Variable Using SNMP*

```
linux1>snmpwalk -t 500 7.1.5.4 public .1.3.6.1.3.95.2.4.1.5
  (mplsTunnelHopIpv4Addr)
95.2.4.1.5.1.5.1 =  Hex: 0A 00 03 05 (10.0.3.5)
95.2.4.1.5.1.5.2 =  Hex: 0A 00 05 0B (10.0.5.11)
95.2.4.1.5.1.5.3 =  Hex: 0A 00 11 0C (10.0.12.17)
95.2.4.1.5.1.5.4 =  Hex: 0C 0C 0C 0C (12.12.12.12)
```

mplsTunnelHopIpv4PrefixLen

This variable represents the prefix length. For IPv4, this is 32 (bits), as demonstrated in Example 8-74.

Example 8-74 *Determining the Prefix Length for Tunnel Hop Addresses*

```
linux1>snmpwalk -t 500 7.1.5.4 public .1.3.6.1.3.95.2.4.1.6
  (mplsTunnelHopIpv4PrefixLen)
95.2.4.1.6.1.5.1 = Gauge: 32
95.2.4.1.6.1.5.2 = Gauge: 32
95.2.4.1.6.1.5.3 = Gauge: 32
95.2.4.1.6.1.5.4 = Gauge: 32
95.2.4.1.6.1.6.1 = Gauge: 32
```

The prefix length is 32 because the IPv4 length is always 32, as specified in RFC 3209.

mplsTunnelHopType

This object represents the hop type, whether strict (1) or loose (2).

For the path list "primary" on 7200a, they are all strict hops, as demonstrated in Example 8-75.

Example 8-75 *Determining Whether Tunnel Hops Are Strict or Loose*

```
linux1>snmpwalk -t 500 7.1.5.4 public .1.3.6.1.3.95.2.4.1.11 (mplsTunnelHopType)
95.2.4.1.11.1.5.1 = 1
95.2.4.1.11.1.5.2 = 1
95.2.4.1.11.1.5.3 = 1
95.2.4.1.11.1.5.4 = 1
95.2.4.1.11.1.6.1 = 1
```

A value of 1 indicates a strict ERO subobject. This can be verified by the CLI output shown in Example 8-76.

Example 8-76 **show ip explicit-paths** *Command Output on 7200a*

```
mpls-7200a#show ip explicit-paths name primary detail
PATH primary (strict source route, path complete, generation 6)
    1: next-address 10.0.3.5
    2: next-address 10.0.5.11
    3: next-address 10.0.17.12
    4: next-address 12.12.12.12 (lasthop)
```

mplsTunnelHopIncludeExclude

Example 8-77 shows the next address, which is "include" by default. If you use "exclude," it appears in the **show** command.

This variable determines whether to include or exclude this hop during CSPF:

- Include (1)
- Exclude (2)

For the path list "primary," they should all be "include," as demonstrated in Example 8-77.

Example 8-77 *Polling the mplsTunnelHopIncludeExclude Variable Using SNMP*

```
linux1> snmpwalk -t 500 7.1.5.4 public .1.3.6.1.3.95.2.4.1.12
   (mplsTunnelHopIncludeExclude)
95.2.4.1.12.1.5.1 = 1
95.2.4.1.12.1.5.2 = 1
95.2.4.1.12.1.5.3 = 1
95.2.4.1.12.1.5.4 = 1
95.2.4.1.12.1.6.1 = 1
```

mplsTunnelHopPathOptionName

This refers to the path option for which the path list applies. You can check the **path-option** statement in the tunnel interface in the output of Example 8-78.

Example 8-78 *Checking for the **path-option** Number Under the tunnel1 Configuration of 7200a*

```
7200a#show running-config interface tunnel1
interface Tunnel1
 description Primary tunnel 7200a->12008a->12008c->7200c
 ip unnumbered Loopback0
 no ip directed-broadcast
 no ip route-cache cef
 tunnel destination 12.12.12.12
 tunnel mode mpls traffic-eng
 tunnel mpls traffic-eng autoroute announce
 tunnel mpls traffic-eng priority 7 7
 tunnel mpls traffic-eng bandwidth  100
 tunnel mpls traffic-eng path-option 5 explicit name primary
 tunnel mpls traffic-eng path-option 6 dynamic
 tunnel mpls traffic-eng record-route
 tunnel mpls traffic-eng fast-reroute
```

The variable should hold the value 5, as demonstrated in Example 8-79.

Example 8-79 *Polling the mplsTunnelHopPathOptionName Variable Via SNMP*

```
linux1>snmpwalk -t 500 7.1.5.4 public .1.3.6.1.3.95.2.4.1.13
  (mplsTunnelHopPathOptionName)
95.2.4.1.13.1.5.1 = 5
95.2.4.1.13.1.5.2 = 5
95.2.4.1.13.1.5.3 = 5
95.2.4.1.13.1.5.4 = 5
95.2.4.1.13.1.6.1 = 5
```

mplsTunnelResourceTable

You can specify tunnel resources such as MaxRate, MinRate, and burst using ResourceTable so that these attributes can be shared by several tunnels. The mplsTunnelResourceTable contains mplsTunnelResourceEntry.

Table 8-10 shows the organization of the mplsTunnelResourceEntry table.

Table 8-10   *Organization of Objects in the mplsTunnelResourceEntry Table*

Object	Syntax	Access	Description
mplsTunnelResource Index	Unsigned32	not-accessible	Uniquely identifies an entry in this table.
mplsTunnelResource MaxRate	MplsBitRate	read-create	Maximum rate in bps.

continues

Table 8-10 *Organization of Objects in the mplsTunnelResourceEntry Table (Continued)*

Object	Syntax	Access	Description
mplsTunnelResource MeanRate	MplsBitRate	read-create	Mean rate in bps.
mplsTunnelResource MaxBurstSize	MplsBurstSize	read-create	Maximum burst size in bytes.
mplsTunnelResource MeanBurstSize	MplsBurstSize	read-create	Mean burst size in bytes.
mplsTunnelResource ExcessBurstSize	MplsBurstSize	read-create	Excess burst size in bytes. Comes from CR-LDP. Is not currently supported by Cisco IOS Software.
mplsTunnelResource Frequency	unspecified(1), frequent(2), veryFrequent(3)	read-create	Granularity of the availability of the committed rate. Comes from CR-LDP. Is not currently supported by Cisco IOS Software.
mplsTunnelResource Weight	Unsigned32 (0...255)	read-create	Relative weight for using excess bandwidth above its committed rate. Comes from CR-LDP. Is not currently supported by Cisco IOS Software.
mplsTunnelResource RowStatus	RowStatus	read-create	Used to create, modify, and/or delete a row in this table.
mplsTunnelResource StorageType	StorageType	read-create	Indicates the storage type for this object.

The values of these variables correspond to the ones seen using the CLI command **show mpls traffic-eng tunnels**, as demonstrated in Example 8-80.

Example 8-80 *Determining Tunnel Resources in Use*

```
7200a#show mpls traffic-eng tunnels tunnel1
...
RSVP Path Info:
     My Address: 4.4.4.4
     Explicit Route: 10.0.3.5 10.0.5.11 10.0.17.12 12.12.12.12
     Record    Route:
     Tspec: ave rate=100 kbits, burst=1000 bytes, peak rate=100 kbits
...
```

Using SNMP, you get the results shown in Example 8-81.

Example 8-81 *Polling the mplsTunnelResourceEntry Table Via SNMP*

```
linux1> snmpwalk -t 500 7.1.5.4 public .1.3.6.1.3.95.2.6 (mplsTunnelResourceEntry)
95.2.6.1.2.1642132836 = 100000 (mplsTunnelResourceMaxRate)
95.2.6.1.3.1642132836 = 100000 (mplsTunnelResourceMeanRate)
95.2.6.1.4.1642132836 = 1000 (mplsTunnelResourceMaxBurstSize)
95.2.6.1.5.1642132836 = 1 (mplsTunnelResourceMeanBurstSize)
95.2.6.1.6.1642132836 = 5 (mplsTunnelResourceExcessBurstSize)
```

NOTE   Remember from Chapter 4 that these values are not enforced in the forwarding plane, they are merely signalled in the control plane.

Summary

This chapter covered the MPLS LSR and the MPLS TE MIBs. The objects covered in each MIB were discussed, along with examples of how they compare to information available on the CLI.

The MPLS MIBs provide an alternative way to access information available through the CLI. Even though the method of accessing some of this information might seem tedious, polling the information using SNMP is how most reports are created. To create a performance report, for example, it might be easy to run the CLI to obtain the output for a handful of routers, but when you have a large network, it's efficient to collect the statistics using SNMP commands embedded within scripts or using tools such as HP OpenView and MRTG. If you are interested in learning more about management aspects of MPLS, references are provided in Appendix B.

This chapter covers the following topics:

- Sample Network for Case Studies
- Different Types of TE Design
- Tactical TE Design
- Online Strategic TE Design
- Offline Strategic TE Design
- Protection Scalability
- Forwarding Adjacency Scalability

CHAPTER 9

Network Design with MPLS TE

So far, this book has covered the detailed aspects of MPLS TE; how it works, and how you configure and manage it. But how do you use MPLS TE in your network design? That's what this chapter covers.

Chapter 1, "Understanding Traffic Engineering with MPLS," discussed the two main ways to think about deploying MPLS TE—tactically and strategically:

- *Tactical* MPLS TE is building MPLS TE LSPs as you need them, to work around congestion.

- *Strategic* MPLS TE is a full mesh of TE tunnels between a given set of routers. Strategic MPLS TE can be further broken down into two pieces:

    — **Online path calculation**—The routers themselves are allowed to determine the path their TE LSPs take.

    — **Offline path calculation**—The path that TE LSPs take is chosen by an external device that has a better view of the network topology and traffic demands than a router does.

This chapter discusses network design using both tactical and strategic approaches.

A design chapter could concentrate on many things. The entire topic of network design can't be covered in a single chapter. Therefore, this chapter focuses on the scalability of various approaches and tools.

Why scalability? Scalability is one of the most important things to think about when designing a network. You need to understand not only how well a particular solution scales and the factors that influence this scalability, but also the limits within which you are trying to scale. A solution that scales wonderfully for a ten-router network might not scale for 100 nodes, and a solution that scales for a 100-node network or a 1000-node network might not scale for 1,000,000 nodes. On the other hand, who has a million routers in their network? This chapter discusses scalability with real-life networks in mind—anywhere from dozens to hundreds of routers in the TE portion of the network.

Also discussed is the scalability of various protection techniques. Protection was covered in Chapter 7, "Protection and Restoration." All that's covered in this chapter is scaling MPLS TE with protection.

Sample Network for Case Studies

In order to demonstrate the applicability of multiple concepts discussed in this chapter, a base network that resembles a medium-sized ISP network is necessary. It has a total of 168 routers in 14 POPs across the continental U.S. Refer to Figure 9-1 for most of the configurations and case studies in this chapter.

Figure 9-1   *Sample Network for Case Studies*

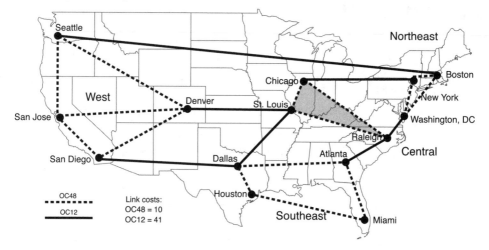

The network is divided into four regions:

- Northeast
- Central
- Southeast
- West

Each region is composed of four or five Points of Presence (POPs). Between POPs in a region, there's OC-48 connectivity; between regions, there's OC-12.

All POPs consist of two WAN routers that terminate the long-haul links between POPs, zero or more distribution routers, and three to 20 customer-facing routers. The WAN routers are called *WRs,* the distribution routers are *DRs,* and the customer routers are *CRs.* The naming scheme is *POPNameRoleNumber.* So the two WAN routers in Denver are DenverWR1 and DenverWR2.

If a POP has more than 11 CRs, it has three DRs; otherwise, it has zero DRs. This was done because some ISP networks use DRs and some don't, so we tried to cut somewhere down the middle. So a POP will look like either Figure 9-2 or Figure 9-3.

Figure 9-2   *POP with 11 or Fewer CRs*

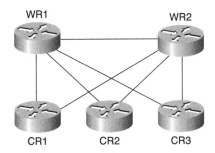

Figure 9-3   *POP with More Than 11 CRs*

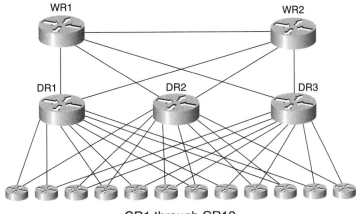

CR1 through CR12

The entire network consists of 28 WRs, 12 DRs, and 128 CRs—a total of 168 routers. It's not the world's largest network, but it's certainly large enough to demonstrate the points made in this chapter.

CR uplinks (to either WR or DR, depending on POP topology) are OC-3 POS links. DR uplinks to WRs (where applicable) are OC-48s.

Because you'll need these numbers later for a case study, Table 9-1 provides the exact count of how many WRs, DRs, and CRs are in each POP.

Table 9-1   *WRs, DRs, and CRs in Each POP*

POP Location	WRs	DRs	CRs
Seattle	2	3	14
San Jose	2	0	11
San Diego	2	0	8
Denver	2	0	3

continues

Table 9-1 *WRs, DRs, and CRs in Each POP (Continued)*

POP Location	WRs	DRs	CRs
Dallas	2	0	5
Houston	2	0	6
St. Louis	2	0	6
Chicago	2	0	7
Atlanta	2	0	9
Raleigh	2	3	12
D.C.	2	3	15
New York	2	3	20
Boston	2	0	8
Miami	2	0	4

All routers are at the same IS-IS level; they're all Level 2 neighbors. However, almost anything you do with IS-IS is possible with OSPF, so if you'd rather read about an OSPF network, just assume that the network is a single OSPF Area 0.

When discussing WR full mesh, it is only necessary for the WRs to be at the same level or area. The POPs can be in separate areas if that's how you'd rather picture them.

LDP on a TE Tunnel

If your network offers MPLS VPN services or otherwise uses MPLS outside the TE cloud, you need to enable LDP (or TDP) on your MPLS TE tunnels. This is not discussed in this chapter; see Chapter 10, "MPLS TE Deployment Tips," for details.

For the sake of simplicity, assume the following about the network:

- An OC-48 link has 2.4 Gbps of capacity and is configured with an IGP metric of 10.
- An OC-12 link has 600 Mbps of capacity and an IGP metric of 41.
- The link between WRs is an OC-48 with a cost of 2.
- All loads specified on a link are not instantaneous load, but instead are measured over a longer interval—at least a few hours. The loads are 95th percentile.

NOTE   Although this topology was designed to look like a typical ISP, resemblance to any specific network, living or dead, is purely coincidental.

Different Types of TE Design

There are two basic types of TE network design—tactical (deploying TE tunnels as needed) and strategic (deploying a full mesh of TE tunnels in some part of your network). They're really two points along a spectrum, which means that depending on your design goals and network policies, you could do one, the other, or something in between.

Figure 9-4 shows the network design spectrum.

Figure 9-4   *Network Design Spectrum*

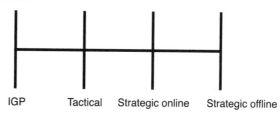

IGP   Tactical   Strategic online   Strategic offline

The four points along the spectrum can be described as follows:

- **IGP**—This is what you have today. All paths to destinations are determined by your routing protocol. Changing traffic flows requires changing link metrics, which might influence traffic you don't want to affect. This kind of network runs either LDP or IP forwarding, or perhaps uses TE for traffic measurement (see Chapter 10).

- **Tactical**—Your traffic is predominantly forwarded along the IGP-calculated path, but you build the occasional TE LSP to carry traffic along a path the IGP didn't select. You might do this to steer traffic away from congestion without having to change link metrics, or you might do this to take advantage of TE's unequal-cost forwarding.

- **Strategic online**—You build a full mesh of TE LSPs between the routers at the edge of your MPLS TE cloud. This might be all the routers at the access layer in your network, it might be all the routers in your core, or it might be some other boundary. TE LSPs used for strategic TE typically are configured to reserve bandwidth in accordance with the amount of bandwidth that will actually go down the TE tunnel; this leads to more-efficient use of your network's capacity. A headend runs CSPF (as described in Chapter 4, "Path Calculation and Setup") to calculate the path that each of its LSPs will take.

- **Strategic offline**—You build a full mesh of TE LSPs, just as in the strategic online case, but the paths that the LSPs take are calculated by an offline path calculation tool. This is the most efficient way to use your network resources. It relies on an offline path calculator to monitor your topology, your traffic patterns, and your LSPs.

It should be clear by now that these are points on a spectrum. For example, there's no reason why you couldn't do a full mesh between most of your routers, but not between pairs of nodes that don't have much traffic between them.

Part of what TE model you pick has to do with what your needs are. And part has to do with your experience and preferences. People coming from an ATM PVC or TDM world might prefer the strategic offline model; people coming from an IP world might feel more comfortable with a tactical or strategic online model. The models are flexible enough that it's easy to move from one point to another; the choice is up to you.

The following sections cover all three models. There's no way to cover all possible features and knobs used in every architecture, but hopefully this chapter gives you plenty to think about.

Tactical TE Design

In the tactical model, you build TE LSPs to work around congestion. The key things to deal with in this model are as follows:

- When you decide to build TE LSPs
- Where you put them
- When you take them down
- What nifty TE features you can use

The following sections sift through all four considerations.

One thing that this section assumes is that you have already configured MPLS TE on every link in your network, as well as in your IGP. In other words, you have everything you need to use MPLS TE tunnels already in place, except for the TE tunnels themselves. When you first decide to roll out MPLS, even if it's not for TE but for VPNs or some other reason, it can't hurt to enable MPLS TE everywhere (IGP and on interfaces) so that when you do need to use it in a tactical manner, it's right there waiting for you.

When You Decide to Build TE LSPs

Consider the sample network shown in Figure 9-1—specifically, the OC-12 link between St. Louis and Denver. Two cases in which that link can be overloaded for a significant amount of time are

- A link failure somewhere else in the network (probably either Boston→Seattle or Dallas→San Diego) pushes more traffic than you'd planned for onto the St. Louis→Denver link. The link failure can be short (a line card crashed), or it can be long (a fiber cut that will take days to fix).

- Something on the other side of that link becomes a major traffic draw. Perhaps you have a customer who has just turned up a major streaming media service, and they're sending a lot of traffic from the East Coast to the West Coast. Maybe there's major breaking news. Maybe a big Denial of Service attack is headed toward the West Coast. All these things are traffic draws.

Suppose a large amount of traffic is going from St. Louis to Denver, as shown in Figure 9-5. It is routed across the St. Louis→Denver link even if the traffic being sent down the link exceeds the link capacity.

Figure 9-5   *Excess Traffic from St. Louis to Denver*

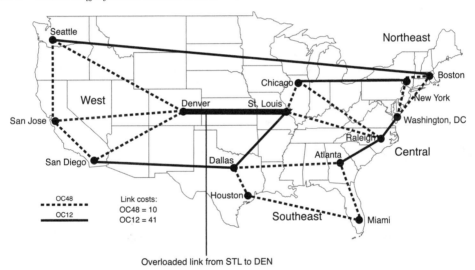

If you discover a link that's full, how long do you wait before working around it with TE LSPs? You don't want TE LSPs to be built the instant a link starts queuing and dropping packets. And if you have an outage that you know will last only a little while (a router reboot or crash, for example), it's not worth working around.

But if you have a significant traffic disruption for a long time (perhaps an hour or more), you should consider using TE-LSPs to see if you temporarily clear up the problem.

There is no hard and fast minimum time you need to wait before using TE-LSPs. It's up to you. You should start applying them to failures of an hour or more, get a feel for how long it takes you to apply them, and then use that to factor into a policy specific to your network. Although it takes far less than an hour to build a TE-LSP (it can be done in seconds!), being too responsive to short-term problems can make you trigger-happy and twitchy, and that's no way to run a network.

Where You Put TE LSPs

By the time you get around to determining where to put TE LSPs, you've already decided there's a problem you're going to work around. So now the question becomes "Where do I place TE-LSPs so that I don't create *another* problem?"

Think about the St. Louis→Denver link shown in Figure 9-1 again. If the load on this link increases to 900 Mbps for a significant amount of time, it's clear that you want to push that traffic somewhere else, because it's an OC-12 link, which has an IP capacity of about only 600 Mbps. So you're dropping 33 percent of your traffic, which is a bad thing.

The first thing you might think of doing is splitting the traffic along two paths. You obviously want to keep using the St. Louis→Denver link directly for as much traffic as you can, because when it's not congested, that's the best path from St. Louis to Denver.

So what you can do is build two TE LSPs. One goes directly across the St. Louis→Denver path, and the other goes St. Louis→Dallas→San Diego→Denver. The load is split roughly equally between the two LSPs, leading to 450 Mbps across the St. Louis→Denver path and 450 Mbps across the St. Louis→Dallas→San Diego→Denver path.

Your network then ends up looking like Figure 9-6.

Figure 9-6 *Two LSPs Between St. Louis and Denver, Each Carrying 450 Mbps*

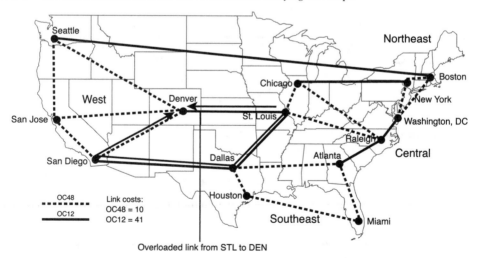

Why Two LSPs?

Recall from Chapter 5, "Forwarding Traffic Down Tunnels," that you never load-share between a TE tunnel path and an IGP path for a tunnel's tail. So if you want to use a TE LSP to get to a particular destination, you also need to build a tunnel across the IGP shortest path so that you'll use both paths.

For the sake of simplicity, assume that you don't have a significant amount of traffic on the Dallas→San Diego link, so it's safe to put 450 Mbps of traffic there for a a short time. But suppose that the load increases on the Dallas→San Diego link so that you don't have 450 Mbps of spare capacity there. What do you do then? One thing to do is build a total of three LSPs from St. Louis to Denver—the first one across the St. Louis→Denver path, the second through St. Louis→Dallas→San Diego→Denver, and the third through St. Louis→ Chicago→New York→Boston→Seattle→Denver. This splits the traffic across the three paths, sending something like 300 Mbps across each LSP, as shown in Figure 9-7.

Figure 9-7   *Three LSPs Between St. Louis and Denver, Each Carrying 300 Mbps*

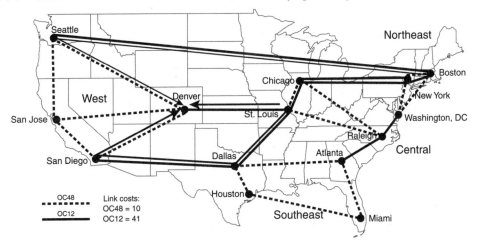

Considering the two-LSP solution, using a 600-Mbps LSP and a 300-Mbps LSP isn't feasible, because putting 600 Mbps of traffic across a link with 600 Mbps of capacity is not a good idea. If even a small burst greater than 600 Mbps occurs, you'll have a lot of delay to deal with. A 450/450 split is better, because no link is full. In the three-LSP case, you can split the traffic into three 300-Mpbs LSPs; either solution might be appropriate given other bandwidth demands on the network.

There are four ways you can control the ratio of traffic distributed between the two LSPs:

1 For equal-cost forwarding, don't reserve any bandwidth or change any administrative weight. Traffic is shared evenly between both LSPs.

2 Have each tunnel reserve bandwidth in accordance with how much traffic is actually supposed to flow across the link. So on each tunnel interface, configure **tunnel mpls traffic-eng bandwidth 450000** to have the tunnel reserve 450 Mbps of bandwidth.

3 Have each tunnel reserve bandwidth in accordance with the *ratio* of traffic share you want them to have. So have each tunnel reserve 1 Kbps, or 2 Kbps, or 47 Mbps, or whatever; it doesn't matter. Because all you're interested in is the ratio, reserve whatever bandwidth you want.

4 Have each tunnel reserve no bandwidth, but set the load-share ratio on the tunnel with **tunnel mpls traffic-eng load-share**. In this example, you'd configure **tunnel mpls traffic-eng load-share 1** on each tunnel.

With only two equal-cost tunnels, it doesn't matter what method you pick. But if you're going to be doing unequal-cost load balancing between two or more tunnels, you should use solutions 2, 3, or 4. Use solution 2 (reserving actual bandwidth) if you want a quick way to look at a midpoint and see how much bandwidth each LSP *should* be carrying. Use solutions 3 or 4 if you don't want to have to worry about accidentally overreserving bandwidth but just want to control the load-share ratios. (Sometimes this is done by controlling bandwidth ratios, and sometimes this is done by directly controlling load-share ratios.)

Laying out LSPs of 300 Mbps and 450 Mbps in a network whose bottleneck is 600 Mbps links can be dangerous; you might still have congestion problems even after you've shifted data around. One way to deal with this is to add more bandwidth, but that takes time. Another way to deal with this problem is to try to optimize your tunnel placement to avoid congestion as much as possible.

Optimizing Tunnel Placement: Step 1

Whereas distributing the traffic over multiple LSPs overcomes the problem of an overloaded link, it might introduce a new, although less-severe, problem—suboptimal forwarding.

In the scenario with three LSPs, consider the East Coast traffic destined for Seattle and San Diego that enters St. Louis. Because two of the three LSPs have Seattle or San Diego as LSP midpoints, any traffic from St. Louis that goes over these LSPs and that is actually destined for Seattle or San Diego first must get to Denver (the tail of all three TE tunnels) before heading back west to Seattle and San Diego.

For example, if traffic were destined for a Web-hosting center in Seattle, and it followed the IGP path from St. Louis, it would go St. Louis→Denver→Seattle. But if you install the three LSPs mentioned in the preceding section, as a result of autoroute, anything destined for Seattle from St. Louis will go over these LSPs to Denver, after which they follow the IGP path to Seattle. Because of load sharing, approximately one-third of your Seattle-bound traffic will go St. Louis→Chicago→New York→Boston→Seattle→Denver over the tunnel and then Denver→Seattle via IGP-based forwarding. This won't cause any loops, because you're following an LSP to Denver and IP routing from Denver back to Seattle.

If you've got lots of extra capacity on the Seattle→Denver link, maybe this isn't something you have to worry about. You still might be concerned with delay. Traffic going Seattle→Denver→Seattle encounters about 50 ms additional delay, which can be substantial if you're talking about real-time traffic.

However, this path is certainly suboptimal.

What Is Optimality?

In order to discuss optimal LSP placement, it's important to first define optimality. Optimality means different things to different people. In this section, optimization is defined as "ensuring that your network traffic takes the path with the lowest possible delay while maximizing the available bandwidth along a path."

Sometimes your delay and bandwidth constraints are mutually exclusive. If you have a choice between a low-delay, low-bandwidth path and a high-delay, high-bandwidth path, what do you do? The choice is up to you. It depends mostly on the type of traffic you're taking on. Generally, though, because most network traffic is TCP and TCP is more sensitive to packet loss than to delay, you'd choose the high-bandwidth, high-delay path. But if you're building a VoIP network, your choice might be different. Of course, your goal should be to never have to make that choice. When you do have to make it, MPLS TE can help you optimize network performance so that your resource shortage affects your users as little as possible.

Of course, you have the same problem if you have traffic destined for San Diego that will go St. Louis→Dallas→San Diego→Denver→San Diego.

How do you improve this?

Take your three TE LSPs and terminating them not on the node at the other end of the St. Louis→Denver link, but instead at the entry point to the Western region. So take the three LSPs already built, and change them. Instead of St. Louis→Chicago→New York→ Boston→Seattle→Denver, make that LSP St. Louis→Chicago→New York→ Boston→Seattle. Do the same with the St. Louis→Dallas→San Diego→Denver LSP: Have it run St. Louis→Dallas→San Diego instead. When traffic comes out of the TE LSP as it enters the West region, the router that is the tail for the TE LSP receives an IP packet and routes it appropriately.

The St. Louis→Denver LSP, of course, needs to stay the same.

Optimizing Tunnel Placement: Step 2

There's another problem that you can solve, too. Even after you make the adjustments described in Step 1, you still have some suboptimal packet paths.

Take a closer look at the 900-Mbps traffic going St. Louis→Denver. There are only four places that 900 Mbps could have come from:

- Originated from St. Louis
- Coming from Chicago
- Coming from Raleigh
- Coming from Dallas

Traffic from Dallas to Denver isn't likely to cross St. Louis, though, because Dallas has a more attractive path through San Diego to anything in the West region. So that leaves three possible ways this Denver-bound traffic (or, indeed, *any* traffic) could have come into St. Louis.

For the sake of simplicity, assume that 300 Mbps of the 900 Mbps Denver-bound traffic originates from St. Louis, 300 Mbps comes from Raleigh, and 300 Mbps comes from Chicago. Because traffic arriving in St. Louis will be pretty evenly distributed across the three LSPs, this means that 100 Mbps of the Chicago-sourced traffic will go over the St. Louis→Chicago→New York→Boston→Seattle path. Put another way, the path for that traffic is Chicago→St. Louis→Chicago→New York→Boston→Seattle. Again, there's no danger of routing loops, because you're forwarding in an LSP, but things are certainly suboptimal.

How do you get around this suboptimality? By building TE LSPs farther away from the source of the congestion.

Assume the following:

- Chicago sends 300 Mb of traffic to St. Louis:
  - 100 Mb is destined for Denver.
  - 100 Mb is destined for Seattle.
  - 100 Mb is destined for San Diego.
- Raleigh sends 300 Mb of traffic to St. Louis:
  - 100 Mb is destined for Denver.
  - 100 Mb is destined for Seattle.
  - 100 Mb is destined for San Diego.
- St. Louis originates 300 Mb of traffic:
  - 100 Mb is destined for Denver.
  - 100 Mb is destined for Seattle.
  - 100 Mb is destined for San Diego.

If you build TE LSPs between the following points, you can individually control each of these 100 Mb traffic streams and place them anywhere in the network you want:

- Chicago to Denver
- Chicago to Seattle
- Chicago to San Diego
- Raleigh to Denver
- Raleigh to Seattle
- Raleigh to San Diego
- St. Louis to Denver
- St. Louis to Seattle
- St. Louis to San Diego

NOTE	In general, the farther you move from the point of congestion, the more exact control you have over your network traffic. The ultimate case of this is a full mesh of TE LSPs between all routers, or at least all routers with a given role in the network. For example, if you have a full mesh of TE LSPs between all the WRs in the network, you have full control over all traffic entering your WAN, at the level of granularity equal to the amount of traffic between any two WRs. See the sections "Online Strategic TE Design" and "Offline Strategic TE Design" for more information on a full mesh of TE LSPs and how to manage it.

As soon as you understand this methodology, it's simple to apply. Based on real-life scenarios, as soon as you discover the source of congestion, you can make modifications in a matter of minutes!

By now, hopefully you've seen some of the power of the tactical TE model; however, you still need to address a few more issues.

When to Remove Your Tactical TE Tunnels

Now that you've built all these nifty TE LSPs to work around problems, are you done? Nope. Because your problem was caused by a temporary event, the problem you're trying to solve will eventually go away. Just like your mother periodically harangued you to clean your room, so too should you periodically clean your network. In fact, two cases when you should consider taking TE LSPs down are

- **When they're no longer needed**—The problem they're solving doesn't exist anymore.
- **When they're causing problems**—A traffic spike somewhere else in the network collides with traffic in a TE LSP.

Determining When TE LSPs Are No Longer Needed

How do you tell if TE LSPs are no longer needed? It's pretty simple. Take the example of the LSPs that were created to work around the congested St. Louis→Denver link. You know that that link has a nominal capacity of 600 Mbps. You know that three TE LSPs are in place to work around the congestion. If the aggregate throughput of these three LSPs falls to significantly less than 600 Mbps (low enough that high traffic rates don't induce delay), you can safely consider bringing down the TE LSPs. However, this requires doing a few things:

- You need to constantly monitor the network to see what new TE LSPs have been installed and whether existing TE LSPs are still useful.

- You need to remember why TE LSPs were put up in the first place!

Tracking the existence of TE LSPs is easy enough, because TE LSPs are interfaces, and you will see them with SNMP's IF-MIB or via **show interfaces** and other such CLI commands.

Remembering why the TE LSPs were put up in the first place is also straightforward, surprisingly enough. Because TE-LSPs are interfaces, you can put a description on them, like any other interface. This description is carried in the RSVP setup information as an LSP is set up.

Determining When TE LSPs Are Causing Problems

TE LSPs can induce artificial congestion—link congestion because of traffic that's there only because some TE LSPs are traversing a non-shortest path across that link.

Remember that the sample network has a TE LSP from St. Louis→Dallas→San Diego that carries 300 Mbps of traffic. But the path that these LSPs follow is made up of OC-12s that are just half-filled. If 400 Mbps of additional traffic starts leaving Atlanta, destined for San Jose, that traffic crosses the Dallas→San Diego link.

If you discover a congested link, the first thing you need to do is check to see if any TE LSPs are crossing that link, and if so, how much bandwidth they're consuming.

If the St. Louis→Denver LSPs haven't been removed, but the Dallas→San Diego link utilization shoots up to 700 Mbps, the first thing to do is check on the Dallas router to see how much the St. Louis→Dallas→San Diego LSP is contributing to the congestion.

You can check this by first determining which LSPs are traversing a given link, as demonstrated in Example 9-1.

Example 9-1 *Determining the LSPs Traversing a Link*

```
STLouisWR1#show mpls traffic-eng tunnels interface out pos5/0 brief
Signalling Summary:
    LSP Tunnels Process:          running
    RSVP Process:                 running
    Forwarding:                   enabled
    Periodic reoptimization:      disabled
```

Example 9-1 *Determining the LSPs Traversing a Link (Continued)*

```
     Periodic auto-bw collection:     disabled
 TUNNEL NAME                      DESTINATION      UP IF      DOWN IF    STATE/PROT
 STLouisWR1_t6                    192.168.1.6      -          PO5/0      up/up
```

Next, you can check one of two things:

- StLouisWR1 (the headend of this tunnel) to see how much traffic is going down the tunnel

- The midpoint

Checking the traffic on the headend is simple—as you know by now, TE tunnels are interfaces. **show interface tunnel1** on the headend router tells you how much traffic is going down the TE tunnel.

You can check the midpoint by finding the incoming label for a particular tunnel and then keeping an eye on the traffic coming in with that label, as demonstrated in Example 9-2.

Example 9-2 *Checking the Midpoint for Traffic Flow*

```
DalWR2#show mpls traffic-eng tunnels name-regexp StLouisWR1 | include InLabel
   InLabel   : POS1/2, 17


DalWR2#show mpls forwarding-table labels 17
Local   Outgoing     Prefix          Bytes tag    Outgoing    Next Hop
tag     tag or VC    or Tunnel Id    switched     interface
17      Pop tag      192.168.1.5 8 [1] 1939835    PO1/1       point2point
```

Keep an eye on the **Bytes tag switched** value, and see if it increases over time. On distributed systems (such as the GSR), you might not see the counters change for several seconds and then make quite a jump; this is normal.

Checking at the headend is preferred, because it is easier, but either method works.

Assume that the St. Louis→Dallas→San Diego LSP is still carrying 300 Mbps of traffic. This is 300 Mbps of artificial congestion, and if you remove it, the Dallas→San Diego link will carry only 400 Mbps of traffic and will be OK. 400 Mbps on an OC-12 is still a 67 percent traffic load, but 67 percent load is better than 117 percent load!

You now have a tough choice to make. How do you solve the St. Louis→Denver problem *and* the brand-new Dallas→San Diego problem? You can probably attack the problem further upstream and break the traffic into small-enough streams that you can balance them properly. At this point, 1.3 Gbps (St. Louis→Denver 900 Mbps + Dallas→San Diego 400 Mbps) needs to be balanced over a total of 1.8 Gbps of bandwidth (OC-12's Boston→ Seattle, St. Louis→Denver, and Dallas→San Diego), so you're running pretty close to the edge already. You might be able to further optimize this problem, though. Use TMS or your favorite traffic-matrix generation tool (see Chapter 10) to figure out what traffic is crossing those links and where it's coming from, and place the LSPs in a way that makes sense. If no single traffic flow can be put onto a single link, split the flow into multiple LSPs.

Hacky? Sure. Difficult to track? Yeah, probably. But this is a workaround to a problem that exists until you get more bandwidth. If you have an OC-192 St. Louis→Denver coming in three days from now, it might not be worth doing all this work in the interim. Or it might be. It depends on how badly your customers are affected and what this means to your business.

On the other hand, if your St. Louis→Denver OC-192 isn't due in for six months, and you can't get any additional capacity until then, clearly the duct-tape approach is far better than nothing.

Remember, one of the things MPLS TE buys you is the capability to prolong the life of your existing capacity, thus putting off the amount of time until you have to buy new circuits. Every month you save on buying capacity can equal tens or hundreds of thousands of dollars. Of course, nobody ever said it was easy.

If placing all these LSPs by hand seems too complex, skip ahead to the discussion of full-mesh TE models; they can manage a lot of that complexity.

Useful TE Features for Tactical TE

MPLS TE has lots of neat features, as covered throughout this book. There's auto bandwidth, Fast Reroute, DiffServ-aware TE, forwarding adjacency, and lots more. But not all of these features are appropriate for the tactical model. Table 9-2 lists the major TE features that might be suitable for a tactical TE deployment.

Table 9-2   *TE Feature Recommendations for Tactical TE Deployment*

Feature	Should You Use It?	Reference
Auto bandwidth	Yes.	Chapter 5
Autoroute	Possibly. It depends on what your needs are. If you need to steer traffic around that's only destined for a particular BGP neighbor, you can use static routes. Autoroute is easier to scale, because you don't have to manage a bunch of static routes, but make sure that what autoroute does is what you want.	Chapter 5

Table 9-2   *TE Feature Recommendations for Tactical TE Deployment (Continued)*

Feature	Should You Use It?	Reference
Forwarding adjacency	Yes, but pay attention. Enabling forwarding adjacency changes not only the traffic patterns for traffic from the TE headend router, but it also influences the path decision other routers make, which can change your traffic flow. FA can solve some problems, but it can create others if you're not careful.	Chapter 5
Fast Reroute	No. It doesn't make sense to FRR-protect every link in your TE cloud if you're not going to be running TE LSPs over most of them. You'd need to configure FRR everywhere, and the nature of tactical TE is that you don't use TE most of the time, so you'd have a large FRR infrastructure deployed that wouldn't get used.	Chapter 7
DiffServ-aware TE	No. Because you might have both IP and MPLS TE traffic in the same queue, administratively reserving space from a subpool can give you a false sense of security.	Chapter 6
Administrative weight	Probably not. In the tactical model, you'll most likely build explicit paths, in which case admin-weight does you no good, but if you see a use for it in your application, by all means go ahead.	Chapter 3
Link attributes and LSP affinities	See administrative weight. The same concerns apply here.	Chapter 3

Online Strategic TE Design

In the section "Tactical TE Design," you saw that the farther away from a congested link TE tunnels are deployed, the more fine-grained your traffic manipulation can be, and the more likely you are to avoid congestion.

The logical progression of this model is to have a full mesh of TE LSPs at some level in the network, typically the WAN core routers. Doing so gives you the most control over the traffic that's entering your WAN, because you can manipulate traffic at all points where it enters the core.

This is the strategic method of deploying MPLS TE.

In this model, you decide where the boundaries of your TE cloud are, and you build a full mesh of TE LSPs between them. These TE-LSPs reserve bandwidth commensurate with what they're actually carrying, rather than reserving only enough bandwidth to have the proper forwarding ratios. The actual bandwidth value is reserved because it makes things simple. As traffic demands between routers change, the traffic demands can be measured and the tunnels changed accordingly. Periodically, these TE-LSPs are resized to account for the amount of traffic they're actually carrying.

The strategic online model has some advantages over the tactical model. Because you're supposed to have LSPs between every node at the edge of the cloud, you won't be constantly stumbling across LSPs that you didn't expect to find. Also, full-mesh models tend to make more optimal use of your bandwidth than tactical ones, which can save you more money.

The full-mesh model definitely has some trade-offs. Table 9-3 compares the strategic model with the tactical model.

Table 9-3   *Tactical Model Versus Strategic Model*

Tactical	Strategic
Reserves bandwidth as necessary to affect unequal-cost load balancing	Reserves bandwidth that matches the actual traffic sent
Small number of tunnels	Larger number of tunnels
Difficult to track what tunnels are where and why they're there	Easier to track, because you know how many tunnels you have and where they go

LSP Scalability

The most important issue on the mind of any self-respecting network engineer is scalability—"How well does this scale?"

The answer to this question depends on where you want to put your TE cloud. In this chapter's sample network architecture, three choices exist:

- Full mesh between WRs
- Full mesh between CRs
- Somehow involving the DRs in the equation

All three of these choices scale the same way (a full mesh is $n * (n - 1)$ LSPs), but their scaling numbers are different. CRs outnumber WRs, which means more TE tunnels, which means more signalling load on your network.

You should also ask a few specific scalability questions:

- How many LSPs can a router be a headend for?
- How many LSPs can a router be a midpoint for?
- How many LSPs can a router be a tailend for?

The question of "how many" is murkier than it seems. For example, how do you decide when you have too many? One way to set this ceiling is to set a limit for network convergence time. Find the maximum number of LSPs at each head/tail/mid role that converge in x amount of time, and that's your scalability limit. Of course, this number of LSPs vary from network to network, because convergence time is affected by things such as router CPU utilization, which in turn is influenced by what else is going on in the network, the size of the network, and so forth.

However, Cisco has put a stake in the ground and has done some initial convergence testing. Appendix B, "CCO and Other References," has a pointer to a document titled "MPLS Traffic Engineering (TE)—Scalability Enhancements," which gives the following scalability guidelines:

- 600 LSPs as a headend
- 10,000 LSPs as a midpoint
- 5000 LSPs as a tail

The number of LSPs as a tail is fairly irrelevant. Because a full-mesh architecture is the basis here, the number of LSPs for which a router is a head and for which it is a tail are the same, so the gating factor in head/tail scalability is the number of headends.

NOTE   It is important to enable **ip rsvp msg-pacing** in order to achieve these large scalability numbers. Although the actual signalling performance depends largely on your topology and network events, message pacing becomes more and more useful as you add more and more TE tunnels in your network. See the section "RSVP Message Pacing" in Chapter 4 for more details on message pacing.

The numbers given here are neither the minimum number of tunnels that can be supported nor the maximum. Scalability depends tremendously on what else the router and the network are doing. Some routers and networks can deal with far more TE tunnels, because they're otherwise relatively unencumbered, and the network is stable. Others can't hit the numbers listed here because the routers are overworked and the network is unstable.

These numbers, however, serve as a starting point. As you'll see in the upcoming discussion of scalability, these numbers are quite large and give you plenty of room to expand your network.

Data and Variables

Before you begin exploring scalability in great depth, review the sample network. The sample network we're using is built out of the pieces listed in Table 9-4.

Table 9-4 *Sample Network Components*

POP	WRs	DRs	CRs
Seattle	2	3	14
San Jose	2	0	11
San Diego	2	0	8
Denver	2	0	3
Dallas	2	0	5
Houston	2	0	6
St. Louis	2	0	6
Chicago	2	0	7
Atlanta	2	0	9
Raleigh	2	3	12
D.C.	2	3	15
New York City	2	3	20
Boston	2	0	8
Miami	2	0	4
TOTALS:	28	12	128

Now that the data is defined, Table 9-5 defines some variables to enable discussion about this data.

Table 9-5 *Variable Definitions*

Variable	Definition	Value
M	Number of LSPs for which a router is a midpoint	See the section "Full Mesh Between WRs"
P	Number of POPs in the network	14
Wp	Number of WRs per POP	2
Wn	Number of WRs in the network	28
Dp	Number of DRs per POP	0 or 3
Dn	Number of DRs in the network	12
Cp	Number of CRs per POP	Between 3 and 20

Table 9-5   *Variable Definitions (Continued)*

Variable	Definition	Value
Cn	Number of CRs in the network	128
Ln	Total number of LSPs in the network	$n * n-1$, where n = Wn in a WR full mesh, and n = CN in a CR full mesh
Lp	Number of LSPs that originate and/or terminate in a given POP	See the section "DR Midpoint Scalability"
Lt	Number of LSPs that transit a POP (those that are neither originated nor terminated in that POP)	See the section "WR Midpoint Scalability"

The factors to consider with scalability differ depending on the role a given router plays in the network. Table 9-6 lists the router types in the sample network.

Table 9-6   *Router Types in the Sample Network*

Router Type	Role	Things That Affect Scalability
CR	Customer router. This is where the network's customers come into.	Number of other CRs in the network (Cn).
DR	Distribution router. Used in large POPs to consolidate CR traffic into fewer links for handoff to WRs.	Number of LSPs that originate, terminate, or both originate *and* terminate in a POP.
WR	WAN router. Connects to other WRs.	Number of LSPs that originate, terminate, or both originate *and* terminate in a POP. Also the number of LSPs that transit through these WRs on their way to other POPs.

The other assumption here is that DRs do not act as transit LSPs for LSPs other than ones involving their POP. In other words, although an LSP from Boston to Raleigh might cross Washington D.C., it will cross only a WR, not a DR.

Full Mesh Between WRs

The first type of strategic TE to look at is a full mesh of TE LSPs between WRs. This design probably makes the most sense, because the WRs are the devices that connect other POPs. WAN links are generally the most expensive links in a network, and as such, you get the most bang for your buck by applying MPLS TE to optimize your bandwidth utilization in the WAN.

As far as the number of LSPs that a router is a headend or tail for, this is easy to figure.

There are 14 POPs, with two WRs each, so Wn = 28.

If the full mesh is between the 28 WRs, Ln = 28 * 27 = 756 LSPs.

The other fact you need is the number of LSPs for which a router can be the midpoint. This is a tricky fact to determine accurately, because this number depends on the degree of connectivity of a given router (the number of physical links it has to neighbors), as well as the bandwidth of that router's links, the router's location in the network, and the overall network topology. However, it's possible to do some rough calculations that give you an approximation of the required load on any router so that you can get an idea of whether MPLS TE will scale to your requirements.

NOTE	You might also be considering a full mesh of DS-TE tunnels, in addition to a full mesh of global-pool TE tunnels. This doubles the size of your signalling load. Simply work through the formulae presented here, and then double them to account for the fact that you have two pools and, therefore, two meshes.

Continue using the sample network that's already established. First, you need to calculate M, the number of LSPs for which a router can be a midpoint. Clearly $M \le Ln$, because you can't have a midpoint for more LSPs than are present in the network. However, to find the value of M, you can start with Ln and subtract the following:

- All LSPs for which a router is a headend ($Wn - 1$)
- All LSPs for which a router is a tail ($Wn - 1$)

because clearly a router will not be a midpoint for LSPs for which it is a head or tail.

So:

$$max(M) = Ln - (2 * (Wn - 1))$$

This is the *maximum* number of LSPs a router can be a midpoint for. However, because not all LSPs go through the same router (does traffic from New York to Boston need to transit through Denver?), M is much smaller. One decent number to consider is the average number of LSPs per router. Let's redefine M as follows:

$$max(M) = \frac{Ln - (2 * (Wn - 1)))}{Wn}$$

This is simply the previous calculation for M divided by the number of WRs in the network.

The result of this calculation varies quite a lot, because links, bandwidth, and connectivity all figure into the equation, but assume that it's stable because it's a nice rough estimate.

In summary, a full mesh of Wn routers has the following characteristics:

- Each router is a headend and tail for $Wn - 1$ LSPs.
- There is a total of $Wn * (Wn - 1)$ LSPs in the network.
- Each router will be a midpoint for approximately $(Ln - (2 * (Wn - 1))) / Wn$ LSPs.

In the sample network of 28 WRs, this means

- Each router is a headend for 27 LSPs and a tail for 27 more.
- There are 756 LSPs in the entire network.
- Each router is a midpoint for approximately 25 LSPs.

You might notice that the scalability numbers for head/tail/mid are much larger than what is stated here. Given the earlier formulae and the presumed limits of 600 heads/5,000 tails/ 10,000 midpoints, the largest MPLS TE network of WRs you can build is a network of roughly 300 POPs with two WRs each. (Each router is a headend for 599 LSPs, a tail for 599 LSPs, and a midpoint for about 597 LSPs.)

Clearly, this is a large network. Not many networks have 300 POPs. You'll hit other scaling limits if you try to get this big with this model—limits such as port density and IGP scaling. But the important point (because this is a book about TE and not about IP design) is that MPLS TE scalability is not the gating factor in your design!

At least, not in a cloud made up of a full mesh of WRs. Are the scaling limits the same with the number of CRs? The formulae are different, so let's look at a CR mesh separately.

Full Mesh Between CRs

A full mesh of TE LSPs between WRs scales quite nicely, as discussed in the preceding section. But what about between CRs?

Why would you want to do a CR full mesh? Perhaps to get more exacting control over your traffic. Also, if some of the CRS are not in the same physical location as their adjacent WRs or DRs, but are instead in remote sub-POPs (so a MAN network), there might be some utility in optimizing the MAN bandwidth. Or maybe you want to do CR-to-CR accounting, or run MPLS VPNs over end-to-end TE tunnels between PEs (which are the CRs). Or maybe you're just curious to see how well TE really scales.

In the CR full mesh, it's important to understand that the CRs are the only routers that are TE headends or tails. DRs and WRs are only midpoints, because in this architecture, traffic enters and exits the network only on CRs. If external connections were brought in on DRs or WRs (such as high-speed customer links or public/private peers), you'd need to include those routers in the mesh. In this architecture, all traffic external to the network enters and exits on CRs.

This network has three different types of routers: CRs, DRs, and WRs. Not all POPs have DRs, but those that do need to consider LSP scalability within the DRs.

It should be obvious what the scaling factor is for CRs. Because the network model discussed here is a full mesh of CRs, and because CRs are only ever headend or tail routers and never midpoints, each CR has to deal with $C_n - 1$ LSPs. Because 128 CRs exist, each one has an LSP to all 127 of the others; this, hopefully, is clear.

NOTE	A CR full mesh of Cn – 1 LSPs implies that a CR has TE tunnels not only to CRs that can be reached across the WAN, but also to CRs within its own POP. This is necessary if you're planning to build inter-POP TE tunnels. If you don't control the traffic flow of intra-POP TE tunnels, you can't know for sure where your bandwidth demands will be, so you can't assume that you'll always get the bandwidth you need.

So far, you're well within the stated scalability limits. A router can be a headend for 600 LSPs and a tailend for 5000, and you're designing for only 127 in either category. The more complicated question in a CR mesh is the DRs and WRs. DRs and WRs are midpoints for some number of TE tunnels. With 128 CRs in a full mesh, that's 16,256 LSPs (128 * 127). Because the stated scalability limit for a midpoint router is 10,000 LSPs, you need to make sure that it's not likely that a midpoint will approach that limit. Intuitively, it's probably not a big deal (what are the odds that a single router will carry 60 percent or more of your network traffic?), but the exercise is well worth going through. The next two sections examine DR and WR scalability in a CR full mesh.

DR Midpoint Scalability

A DR needs to care about the number of LSPs that originate, terminate, or both originate *and* terminate in a POP. Table 9-7 breaks down these numbers separately.

Table 9-7 *Different LSP Types to Consider in DR Scalability*

Type of LSP	Rationale	Formula
Originates and terminates in the same POP	Part of the full mesh is full-mesh connectivity between CRs in their own POPs	$Cp * (Cp - 1)$
Originates *or* terminates in a given POP	LSPs coming in from other CRs into a given POP	$(Cn - Cp) * Cp$
	LSPs originating in this POP and terminating elsewhere	$Cp * (Cn - Cp)$

You can combine the last two terms into $\{[(Cn - Cp) * Cp] * 2\}$. What you have so far, then, is

$$Cp * (Cp - 1) + [(Cn - Cp) * Cp] * 2$$

This ultimately reduces to $Cp (2Cn - Cp - 1)$.

This is the formula for Lp, the number of LSPs that originate and/or terminate in a given POP. So:

$$Lp = Cp (2Cn - Cp - 1)$$

But you're not done yet. Because the assumption is an even distribution of load, you need to divide the results from the preceding calculation by the number of DRs to get the number of LSPs *per DR* in the POP. The formula then becomes

$$\frac{Lp}{Dp}$$

For demonstration purposes, let's plug some real numbers into this.

This calculation obviously makes sense only when DRs are present in a POP, so you know Dp will always be 3.

> Cn is 128.
> Cp varies, depending on the size of the POP.

Because only three POPs have DRs, here are the calculations for each POP.

In Seattle, Cp is 14. So the formula P(2N – P – 1) / 3 becomes

$$\frac{14 * (256 - 14 - 1)}{3} = {\sim}1125$$

So each Seattle DR will be a midpoint for approximately 1125 LSPs. This is no big deal, because the scalability limit we're working under has a ceiling of 10,000.

In Raleigh, Cp is 12. This means that each DR is a midpoint for approximately 972 LSPs.

In New York, Cp is 20. This is the largest POP in the network. Even here, a DR is a midpoint for approximately 1567 LSPs.

So it should be obvious that DR LSP scalability is a nonissue. But what about WRs?

WR Midpoint Scalability

WRs are a little tricky. Why? Because WRs do double duty. Because no physical connections exist between the DRs in this network, all LSPs that originate and/or terminate in a given POP also go through the WRs. This is the same equation as for the DRs in POP, but spread over the number of WRs rather than DRs:

$$\frac{Lp}{Wp}$$

Wp is the number of WRs per POP; in this network, it's 2. So the formula for the number of LSPs for which a WR is a midpoint then becomes

$$\frac{Lp}{2}$$

This is the number of LSPs that originate or terminate in a POP (Lp) divided by the number of WRs in that pop (2).

But there's more to the calculations than just that. A significant number of LSPs (called *transit LSPs*) go through WRs that are not in their own POP (*transit WRs* and *transit POPs*). This is because if you build an LSP from a CR in St. Louis to a CR in Seattle, those LSPs have to go through other POPs to get there. And because the WRs are the ones with the WAN links, LSPs have to transit WRs that are not in the headend or tailend POP.

But how many LSPs will a given WR see? The real answer to this question is difficult to calculate. It has to account for bandwidth availability at every hop, because a major function of full-mesh TE LSPs is to consume bandwidth, thereby finding the best path through the network. And because LSPs make path determination based on bandwidth, they might build paths across some arbitrary path in the network. For example, you can have an LSP from StLouisCR1 to MiamiCR1 via Raleigh→Atlanta→Miami and an LSP from StLouisCR2 to MiamiCR2 via Dallas→Houston→Miami. And at every transit POP, an LSP might go in one WR and out the same WR, or in one WR and out the other WR. And things get even more complex, as you will see in the section "The Packing Problem."

Because the path an LSP can take depends on available bandwidth, and because available bandwidth depends on what other LSPs are already in the network, this leads to rather complex calculations. See the section "Offline Strategic TE Design" for more details.

Even if you assume that there are no bandwidth issues, this is still a difficult problem. Assume for a second that all LSPs follow the IGP shortest path from head to tail. Of course, if this were really the case, this obviates the need for MPLS TE, but make the assumption nonetheless. Where does that leave you?

You'd have to run SPF for every POP to every other POP, to see which POPs' traffic would transit other POPs on the way to their destination. Because you have 14 POPs, that's 14 SPFs. And then you'd have to figure out how many LSPs from a headend POP to a tailend POP there would actually be, because this varies depending on the number of CRs in both POPs. This is a much simpler problem to solve, but it's still too big to tackle here.

Let's simplify the problem some more, so we can get an approximate answer. You know that there are Ln LSPs in the network. This means that any one WR will never transit for more than Ln LSPs. So, in other words:

$$Lt <= Ln$$

Remember, Lt is the number of LSPs that transit a POP. So you can make this number smaller. You've already accounted for LSPs that originate or terminate in WR's own POP (Lp). So the term can be refined to

$$Lt <= Ln - Lp$$

You can take this further by realizing that a WR in a given POP will never be transit not only for intra-POP LSPs (LSPs in its own POP), but also for intra-POP LSPs in all other POPs.

So take the sum of Lp for *all* POPs—in other words, $(Cp * (Cp - 1))$ across all POPs. If you let X be the set of Cp for each POP, you're now looking at this:

$$L <= Ln - \sum_{i=1}^{P} x_i * (x_i - 1)$$

To make this data easier to visualize, check out Table 9-8.

Table 9-8   *Number of LSPs that Originate or Terminate in a Given POP*

POP	Cp	Lp (Cp * (Cp – 1))
Seattle	14	182
San Jose	11	110
San Diego	8	56
Denver	3	6
Dallas	5	20
Houston	6	30
St. Louis	6	30
Chicago	7	42
Atlanta	9	72
Raleigh	12	132
D.C.	15	210
NYC	20	380
Boston	8	56
Miami	4	12
TOTALS:	128	1338

Furthermore, because there are Wn WRs in the network, the formula becomes

$$Lt <= Ln - \frac{\sum_{i=1}^{P} x_i * (x_i - 1)}{Wn}$$

Why are you dividing by Wn? Because you're assuming that the number of LSPs is divided equally across all WRs. This is not a terribly valid assumption, because it assumes that all LSPs cross only one transit WR (not including WRs in the originating or terminating POP). In real life, an LSP crosses anywhere from one to 24 WRs.

24? Yes. Because you're not counting WRs in the originating or terminating POPs, that leaves you with 28 – 2 – 2 = 24 WRs that an LSP can possibly pass through. 24 is the absolute worst case, though. 24 WRs would be an LSP that went from St. Louis to Denver along the path St. Louis→Dallas→Houston→Miami→Atlanta→Raleigh→Chicago→ New York→D.C.→Boston→Seattle→San Jose→San Diego→Denver and hits both WRs in every POP along the way.

This, you will agree, is astoundingly suboptimal. But it is possible.

So you should really multiply Wn by some constant, which is the average number of transit WRs that an LSP will touch.

The problem with finding this number is that it requires a fair bit of work to find, and if you could find that number, you could probably also solve some of the other hard problems we've deliberately tried to avoid.

Assume that the average LSP transits through three WRs. Call this number T, the number of transit routers an LSP goes through. T could be through three POPs (WR1 to WR2 to WR1) or two POPs (WR1 to WR2). This number is based on real-world experience with LSPs in ISP networks; feel free to substitute your own number if you like. The calculations here, however, use T = 3.

This means that

$$Lt <= Ln - \frac{\left[\sum_{i=1}^{P} x_i * (x_i-1)\right] * T}{Wn}$$

Lt is the number of LSPs that cross a WR but that neither terminate nor originate in that POP. But to fully account for the number of LSPs a WR will be a midpoint for, you need to account for Lp again. So the final equation becomes

$$Lt <= Ln - \frac{\left[\sum_{i=1}^{P} x_i * (x_i-1)\right] * T}{Wn} + \frac{Lp}{Wp}$$

Because Cp varies per POP, you should do this calculation once per POP. You could probably come up with the average Cp value across all POPs and just use that for each POP, but it's not that much work to calculate this number for each POP. In fact, for this example, you don't have to do any work, because it's already done for you, in Table 9-9.

Table 9-9 shows the estimated number of midpoint LSPs per WR, per POP.

Table 9-9   *Number of Midpoint LSPs Per WR*

POP	Midpoint LSPs Per WR
Seattle	3285
San Jose	2940
San Diego	2586
Denver	1976
Dallas	2223
Houston	2345
St. Louis	2345
Chicago	2466

Table 9-9   *Number of Midpoint LSPs Per WR (Continued)*

POP	Midpoint LSPs Per WR
Atlanta	2705
Raleigh	3056
D.C.	3398
New York	3948
Boston	2586
Miami	2100

So, as you can see (if you've stayed awake this far!), you're comfortably under the scalability limits for WR midpoints, which is 10,000 LSPs.

This might be clearer with a summarization of all the data in one big table (see Table 9-10). For each POP, there are three columns—WR, DR, and CR. The number in each column is the number of LSPs each router in that POP has to deal with:

- For WRs, this number is the number of LSPs for which the WR is a midpoint.

- For DRs, this number is the number of LSPs for which the DR is a midpoint.

- For CRs, this number is the number of LSPs for which a router is a headend and also the number of LSPs for which the router is a tail.

- At the top of each column is the number that is the scalability limit for that column—10,000 LSPs as a midpoint for WRs and DRs, and 600 headend LSPs at the CRs.

Table 9-10   *Comparing Scalability Limits to Estimated LSP Numbers*

Scalability Limit POP	10,000 WR	10,000 DR	600 CR
Seattle	3285	1125	127
San Jose	2940	N/A	127
San Diego	2586	N/A	127
Denver	1976	N/A	127
Dallas	2223	N/A	127
Houston	2345	N/A	127
St. Louis	2345	N/A	127
Chicago	2466	N/A	127
Atlanta	2705	N/A	127
Raleigh	3056	972	127
D.C.	3398	N/A	127
New York	3948	1567	127

continues

Table 9-10 *Comparing Scalability Limits to Estimated LSP Numbers (Continued)*

Scalability Limit POP	10,000 WR	10,000 DR	600 CR
Boston	2586	N/A	127
Miami	2100	N/A	127

As you can see, you are well under the scalability limits in all cases. Now, some assumptions were made that might not be true (especially in the case of T in the WR calculations), but they are accurate enough to make our point, which is that MPLS TE is not the gating factor in scaling your network.

Other Growth Factors

In the tactical architecture, you read about periodically cleaning up after yourself. The strategic architecture doesn't really have housecleaning per se, but it does have a few things you need to be concerned about. These things are mostly a concern if you're going to do online path calculation; if you do offline path calculation, the path calculation tool itself should help take care of these details.

You should consider three principal things when talking about online tactical housecleaning:

- Tunnel reoptimization
- Tunnel resizing
- Multiple parallel LSPs

These topics are discussed in the following sections.

Tunnel Reoptimization

The first thing you need to consider is tunnel reoptimization. Reoptimization in this context is the recalculation of CSPF for all LSPs, to see if there is a more optimal path across the network they can take. Why is this important?

Consider the network shown in Figure 9-8.

Figure 9-8   *Sample Network for the Reoptimization Example*

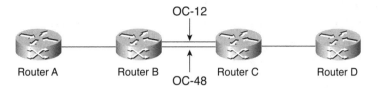

At time 0, Router A has a 400-Mbps LSP to Router D that goes across the OC-48 link between Router B and Router C.

Sometime after this LSP is up (call it time 1), the OC-48 link goes down for some reason. No problem. The 400-Mbps LSP just reroutes over the OC-12, and all is well.

At time 2, the OC-48 link comes up.

What happens next? Eventually, you'd like the A→D LSP to move back to the OC-48 link, because it has more headroom and can better handle a burst of traffic. But without reoptimization of some kind, the A→D LSP will stay across the OC-12 link until either the OC-12 link or the A→D LSP goes down for some reason.

So you need some kind of reoptimization, to tell the headend to try to find new paths for the LSPs, if there are better ones than those it is currently using. There are three kinds of reoptimization events:

- Periodic reoptimization
- Event-driven reoptimization
- Manual reoptimization

Periodic Reoptimization

Periodically, an LSP headend tries to calculate new paths for all its LSPs. If a better path is found, the headend signals the new LSP and installs the new outgoing label; this is make-before-break.

The default periodic reoptimization timer is 1 hour (3600 seconds). In a CR full mesh in our sample network, every hour, a router recalculates paths for all 127 of its LSPs. This periodic interval can be tuned using the global command **mpls traffic-eng reoptimize timers frequency**. You can go quite low with this timer; some networks tune it down to 60 seconds or less. The reoptimization timer can be set to no less than 30 seconds; trying to set a nonzero value less than 30 will result in a configured value of 30.

You can also disable periodic reoptimization. If you set the periodic reoptimization timer to 0, the tunnel's LSPs will never be reoptimized.

You can see how much more time you have to go until the reoptimization timer kicks in with **show mpls traffic-eng tunnels summary**, as demonstrated in Example 9-3.

Example 9-3 **show mpls traffic-eng tunnels summary** *Output Shows the Time to Reoptimization*

```
gsr3#show mpls traffic-eng tunnels summary
Signalling Summary:
    LSP Tunnels Process:            running
    RSVP Process:                   running
    Forwarding:                     enabled
    Head: 2 interfaces, 1 active signalling attempts, 1 established
          6 activations, 5 deactivations
    Midpoints: 0, Tails: 0
    Periodic reoptimization:        every 3600 seconds, next in 3599 seconds
    Periodic auto-bw collection:    every 300 seconds, next in 89 seconds
```

Why tune down to 60 seconds or less? Suppose you have strict SLAs that result in financial penalties if they're not met. This means that you have a strong incentive to try to find the shortest path possible for your LSP as quickly as you can. For the network shown in Figure 9-8, you want LSPs to take the OC-12 link only if they have to and revert to the OC-48 link as quickly as possible. So this is an incentive to make the reoptimization timer as low as possible.

But you run into scalability issues here. If you ask the router to reoptimize all its LSPs every 30 seconds, and the time to run CSPF for all that router's LSPs is more than 30 seconds, you're in trouble. Tunnel CSPF run times are typically in the low milliseconds (about 20 to 40 ms, depending on the size of your network), so you can fit quite a lot of LSPs in this time. But still, running that often might suck up too much CPU and cause other problems.

This problem makes for a nice segue into its solution—event-driven reoptimization.

Event-Driven Reoptimization

The problem with periodic reoptimization is that *all* LSPs are recalculated every time the reoptimization timer goes off. And if you tune the reoptimization timer pretty low, almost all the time your per-LSP CSPF is run, no new paths will be found, because the odds of a link flapping somewhere in your TE network (usually your core) in the last 30 seconds are quite low.

What you'd rather do is recalculate LSP paths only if something changes in the network. From this perspective, there are two kinds of changes—links going up and links going down. The network considers one node going down to be the same thing as all the links on that node going down.

NOTE   Link flaps are not the only things a router needs to care about. If you are using LSPs that consume bandwidth, and a large-bandwidth LSP goes down, that might free up enough bandwidth to make a more optimal path for one or more of the remaining LSPs. However, doing event-driven reoptimization based on link bandwidth is complex, mostly because a change in bandwidth might trigger a reoptimization, which would trigger a change in bandwidth, which would trigger reoptimization, and so on. In other words, event-driven reoptimization in which the result of the reoptimization triggers an event is something that is difficult to get right.

However, periodic reoptimization doesn't have this issue, because it's not event-driven. So even if you enable event-driven linkup reoptimization, you probably still want to use periodic reoptimization as well, to safely pick up on any significant bandwidth changes in the network.

Links going down don't need to trigger reoptimization. Any LSPs that cross those links will be rerouted when they receive failure notification via RSVP or the IGP, and any LSPs not crossing a failed link don't need to care about a link going down.

But what about when links come up? When a link comes up, this represents new resources that existing LSPs can take advantage of. LSPs that are currently down (because they can't find the resources they want) try to find new paths every 30 seconds, so no worries there.

What about LSPs that are up but that don't follow the most optimal path? You'd like to run reoptimization checks for these LSPs only when a link (or multiple links) somewhere in the network comes up, because only then would these LSPs be able to find a better path.

Event-driven link-up reoptimization can be enabled with **mpls traffic-eng reoptimize events link-up**. If you turn this on, whenever a link comes up somewhere in the network, CSPF for all existing LSPs is run to see if they can get a more optimal path through the network using the link that's just come up.

This can be dangerous if you have a link that flaps (goes up or down) more often than you'd run the reoptimize timer. Suppose you want to turn the reoptimize timer down to 60 seconds, but you use **events link-up** instead. If you have a link that flaps every 5 seconds (down for 5 seconds, up for 5 seconds, etc.), you'll run six times as many reoptimizations as you would without this command. You might also end up with more RSVP signalling, depending on whether the reoptimization on linkup moves LSPs onto the link that just came up.

Not to worry, though. Because link availability information is flooded in the IGP, you can fall back on the IGP's safety mechanisms to prevent this. IS-IS and OSPF both have timers you can tweak to control constant link advertisement and withdrawal in this type of situation. These knobs apply to the TE information for that link as well. Relying on the IGP only makes things a little worse than they would be without MPLS TE (you run an IGP SPF *and* many tunnel CSPFs), but not much worse, and then only in pathological failure conditions.

How do you know if a tunnel is following a suboptimal path? Use the command **show mpls traffic-eng tunnels suboptimal constraints current**. Like many other **show mpls traffic-eng tunnels** commands, this can be used with or without the **brief** keyword, as demonstrated in Example 9-4.

Example 9-4 *Determining Whether the Tunnel Is Following a Suboptimal Path Using* **show mpls traffic-eng tunnels suboptimal constraints current brief**

```
gsr3#show mpls traffic-eng tunnels suboptimal constraints current brief
Signalling Summary:
    LSP Tunnels Process:              running
    RSVP Process:                     running
    Forwarding:                       enabled
    Periodic reoptimization:          every 3600 seconds, next in 967 seconds
    Periodic auto-bw collection:      every 300 seconds, next in 157 seconds
TUNNEL NAME                     DESTINATION      UP IF     DOWN IF   STATE/PROT
Tunnel1 from GSR3 to GSR7       192.168.1.7      -         PO2/1     up/up
Displayed 1 (of 2) heads, 0 (of 0) midpoints, 0 (of 0) tails
```

Table 9-11 describes the three types of constraints you can display.

Table 9-11 *Three Constraint Options for* **show mpls traffic-eng tunnels suboptimal constraints**

Command Option	Description
none	Shows tunnels that are taking a longer path than the IGP path to the destination—that is, tunnels that diverge from the IGP shortest path, presumably because of bandwidth constraints, explicit path configuration, or other such TE mechanisms.
	Note that this command actually is **show mpls traffic-eng tunnels suboptimal constraints none**. The word **none** is part of the command, not an indication that there is no keyword there!
current	Shows tunnels that are taking a path to the destination that's longer than the currently available shortest path. Tunnels that match this command would change the path they took if the command **mpls traffic-eng reoptimize** were used right then.
max	Shows tunnels that are taking a path longer than they could be because of resource consumption by other tunnels. Any tunnels that show up in this command are reoptimized onto a shorter path.

Manual Reoptimization

Assume that after careful study, you decide to leave the periodic reoptimization timer at its default of 1 hour and to not enable link-up reoptimization. Most of the time, you're fine with that. But occasionally, you find a particular LSP that needs reoptimization urgently and that can't wait for the timer to expire. What do you do then? You could shut down the tunnel and bring it back up again, but that disrupts traffic.

A better way to do this is via the EXEC command **mpls traffic-eng reoptimize mpls traffic-eng reoptimize**, which by itself reoptimizes all tunnels for which a router is a headend. You can also reoptimize a single tunnel with **mpls traffic-eng reoptimize** *tunnel-interface*.

Tunnel Resizing

Tunnel *resizing* is slightly different from the tunnel reoptimization discussed in the previous sections. Reoptimization involves finding a new path for an existing tunnel. Resizing involves changing the bandwidth requirement on tunnels, based on demand. Of course, changing the bandwidth requirements might also change the path a tunnel takes.

There are two ways bandwidth requirements can change—they can go up or down. Obviously, you need to care about both types of events.

You still have a few questions to be answered. The first is "How often do I resize my tunnels?", and the second is "What size do I make my new tunnels?"

When determining how often to resize new tunnels, you want to be careful not to resize too often, because this makes TE look more like a microscale thing than a macroscale thing. Resizing every 10 minutes, for example, is too often.

On the other hand, you don't want to resize too infrequently. If you don't resize in a timely fashion, you'll have a TE LSP topology that's out of sync with the real world.

There is no clear-cut answer to how often you resize your tunnels. Like so many things, the answer is "It depends." Here are some questions to ask:

- What do your traffic patterns look like?
- Do you have clearly defined busy periods in which your traffic patterns obviously increase and decrease?
- Do you have daily, twice-daily, or weekly traffic patterns?

You'll have to investigate. In the absence of any sense of where to start, you might want to start by resizing every 8 hours to see if that fits your traffic demands. Getting this resize interval right takes a fair bit of work to get started, but as soon as you have a better handle on your traffic, it gets easier.

You might not resize TE tunnels on a fixed interval. Maybe you want to resize every 2 hours from 6 a.m. to 6 p.m. and every 4 hours from 6 p.m. to 6 a.m. The choice is up to you.

So now that you know you need to resize your LSPs, how do you actually *do* this? There are two ways. One is to use an offline tool, and the other is to have the router itself make the resize decision. Using an offline tool is covered in the next section, so we won't deal with it here.

How do you have the router resize tunnels automatically? By using auto bandwidth. See the section "Automatic Bandwidth Adjustment" in Chapter 5 for a discussion of how auto bandwidth works. Auto bandwidth has reasonable defaults for how often and how accurately it resizes tunnels, but like everything else, it's a good idea to keep an eye on things and tune your network as you see fit.

Multiple Parallel LSPs

As mentioned in the discussion of tunnel numbering, sometimes you might want parallel tunnels between two routers. You might find parallel tunnels effective if you want to send more traffic between those routers than you can fit on any single path between CRs. Or if the only path you can find between two routers goes quite out of the way, splitting that traffic across two tunnels can help alleviate the problem.

The basic idea behind multiple tunnels was covered in the tactical discussion earlier. But how do you apply it to a full-mesh (strategic) architecture?

This is actually pretty tricky in an online strategic model. You need some way to decide that traffic heading toward a particular destination is more than the available physical bandwidth. Auto bandwidth doesn't have such a facility.

At first glance, you might think that all you need to do is monitor both the reserved bandwidth for an LSP and the actual traffic going down an LSP, and change the reserved bandwidth when the two values get too far out of sync. The problem with this approach, though, is that it can't always help you. TCP, which is the majority of Internet traffic, adjusts itself to fit the available bandwidth. This means that if you build a TE LSP across a link that is a bottleneck (either it's a lower-speed link or it's close to maximum utilization), the traffic down the TE LSP decreases to fit in the congested link. To do this right, you need to monitor your network for links that are close to maximum utilization and move TE LSPs off those links, to allow the TCP traffic inside those LSPs to open up to as much bandwidth as it can take.

Doing this monitoring and readjusting is nontrivial. This problem was touched on earlier, in the section "Determining When TE LSPs Are Causing Problems." It's something you need to be aware of if you plan to use MPLS TE on a large scale.

Offline Strategic TE Design

The online strategic discussion covered a lot of things that are inherent to either full-mesh architecture. But the online strategic architecture is not very good at a few things that the offline strategic architecture can handle better.

The most important thing to consider is what's known as the *packing problem*. A packing problem is a type of problem that deals with optimal use of resources. It's worth spending some serious time on this next section if you don't understand it at first pass, because you need to understand the impact this problem has on your network.

Packing Problem

Consider the two links between the two LSRs shown in Figure 9-9. Each link is an OC-3, with a maximum of 150 Mbps of reservable bandwidth. Link 1 has an available bandwidth of 60 Mbps (90 Mbps has already been reserved), and Link 2 has an available bandwidth of 40 Mbps (110 Mbps has already been reserved). Both links have the same IGP cost.

Figure 9-9   *Packing Problem*

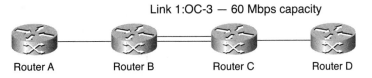

Link 1:OC-3 — 60 Mbps capacity

Router A   Router B   Router C   Router D

Link 2:OC-3 — 40 Mbps capacity

Two tunnels that need to be placed want to get from Router A to Router D. Tunnel1 wants 60 Mbps of bandwidth; Tunnel2 wants 40 Mbps. What happens?

If Tunnel1 comes up first, all is well. Tunnel1 consumes all 60 of the 60 Mbps on Link 1, and Tunnel2 goes to the only other place it can—Link 2. At this point, both links are 100 percent fully reserved, and both LSPs are happy.

However, if Tunnel2 comes up first, it consumes 40 Mbps of the 60 Mbps on Link 1, leaving Link 1 with 20 Mbps of capacity and Link 2 with 40 Mbps. So where does Tunnel1 go? It can't fit on either of these links. If these links are the only way Tunnel1 can get to its destination, Tunnel1 won't come up.

The problem here is that one of the tiebreakers to decide where to place an LSP is to pick the link with the maximum amount of bandwidth available (see Chapter 4). This is often known as *max-fill LSP placement*. It refers to the tiebreaker of finding the link that has the maximum possible bandwidth.

So one possible fix for this problem is to try to place LSPs on links that have the *least* amount of available bandwidth; this is *min-fill*. Cisco IOS Software doesn't allow you to select anything other than max-fill for LSP placement, but as you'll see, min-fill isn't really any better than max-fill.

If you did this for the situation just described, all would be happy. The 40-Mbps LSP would place itself on the 40-Mbps link, and the 60-Mbps LSP would place itself on the 60-Mbps link, regardless of order.

But min-fill doesn't solve all problems.

Assume that the network topology is slightly more complicated and has two links but three LSPs. These LSPs want bandwidth of 20, 30, and 40 Mbps, respectively. Table 9-12 examines min-fill and max-fill algorithms for the different orders tunnels can come up in.

There are six (3 factorial, or 3 * 2 * 1) different orders in which the tunnels can attempt to come up, and two algorithms to try with each order.

The notation used here is as follows:

- **min (20,30,40)**—Placing LSPs in the order 20, 30, 40, using the min-fill algorithm
- **{40,60}**—The amount of bandwidth available on each link
- **{F}**—Failure. None of the three LSPs could be successfully placed

Table 9-12 *min-fill and max-fill Algorithms for the Different Orders in Which Tunnels Can Appear*

	Start	After the First LSP Is Placed	After the Second LSP Is Placed	After the Third LSP Is Placed
min (20,30,40)	{40,60}	{20,60}	{20,30}	{F}
max (20,30,40)	{40,60}	{40,40}	{10,40}	{10,0}
min (20,40,30)	{40,60}	{20,60}	{20,20}	{F}
max (20,40,30)	{40,60}	{40,40}	{0,40}	{0,10}
min (30,20,40)	{40,60}	{10,60}	{10,40}	{10,0}
max (30,20,40)	{40,60}	{40,30}	{20,30}	{F}
min (30,40,20)	{40,60}	{10,60}	{10,20}	{10,0}
max (30,40,20)	{40,60}	{40,30}	{0,30}	{0,10}
min (40,20,30)	{40,60}	{0,60}	{0,40}	{0,10}
max (40,20,30)	{40,60}	{40,20}	{20,20}	{F}
min (40,30,20)	{40,60}	{0,60}	{0,30}	{0,10}
max (40,30,20)	{40,60}	{40,20}	{10,20}	{10,0}

Stare at this table for a moment. The following facts should become obvious:

- There are two orders for which min-fill works and max-fill doesn't.
- There are two orders for which max-fill works and min-fill doesn't.
- There are two orders for which both max-fill and min-fill work.

In every case, either min-fill or max-fill can find a solution to the problem and successfully place the LSPs. However, for tunnels coming up in different orders, sometimes min-fill works, and sometimes max-fill works.

What you haven't seen yet is that it's possible that LSPs can come up in an order in which neither max-fill nor min-fill works, but those same LSPs could be placed successfully with either algorithm if the LSPs came up in just the right order.

Consider a still more complicated example—links of capacity 66 and 75, and LSPs of size 21, 22, 23, 24, 25, and 26. It's clear that if you placed these LSPs by hand, they could be placed so that all LSPs fit on all links. In fact, there are 36 factorial $(3)^2$ possible ways that these could be placed by hand and still work.

There are 1440 possible outcomes here (6! permutations of LSPs times 2 placement algorithms). For brevity, they are not all listed, but the following tables show three possible outcomes:

- Table 9-13 shows the results when a min-fill algorithm works but max-fill fails.
- Table 9-14 shows the results when max-fill works but min-fill fails.
- Table 9-15 shows the results when neither min-fill nor max-fill works.

Table 9-13   *min-fill Works, But max-fill Fails*

LSPs Placed in This Order	0	21	22	23	24	25	26
min-fill	{66,75}	{45,75}	{23,75}	{0,75}	{0,51}	{0,26}	{0,0}
max-fill	{66,75}	{66,54}	{44,54}	{44,31}	{20,31}	{20,6}	{F}

Table 9-14   *max-fill Works, But min-fill Fails*

LSPs Placed in This Order	0	26	23	25	22	24	21
min-fill	{66,75}	{40,75}	{17,75}	{17,50}	{17,28}	{17,4}	{F}
max-fill	{66,75}	{66,49}	{43,49}	{43,24}	{21,24}	{21,0}	{0,0}

Table 9-15   *Both min-fill and max-fill Fail*

LSPs Placed in This Order	0	26	25	24	23	22	21
min-fill	{66,75}	{40,75}	{15,75}	{15,50}	{15,27}	{15,6}	{F}
max-fill	{66,75}	{66,49}	{41,49}	{41,24}	{18,24}	{18,2}	{F}

As you can see, min-fill and max-fill can't guarantee a solution to this packing problem. To work around this problem, you can use a few techniques:

- Use tunnel priority to give larger trunks better priority. The idea here is to divide your tunnel bandwidths into four or five bands, grouped by size. Maybe 0 to 50-Mbps tunnels go in one band, 51 to 150-Mbps in another, 151 to 500-Mbps in another, and 501-Mbps+ in another.

  Give the larger tunnels a better (that is, *lower*) setup and holding priority with the command **tunnel mpls traffic-eng priority**. This means that bandwidth-hungry LSPs will push smaller LSPs out of the way, and these smaller LSPs will then coalesce around the larger ones. See Chapter 3, "Information Distribution," for information on the mechanics of tunnel priority.

- The packing problem gets worse as your LSPs get larger. The larger your LSPs are relative to the size of your links, the more likely you are to waste bandwidth. If you have a 100 Mb link and four LSPs of 30 Mb, you can place only three of them across that link, and you have 10 Mb of unused bandwidth. If you have two 60 Mb LSPs instead, you can place only one of them, leaving 40 Mb wasted. Consider making it a rule not to have any LSPs that are more than a fixed percentage of the minimum link size they might cross. If this rule means that you never have any LSPs of more than 300 Mbps in your network, for example, and you need 500 Mbps of LSP bandwidth from one router to another, build two LSPs. It's up to you whether you build them both as 250 Mbps, or one as 300 Mbps and one as 200 Mbps. As long as you fit within CEF's load-balancing rules (see Chapter 5), you're OK.

- Use an offline tool to find the paths your LSPs should take. This is the most efficient solution in terms of network utilization. It's also the most complicated. Not everybody buys into this approach, because it involves an external box that builds your network for you. But even those who don't use external path placement tools agree that external placement is more efficient than having the headend place each LSP.

Using an Offline Tool for LSP Placement

An offline tool can do a much better job of placing LSPs than a router can. Why? Because whereas a router is aware of what traffic requirements *its* tunnels have, an offline tool is aware of the traffic requirements of *all* LSPs. For example, consider the packing problem just discussed with LSPs of {21, 22, 23, 24, 25, 26}. None of those LSPs are aware of the others, so you've got a good chance of ending up with suboptimal LSP placement. It comes down to a race condition. If things happen in just the right order, you'll be OK. It helps to divide LSPs into bands (the first of the three options mentioned in the preceding section), but you can still get into contention *within* a band. In fact, if you follow the suggestion of having a priority band for tunnels of bandwidth 0 to 50, you haven't changed anything for the LSPs in the preceding examples.

An offline tool, which knows all the demands in all the LSPs, can come up with a more efficient method of placing LSPs. However, an offline tool has to deal with a specific type of problem known as a *bin-packing problem*. Bin-packing problems are known to be NP-complete (if you're not a mathematician, NP-complete means "really, really hard"), but you can come up with alternative approaches involving specific heuristics that make an offline tool better at placing LSPs than can be done by having the routers calculate their own LSP paths.

Discussing the specifics of offline tools and their capabilities would take another chapter. Or book. Or several. You should contact specific tool vendors to figure out if an offline tool is right for you. Here are two of the vendors that make such tools:

- **WANDL**—www.wandl.com
- **OPNET**—www.opnet.com

Of course, you're free to write your own, especially if you have specific needs not addressed by commercial tools. Just make sure that you understand how complex this problem is before you start working on it!

Protection Scalability

This section covers how to use Fast Reroute (FRR) link, node, and path protection in your network—specifically, how well it scales.

There's quite a lot to FRR. But the biggest piece people want to get their hands on, after understanding how protection works, is how it scales. If I do link protection everywhere in my network, how many extra LSPs does that give me? What about node protection? Or path protection?

Luckily, the formulae for link/node/path protection are pretty simple. All you need to do is determine the number of additional LSPs each node will have to deal with. You can then add this back into the full-mesh scalability numbers generated earlier in the chapter and see how your design stacks up against your scalability limits.

Before defining any formulae, though, you need to define some variables. In addition to the variables already defined in the full-mesh scalability discussion, you need to add the following:

- **D**—Degree of connectivity. This is the average number of directly attached links configured for TE on a router. So if a router has three links, its degree of connectivity is 3. It is sometimes also useful to talk about the average degree of connectivity among a certain set of routers. D means either the degree of connectivity for a specific node or the average degree of connectivity for all nodes, depending on context. The implicit assumption here is that all routers in the network have the same degree of connectivity. This is generally not true in most networks, but it's a reasonable starting point for these simple calculations.

- **Rn**—Number of routers in the MPLS TE portion of the network. If you do a WR full mesh of TE tunnels, for example, Rn = Wn. But if you do a full mesh of CR routers, Rn = Cn + Dn + Wn.

- **Fn**—Number of FRR LSPs that need to exist in the network as a result of a particular type of protection.

Two pieces to talk about when considering protection (discussed in the next few sections) are as follows:

- The approximate number of LSPs that are added to the network as a whole when a particular type of protection is enabled.

- The number of LSPs that a given router has to deal with.

Link Protection

For link protection, the number of additional LSPs in the network is approximately D * Rn—the average degree of connectivity per node, multiplied by the number of nodes in the cloud. From real-world experience, D tends to be somewhere in the neighborhood of 3 to 5. So if you're doing a WR full mesh, and Wn = 28 (therefore, Rn = 28), you're talking about Fn being somewhere between 84 and 112 additional LSPs in the entire network.

One assumption made here is that it takes only one backup tunnel to protect a link. If your network topology requires you to build two or three or x backup tunnels to protect a link, you're really talking about $x * D * Rn$ LSPs. This is still not much signalling. If x gets big enough that the number of backup LSPs starts taking significant resources, you probably have underlying network issues.

Another assumption is that you're FRR-protecting every link. If you don't need to protect all the links in your network, of course, the number of protection LSPs will go down.

Protecting a CR full mesh requires protecting all the links those CR LSPs might traverse. So in this case, Rn = Wn + Dn + Cn = 168, and if D still varies between 3 and 5, Fn is an additional 504 to 840 LSPs. In the entire network. Still not a big deal.

The additional load on a given router is 2 * D. If a router has six links, it is a headend for six protection LSPs and a tail for six protection LSPs. Scalability as a TE tail is generally not a concern, as was illustrated earlier in this chapter. All you have to deal with, then, are the additional six LSPs this node is a headend for, and there's not much work there, either.

But how many LSPs is a node a midpoint for? This depends on the LSP length (that is, how far they have to diverge from the shortest path to arrive at the next-next hop).

Certainly an LSP is a midpoint for no more than Fn LSPs. But the number will be far less than that. It's hard to come up with an accurate rule for generating this number because networks are so different, but a reasonable approximation is

$$((Ln * T) / Rn) - (2 * D)$$

where Ln = Rn * D and T is the fudge factor that we used earlier in this chapter. Note that this equation reduces to $(D * T) - (2 * D)$.

For a WR full mesh (28 nodes) and T = 3, with D = 3 to 5, a node is a midpoint for 3-5 protection LSPs. Not a big deal at all.

Node Protection

In node protection, each node needs an LSP not to its neighbors, but to the neighbors of its neighbors. So the total number of LSPs added to the network (Ln) is Rn*D*(D-1). In a WR full mesh, this means that Fn ranges somewhere around (28 * 3 * 2) = 168 through (28 * 5 * 4) = 560 LSPs.

The equation for Fn is the same as it was in link protection; the only difference is in the value of Ln. The equation is still

$$((Ln * T) / Rn) - (2 * D)$$

In node protection, though, remember that Ln = Rn*D*(D-1), rather than Rn*D. That means that this equation reduces to $(D * (D - 1) * T) - (2 * D)$.

Assuming that T = 3 and D is 3 to 5, the number of node-protection LSPs for which a node is a midpoint is between 12 and 50. Still not a big deal either way.

Path Protection

Path protection is the easiest to calculate. If you have Ln LSPs in a network, and you calculate fully diverse paths for each one, you have a total of 2 * Ln LSPs in the network; for each LSP, you have one additional (protection) LSP. So Fn = Ln. Again employing a fudge-factor T value of 3, it's safe to assume that a router is a midpoint for approximately (Fn * T) / Rn LSPs. This can be further refined, as with the link and node protection cases, by subtracting the LSPs that a node is a headend or tail for. If you assume that each node has the same number of LSPs as head and tail, a router is a midpoint for somewhere around $((Fn * T) / Rn) - (Ln / Rn)$ LSPs.

Where path protection gets tricky is if you need more than one LSP to protect a primary LSP. Maybe you can't get enough bandwidth to match the entire LSP (or whatever portion of it you're protecting) in one path. Cisco IOS Software doesn't implement path protection, but as you will see, it scales so poorly that it's not a very attractive solution on a network of any reasonable size. Consider the network shown in Figure 9-10.

Figure 9-10 *Primary LSP Requiring Multiple LSPs*

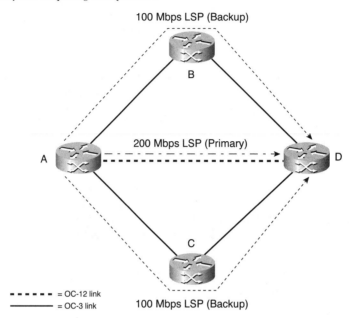

The LSP from A to D is 200 Mbps, but there are only OC-3 links to protect it over. If you want to protect all the bandwidth, you have to build two LSPs of 100 Mbps—one across each path.

So in this case, Fn > Ln. If the entire network happens to look like this, Fn > Fn.

How much greater? It depends. It could be two to three times greater. But no matter whether Fn = 1 * Ln or Fn = 3 * Ln or Fn = 100 * Ln (not likely!).

Actual Data for Determining Scalability

So how well does this stuff scale in real life? Good question. Let's look at some data.

In some topologies, in order to protect your network fully using link or node protection, you could have *more* protection LSPs than primary LSPs. This happens when you have either a small number of nodes or a high degree of connectivity. Assume that the *break-even point* is the point at which the number of protection LSPs and primary LSPs are equal, for a given protection scheme. So a network in which you have 12 LSPs, but you need 36 LSPs to enact full node protection, does not break even. A network in which you have 110 primary LSPs and 99 protection LSPs meets the break-even point.

The definition of this break-even point is somewhat arbitrary. You might decide that a protection scheme is good only if the number of protection LSPs is no more than 50 percent of the number of primary LSPs. Or 20 percent. Or some other percentage. But given the following data, it's easy to see that you'll reach that point eventually.

NOTE   Of course, the break-even scalability point isn't the only reason to consider a particular type of protection. You also need to consider things such as where your failures occur, how often they happen, how much data you have to protect, and so forth.

Given the formula and assumptions here, the break-even point for link protection is at four nodes, and node protection is at ten nodes.

It should be obvious that path protection is always just at the break-even point, because Fn = Ln. This assumes that multiple LSPs are not protecting a single LSP.

Table 9-16 shows different numbers of nodes, the total number of LSPs used in the network (assuming that all links in the TE portion of the network are to be protected), and the number of protection LSPs used. In this table, the average degree of connectivity (D) is 3.

Table 9-16   *Link, Node, and Path Protection Scalability*

Number of Nodes (Rn)	Number of Primary LSPs (Rn * (Rn – 1))	Number of LSPs Used in Link Protection	Number of LSPs Used in Node Protection	Number of LSPs Used in Path Protection
1	0	3	9	0
10	90	30	90	90
20	380	60	180	380
30	870	90	270	870
40	1560	120	360	1560
50	2450	150	450	2450
60	3540	180	540	3540
70	4830	210	630	4830
80	6320	240	720	6320
90	8010	270	810	8010
100	9900	300	900	9900
110	11,990	330	990	11,990
120	14,280	360	1080	14,280
130	16,770	390	1170	16,770

continues

Table 9-16 *Link, Node, and Path Protection Scalability (Continued)*

Number of Nodes (Rn)	Number of Primary LSPs (Rn * (Rn – 1))	Number of LSPs Used in Link Protection	Number of LSPs Used in Node Protection	Number of LSPs Used in Path Protection
140	19,460	420	1260	19,460
150	22,350	450	1350	22,350

The number of LSPs used in node protection is the formula Rn * D * (D – 1) plus the number of LSPs in link protection (Rn * D). So the entire formula is

$$Rn * D * (D - 1) + Rn * D$$

which reduces to $Rn * D^2$.

Why do you need both link and node protection? Because if you have LSPs that terminate on a directly connected neighbor, you can't node-protect that neighbor; you need to link-protect it. You might not always need to link-protect every node (not all nodes are TE tunnel tails), but the number of additional LSPs is so small that it's not worth calculating and trying to factor out here.

Figure 9-11 shows a graph of link, node, and path scalability. Figure 9-12 shows a graph of only the link and node scalability numbers, because it's easier to see the difference between these two if path protection isn't in the way. It's important to note, however, that the graphs in both figures use the exact same data. The reason it's hard to see link and node protection numbers on the path protection graph is because of how poorly path protection scales to large numbers.

Figure 9-11 *Link/Node/Path Scalability Graph*

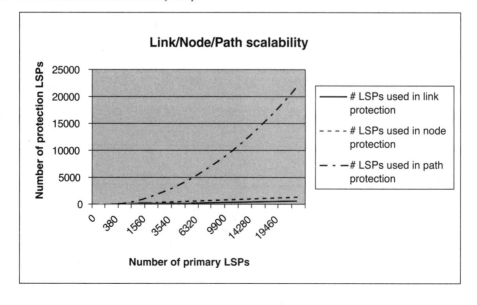

Figure 9-12 *Link/Node Scalability Graph*

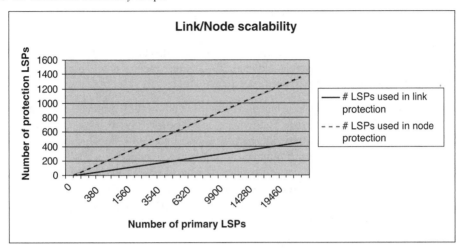

As you can see, both link and node protection scale quite nicely, while path protection quickly creates a large number of protection LSPs. Path protection has other issues as well, so it's not very suitable for deployment on large TE networks.

Forwarding Adjacency Scalability

Chapter 5 covered the basic configuration of forwarding adjacency, along with why you might want to use it. But you need to be careful. Forwarding adjacency in a network with a large number of LSPs can grow pretty quickly.

The increase in the number of LSPs is because of the fact that every LSP that has forwarding adjacency enabled is advertised into the IGP as a link. If you have a full mesh of TE tunnels between 128 CRs, this means that every node in the same IGP level, which previously had to deal with fewer than 500 links in the IGP, now has to deal with an additional 16,256 (128 * 127) links, bringing the total IGP size to almost 17,000 links!

17,000 is a lot. It could easily be more than your IGP can handle. Keep this in mind as you consider deploying forwarding adjacency. You might have to deploy forwarding adjacency only where it's needed, and give up some of its optimality in the name of scalability.

Summary

This chapter was somewhat of a departure from the other chapters in this book. Rather than talking about things like configurations and debugs, this chapter concentrated mostly on scalability. Both tactical and strategic TE deployment methodologies were discussed, with a major focus on the scalability of strategic TE deployment in a full mesh. The scalability of various FRR protection methods (link, node, and path) was also discussed.

It is important to realize that the scalability of a particular TE deployment methodology is not the only reason you pick that methodology. You need to consider all sorts of other factors, including network stability, SLAs and uptime goals, and many other things.

The most important thing you can take away from this chapter is that you have two ways to deploy MPLS TE—strategic and tactical—and that they're both valid. Both methods are being used successfully in networks today.

The same thing applies to protection. Whether you use link protection or node protection, your scalability isn't at risk. Your choice of protection scheme has more to do with what types of problems your network is likely to encounter (link flaps? router outages? both? how often?) and how much time you want to put into applying a backup strategy. You can do things as simple as dynamically placed link protection LSPs whose paths are calculated by the routers doing the protection, or as complicated as bandwidth-aware node protection with LSP paths calculated by an offline tool. It's up to you. Hopefully, this chapter has opened your eyes to some of the possibilities, caveats, and mind-sets involved.

This chapter covers the following topics:

- Bandwidth and Delay Measurements
- Fine-Tuning MPLS TE Parameters
- Migrating IS-IS from Narrow to Wide Metrics
- TE and Multicast
- Tunnel Identification Schemes
- Combining MPLS TE with MPLS VPNs
- Deployment Possibilities

CHAPTER 10

MPLS TE Deployment Tips

By now, you've probably read Chapter 9, "Network Design with MPLS TE." So hopefully you have a grip on some of the different ways MPLS TE can be deployed and how it scales. This chapter takes a look not at the theoretical side of things, but at some of the real-world aspects of MPLS TE deployment. This chapter covers several things that are useful to understand when considering MPLS TE deployment in the real world. Here are the specific things that are covered:

- Bandwidth and delay measurements
- Tuning timers and tweaking knobs
- Migrating IS-IS from narrow to wide metrics
- TE and multicast coexistence
- Tunnel identification schemes
- Combining MPLS TE and MPLS VPNs
- Deployment possibilities

Consider this chapter an assortment of tools for your MPLS TE toolbox. You might not use all of them (if you don't run multicast, or MPLS VPNs, or IS-IS), so feel free to read only the parts that are of interest to you.

Bandwidth and Delay Measurements

As you know by now, MPLS TE is mostly about moving traffic around on your network, away from congested points and onto less-congested paths.

But what traffic do you move? From where? To where?

In order to move traffic away from spots that would otherwise be congested, you first need to know how much traffic you want to send across the network. You also need to know something about the properties of the paths onto which you'd move traffic.

To make these determinations, you need accounting and measurement tools, some of which you can find in Cisco IOS Software. Here are some of the many different measurement tools provided by Cisco IOS Software that you can use to figure out where your congestion lies:

- Physical interface statistics
- IP accounting
- CEF accounting
- BGP policy accounting
- NetFlow accounting
- Traffix Matrix Statistics (TMS)
- Using TE tunnels for traffic measurement
- Service Assurance Agent (SAA)

All these tools do different things, however, so they might not give you all the information you need to figure out how much traffic is going where in your network.

The most important thing you need to know about your network traffic is how much of it there is. This chapter covers NetFlow, TMS, and a method of using TE tunnels to measure traffic demand.

Another thing that's useful to measure is the delay and jitter from one point in the network to another. You can measure delay and jitter using SAA, which is also covered in this chapter.

The first four measurement tools (interface statistics, IP accounting, CEF accounting, and BGP policy accounting) are not covered in this chapter or this book. Check www.cisco.com for more information about those specific tools.

In order to successfully place TE tunnels in your network, the first thing you need to do is decide what the border of your TE tunnel network will be—whether you have TE tunnels edge-to-edge, or only within the core.

As soon as you've decided where TE tunnels will be placed, start thinking of this area of your network as the TE cloud. If you're going to apply a strategic full mesh of some kind, whether edge-to-edge or only in the WAN, you need to get an idea of what traffic is going into this cloud, where it's entering, and where it's leaving. This is commonly known as a *traffic matrix*. Figure 10-1 shows the TE cloud within a small sample network used in the TMS discussion.

A traffic matrix is a measurement of how much traffic is going from an entry point in the TE cloud to an exit point from that TE cloud. Table 10-1 shows a possible traffic matrix for the network shown in Figure 10-1.

Figure 10-1 *TE Cloud Within a Network*

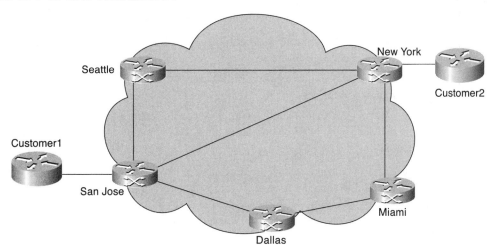

Table 10-1 *Traffic Matrix for Figure 10-1*

From →	Seattle	San Jose	Dallas	New York	Miami
To ↓					
Seattle	N/A	500 Mbps	100 Mbps	300 Mbps	200 Mbps
San Jose	525 Mbps	N/A	175 Mbps	400 Mbps	225 Mbps
Dallas	75 Mbps	350 Mbps	N/A	200 Mbps	50 Mbps
New York	250 Mbps	600 Mbps	190 Mbps	N/A	160 Mbps
Miami	50 Mbps	200 Mbps	100 Mbps	230 Mbps	N/A

Note that traffic can be asymmetric—for example, 50 Mbps from Seattle to Miami, but 200 Mbps from Miami to Seattle. This is perfectly valid, and MPLS TE is quite capable of dealing with asymmetric bandwidth demands.

Generating a traffic matrix is the first step in building a backbone that can carry your traffic efficiently.

But how do you build that traffic matrix? Many ways exist, but the main three are covered here:

- NetFlow
- TMS
- TE tunnels

NetFlow

NetFlow is deployed pretty extensively in networks. You can use NetFlow for two things:

- Determining what your network traffic patterns look like *before* you add MPLS Traffic Engineering to the mix

- Determining what your network traffic patterns look like *after* you add MPLS Traffic Engineering to the mix

NetFlow gathers information about traffic flows—different protocol types, packet sizes, flow lengths, and so on. NetFlow monitors IP packets going through a router to gather this information.

NetFlow does not currently gather any information about packets that already have a label on them, but NetFlow *can* be used to measure IP packets that enter a TE tunnel headend and are sent down TE tunnels. Because TE tunnels are just interfaces, any traffic going out TE tunnel interfaces is captured for NetFlow analysis if NetFlow is enabled on the interface the traffic came in on.

You can then export this data to a collector, such as Cisco's NetFlow Flow Collector, and feed this data to an analyzer such as Cisco's NetFlow FlowAnalyzer. When all is said and done, you have a pretty accurate picture of what kind of traffic exists on your network and where it's going.

Rolling out NetFlow in its full glory is a nontrivial task. NetFlow also has lots of uses besides traffic planning, such as billing and Denial of Service (DoS) tracking. All of those uses are pretty nifty but are beyond the scope of this book.

The bottom line is that because you can use NetFlow for planning purposes, you can use it to help plan TE layout. And because NetFlow tracks traffic sent out a TE tunnel interface just like it tracks traffic going out any other type of interface, you can use NetFlow to get an idea of what sort of traffic is flowing across your network even after you deploy TE tunnels. For more information on NetFlow, see Appendix B, "CCO and Other References."

Traffic Matrix Statistics

Not surprisingly, TMS is pretty good at building a traffic matrix. TMS is a simple, low-overhead method of gathering statistics about packets entering and traversing your network. It is an extension to CEF accounting that lets you collect information about the number of packets and bytes destined for a particular nonrecursive prefix. Both TMS and NetFlow count traffic, but TMS sacrifices some of NetFlow's granularity in exchange for a lower-overhead method of gathering the same kind of information. TMS works with both IP packets and MPLS-labeled packets.

TMS allows you to gather information about the following:

- The number of packets and bytes switched toward a given nonrecursive prefix
- Information about "internal" and "external" traffic (discussed later)
- BGP next-hop and neighbor AS information for a given destination network

You can gather this information for both IP packets and labeled packets.

TMS is based on Cisco Express Forwarding (CEF). CEF uses the concept of a *nonrecursive prefix*. A nonrecursive prefix is essentially a route that was not learned via BGP. IGP-learned routes, static routes, and directly connected routes are all examples of nonrecursive prefixes. A few nonrecursive prefixes are not in the routing table (CEF has the concept of a *host adjacency,* which is a /32 prefix installed for a host on a broadcast network, such as Ethernet), but generally speaking, nonrecursive prefixes are non-BGP routes.

You can see a router's nonrecursive prefixes using **show ip cef non-recursive**, as shown in Example 10-1.

Example 10-1 *Output of* **show ip cef non-recursive**

```
gsr1#show ip cef non-recursive
Prefix              Next Hop           Interface
2.3.4.0/24          attached           POS0/1
3.3.3.3/32          attached           Null0
4.4.4.4/32          attached           Null0
172.27.232.0/21     attached          Ethernet0
172.27.232.6/32     172.27.232.6  Ehernet0
172.27.235.66/32    172.27.235.66 Ethernet0
172.27.235.85/32    172.27.235.85      Ethernet0
192.168.1.12/32     2.3.4.12           POS0/1
```

Example 10-2 shows the routing table that matches up to these nonrecursive prefixes.

Example 10-2 *Routing Table for Example 10-1*

```
gsr1#show ip route
Codes: C - connected, S - static, I - IGRP, R - RIP, M - mobile, B - BGP
       D - EIGRP, EX - EIGRP external, O - OSPF, IA - OSPF inter area
       N1 - OSPF NSSA external type 1, N2 - OSPF NSSA external type 2
       E1 - OSPF external type 1, E2 - OSPF external type 2, E - EGP
       i - IS-IS, L1 - IS-IS level-1, L2 - IS-IS level-2, ia - IS-IS inter area
       * - candidate default, U - per-user static route, o - ODR

Gateway of last resort is 172.27.232.6 to network 0.0.0.0

     2.0.0.0/24 is subnetted, 1 subnets
C       2.3.4.0 is directly connected, POS0/1
     3.0.0.0/32 is subnetted, 1 subnets
S       3.3.3.3 is directly connected, Null0
     4.0.0.0/32 is subnetted, 1 subnets
S       4.4.4.4 is directly connected, Null0
     172.27.0.0/21 is subnetted, 1 subnets
```

continues

Example 10-2 *Routing Table for Example 10-1 (Continued)*

```
C       172.27.232.0 is directly connected, Ethernet0
        192.168.1.0/32 is subnetted, 2 subnets
i L2    192.168.1.12 [115/10] via 2.3.4.12, POS0/1
C       192.168.1.1 is directly connected, Loopback0
S*   0.0.0.0/0 [1/0] via 172.27.232.6
```

CEF's nonrecursive accounting lets you track traffic destined for these nonrecursive prefixes, even if your network traffic is destined for a BGP-learned route that is using that nonrecursive prefix as a next hop.

TMS adds some more accounting granularity to CEF's nonrecursive accounting, as well as adding the concept of *internal* and *external* interfaces. The internal/external distinction is an administrative one. You can flag interfaces coming from outside your network (or, in this case, from outside your MPLS TE cloud) as *external* and account for those packets separately from traffic flowing on internal interfaces.

Figure 10-2 flags the interfaces from inside the cloud as internal (I) interfaces and the customer-facing interfaces as external (E).

Figure 10-2 *Network with Internal and External Interfaces*

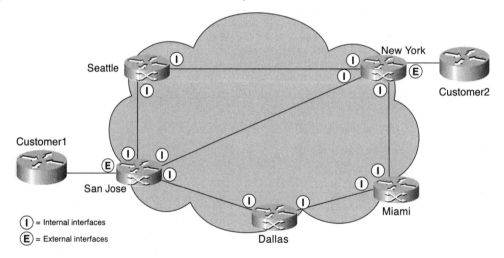

TMS, unlike NetFlow, does not export its data to a server. Rather than using NetFlow's "push" model, where data is pushed from a router to a NetFlow collector, TMS stores its data on the router and allows network administrators to collect data when they want to.

Configuring TMS

TMS is simple to configure. You do two things to enable TMS:

- Enable **ip cef accounting non-recursive** globally

- Optionally, configure an interface with **ip cef accounting non-recursive** {**internal** | **external**}

That's all you need to do. Interfaces are set to **ip cef accounting non-recursive internal** by default, so you only need to change the configuration for external interfaces. However, TMS data collection isn't enabled unless you configure **ip cef accounting non-recursive** globally.

Displaying TMS Data

You have two ways to display TMS data. One is via **show ip cef**, as demonstrated in Example 10-3.

Example 10-3 *Output of* **show ip cef** *Showing TMS Data*

```
Seattle#show ip cef 192.168.1.15
192.168.1.15/32, version 15, epoch 0, per-destination sharing
0 packets, 0 bytes
  tag information set
    local tag: 18
  via 192.168.22.15, Serial1/0, 0 dependencies
    next hop 192.168.22.15, Serial1/0
    valid adjacency
    tag rewrite with Se1/0, point2point, tags imposed: {0}
  5 packets, 500 bytes switched through the prefix
  tmstats: external 0 packets, 0 bytes
           internal 5 packets, 500 bytes
  30 second output rate 0 Kbits/sec
```

The four highlighted lines at the end of Example 10-3 show the TMS information recorded for a given nonrecursive prefix (in this case, 192.168.1.15). They're pretty straightforward. They show the total number of bytes and packets destined for a specific prefix, as received on both external and internal interfaces.

You can also access TMS information by retrieving data files directly from the router. TMS stores its data in a few different files:

- **tmstats_ascii**—Collects information about destination nonrecursive (IGP-learned) prefixes and the traffic forwarded toward them. This file also collects information about MPLS TE tunnel traffic.

- **tmstats_binary**—Collects the same information as tmstats_ascii, but in a more compact binary format. tmstats_binary is not covered in this chapter, because it contains the same information that's in tmstats_ascii.

- **tmasinfo**—Collects information about a particular nonrecursive IGP prefix/mask, the recursive destination IP addresses behind that IGP prefix (as learned via BGP), and the neighbor AS traversed to get to that destination IP address.

The TMS data files are in system:/vfiles/, which is a little-known ephemeral file system within Cisco IOS Software DRAM. Later examples show how you can access these files.

By now, you might be getting an idea of how and where TMS is useful. By tracking the amount of traffic destined for a particular nonrecursive prefix (say, a BGP next hop that's the exit point from your MPLS TE cloud), you can build a matrix of input and output traffic and use it to size your TE tunnels.

The following example takes a detailed look at exactly what data TMS saves and how it can be used to build a traffic matrix.

Consider the network shown in Figure 10-3.

Figure 10-3 *Simple TMS Network*

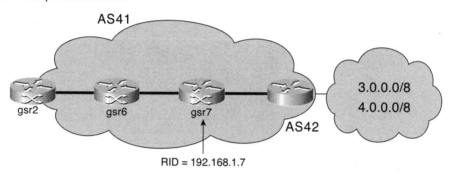

All three GSRs are in the same AS—41.

AS42 is advertising a full BGP table to gsr7. 3.0.0.0/8 and 4.0.0.0/8 are two such routes learned from AS 42. gsr7 has gsr2 and gsr6 as IBGP neighbors. It is setting next-hop-self on the BGP routes it advertises to gsr2 and gsr6. gsr7's RID is 192.168.1.7.

gsr2 is sending traffic to 3.3.3.3 and 4.4.4.4, which are located in AS42.

gsr6 is doing TMS on the interface facing gsr2. Example 10-4 shows the configuration for this interface on gsr6.

Example 10-4 *Configuration for the gsr6 Interface Between gsr6 and gsr2*

```
!
ip cef accounting non-recursive
!
interface POS3/3
 ip address 192.168.11.6 255.255.255.0
end
!
```

As mentioned earlier, TMS stores the data it gathers in some files in system:/vfiles/. Example 10-5 shows these files.

Example 10-5 *TMS Data in system:/vfiles/*

```
gsr6#dir system:/vfiles/
Directory of system:/vfiles/

  15  -r--          0            <no date>  tmasinfo
  13  -r--          0            <no date>  tmstats_ascii
  14  -r--          0            <no date>  tmstats_binary
```

One thing to note is that the file size (the third column in Example 10-5) always shows 0. Data is not actually stored in a file; it is dynamically generated as you access the file itself.

As Example 10-6 demonstrates, gsr6's routing table has four connected routes (two network routes, two subnet routes), one static route, and three IS-IS routes (one network, two subnet). gsr6 also has 80,627 BGP routes.

Example 10-6 *Routing Table for gsr6*

```
gsr6#show ip route summary
Route Source    Networks    Subnets    Overhead    Memory (bytes)
connected       2           2          560         640
static          1           0          64          160
isis            1           2          464         480
  Level 1: 0 Level 2: 3
bgp 3402        70910       9717       5160128     12255304
  External: 0 Internal: 80627 Local: 0
internal        824                                965728
Total           71738       9721       5161228     13223008
```

As you can see in Example 10-7, the contents of tmstats_ascii contain the prefixes (directly connected and learned via IGP) shown in Example 10-6.

Example 10-7 *tmstats_ascii File Information About All IGP Routes*

```
gsr6#more system:/vfiles/tmstats_ascii
VERSION 1 |ADDR 172.27.235.75 |AGGREGATION TrafficMatrix.ascii | SYSUPTIME 541175 |
   routerUTC 3212749402 |NTP unsynchronized |DURATION 0|
p| 192.168.1.7/32 |444745 |698 58464 |0 |0
p| 192.168.1.2/32 |444745 |0 |0 |0 |0
p| 192.168.1.6/32 |444745 |0 |0 |0 |0
p| 192.168.12.0/24 |444745 |0 |0 |0 |0
p| 192.168.13.0/24 |444745 |0 |0 |0 |0
p| 192.168.11.0/24 |530312 |713 |47040 |0 |0
```

The highlighted line in Example 10-7 shows the TMS entry for gsr7's router ID. All traffic destined for the IP address 192.168.1.7, as well as traffic destined for all recursive prefixes (BGP prefixes) that resolve to 192.168.1.7, are counted in this line.

All the fields in the highlighted line of output are documented in the next section, but the important ones are as follows:

- The IP address (192.168.1.7/32)

- The number of packets switched toward that prefix (698)

- The total number of bytes in those 698 packets (58464, an average of about 84 bytes per packet)

The byte and packet counters go up whenever a packet is switched toward 192.168.1.7, even if a packet is destined for a BGP route whose next hop is 192.168.1.7.

Example 10-8 shows that the tmasinfo file provides a mapping of all BGP routes to their next hop. The tmasinfo file contains information about all of its 80,627 BGP routes. The output shown here has been truncated for brevity. It makes for pretty boring reading after the first 1200 pages anyway.

Example 10-8 *tmasinfo File Mapping Information About BGP/Next-Hop Routes*

```
gsr6#more system:/vfiles/tmasinfo
VERSION 1 |ADDR 172.27.235.75 |AGGREGATION ASList.ascii |SYSUPTIME 541237 |
  routerUTC 3212749464 |DURATION 0
192.168.1.7/32 |42 |3.0.0.0/8
192.168.1.7/32 |42 |4.0.0.0/8
192.168.1.7/32 |42 |4.0.37.184/30
192.168.1.7/32 |42 |4.2.47.0/25
192.168.1.7/32 |42 |4.2.55.0/24
192.168.1.7/32 |42 |6.0.0.0/8
...
...
```

Note that tmasinfo has no traffic counters; its job is to present the BGP portion of the routing table should you care to examine it. The highlighted lines in Example 10-8 show the tmasinfo entries for 3.0.0.0/8 and 4.0.0.0/8, which are the prefixes that gsr2 is sending traffic toward. The three columns in each of the highlighted lines are the BGP next hop, the next hop AS for that route, and the route itself. These columns are more fully explained in the next section.

Understanding TMS Data Files

tmstats_ascii and tmasinfo share a common header format, even though the data these files carry is different. Table 10-2 breaks down the common header format.

Table 10-2 *TMS Common Header Format*

Field	Description
VERSION 1	The TMS data version—currently 1.
ADDR *address*	The router ID of the router generating the TMS data file.
AGGREGATION *name*	The type of aggregation being performed. tmstats_ascii always says TrafficMatrix.ascii, and tmasinfo always says ASList.ascii.
SYSUPTIME *time*	System uptime in milliseconds.
NTP [**synchronized** | **unsynchronized**]	Seen only in tmstats_ascii. Tells you whether the router is synchronized with an NTP server.
routerUTC *time*	The time of data collection in seconds since 1900/01/01. Because data is gathered by examining this file, the routerUTC timestamp is what time the router thought it was when it started displaying the file in question.
DURATION *time*	The time needed to capture the data, in seconds. This is almost always 0. This time is provided in case it takes a significant amount of time to build the various data files so that you can extrapolate how much traffic might not have been recorded by TMS.

Then there's the data itself. tmasinfo and tmstats_ascii have different formats for the data they contain. Table 10-3 describes each line of tmstats_ascii from the highlighted line of Example 10-7.

Table 10-3 *tmstats_ascii Data Information*

Line	Description
p	Denotes that information in this line applies to an IP prefix rather than a TE tunnel. "p" shows up in the first column if a packet has been received as IP or with a label that was distributed with TDP or LDP. Packets that are received as part of an MPLS TE tunnel are marked with a "t" instead (see Table 10-5).
192.168.1.7/32	IGP prefix being accounted for.
444745	Amount of time (in milliseconds) since the record for this prefix was first created. If the prefix leaves the routing table, all accounting data is lost; when the prefix comes back, the counter starts again.
698	Number of packets received on all internal TMS interfaces for this prefix.
58464	Number of bytes received on all internal TMS interfaces for this prefix.
0	Number of packets received on all external TMS interfaces for this prefix.
0	Number of bytes received on all external TMS interfaces for this prefix.

Table 10-4 describes each line of tmasinfo from Example 10-8.

Table 10-4 *tmasinfo Data Information*

Line	Description
192.168.1.7/32	BGP next hop.
42	For the prefix specified in the next column, the next-hop AS in this route's AS path.
3.0.0.0/8	Prefix learned from the next-hop AS.

Given this information, it is easy to determine how much traffic entered the router on all external interfaces, how much traffic entered the router on all internal interfaces, and where traffic exited.

tmstats_ascii has enough information to do per-exit-point accounting. This gives you your traffic matrix—you know the amount of traffic destined for a particular nonrecursive prefix and the amount of time in which that traffic has arrived, and you can easily compute the traffic rate. In the preceding example, with 698 packets heading toward 192.168.1.7 in the last 444745 milliseconds, this means that the average traffic rate is about 1.5 pps. This isn't the busiest network in the world, but it's good enough to serve as an example here.

Because TMS is pull-based, you can let statistics accumulate on the router for as long as you like. The packet and byte counters are 64-bit counters. So even on an OC-48, which runs at approximately 2.5 Gbps, you only need to pull TMS data once every (2^{64} / (2.5 * 10^9)) seconds, or 234 years, before the counters wrap.

Now for the bad news. TMS stats are stored in a CEF loadinfo structure. CEF is a switching path based on the routing table. This means that when the routing table changes, the CEF table changes. So any data accumulated by CEF counters disappears if the corresponding route disappears. And when the route comes back, the TMS data structure counters are all zeroed out. This means that TMS is good for long-term data collection about general trends, but it's not the device you want to use if you need to make sure that you're measuring every single packet that has ever crossed the interface.

TMS can also track packets sent through TE tunnels. At TE midpoints, tmstats_ascii displays a line like the following:

```
t | 192.168.1.22 21 | 547059 | 44 | 3696 | 0 | 0
```

This information is similar to the information recorded if tmstats_ascii is dealing with packets not destined down a TE tunnel.

Table 10-5 describes the information from the tmstats_ascii output.

Table 10-5   *TE Tunnel Tracking Information from tmstats_ascii*

Field	Description
t	TE tunnel
192.168.1.22	RID of the tunnel tail
21	Tunnel ID
547059	Router uptime at which TE LSP was created
44	Number of packets received on all internal TMS interfaces for this prefix
3696	Number of bytes received on all internal TMS interfaces for this prefix
0	Number of packets received on all external TMS interfaces for this prefix
0	Number of bytes received on all external TMS interfaces for this prefix

Getting TMS Information off the Router

There are three ways to get tmstats_ascii, tmstats_binary, and tmasinfo off the router:

- Use **more file system:/vfiles/**{*filename*} (this is not recommended for retrieving the TMS binary file).

- Use **copy system:/vfiles/tmstats_ascii** {**rcp** | **ftp** | **tftp**} from the CLI to copy the TMS file to a server for analysis.

- Use the FTP client MIB to achieve the same thing as the CLI.

As soon as you've got the TMS info off the router, build a traffic matrix like the one shown in Table 10-1. As soon as you've got that matrix, go forth and build TE tunnels! Search CCO for "traffic matrix statistics," or see Appendix B for more information on TMS.

Using TE Tunnels for Traffic Measurement

So far, you've learned how to use a few Cisco IOS Software accounting tools to measure traffic demands. There is another way that doesn't require rolling out a specific traffic-measurement tool, or any management devices other than what you're already using to monitor router interfaces.

If you want to find out how much traffic is going from one router to another, just build an MPLS TE tunnel between the two routers. If you do that, and you enable autoroute on the tunnel interface, all traffic destined for the tunnel tail or anything behind it traverses the tunnel. Because the tunnel is just an interface, you simply have to check the traffic rate on the interface to see the amount of traffic going from the tunnel headend to the tunnel tail.

The recipe is pretty simple:

Step 1   Deploy 0-bandwidth tunnels with a dynamic path option from ingress node to egress (where ingress and egress are the ingress and egress of your TE cloud).

Step 2   Monitor these interfaces as you would any other interface (using IF-MIB or **show interfaces**).

Step 3   Optionally, resize the tunnels to reflect the amount of bandwidth they're carrying. If you do this, you'll find you've deployed TE tunnels using the strategic online methodology.

It's that easy!

In Figure 10-4, tracking interface utilization on Tunnel0 gives you the amount of traffic destined for Router D and Networks 1, 2, and 3 (because they are behind Router D).

Figure 10-4   *Sample Network for Tracking Tunnel Utilization*

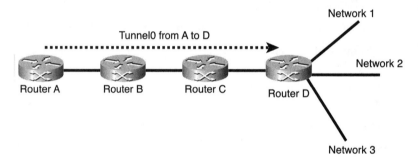

Some existing networks use MPLS TE just to do measurement, without steering traffic down paths other than what the IGP would take. The advantages of doing your measurements using MPLS TE are that you have

- No external data collection box, other than what you're already using to monitor interfaces

- No performance impact, because the per-destination accounting is a by-product of the TE implementation

One thing to keep in mind is that your load-balancing capabilities change. With IP, you inherently load-share traffic across equal-cost paths; with TE, you have to explicitly configure more than one LSP if you want to share traffic across different paths. If you configure a single TE tunnel between two routers and enable autoroute on that tunnel, all traffic between those two routers takes that single tunnel, which of course follows a single physical path. If the traffic between those two routers would normally take multiple equal-cost paths, to achieve the same effect with MPLS TE, you need to configure multiple TE tunnels, across all paths from headend to tail, which that IP traffic would take.

Service Assurance Agent

Bandwidth is only half the story. You've also got to care about delay. Referring back to Figure 10-1, if you want to get from Seattle to San Jose, and you have enough bandwidth only by going via Miami, you probably don't want to take that path. You might prefer to take the path with less available bandwidth, because the cost of obtaining the necessary bandwidth is too much delay.

Cisco IOS Software has a powerful facility for measuring delay called Service Assurance Agent (SAA). You can use SAA to get the measurements for one-way or round-trip delay on a circuit, as well as other performance measurements (HTTP response, DNS response, jitter, and so on), all on a per-DSCP basis.

SAA does a lot more than what is covered in this chapter, but you have enough here to get you started:

- Basic SAA theory and operation
- How to measure two-way delay using ICMP
- How to measure one-way delay using specialized SAA probes

What Is SAA?

SAA grew out of a project known as the Response Time Reporter (RTR). Although officially now named SAA, the RTR configuration syntax is still used.

The basic idea behind SAA is that it can measure the latency of several types of network traffic between any two points. SAA can do this by sending ICMP echo requests, HTTP GET requests, FTP file requests, and several other types of requests.

SAA is made up of two things—probes and responders. They are fairly self-explanatory. A *probe* is something that sends out packets that measure properties of a network, and a *responder* is something that responds to a probe. The device that sends the probe is sometimes called the *client,* and the responder is sometimes called the *server.*

There are several different types of probes. SAA can send probes that measure things as basic as ICMP and as complex as one-way jitter, FTP, HTTP, DLSW, DNS, and DHCP. Complete SAA operations aren't covered in this book, but this section covers ICMP and jitter probes, which is enough to get you started with SAA.

Not all devices can respond to all SAA probes. For example, an ICMP probe is just a ping (an ICMP echo request). An HTTP probe is much the same. It fetches a specific Web page and reports back on how long it took to retrieve the page. You can't send an HTTP probe to a device that's not running a Web server (obviously).

Some probes are meant to be responded to by a specific SAA responder. Specifically, there is a one-way jitter probe that relies on two things:

- The device that is the other end of the probe can recognize and respond to specialized SAA jitter probes.
- The device sending the probe and the device responding to the probe have their clocks synchronized via NTP.

One-way and two-way probes are covered more in the next two sections.

Two basic uses for SAA are

- Measuring delay and jitter between two points in the network (from one POP to another across the WAN, or from a dialup server to a Web farm, for example)
- Measuring delay and jitter between two directly connected routers

The second use is a degenerate case of the first, but in the context of MPLS TE, these two cases have two different applications, so they're listed separately.

It's useful to be able to measure end-to-end delay to get an idea of whether you're violating your Service-Level Agreements (SLAs) to your users. Most networks offer some guarantee on the maximum latency encountered in a network, and SAA is one way to measure that latency.

Those who are serious about SAA measurements often deploy a dedicated SAA router in each POP. A small but powerful router such as the Cisco 3620 can deal with dozens or hundreds of SAA probes, so it's easy to set up a mesh of probes between each POP.

Another way to use SAA is to determine the one-way delay on a link between two routers, as opposed to determining the one-way delay between two arbitrary points in the network. Simply run one-way delay probes between two directly connected neighbors on a physical link rather than across the network.

This gives you a number you can use with the physical-interface command **mpls traffic-eng administrative-weight**. If you want to build delay-sensitive tunnels (see Chapter 3, "Information Distribution"), take the one-way delay, multiply by 10, and set that to the interface administrative weight.

So if you know that a circuit from Dallas to Miami has an unloaded one-way delay of 22 ms, set the administrative weight on the interface to 220.

Multiplying by 10 gives you some room to play with. If you have two links with a delay of 22 ms, but you'd rather prefer one to the other, give one a cost of 220 and the other a cost of 221, or anything up to 229.

SAA can be monitored, maintained, and controlled using Cisco's Internetwork Performance Monitor (IPM) software or via MIBs, but it can also be dealt with purely from the CLI. SAA is geared toward being managed by a MIB. (The CLI output is pretty much an exact duplicate of what's in the MIB, even when it would be nice if the CLI prettied up the output a bit.) But it's certainly possible to use SAA purely from the CLI, especially for something as simple as determining the delay between two points.

If you're going to use the CLI, it's a good idea to read the Cisco Response Time Monitoring (RTTMON) (CISCO-RTTMON-MIB), because it explains a lot about what information the MIB can get for you.

Measuring Two-Way Delay

Measuring two-way delay is just about as simple as it gets. You configure SAA to send an ICMP echo request to a particular destination, and SAA reports back the round-trip time. If you want to find the one-way delay, simply assume that the network is symmetric and divide the reported delay number by 2.

The basic SAA configuration is simple. The following two global configuration lines define an SAA probe:

```
rtr probe-number
  type echo protocol ipIcmpEcho target-addr [source-ipaddr ipaddr]
```

The first line, **rtr 1**, defines the probe. The probe number is simply a number you assign. You can build dozens or hundreds of probes on a router; you number each one separately. You can give RTR probes a number up to 2,147,483,647. If you're going to build an RTR probe for each TE tunnel, just make the RTR probe number the same as the tunnel interface number to keep things straight.

Configuring **rtr** *probe-number* puts you into a submode called **config-rtr**. In that submode, you create an echo probe of type **ipIcmpEcho**, giving it a target IP address and an optional source IP address. This defines a probe that is simply a ping.

After defining the probe, you need to tell it when to run. You have lots of options here (see Appendix B for more information), but the most basic configuration is

```
rtr schedule probe-number start-time now
```

This is done in global configuration mode. It tells the router to periodically initiate the probe, starting now. By default, each probe is sent out every 60 seconds. You can change the probe frequency with the **frequency** *seconds* command:

```
rtr 3
  type echo protocol ipIcmpEcho 192.168.1.14
  frequency 10
```

There's no need to configure an SAA Responder for an ICMP echo probe, because the probe sent out is just a regular ICMP ping.

You can examine the results of an SAA probe with the command **show rtr distributions-statistics** *probe-number,* as shown in Example 10-9.

Example 10-9 **show rtr distributions-statistics 1** *Command Output*

```
vxr15#show rtr distributions-statistics 1
        Captured Statistics
Entry    = Entry Number
StartT   = Start Time of Entry (hundredths of seconds)
Pth      = Path Index
Hop      = Hop in Path Index
Dst      = Time Distribution Index
Comps    = Operations Completed
OvrTh    = Operations Completed Over Thresholds
SumCmp   = Sum of Completion Times (milliseconds)
SumCmp2L = Sum of Completion Times Squared Low 32 Bits (milliseconds)
SumCmp2H = Sum of Completion Times Squared High 32 Bits (milliseconds)
TMax     = Completion Time Maximum (milliseconds)
TMin     = Completion Time Minimum (milliseconds)


Entry StartT  Pth Hop Dst Comps   OvrTh   SumCmp    SumCmp2L   SumCmp2H   TMax   TMin
1     1568    1   1   1   105     0       64541     59035203   0          1662   127
```

Another way to display this information is with the command **show rtr distributions-statistics** *probe-number* **full**, as shown in Example 10-10.

Example 10-10 **show rtr distributions-statistics 1 full** *Command Output*

```
vxr15#show rtr distributions-statistics 1 full
        Captured Statistics
Entry Number: 1
Start Time Index: 20:20:03.000 EST Wed Apr 3 2002
Path Index: 1
Hop in Path Index: 1
Time Distribution Index: 1
Operations Completed: 105
Operations Completed Over Thresholds: 0
Sum of Completion Times (milliseconds): 64541
Sum of Completion Times Squared Low 32 Bits (milliseconds): 59035203
Sum of Completion Times Squared High 32 Bits (milliseconds): 0
Completion Time Maximum (milliseconds): 1662
Completion Time Minimum (milliseconds): 127
```

Examples 10-9 and 10-10 contain the same information; it's just formatted differently. In either case, the interesting information is highlighted. You see

- The number of operations completed (105)
- The sum of completion times (64,541 ms)
- The sum of squared completion times (59,035,203 ms)
- The maximum and minimum completion times (1662 ms and 127 ms, respectively)

The sum of completion times squared is a 64-bit value, stored as two 32-bit values.

Because this is output from an ICMP echo probe, the completion time here is just how long it took the probed device to respond. Not only can you calculate the mean response time (1.66 ms), but you also have the sum of squares, so you can do more advanced statistics on the response time.

Measuring One-Way Delay

Measuring two-way delay isn't always the best way to figure out your network delay. What you really want is one-way delay. You can always configure a two-way delay and divide by 2, but this assumes that the delay is the same in both directions. Networks can have different delays in different directions, because of buffering issues, L2 circuit routing, and so on.

Fortunately, SAA lets you configure a probe that measures one-way delay. The probe configuration here is much like the ICMP probe you've already seen:

```
rtr probe-numer
  type jitter dest-ipaddr dest-addr dest-port dest-port
```

The main difference here is that the probe is of type **jitter**.

You also need to tell the router to actually send the probe. This doesn't change from the ICMP probe:

```
rtr schedule probe-number start-time now
```

There's one more thing you need to do, and that's to configure the SAA Responder. An SAA one-way probe works by putting a timestamp in the packet it sends, sending a probe, and getting a response to its probe that has the timestamp at which the probe was received.

To configure an SAA Responder, you simply use the global command **rtr responder** on the device that is the probe's *dest-addr*. As soon as the responder is enabled, it responds to all probes sent its way.

Because the one-way jitter probe relies on a timestamp, both the probing device and the responding device must have their clocks synchronized; this is generally done using Network Time Protocol (NTP).

As soon as a jitter probe is running, you can see the results of that probe with the command **show rtr collection-statistics** *probe-number,* as shown in Example 10-11.

Example 10-11 show rtr collection-statistics 2 *Command Output*

```
vxr15#show rtr collection-statistics 2
        Collected Statistics

Entry Number: 2
Target Address: 192.168.1.14, Port Number: 2000
Start Time: 20:22:03.000 EST Wed Apr 3 2002
Latest Oper Sense: Unknown
RTT Values:
```

continues

Example 10-11 **show rtr collection-statistics 2** *Command Output (Continued)*

```
NumOfRTT: 244    RTTSum: 70434    RTTSum2: 23198478
Packet Loss Values:
PacketLossSD: 0 PacketLossDS: 0
PacketOutOfSequence: 0  PacketMIA: 36   PacketLateArrival: 0
InternalError: 0       Busies: 11
Jitter Values:
NumOfJitterSamples: 216
MinOfPositivesSD: 35     MaxOfPositivesSD: 40
NumOfPositivesSD: 218    SumOfPositivesSD: 7942   Sum2PositivesSD: 289520
MinOfNegativesSD: 0      MaxOfNegativesSD: 0
NumOfNegativesSD: 0      SumOfNegativesSD: 0      Sum2NegativesSD: 0
MinOfPositivesDS: 1      MaxOfPositivesDS: 47
NumOfPositivesDS: 29     SumOfPositivesDS: 266    Sum2PositivesDS: 9806
MinOfNegativesDS: 1      MaxOfNegativesDS: 1
NumOfNegativesDS: 29     SumOfNegativesDS: 29     Sum2NegativesDS: 29
Interarrival jitterout: 0       Interarrival jitterin: 0
One Way Values:
NumOfOW: 244
OWMinSD: 60     OWMaxSD: 443    OWSumSD: 54182   OWSum2SD: 14670634
OWMinDS: 59     OWMaxDS: 108    OWSumDS: 16252   OWSum2DS: 1135116
```

DS means "from destination to source," and SD means "from source to destination." When you configure a one-way probe, SAA automatically measures in both directions—from the client to the responder and from the responder to the client.

Of particular interest is the set of data highlighted in the output of Example 10-11. Both Round-Trip Time (RTT, in the RTT Values: section) and one-way delay values (in the One Way Values: section) are measured; jitter is also measured. Although jitter is important for understanding the impact on VoIP and other real-time services in your network, for MPLS TE the most useful data is the one-way delay. Table 10-6 shows the breakdown of the data in the One Way Values: section.

Table 10-6 *One Way Values: Section Definition*

Data	Value
NumOfOW	Number of successful one-way probes since the current probe was configured
OWMinSD	Minimum one-way delay from the source (the client) to the destination (the server, or SAA Responder)
OWMaxSD	Maximum one-way delay from the source to the destination
OWSumSD	Sum of one-way delay times from the source to the destination
OWSum2SD	Sum of squares of the one-way delay times from the source to the destination

The data that ends in DS (OWMinDS, OWMaxDS, and so on) is the same information, but from the server to the client.

To compute the mean one-way delay from client to server, simply divide OWSumSD by NumOfOW. In Table 10-6, the mean one-way delay from client to server is 54182 ms / 244 probes, or 222.06 ms.

Configuring DSCP in an SAA Probe

You can control the DSCP byte in any SAA probes. This is useful if you've made different latency guarantees for different classes of service, because you should then be measuring latency in each class. You configure the DSCP using the **tos** keyword, which controls the entire DSCP byte.

Table 10-7 shows each ToS setting you'd use to configure a particular DSCP setting. See the "DiffServ and IP Packets" section in Chapter 6, "Quality of Service with MPLS and MPLS TE," for more information on DSCP. The ToS byte can be configured in either hex or decimal; Table 10-7 shows the hexadecimal configuration.

Table 10-7   *Mapping the ToS Byte to DSCP Values*

DSCP Class Name	ToS Value
Default	0x00
CS1	0x20
CS2	0x40
CS3	0x60
CS4	0x80
CS5	0xA0
CS6	0xC0
CS7	0xE0
AF21	0x48
AF22	0x50
AF23	0x58
AF31	0x68
AF32	0x70
AF33	0x78
AF41	0x88
AF42	0x90
AF43	0x98
EF	0xE8

For example, to create an ICMP echo probe in the EF class, you'd use the configuration shown in Example 10-12.

Example 10-12 *Sample Configuration for an ICMP Echo Probe with EF DSCP*

```
rtr 4
 type echo protocol ipIcmpEcho 192.168.1.14
 tos 0xE8
```

This section has only scratched the surface of what SAA can do. See Appendix B for more information on SAA and its capabilities.

Fine-Tuning MPLS TE Parameters

So far, this chapter has covered network measurements. You have read about both traffic (bandwidth) measurements and delay measurements. Delay and bandwidth measurements help you place tunnels initially or move them around subsequently.

As soon as your tunnels are operational, you might need to customize MPLS TE according to your needs. Cisco IOS Software provides a lot of latitude for you to fine-tune MPLS TE to better suit your network. The default values of the different timers should in most cases be fine. Just in case they are not, knobs are provided for you to tune. This might become more evident as your network grows and traffic increases.

This section doesn't cover all the possible configuration options, just the major ones you might need to deal with as your network and your demands change.

Headend Configuration Knobs

There are three main things you can tweak on a TE tunnel headend, as described in the following sections. These are things you might find you need to change as your network grows or your service requirements change.

mpls traffic-eng reoptimize timers frequency *0-604800* Command

What it does: Sets how often the LSPs on a headend are reoptimized. See the "Tunnel Reoptimization" section in Chapter 4, "Path Calculation and Setup," for more details on this command.

Default setting: 3600 seconds (1 hour)

When to tune it: Lower this number if you want to increase the likelihood of an LSP's finding its way onto a shorter path shortly after a link has come up. A better way to solve this problem, though, might be to use the **mpls traffic-eng reoptimize events link-up** command, although you need to be careful about flapping links. Setting **mpls traffic-eng reoptimize timers frequency** to 0 disables periodic reoptimization. See the "Tunnel Reoptimization" section in Chapter 9 for more information.

Recommendation: Change it if you like, especially if you're not on a Cisco IOS Software release that supports **mpls traffic-eng reoptimize events link-up**. Just be sure to keep an eye on your CPU so that if you've got a headend with a large number of LSPs, it doesn't spend too many cycles on reoptimization.

mpls traffic-eng reoptimize events link-up Command

What it does: In addition to periodically running CSPF for all LSPs regardless of whether anything has changed, enabling this knob runs reoptimization when a link in the TE database has come up.

Default setting: Disabled

When to tune it: Turn this on if you want to converge on a new link as quickly as possible.

Recommendation: This command is generally a good thing to enable, but if you have a link in your network that's constantly flapping, using this command can cause all tunnels to be reoptimized every time that link comes up. This is a useful command to have, so you should definitely consider using it, but be mindful of the impact it can have when you have a problem in your network.

Also, when you enable this command, you might think that you can now disable periodic reoptimization, because event-driven reoptimization will catch all linkup events. This is not quite true. You should still run periodic reoptimization, because conditions exist that might result in a more-optimal LSP path but that this command won't catch (such as a significant increase in available bandwidth on an interface). However, you can run less-frequent periodic reoptimization, because the majority of events that significantly change the network topology are related to links going up and down.

mpls traffic-eng topology holddown sigerr *0-300* Command

What it does: When certain PathErr messages are received because a link went down, those links are marked as unavailable in the TE-DB for some amount of time. This holddown is to prevent headends from being told that the link is down via RSVP when the headends have not yet received an IGP update about the link's being down. If the links were not marked as unavailable in the TE-DB, when the headends try to find another LSP for the tunnel, because the IGP update has not arrived yet, the headends might choose a path over the very link that went down in the first place. This timer is the difference between the amount of time it takes for an RSVP message to get back to the headend and the amount of time the IGP takes to propagate the same information.

Default setting: 10 seconds

When to tune it: Increase this time if it takes your IGP longer than 10 seconds to converge; decrease it if your network has links that flap a lot and your IGP converges quickly when these links change state.

Recommendation: Make sure this number is no lower than the time it takes your IGP to converge. It's probably a good idea to set it to at least 2 * IGP convergence, to give things time to settle down. Your IGP should converge in a small number of seconds, but if you find that your IGP converges in more than 5 seconds, you should think about increasing this value slightly.

Midpoint Configuration Knobs

In addition to having things you can configure on the headend, you can also tweak a few things at a midpoint should you so desire.

mpls traffic-eng link-management timers bandwidth-hold *1-300* Command

What it does: When a Path message comes through, the bandwidth it asks for is temporarily set aside until the corresponding Resv is seen. **mpls traffic-eng link-management timers bandwidth-hold** is Link Manager's timeout on the Path message. When this timeout pops, the bandwidth is no longer held, and it is available for other LSPs to reserve. If the Resv message for the first LSP comes back after the timeout expires, the LSP is still set up. But if a second LSP had come along in the meantime and requested bandwidth after the timeout, that second LSP might have taken bandwidth that the first LSP wanted to use, resulting in a failure of the first LSP.

Default setting: 15 seconds

When to tune it: If you have a big-enough network that Path messages really take 15 seconds or longer to get the corresponding Resv back, you might want to increase this timer. 15 seconds is quite a long time, though, and if you have 15 seconds of setup delay along a path, you likely have underlying problems. Either that, or you have an end-to-end path that's more than 830,000 miles long! Setting this timer lower than the default might help avoid backoff and resignalling if you have LSPs that are churning faster than every 15 seconds. This generally indicates a problem as well, because LSP lifetime should be measured in days, not seconds. The higher this timeout value is set, the more likely you are to have collisions over the same resources if and only if Resv messages are taking a long time to come back.

Recommendation: Leave this knob alone unless you have extenuating circumstances.

mpls traffic-eng link-management timers periodic-flooding *0-3600* Command

What it does: Periodically, if the link bandwidth has changed but has not yet been flooded, the changed information is flooded anyway to bring the rest of the network in sync with the router advertising the links.

Default setting: 180 seconds (3 minutes)

When to tune it: If you have links that are always close to full, and you have lots of relatively little LSPs (LSPs that are small enough that the appearance or disappearance of an LSP will not cross a flooding threshold), tuning this number down might help.

Another option this command gives you is to be able to minimize IGP flooding. If you'd like to keep IGP flooding to an absolute minimum, you could set this timer to 0 and let flooding thresholds and link flaps take care of all the flooding. It's probably a good idea not to disable this command, but instead to stretch it out to something like the full 3600 seconds so that TE information is occasionally flooded to anyone who might have overly stale information.

Recommendation: This is another knob to leave alone, at least to start. If you find that your headends are often out of sync with the bandwidth available on your links, you might want to lower this timer so that it floods more often, but do so cautiously; lots of TE tunnel churn can lead to increased IGP flooding.

mpls traffic-eng flooding thresholds {up | down} *0-100*... Command

What it does: Controls how much available link bandwidth needs to change (in both the up and down directions) for information about that link's bandwidth to be reflooded throughout the network. (See Chapter 3 for a detailed explanation.)

Default setting: 15, 30, 45, 60, 75, 80, 85, 90, 95, 96, 97, 98, 99, and 100 percent, in both the up and down directions

When to tune it: These flooding thresholds are more sensitive to links as they get full. If you have lots of LSPs that reserve 90 percent or more of a link and LSPs that reserve less than 5 percent of a link, you might want to increase the lower-end thresholds to something like 1,2,3,4,5,7,10,12,15.

Recommendation: Yet another knob that is good to know about but bad to fiddle with. Unless you're aware of the sizes and behaviors of your LSPs, you can easily do more harm (lots of unnecessary IGP flooding) than good with this command.

Migrating IS-IS from Narrow to Wide Metrics

As discussed in Chapter 3, IS-IS needs wide metrics enabled in order for MPLS TE to work. However, if you're running IS-IS already, chances are you're not running with wide metrics enabled. You might also have some devices in the network that don't understand wide metrics at all. The tricky bit in migrating from narrow to wide metric support is that you need to do so with as little service disruption as possible. If you just go to some routers and turn on **metric-style wide**, routers that don't understand wide-style metrics will not understand the IS-IS advertisements from the wide-style routers, and your network will break. So the goal here is to enable wide metrics with as little service disruption as possible.

The resolution of this problem is fairly simple if you follow the steps covered next.

Assuming that all routers start at narrow metrics only (the default), you have a couple of choices:

- Moving from narrow to wide metrics in two steps
- Moving from narrow to wide metrics in three steps

Moving from Narrow to Wide Metrics in Two Steps

Moving from narrow to wide metrics in two steps is the shorter of the two migration strategies:

Step 1   Configure all routers to both advertise and accept both old and new TLVs with the command **metric-style transition**. If not all routers in your network understand wide metrics, you'll have to stay at **metric-style transition** until you can get those routers to code that understands wide metrics.

Step 2   Configure all routers to both advertise and accept only new-style TLVs by using **metric-style wide** instead of **metric-style transition**.

The advantage of configuring all routers to both advertise and accept both old and new TLVs is that you have only two steps to go through, so you can migrate to TE faster, with less maintenance windows devoted to migration. The downside is that when you both advertise and accept old- and new-style TLVs, the size of your link-state database (LSDB) doubles. This is not a concern on most networks, but if your network is extremely large, this might be an issue for you. Check the Holding column of the IS-IS Update entry in **show processes memory**, as demonstrated in Example 10-13.

Example 10-13 *Checking the LSDB Size with the* **show process memory** *Command*

```
gsr3#show processes memory | include IS-IS Update | PID
  PID TTY  Allocated     Freed   Holding   Getbufs   Retbufs Process
  126   0   10882888   2950160    219460         0         0 IS-IS Update
```

If doubling this number is of concern to you, consider the other method of transitioning from narrow to wide metrics.

Moving from Narrow to Wide Metrics in Three Steps

This method is longer, but it sidesteps the problem of doubling the size of your LSDB. The steps to do this are as follows:

Step 1   Configure all routers to advertise only old-style TLVs but accept both old and new using the command **metric-style narrow transition**.

Step 2   Configure all routers to advertise new-style TLVs and accept both using the command **metric-style wide transition**.

Step 3   Configure all routers to advertise new-style TLVs and accept only new-style TLVs using the command **metric-style wide**.

This avoids doubling the size of your database, but at the expense of one additional migration step. The choice is up to you. As long as you end up at **metric-style wide**, it doesn't matter how you get there.

The section "Migrating an IS-IS Network to a New Technology" in the "Multiprotocol Label Switching Overview," which you can find on www.cisco.com (also see Appendix B), provides excellent coverage of how to do this.

TE and Multicast

Multicast packets are not sent over TE tunnels, but over the underlying physical infrastructure. This can cause problems with multicast's Reverse-Path Forwarding (RPF) lookup when autoroute is enabled.

Multicast does its forwarding by doing an RPF lookup on the source address of every multicast packet. It forwards that packet only if it came in on the interface that the routing table says is the shortest path to the source.

The problem with this and TE, though, is that if you enable autoroute, your routing table points to a bunch of routes out a TE tunnel, but packets never come in on TE tunnels! Multicast breaks! Bad!

With autoroute disabled, things look like Example 10-14.

Example 10-14 *Routing and RPF Information with No MPLS TE*

```
gsr3#show ip route 192.168.1.7
Routing entry for 192.168.1.7/32
  Known via "isis", distance 115, metric 45, type level-2
  Redistributing via isis
  Last update from 192.168.11.6 on POS2/1, 00:00:26 ago
  Routing Descriptor Blocks:
  * 192.168.11.6, from 192.168.1.7, via POS2/1
      Route metric is 45, traffic share count is 1

gsr3#show ip rpf 192.168.1.7
```

continues

Example 10-14 *Routing and RPF Information with No MPLS TE (Continued)*

```
RPF information for ? (192.168.1.7)
  RPF interface: POS2/1
  RPF neighbor: ? (0.0.0.0)
  RPF route/mask: 192.168.1.7/32
  RPF type: unicast (isis lab)
  RPF recursion count: 0
  Doing distance-preferred lookups across tables
```

In the preceding output, you can see that both the unicast IP route and the RPF entry for 192.168.1.7 are out POS2/1. This is good.

With autoroute enabled on Tunnel1, RPF breaks, as Example 10-15 confirms.

Example 10-15 *Routing and RPF Information with MPLS TE Enabled and Without* **mpls traffic-eng multicast-intact** *Configured*

```
gsr3#show ip route 192.168.1.7
Routing entry for 192.168.1.7/32
  Known via "isis", distance 115, metric 45, type level-2
  Redistributing via isis
  Last update from 192.168.1.7 on Tunnel1, 00:00:11 ago
  Routing Descriptor Blocks:
  * 192.168.1.7, from 192.168.1.7, via Tunnel1
      Route metric is 45, traffic share count is 1

gsr3#show ip rpf 192.168.1.7
RPF information for ? (192.168.1.7) failed, no route exists
```

Luckily, there's an easy solution to this problem. Under your IGP configuration (both OSPF and IS-IS support this), configure **mpls traffic-eng multicast-intact**. This builds the RPF table using the routing table that would be used if you *didn't* have TE tunnels. Problem solved.

The configuration is simple, as Example 10-16 shows.

Example 10-16 *Configuring* **mpls traffic-eng multicast-intact**

```
router ospf 1
  log-adjacency-changes
  passive-interface Ethernet0
  network 0.0.0.0 255.255.255.255 area 0
  mpls traffic-eng router-id Loopback0
  mpls traffic-eng area 0
  mpls traffic-eng multicast-intact
```

The result of configuring **mpls traffic-eng multicast-intact** is that both the unicast routing table and the RPF table are correct, as shown in Example 10-17.

Example 10-17 *Routing and RPF Information with MPLS TE Enabled and* **mpls traffic-eng multicast-intact** *Configured*

```
gsr3#show ip route 192.168.1.7
Routing entry for 192.168.1.7/32
  Known via "isis", distance 115, metric 45, type level-2
  Redistributing via isis
  Last update from 192.168.1.7 on Tunnel1, 00:00:14 ago
  Routing Descriptor Blocks:
  * 192.168.1.7, from 192.168.1.7, via Tunnel1
      Route metric is 45, traffic share count is 1

gsr3#show ip rpf 192.168.1.7
RPF information for ? (192.168.1.7)
  RPF interface: POS2/1
  RPF neighbor: ? (0.0.0.0)
  RPF route/mask: 192.168.1.7/32
  RPF type: unicast (isis lab)
  RPF recursion count: 0
  Doing distance-preferred lookups across tables
```

As you can see, the unicast route for 192.168.1.7 now points down Tunnel1, but the RPF information for that same prefix points down the physical interface, POS2/1. This is as it should be. Multicast traffic now flows properly on your network.

Tunnel Identification Schemes

Chapter 9 discussed tunnel scalability and showed that you can build rather large networks with MPLS TE. Showing that the network can handle as many tunnels as you need it to is one thing. Showing how you actually *support* this setup is quite another.

One question that gets asked a lot is "How do I number my TE tunnels?" All TE tunnels on a router have a number—Tunnel0, Tunnel1, and so on.

The easiest method to assign a number to your tunnel is to assign each tunnel tailend a unique number. This number needs to be tracked in any provisioning systems you have, just like you track IP addresses or anything else. Then each router that terminates a tunnel on that particular tailend uses the assigned tunnel number to do so.

Assume that you're provisioning a full mesh between CRs (see Chapter 9, in the section "Sample Network for Case Studies") and that you assign DenverCR1 the number 1. This means that when you build a TE tunnel from DenverCR2 to DenverCR1, it's named Tunnel1. When you build a TE tunnel from SanDiegoCR3 to DenverCR1, the tunnel on SanDiegoCR3 is also called Tunnel1. And so forth.

Even better, leave yourself some room to grow. Rather than assigning tunnels Tunnel1, Tunnel2, Tunnel3, and so on, do it in multiples of 10. DenverCR1 gets Tunnel10, DenverCR2 gets Tunnel20, and so on.

This method of tunnel number assignment is effective if you want to load-share between routers, where you expand upward past the multiple of 10. So if two TE tunnels exist from BostonCR7 to DenverCR1, call them Tunnel10 and Tunnel11.

Tunnel numbers can range from 0 to 65,535. Even if you allocate tunnel numbers in blocks of 10 (all tunnels to DenverCR1 are Tunnel10, all tunnels to DenverCR2 are Tunnel20, and so on), you still have room for more than 6500 routers in your numbering space! So that's plenty of room.

Another useful thing you can do is put a description on a tunnel.

The **description** command is not TE-specific; it is a property you can give to any interface. Example 10-18 shows the basic configuration.

Example 10-18 *Configuring a Tunnel Description*

```
interface Tunnel1
 description Tunnel1 from GSR3 to GSR7
 ip unnumbered Loopback0
 no ip directed-broadcast
 load-interval 30
 tunnel destination 192.168.1.7
 tunnel mode mpls traffic-eng
 tunnel mpls traffic-eng autoroute announce
 tunnel mpls traffic-eng path-option 10 dynamic
end
```

If you don't give a tunnel a description, the tunnel name that's carried in the RSVP messages is a concatenation of the headend router name and tunnel number, as shown in Example 10-19.

Example 10-19 *Tunnel Name When No Description Is Configured*

```
gsr6#show mpls traffic-eng tunnels role middle brief
Signalling Summary:
    LSP Tunnels Process:         running
    RSVP Process:                running
    Forwarding:                  enabled
TUNNEL NAME                  DESTINATION     UP IF    DOWN IF   STATE/PROT
gsr3_t1                      192.168.1.7     PO1/0    PO1/1     up/up
Displayed 0 (of 1) heads, 1 (of 1) midpoints, 0 (of 0) tails
```

As the output in Example 10-19 reveals, this is Tunnel1 from gsr3. If you put a description on the tunnel interface, the output then looks like Example 10-20.

Example 10-20 *Tunnel Name When a Description Is Configured*

```
gsr6#show mpls traffic-eng tunnels role middle brief
Signalling Summary:
    LSP Tunnels Process:         running
    RSVP Process:                running
    Forwarding:                  enabled
TUNNEL NAME                  DESTINATION      UP IF     DOWN IF   STATE/PROT
Tunnel1 from GSR3 to GSR7    192.168.1.7      PO1/0     PO1/1     up/up
Displayed 0 (of 1) heads, 1 (of 1) midpoints, 0 (of 0) tails
```

You can also display tunnels by name or by a regular expression that matches a name, as shown in Example 10-21.

Example 10-21 **show mpls traffic-eng tunnels role middle name-regexp** *Command Output Using a Regular Expression Displays the Tunnel Description*

```
gsr6#show mpls traffic-eng tunnels role middle name-regexp GSR3
LSP Tunnel Tunnel1 from GSR3 to GSR7 is signalled, connection is up
  InLabel  : POS1/0, 18
  OutLabel : POS1/1, implicit-null
  RSVP Signalling Info:
      Src 192.168.1.3, Dst 192.168.1.7, Tun_Id 1, Tun_Instance 2
    RSVP Path Info:
      My Address: 192.168.11.6
      Explicit Route: 192.168.12.7 192.168.1.7
      Record    Route:  NONE
      Tspec: ave rate=9 kbits, burst=1000 bytes, peak rate=9 kbits
    RSVP Resv Info:
      Record    Route:  NONE
      Fspec: ave rate=9 kbits, burst=1000 bytes, peak rate=Inf
```

The regular expression is a standard Cisco regular expression—the same kind you'd use in BGP, for example. You can find more information on standard Cisco regular expressions by doing a general search at www.cisco.com for the document titled "Regular Expressions."

Combining MPLS TE with MPLS VPNs

One thing that's not been discussed so far is how to use MPLS TE in conjunction with other MPLS services. One of the most popular MPLS applications is MPLS VPNs.

MPLS VPNs use a label of their own (a *service label*) that is carried across your network by one or more *IGP labels*. TE can provide the IGP label, as can LDP.

There's nothing particularly special about using TE LSPs to carry VPN traffic. You use the standard MPLS TE mechanisms to route traffic down a TE tunnel (static routes or autoroute), and MPLS VPNs resolve via a next hop. Both mechanisms end up resolving via the tunnel.

Consider the network shown in Figure 10-5.

Figure 10-5 *Sample Network for the TE+VPN Example*

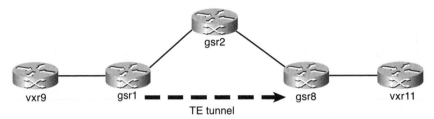

gsr1 and gsr8 are PEs; vxr9 and vxr11 are CEs in the same VPN. gsr2 is just there as a midpoint for the TE LSP. Example 10-22 shows the VPN and TE portions of gsr1's configuration.

Example 10-22 *gsr1 Configuration: VPN and TE Portions*

```
ip vrf test
 rd 100:1
 route-target export 100:1
 route-target import 100:1
...
mpls traffic-eng tunnels
...
interface Tunnel1
 ip unnumbered Loopback0
 no ip directed-broadcast
 tunnel destination 192.168.1.8
 tunnel mode mpls traffic-eng
 tunnel mpls traffic-eng autoroute announce
 tunnel mpls traffic-eng path-option 10 dynamic
 !
...
interface POS0/1
 description interface to vxr9
 ip vrf forwarding test
 ip address 192.168.32.1 255.255.255.0

 !
```

Because Tunnel1 has autoroute enabled, gsr8 (whose loopback address/RID is 192.168.1.8) is automatically reachable via that tunnel, as shown in Example 10-23.

Example 10-23 *Verifying That gsr8 Is Reachable Via Tunnel1*

```
gsr1#show ip route 192.168.1.8
Routing entry for 192.168.1.8/32
  Known via "isis", distance 115, metric 20, type level-2
  Redistributing via isis
  Last update from 192.168.1.8 on Tunnel1, 00:30:24 ago
  Routing Descriptor Blocks:
  * 192.168.1.8, from 192.168.1.8, via Tunnel1
      Route metric is 20, traffic share count is 1
```

The outgoing tunnel label is 16, as shown in Example 10-24.

Example 10-24 *Determining the Outgoing Tunnel Label*

```
gsr1#show mpls traffic-eng tunnels Tunnel1

Name: gsr1_t1                        (Tunnel1) Destination: 192.168.1.8
  Status:
    Admin: up        Oper: up     Path: valid      Signalling: connected

    path option 10, type dynamic (Basis for Setup, path weight 20)

  Config Parameters:
    Bandwidth: 0        kbps (Global) Priority: 7  7   Affinity: 0x0/0xFFFF
    AutoRoute: enabled   LockDown: disabled Loadshare: 0       bw-based
    auto-bw: disabled(0/24) 0  Bandwidth Requested: 0

  InLabel  :  -
  OutLabel : POS0/0, 16
```

As Example 10-25 confirms, this label has been installed in the Forwarding Information Base (FIB).

Example 10-25 *Confirming That the Outgoing Tunnel Label Is Installed in the FIB*

```
gsr1#show ip cef 192.168.1.8
192.168.1.8/32, version 86
0 packets, 0 bytes
  tag information set
    local tag: 28
    fast tag rewrite with Tu1, point2point, tags imposed {16}
  via 192.168.1.8, Tunnel1, 1 dependency
    next hop 192.168.1.8, Tunnel1
    valid adjacency
      tag rewrite with Tu1, point2point, tags imposed {16}
```

Next, look at the VPN information in Example 10-26, which makes things simple; only two
routes exist in the VPN routing table.

Example 10-26 *VPN Information*

```
gsr1#show ip route vrf test
Codes: C - connected, S - static, I - IGRP, R - RIP, M - mobile, B - BGP
       D - EIGRP, EX - EIGRP external, O - OSPF, IA - OSPF inter area
       N1 - OSPF NSSA external type 1, N2 - OSPF NSSA external type 2
       E1 - OSPF external type 1, E2 - OSPF external type 2, E - EGP
       i - IS-IS, L1 - IS-IS level-1, L2 - IS-IS level-2, ia - IS-IS inter area
       * - candidate default, U - per-user static route, o - ODR

Gateway of last resort is not set

B    192.168.27.0/24 [200/0] via 192.168.1.8, 00:39:42
C    192.168.32.0/24 is directly connected, POS0/1
```

As Example 10-27 shows, gsr1 has learned that 192.168.27.0/24 in the VPN routing and
forwarding instance (VRF) called **test** has a next hop of 192.168.1.8 and an outgoing label
of 21.

Example 10-27 *Information Learned Via BGP for the **test** VRF on gsr1*

```
gsr1#show ip bgp vpnv4 vrf test label
   Network          Next Hop        In label/Out label
Route Distinguisher: 100:1 (test)
   192.168.27.0     192.168.1.8     nolabel/21
   192.168.32.0     0.0.0.0         31/aggregate(test)
```

Consider the following points:

- gsr1 uses label 16 out interface POS0/0 to reach 192.168.1.8—the tunnel1 interface.
- gsr1 uses label 21 to reach 192.168.27.0/24 in the VRF test.
- The next hop for 192.168.27.0/24 is 192.168.1.8.

Given these points, it only makes sense that you'd use label 16 (the TE LSP) to get to gsr8,
right?

Right. And that's exactly how it works, as Example 10-28 confirms.

Example 10-28 *CEF Table for VRF Routes, Using a TE Tunnel*

```
gsr1#show ip cef vrf test 192.168.27.0
192.168.27.0/24, version 7
0 packets, 0 bytes
  tag information set
    local tag: VPN route head
    fast tag rewrite with Tu1, point2point, tags imposed {16 21}, wccp tag 92
  via 192.168.1.8, 0 dependencies, recursive
    next hop 192.168.1.8, Tunnel1 via 192.168.1.8/32
    valid adjacency
    tag rewrite with Tu1, point2point, tags imposed {16 21}
```

The {16 21} means that gsr1 puts two labels on the packet—16 on the top and 21 under that. This means that when the packet leaves gsr1 destined for vxr11, it looks like Figure 10-6.

Figure 10-6 *VPN Packets in a TE Tunnel*

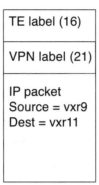

Static routes also work. If you disable autoroute on Tunnel1 and install **ip route 192.168.1.8 255.255.255.255 Tunnel1** on gsr1, things look much the same, as you can see in Example 10-29.

Example 10-29 *Routing and CEF Entries Using Static Routes*

```
gsr1#show ip route 192.168.1.8
Routing entry for 192.168.1.8/32
  Known via "static", distance 1, metric 0 (connected)
  Routing Descriptor Blocks:
  * directly connected, via Tunnel1
      Route metric is 0, traffic share count is 1

gsr1#show ip cef 192.168.1.8
192.168.1.8/32, version 115, attached
0 packets, 0 bytes
  tag information set, unshareable
    local tag: 28
    fast tag rewrite with Tu1, point2point, tags imposed {16}
  via Tunnel1, 1 dependency
    valid adjacency
    tag rewrite with Tu1, point2point, tags imposed {16}

gsr1#show ip cef vrf test 192.168.27.0
192.168.27.0/24, version 7
0 packets, 0 bytes
  tag information set
    local tag: VPN route head
    fast tag rewrite with Tu1, point2point, tags imposed {16 21}, wccp tag 92
  via 192.168.1.8, 0 dependencies, recursive
    next hop 192.168.1.8, Tunnel1 via 192.168.1.8/32
    valid adjacency
    tag rewrite with Tu1, point2point, tags imposed {16 21}
```

Any traffic that needs to get from gsr1 to gsr8 uses the TE LSP. It doesn't matter whether that traffic is IP or MPLS; if it needs to get to 192.168.1.8 or something that resolves via that address, that traffic is sent down the TE LSP.

A TE Tunnel Per VRF

Rather than taking advantage of MPLS's LSP hierarchy, some people want to build a TE LSP *per VPN* between a pair of CEs. In other words, rather than letting all VPN traffic between gsr1 and gsr8 share the same tunnel, they want each VPN to have its own LSP.

A TE tunnel per VRF is often not a good idea. If you have more traffic between gsr1 and gsr8 than you can fit in a single LSP (such as if you want to make a 200 Mb reservation and you have two OC-3s between gsr1 and gsr8), build two TE LSPs. But the idea here is that TE LSPs transport core traffic; they're not really for per-user traffic. Also, besides scaling horribly, a per-VPN LSP makes little to no sense. What does it buy you? Yes, each customer is in its own TE LSP, but so what? That's like building a network to carry OC-3s by laying dozens of strands of dark fiber, each carrying its own OC-3, rather than grooming 64 OC-3s into a single OC-192. Hierarchy is *good*. Use it.

On the other hand, there might be the occasional legitimate reason to have separate TE tunnels for services between the same pair of routers. For example, if you want to offer strict QoS guarantees for a VPN service, it might be easier to do this with multiple TE tunnels. Just make sure that before you start provisioning TE tunnels on a per-service basis, you have both a justification for doing so and a handle on the scalability aspects.

LDP on a Tunnel Interface

You might have noticed in the previous section that Tunnel1 on gsr1 has **mpls ip** enabled. This turns on TDP or LDP on the tunnel interface.

This is not strictly necessary in the network illustrated in Figure 10-5, but it is necessary when the TE tunnel does not run from PE to PE, but instead from P to P. Expanding the network shown in Figure 10-5 to something like Figure 10-7, where gsr1 and gsr8 are PEs, but gsr2 and gsr5 have TE LSPs to each other, you need TDP or LDP over the TE tunnel.

Figure 10-7 *Expansion of the Network Shown in Figure 10-5, with the Need for TDP or LDP Over the TE Tunnel*

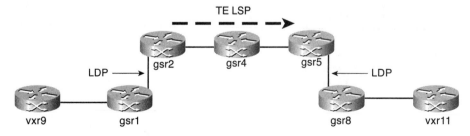

Enabling TDP or LDP on the TE tunnel with the command **mpls ip** is necessary here. If you think about the packet path, packets leave gsr1 with an LDP-derived label on them. This labeled packet gets to gsr2. gsr2 needs to take this packet and put it down the TE tunnel that terminates on gsr5.

Figure 10-8 shows what the packet at each hop looks like.

Figure 10-8 *Packet Path and Label Stacks Without LDP Over the TE Tunnel*

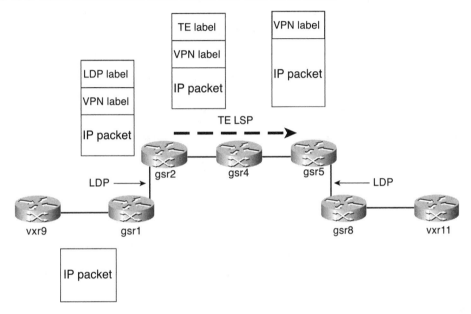

gsr5 isn't the egress PE, so it doesn't know what to do with the VPN label. As a result, it drops or misroutes the packet. For this reason, an LDP label must exist on the packet when it gets to gsr5. You can't have just a TE label and a VPN label, because by the time the packet gets to gsr5, the TE label will have been removed already because of penultimate hop popping, and the only label gsr5 would see is a VPN label.

With LDP on the TE tunnel, the packet at each hop then looks like Figure 10-9.

Figure 10-9 *Packet Path and Label Stacks with TE Over the LDP Tunnel*

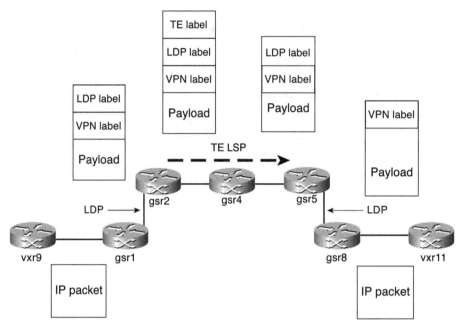

gsr2 and gsr5 form an LDP neighbor relationship so that gsr2 can do the following:

- Swap the incoming top label (from gsr1) for the LDP label that gsr5 wants to see
- Push the TE LSP on the packet and send the packet down the TE LSP

When gsr5 gets the packet, it will only have the LDP label on it. gsr5 will switch the packet according to the value in that label and, therefore, forward the packet to gsr8.

Thus the need for LDP. Or TDP; it works the same way. You just configure **mpls ip** on a TE tunnel interface, just like you would on any other interface.

And, of course, you almost always have a TE tunnel from gsr5 to gsr2, also with the same **mpls ip** configuration. If for some reason you have only a TE LSP from gsr1 to gsr5, you need to tell gsr5 to listen to the LDP hello messages that gsr5 is sending. You do that by configuring **mpls ldp discovery targeted-hello accept** on gsr5. This command can take an ACL specifying the RID of the peers you're willing to accept targeted hellos from; it's a good idea to use the ACL so that you don't open yourself to forming LDP sessions with devices you shouldn't.

You should generally have tunnels in both directions, so you shouldn't need to configure **mpls ldp discovery targeted-hello accept** anywhere in your network.

Deployment Possibilities

One thing that you haven't seen yet is an example of how MPLS TE can be applied to solve specific problems in a network.

This section covers just that—the application of MPLS TE to solve different types of problems. This section has three main pieces:

- Applications of tactical TE (two examples)
- Using MPLS TE only for protection
- Using MPLS TE for unequal-cost one-hop load balancing

Why is there no example of strategic (full-mesh) TE? It's not that strategic TE isn't useful, and it's certainly not that strategic TE isn't being deployed in the real world. It's that as soon as you have strategic TE, there's not much to it besides maintenance tasks—periodically changing your tunnel layout in accordance with traffic demands. Although this process is not trivial, the choices you can make in this area were covered fairly well in Chapter 9. This section instead covers a few applications of MPLS TE to solve specific problems, rather than the full general solution that strategic TE gives you.

Applications of Tactical TE

Throughout this book, you have read about the possibility of using tactical TE to solve specific congestion problems. Here are two real-world examples the authors have dealt with in which tactical TE was effectively used to solve problems.

Although these examples are real-world, done on actual networks with actual routers and by actual customers, we don't disclose the customer names. Let's call them FooNet and BarNet. The topologies have been changed somewhat, but the basic application of MPLS TE, and its effectiveness as a solution, remain the same.

FooNet: Bandwidth on Order

FooNet is a large national U.S. ISP. The northeast portion of their backbone network looks like a ring of routers, as shown in Figure 10-10.

Figure 10-10 *FooNet's Northeast Backbone*

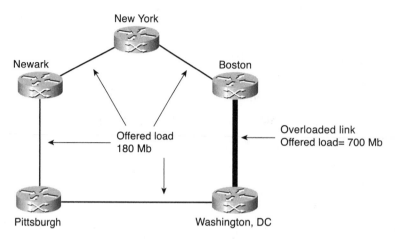

All links in this network are OC-12, and OC-48s are on order. Most of the links are running at about 30 percent utilization (a load of 180 Mb), except for the link from Boston to Washington. The Boston→Washington link is 100 percent full, and it constantly drops packets. It turns out that the offered load on the Boston→Washington link is a persistent 700 Mb, and as you probably know, an OC-12 has a nominal capacity of about 600 Mbps. Of course, 700 Mbps is bigger than 600 Mbps. This results in roughly 14 percent packet loss for any traffic that tries to cross the link from Boston to Washington. Traffic demands aren't going away anytime soon, and the OC-48s that can eliminate this problem aren't due to arrive for months.

What to do? They can't send all Boston→Washington traffic via New York, because all links in the picture are the same speed. Doing that would only congest the Boston→New York→Newark →Pittsburgh→Washington path. Adjusting link metrics is tricky, too. Changing link metrics would affect not just the traffic in this small corner of their network, but also how traffic from other parts of the network enters the Northeast. It's certainly possible to solve this problem with link metric adjustment, but it's not easy.

The solution is MPLS TE. They simply build two TE tunnels from Boston to Washington— one via the directly connected link, and one in the other direction. Autoroute is enabled on both tunnels. The directly connected TE tunnel (called the short tunnel) and the other tunnel (called the long tunnel) are shown in Figure 10-11.

NOTE   Why two TE tunnels? Recall from Chapter 5, "Forwarding Traffic Down Tunnels," in the "Load Sharing" section, that a router does not load-share between an IGP path and a TE tunnel for the same destination. If all FooNet did were to build the long tunnel, all traffic to Washington would be sent down that tunnel, and that wouldn't solve the problem. So, two tunnels.

Figure 10-11 *Applying MPLS TE to FooNet*

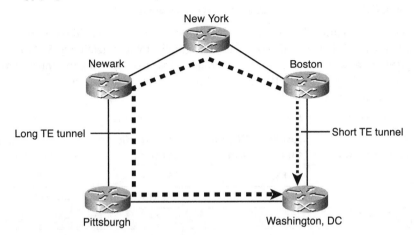

Because the short tunnel is a lower-latency path than the long tunnel, it's desirable to send as much traffic as possible down the short tunnel. The tunnels are set up in a 3:1 ratio—the short tunnel reserves 3 times as much bandwidth as the long tunnel. This has the net effect of taking the 700 Mb of traffic from Boston to Washington and sending 25 percent of it (185 Mb) down the long tunnel and 75 percent of it (525 Mb) down the short tunnel (see Figure 10-12).

Figure 10-12 *Unequal Bandwidth Distribution in FooNet*

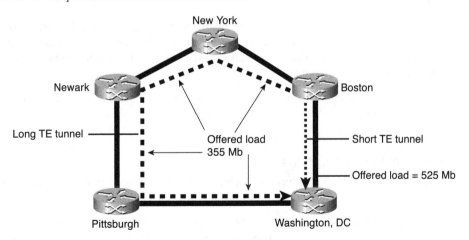

Although 525 Mb is still a little full for an OC-12 (88 percent utilization—a link that, when full, has increased delays and periodic drops because of bursts), 88 percent full is a lot better than 117 percent full (700 Mb over a 600-Mbps link). And the long path, which went from

a utilization of 180 Mb to 355 Mb, is now slightly over 50 percent full, which is empty enough that traffic down that path still receives good service.

Why 3:1? Splitting the bandwidth 50:50 down each tunnel would send 350 Mb of additional traffic across the long path, bringing its total utilization to 530 Mb. This isn't good, because this would come dangerously close to congesting the entire Northeast network! Consider Table 10-8, which shows possible load-sharing ratios and the traffic pattern that results from them.

Table 10-8   *Possible Load-Sharing Ratios and the Resulting Traffic Patterns*

Ratio (Short:Long)	Additional Traffic on Long Path	Total Traffic on Long Path	Total Traffic on Short Path
1:1	350 Mb	530 Mb	350 Mb
2:1	233 Mb	413 Mb	467 Mb
3:1	175 Mb	355 Mb	525 Mb
4:1	140 Mb	320 Mb	560 Mb
7:1	88 Mb	268 Mb	612 Mb

3:1 also has the advantage of fitting exactly into CEF's load-sharing limits. Also covered in Chapter 5, the 2:1 and 4:1 ratios would really end up as something like 10:5 and 13:3, respectively. This isn't a big deal, but because either 3:1 or 4:1 seems to be acceptable in this situation, you might as well go with the one that fits best into the load-sharing algorithm.

Also, because this is a tactical TE situation, the actual bandwidth that is reserved on these tunnels doesn't matter. All that matters is the *ratio* of bandwidths between the two tunnels. So, for simplicity's sake, the long tunnel reserves 1 kbps of bandwidth, and the short tunnel reserves 3 kbps of bandwidth.

When the OC-48s come in, the tunnels are removed. There's no need for TE if you're trying to put 700 Mb down a link that has a capacity of 2.5 Gb.

BarNet: Same Problem, More Paths

You've seen how FooNet solved its problem. Nice, elegant, and simple. Now look at a more complex scenario—BarNet—and see how TE also solves that problem.

BarNet has the same fundamental problem as FooNet—links are being asked to carry more than they can hold. Figure 10-13 shows BarNet's network.

Figure 10-13 *BarNet's International Links*

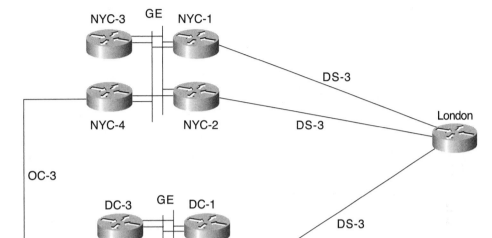

The New York (NYC) POP has four routers, as does the Washington (DC) POP. Between routers in each POP are two Gigabit Ethernet segments. The DS-3s from NYC-1 to London and NYC-2 to London are both overloaded—60 Mb of offered load is being put down each 45-Mbps link. That's 133 percent oversubscription, which is definitely not a good thing. All other links are effectively empty, including the DS-3 from DC-2 to London. The goal is to move some of the traffic from the NYC DS-3s to the DC DS-3.

The first pass at a solution is to build a TE tunnel from NYC-1 to London across the short path and another across the long path, and a similar pair of TE tunnels from NYC-2 to London. Figure 10-14 shows this first-pass solution.

Bandwidth is reserved in a 1:1 ratio so that 30 Mb of the 60 Mb of London-bound traffic is sent across the link between NYC-2 and London and the remaining 30 Mb is sent across the link between DC-2 and London. A 2:1 ratio would also work here, sending 40 Mb across the NYC-2→London link and 20 Mb across the DC-2→London link.

This solution works, but it's inefficient. Traffic can enter the NYC POP via NYC-4 (which is connected to other POPs and routers, although that's not shown in the figure), get forwarded via IP to NYC-2, and get encapsulated in a tunnel that goes the long way to London—via NYC-4. So packets end up crossing NYC-4, and the Gigabit Ethernet switches twice.

Figure 10-14 *First Pass at Fixing BarNet's Problem*

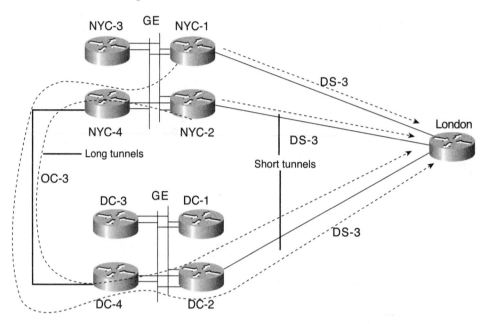

Is this a problem? No, not really. It adds some delay, but only minimal delay; coming into and out of a local subnet twice wouldn't even be noticed when compared to the delay of an international DS-3. Traceroutes would show NYC-4 twice, which might or might not be a consideration.

It turns out that BarNet is satisfied with running the tunnels shown in Figure 10-14. A more optimal solution would be to also run tunnels from NYC-3 and NYC-4 to London so that traffic won't have to hairpin through NYC-2. Given the relatively massive amount of bandwidth available in the POP and the minimal delay required to go into and out of the same router and across a LAN link, optimizing this tunnel further wouldn't have much of a noticeable impact on user traffic.

A lot can be done with the tactical methodology. It all depends on how much work you want to put into it. In the BarNet case especially, all sorts of little optimizations can be made, such as experimenting with where the TE tunnels terminate, which necessitates playing with the autoroute metric or perhaps using static routes. Those applications aren't covered here, because there are probably a dozen little things that can be done differently in this picture that might make things more efficient. None of them have the immediate payoff of the simple solution, though.

The point to take away from all this is that tactical MPLS TE can and does work. The basic tenet is simple: If you add some TE tunnels to the router that is the headend of a congested link, you gain a large amount of control over where you can put traffic that might have run across that link. Just remember to pay close attention to make sure you don't create a problem somewhere else. Also remember to remove these tunnels when they're no longer needed.

TE for Protection

Some networks have no need to send traffic across paths other than the IGP shortest path. For these networks, there might be little to no advantage to deploying MPLS TE in either a strategic or tactical design. A full mesh of TE tunnels doesn't really have a problem to solve, and similarly, there's so much bandwidth in the network that there's little chance of tactical TE's being of any significant use.

There's still something MPLS TE can buy you. You can use MPLS TE purely for protection. As you saw in Chapter 7, "Protection and Restoration," MPLS TE's Fast Reroute (FRR) can be used in place of SONET's Automatic Protection Switching (APS). FRR has several advantages over APS. These are discussed in Chapter 7 and therefore aren't discussed here.

Using MPLS TE purely for protection might seem like a hack, or perhaps an improper use of TE. It's not. Just as any technology evolves over time, MPLS TE has evolved from a tool purely used to send traffic along paths other than the IGP shortest path into a tool that can be used to minimize packet loss much quicker than the IGP can, without the tremendous expense (in both circuits and equipment) of APS.

The idea here is simple. Create one-hop TE tunnels (that is, tunnels between two directly connected routers) that reserve minimal bandwidth, and then protect the links these tunnels go over with FRR link protection.

Consider the network shown in Figure 10-15. It is a full mesh of OC-48 circuits between routers. There is a link from Router A to Router B, from Router A to Router C, and from Router B to Router C.

Figure 10-15 *Simple Network Without Any Protection*

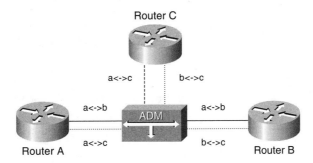

This is a simplified SONET network; there's only one ADM. In real life, there would probably be more than one ADM in a SONET network, but the protection principles are the same.

Currently, this network has no protection capabilities. Protection is often a desirable thing, because it minimizes packet loss. This becomes more and more important the more SLAs you have and the more VoIP traffic you carry.

There are two ways to protect the traffic in this network. One is with APS, and the other is with FRR. First we'll take a quick look at APS so that you can contrast it with FRR. The next section assumes that you know how APS works. For more information on APS, see Appendix B.

SONET APS

Figure 10-16 shows a simplified APS network. It's the same network as in Figure 10-15, but with APS Working and Protect (W and P) circuits between all routers.

Figure 10-16 *Simple APS Setup*

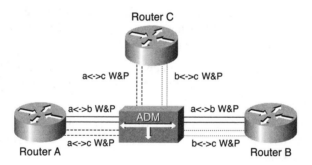

Figure 10-16 shows a Working circuit and a Protect circuit between each pair of routers. There's a Working circuit and a Protect circuit between Router A and Router B, between Router A and Router C, and between Router B and Router C. This is a total of six circuits (A↔B Working, A↔B Protect, A↔C Working, A↔C Protect, B↔C Working, B↔C Protect) consuming 12 router interfaces.

If any one of the Working circuits goes down, the router quickly detects this failure and switches over to the Protect circuit. However, if one of the routers in this picture fails, APS doesn't do any good, because both Working and Protect terminate on the same router. FRR link protection has the same problem, but FRR node protection can alleviate this problem (although not in this simple picture).

If you would deploy APS as shown in Figure 10-16, you can easily use link protection to replace APS.

Using Link Protection Instead of APS

APS definitely has advantages over no protection at all, but at a cost. Look at how you might replace APS with MPLS TE Fast Reroute to achieve the same or better protection.

Figure 10-15 is the basic unprotected version of this network. Figure 10-17 shows what this network looks like from a routing perspective, with the ADM removed.

Figure 10-17 *Routing View of Figure 10-15*

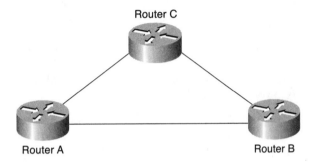

Adding MPLS TE for FRR to this network means adding a total of 12 LSPs—six protected LSPs and six protection LSPs. Two things to remember here are

- Using MPLS TE purely for link protection means building one-hop LSPs (to the router on the other end of a directly connected link).

- TE LSPs are unidirectional, so you need two LSPs for a given link—one from each router to the other one.

This means that there are six one-hop primary LSPs:

- Router A to Router B
- Router B to Router A
- Router A to Router C
- Router C to Router A
- Router B to Router C
- Router C to Router B

Figure 10-18 shows these LSPs.

Figure 10-18 *Six Primary LSPs*

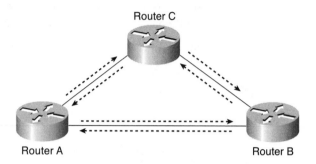

Of course, these LSPs by themselves do no good. It's only when you protect them that they add any value to your network.

In addition to the six primary LSPs, this network needs six protection LSPs. The protection LSPs are all doing link protection, and as such, they must terminate on the router at the other end of the protected link. Figure 10-19 shows the necessary protection LSPs. These LSPs have the same sources and destinations as the primary LSPs, but take different paths from the primary LSPs to get to the tunnel tails.

Figure 10-19 *Six Protection LSPs*

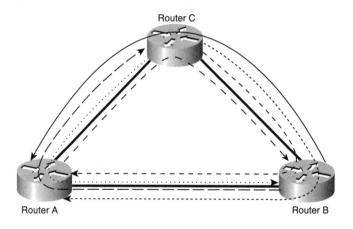

Put all together, there are a total of 12 LSPs in the network, as shown in Figure 10-20.

Figure 10-20 *12 LSPs*

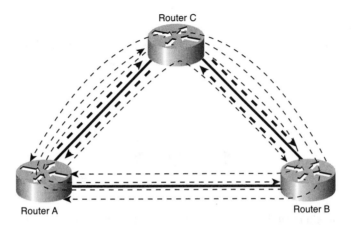

That's all you need to protect the directly connected links. Sure, the picture looks a little messy. But look back at Figure 10-15; each router has only two connections to the ADM instead of four. So if you do the extra work of dealing with the 12 LSPs (six protected, six protection), you have cut your necessary port requirements in half. This effectively doubles your port density. Are 12 LSPs too much to pay for this? The choice is up to you.

TE for Unequal-Cost One-Hop Load Balancing

As you've already read (in Chapter 5), MPLS TE gives you the ability to do unequal-cost load balancing between two or more TE tunnels. Much like using FRR to replace APS, you can use MPLS TE one-hop tunnels to achieve unequal-cost load balancing between directly connected routers.

Suppose you have a setup like the one shown in Figure 10-21.

Figure 10-21 *Two Parallel Links of Different Bandwidths*

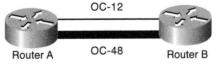

If you want to send traffic from Router A to Router B across both links, how do you do it? With IP, it's difficult to load-balance properly between these two links. If you give both links the same cost, they'll both carry the same amount of traffic. This means that if you have 2 Gb of traffic to go from Router A to Router B, you'll end up sending 1 Gb over the

OC-48 link (leaving ~1.5 Gb of unused bandwidth) and 1 Gb over the OC-12 link (which is about 400 Mb more than the OC-12 link can handle).

There's a simple solution to this problem. All you have to do is build two TE tunnels from A to B—one across the OC-12 and one across the OC-48. Load-balance between the two in a 4:1 ratio, and you'll end up sending approximately 500 Mb down the OC-12 and 2 Gb down the OC-48, as shown in Figure 10-22.

Figure 10-22 *Load Sharing Over Links of Disparate Bandwidth with One-Hop TE Tunnels*

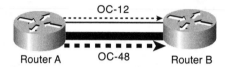

As you might recall from the FooNet case study or the "Load Sharing" section of Chapter 5, you won't get exactly 4:1, but more like 12:4 (so, 3:1). Even though the ratios aren't perfect, you still end up with a much neater solution than if you tried to solve the problem using IP.

Summary

This chapter demonstrated some of the things you can do with MPLS TE. The previous chapter discussed how you can scale MPLS TE across your network. Between these two chapters, you should have plenty of tools, knobs, options, and information with which to design and deploy your network.

This chapter covers the following topics:

- Common Configuration Mistakes
- Tools for Troubleshooting MPLS TE Problems
- Finding the Root Cause of the Problem

CHAPTER 11

Troubleshooting MPLS TE

The other chapters in this book cover various aspects of MPLS TE—signalling, forwarding, design, and deployment. However, this book would be seriously lacking if it didn't discuss troubleshooting as the final thing you need to understand before deploying MPLS TE. If you can deploy and design something, that's great, but if you can't troubleshoot it after you've rolled it out, you're just asking for trouble.

When it comes to troubleshooting, for any problem ranging from a car stalling when idling to MPLS TE tunnels not coming up, the basic rules for handling the problem are essentially the same:

- **Get organized**—Gather the data required to solve the problem and become well versed in the tools available for gathering the required information. This chapter describes the commonly used **show** and **debug** commands that are used to troubleshoot MPLS TE problems, where to use these commands, and when to use them.

- **Be systematic**—Don't jump to Step 3 without going through Steps 1 and 2 first.

- **Break up large problems into smaller ones**—Use the "divide and conquer" approach when the problem is large enough to be broken into subproblems.

This chapter assumes that you are well versed in the various components of MPLS TE introduced throughout this book. Troubleshooting MPLS TE also requires in-depth knowledge of your Interior Gateway Protocol (IGP), either OSPF or IS-IS. The next component that is useful for troubleshooting MPLS TE problems is knowledge of how MPLS forwarding works with Cisco Express Forwarding (CEF) (introduced in Chapter 2, "MPLS Forwarding Basics"). Last but not least is familiarity with the Cisco command-line interface (CLI).

All the examples in this chapter are based on the sample topology shown in Figure 11-1.

Figure 11-1 shows the IP addressing used in this sample network. The router IDs (RIDs), which are also the loopback addresses, are in parentheses above or below the routers. For example, 7200a's RID is 4.4.4.4.

The subnet address of each link is of the form 10.0.*x.y,* and each link has a 24-bit mask. For example, the link between 7200a and 12008a is 10.0.3.0/24, the IP address of 7200a's side of the link is 10.0.3.4 (because 7200a's RID is 4.4.4.4), and 12008a's side of the link has the address 10.0.3.5 (because 12008a's RID is 5.5.5.5).

Figure 11-1 *IP Addressing Used in the Sample Network*

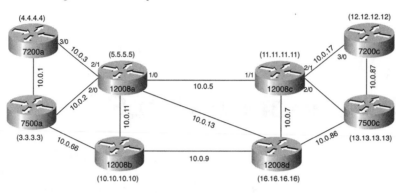

(y.y.y.y)   Router ID
10.0.x.y/24   Link IP subnet (example 10.0.3), y is from router-id,
              7200a address on 10.0.3 subnet is 10.0.3.4 because y=4

Most of the troubleshooting scenarios revolve around a single TE tunnel. 7200a is the headend of this tunnel, tunnel1, which is referred to as the *primary tunnel*. 7200c is the tunnel's tail. The rest of the LSRs shown are potential midpoints for this tunnel.

When there are no failures in the sample network, the primary tunnel path is 7200a→12008a→12008c→7200c. This is shown in the highlighted text of Example 11-1.

Example 11-1 *Configuration of the Primary Tunnel—tunnel1 on 7200a*

```
7200a#show running-config interface tunnel1
Building configuration...

Current configuration : 425 bytes
!
interface Tunnel1
 description Primary tunnel 7200a->12008a->12008c->7200c
 ip unnumbered Loopback0
 no ip directed-broadcast
 tunnel destination 12.12.12.12
 tunnel mode mpls traffic-eng
 tunnel mpls traffic-eng autoroute announce
 tunnel mpls traffic-eng priority 7 7
 tunnel mpls traffic-eng bandwidth  100
 tunnel mpls traffic-eng path-option 5 explicit name primary
 tunnel mpls traffic-eng path-option 6 dynamic
end

7200a#show ip explicit-paths name primary
PATH primary (strict source route, path complete, generation 6)
    1: next-address 10.0.3.5
    2: next-address 10.0.5.11
    3: next-address 10.0.17.12
    4: next-address 12.12.12.12
```

Example 11-1 *Configuration of the Primary Tunnel—tunnel1 on 7200a (Continued)*

```
7200a#show mpls traffic-eng tunnels tunnel1

Name: Primary tunnel 7200a->12008a->12... (Tunnel1) Destination: 12.12.12.12
  Status:
    Admin: up          Oper: up      Path: valid       Signalling: connected

    path option 5, type explicit primary (Basis for Setup, path weight 3)
    path option 6, type dynamic

  Config Parameters:
    Bandwidth: 100      kbps (Global) Priority: 7  7   Affinity: 0x0/0xFFFF
    Metric Type: TE (default)
    AutoRoute: enabled   LockDown: disabled  Loadshare: 100      bw-based
    auto-bw: disabled

  InLabel  :  -
  OutLabel : POS3/0, 12325
  RSVP Signalling Info:
       Src 4.4.4.4, Dst 12.12.12.12, Tun_Id 1, Tun_Instance 38
    RSVP Path Info:
      My Address: 4.4.4.4
      Explicit Route: 10.0.3.5 10.0.5.11 10.0.17.12 12.12.12.12
      Record   Route:   NONE
      Tspec: ave rate=100 kbits, burst=1000 bytes, peak rate=100 kbits
    RSVP Resv Info:
      Record   Route:   NONE
      Fspec: ave rate=100 kbits, burst=1000 bytes, peak rate=Inf
  Shortest Unconstrained Path Info:
    Path Weight: 3 (TE)
    Explicit Route: 10.0.3.5 10.0.5.11 10.0.17.12 12.12.12.12
  History:
    Tunnel:
      Time since created: 4 hours, 52 minutes
      Time since path change: 9 minutes, 29 seconds
    Current LSP:
      Uptime: 9 minutes, 29 seconds
    Prior LSP:
      ID: path option 5 [34]
      Removal Trigger: path verification failed
```

The IGP used in the sample network is OSPF. As a result, some of the commands used during troubleshooting might be OSPF-specific. However, IS-IS commands are also shown where appropriate.

Common Configuration Mistakes

By now, you should understand how to configure MPLS TE. Although a basic MPLS TE configuration is simple, there are lots of things to type, and it's easy to get one or two things wrong. This section presents problems that can arise from common configuration mistakes.

Portions of the configuration are highlighted to call your attention to potential problem areas. MPLS TE configuration can be divided into two parts:

- Common configuration (needed on all participating LSRs)
- Headend configuration (needed at the tunnel headends only)

Common Configuration on All MPLS TE Routers

Common configuration has three parts:

- Global configuration
- Interface-level configuration
- Routing protocol configuration

Global Configuration

Two commands are required on LSRs that are participating in MPLS TE:

```
ip cef {distributed}
mpls traffic-eng tunnels
```

These commands, and the effects of not having them, are covered in the following two sections.

ip cef {distributed} Command

The **ip cef** command configures CEF forwarding on the LSR. Some platforms, such as the 7500 or 12000 series of routers, use distributed forwarding line cards, and as such, should be configured with **ip cef distributed**.

If the LSR is a 12000 series router, CEF is the only forwarding mechanism. CEF is also the default forwarding method in Cisco IOS Software Release 12.0 and later, so **ip cef {distributed}** might not show up in your configuration. By and large, you should be running CEF on every device in your network.

MPLS TE tunnels don't come up if you don't have CEF enabled on your router. Example 11-2 shows the MPLS Traffic Engineering state when CEF is turned on.

Example 11-2 *MPLS TE Tunnels State When CEF Is Enabled*

```
7200a#show mpls traffic-eng tunnels brief
Signalling Summary:
    LSP Tunnels Process:            running
    RSVP Process:                   running
    Forwarding:                     enabled
    Periodic reoptimization:        every 3600 seconds, next in 3134 seconds
    Periodic FRR Promotion:         every 300 seconds, next in 134 seconds
    Periodic auto-bw collection:    disabled
TUNNEL NAME                     DESTINATION      UP IF    DOWN IF    STATE/PROT
Primary tunnel 7200a->12008a... 12.12.12.12        -       PO3/0      up/up
Displayed 1 (of 1) heads, 0 (of 0) midpoints, 0 (of 0) tails
```

As you can see from the highlighted text in Example 11-2, the primary tunnel is up/up, and forwarding is enabled. Example 11-3 shows what you see when CEF is disabled.

Example 11-3 *MPLS TE Tunnels State After CEF Is Disabled*

```
7200a#configure terminal
Enter configuration commands, one per line.  End with CNTL/Z.
7200a(config)#no ip cef
7200a(config)#end
00:27:50: %SYS-5-CONFIG_I: Configured from console by console
00:28:01: %LINEPROTO-5-UPDOWN: Line protocol on Interface Tunnel1, changed state to
    down
7200a#show mpls traffic-eng tunnels brief
Signalling Summary:
    LSP Tunnels Process:            running
    RSVP Process:                   running
    Forwarding:                     disabled
    Periodic reoptimization:        every 3600 seconds, next in 2025 seconds
    Periodic FRR Promotion:         every 300 seconds, next in 225 seconds
    Periodic auto-bw collection:    disabled
TUNNEL NAME                     DESTINATION      UP IF    DOWN IF    STATE/PROT
Primary tunnel 7200a->12008a... 12.12.12.12        -       unknown    up/down
Displayed 1 (of 1) heads, 0 (of 0) midpoints, 0 (of 0) tails
```

As you can see from Example 11-3, tunnel1 goes down immediately after CEF is disabled. The forwarding state is **disabled**, and the primary tunnel is **up/down**. You can use **show ip cef summary** to check if CEF is enabled on your router. Example 11-4 shows the output of **show ip cef summary** when CEF is turned on.

Example 11-4 **show ip cef summary** *When CEF Is Turned On*

```
mpls-7200a#show ip cef summary
IP CEF with switching (Table Version 631), flags=0x0, bits=8
  51 routes, 0 reresolve, 0 unresolved (0 old, 0 new), peak 2
  51 leaves, 52 nodes, 61808 bytes, 235 inserts, 184 invalidations
  3 load sharing elements, 1032 bytes, 3 references
  universal per-destination load sharing algorithm, id B7E4AF56
  2(1) CEF resets, 268 revisions of existing leaves
  405 in-place/0 aborted modifications
```

continues

Example 11-4 show ip cef summary *When CEF Is Turned On (Continued)*

```
    Resolution Timer: Exponential (currently 1s, peak 1s)
    refcounts:  13711 leaf, 13568 node

    Table epoch: 0 (51 entries at this epoch)

Adjacency Table has 9 adjacencies
```

Example 11-5 shows the output of **show ip cef summary** when CEF is turned off.

Example 11-5 show ip cef summary *When CEF Is Turned Off*

```
mpls-7200a#show ip cef summary
IP CEF without switching (Table Version 563), flags=0x0, bits=8
  0 routes, 0 reresolve, 0 unresolved (0 old, 0 new), peak 1
  0 leaves, 0 nodes, 0 bytes, 175 inserts, 175 invalidations
  0 load sharing elements, 0 bytes, 0 references
  universal per-destination load sharing algorithm, id B7E4AF56
  2(1) CEF resets, 258 revisions of existing leaves
  397 in-place/0 aborted modifications
  Resolution Timer: Exponential (currently 1s, peak 1s)
  refcounts:  0 leaf, 0 node

  Table epoch: 0

%CEF not running
```

As you can see, when CEF is not running, this is indicated in a few places.

mpls traffic-eng tunnels Command

Configuring **mpls traffic-eng tunnels** at the global level starts various internal subsystems that comprise MPLS TE. They are collectively referred to as the *LSP Tunnels Process*. Example 11-6 shows what the LSP Tunnels Process state looks like when you have the **mpls traffic-eng tunnels** command on the router at the global level.

Example 11-6 *LSP Tunnels Process State When* mpls traffic-eng tunnels *Is Configured at the Global Level*

```
7200a#show mpls traffic-eng tunnels brief | include Process
Signalling Summary:
    LSP Tunnels Process:               running
    RSVP Process:                      running
```

As you can see from the highlighted text in Example 11-6, the LSP Tunnels Process shows **running**. Example 11-7 shows what you see if **mpls traffic-eng tunnels** is not configured at the global level.

Example 11-7 *LSP Tunnels Process State When* **mpls traffic-eng tunnels** *Is Not Configured at the Global Level*

```
7200a#configure terminal
Enter configuration commands, one per line.  End with CNTL/Z.
7200a(config)#no mpls traffic-eng tunnels
7200a(config)#end
00:49:32: %SYS-5-CONFIG_I: Configured from console by console
00:49:51: %LINEPROTO-5-UPDOWN: Line protocol on Interface Tunnel1, changed state to
  down
7200a#show mpls traffic-eng tunnels brief | include Process
    LSP Tunnels Process:              not running, disabled
    RSVP Process:                     running
```

As you might expect, tunnel1 goes down, and the LSP tunnels process shows **not running, disabled**.

Interface-Level Configuration

The following two interface-level commands are required for MPLS TE:

```
mpls traffic-eng tunnels
ip rsvp bandwidth {bandwidth}[{bandwidth}] [sub-pool bandwidth]
```

NOTE   Configuring **ip rsvp bandwidth** is not strictly necessary, because you can build an MPLS TE network entirely out of zero-bandwidth tunnels (those that don't have any bandwidth requirements) if you want to. However, reserving bandwidth is such a common use of MPLS TE that bandwidth configuration is essentially mandatory. If you know you don't need to advertise any reservable bandwidth, you can disregard the **ip rsvp bandwidth** command.

For all nonzero-bandwidth tunnels, you need to configure the **ip rsvp bandwidth** statement on each MPLS TE interface. In addition, the configured bandwidth needs to be large enough to satisfy the bandwidth requested by the primary tunnel if you want the primary tunnel to choose this interface.

The **mpls traffic-eng tunnels** command has to be configured on both sides of a link at the interface level. Failure to do so results in the link not being flooded in the IGP, which causes Path Computation's (PCALC's) bidirectionality check to fail, and the link in question will never be used for any TE tunnels in either direction.

Omitting either of these two configurations at the interface level will make the link unavailable to headends when they do their CSPF computation. This could have two undesirable results:

- Tunnels that are configured with only an explicit path option that uses this link do not come up.

- Tunnels that have a second path option configured (either explicit or dynamic) are rerouted using the second path option, which might not be as desirable in some cases.

The way 7200a has been configured (see Example 11-1), it falls into the second category, because it has a second path option—path option 6 configured under the tunnel1 interface.

If you remove the **mpls traffic-eng tunnels** command on interface POS1/1 of 12008c, as shown in Figure 11-2, 7200a reroutes the primary tunnel.

Figure 11-2 *Removing* **mpls traffic-eng tunnels** *from Interface POS1/1 on 12008c*

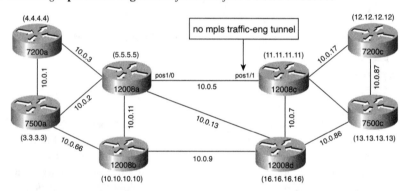

This is demonstrated in the following four steps. First, **debug mpls traffic-eng tunnels events detail** is enabled on the headend, as shown in Example 11-8. You can see what happens in Example 11-10.

Example 11-8 *Turning on* **debug mpls traffic-eng tunnels events detail** *on 7200a*

```
7200a#debug mpls traffic-eng tunnels events detail
MPLS traffic-eng tunnels system events debugging is on (detailed)
```

Next, **mpls traffic-eng tunnels** is removed from interface POS1/1 on 12008c, as shown in Example 11-9.

Example 11-9 *Removing* **mpls traffic-eng tunnels** *on Interface POS1/1 on 12008c*

```
12008c#configure terminal
12008c(config)#interface pos 1/1
12008c(config-if)#no mpls traffic-eng tunnels
```

7200a realizes that the link is no longer in the TE database, and then 7200a falls back to the next configured path option, rerouting the LSP, as shown in Example 11-10.

Example 11-10 *Output of* **debug mpls traffic-eng tunnel events detail** *Shows the Tunnel Being Rerouted*

```
*Apr  3 21:52:46.382: LSP-TUNNEL: received event: TPDB--link down
  [10.0.5.11 -> 10.0.5.5]
*Apr  3 21:52:46.382: LSP-TUNNEL: posting action(s) to all-tunnels:
*Apr  3 21:52:46.382:                    verify all LSPs
*Apr  3 21:52:46.382: LSP-TUNNEL: scheduling pending actions on all-tunnels
*Apr  3 21:52:46.386: LSP-TUNNEL: receiving LSA change events for node 11.11.11.
11 (0.0.0.0, ospf 100  area 0)
*Apr  3 21:52:46.386: LSP-TUNNEL: received event: TPDB--link bw chg
  [10.0.17.11 -> 10.0.17.12]
*Apr  3 21:52:46.386: LSP-TUNNEL: posting action(s) to all-tunnels:
*Apr  3 21:52:46.386:                    LSP path lookup
*Apr  3 21:52:46.386: LSP-TUNNEL: processing actions list...
*Apr  3 21:52:46.386: LSP-TUNNEL: applying actions to all-tunnels, as follows:
*Apr  3 21:52:46.386:                    verify all LSPs, LSP path lookup
*Apr  3 21:52:46.386: LSP-TUNNEL: done COMPLETE processing of actions list
```

As you can see from the highlighted output of Example 11-11, the primary tunnel now uses path option 6 (dynamic), and the ERO has changed from what you saw in Example 11-1.

Example 11-11 *Primary Tunnel Is Now Dynamic Path Option 6 After the Reroute*

```
7200a#show mpls traffic tunnels tunnel1

Name: Primary tunnel 7200a->12008a->12... (Tunnel1) Destination: 12.12.12.12
  Status:
    Admin: up         Oper: up     Path: valid      Signalling: connected

    path option 6, type dynamic (Basis for Setup, path weight 4)
    path option 5, type explicit primary

  Config Parameters:
    Bandwidth: 100       kbps (Global)  Priority: 7  7   Affinity: 0x0/0xFFFF
    Metric Type: TE (default)
    AutoRoute: enabled   LockDown: disabled  Loadshare: 100      bw-based
    auto-bw: disabled

  InLabel  :  -
  OutLabel : POS3/0, 12325
  RSVP Signalling Info:
      Src 4.4.4.4, Dst 12.12.12.12, Tun_Id 1, Tun_Instance 53
    RSVP Path Info:
      My Address: 4.4.4.4
      Explicit Route: 10.0.3.5 10.0.13.16 10.0.7.11 10.0.17.12
                      12.12.12.12
      Record   Route:   NONE
```

Routing Protocol Configuration

For all LSRs participating in MPLS TE, you also need to configure your IGP:

- OSPF:

    ```
    mpls traffic-eng area area 0-4294967295
    mpls traffic-eng router-id interface
    ```

- IS-IS:

    ```
    mpls traffic-eng {level1 | level2}
    mpls traffic-eng router-id interface
    metric-style wide [transition][{level-1 | level-1-2 | level-2}]
    ```

Table 11-1 shows the potential problems that arise from misconfiguring these commands.

Table 11-1   *Effects of Misconfiguring the Routing Protocol for MPLS TE*

Command Parameter	Effect of Misconfiguration
mpls traffic-eng area in OSPF	Configuring the wrong area or omitting this command leads to headends not receiving the required OSPF-TE flooding. Headends will not use the MPLS TE links configured on this router.
**mpls traffic-eng {level1	level2}**	Configuring the wrong level or omitting this command leads to headends not receiving the required IS-IS-TE flooding. Headends will not use the MPLS TE links configured on this router.
mpls traffic-eng router-id in either OSPF or IS-IS	Omitting this command leads to headends not sending/receiving the required IGP flooding. Headends will not use the MPLS TE links configured on this router.
metric-style wide or **metric-style transition** in IS-IS	Omitting this command leads to headends not receiving the required IS-IS-TE flooding. Headends will not use the MPLS TE links configured on this router. You need either **metric-style wide** or **metric-style transition**. **metric-style wide** is recommended. See Chapter 3 for a discussion of metric styles and Chapter 10 for a discussion of how to migrate from narrow to wide metrics.

Headend Configuration

As you know by now, a TE tunnel is configured at the headend LSR only.

Example 11-12 shows the configuration for Tunnel1 in the sample network. The most important TE commands are highlighted.

Example 11-12 *Headend Tunnel Configuration on 7200a*

```
7200a#show running-config interface tunnel 1
Building configuration...

Current configuration : 425 bytes
!
interface Tunnel1
 description Primary tunnel 7200a->12008a->12008c->7200c
 ip unnumbered Loopback0
 no ip directed-broadcast
 tunnel destination 12.12.12.12
 tunnel mode mpls traffic-eng
 tunnel mpls traffic-eng autoroute announce
 tunnel mpls traffic-eng priority 7 7
 tunnel mpls traffic-eng bandwidth 100
 tunnel mpls traffic-eng path-option 5 explicit name primary
 tunnel mpls traffic-eng path-option 6 dynamic
end

7200a#show ip explicit-paths name primary
PATH primary (strict source route, path complete, generation 6)
    1: next-address 10.0.3.5
    2: next-address 10.0.5.11
    3: next-address 10.0.17.12
    4: next-address 12.12.12.12
```

Table 11-2 lists the effects of misconfiguring the highlighted commands in Example 11-12.

Table 11-2   *Effects of Misconfiguring Tunnel Parameters at the Headend*

Command Parameter	Effect of Misconfiguration
ip unnumbered Loopback0	If this command is omitted, the tunnel does not have an IP address, and the tunnel interface is not used in the routing table. As a result, no traffic is sent through this tunnel.
tunnel destination	In addition to the tunnel destination's being configured to the correct tail LSR, the tunnel destination has to be the TE-ID of that tail. In the sample network, 12.12.12.12 is the 7200c's (tail) TE-ID. If you use an interface address on 7200c, such as 10.0.17.12, the primary tunnel does not come up.
autoroute announce	If you don't use **autoroute announce** or point static routes over the TE tunnel, no traffic goes over the tunnel. Although **autoroute announce** is not mandatory, and other ways exist to steer traffic down a tunnel, it is extremely common.
bandwidth	If the bandwidth you advertise on interfaces doesn't satisfy the bandwidth you configure on a TE tunnel interface, the tunnel does not come up.

continues

Table 11-2 *Effects of Misconfiguring Tunnel Parameters at the Headend (Continued)*

Command Parameter	Effect of Misconfiguration
explicit name primary	If you want the tunnel to try the explicit path and use the dynamic path (less control) only if the explicit path is unavailable, you need to make sure you actually define the explicit path.
next-address	Make sure all the next-address statements are correct. If you use RIDs in the **next-address** statement instead of the interface address and you have multiple links between two nodes, the headend might not choose the link you want it to go over—it might choose one of the other links. You might want to use interface addresses to control which links this tunnel goes over.

Tools for Troubleshooting MPLS TE Problems

This section provides a quick overview of some of the commands that are useful for troubleshooting MPLS TE problems. Table 11-3 summarizes these commands. Not all **debug** or **show** commands are shown here; there are too many to list. However, these are the major ones.

Table 11-3 *Useful Commands for MPLS TE Troubleshooting*

Command	Where to Use It	Description
show running-config [*modifier*]	Headend, midpoint, tail	This command can be used to verify the different configurations on any LSR regardless of the LSR's role.
show mpls traffic-eng tunnel summary [*modifier*]	Headend, midpoint, tail	This command displays the following information: • If the LSP tunnel process is running • If the RSVP process is running • If forwarding is enabled • Periodic reoptimization • Periodic FRR promotion • Periodic auto bandwidth collection • Role of this LSR for various LSPs (how many LSPs this LSR is headend/midpoint/tail for)
show ip cef summary	Headend, midpoint, tail	Used to check if CEF is enabled on an LSR.

Table 11-3   *Useful Commands for MPLS TE Troubleshooting (Continued)*

Command	Where to Use It	Description
show ip interface brief	Headend, midpoint, tail	On the headend, checks both the tunnel state and the outbound interfaces. At the midpoints and tail, displays the state of inbound/outbound physical interfaces.
show mpls traffic-eng tunnels brief	Headend, midpoint, tail	Can be used to obtain any information that is available using **show mpls traffic-eng summary**. In addition, you can use it to check the state of any tunnels for which this router is a head, mid, or tail.
show mpls traffic-eng tunnels *tunnel*	Headend	Although this command can be executed on midpoints and tail, it is one of the most useful commands for determining why a tunnel is not coming up.
**show mpls traffic-eng link-management [interfaces	admission-control	advertisements	statistics]**	Midpoint, tail	Used to check the advertisements out a link at midpoints or the tail.
**show ip rsvp [interface	sender	request	reservation]**	Headend, midpoint, tail	Checks signalling details and whether RSVP is configured on interfaces.
show ip rsvp counters	Headend, midpoint, tail	Checks how many signalling attempts were made, how many times an RSVP session was established, and the number of activations and deactivations.
**show mpls traffic-eng topology [TE-ID	path	area	level-1	level-2]**	Headend	Even though the contents of the topology should be the same everywhere, this command should be executed at the headend to examine the contents of the TE database (TE-DB) to verify CSPF manually.
show ip ospf database opaque-area	Headend, midpoint, tail	Used to check the actual TE-LSAs received by this LSR.
show isis mpls traffic-eng advertisements	Headend, midpoint, tail	Used to check the actual TE-LSAs received by this LSR.

continues

Table 11-3 *Useful Commands for MPLS TE Troubleshooting (Continued)*

Command	Where to Use It	Description
debug ip rsvp [path | resv]	Headend, midpoint, tail	Used to obtain RSVP signalling information between neighbors.
debug mpls traffic-eng path lookup	Headend	Shows the verification of an explicit path prior to signalling that path.
debug mpls traffic-eng path spf	Headend	Shows the CSPF process that the headend goes through when operating on the path-option dynamic.

The following section provides detailed information on how to go about finding what exactly is wrong and how to fix it.

Finding the Root Cause of the Problem

The section "Common Configuration Mistakes" discussed the effects of configuring certain things incorrectly. The section "Tools for Troubleshooting MPLS TE Problems" provided a quick overview of commands that are useful for troubleshooting MPLS TE problems.

Sometimes, the problem's not so easy to spot. This section goes into detail about what you should look for when something goes wrong, how to look for it, and what you can do to fix it.

If you have an MPLS TE problem, you generally start looking at the problem from the headend of the TE tunnel. From the headend, you find only two possible categories of problems—your tunnel is either down or up.

MPLS TE problems can broadly be broken up into the following:

- **Tunnel-down problems**—Your tunnel either won't come up or won't stay up.
- **Tunnel-up problems**—Your tunnel is up, but traffic either is not being routed over the tunnel or is being routed down the tunnel without reaching its destination.

If your tunnel is down, you need to focus on the section "Tunnel-Down Problems"; if your tunnel is up, you need to focus on the "Tunnel-Up Problems" section. Generally speaking, the most interesting MPLS TE problems are the ones in which the tunnel doesn't come up. If the tunnel's up and things still aren't working, you probably have either a routing problem or a forwarding problem.

Tunnel-Down Problems

"My TE tunnel won't come up" is the most common MPLS TE problem. Of course, if the tunnel does not come up, no traffic can be forwarded down that tunnel.

There are three basic reasons why a TE tunnel won't come up:

- Because it is administratively shut down
- Because PCALC failed
- Because the tunnel could not be signalled using RSVP

The steps for fixing a tunnel-down problem are shown in Figure 11-3.

Figure 11-3 *MPLS TE Troubleshooting Flow Chart*

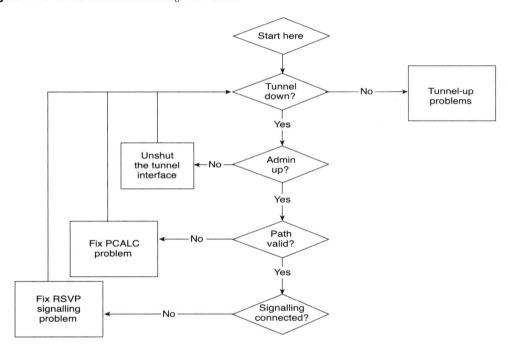

Tunnel Admin Down

Example 11-13 shows how you can determine if the tunnel is administratively shut down and then fix it.

Example 11-13 *Admin Down Tunnel*

```
7200a#show ip interface brief | include Tunnel1
Tunnel1                    4.4.4.4        YES unset  administratively down down

7200a#show mpls traffic-eng tunnels brief
Signalling Summary:
    LSP Tunnels Process:        running
    RSVP Process:               running
    Forwarding:                 enabled
    Periodic reoptimization:    every 3600 seconds, next in 137 seconds
```

continues

Example 11-13 *Admin Down Tunnel (Continued)*

```
       Periodic FRR Promotion:          every 300 seconds, next in 137 seconds
       Periodic auto-bw collection:     disabled
 TUNNEL NAME                            DESTINATION      UP IF     DOWN IF    STATE/PROT
 Primary tunnel 7200a->12008a...  12.12.12.12       -          unknown    admin-down
 Displayed 1 (of 1) heads, 0 (of 0) midpoints, 0 (of 0) tails


 7200a#show mpls traffic-eng tunnels tunnel 1 | include Admin
     Admin: admin-down Oper: down    Path: not valid   Signalling: Down
```

Then you unshut the tunnel. If the only reason the tunnel was down was because it was administratively shut down, the tunnel comes up. As you can see in Example 11-14, the tunnel on 7200a comes up when you use **no shutdown** on the tunnel interface.

Example 11-14 *Doing **no shutdown** on the Tunnel1 Interface of 7200a Brings the Tunnel Up*

```
7200a#configure terminal
Enter configuration commands, one per line.  End with CNTL/Z.
7200a(config)#interface Tunnel 1
7200a(config-if)#no shutdown
7200a(config-if)#end
23:53:27: %SYS-5-CONFIG_I: Configured from console by console
23:53:28: %LINK-3-UPDOWN: Interface Tunnel1, changed state to up
23:53:29: %LINEPROTO-5-UPDOWN: Line protocol on Interface Tunnel1, changed state
    to up
```

Remember that TE tunnels are treated much like any other interface on the router—if you shut them down, they won't be used.

PCALC Problems

If the tunnel is not administratively shut down but is still not up, the next thing to check for is to see if the path is valid. You can again use the **show mpls traffic-eng tunnel** [*tunnel*] command to see if the path is valid. Example 11-15 shows the output of **show mpls traffic-eng tunnel tunnel1** under normal circumstances.

Example 11-15 **show mpls traffic-eng tunnel tunnel1** *on 7200a Under Normal Circumstances*

```
7200a#show mpls traffic-eng tunnels tunnel1

Name: Primary tunnel 7200a->12008a->12... (Tunnel1) Destination: 12.12.12.12
  Status:
    Admin: up        Oper: up      Path: valid       Signalling: connected

    path option 5, type explicit primary (Basis for Setup, path weight 3)
    path option 6, type dynamic

  Config Parameters:
    Bandwidth: 100      kbps (Global) Priority: 7  7   Affinity: 0x0/0xFFFF
    Metric Type: TE (default)
```

Example 11-15 show mpls traffic-eng tunnel tunnel1 *on 7200a Under Normal Circumstances (Continued)*

```
    AutoRoute: enabled   LockDown: disabled Loadshare: 100     bw-based
    auto-bw: disabled

 InLabel  :  -
 OutLabel : POS3/0, 12305
 RSVP Signalling Info:
      Src 4.4.4.4, Dst 12.12.12.12, Tun_Id 1, Tun_Instance 260
   RSVP Path Info:
     My Address: 4.4.4.4
     Explicit Route: 10.0.3.5 10.0.5.11 10.0.17.12 12.12.12.12
     Record   Route:   NONE
     Tspec: ave rate=100 kbits, burst=1000 bytes, peak rate=100 kbits
   RSVP Resv Info:
     Record   Route:   NONE
     Fspec: ave rate=100 kbits, burst=1000 bytes, peak rate=Inf
 Shortest Unconstrained Path Info:
   Path Weight: 3 (TE)
   Explicit Route: 10.0.3.5 10.0.5.11 10.0.17.12 12.12.12.12
 History:
   Tunnel:
     Time since created: 1 days, 1 minutes
     Time since path change: 1 minutes, 9 seconds
   Current LSP:
     Uptime: 1 minutes, 9 seconds
   Prior LSP:
     ID: path option 5 [259]
     Removal Trigger: tunnel shutdown
```

In this case, the path is valid.

The text at the bottom of the output is highlighted to call your attention to the History section of the output. The History section is a good place to start looking if path is invalid. As you can see, it has the reason why the tunnel was last removed—because of tunnel shutdown.

You'll find several cases that might cause the path to be invalid:

- **Case A**—Multiple constraints are placed on the tunnel. Removing some of them brings the tunnel up.

- **Case B**—One or more constraints on the tunnel, and only when you remove all of them does the tunnel come up.

- **Case C**—There are no paths to the destinations, constrained or unconstrained, and even when you remove all the constraints on the tunnel, it still stays down.

NOTE   *Constraints* are things configured on the headend that can cause the TE tunnel path to diverge from the IGP shortest path. Specifically, the available TE constraints are bandwidth, affinity/link attributes, priority, and path option. An *unconstrained path* is the path that the TE tunnel would take with no constraints—essentially, the IGP path.

Case A: Removing Some Constraints Brings Up the Tunnel

Consider Example 11-16, in which the path is invalid.

Example 11-16 *Path on tunnel1 on 7200a Is Invalid*

```
7200a#show mpls traffic-eng tunnels tunnel1

Name: Primary tunnel 7200a->12008a->12... (Tunnel1) Destination: 12.12.12.12
  Status:
    Admin: up      Oper: down   Path: not valid   Signalling: Down
    path option 5, type explicit primary

  Config Parameters:
    Bandwidth: 100      kbps (Global)  Priority: 7  7   Affinity: 0x0/0xFFFF
    Metric Type: TE (default)
    AutoRoute: enabled   LockDown: disabled  Loadshare: 100      bw-based
    auto-bw: disabled

  Shortest Unconstrained Path Info:
    Path Weight: 3 (TE)
    Explicit Route: 10.0.3.5 10.0.5.11 10.0.17.12 12.12.12.12
  History:
    Tunnel:
      Time since created: 1 days, 44 minutes
      Time since path change: 23 minutes, 5 seconds
    Prior LSP:
      ID: path option 5 [260]
      Removal Trigger: path verification failed
      Last Error: PCALC:: Can't use link 10.0.3.5 on node 5.5.5.5
```

You need to notice a few facts from the highlighted output of Example 11-16:

- The tunnel is operationally down, and the path is invalid.

- Only one path option is configured on the tunnel, and it is explicit.

- The shortest unconstrained path matches the explicitly specified path that was shown earlier, in Example 11-1.

- The **Last Error** field in the History section says **PCALC:: Can't use link 10.0.3.5 on node 5.5.5.5**.

If the shortest unconstrained path is the same as the specified explicit path and the path is invalid, this can mean only one thing—the constraints placed on the tunnel cannot be satisfied along the explicitly specified path.

You can do one of the following things to fix this problem:

- Remove the bandwidth constraints and keep the explicit path option
- Keep the bandwidth constraints and remove the explicit path option that brings up the tunnel

---

NOTE   Using an explicit path option is also a type of constraint, because you are asking the headend to build the tunnel using an explicitly specified path list.

Removing Bandwidth Constraints While Keeping the Explicit Path Option

Tunnel1 comes up after you remove the bandwidth constraint but use the same explicit path option. Example 11-17 demonstrates this.

Example 11-17 *Removing Bandwidth Constraints on tunnel1*

```
7200a#show running-config interface tunnel1
Building configuration...

Current configuration : 378 bytes
!
interface Tunnel1
 description Primary tunnel 7200a->12008a->12008c->7200c
 ip unnumbered Loopback0
 no ip directed-broadcast
 tunnel destination 12.12.12.12
 tunnel mode mpls traffic-eng
 tunnel mpls traffic-eng autoroute announce
 tunnel mpls traffic-eng priority 7 7
 tunnel mpls traffic-eng bandwidth 100
 tunnel mpls traffic-eng path-option 5 explicit name primary
end

7200a#show ip explicit-paths name primary
PATH primary (strict source route, path complete, generation 6)
    1: next-address 10.0.3.5
    2: next-address 10.0.5.11
    3: next-address 10.0.17.12
    4: next-address 12.12.12.12

7200a#configure terminal
Enter configuration commands, one per line.  End with CNTL/Z.
7200a(config)#interface tunnel1
7200a(config-if)#no tunnel mpls traffic-eng bandwidth  100
7200a(config-if)#end
7200a#
1d05h: %LINEPROTO-5-UPDOWN: Line protocol on Interface Tunnel1, changed state to up
1d05h: %SYS-5-CONFIG_I: Configured from console by console
```

Keeping Bandwidth Constraints While Removing the Explicit Path Option

Instead of removing the bandwidth, as in Example 11-17, if you add a second path option (dynamic), tunnel1 comes up. This is demonstrated in Example 11-18.

Example 11-18 *Adding a Dynamic Path Option to tunnel1 Brings Up the Tunnel*

```
mpls-7200a#configure terminal
Enter configuration commands, one per line.  End with CNTL/Z.
mpls-7200a(config)#interface tunnel1
mpls-7200a(config-if)#tunnel mpls traffic-eng path-option 6 dynamic
3d02h: %LINEPROTO-5-UPDOWN: Line protocol on Interface Tunnel1, changed state to up
```

NOTE	The reason for adding another path option is because the tunnel has only one path option (refer to Example 11-17), and removing it would leave the tunnel with no path options, which certainly would not bring up the tunnel. Also, there is no need to remove the explicit path option, because Cisco IOS Software attempts the next path option in sequence when the current one fails.

If the tunnel does not come up after one of the two constraints (bandwidth or explicit path option) is removed, you can conclude that either there's a problem along the specified explicit path, or you're requesting too much bandwidth. This means you've got a problem that falls into either Case B or Case C.

If the tunnel comes up after you remove both the explicit path and the bandwidth constraints, you have a Case B problem; if it continues to stay down, you have a Case C problem.

As you can see from the highlighted text in Example 11-18, the tunnel comes up the moment you add another path-option while retaining the bandwidth. This means that somewhere along the explicitly specified path there is insufficient bandwidth to satisfy a 100 kbps reservation.

The output of **show mpls traffic-eng tunnels tunnel1** in Example 11-16 shows this:

```
Last Error: PCALC:: Can't use link 10.0.3.5 on node 5.5.5.5
```

This is confusing, because it seems as though 7200a is complaining about not being able to use 10.0.3.5 (POS2/1) on 5.5.5.5 (12008a). In reality, 7200a is trying to tell you that it can't use the hop that comes after 10.0.3.5, which is 10.0.5.11. Think of this error as indicating the last known usable link in the configured explicit path; something past this link is not acceptable, given the headend configuration. Because for RSVP the nodes do accounting for downstream links, you need to look at the interface of POS1/0 (10.0.5.5) on 12008a.

You can check the TE database to see what is being advertised for the next hop that comes after 10.0.3.5 by 12008a. Example 11-19 shows you how to do this.

Example 11-19 *Checking the Contents of the TE Database for 10.0.5.5 Advertisement*

```
7200a#show mpls traffic-eng topology 11.11.11.11
    link[3]: Point-to-Point, Nbr IGP Id: 11.11.11.11, nbr_node_id:4, gen:26
        frag_id 1, Intf Address:10.0.5.5, Nbr Intf Address:10.0.5.11
        TE metric:1, IGP metric:1, attribute_flags:0x0
        physical_bw: 622000 (kbps), max_reservable_bw_global: 0 (kbps)
        max_reservable_bw_sub: 0 (kbps)

                                    Global Pool      Sub Pool
                  Total Allocated   Reservable       Reservable
                  BW (kbps)         BW (kbps)        BW (kbps)
                  ---------------   -----------      ----------
        bw[0]:            0                 0                0
        bw[1]:            0                 0                0
        bw[2]:            0                 0                0
        bw[3]:            0                 0                0
        bw[4]:            0                 0                0
        bw[5]:            0                 0                0
        bw[6]:            0                 0                0
        bw[7]:            0                 0                0
```

As you can see from the highlighted text in Example 11-19, the maximum reservable bandwidth for link 10.0.5.0/24 on 12008a is 0. Because the tunnel needs 100 kbps, PCALC is failing.

Example 11-20 shows the configuration of interface POS1/0 on 12008a, which confirms that the bandwidth statement is missing from the interface configuration. Adding it back brings up tunnel1.

Example 11-20 *Checking and Fixing the Configuration of Interface POS1/0 on 12008a*

```
12008a#show running-config interface pos 1/0
Building configuration...

Current configuration : 181 bytes
!
interface POS1/0
 ip address 10.0.5.5 255.255.255.0
 no ip directed-broadcast
 mpls label protocol ldp
 mpls traffic-eng tunnels
 crc 32
 clock source internal
 pos ais-shut
end
! ↑ Missing ip rsvp bandwidth command

12008a#configure terminal
Enter configuration commands, one per line.  End with CNTL/Z.
12008a(config)#interface pos 1/0
12008a(config-if)#ip rsvp bandwidth

7200a#
00:57:28: %LINEPROTO-5-UPDOWN: Line protocol on Interface Tunnel1, changed state
  to up
```

Case B: Removing All Constraints Brings Up the Tunnel

Example 11-21 fits the description of Case B. Only the unconstrained path is available, but not along the explicitly specified path.

Example 11-21 *Case B: Removing All Constraints Brings Up the Tunnel*

```
7200a#show mpls traffic-eng tunnels tunnel1

Name: Primary tunnel 7200a->12008a->12... (Tunnel1) Destination: 12.12.12.12
  Status:
    Admin: up        Oper: down   Path: not valid   Signalling: Down
    path option 5, type explicit primary

  Config Parameters:
    Bandwidth: 100      kbps (Global) Priority: 7  7   Affinity: 0x0/0xFFFF
    Metric Type: TE (default)
    AutoRoute: enabled   LockDown: disabled Loadshare: 100       bw-based
    auto-bw: disabled

  Shortest Unconstrained Path Info:
    Path Weight: 4 (TE)
    Explicit Route: 10.0.3.5 10.0.13.16 10.0.7.11 10.0.17.12
                    12.12.12.12
  History:
    Tunnel:
      Time since created: 1 hours, 4 minutes
      Time since path change: 31 seconds
    Prior LSP:
      ID: path option 5 [127]
      Removal Trigger: path verification failed
      Last Error: PCALC:: No addresses to connect 10.0.3.5 to 10.0.5.11
```

For cases involving an explicit path option, you can try to narrow down the problem by first checking every hop in the explicit hop list. You can also try to back down the tunnel: Move the tail one hop back each time to see if the tunnel comes up. If the tunnel comes up when you move the tail to a previous hop, you can conclude that there is a problem between that hop and the next hop, and you can start scrutinizing that hop carefully.

Case C: The Tunnel Remains Down Even After All Constraints Are Removed

Finally, for Case C, consider Example 11-22.

Example 11-22 *Case C: The Tunnel Remains Down Even After All Constraints Are Removed*

```
7200a#show mpls traffic-eng tunnels tunnel1

Name: Primary tunnel 7200a->12008a->12... (Tunnel1) Destination: 12.12.12.12
  Status:
    Admin: up        Oper: down   Path: not valid   Signalling: Down
```

Example 11-22 *Case C: The Tunnel Remains Down Even After All Constraints Are Removed (Continued)*

```
  path option 6, type dynamic

Config Parameters:
  Bandwidth: 0       kbps (Global)  Priority: 7  7   Affinity: 0x0/0xFFFF
  Metric Type: TE (default)
  AutoRoute: enabled   LockDown: disabled  Loadshare: 0       bw-based
  auto-bw: disabled

Shortest Unconstrained Path Info:
  Path Weight: UNKNOWN
  Explicit Route:  UNKNOWN
History:
  Tunnel:
    Time since created: 1 hours, 14 minutes
    Time since path change: 4 minutes, 3 seconds
  Prior LSP:
    ID: path option 5 [147]
    Removal Trigger: path verification failed
  Path Option 6:
    Last Error: PCALC:: No path to destination, 12.12.12.12
```

Example 11-22 provides little information as to what might be wrong. The **Shortest Unconstrained Path Info:** shows the explicit route as **UNKNOWN**, and the last error says **No path to destination, 12.12.12.12**. This output shows only one active path option, and it is dynamic.

With an explicitly specified path, it is easy to check for MPLS TE information at each hop, because you specify the hops that should be used. If something goes wrong, it would have to be somewhere along this path.

However, with the dynamic path option, if there are multiple ways to get to the tail from the head, there is no obvious path where you can start looking for errors. To troubleshoot this type of problem, you must know the topology of your network very well!

For example, you need to know the IGP path between the headend and the tail. As soon as you know that, you should remove the constraints that are placed on the tunnel and see if the tunnel comes up. If you remove all constraints, the headend should follow the IGP best path to get to the tail. If the tunnel does not come up, you can start looking for information in the TE-DB, check the information distribution, and check the configuration of each node along that path, just as you'd do with the explicit path option.

NOTE   One thing you need to be aware of is what forwarding adjacency can do to your shortest path. If you advertise forwarding adjacencies into your IGP, the path that IP packets will follow across the network is not necessarily the path that unconstrained TE tunnels would follow.

One way to determine the IGP shortest path to the tail is to turn off autoroute and forwarding adjacency (FA) at the headend and at all the midpoints so that traffic truly uses the IGP path to the tunnel's tail if you, for example, run traceroute from the headend to the tail. But, turning off FA or autoroute at the midpoints might affect other traffic in your network and thus is not a viable option. Consider Example 11-23. 7200a has only one tunnel that is currently down. No other tunnels downstream will sway traffic from 7200a to 7200c in a non-IGP path.

Example 11-23 *IGP Shortest Path from 7200a to 7200c*

```
7200a#show ip route 12.12.12.12
Routing entry for 12.12.12.12/32
  Known via "ospf 100", distance 110, metric 4, type intra area
  Last update from 10.0.3.5 on POS3/0, 04:39:01 ago
  Routing Descriptor Blocks:
  * 10.0.3.5, from 12.12.12.12, 04:39:01 ago, via POS3/0
      Route metric is 4, traffic share count is 1

7200a#traceroute 12.12.12.12

Type escape sequence to abort.
Tracing the route to 12.12.12.12

  1 10.0.3.5 0 msec 0 msec 0 msec
  2 10.0.5.11 0 msec 0 msec 0 msec
  3 10.0.17.12 0 msec *  0 msec
```

Notice in the highlighted text of the **traceroute** output that there is no label information for each hop. Not having labels in the traceroute output is not always a guarantee that there are no tunnels on the way to the destination. You could have many one-hop tunnels from 7200a to 7200c that make the traffic from 7200a→7200c follow the non-IGP best path and still don't show labels in the output of a traceroute from 7200a to 7200c. However, if you see labels in a traceroute, and you see the traceroute taking a path that does not come across as the IGP shortest path, this should make you suspicious of midpoint tunnels that have autoroute or FA configured on them.

Of course, you also see labels in a traceroute if you have LDP/TDP turned on somewhere in the path. Example 11-24 shows a traceroute from 7200a to 7200c when the traffic is going down a TE tunnel that has autoroute configured on 12008a, causing the packets from 7200a to take the non-IGP shortest path. Traceroute provides you with information about the path that the packet takes to reach the destination. Traceroute is safe to use only if you know that nothing downstream will make the traceroute packets take the non-IGP best path. Although **show mpls traffic-eng topology path destination** *tunnel-dest* shows you what

CSPF thinks is the shortest unconstrained path to the destination, there is no substitute in such cases for knowing what path a packet should take in the absence of MPLS TE.

Example 11-24 **traceroute** *from 7200a to 7200c When a Tunnel Is Present on 12008a with Autoroute*

```
7200a#traceroute 12.12.12.12

Type escape sequence to abort.
Tracing the route to 12.12.12.12

  1 10.0.3.5 0 msec 0 msec 0 msec
  2 10.0.11.10 [MPLS: Label 12334 Exp 0] 0 msec 0 msec 0 msec
  3 10.0.9.16 [MPLS: Label 12332 Exp 0] 4 msec 0 msec 0 msec
  4 10.0.86.13 [MPLS: Label 18 Exp 0] 0 msec 0 msec 0 msec
  5 10.0.87.12 4 msec *  0 msec
```

Going back to Case C (Example 11-23), you should start checking the MPLS TE state at each hop in the traceroute. Example 11-25 shows that the global MPLS settings are fine because the LSP and RSVP processes are running, and forwarding is enabled.

Example 11-25 *Checking the MPLS TE State at First Hop 12008a*

```
12008a#show mpls traffic-eng tunnels summary
Signalling Summary:
    LSP Tunnels Process:              running
    RSVP Process:                     running
    Forwarding:                       enabled
    Head: 4 interfaces, 2 active signalling attempts, 2 established
          49 activations, 47 deactivations
    Midpoints: 1, Tails: 0
    Periodic reoptimization:      every 3600 seconds, next in 1347 seconds
    Periodic FRR Promotion:       every 300 seconds, next in 147 seconds
    Periodic auto-bw collection:  disabled
```

Example 11-26 checks the link management information for inbound interface POS2/1 and outbound interface POS1/0. The output of **show mpls traffic-eng link-management interface** tells you that MPLS TE is on, RSVP is on, the interface is admin-up, and TE information has been flooded on this interface.

Example 11-26 *Checking Inbound and Outbound Interface Link Management States*

```
12008a#show mpls traffic-eng link-management interface pos 2/1

12008a#show mpls traffic-eng link-management interface pos 1/0
System Information::
    Links Count:          5
Link ID::  PO1/0 (10.0.5.5)
    Link Status:
        Physical Bandwidth:    622000 kbits/sec
        Max Res Global BW:     466500 kbits/sec (reserved: 0% in, 0% out)
        Max Res Sub BW:        0 kbits/sec (reserved: 100% in, 100% out)
        MPLS TE Link State:    MPLS TE on, RSVP on, admin-up, flooded
```

continues

Example 11-26 *Checking Inbound and Outbound Interface Link Management States (Continued)*

```
          Inbound Admission:     allow-all
          Outbound Admission:    allow-if-room
          Admin. Weight:         1 (IGP)
          IGP Neighbor Count:    1
          IGP Neighbor:          ID 11.11.11.11, IP 10.0.5.11 (Up)
    Flooding Status for each configured area [1]:
          IGP Area[1]:  ospf 100  area 0:  flooded
```

However, no output is generated for interface POS2/1. This means that you need to check the configuration of interface POS2/1. This is shown in Example 11-27.

As you can see, the **mpls traffic-eng tunnels** command is missing from this interface, causing all the grief.

Example 11-27 *Checking the Configuration of Inbound Interface POS2/1*

```
12008a#show running-config interface pos2/1
Building configuration...

Current configuration : 199 bytes
!
interface POS2/1
 ip address 10.0.3.5 255.255.255.0
 no ip directed-broadcast
 encapsulation ppp
 crc 16
 clock source internal
 pos ais-shut
 pos report prdi
 ip rsvp bandwidth 155000 155000
end
```

Example 11-28 shows **mpls traffic-eng tunnels** being added back to interface POS2/1.

Example 11-28 *Adding* **mpls traffic-eng tunnels** *on Interface POS2/1*

```
12008a#configure terminal
Enter configuration commands, one per line.  End with CNTL/Z.
12008a(config)#interface pos2/1
12008a(config-if)#mpls traffic-eng tunnels
```

This causes tunnel1 on 7200a to come back up, as shown in Example 11-29.

Example 11-29 *Tunnel1 on 7200a Comes Back Up*

```
7200a#
12:39:03: %LINEPROTO-5-UPDOWN: Line protocol on Interface Tunnel1, changed state
  to up
```

When the unconstrained path is invalid, as in Case C, you might have to make sure that the information distribution—OSPF/IS-IS flooding—population of the TE-DB is correct. The next section describes how you go about doing this.

Validating Information Distribution

Chapter 3, "Information Distribution," provided in-depth coverage of how MPLS TE resource information is flooded using OSPF and IS-IS. This section goes over how you verify that the information distribution has taken place properly and that the TE-DB has the correct information. This can be broken up into five pieces:

- Reading the TE-DB
- Looking for TE information in the OSPF database
- Looking for TE information in the IS-IS database
- Checking the Link Manager for what was flooded
- Checking RSVP bandwidth information

Reading the TE-DB

The output of **show mpls traffic-eng topology** can be rather cumbersome if you don't use the command in conjunction with output modifiers. Here are some ways to limit the output produced:

- Look at only the entries (corresponding to LSAs) that were originated by a certain node by simply adding the MPLS TE ID. For example, **show mpls traffic-eng topology 5.5.5.5** shows you the entries in the TE-DB that were built from LSAs sent by 12008a. Example 11-30 demonstrates this on 7200a.

- Use the **path** keyword to show the entire path from the current router to a given tunnel destination. For example, to see information related to destination 12.12.12.12, you can use **show mpls traffic-eng topology path destination 12.12.12.12** (as shown in Example 11-32), optionally taking into account the constraints placed on interface Tunnel1. This is shown in Example 11-34.

Example 11-30 *TE-DB Entries Built on LSAs from 12008a (5.5.5.5)*

```
7200a#show mpls traffic-eng topology 5.5.5.5
...output omitted...
    link[2]: Point-to-Point, Nbr IGP Id: 10.10.10.10, nbr_node_id:7, gen:52
        frag_id 0, Intf Address:10.0.11.5, Nbr Intf Address:10.0.11.10
        TE metric:1, IGP metric:1, attribute_flags:0x0
        physical_bw: 622000 (kbps), max_reservable_bw_global: 466500 (kbps)
        max_reservable_bw_sub: 0 (kbps)

                              Global Pool      Sub Pool
            Total Allocated   Reservable       Reservable
```

continues

Example 11-30 *TE-DB Entries Built on LSAs from 12008a (5.5.5.5) (Continued)*

```
              BW (kbps)          BW (kbps)          BW (kbps)
           ---------------    -----------        ----------
      bw[0]:            0          466500                   0
      bw[1]:            0          466500                   0
      bw[2]:            0          466500                   0
      bw[3]:            0          466500                   0
      bw[4]:            0          466500                   0
      bw[5]:            0          466500                   0
      bw[6]:            0          466500                   0
      bw[7]:            0          466500                   0
...output omitted...
```

Example 11-30 examines the TE-DB for just the entries built from 12008a LSAs, but it has been trimmed to show the entry for only one link. Focus on the highlighted output. The **Intf Address** and **Nbr Intf Address** fields give the IP addresses of the advertising router and its IGP neighbor on that link, respectively.

The **physical bw** field gives you the link's actual physical bandwidth, or whatever you've configured with the **bandwidth** command (not the **ip rsvp bandwidth** command) on the interface. In Example 11-30, it is **622000 (kbps)** for the 12008a→12008c link. An important thing to note about the physical bandwidth is that even though you might want to oversubscribe a link by configuring the RSVP bandwidth to be, say, 4 times OC-12, the headend does not allow you to configure a single tunnel request for more than the interface's physical bandwidth, which, in this case, is OC-12.

The output in Example 11-30 is useful when you want to check the bandwidth, affinity, and TE metric information. Also keep in mind that the bandwidth is advertised on a per-priority basis. So, if your tunnel is requesting bandwidth of 100 Kb and the headend's tunnel setup/holding priority is 5, you should check the bw[5] row of the output.

Let us say you suspect that MPLS TE is not enabled on a certain link on 12008a, you can use output modifiers, as shown in Example 11-31, rather than combing through all the output by hand. This allows you to quickly check if a given link has even been advertised.

Example 11-31 *Checking for All MPLS-TE Links Advertised by 12008a*

```
7200a#show mpls traffic-eng topology 5.5.5.5 | include link
      link[0]: Broadcast, DR: 100.100.100.100, nbr_node_id:-1, gen:50
      link[1]: Point-to-Point, Nbr IGP Id: 3.3.3.3, nbr_node_id:8, gen:50
      link[2]: Point-to-Point, Nbr IGP Id: 10.10.10.10, nbr_node_id:7, gen:53
      link[3]: Point-to-Point, Nbr IGP Id: 11.11.11.11, nbr_node_id:4, gen:50
      link[4]: Point-to-Point, Nbr IGP Id: 4.4.4.4, nbr_node_id:9, gen:50
```

Example 11-32 shows how to use the **path** keyword to get destination-based information from the TE-DB.

Example 11-32 *Using the* **path destination** *Keywords to Get Destination-Based Information from TE-DB*

```
7200a#show mpls traffic-eng topology path destination 12.12.12.12
Query Parameters:
  Destination: 12.12.12.12
    Bandwidth: 0
   Priorities: 0 (setup), 0 (hold)
     Affinity: 0x0 (value), 0xFFFFFFFF (mask)
Query Results:
  Min Bandwidth Along Path: 116250 (kbps)
  Max Bandwidth Along Path: 466500 (kbps)
  Hop  0: 10.0.3.4      : affinity 00000000, bandwidth 116250 (kbps)
  Hop  1: 10.0.5.5      : affinity 00000000, bandwidth 466500 (kbps)
  Hop  2: 10.0.17.11    : affinity 00000000, bandwidth 116250 (kbps)
  Hop  3: 12.12.12.12
```

This is a quick way to check the path from 7200a to 12.12.12.12, as determined by what's in the TE-DB.

If you want to find any paths from 7200a to 7200c that have 120,000 Kb bandwidth, you can add constraints using the keywords **bandwidth**, **priority**, and **affinity**. Example 11-33 demonstrates this for **bandwidth**.

Example 11-33 *Using the* **path destination bandwidth** *Keywords to Get Destination-Based Information from TE-DB with Bandwidth Constraints*

```
7200a#show mpls traffic-eng topology path destination 12.12.12.12 bandwidth 120000
Query Parameters:
  Destination: 12.12.12.12
    Bandwidth: 120000
   Priorities: 0 (setup), 0 (hold)
     Affinity: 0x0 (value), 0xFFFFFFFF (mask)
Query Results:
% No matching path to destination, 12.12.12.12
```

As you can see, asking for 120,000 Kb yields no paths to destination 12.12.12.12.

On the other hand, if you want to apply the attributes of tunnel1 to see what paths are available, you can use the **tunnel** keyword, as shown in Example 11-34.

Example 11-34 *Checking the TE-DB Against Tunnel1 Attributes*

```
7200a#show mpls traffic-eng topology path tunnel1
Query Parameters:
  Destination: 12.12.12.12
    Bandwidth: 100
   Priorities: 7 (setup), 7 (hold)
     Affinity: 0x0 (value), 0xFFFF (mask)
Query Results:
  Min Bandwidth Along Path: 116150 (kbps)
  Max Bandwidth Along Path: 466400 (kbps)
  Hop  0: 10.0.3.4      : affinity 00000000, bandwidth 116150 (kbps)
  Hop  1: 10.0.5.5      : affinity 00000000, bandwidth 466400 (kbps)
  Hop  2: 10.0.17.11    : affinity 00000000, bandwidth 116150 (kbps)
  Hop  3: 12.12.12.12
```

As you can see from the highlighted output of Example 11-34, the attributes of tunnel1 are used to filter the content of the TE-DB.

Looking for TE Information in the OSPF Database

If you find an incorrect entry in the TE-DB, the first thing you should check is the IGP database. If the IGP database and the TE-DB show different information, you have found the problem.

For OSPF, you can check the received OSPF opaque-area LSAs. This is shown in Example 11-35.

Example 11-35 *OSPF Opaque-Area Database Contents*

```
7200a#show ip ospf database opaque-area adv-router 5.5.5.5

               OSPF Router with ID (4.4.4.4) (Process ID 100)

               Type-10 Opaque Link Area Link States (Area 0)

  LS age: 1252
  Options: (No TOS-capability, DC)
  LS Type: Opaque Area Link
  Link State ID: 1.0.0.0
  Opaque Type: 1
  Opaque ID: 0
  Advertising Router: 5.5.5.5
  LS Seq Number: 8000012F
  Checksum: 0xD6A
  Length: 132
  Fragment number : 0

    MPLS TE router ID : 5.5.5.5

    Link connected to Point-to-Point network
      Link ID : 10.10.10.10
      Interface Address : 10.0.11.5
      Neighbor Address : 10.0.11.10
      Admin Metric : 1
      Maximum bandwidth : 77750000
      Maximum reservable bandwidth : 58312500
      Number of Priority : 8
      Priority 0 : 58312500    Priority 1 : 58312500
      Priority 2 : 58312500    Priority 3 : 58312500
      Priority 4 : 58312500    Priority 5 : 58312500
      Priority 6 : 58312500    Priority 7 : 57062500
      Affinity Bit : 0x0
```

The highlighted text in the output of Example 11-35 corresponds to that shown in Example 11-30, except that the bandwidth numbers from the OSPF database are in bytes per second, whereas the numbers in the TE-DB are in kilobits per second. 77,750,000 bytes per second is 622,000 kilobits per second, and 58,312,500 bytes per second is 466,500 kilobits per second.

Looking for TE Information in the IS-IS Database

This is similar to what you saw in the OSPF database. Because the sample network is configured for OSPF and not IS-IS, the output shown in this section was taken from a different sample network.

You can obtain the TE information in the IS-IS database using the **show isis database verbose** command, which is similar to the **show ip ospf database opaque-area** command. It displays the TE TLVs received, as demonstrated in Example 11-36.

Example 11-36 **show isis database verbose gsr2.00-00** *Command Output*

```
gsr1#show isis database verbose gsr2.00-00

IS-IS Level-2 LSP gsr2.00-00
LSPID                   LSP Seq Num  LSP Checksum  LSP Holdtime     ATT/P/OL
gsr2.00-00              0x000000E5   0xA79C        802              0/0/0
  Area Address: 47
  NLPID:        0x81 0xCC
  Hostname: gsr2
  Router ID:    192.168.1.2
  IP Address:   192.168.1.2
  Metric: 10        IP 192.168.6.0/24
  Metric: 10        IP 192.168.6.0 255.255.255.0
  Metric: 10        IS gsr4.02
  Metric: 10        IS gsr1.00
  Metric: 10        IS-Extended gsr4.02
    Affinity: 0x00000000
    Interface IP Address: 192.168.6.2
    Physical BW: 622000000 bits/sec
    Reservable Global Pool BW: 466500000 bits/sec
    Global Pool BW Unreserved:
      [0]: 466500000 bits/sec, [1]: 466500000 bits/sec
      [2]: 466500000 bits/sec, [3]: 466500000 bits/sec
      [4]: 466500000 bits/sec, [5]: 466500000 bits/sec
      [6]: 466500000 bits/sec, [7]: 466500000 bits/sec
```

The **IS-Extended** text refers to the IS-IS extension TLV for MPLS TE. Inside the IS-Extended TLV is the same information you'd find in the TE-DB.

Checking the Link Manager for What Was Flooded

In addition to checking the TE-DB for the information it holds (based on the information it received), you can see what was actually advertised by a given router. Example 11-37 shows this output.

Example 11-37 *Link Management Advertisements on 12008a*

```
12008a#show mpls traffic-eng link-management advertisements
Flooding Status:      ready
Configured Areas:     1
IGP Area[1] ID:: ospf 100  area 0
  System Information::
```

continues

Example 11-37 *Link Management Advertisements on 12008a (Continued)*

```
         Flooding Protocol:     OSPF
      Header Information::
         IGP System ID:         5.5.5.5
         MPLS TE Router ID:     5.5.5.5
         Flooded Links:         6
   ...output omitted...
      Link ID::  2
         Link Subnet Type:      Point-to-Point
         Link IP Address:       10.0.11.5
         IGP Neighbor:          ID 10.10.10.10, IP 10.0.11.10
         TE metric:             1
         IGP metric:            1
         Physical Bandwidth:    622000 kbits/sec
         Res. Global BW:        466500 kbits/sec
         Res. Sub BW:           0 kbits/sec
         Downstream::
                                  Global Pool    Sub Pool
                                  -----------    ----------
            Reservable Bandwidth[0]:    466500            0 kbits/sec
            Reservable Bandwidth[1]:    466500            0 kbits/sec
            Reservable Bandwidth[2]:    466500            0 kbits/sec
            Reservable Bandwidth[3]:    466500            0 kbits/sec
            Reservable Bandwidth[4]:    466500            0 kbits/sec
            Reservable Bandwidth[5]:    466500            0 kbits/sec
            Reservable Bandwidth[6]:    466500            0 kbits/sec
            Reservable Bandwidth[7]:    456500            0 kbits/sec
         Attribute Flags:       0x00000000
   ...output omitted...
```

As you can see, the highlighted output in Example 11-37 matches what you saw in the
TE-DB for the link2 entry from 12008a (5.5.5.5) in Example 11-30.

The **show mpls traffic-eng link-management advertisements** command is basically used
to get an idea of whether a certain interface was advertised at all and, if so, what resources
(bandwidth and link attributes) are associated with each link. Note that link management
output is only relevant on the router that controls those links, i.e. the router that does
admission control and flooding for those links.

Checking RSVP Bandwidth Information

Another way to get a snapshot of all the interface bandwidth on a router is to use the **show
ip rsvp interface** command. Example 11-38 shows this output.

Example 11-38 *Snapshot of Link Bandwidth on 12008a*

```
12008a#show ip rsvp interface
interface    allocated   i/f max   flow max sub max
PO0/0        0G          1866M     1866M    0G
PO1/0        100K        466500K   466500K  0G
PO1/1        10M         466500K   466500K  0G
PO2/0        0G          116250K   116250K  0G
```

Example 11-38 *Snapshot of Link Bandwidth on 12008a (Continued)*

```
PO2/1        0G          155M        155M        0G
Fa4/0        0G          0G          0G          0G
Tu1          0G          0G          0G          0G
Tu2          0G          0G          0G          0G
Tu3          0G          0G          0G          0G
```

Several **show** commands related to TE information distribution were presented in this section. The **show** commands essentially provide the current state information. However, if you want to catch the LSAs as they leave a router or as they arrive at a router, you can use **debug** commands. Table 11-4 gives you the **show** commands and the equivalent **debug** commands. As with any **debug** commands, be aware that it is not wise to turn them on in a production environment unless you know it produces a small amount of data. Turning off **logging console** and turning on **logging buffered** is also advised when you use debugs, especially in a production network.

Table 11-4   **show** *and the Equivalent* **debug** *Commands for Checking Information Distribution*

show Command	debug Command
show mpls traffic-eng link-management advertisements	**debug mpls traffic-eng link-management advertisements**
show ip ospf database opaque-area	**debug ip ospf mpls traffic-eng advertisements**
show isis mpls traffic-eng advertisements	**debug isis mpls traffic-eng advertisements**

This concludes the PCALC section. The next section assumes that the path is valid, but that you are having an RSVP signalling problem.

RSVP Signalling Problems

When the headend shows that the path is valid, but the tunnel is down, it is because of a signalling problem. How do you identify a problem in signalling? What are the symptoms of a signalling problem?

The first sign, of course, is that the tunnel is down. As with troubleshooting PCALC problems, the output of **show mpls traffic-eng tunnels** [tunnel] plays a key role in determining the cause of a tunnel's being down. Example 11-39 shows you a portion of the output from Example 11-22.

Example 11-39 *RSVP Signalling Status in the* **show mpls traffic-eng tunnels tunnel1** *Command*

```
7200a#show mpls traffic-eng tunnels tunnel1

Name: Primary tunnel 7200a->12008a->12... (Tunnel1) Destination: 12.12.12.12
  Status:
    Admin: up        Oper: down   Path: not valid   Signalling: Down
    path option 6, type dynamic
```

The **Signalling** field can have one of the following values:

- Down
- RSVP Signalling Proceeding
- Connected

In all the output shown earlier in this chapter, you saw only signalling being **Down** or **Connected**.

If the tunnel is either admin down or the path is invalid, the signalling state shows **Down**.

When a Path message is sent out, the signalling state goes into **RSVP signalling proceeding**. When the corresponding Resv message is received, the signalling state goes to **Connected**.

Most of the time, you don't see the signalling proceeding state, because signalling happens relatively quickly. However, there are certainly cases in which you see it—if there's lots of signalling traffic, or if a problem downstream is causing Path or Resv messages to be dropped. For example, if you see a tunnel in RSVP signalling proceeding, and it stays in that state for more than a second or two, it's probably worth investigating.

Example 11-40 shows tunnel1 on 7200a in RSVP signalling proceeding.

Example 11-40 *7200a in Signalling Proceeding State*

```
7200a#show mpls traffic-eng tunnels tunnel1

Name: Primary tunnel 7200a->12008a->12... (Tunnel1) Destination: 12.12.12.12
  Status:
    Admin: up        Oper: down   Path: valid Signalling: RSVP signalling
 proceeding

    path option 5, type explicit primary (Basis for Setup, path weight 3)
    path option 6, type dynamic
...output omitted...
```

As you can see from the highlighted output, the tunnel is operationally down, the path is valid, and signalling shows **RSVP signalling proceeding**.

You can check the output of **show ip rsvp counter** to see how many RSVP messages were sent and received across all RSVP-enabled interfaces. Of course, if you are troubleshooting an RSVP problem and you want to start looking at the counters, it is a good idea to clear the counters first using the **clear ip rsvp counters** command. This is shown in Example 11-41.

Example 11-41 *Clearing RSVP Counters Before Checking Them*

```
7200a#clear ip rsvp counters
Clear rsvp counters [confirm]
```

Example 11-42 shows the RSVP counters immediately after they are cleared.

Example 11-42 *RSVP Counters Right After They Are Cleared*

```
7200a#show ip rsvp counters interface pos 3/0
POS3/0                  Recv    Xmit                      Recv    Xmit
   Path                   0       0   Resv                  0       0
   PathError              0       0   ResvError             0       0
   PathTear               0       0   ResvTear              0       0
   ResvConfirm            0       0   ResvTearConfirm       0       0
   UnknownMsg             0       0   Errors                0       0
```

Example 11-43 shows the RSVP counters a few minutes after they are cleared.

Example 11-43 *RSVP Counters a Few Minutes After They Are Cleared*

```
7200a#show ip rsvp counters interface pos 3/0
POS3/0                  Recv    Xmit                      Recv    Xmit
   Path                   0       6   Resv                  0       0
   PathError              0       0   ResvError             0       0
   PathTear               0       0   ResvTear              0       0
   ResvConfirm            0       0   ResvTearConfirm       0       0
   UnknownMsg             0       0   Errors                0       0
```

As you can see from the highlighted output, 7200a has sent six Path messages but has not received any Resv messages. This is what is causing the signalling state to remain in proceeding.

The way to troubleshoot this type of problem is to methodically follow Path messages as they leave the headend and go all the way to the tail. If the Path messages are making it to the tail, follow the Resv messages upstream to the headend. To see the RSVP Path and Resv messages, you need to use the **debug ip rsvp** command. Example 11-44 shows the Path message leaving the headend 7200a.

NOTE   We recommend that you use **service timerstamps debug datetime msec,** as this gives debug messages millisecond resolution, which makes it easier to tell one RSVP message from the next.

Example 11-44 *Path Message Leaving 7200a*

```
7200a#debug ip rsvp path
RSVP debugging is on
7200a#
*Apr  5 23:40:57.421: RSVP: Outgoing path message 4.4.4.4_1614-
   >12.12.12.12_1_4.4.4.4 (on POS3/0)
*Apr  5 23:40:57.421: RSVP session 12.12.12.12_1_4.4.4.4: send path multicast on
   POS3/0
```

continues

Example 11-44 *Path Message Leaving 7200a (Continued)*

```
*Apr  5 23:40:57.421: RSVP:     version:1 flags:0000 type:PATH cksum:0EAA ttl:254
  reserved:0 length:236
*Apr  5 23:40:57.421:  SESSION             type 7 length 16:
*Apr  5 23:40:57.421:   Tun Dest:   12.12.12.12  Tun ID: 1  Ext Tun ID: 4.4.4.4
*Apr  5 23:40:57.421:  HOP                 type 1 length 12:
*Apr  5 23:40:57.421:   Hop Addr: 10.0.3.4 LIH: 0x0
*Apr  5 23:40:57.421:  TIME_VALUES         type 1 length 8 :
*Apr  5 23:40:57.421:   Refresh Period (msec): 30000
*Apr  5 23:40:57.421:  EXPLICIT_ROUTE      type 1 length 36:
*Apr  5 23:40:57.421:   10.0.3.5 (Strict IPv4 Prefix, 8 bytes, /32)
*Apr  5 23:40:57.421:   10.0.5.11 (Strict IPv4 Prefix, 8 bytes, /32)
*Apr  5 23:40:57.421:   10.0.17.12 (Strict IPv4 Prefix, 8 bytes, /32)
*Apr  5 23:40:57.421:   12.12.12.12 (Strict IPv4 Prefix, 8 bytes, /32)
*Apr  5 23:40:57.421:  LABEL_REQUEST       type 1 length 8 : 00000800
*Apr  5 23:40:57.421:  SESSION_ATTRIBUTE   type 7 length 52:
*Apr  5 23:40:57.421:   Setup Prio: 7, Holding Prio: 7
*Apr  5 23:40:57.421:   Flags: SE Style
*Apr  5 23:40:57.421:   Session Name: Primary tunnel 7200a->12008a->12008c->7200c
*Apr  5 23:40:57.421:  SENDER_TEMPLATE     type 7 length 12:
*Apr  5 23:40:57.421:   Tun Sender: 4.4.4.4 LSP ID: 1614
*Apr  5 23:40:57.421:  SENDER_TSPEC        type 2 length 36:
*Apr  5 23:40:57.421:   version=0, length in words=7
*Apr  5 23:40:57.421:   service id=1, service length=6
*Apr  5 23:40:57.421:   parameter id=127, flags=0, parameter length=5
*Apr  5 23:40:57.421:   average rate=12500 bytes/sec, burst depth=1000 bytes
*Apr  5 23:40:57.421:   peak rate  =12500 bytes/sec
*Apr  5 23:40:57.421:   min unit=0 bytes, max unit=0 bytes
*Apr  5 23:40:57.421:  ADSPEC              type 2 length 48:
*Apr  5 23:40:57.421:   version=0  length in words=10
*Apr  5 23:40:57.421:  General Parameters  break bit=0  service length=8
*Apr  5 23:40:57.421:                                         IS Hops:1
*Apr  5 23:40:57.421:               Minimum Path Bandwidth (bytes/sec):19375000
*Apr  5 23:40:57.421:                         Path Latency (microseconds):0
*Apr  5 23:40:57.421:                                      Path MTU:4470
*Apr  5 23:40:57.421:  Controlled Load Service  break bit=0  service length=0
*Apr  5 23:40:57.421:
```

As you can see from the output of Example 11-44, the path message left 7200a.

Before trying to check if it made it into next hop 12008a, you should know that the **debug ip rsvp** messages produce large amounts of output. This is because RSVP is a soft-state protocol—refresh messages keep going back and forth. If you have many tunnels going through a midpoint, it becomes hard to sift through the output to try to find the Path or Resv message you are looking for.

Fortunately, you can simplify this by using IP extended access lists. The extended access list is used differently in debugging RSVP messages than when you use it to filter packets in the forwarding path. Here is the syntax if you want to use an extended access list to filter out unwanted RSVP debug output:

```
access-list {100-199} permit udp host {tunnel source} [eq {tunnel-id}] host
  {tunnel dest} [eq {LSP-ID}]
```

The access list has to be 100 through 199 for it to be an IP extended access list. Even though RSVP messages have their own protocol type, the access list you specify is listed as UDP. This is because the Cisco IOS Software allows you to specify a port number for UDP after the source or destination address. When a UDP access list is used in RSVP debugs, the source and destination port numbers are interpreted to mean tunnel-id and LSP ID, respectively.

The tunnel source is the headend's TE-ID. For a Path message coming from 7200a for tunnel1, the *tunnel source* needs to be 4.4.4.4, and the tunnel destination should be the tail's TE-ID—12.12.12.12.

The [**eq** {*tunnel-id*}] and the [**eq** {*LSP-ID*}] are useful if you have many tunnels going from the same headend to the same tail. Example 11-45 shows extended access list 101 being defined to be used in the RSVP debug.

Example 11-45 *Checking if the Path Message Made It to First Hop 12008a*

```
12008a#configure terminal
12008a(config)#access-list 101 permit udp host 4.4.4.4 host 12.12.12.12
```

debug ip rsvp path 101 detail is turned on after that. It uses IP extended access list 101, as shown in Example 11-46.

Example 11-46 *Turning on* **debug ip rsvp path 101**

```
12008a#debug ip rsvp path 101
RSVP debugging is on
*Apr  5 23:30:35.576: RSVP:      version:1 flags:0000 type:PATH cksum:0000
   ttl:254 reserved:0 length:236
*Apr  5 23:30:35.576:  SESSION            type 7 length 16:
*Apr  5 23:30:35.576:   Tun Dest:   12.12.12.12  Tun ID: 1  Ext Tun ID: 4.4.4.4
*Apr  5 23:30:35.576:  HOP                type 1 length 12:
*Apr  5 23:30:35.576:   Hop Addr: 10.0.3.4 LIH: 0x0
*Apr  5 23:30:35.576:  TIME_VALUES        type 1 length 8 :
*Apr  5 23:30:35.576:   Refresh Period (msec): 30000
*Apr  5 23:30:35.576:  EXPLICIT_ROUTE     type 1 length 36:
*Apr  5 23:30:35.576:   10.0.3.5 (Strict IPv4 Prefix, 8 bytes, /32)
*Apr  5 23:30:35.576:   10.0.5.11 (Strict IPv4 Prefix, 8 bytes, /32)
*Apr  5 23:30:35.576:   10.0.17.12 (Strict IPv4 Prefix, 8 bytes, /32)
*Apr  5 23:30:35.576:   12.12.12.12 (Strict IPv4 Prefix, 8 bytes, /32)
*Apr  5 23:30:35.576:  LABEL_REQUEST      type 1 length 8 : 00000800
*Apr  5 23:30:35.576:  SESSION_ATTRIBUTE  type 7 length 52:
*Apr  5 23:30:35.576:   Setup Prio: 7, Holding Prio: 7
*Apr  5 23:30:35.576:   Flags: SE Style
*Apr  5 23:30:35.576:   Session Name: Primary tunnel 7200a->12008a->12008c>7200c
*Apr  5 23:30:35.576:  SENDER_TEMPLATE    type 7 length 12:
*Apr  5 23:30:35.576:   Tun Sender: 4.4.4.4 LSP ID: 1618
*Apr  5 23:30:35.576:  SENDER_TSPEC       type 2 length 36:
*Apr  5 23:30:35.576:   version=0, length in words=7
*Apr  5 23:30:35.576:   service id=1, service length=6
*Apr  5 23:30:35.576:   parameter id=127, flags=0, parameter length=5
*Apr  5 23:30:35.576:   average rate=12500 bytes/sec, burst depth=1000 bytes
```

continues

Example 11-46 *Turning on* **debug ip rsvp path 101** *(Continued)*

```
*Apr  5 23:30:35.576:   peak rate    =12500 bytes/sec
*Apr  5 23:30:35.576:   min unit=0 bytes, max unit=0 bytes
*Apr  5 23:30:35.576:  ADSPEC              type 2 length 48:
*Apr  5 23:30:35.576:  version=0  length in words=10
*Apr  5 23:30:35.576:  General Parameters  break bit=0  service length=8
*Apr  5 23:30:35.576:                              IS Hops:1
*Apr  5 23:30:35.576:            Minimum Path Bandwidth (bytes/sec):19375000
*Apr  5 23:30:35.576:                  Path Latency (microseconds):0
*Apr  5 23:30:35.576:                              Path MTU:4470
*Apr  5 23:30:35.576:  Controlled Load Service  break bit=0  service length=0
*Apr  5 23:30:35.576:
*Apr  5 23:30:35.576: RSVP 4.4.4.4_1618-12.12.12.12_1: PATH message arrived
    from PHOP 10.0.3.4 on POS2/1
*Apr  5 23:30:45.320: RSVP: Outgoing path message 4.4.4.4_1618->12.12.12.12
 _1_4.4.4.4 (on POS1/0)
*Apr  5 23:30:45.320: RSVP:     version:1 flags:0000 type:PATH cksum:3BC1
    ttl:253 reserved:0 length:228
*Apr  5 23:30:45.320:  SESSION              type 7 length 16:
*Apr  5 23:30:45.320:   Tun Dest:   12.12.12.12  Tun ID: 1  Ext Tun ID: 4.4.4.4
*Apr  5 23:30:45.320:  HOP                  type 1 length 12:
*Apr  5 23:30:45.320:   Hop Addr: 10.0.5.5 LIH: 0x0
*Apr  5 23:30:45.320:  TIME_VALUES          type 1
*Apr  5 23:30:45.320:   Refresh Period (msec): 30000
*Apr  5 23:30:45.320:  EXPLICIT_ROUTE       type 1 length 28:
*Apr  5 23:30:45.320:   10.0.5.11 (Strict IPv4 Prefix, 8 bytes, /32)
*Apr  5 23:30:45.320:   10.0.17.12 (Strict IPv4 Prefix, 8 bytes, /32)
*Apr  5 23:30:45.320:   12.12.12.12 (Strict IPv4 Prefix, 8 bytes, /32)
*Apr  5 23:30:45.320:  LABEL_REQUEST        type 1 length 8 : 00000800
*Apr  5 23:30:45.320:  SESSION_ATTRIBUTE    type 7 length 52:
*Apr  5 23:30:45.320:   Setup Prio: 7, Holding Prio: 7
*Apr  5 23:30:45.320:   Flags: SE Style
*Apr  5 23:30:45.320:   Session Name: Primary tunnel 7200a->12008a->12008c->7200c
*Apr  5 23:30:45.320:  SENDER_TEMPLATE      type 7 length 12:
*Apr  5 23:30:45.320:   Tun Sender: 4.4.4.4  LSP ID: 1618
```

As you can see from the highlighted output of Example 11-46, the Path message arrives on interface POS2/1 and goes out on interface POS1/0. You know these messages belong to the same session because both the incoming and outgoing message carry the same Tunnel Sender, Tunnel Destination, Tunnel ID, and LSP ID. You might have noted that the same RSVP message showed up twice in Example 11-46. The first RSVP message is the message the router received; the second one is the message it sent. There are a few differences between the two messages, such as the HOP object and the contents of the EXPLICIT_ROUTE object. This sample network has only a single tunnel, whose LSP ID is 1618. Tracking RSVP messages that carry this LSP ID means that they all belong to the same tunnel. Now you need to check the same thing at the next hop 12008c. Example 11-47 shows this on 12008c.

Example 11-47 *Checking on 12008c to See if the Path Message Made It*

```
12008c#show clock
*23:31:18.236 UTC Fri Apr 5 2002
12008c#debug ip rsvp 101
RSVP debugging is on
...
...
12008c#show clock
*23:32:25.396 UTC Fri Apr 5 2002
```

You can see from the highlighted output of Example 11-47 that 12008c is not receiving the Path message. Path messages by default arrive every 30 seconds, plus or minus 50 percent jitter. This is what is preventing the tunnel from being set up.

After the signalling problem is fixed, the Path message arrives on the tail 7200c, which sends a Resv message that arrives on 7200a, and tunnel1 on 7200a finally comes up. Example 11-48 shows the Resv message arriving at 7200a and tunnel1 coming up.

Example 11-48 *Resv Message*

```
7200a#debug ip rsvp resv
RSVP debugging is on
*Apr  6 00:26:10.781: RSVP:      version:1 flags:0000 type:RESV cksum:0000
   ttl:255 reserved:0 length:108
*Apr  6 00:26:10.781:  SESSION            type 7 length 16:
*Apr  6 00:26:10.781:   Tun Dest:   12.12.12.12  Tun ID: 1  Ext Tun ID: 4.4.4.4
*Apr  6 00:26:10.781:  HOP               type 1 length 12:
*Apr  6 00:26:10.781:   Hop Addr: 10.0.3.5 LIH: 0x0
*Apr  6 00:26:10.781:  TIME_VALUES        type 1 length 8 :
*Apr  6 00:26:10.781:   Refresh Period (msec): 30000
*Apr  6 00:26:10.781:  STYLE    type 1 length 8 :
*Apr  6 00:26:10.781:   RSVP_SE_OPTION
*Apr  6 00:26:10.781:  FLOWSPEC              type 2 length 36:
*Apr  6 00:26:10.781:   version = 0 length in words = 7
*Apr  6 00:26:10.781:   service id = 5, service length = 6
*Apr  6 00:26:10.781:   tspec parameter id = 127, tspec flags = 0, tspec
   length= 5
*Apr  6 00:26:10.781:   average rate = 12500 bytes/sec, burst depth = 1000 bytes
*Apr  6 00:26:10.781:   peak rate    = 2147483647 bytes/sec
*Apr  6 00:26:10.781:   min unit = 0 bytes, max unit = 0 bytes
*Apr  6 00:26:10.781:  FILTER_SPEC        type 7 length 12:
*Apr  6 00:26:10.781:   Tun Sender: 4.4.4.4, LSP ID: 1618
*Apr  6 00:26:10.781:  LABEL            type 1 length 8 : 00003025
*Apr  6 00:26:10.781:
*Apr  6 00:26:10.781: RSVP 4.4.4.4_1623-12.12.12.12_1:
   RESV message arrived from 10.0.3.5 on POS3/0
*Apr  6 00:26:10.781: RSVP session 12.12.12.12_1_4.4.4.4: Reservation is new
1d03h: %LINEPROTO-5-UPDOWN: Line protocol on Interface Tunnel1, changed state to up
```

If your signalling state shows connected, you no longer have a tunnel-down problem. The next section talks about problems related to forwarding after the TE tunnel is up.

Tunnel-Up Problems

As discussed earlier, tunnel-up problems are either routing problems or forwarding problems.

For troubleshooting MPLS forwarding problems, it is important to know what labels are exchanged in the control plane so that you know what labels each hop expects to see in the forwarding plane. Figure 11-4 shows the labels exchanged (from right to left) and packets being forwarded over the tunnel from left to right. 7200a imposes a label of 12325 on the packet as it switches it down the TE tunnel. 12008a label-swaps it to 12330, and 12008c pops the label and sends it to 7200c, the tunnel's tail.

Figure 11-4 *Labels Exchanged Over the Tunnel and Packet Forwarding Over the Tunnel*

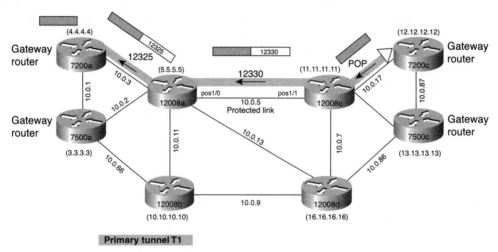

Forwarding problems can be categorized as follows:

- Traffic doesn't enter the tunnel.
- Traffic enters the tunnel but gets lost somewhere downstream.

Traffic Doesn't Enter the Tunnel

Just because your tunnel is up doesn't mean traffic will flow over it. After the tunnel is up, traffic might not go through the tunnel if you don't have the following configured on the headend:

- **ip unnumbered loopback0** under the tunnel interface
- Static route pointing down the tunnel, or
- Autoroute announce, or

- Forwarding adjacency (FA), or

- Policy-based routing (PBR)

If you don't have **ip unnumbered loopback0** under the tunnel interface, the tunnel does not have a source IP address. As a result, it will not be installed in the routing table as an outgoing interface.

If you remember from Chapter 5, "Forwarding Traffic Down Tunnels," you have to use either static routes, autoroute announce, FA, or PBR, or no traffic will use the tunnel, even if it is signalled up.

Verifying Routing and Forwarding Tables

For static routes, autoroute, or FA, the easiest way to check what prefixes are mapped over the tunnel is to use **show ip cef** {*tunnel*}. This is shown in Example 11-49.

Example 11-49 *Using CEF to See What Is Mapped onto the Tunnel*

```
7200a#show ip cef tunnel1
Prefix              Next Hop           Interface
1.1.1.1/32          0.0.0.0            Tunnel1
2.2.2.2/32          0.0.0.0            Tunnel1
10.0.18.0/24        10.0.3.5           POS3/0
                    0.0.0.0            Tunnel1
10.0.87.0/24        10.0.3.5           POS3/0
                    0.0.0.0            Tunnel1
10.1.1.1/32         0.0.0.0            Tunnel1
10.1.1.2/32         0.0.0.0            Tunnel1
12.12.12.12/32      0.0.0.0            Tunnel1
66.66.66.0/24       0.0.0.0            Tunnel1
171.68.0.0/16       12.12.12.12        Tunnel1
171.68.1.0/24       0.0.0.0            Tunnel1
```

It is important to look at the CEF table and not the routing table, because the forwarding might have been recursively resolved to the tunnel interface, whereas the routing table does not actually point down the tunnel interface for a certain prefix.

Example 11-50 shows the routing entry for prefix 171.68.0.0. The match is highlighted in the output.

Example 11-50 *Routing Table Entry for 171.68.0.0*

```
7200a#show ip route 171.68.0.0
Routing entry for 171.68.0.0/16, 2 known subnets
  Variably subnetted with 2 masks

O E2    171.68.1.0/24 [110/20] via 10.0.3.5, 00:02:04, POS3/0
B       171.68.0.0/16 [200/0] via 12.12.12.12, 00:01:09
```

Example 11-51 shows the CEF table entry for 171.68.0.0.

Example 11-51 *Checking the CEF Table for 171.68.0.0*

```
7200a#show ip cef 171.68.0.0
171.68.0.0/16, version 432, epoch 0
0 packets, 0 bytes
  tag information from 12.12.12.12/32, shared, unshareable
    local tag: 37
    fast tag rewrite with Tu1, point2point, tags imposed {12325}
  via 12.12.12.12, 0 dependencies, recursive
    next hop 12.12.12.12, Tunnel1 via 12.12.12.12/32
    valid adjacency
    tag rewrite with Tu1, point2point, tags imposed {12325}
```

The reason that the routing table entry for 171.68.0.0 doesn't point down Tunnel1 is because only its next hop 12.12.12.12 is mapped onto Tunnel1. As a result, the CEF entry recursively resolves 171.68.0.0 to Tunnel1, whereas the routing table does not. Example 11-52 shows that 12.12.12.12 is mapped onto Tunnel1 statically.

Example 11-52 *12.12.12.12 Is Statically Routed Over Tunnel1*

```
7200a#show ip route 12.12.12.12
Routing entry for 12.12.12.12/32
  Known via "static", distance 1, metric 0 (connected)
  Routing Descriptor Blocks:
  * directly connected, via Tunnel1
      Route metric is 0, traffic share count is 1
```

If you have autoroute turned on for Tunnel1, you can also check to see if it is being announced using **show mpls traffic-eng autoroute**, as shown in Example 11-53.

Example 11-53 *Checking if Autoroute Is Enabled for the Tunnel*

```
7200a#show mpls traffic-eng autoroute
MPLS TE autorouting enabled
  destination 12.12.12.12 has 1 tunnels
    Tunnel1     (load balancing metric 20000000, nexthop 12.12.12.12)
                (flags: Announce)
```

The same applies with FA. If you have FA configured on Tunnel1 instead of autoroute, you can use **show mpls traffic-eng forwarding-adjacency**, as shown in Example 11-54.

Example 11-54 *Checking if FA Is Enabled for the Tunnel*

```
pls-7200a#show mpls traffic-eng forwarding-adjacency
  destination 12.12.12.12 has 1 tunnels
    Tunnel1     (load balancing metric 20000000, nexthop 12.12.12.12)
                (flags:  Forward-Adjacency, holdtime 0)
```

Verifying That Traffic Is Really Going Down the Tunnel

If everything checks out, how do you know that traffic is actually entering the tunnel? You can check this by following these two steps:

- Check the interface tunnel accounting

- Check output counters or accounting on the outbound (downstream) physical interface to make sure the traffic is actually leaving the router

Before you check the interface tunnel accounting, it is a good idea to clear the counters, as shown in Example 11-55.

Example 11-55 *Clearing Tunnel1 Counters*

```
mpls-7200a#clear counters tunnel 1
Clear "show interface" counters on this interface [confirm]
3d04h: %CLEAR-5-COUNTERS: Clear counter on interface Tunnel1 by console
```

Next, send 1000 pings to the tail 12.12.12.12, as shown in Example 11-56.

Example 11-56 *Sending 1000 Pings to 7200c (12.12.12.12)*

```
7200a#ping ip
Target IP address: 12.12.12.12
Repeat count [5]: 1000
Datagram size [100]:
Timeout in seconds [2]:
Extended commands [n]:
Sweep range of sizes [n]:
Type escape sequence to abort.
Sending 1000, 100-byte ICMP Echos to 12.12.12.12, timeout is 2 seconds:
!!!!!!!!!!!!!!!!!!!!!!!!!!!!!!!!!!!!!!!!!!!!!!!!!!!!!!!!!!!!!!!!!!!!!!!!!!!!
!!!!!!!!!!!!!!!!!!!!!!!!!!!!!!!!!!!!!!!!!!!!!!!!!!!!!!!!!!!!!!!!!!!!!!!!!!!!
!!!!!!!!!!!!!!!!!!!!!!!!!!!!!!!!!!!!!!!!!!!!!!!!!!!!!!!!!!!!!!!!!!!!!!!!!!!!
!!!!!!!!!!!!!!!!!!!!!!!!!!!!!!!!!!!!!!!!!!!!!!!!!!!!!!!!!!!!!!!!!!!!!!!!!!!!
!!!!!!!!!!!!!!!!!!!!!!!!!!!!!!!!!!!!!!!!!!!!!!!!!!!!!!!!!!!!!!!!!!!!!!!!!!!!
!!!!!!!!!!!!!!!!!!!!!!!!!!!!!!!!!!!!!!!!!!!!!!!!!!!!!!!!!!!!!!!!!!!!!!!!!!!!
!!!!!!!!!!!!!!!!!!!!!!!!!!!!!!!!!!!!!!!!!!!!!!!!!!!!!!!!!!!!!!!!!!!!!!!!!!!!
!!!!!!!!!!!!!!!!!!!!!!!!!!!!!!!!!!!!!!!!!!!!!!!!!!!!!!!!!!!!!!!!!!!!!!!!!!!!
!!!!!!!!!!!!!!!!!!!!!!!!!!!!!!!!!!!!!!!!!!!!!!!!!!!!!!!!!!!!!!!!!!!!!!!!!!!!
!!!!!!!!!!!!!!!!!!!!!!!!!!!!!!!!!!!!!!!!!!!!!!!!!!!!!!!!!!!!!!!!!!!!!!!!!!!!
!!!!!!!!!!!!!!!!!!!!!!!!!!!!!!!!!!!!!!!!!!!!!!!!!!!!!!!!!!!!!!!!!!!!!!!!!!!!
!!!!!!!!!!!!!!!!!!!!!!!!!!!!!!!!!!!!!!!!!!!!!!!!!!!!!!!!!!!!!!!!!!!!!!!!!!!!
!!!!!!!!!!!!!!!!!!!!!!!!!!!!!!!!!!!!!!!!!!!!!!!!!!!!!!!!!!!!!!!!!!!!!!!!!!!!
!!!!!!!!!!!!!!!!!!!!!!!!!!!!!!!!!!!!!!!!!!!!!!!!!!!!!!!!!!!!!!!!!!!!!!!!!!!!
!!!!!!!!!!!!!!!!!!!!!!!!!
Success rate is 100 percent (1000/1000), round-trip min/avg/max = 1/1/4 ms
```

The next step is to check the interface accounting for Tunnel1 to see how many packets went over the tunnel. This is shown in Example 11-57.

Example 11-57 *Checking the Accounting for Tunnel1*

```
7200a#show interfaces tunnel1 accounting
Tunnel1 Primary tunnel 7200a->12008a->12008c->7200c
                 Protocol    Pkts In    Chars In    Pkts Out    Chars Out
                       IP          0           0        1000       108000
```

As you can see from the highlighted output, the **Pkts Out** field for the Tunnel1 accounting shows 1000 packets. The same is reflected on interface POS3/0, as shown in Example 11-58. Notice for interface POS3/0 that the packets out are Tag or MPLS packets.

Example 11-58 *Checking the Accounting for Interface POS3/0 (the Outbound Physical Interface)*

```
7200a#show interfaces pos 3/0 accounting
POS3/0
                 Protocol    Pkts In    Chars In    Pkts Out    Chars Out
                       IP       1036      107881          45         3804
                      CDP          2         696           3         1047
                      Tag          0           0        1000       108000
```

Also, if a prefix is being forwarded down a tunnel, the CEF entry for that destination should look as shown in Example 11-59.

Example 11-59 *CEF Entry for the Destination Mapped onto the Tunnel*

```
7200a#show ip cef 12.12.12.12
12.12.12.12/32, version 521, epoch 0
0 packets, 0 bytes
  tag information set, shared
    local tag: 37
    fast tag rewrite with Tu1, point2point, tags imposed {12325}
  via 0.0.0.0, Tunnel1, 1 dependency
    next hop 0.0.0.0, Tunnel1
    valid adjacency
    tag rewrite with Tu1, point2point, tags imposed {12325}
```

Traffic Enters the Tunnel But Gets Lost

If the traffic left the headend, but does not make it to the destination properly, it is getting blackholed somewhere.

To troubleshoot this, you have to determine where traffic is getting lost. You can determine the location of the black hole by

- Using **traceroute** to the tunnel destination
- Using interface accounting

Example 11-60 shows the output of traceroute from 7200a to 7200c (12.12.12.12).

Example 11-60 **traceroute** *from 7200a to 7200c*

```
7200a#traceroute 12.12.12.12

Type escape sequence to abort.
Tracing the route to 12.12.12.12

  1 10.0.3.5 [MPLS: Label 12325 Exp 0] 4 msec 0 msec 0 msec
  2 10.0.5.11 [MPLS: Label 12330 Exp 0] 0 msec 0 msec 0 msec
  3 10.0.17.12 0 msec *  0 msec
```

From the traceroute results, you can conclude that the packet should reach 12008a (the first hop) with a label of 12325 and should reach 12008c (the second hop) with a label of 12330. The output of Example 11-60 is what you see when things are normal. For example, if 12008a were blackholing the packets, you would only see the output in row 1, followed by rows of asterisks. If you see asterisks in the second row, does this mean that the packet left 12008a and did not reach 12008c, or does it mean that the packets did not even leave 12008a? Traceroute does not help you answer this question. You have to resort to looking at the interface accounting for incoming and outgoing interfaces of each hop. The recommended steps are as follows:

Step 1   Turn off autoroute announce and FA at the headend. Having them on not only causes many packets to be lost, but also obstructs troubleshooting.

Step 2   Pick a single destination, and statically route it over the tunnel.

Step 3   Send large numbers of packets using extended pings from the headend. This helps when you are looking at interface accounting information. Rapidly incrementing counters indicate the receipt and transmission of packets.

Step 4   At the midpoints, check the **show mpls forwarding labels** [*in-label*] command to check if the tag-switched bytes counter is incrementing. It is insufficient to see interface counters incrementing, because this is not a good indication of forwarding labeled packets. Using **show mpls forwarding** only applies to packets that are coming in with a label and leaving with a label. For MPLS→IP packets, you still need to use interface accounting counters. Example 11-62 demonstrates the use of **show mpls forwarding** at tunnel midpoint 12008a.

Step 5   Shut down the tunnel. If the packets are being blackholed even after the tunnel is shut down, it is not an MPLS TE problem.

As always, clear the counters first, as shown in Example 11-61.

Example 11-61 *Clearing MPLS Counters*

```
12008a#clear mpls counters
Clear "show mpls forwarding-table" counters [confirm]
12008a#
1w0d: %TFIB-5-CLEAR_COUNTERS: Clear tagswitch forwarding counters by console
```

From Example 11-59, you know that packets forwarded down the tunnel have a label value of 12,325 as they leave 7200a and go toward 12008a. So, as shown in Example 11-62, you have to check the MPLS forwarding table for entry 12325. As you can see from the high-lighted output, **Bytes tag switched** is 108,000, which equals 1000 packets of size 108 (bytes).

Example 11-62 *Checking MPLS Forwarded Packets at 12008a for Tunnel1 on 7200a*

```
12008a#show mpls forwarding-table labels 12325 detail
Local  Outgoing    Prefix        Bytes tag Outgoing    Next Hop
tag    tag or VC   or Tunnel Id  switched  interface
12325  12330       4.4.4.4 1 [1623]  108000  PO1/0       point2point
               MAC/Encaps=4/8, MTU=4470, Tag Stack{12330}
               0F008847 0302A000
               No output feature configured
```

NOTE   If you are using pings to test a tunnel that you just provisioned, just because you don't see the pings succeeding does not mean that there is a problem with the tunnel. Tunnels are unidirectional, and forwarding might be broken in the return path, but not in the forward path. Turn on **debug ip icmp** on the tail to see if ICMP packets are received or not.

Summary

Troubleshooting MPLS TE, like any other kind of troubleshooting, needs to be done very systematically. You need a good grasp of how MPLS TE works in order to troubleshoot. You should know the tools for the job—the **show** and **debug** commands.

TE problems can be broadly divided into tunnel-down problems and forwarding problems. This chapter described in great detail how to troubleshoot these problems, including which **show** or **debug** commands to use and when to use them. With this, you should be able to tackle most of the basic TE problems you run into, if not all.

MPLS TE Command Index

We thought it would be nice to have a complete list of MPLS TE commands in one place. This is our stab at it. A command list is a tricky thing to build; the list of available commands varies with the Cisco IOS Software train and code version you're using. And by the time you take this book off the shelf, it will already be five months or more out of date; such is the nature of the beast. But this appendix gives you a good grip on most of what's out there. It also gives you a feel for where new commands are likely to crop up.

This appendix is divided into the following sections:

- **show** commands
- EXEC commands
- Global configuration commands
- Physical interface configuration commands
- Tunnel interface configuration commands
- IGP configuration commands
- RSVP commands
- **debug** commands
- Explicit path configuration

Each command is listed with any modifiers it takes, the defaults for those modifiers (for configuration commands), and a one-line description of what the command does for you.

MPLS TE commands are fairly hierarchical—more so than most Cisco IOS Software commands. This makes for a lot of typing, but it also makes it extremely easy for you to add commands later and have a logical place to put them.

The conventions used to present command syntax in this book are the same conventions used in the Cisco IOS Software Command Reference. The Command Reference describes these conventions as follows:

- Vertical bars (|) separate alternative, mutually exclusive elements.
- Square brackets ([ ]) indicate an optional element.
- Braces ({ }) indicate a required choice.
- Braces within brackets ([{ }]) indicate a required choice within an optional element.

- **Boldface** indicates commands and keywords that are entered literally as shown. In configuration examples and output (not general command syntax), boldface indicates commands that are manually input by the user (such as a **show** command).

- *Italic* indicates arguments for which you supply actual values.

As always, the best way to get a completely accurate list of what commands are available is to load an image onto a router and use the **?** key to walk yourself through the command-line interface (CLI). Of course, not all debugs are suitable for use on a production network. Make sure you have a grip on what kind and level of output the debugs will give you before you use them for the first time on a production network. The command list in this appendix was generated from a prerelease version of Cisco IOS Software Release 12.0(22)S; your mileage, as always, might vary.

show Commands

All MPLS TE **show** commands start with **show mpls traffic-eng**.

Command	Modifiers	Usage
...autoroute	[*dest address*]	Shows which tunnels have autoroute configured and are announcing information to the routing protocol.
...fast-reroute database	[{*network* [*mask* | *masklength*] | **labels low label** [**-high label**] | **interface** *ifname* [**backup-interface** *ifname*] | **backup-interface** *ifname*}] [**state** {**active** | **ready** | **partial**}] [**role** {**head** | **middle**}] [**detail**]	Shows information about the FRR database—which tunnels are protected, the status of protection tunnels, and so forth.
...fast-reroute log reroutes	None	Shows a log of FRR events on a headend.
...forwarding-adjacency	[*dest address*]	Shows information about tunnels with forwarding adjacency configured.

(Continued)

Command	Modifiers	Usage
...link-management	[**admission-control** [*interface-name*] | **advertisements** | **bandwidth-allocation** [*interface-name*] | **igp-neighbors** [*interface-name* | **igp-id** {**ospf** *ospf-id* | **isis** *isis-id*} | **ip** *node-address*] | **interfaces** [*interface-name*] | **statistics** [*interface-name*] | **summary** [*interface-name*]]	Shows information about MPLS TE's link manager, which deals with things such as deciding when to flood and which tunnel requests to admit.
...topology	[*ip address* | **area** | **brief** | **igp-id** | **level-1** | **level-2** | **path**]	Gives information about the MPLS topology database. In particular, **show mpls traffic-eng topology path** is useful because it shows you the path a tunnel takes if you reoptimize it. This command is useful for troubleshooting as well.
...tunnels	[*tunnel name* | **accounting** | **backup** | **brief** | **destination** | **down** | **interface** | **name** | **name-regexp** | **property** | **protection** | **role** | **source-id** | **statistics** | **suboptimal** | **summary** | **up**]	This is a rather complex command (lots of its options have suboptions), and it lists a lot of information. This command gives you information about what tunnels touch this router, and whether the router is a headend, midpoint, or tailend to those tunnels. Of particular use is **show mpls traffic-eng tunnels suboptimal**, which has a set of options after it that show you how far from various ideas of best case your tunnels stray. **show mpls traffic-eng tunnels** by itself is an extremely useful command, and one with which you'll want to be familiar.

EXEC Commands

Command	Modifier	Use
mpls traffic-eng reoptimize	[*tunnel-name*]	Forces a tunnel to recalculate CSPF. It can force a reopt for either one tunnel or all tunnels (the default).

Global Configuration Commands

To enable MPLS TE SNMP traps, use the following global command.

Command	Modifiers	Default	Use
snmp-server enable traps mpls traffic-eng	{**down** | **reroute** | **up**}	Disabled	Enables MPLS TE traps for tunnel down, tunnel reroute, or tunnel up events. If you enable **snmp-server enable traps mpls traffic-eng**, all three traps are enabled.

All other commands in global configuration mode start with **mpls traffic-eng**.

Command	Modifiers	Default	Use
...auto-bw timers	[**frequency** *1- 604800 seconds*]	300 seconds	Determines how often tunnel bandwidth is polled for all interfaces with auto bandwidth enabled.
...link-management timers bandwidth-hold	1-300 seconds	15 seconds	Determines how long bandwidth requested in a Path message is set aside in anticipation of the Resv message.
...link-management timers periodic-flooding	0-3600 seconds	180 seconds	Determines how often unflooded changed link information is flooded.
...logging lsp	[**path-errors** | **preemption** | **reservation-errors** | **setups** | **teardowns**] {*1-199 ACL* | *1300-2690 ACL*}	Disabled	Enables logging of various LSP-related events.

(Continued)

Command	Modifiers	Default	Use
...logging tunnel lsp-selection	*[1-199 ACL	1300-2690 ACL]*	Disabled	Enables the logging of LSP selection events on TE tunnels—when a TE tunnel goes up and down, and which path option was used.
...path-selection metric	{**igp**	**te**}	TE	Tells all tunnels on a headend to use either the IGP metric or the TE metric for path selection.
...path-selection overload allow	{**head**	**middle**	**tail**}	Disabled	Allows PCALC to use nodes signalled as overloaded in the path calculation for an LSP.
...reoptimize events link-up	None	Disabled	With this enabled, try to reoptimize all TE tunnels on a box whenever a link comes up in the network.
...reoptimize timers frequency	*0-604800 seconds*	3600 seconds	Determines how often to reoptimize each up tunnel to see if there's a better path it could take. Setting a time of 0 disables reoptimization.
...signalling advertise implicit-null	{*1-99 ACL*}	Disabled	Advertises implicit null rather than explicit null for any tunnels for which this router is a tail.
...signalling interpret explicit-null verbatim	None	Disabled	Controls whether a received explicit null signaled value is interpreted as explicit null or implicit null.
...topology holddown sigerr	*0-300 seconds*	10 seconds	When RSVP signalling says that a link is down, this governs how long that link can be disregarded for CSPF purposes.
...tunnels	None	Off	Starts the basic MPLS TE process.

Physical Interface Configuration Commands

All commands in this section begin with **mpls traffic-eng** and are configured on the physical interface.

Command	Modifiers	Default	Use
...administrative-weight	*0-4294967295*	Admin weight takes the same value as the IGP cost.	Use this to engender delay-sensitive metrics.
...attribute-flags	*0x0-0xFFFFFFFF*	0x0	Sets the attribute flags on an interface.
...backup-path	*tunnel-name*	Off	Sets the tunnel interface that protects this physical interface, for FRR link protection.
...flooding thresholds	{**down** | **up**} *0-100 ...*	Up: 15 30 45 60 75 80 85 90 95 96 97 98 99 100 Down: 100 99 98 97 96 95 90 85 80 75 60 45 30 15	Bandwidth threshold that, when crossed, triggers IGP flooding of the TE information about this link.
...tunnels	None	Off	Enables MPLS TE on an interface.

In addition, three particularly useful MPLS commands are configured on a physical interface but are not options of **mpls traffic-eng**. They are as follows.

Command	Modifiers	Default	Use
mpls accounting experimental	{**input** | **output**}	Neither	Counts MPLS packets by EXP, in either the in (Rx) or out (Tx) direction—or both, if you configure them both. You can view these counts with **show interface** *interface* **mpls-exp**.
mpls netflow egress	None	Off	Netflow normally works on packets that have come into the router as IP. This command allows you to account for packets that come into the router as MPLS, but have their label stack removed and leave as IP.

(Continued)

Command	Modifiers	Default	Use
ip rsvp bandwidth	[*1-10000000 reservable BW* [**sub-pool** *1-10000000 reservable BW*]]	Off	Configures the amount of reservable bandwidth on an interface; see Chapter 3, "Information Distribution."

Tunnel Interface Configuration Commands

Command	Modifiers	Default	Use
tunnel mode mpls traffic-eng	None	Off	Configures a tunnel interface to be an MPLS TE tunnel.

All other commands in this section are configured on a tunnel interface and start with **tunnel mpls traffic-eng**.

Command	Modifiers	Default	Use
...affinity	*0x0-0xFFFFFFFF* [**mask** *0x0-0xFFFFFFFF*]	0x0 affinity, 0xFFFF mask	Sets the tunnel affinity for certain link attributes; see Chapter 3.
...auto-bw	[**collect-bw** | **frequency** | **max-bw** | **min-bw**]	Disabled	Enables auto bandwidth on a TE headend, allowing a tunnel to periodically resize itself to match bandwidth demands.
...autoroute announce	None	Off	Announces the TE tunnel to the IGP for IGP SPF purposes; see Chapter 5, "Forwarding Traffic Down Tunnels."
...autoroute metric	{*1-4294967295* | **absolute** *1-4294967295* | **relative** *-10 - 10*}	**...autoroute metric relative 0** (effectively, off)	Influences the metric with which this link is announced to the IGP.
...bandwidth	[**sub-pool**] *1-4294967295>*	0	Tells the tunnel how much bandwidth to look for and reserve in the network; see Chapter 3, "Protection and Restoration."

continues

(Continued)

Command	Modifiers	Default	Use
...fast-reroute	None	Off	Tells the tunnel to ask the network for protection; see Chapter 7, "Protection and Restoration."
...forwarding-adjacency	[**holdtime** *0-4294967295 milliseconds*]	Off	Advertises the link into the network's IGP; see Chapter 5.
...load-share	*0-1000000*	Not set	Sets the load share value used to determine load sharing between parallel tunnels; see Chapter 5.
...path-option	*1-1000 preference* {**dynamic** | **explicit** {**identifier** *id* | **name** *name*}} [**lockdown**]	None set	Applies constraints to the path that the tunnel can calculate; see Chapter 4, "Path Calculation and Setup."
...path-selection metric	{**igp** | **te**}	te	Just like the global command **mpls traffic-eng path-selection**, but it lets you perform path selection on a per-tunnel basis.
...priority	{*0-7 setup*} [*0-7 holding*]	Setup and holding are both 7	Controls the tunnel's setup and holding priority; see Chapter 3.
...record-route	None	Off	Tells the tunnel to add the RECORD_ROUTE object to its PATH message. This is useful for diagnostic purposes.

IGP Configuration Commands

These commands are performed under either **router ospf** or **router isis**. Some commands are OSPF only, and others are IS-IS only. All commands start with **mpls traffic-eng**.

Command	Modifiers	Default	Use
...area	{*0-4294967295*}	Not set	OSPF only. Determines in which area to enable MPLS TE.

(Continued)

Command	Modifiers	Default	Use
...level-1	None	Not set	IS-IS only. Determines at which level to enable MPLS TE.
...level-2	None	Not set	IS-IS only. Same as **level-1**.
...interface	{*interface-name* **area** *area-number*}	Not set	OSPF only. This is used when you have a virtual link in area *X* across a physical link, and you want to advertise that link into area *Y*.
...multicast-intact	None	Not set	Allows multicast to use the real physical interface, not a tunnel interface, for RPF purposes; see Chapter 10, "MPLS TE Deployment Tips."
...router-id	*{interface-name}*	Not set	Sets the MPLS TE RID carried in OSPF or IS-IS advertisements.
...scanner interval	*1-60 seconds*	5 seconds	IS-IS only. The **...scanner interval** and **scanner max-flash** knobs control how information is copied from the IS-IS database to the TE database.
...scanner max-flash	*1-200 LSPs*	15	

RSVP Commands

Two types of RSVP commands are applicable to MPLS TE: global configuration commands and interface configuration commands.

The global configuration commands are as follows.

Command	Modifiers	Default	Use
ip rsvp msg-pacing	[**period msec** [**burst msgs** [*max_size qsize*]]]	Off	If you have large numbers of RSVP messages to send, message pacing throttles message transmission so that the router on the other end of the link is not overwhelmed with signalling messages.
ip rsvp signalling hello	{**statistics**}	Off	Enables RSVP hellos.

The interface configuration command (which is also covered in the section "Physical Interface Configuration Commands") is as follows.

Command	Modifiers	Default	Use
ip rsvp bandwidth	[*1-10000000 reservable BW* [**sub-pool** *1-10000000 reservable BW*]]	Off	Configures the amount of reservable bandwidth on an interface; see Chapter 3.

debug Commands

All these commands begin with **debug mpls traffic-eng**.

Command	Modifiers	Use
...areas	None	Debugs MPLS as it covers different areas.
...autoroute	None	Debugs autoroute functionality.
...forwarding-adjacency	None	Debugs forwarding adjacency functionality.
...link-management	{**admission-control** | **advertisements** | **bandwidth-allocation** | **errors** | **events** | **igp-neighbors** | **links** | **preemption** | **routing**}	Allows you to debug various Link Manager activities.
...load-balancing	None	Debugs the processing of unequal-cost load balancing.
...path	{*0-4294967295* | **lookup** | **spf** | **verify**}	Debugs various parts of the path calculation, optionally for a specific TE tunnel.
...topology	{**change** | **lsa**}	Debugs topology changes and LSA reception events.
...tunnels	{**auto-bw** | **errors** | **events** | **fast-reroute** | **labels** | **reoptimize** | **signalling** | **state** | **timers**}	Debugs different pieces of MPLS TE tunnel processing.

Explicit Path Configuration

One other command set is used in MPLS TE, but it doesn't fit into any of the preceding categories all that well.

Command	Modifiers	Use
ip explicit-path	{**identifier** *identifier* | **name** *name*} [**disable** | **enable**]	Configures an explicit path.

This puts you into a submode called cfg-ip-expl-path, where your configuration choices are as follows.

Command	Modifiers	Use
append-after	{*previous-index* {**exclude-address** *ip-addr* | **next-address** [*loose* | *strict*] *ip-addr*}}	Adds a **path-option** statement after an existing **path-option** statement.
exclude-address	{*ip-addr*}	An address (router ID or interface address) to avoid while doing CSPF for this path option.
index	{*index* {**exclude-address** *ip-addr* | **next-address** [*loose* | *strict*] *ip-addr*}}	Much like the **append-after** command, except that *index* overwrites whatever is already configured at a given level in the path option.
list	None	Unusual for configuration mode, this command doesn't configure anything. Instead, it lists the addresses you already have configured in the path option, and their indices.
next-address	{[**loose** | **strict**] *ip-addr*}	Gives the next address in the path you'd like to take. **exclude-address** and **next-address** are mutually exclusive. If you use them both in the same explicit path, the path is not successfully calculated.
no	{**index** *index*}	Removes a given index number.

For more documentation on and examples of this command, see Chapter 4.

CCO and Other References

This appendix contains all the URLs mentioned in this book, as well as pointers to other resources that might be of use.

Here are a few notes on this appendix:

- This appendix is laid out by chapter number. Things are just easier that way.

- Some of the references have comments, and others don't. That's because some of the things referenced are self-explanatory, and others aren't.

- Some things (particularly other Cisco Press books) are referenced more than once in this book. This is because we figured that the more we point to other people's work, the less we have to do of our own! Nevertheless, if we mentioned a particular reference more than once in this book, we mention it only once in this appendix.

- Some of these URLs are long and cumbersome, especially the CCO (Cisco Connection Online, located at www.cisco.com, a.k.a cco.cisco.com). To this end, we have done two things to help you:

    — Provided document titles—This makes them easier to find using CCO's search function. Plug the document title in, and the document referred to should be one of the top few hits.

    — Provided you with a web page—www.ciscopress.com/1587050315. This web page contains all the references from this appendix, so there's no need to copy URLs from this book to your computer.

- CCO has different login privilege levels, depending on whether you're a registered Cisco customer, a reseller, a partner, or an employee. You can retrieve any of these documents without even being logged into CCO. However, you might likely find more information available to you if you log in and search, so consider this appendix a starting point rather than an exhaustive list.

- Things change. Documentation gets updated, URLs can change, and so forth. If you can't find the document you're looking for, search for the title. Chances are it's either there somewhere or it's been supplanted by something with a similar name.

Resources for Chapter 1, "Understanding Traffic Engineering with MPLS"

Table B-1 provides information about resources related to Chapter 1's topics.

Table B-1   *Chapter 1 Resources*

URL	Title	Description
www.ietf.org/html.charters/ mpls-charter.html	"Multiprotocol Label Switching (MPLS)"	This is the IETF MPLS working group page. It contains information on drafts and RFCs that have come from this group, as well as other exciting information. If you're looking for the latest status on a standard or specification, go here first.
www.cisco.com/warp/ public/cc/so/neso/vpn/ unvpnst/atomf_ov.htm	"Any Transport Over MPLS—Technical Overview"	A technical overview of Layer 2 VPN services.

Resources for Chapter 2, "MPLS Forwarding Basics"

Table B-2 provides information about resources related to Chapter 2's topics.

Table B-2   *Chapter 2 Resources*

URL/Author(s)	Title	Description	Additional Publication Information
www.cisco.com/go/mpls/	"Cisco IOS MPLS"	A one-stop shop for MPLS information, including business-facing stuff, customer profiles, and other such marketing issues.	
Davie, B. and Y. Rekhter	*MPLS: Technology and Applications*	For a while, this was the only MPLS book you could get. It's still one of the better books to cover both the basics and the history. It was written by two MPLS designers who were there from the start.	Published in 2000 by Morgan Kaufmann
www.cisco.com/univercd/cc/td/doc/product/wanbu/bpx8600/mpls/9_3_1/mpls01.htm	"Introduction to MPLS"	This document is an introduction to IP+ATM on the ATM switch (BPX, MGX) platform. It's a good place to start if you're into MPLS and ATM integration, which we hardly spent any time on in this book.	
www.cisco.com/univercd/cc/td/doc/product/wanbu/bpx8600/mpls/9_3_1/mpls02.htm	"Integrating MPLS with IP and ATM"	Along the same lines and in the same collection as the "Introduction to MPLS" document, only more detailed. Contains the entire 9.3.1 doc set.	
www.cisco.com/univercd/cc/td/doc/product/wanbu/bpx8600/mpls/9_3_1/	Release 9.3.10	A good resource, albeit decidedly ATM-centric.	

continues

Table B-2 *Chapter 2 Resources (Continued)*

URL/Author(s)	Title	Description	Additional Publication Information
www.cisco.com/ networkers/nw01/ pres/#8		The presentations from Cisco's Networkers 2001. Check out the Introduction to MPLS, OSPF, and IS-IS presentations if you need more details on those topics. There are probably other Networkers presentations at www.cisco.com/networkers/ nw02/, /nw03/, and so forth, as they happen (typically in late summer or early fall of a given year).	
www.cisco.com/ univercd/cc/td/doc/ product/software/ ios122/122newft/ 122t/122t2/ ldp_221t.htm	"MPLS Label Distribution Protocol (LDP)"	A basic guide to LDP, focusing mainly on configuration and debugs.	
Andersson, L., P. Doolan, N. Feldman, A. Fredette, and R. Thomas	RFC 3036: "LDP Specification"	The RFC that defines LDP. Not for the faint of heart or those low on time, but it explains how everything in LDP is supposed to work.	Published in January 2001
Bollapragada, V., C. Murphy, and R. White	*Inside Cisco IOS Software Architecture*	More than you ever wanted to know about router internals, including things such as CEF. Although it contains no MPLS coverage (so nothing in the way of LFIB/TFIB/label switching), it's still a valuable reference to see how things actually work.	Published in 2000 by Cisco Press

Resources for Chapter 3, "Information Distribution"

Table B-3 provides information about resources related to Chapter 3's topics.

Table B-3   *Chapter 3 Resources*

URL	Title	Description
www.cisco.com/univercd/ cc/td/doc/product/software/ ios121/121newft/121t/ 121t3/traffeng.htm	"MPLS Traffic Engineering and Enhancements"	From September of 2000. It doesn't cover any then-nonexistent stuff like DS-TE and FRR, but it's a good configuration guide and command reference for the basics.
www.cisco.com/warp/ public/97/tlvs_5739.html	"Intermediate System-to-Intermediate System (IS-IS) TLVs"	Covers all the defined (not necessarily implemented) IS-IS TLVs, including the ones used for MPLS TE—22 and 135.
www.ietf.org/rfc/ rfc2370.txt?number=2370	"The OSPF Opaque LSA Option"	Defines opaque LSAs for OSPF, including the Type 10 LSA that carries MPLS TE information in OSPF.
http://search.ietf.org/ internet-drafts/draft-katz-yeung-ospf-traffic-06.txt	"Traffic Engineering Extensions to OSPF"	Defines the sub-TLVs used inside a Type 10 opaque LSA to carry MPLS TE information. Might have expired and/or been ratified as an RFC by the time you read this.
http://search.ietf.org/ internet-drafts/draft-ietf-isis-traffic-04.txt	"IS-IS Extensions for Traffic Engineering"	Defines the new IS-IS TLVs and sub-TLVs necessary to carry MPLS TE information in IS-IS. Might have expired and/or been ratified as an RFC by the time you read this.

Resources for Chapter 4, "Path Calculation and Setup"

Table B-4 provides information about resources related to Chapter 4's topics.

Table B-4 *Chapter 4 Resources*

URL/Author(s)	Title	Description	Additional Publication Information
Perlman, R.	*Interconnections: Bridges, Routers, Switches, and Internetworking Protocols*	A must-have in anyone's networking library. Radia's explanation of SPF (pages 317–319), although not exactly the same as a CSPF algorithm, is a particularly good introduction to the Dijkstra algorithm.	Published in 1999 by Addison-Wesley
www.ietf.org/rfc/ rfc2205.txt?number= 2205	"Resource ReSerVation Protocol (RSVP)— Version 1 Functional Specification"	The basic RSVP specification.	
www.ietf.org/rfc/ rfc3209.txt?number= 3209	"RSVP-TE: Extensions to RSVP for LSP Tunnels"	Extensions to RSVP to signal TE tunnels.	
www.ietf.org/rfc/ rfc2210.txt?number= 2210	"The Use of RSVP with IETF Integrated Services"	This RFC defines the SENDER_TSPEC, FLOWSPEC, and ADSPEC objects used to signal QoS requirements (primarily bandwidth) in MPLS TE tunnels.	

Resources for Chapter 5, "Forwarding Traffic Down Tunnels"

Table B-5 provides information about resources related to Chapter 5's topics.

Table B-5   *Chapter 5 Resources*

URL	Title	Description
www.cisco.com/warp/public/ cc/techno/protocol/tech/ plicy_wp.htm	"Policy-Based Routing"	A white paper on the uses and benefits of PBR.
www.cisco.com/univercd/cc/ td/doc/product/software/ ios120/12cgcr/qos_c/qcpart1/ qcpolicy.htm	"Configuring Policy-Based Routing"	A basic guide to configuring PBR.
www.cisco.com/warp/public/ 105/46.html	"How Does Load-Balancing Work?"	Although this paper is a bit dated (circa 11.1CC), its information might still be useful if you're trying to find out more about CEF and its load-balancing capabilities.
www.cisco.com/warp/public/ cc/pd/ifaa/pa/much/prodlit/ loadb_an.htm	"Load Balancing with Cisco Express Forwarding"	Although this paper is a bit dated (circa 11.1CC), its information might still be useful if you're trying to find out more about CEF and its load-balancing capabilities.
www.cisco.com/univercd/cc/ td/doc/product/software/ ios120/120newft/120limit/ 120st/120st16/fs_tefa.htm	"MPLS Traffic Engineering Forwarding Adjacency"	This document describes the configuration and capabilities of forwarding adjacency.

Resources for Chapter 6, "Quality of Service with MPLS TE"

Table B-6 provides information about resources related to Chapter 6's topics.

Table B-6   *Chapter 6 Resources*

URL	Title	Description
www.cisco.com/go/qos/	"Cisco IOS Quality of Service"	A good place to start with QoS in general. Because MPLS QoS and IP QoS are fairly closely related, learning more about IP QoS can help you understand MPLS QoS.
www.cisco.com/univercd/cc/ td/doc/product/software/ ios120/12cgcr/qos_c/ qcintro.htm	"Introduction: Quality of Service Overview"	As the title says, this is an introduction to and overview of QoS.
www.cisco.com/univercd/cc/ td/doc/product/wanbu/ bpx8600/mpls/9_3_1/ mpls04.htm	"Quality of Service in MPLS Networks"	Despite its name, this document emphasizes the IP+ATM side of things. Still, it's a good guide to some of the MPLS QoS issues you might face.
www.cisco.com/warp/public/ cc/pd/iosw/prodlit/ mpios_wp.htm	"Cisco IOS MPLS Quality of Service"	A good starting point for understanding MPLS QoS.
www.cisco.com/univercd/cc/ td/doc/product/software/ ios120/120newft/120limit/ 120xe/120xe5/mqc/mcli.htm	"Modular Quality of Service Command-Line Interface"	A basic guide to MQC. MQC provides different mechanisms on different platforms and IOS versions, but this reference gives you the platform-independent basics.
www.cisco.com/warp/public/ cc/pd/iosw/prodlit/ dlypl_pg.htm	"Deploying MPLS QoS"	As the title says, this is a presentation on deploying MPLS QoS.
www.cisco.com/univercd/cc/ td/doc/product/software/ ios122/122newft/122t/122t4/ ft_ds_te.htm	"Diff-Serv-aware MPLS Traffic Engineering (DS-TE)"	A configuration and usage guide for DS-TE.
www.cisco.com/univercd/cc/ td/doc/product/software/ ios122/122newft/122t/122t8/ ftcsc8.htm	"MPLS VPN Carrier Supporting Carrier"	A basic document that discusses Cisco's CSC feature.

Resources for Chapter 7, "Protection and Restoration"

Table B-7 provides information about resources related to Chapter 7's topics.

Table B-7   *Chapter 7 Resources*

URL	Title	Description
www.cisco.com/univercd/cc/ td/doc/product/software/ ios120/120newft/120limit/ 120st/120st16/frr.htm	"MPLS Traffic Engineering Fast Reroute—Link Protection"	Basic configuration documentation for FRR link protection.
draft-ietf-mpls-rsvp-lsp-fastreroute-00.txt	"Fast Reroute Extensions to RSVP-TE for LSP Tunnels"	This draft defines different FRR techniques, including the one Cisco uses (referred to here as Facility backup or bypass tunnel). As with all drafts, the version number might have changed, or this might be an RFC by the time you look for it.

As of this writing, FRR node protection hasn't yet been released, so there is no CCO documentation to refer to. Try searching CCO for "MPLS node FRR" or something similar, and you're bound to find node protection configuration documentation.

Resources for Chapter 8, "MPLS TE Management"

Table B-8 provides information about resources related to Chapter 8's topics.

Table B-8 *Chapter 8 Resources*

URL/Author(s)	Title	Description	Additional Publication Information
www.cisco.com/ univercd/cc/td/doc/ product/software/ ios122/122newft/122t/ 122t2/lsrmibt.htm	"MPLS Label Switching Router MIB"	Documentation on the LSR MIB.	
www.cisco.com/ univercd/cc/td/doc/ product/software/ ios122/122newft/122t/ 122t2/te_mib12.htm	"MPLS Traffic Engineering (TE) MIB"	Documentation on the TE MIB.	
Nadeau, Thomas D.	*MPLS Network Management: MIBs, Tools and Techniques*	As the title says, a guide to MPLS network management. Written by the primary author of several MPLS MIBs.	Published by Morgan Kaufmann in 2002
Della Maggiora, Paul L. (editor), Christopher E. Elliott, James M. Thompson, Robert L. Pavone, Jr., and Kent J. Phelps	*Performance and Fault Management*	A general text on network management. It's helpful for those who want to under-stand more about network management practices.	Published in 2000 by Cisco Press. Part of the Cisco Press Core series.
Stallings, William	*SNMP, SNMPv2, SNMPv3, and RMON 1 and 2*	One of the classic SNMP (and RMON) texts.	Published by Addison-Wesley in 1999
RFC 1555	"Structure and Identification of Management Information for TCP/IP-Based Internets"	This, and the three remaining RFCs, define both SNMP and MIBs.	
RFC 1157	"A Simple Network Management Protocol (SNMP)"		

Table B-8   *Chapter 8 Resources (Continued)*

URL/Author(s)	Title	Description	Additional Publication Information
RFC 1212	"Concise MIB Definitions"		
RFC 1213	"Management Information Base for Network Management of TCP/IP-Based Internets: MIB II"		

Resources for Chapter 9, "Network Design with MPLS TE"

Table B-9 provides information about resources related to Chapter 9's topics.

Table B-9   *Chapter 9 Resources*

URL	Title	Description
www.cisco.com/univercd/cc/ td/doc/product/software/ ios120/120newft/120limit/ 120st/120st14/scalable.htm	"MPLS Traffic Engineering (TE)—Scalability Enhancements"	This paper discusses the scalability numbers stated in Chapter 9—600 headend tunnels, 10,000 midpoint, and 5000 tail.

Resources for Chapter 10, "MPLS TE Deployment Tips"

Table B-10 provides information about resources related to Chapter 10's topics.

Table B-10   *Chapter 10 Resources*

URL	Title	Description
www.cisco.com/go/netflow/	"Cisco IOS Netflow"	A fine place to start when you're looking for NetFlow information.
www.cisco.com/univercd/cc/ td/doc/product/software/ ios121/121newft/121t/121t5/ egress.htm	"MPLS Egress NetFlow Accounting"	A configuration guide for how and where to use the command **mpls netflow egress**.
www.cisco.com/univercd/cc/ td/doc/product/software/ ios121/121newft/121t/121t5/ tms.htm	"Traffic Matrix Statistics"	An overview and configuration guide for TMS.
www.cisco.com/univercd/cc/ td/doc/product/software/ ios122/122cgcr/fswtch_c/ swprt1/xcfcef.htm	"Cisco Express Forwarding Overview"	Useful for its discussion of CEF and TMS interaction.
www.cisco.com/univercd/cc/ td/doc/product/software/ ios120/120newft/120t/120t5/ saaoper.htm	"Service Assurance Agent"	A basic SAA configuration guide.
www.cisco.com/univercd/cc/ td/doc/product/software/ ios120/120newft/120t/120t7/ te120_7t.htm	"MPLS Traffic Engineering"	Particularly useful is the section "Transitioning an IS-IS Network to a New Technology," which talks about migrating from narrow to wide metrics.
www.cisco.com/warp/public/ 127/sonet_aps_tech_tips.html	"A Brief Overview of SONET APS Technology"	As the title says, this is an overview of APS.

Resources for Chapter 11, "Troubleshooting MPLS TE"

Table B-11 provides information about resources related to Chapter 11's topics.

Table B-11 *Chapter 11 Resources*

URL	Title	Description
www.cisco.com/warp/public/ 105/mpls_tsh.html	"MPLS Troubleshooting"	Covers basic MPLS trouble-shooting steps. It's not TE-specific, but it's a good place to start.

Remember that most command documentation comes with a troubleshooting section, and that the MPLS and MPLS TE debugs are documented. See Appendix A, "MPLS TE Command Index," for more ideas on where to start.

INDEX

M

S

U

V-Z

Hey, you've got enough worries.

Don't let IT training be one of them.

Get on the fast track to IT training at InformIT,
your total Information Technology training network.

 | **www.informit.com** |

■ Hundreds of timely articles on dozens of topics ■ Discounts on IT books from all our publishing partners, including Cisco Press ■ Free, unabridged books from the InformIT Free Library ■ "Expert Q&A"—our live, online chat with IT experts ■ Faster, easier certification and training from our Web- or classroom-based training programs ■ Current IT news ■ Software downloads ■ Career-enhancing resources

Train with authorized Cisco Learning Partners.

Discover all that's possible on the Internet.

One of the biggest challenges facing networking professionals is how to stay current with today's ever-changing technologies in the global Internet economy. Nobody understands this better than Cisco Learning Partners, the only companies that deliver training developed by Cisco Systems.

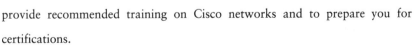

Just go to **www.cisco.com/go/training_ad**. You'll find more than 120 Cisco Learning Partners in over 90 countries worldwide.* Only Cisco Learning Partners have instructors that are certified by Cisco to provide recommended training on Cisco networks and to prepare you for certifications.

To get ahead in this world, you first have to be able to keep up. Insist on training that is developed and authorized by Cisco, as indicated by the Cisco Learning Partner or Cisco Learning Solutions Partner logo.

Visit **www.cisco.com/go/training_ad** today.

CISCO SYSTEMS

EMPOWERING THE
INTERNET GENERATION™

IF YOU'RE USING

CISCO PRODUCTS,

YOU'RE QUALIFIED

TO RECEIVE A

FREE SUBSCRIPTION

TO CISCO'S

PREMIER PUBLICATION,

PACKET™ MAGAZINE.

Packet delivers complete coverage of cutting-edge networking trends and innovations, as well as current product updates. A magazine for technical, hands-on Cisco users, it delivers valuable information for enterprises, service providers, and small and midsized businesses.

Packet is a quarterly publication. To start your free subscription, click on the URL and follow the prompts: www.cisco.com/go/packet/subscribe

CISCO SYSTEMS

CISCO SYSTEMS/PACKET MAGAZINE
ATTN: C. Glover
170 West Tasman, Mailstop SJ8-2
San Jose, CA 95134-1706

Place Stamp Here

☐ **YES!** I'm requesting a **free** subscription to *Packet™* magazine.

☐ No. I'm not interested at this time.

☐ Mr.
☐ Ms.

First Name (Please Print)   Last Name

Title/Position (Required)

Company (Required)

Address

City   State/Province

Zip/Postal Code   Country

Telephone (Include country and area codes)   Fax

E-mail

Signature (Required)   Date

☐ I would like to receive additional information on Cisco's services and products by e-mail.

1. Do you or your company:
- A ☐ Use Cisco products
- B ☐ Resell Cisco products
- C ☐ Both
- D ☐ Neither

2. Your organization's relationship to Cisco Systems:
- A ☐ Customer/End User
- B ☐ Prospective Customer
- C ☐ Cisco Reseller
- D ☐ Cisco Distributor
- E ☐ Integrator
- F ☐ Non-Authorized Reseller
- G ☐ Cisco Training Partner
- I ☐ Cisco OEM
- J ☐ Consultant
- K ☐ Other (specify):

3. How many people does your entire company employ?
- A ☐ More than 10,000
- B ☐ 5,000 to 9,999
- C ☐ 1,000 to 4,999
- D ☐ 500 to 999
- E ☐ 250 to 499
- F ☐ 100 to 249
- G ☐ Fewer than 100

4. Is your company a Service Provider?
- A ☐ Yes
- B ☐ No

5. Your involvement in network equipment purchases:
- A ☐ Recommend
- B ☐ Approve
- C ☐ Neither

6. Your personal involvement in networking:
- A ☐ Entire enterprise at all sites
- B ☐ Departments or network segments at more than one site
- C ☐ Single department or network segment
- F ☐ Public network
- D ☐ No involvement
- E ☐ Other (specify):

7. Your Industry:
- A ☐ Aerospace
- B ☐ Agriculture/Mining/Construction
- C ☐ Banking/Finance
- D ☐ Chemical/Pharmaceutical
- E ☐ Consultant
- F ☐ Computer/Systems/Electronics
- G ☐ Education (K–12)
- U ☐ Education (College/Univ.)
- H ☐ Government—Federal
- I ☐ Government—State
- J ☐ Government—Local
- K ☐ Health Care
- L ☐ Telecommunications
- M ☐ Utilities/Transportation
- N ☐ Other (specify):

CPRESS

PACKET

Packet magazine serves as the premier publication linking customers to Cisco Systems, Inc. Delivering complete coverage of cutting-edge networking trends and innovations, *Packet* is a magazine for technical, hands-on users. It delivers industry-specific information for enterprise, service provider, and small and midsized business market segments. A toolchest for planners and decision makers, *Packet* contains a vast array of practical information, boasting sample configurations, real-life customer examples, and tips on getting the most from your Cisco Systems' investments. Simply put, *Packet* magazine is straight talk straight from the worldwide leader in networking for the Internet, Cisco Systems, Inc.

We hope you'll take advantage of this useful resource. I look forward to hearing from you!

Cecelia Glover
Packet Circulation Manager
packet@external.cisco.com
www.cisco.com/go/packet

PACKET